19th SIGMORPHON Workshop on Computational Research in Phonetics Phonology, and Morphology (SIGMORPHON 2022)

Online
14 July 2022

ISBN: 978-1-7138-5638-2

Printed from e-media with permission by:

Curran Associates, Inc.
57 Morehouse Lane
Red Hook, NY 12571

Some format issues inherent in the e-media version may also appear in this print version.

Association for Computational Linguistics
209 N. Eighth Street
Stroudsburg, Pennsylvania 18360

Phone: 1-570-476-8006
Fax: 1-570-476-0860

acl@aclweb.org

Additional copies of this publication are available from:

Curran Associates, Inc.
57 Morehouse Lane
Red Hook, NY 12571 USA
Phone: 845-758-0400
Fax: 845-758-2633
Email: curran@proceedings.com
Web: www.proceedings.com

SIGMORPHON 2022

19th SIGMORPHON Workshop on Computational Research in Phonetics, Phonology, and Morphology

Proceedings of the Workshop

July 14, 2022

Order copies of this and other ACL proceedings from:

Association for Computational Linguistics (ACL)
209 N. Eighth Street
Stroudsburg, PA 18360
USA
Tel: +1-570-476-8006
Fax: +1-570-476-0860
acl@aclweb.org

Organizing Committee

Co-Chair

Garrett Nicolai, University of British Columbia
Eleanor Chodroff, University of York

SIGMORPHON Officers

President: Garrett Nicolai, University of British Columbia
Secretary: Miikka Silfverberg, University of British Columbia
At Large: Eleanor Chodroff, University of York
At Large: Sandra Kübler, Indiana University
At Large: Çağrı Çöltekin, University of Tübingen

Program Committee

Reviewers

Khuyagbaatar Batsuren, National University of Mongolia
Canaan Breiss, MIT
Jane Chandlee, Haverford College
Çağrı Çöltekin, University of Tübingen
Daniel Dakota, Indiana University
Aniello De Santo, University of Utah
Ewan Dunbar, University of Toronto
Indranil Dutta, Jadavpur University
Micha Jacobs, University of Buffalo
Adam Jardine, Rutgers University
Greg Kobele, Universität Leipzig
Jordan Kodner, Stony Brook University
Sandra Kübler, Indiana University
Andrew Malouf, San Diego State University
Arya McCarthy, Johns Hopkins University
Kemal Oflazer, CMU Qatar
Gerald Penn, University of Toronto
Jelena Prokic, Universiteit Leiden
Jonathan Rawski, San Diego State University
Brian Roark, Google AI
Morgan Sonderegger, McGill University
Miikka Silfverberg, University of British Columbia
Kairit Sirts, University of Tarfu
Ekaterina Vylomova, University of Melbourne
Adam Wiemerslage, University of Colorado, Boulder
Adina Williams, Facebook AI Research
Colin Wilson, Johns Hopkins University
Anssi Yli-Jyrä, University of Helsinki
Changbing Yang, University of British Columbia

Keynote Talk: Parsing continuous speech into lexically bound phonetic sequences

Laura Gwilliams
University of California, San Francisco

Abstract: Speech consists of a continuously-varying acoustic signal. Yet human listeners experience it as sequences of discrete speech sounds, which are used to recognise words. To examine how the human brain appropriately sequences the speech signal, we recorded two-hour magnetoencephalograms from 21 subjects listening to short narratives. Our analyses show that the brain continuously encodes the three most recently heard speech sounds in parallel, and maintains this information long past the sensory input. Each speech sound has a representation that evolves over time, jointly encoding both its phonetic features and time elapsed since onset. This allows the brain to represent the relative order and phonetic content of the phonetic sequence. These dynamic representations are active earlier when phonemes are more predictable, and are sustained longer when lexical identity is uncertain. The flexibility in the dynamics of these representations paves the way for further understanding of how such sequences may be used to interface with higher order structure such as morphemes and words.

Bio: Laura Gwilliams received her PhD in Psychology with a focus in Cognitive Neuroscience from New York University in May 2020. Currently she is a post-doctoral researcher at UCSF, using MEG and ECoG data to understand how linguistic structures are parsed and composed while listening to continuous speech. The ultimate goal of Laura's research is to describe speech comprehension in terms of what operations are applied to the acoustic signal; which representational formats are generated and manipulated (e.g. phonetic, syllabic, morphological), and under what processing architecture.

Keynote Talk: Deep Phonology: Modeling language from raw acoustic data in a fully unsupervised manner

Gasper Begus
University of California, Berkeley

Abstract: In this talk, I propose that language and its acquisition can be modeled from raw speech data in a fully unsupervised manner with Generative Adversarial Networks (GANs) and that such modeling has implications both for the understanding of language acquisition and for the understanding of how deep neural networks learn internal representations. I propose a technique that allows us to "wug-test" neural networks trained on raw speech, analyze intermediate convolutional layers, and test a causal relationship between meaningful units in the output and latent/intermediate representations. I further propose an extension of the GAN architecture in which learning of meaningful linguistic units emerges from a requirement that the networks output informative data and includes both the perception and production principles. With this model, we can test what the networks can and cannot learn, how their biases match human learning biases in behavioral experiments, how speech processing in the brain compares to intermediate representations in deep neural networks (by comparing acoustic properties in intermediate convolutional layers and the brainstem), how symbolic-like rule-like computation emerges in internal representations, and what GAN's innovative outputs can teach us about productivity in human language. This talk also makes a more general case for probing deep neural networks with raw speech data, as dependencies in speech are often better understood than those in the visual domain and because behavioral data on speech (especially the production aspect) are relatively easily accessible.

Bio: Gašper Beguš an Assistant Professor at the Department of Linguistics at UC Berkeley where he directs the Berkeley Speech and Computation Lab. Before coming to Berkeley, he was an Assistant Professor at the University of Washington and before that he graduated with a Ph.D. from Harvard. His research focuses on developing deep learning models for speech data. More specifically, he trains models to learn representations of spoken words from raw audio inputs. He combines machine learning and statistical modeling with neuroimaging and behavioral experiments to better understand how neural networks learn internal representations in speech and how humans learn to speak.

Table of Contents

Program

Thursday, July 14, 2022

08:45 - 09:00 *Opening Remarks*

09:00 - 10:00 *Invited Talk 1: Laura Gwilliams: Parsing continuous speech into lexically bound phonetic sequences*

10:00 - 10:30 *Morning Break*

10:30 - 11:30 *Morning Session: Phonology and Phonetics*

Multidimensional acoustic variation in vowels across English dialects
James Tanner, Morgan Sonderegger and Jane Stuart-Smith

On Building Spoken Language Understanding Systems for Low Resourced Languages
Akshat Gupta

Domain-Informed Probing of wav2vec 2.0 Embeddings for Phonetic Features
Patrick Cormac English, John D. Kelleher and Julie Carson-Berndsen

Investigating phonological theories with crowd-sourced data: The Inventory Size Hypothesis in the light of Lingua Libre
Mathilde Hutin and Marc Allassonnière-Tang

11:30 - 12:30 *Lunch*

12:30 - 13:30 *Invited Talk 2: Gasper Begus: Deep Phonology: Modeling language from raw acoustic data in a fully unsupervised manner*

13:30 - 15:00 *Morning Session: Morphosyntax*

A Masked Segmental Language Model for Unsupervised Natural Language Segmentation
C.M. Downey, Fei Xia, Gina-Anne Levow and Shane Steinert-Threlkeld

Trees probe deeper than strings: an argument from allomorphy
Hossep Dolatian, Shiori Ikawa and Thomas Graf

Thursday, July 14, 2022 (continued)

Logical Transductions for the Typology of Ditransitive Prosody
Mai Ha Vu, Aniello De Santo and Hossep Dolatian

Subword-based Cross-lingual Transfer of Embeddings from Hindi to Marathi and Nepali
Niyata Bafna and Zdeněk Žabokrtský

Morphotactic Modeling in an Open-source Multi-dialectal Arabic Morphological Analyzer and Generator
Nizar Habash, Reham Marzouk, Christian Khairallah and Salam Khalifa

Unsupervised morphological segmentation in a language with reduplication
Simon Todd, Annie Huang, Jeremy Needle, Jennifer Hay and Jeanette King

15:00 - 15:30 *Afternoon Break*

15:30 - 17:45 *Shared Task Session*

17:45 - 18:00 *Closing Statements*

On Building Spoken Language Understanding Systems for Low Resourced Languages

Akshat Gupta
J.P.Morgan AI Research
New York, USA
akshat.x.gupta@jpmorgan.com

Abstract

Spoken dialog systems are slowly becoming and integral part of the human experience due to their various advantages over textual interfaces. Spoken language understanding (SLU) systems are fundamental building blocks of spoken dialog systems. But creating SLU systems for low resourced languages is still a challenge. In a large number of low resourced language, we don't have access to enough data to build automatic speech recognition (ASR) technologies, which are fundamental to any SLU system. Also, ASR based SLU systems do not generalize to unwritten languages. In this paper, we present a series of experiments to explore extremely low-resourced settings where we perform intent classification with systems trained on as low as one data-point per intent and with only one speaker in the dataset. We also work in a low-resourced setting where we do not use language specific ASR systems to transcribe input speech, which compounds the challenge of building SLU systems to simulate a true low-resourced setting. We test our system on Belgian Dutch (Flemish) and English and find that using phonetic transcriptions to make intent classification systems in such low-resourced setting performs significantly better than using speech features. Specifically, when using a phonetic transcription based system over a feature based system, we see average improvements of 12.37% and 13.08% for binary and four-class classification problems respectively, when averaged over 49 different experimental settings.

1 Introduction

Spoken Language Understanding (SLU) systems form an integral part of any spoken dialog system. A traditional SLU pipeline is made up of two modules (Figure 1) - a speech to text module which converts input audio into textual transcripts, and a natural language understanding (NLU) module which aims to understand the semantic content in the user utterance from the textual transcripts (Tur and De Mori, 2011; Lugosch et al., 2019). The conventional two-module SLU pipeline is prone to making speech recognition errors which propagate through the system. To minimize these errors, a lot of recent research has been focused on creating end-to-end spoken language understanding (E2E-SLU) systems (Qian et al., 2017; Serdyuk et al., 2018).

Building E2E-SLU systems requires an even larger amount of task-specific annotated data when compared to the two-module split SLU pipelines (Lugosch et al., 2019; Bastianelli et al., 2020; Wu et al., 2020). While high resourced languages like English are moving towards E2E-SLU, the challenges presented by low resourced languages are very different. Low resourced languages operate in a regime where we have access to only tens or hundreds of labelled utterances, which are not enough to build robust E2E-SLU systems. Creating robust automatic speech recognition (ASR) systems for low resourced languages is itself a challenge as these require large amounts of manual annotation. For many low resourced languages, we might not even have ASR technologies. Creating ASR technologies for unwritten languages or languages that have only a few hundred or a few thousand speakers alive is not even a viable option. But can we create spoken dialog systems for such languages?

'*Low-resourced-ness*' of a particular language is a very broad term often used loosely to describe various types of inadequacies when creating language technologies. It affects creating speech technologies in mainly two ways. For the purpose of this paper, we explicitly define and differentiate between these two scenarios. The first scenario is what we call *language-specific low-resourced-ness*, where we do not have enough resources to create robust, language specific speech recognition technologies. Speech recognition systems are fundamental to creating various kinds of speech technologies includ-

19th SIGMORPHON Workshop on Computational Research in Phonetics, Phonology, and Morphology, pages 1 - 11
July 14, 2022 ©2022 Association for Computational Linguistics

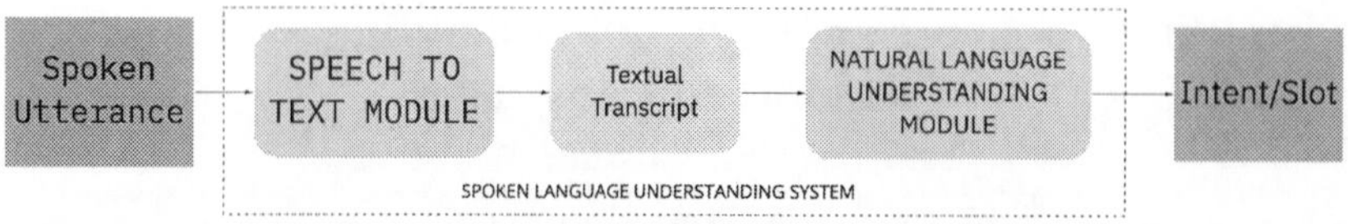

Figure 1: A traditional spoken language understanding system consisting of a speech-to-text system followed by a natural language understanding module.

ing dialog systems, speech emotion recognition systems, keyword spotting systems, speaker recognition and diarization systems. When creating dialog systems, ASR systems allow us to convert input speech to text, after which text based language models like BERT (Devlin et al., 2018) can be used to understand the content of speech and build NLU modules. This allows us to create SLU systems with smaller amounts of task-specific annotated data. But in settings where we do not have access to speech recognition systems, it becomes important to have enough annotated task-specific data to compensate for the lack of ASR systems and text-based language models. This introduces the second source of 'low-resourced-ness', which we call *task-specific low-resourced-ness* - where we do not have enough annotated data for a particular task. Two challenges occur in this scenario - one where we do not have enough speakers to create a task-sepcific speech corpus, and another where we do not have enough recordings per speaker. Not having enough annotated data for a particular task, when combined with lack of speech recognition technologies compounds the problem of creating speech technologies for such languages. We work in this compounded low-resource setting, where we assume language specific and task-specific low-resourced-ness.

In this paper, we present a series of experiments to empirically re-create language-specific and task-specific low-resourced-ness scenarios and work in the compounded setting where we tackle both challenges at the same time. As we assume language specific low-resourced-ness, we work in a setting where we don't have access to language specific ASR systems. One way to tackle this setting is to use an ASR system built for a higher resourced language and use the transcriptions generated to perform downstream tasks as used in (Buddhika et al., 2018; Karunanayake et al., 2019b,a). It was later shown in (Gupta et al., 2021; Yadav et al., 2021) that using language and speaker independent systems trained on many languages to extract speech features works much better than using ASR systems built for a different language, as a different language usually contains a different set of phonemes with a different phone to phoneme set mapping. When this setting is compounded by task-specific low-resourced-ness, we are at an extremely low resourced setting where each data point becomes valuable. To simulate this setting, we pose an I-class intent classification problem ($I = 2, 4$) where we have a varying number speakers (S) available for recording training data. Each speaker provides only k-utterances per intent for training. In this k-shot setting, we evaluate our system in a granular manner for very small values of S and k. Specifically, we evaluate our system for $S = 1, 2, 3, 4, 5, 6, 7$ number of speakers, where each speaker records $k = 1, 2, 3, 4, 5, 6, 7$ utterances per intent. We evaluate our SLU system on robust test sets containing hundreds of utterances collected from multiple speakers which are not present in the training set.

We find that using language independent or multilingual speech recognition systems performs significantly better in such low-resourced settings. Furthermore, what works even better is to generate a language independent symbolic representation of input speech and create NLU systems for this symbolic representation. This hints that creating SLU systems for even extremely low-resourced settings is likely trace conventional SLU pipelines where we represent input speech symbolically in the form of text and then build NLU blocks on top of this. The symbolic representation of speech used here is the phonetic transcription. We find that using a phonetic transcription based system is significantly better than using speech features for classification for low-resourced settings. We see average improvements of 12.37% and 13.08% for binary and four-class classification problems respectively, when averaged over 49 different experimental settings, for Belgian Dutch (Flemish) language.

2 Related Work

English has been the most widely studied language for creating SLU systems. Various datasets have been released to aid this development (Hemphill et al., 1990; Saade et al., 2018; Lugosch et al., 2019; Bastianelli et al., 2020). There have been many previous works on creating SLU systems in a two-module split fashion (Gorin et al., 1997; Mesnil et al., 2014). A typical SLU pipeline, as shown in Figure 1, consists of an ASR system that converts input speech to text and an NLU module that processes the input text to understand the user query. As with any system composed of multiple modules, errors that occur in one part of the system propagate through the system. To prevent this, a large amount of recent work has been focused on creating E2E-SLU systems (Qian et al., 2017; Serdyuk et al., 2018; Chen et al., 2018). The caveat with making such systems to work is that they require an even larger amount of task-specific annotated data, which is usually not a luxury available to low-resourced languages.

Apart from English, there are many other spoken dialog datasets available for various languages including French (Devillers et al., 2004; Saade et al., 2018), Dutch (Tessema et al., 2013; Ons et al., 2014; Renkens et al., 2014), Chinese Mandarin (Zhu et al., 2019; Guo et al., 2021), Sinhala and Tamil (Karunanayake et al., 2019b), and cross-lingual SLU datasets exist for English, Spanish and Thai (Schuster et al., 2019). In this paper, we work with two languages - Belgian Dutch (Flemish) (Tessema et al., 2013; Ons et al., 2014; Renkens et al., 2014) and English (Lugosch et al., 2019).

One of the major bottlenecks in creating SLU systems for low-resourced languages is the creation of ASR systems in such low data scenario. This scenario is what we refer to as a language-specific low-resourced setting. Previous works have tried to use English-based ASR systems for languages like Tamil and Sinhala. In these sytems, input speech in Sinhala/Tamil is converted into English script using an English speech recognition system that is then processed by an NLU system (Buddhika et al., 2018; Karunanayake et al., 2019b,a). We use a similar idea as baseline and use Wav2Vec (Schneider et al., 2019; Baevski et al., 2020) to extract speech features for Flemish. Wav2Vec is a self-supervised speech recognition system trained on large amounts of unlabelled speech data which boasts to learn superior language representations for English. In this work, we use Wav2Vec 2.0 (Baevski et al., 2020) to extract speech features.

A series of recent works (Gupta et al., 2020b,a, 2021; Yadav et al., 2021) replace the ASR module in the SLU pipeline by a universal phone recognition system called Allosaurus (Li et al., 2020). Allosaurus is a universal phonetic transcription system that creates language and speaker independent representations of input speech. Allosaurus is trained to recognize and transcribe input speech into a series of phones contained in the utterance, providing superior representations of input audio which can also be used for languages linguistically distant from high resourced languages like English. (Yadav et al., 2021) show that using embeddings generated from Allosaurus to encode speech content outperforms previous state-of-the-art methods for Sinhala and Tamil by large margins, while maintaining high performance on high resourced languages like English (99.08% classification accuracy for a 31-class intent classification problem). But the performance drops as the dataset size decreases and is not optimal for the task-specific low resourced settings that we are dealing with in this paper. To tackle this, we convert input speech into phonetic transcriptions using Allosaurus as proposed in (Gupta et al., 2020a) for our compounded low resourced setting.

In our paper, we explore a novel and rather unexplored language-specific low-resourced setting compounded with task-specific low-resourced-ness. Our aim it to push the limits and demonstrate performance of using existing technologies in extremely low resourced settings, where each data point becomes crucial.

3 Dataset

In our paper, we work with two languages - Belgian Dutch (Flemish) and English. We use two popular SLU datasets for our experiments - the Fluent Speech Commands (FSC) dataset (Lugosch et al., 2019) for the English language and the Grabo dataset (Tessema et al., 2013; Ons et al., 2014; Renkens et al., 2014) for Flemish.

The primary reason behind the choice of the datasets was that each utterance in the two datasets had clear speaker identities associated with each utterance. Our aim is to test true low resourced settings where getting speaker recordings is extremely hard. Intent recognition datasets in other languages like French (Devillers et al., 2004; Saade et al.,

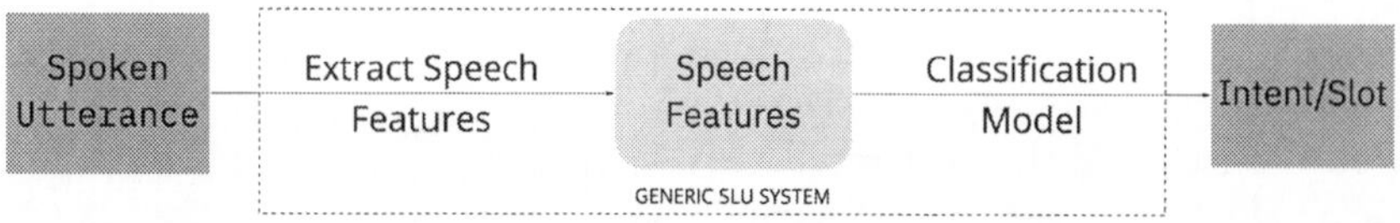

Figure 2: A generic SLU system for language-specific low-resourced setting where we do not have access to speech recognition technologies.

Dataset	Number of Intents	Chosen Intents	Speakers in Validation Set	Utterances in Validation Set	Speakers in Test Set	Utterances in Test Set
FSC (English)	2	'bring newspaper', 'activate washroom lights'	10	194	10	232
FSC (English)	4	'bring newspaper', 'activate washroom lights', 'change language to German', 'decrease volume'	10	519	10	634
Grabo (Flemish)	2	approach', 'lift'	2	106	2	108
Grabo (Flemish)	4	approach', 'lift', 'point', 'grab'	2	212	2	216

Table 1: Validation and Test Set statistics for chosen intents for the FSC and Grabo dataset.

2018), Chinese Mandarin (Zhu et al., 2019; Guo et al., 2021), Sinhala and Tamil (Karunanayake et al., 2019b) do not maintain speaker identities and hence were not suitable for our work. Maintaining a mapping of (anonymized) speaker identities allowed us to create validation and test sets with no speaker overlap with the training set. This allows us to do the most robust evaluation of our systems. Moreover, these datasets also allow us to create large test sets such that the results are robust enough to evaluate the system performance and yet have no overlapping speakers with the training set. We choose Flemish as our low-resourced language since Flemish is not used to train Allosaurus or Wav2Vec 2.0.

FSC is a large and well maintained SLU dataset for the English language. The dataset contains 19 hours of speech data collected from 97 different speakers. The dataset contains commands suitable for a smart home system. An example command would be asking the system to 'change language to Chinese' or to 'turn off the lights in the kitchen'. Each utterance has a clear, anonymized speaker identity associated with it. This allows us to create large validation and test sets with no speakers overlap with the training set. The intents chosen for our experiments and the corresponding number of samples in the validation and test sets are shown in Table 1.

The Grabo dataset contains 11 speakers and is much smaller than FSC. The dataset consists of commands given to a robot such as 'moving right' or 'drive backwards fast'. We use speaker IDs 2-8 to create the training set, speakers 9 and 10 for the validation set, and speakers 11 and 12 for the test set. Thus there is no speaker overlap between the training, validation and test sets. The chosen intents and the validation and test set statistics are shown in Table 1.

4 System and Model

To simulate a language-specific low-resourced setting, we do not use a language specific ASR system. We tackle this challenge by exploring two experimental settings. First we use a generic SLU pipeline as shown in Figure 2. The first step in this pipeline is to extract speech features. We use Wav2Vec 2.0 to extract speech features for Flemish, which represents using a speech recognition system built for a different language. Then, we use the SLU system proposed in (Gupta et al., 2020a) as shown in Figure 3. It replaces a language specific ASR system with Allosaurus (Li et al., 2020), which is a universal phonetic transcription system. We use Allosaurus to convert input speech to phonetic transcriptions. We then build an NLU system from these phonetic transcriptions to perform intent recognition.

The model used in this work is very similar to the model used in (Gupta et al., 2020a) which is a character level model built for a sequence of phones generated by Allosaurus. The model creates its own embeddings using the annotated task-specific dataset and uses Convolutional Neural Networks (CNN) (LeCun et al., 1998) to extract contextual information from phonetic input, and a Long-Short

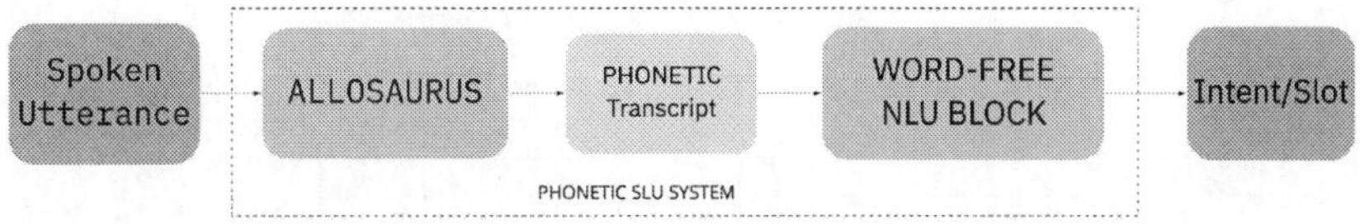

Figure 3: Phonetic transcription based SLU system as proposed in (Gupta et al., 2020a).

Term Memory (LSTM) (Hochreiter and Schmidhuber, 1997) network to make utterance level decision and account for sequential information. This model achieved state-of-the-art intent classification performance for low-resourced languages like Tamil and Sinhala when used without language specific ASR. We keep the model used across experiments constant to identify difference in performance occurring due to difference in feature extraction methods.

We reduce the model size to account for the scarcity of data. We use a 256-dimensional embedding layer with just one CNN layer of kernel size 3 and one or two LSTM layers of hidden dimension 256 depending on the dataset size. For the case of the generic SLU, the embeddings are removed and input feature dimension is dependent on the features extracted. For Wav2Vec 2.0, the feature dimensions are 768. A detailed description of model architecture is provided in the appendix A. Batch normalization (Ioffe and Szegedy, 2015) layer is removed because there are scenarios where we are working with a training set of as low as 2 samples, which are not enough to learn batch statistics and give unstable performance.

5 Experiments

In this paper, we try to emulate a real world low-resourced data collection scenario. A challenging aspect of building SLU systems for low resourced languages is having access to language specific ASR systems. To tackle this, we experiment with two alternatives. We first use a speech recognition systems created for a higher resourced language (English) to extract speech features and use those features for intent recognition on Flemish data (Section 5.1). Then, we create an intent recognition system using a phonetic transcription generated by Allosaurus (Section 5.2). The input audio is converted to language independent phonetic transcriptions, and intent classification is done using the phonetic transcriptions generated.

Data collection is expensive and difficult, even more so in extremely low resourced languages. For example, Canadian Indigenious languages like Inuktitut or Siksika have only a few thousand living speakers. Native speakers of such languages are hard to catch hold of for data collection process. This makes every data point collected crucial. This task-specific low-resourced setting compounds the difficulty in making speech technologies for low-resourced languages.

We pose two I-class intent classification problems, where $I = 2, 4$. The columns of each of the Tables 2-9 in the following sections show results for different values of k, where k is the number of utterances recorded by a speaker per intent. This means that if $k = 3$, each speaker provided 3 recordings for each intent, which amounts to a total of $3 * I$ recordings per speaker. In general, each speaker records $k * I$ audios, where k is the number of audios recorded by a speaker per intent, and I is the number of intents. The rows for each of the tables represent the number of speakers (S) involved in creating the dataset. The total training dataset size is $S * k * I$. All data points in all the following tables represent an average classification accuracy over 3 different random selections of dataset and training the model from scratch on top of it.

5.1 Experiments with Wav2Vec Features

First, we use Wav2Vec 2.0 (Baevski et al., 2020) to extract representations of input speech and use those to perform intent classification on Flemish data. The results for the binary classification setting are shown in Table 2 and for the four-class classification setting is shown in Table 3.

One obvious trend to notice here is that increasing the number of total training samples in general increases the accuracy of the models. This trend is consistently seen in the four-class classification results (Table 3). We also notice a saturation in performance on increasing the number of utterances per speaker. This usually occurs around $k = 4, 5$. For each value of S, we see that adding number of recordings for the same speaker increases the performance significantly, but the rate of this increase starts to reduce when we have $4 - 5$ utterances per

	$k=1$	$k=2$	$k=3$	$k=4$	$k=5$	$k=6$	$k=7$
$S=1$	72.53	74.69	69.44	72.83	74.07	74.38	74.07
$S=2$	69.75	74.69	67.90	63.27	78.70	67.59	69.13
$S=3$	68.20	76.85	82.40	80.86	76.85	74.38	72.83
$S=4$	78.39	64.50	69.13	71.60	75.92	76.85	75.30
$S=5$	70.98	74.07	75.92	78.39	82.09	78.70	76.23
$S=6$	79.62	75.61	87.03	83.95	84.56	83.33	93.82
$S=7$	75.00	76.85	89.19	85.49	91.66	91.97	94.44

Table 2: Two class classification results for the Grabo dataset with 768 dimensional features from Wav2Vec 2.0.

	$k=1$	$k=2$	$k=3$	$k=4$	$k=5$	$k=6$	$k=7$
$S=1$	35.49	37.03	37.19	37.80	39.96	40.12	42.28
$S=2$	39.19	45.21	45.21	45.83	48.76	49.69	53.08
$S=3$	41.82	47.83	53.70	61.57	55.55	63.88	67.59
$S=4$	49.22	45.06	51.23	52.93	60.80	65.27	64.50
$S=5$	44.59	53.39	56.32	66.04	64.96	70.83	66.82
$S=6$	48.14	52.77	58.64	71.91	74.07	74.69	75.30
$S=7$	52.77	56.66	67.12	72.83	79.62	80.09	76.69

Table 3: Four class classification results for the Grabo datasetwith 768 dimensional features from Wav2Vec 2.0.

	$k=1$	$k=2$	$k=3$	$k=4$	$k=5$	$k=6$	$k=7$
$S=1$	75.30	81.17	73.45	79.93	76.23	82.40	78.39
$S=2$	84.87	85.49	93.82	89.81	87.65	91.35	89.50
$S=3$	79.94	95.37	87.65	92.90	90.12	94.75	92.59
$S=4$	83.33	90.74	93.20	95.06	88.58	95.37	92.28
$S=5$	86.11	92.59	92.90	91.35	96.29	94.75	97.83
$S=6$	91.04	91.97	92.28	94.13	96.91	91.97	92.28
$S=7$	85.80	90.74	90.74	90.43	94.44	91.66	95.06

Table 4: Two class classification results for the GRABO (Flemish) dataset using phonetic transcriptions.

	$k=1$	$k=2$	$k=3$	$k=4$	$k=5$	$k=6$	$k=7$
$S=1$	47.83	50.61	50.92	53.85	50.77	52.31	50.00
$S=2$	56.48	64.50	66.82	65.89	67.74	72.22	68.82
$S=3$	59.87	63.58	68.36	69.90	69.75	72.22	70.52
$S=4$	63.88	64.19	68.36	67.43	72.22	71.75	73.76
$S=5$	64.66	67.28	69.44	74.84	72.22	77.31	76.69
$S=6$	66.51	69.59	77.93	77.46	79.62	80.55	82.56
$S=7$	68.51	80.55	81.01	82.09	85.33	85.64	88.73

Table 5: Four class classification results for the GRABO (Flemish) dataset using phonetic transcriptions.

speaker.

5.2 Experiments with Phonetic Transcriptions using Allosaurus

The performance in the compounded low-resourced intent classification setting using Wav2Vec features as seen in the previous was encouraging. In this section, we use Allosaurus to generate phonetic transcriptions of user audio, using the pipeline shown in Figure 3. We then build intent classification systems on top of these phonetic transcriptions. The results for the binary classification setting are shown in Table 4 and for the four-class classification setting in Table 5.

We consistently see better classification performances for almost all experiments when using phonetic transcriptions. We see an average improvement of 12.37% for the binary classification problem and 13.08% for the four-class classification problem, when averaged over 49 different experiments performed in each I-class classification problem. Each experiment represents a accuracy averaged over 3 different random selections of the dataset. Note that the test sets in all the experiments for the binary classification problem are exactly the same with no speaker overlap with the training or the validation set, irrespective of the size of the training set. The same is true for the four-class classification problem.

For the binary classification in Flemish, we see that the improvement in performance when using phonetic transcription becomes more significant as the dataset size reduces. This can be observed when we look at the first 3 columns of Table 4 when compared to Table 2. For example, when $S = 7$ and $k \in [5, 7]$, the performance of the Wav2Vec system is comparable to the phonetic transcription based system. In all other experiments, the phonetic transcription based system outperforms the Wav2Vec feature based system. Table 4 also shows that using just 2-3 speakers are enough to learn generalizable speaker independent features when using Allosaurus phonetic transcription, which allows the classification performance on the test set to be in the 90's. A similar performance requires 6-7 speakers when using Wav2Vec features as shown in Table 2. This can be seen if we look at a system developed with 3 speakers recording 4 utterances each using phonetic transcriptions in Table 4, it is comparable to a 7 speaker system where each speaker records 7 utterances per intent when using Wav2Vec features (Table 2) . We attribute this effect to Allosaurus that creates speaker independent embeddings of input audio. These embeddings when projected to the space of a universal set of phones is more robust to speaker variations.

The performance improvement observed for Flemish when using phonetic transcriptions gets amplified in the four-class classification problem. We see significant improvements when using phonetic transcriptions for all experiments. We see an average improvement of 13.08% over the 49 exper-

	$k=1$	$k=2$	$k=3$	$k=4$	$k=5$	$k=6$	$k=7$
$S=1$	72.84	82.32	84.48	86.20	79.45	83.90	86.78
$S=2$	84.05	89.79	91.23	86.20	94.10	94.10	95.11
$S=3$	77.29	87.78	93.82	95.40	98.27	96.55	97.98
$S=4$	84.33	89.51	93.10	94.97	98.41	98.85	98.13
$S=5$	86.20	89.65	95.25	97.27	98.13	98.70	98.27
$S=6$	86.06	95.25	96.55	98.56	98.70	97.70	99.13
$S=7$	96.69	95.97	96.26	98.70	99.13	98.85	98.85

Table 6: Two class classification results for the FSC (English) Dataset using speech features extracted from Wav2Vec 2.0.

	$k=1$	$k=2$	$k=3$	$k=4$	$k=5$	$k=6$	$k=7$
$S=1$	38.53	42.79	50.36	58.41	59.20	56.15	62.19
$S=2$	46.58	53.73	62.56	64.30	75.23	77.97	84.01
$S=3$	48.63	58.25	75.44	85.80	81.65	81.80	92.74
$S=4$	51.84	76.39	77.70	87.22	89.53	94.00	96.89
$S=5$	77.86	81.59	86.33	91.48	95.58	96.79	96.31
$S=6$	72.02	90.37	81.75	95.58	95.58	95.58	97.05
$S=7$	65.87	85.06	92.32	94.21	95.26	97.21	94.79

Table 7: Four class classification results for the FSC (English) Dataset using speech features extracted from Wav2Vec 2.0.

iments when using phonetic transcriptions. This improvement is large when the amount of data is small which we can check by comparing the first three columns of Tables 3 and 5. If we calculate the improvement when $S \leq 3$ and $k \leq 3$, which we call the 3×3 matrix of the tables, we get an average improvement of 16.25% over the 9 experimental settings. But we also see significant improvement when the amount of data is larger. For example, phonetic transcription based system performs significant better for 7 speakers and 7 recording per speaker when compared to the Wav2Vec features based system. Thus, as the task complexity increases, we see that using phonetic transcriptions is a significantly better option when compared to features from speech-to-text systems created for a different language.

The pipeline proposed in Figure 3 is analogous to the traditional SLU pipline as shown in 1. High resourced languages allows the use of ASR systems which project speech, which is a very long sequence of high dimensional input into a much shorter, 1-dimensional sequence of characters. Thus, ASR systems try to give a 1-dimensional symbolic representation to input speech. This sequence of characters is usually grouped into words or sub-words, which we refer to as tokens in general, and are then projected back into a higher dimensional space as word-embeddings, encoding meaning and context. This is usually done using pre-trained models like BERT

	$k=1$	$k=2$	$k=3$	$k=4$	$k=5$	$k=6$	$k=7$
$S=1$	91.98	93.27	95.56	95.27	95.85	96.71	96.56
$S=2$	95.13	97.99	97.99	98.56	98.56	98.14	97.28
$S=3$	95.85	98.28	97.85	97.65	99.14	99.71	99.28
$S=4$	97.28	98.42	98.14	98.88	98.99	98.85	98.71
$S=5$	98.56	97.56	98.99	98.71	99.28	98.85	99.28
$S=6$	96.71	97.85	98.42	98.56	98.56	98.71	99.58
$S=7$	97.42	99.57	99.42	99.71	99.85	99.57	99.42

Table 8: Two class classification results for the FSC (English) using phonetic transcriptions.

	$k=1$	$k=2$	$k=3$	$k=4$	$k=5$	$k=6$	$k=7$
$S=1$	61.06	62.06	62.79	70.59	69.75	72.29	72.21
$S=2$	65.04	63.99	72.05	77.18	80.06	78.64	81.84
$S=3$	67.13	74.72	75.35	77.91	83.72	85.55	85.29
$S=4$	68.60	79.74	77.18	84.66	84.51	88.54	87.75
$S=5$	72.05	79.59	80.58	87.85	88.27	91.57	92.67
$S=6$	70.80	82.20	83.41	90.16	89.84	91.05	92.83
$S=7$	75.56	80.48	86.65	89.48	91.10	90.99	93.98

Table 9: Four class classification results for the FSC (English) dataset using phonetic transcriptions.

(Devlin et al., 2018), where the different layers of the model encode and understand various possible meanings and contexts in which a token can be used (Tenney et al., 2019). Thus, these pre-trained models can be seen as functions that map an input token into vectors that encode all possible ways the token has been used in the dataset the model is trained on.

The projection by ASR systems into a lower dimensional space of characters causes loss of information and results in errors which is not always compensated by the re-projection of words into the space of word-embeddings, which is why recent research in high resourced languages is moving towards creating E2E models. But this process of projecting high-dimensional and long speech input into a much smaller transcription of symbols, and then re-projecting into the space of word-embeddings encoding meaning and context allows us to create SLU systems with a very small amount of annotated task-specific data.

Our experiments show that the analogous process of projecting down speech into a symbolic transcription of phones and then re-projecting the symbols into a vector space of symbolic embeddings created from the phonetic transcription data performs significantly better than using high dimensional feature representations of input speech, as done with Wav2Vec in section 5.1. The large size of Wav2Vec vectors (768) requires a larger amount of task-specific data to infer content and meaning of input utterances when compared to using phonetic transcription. Using phonetic transcriptions also allow us to create our own vector spaces of symbolic embeddings which are very specific to our dataset and encode the meaning and context in which each phone has been used for the particular task. This is why the pipeline that uses phonetic transcriptions outperforms Wav2Vec based embeddings. (Yadav et al., 2021) show that this is true even when Allosaurus embeddings are compared to phonetic transcriptions generated by Allosaurus. As the amount of available data decreases, intent classification systems built using phonetic transcriptions begin to outperform systems based on Allosaurus embeddings, thus showing that projecting input speech into phonetic transcriptions is the most exhaustive way to use the scarce amount of labelled data in the compounded low-resourced settings.

We verify this by performing the same set of experiment on the English dataset (FSC). We first use Wav2Vec features to extract input speech. The binary classification, the results are shown in Table 6 and for the four-class classification problem, the results are shown in Table 7. Note that Wav2Vec is specifically trained on large amounts of English speech data and thus the features extracted from Wav2Vec are likely to perform much better for English than they worked for Flemish. This experimental setting is thus not a language-specific low-resourced setting anymore, and only a task-specific low-resourced setting. We then create an intent classification system using phonetic transcriptions, as shown in Table 8 and 9. We see an average improvement of 5.42% for the binary classification problem and 2.09% for the four-class classification problem, when averaged over 49 experiments. These improvements are amplified when we compare the 3×3 matrices (when $S \leq 3$ and $k \leq 3$,) for the two classification problems between Wav2Vec based and phonetic transcription based methods. We find an average improvement of 11.14% for the binary classification problem and an average improvement of 14.15% for the four-class classification problem, when averaged over 9 experiments. This shows that a phonetic transcription based SLU pipeline outperforms a speech feature-based pipeline in the low-resourced scenarios, especially when we lack language specific speech recognition technologies.

6 Conclusion

In this paper, we provide a series of experiments to empirically recreate a real-world, low-resourced, SLU system building scenario. We work in the compounded setting of language-specific low-resourced-ness and task-specific low-resourced-ness. The challenge posed by a language-specific low-resourced setting is the absence speech recognition technologies. We bypass this in two ways - firstly, we use a speech recognition system built for a different higher resourced language. Secondly, we use a universal phone recognition system to convert input speech to phonetic transcriptions. To simulate the task-specific low-resource scenario, we present intent classification results at a granularity where we see the effects of changing the number of speakers and the utterances recorded by each speaker. We simulate these settings for Belgian Dutch (Flemish) and English.

We find that using Allosaurus, a universal phone recognition system that creates language and speaker independent representations of input speech, performs better than using Wav2Vec for Flemish dataset. When using Allosaurus, we convert input speech into phonetic transcriptions and use these transcriptions to build NLU models. We find that using phonetic transcription based model performs better than using Wav2Vec features. For Flemish, we see an average improvement of 12.37% for a binary classification problem and an average improvement of 13.08% for a four-class classification over using Wav2Vec features, when averaged over 49 different experimental settings. All results are calculated on a large test set containing hundreds of utterances that has no speaker overlap with the training or validation set. Also, we find that as the dataset size decreases, phonetic transcription based method consistently outperform Wav2Vec feature based methods. Phonetic transcription based models also need fewer speakers to generalize to a test set with no speaker overlap.

Finally, we recommend converting input speech into phonetic transcriptions as an intermediate step for creating SLU systems in such low resourced settings. Doing such conversion allows us to create a task-specific embedding space that uses the small annotated dataset most efficiently.

Disclaimer. This paper was prepared for informational purposes by the Artificial Intelligence Research group of JPMorgan Chase Co and its affiliates ("JP Morgan"), and is not a product of the

Research Department of JP Morgan. JP Morgan makes no representation and warranty whatsoever and disclaims all liability, for the completeness, accuracy or reliability of the information contained herein. This document is not intended as investment research or investment advice, or a recommendation, offer or solicitation for the purchase or sale of any security, financial instrument, financial product or service, or to be used in any way for evaluating the merits of participating in any transaction, and shall not constitute a solicitation under any jurisdiction or to any person, if such solicitation under such jurisdiction or to such person would be unlawful.

References

Alexei Baevski, Yuhao Zhou, Abdelrahman Mohamed, and Michael Auli. 2020. wav2vec 2.0: A framework for self-supervised learning of speech representations. *Advances in Neural Information Processing Systems*, 33:12449–12460.

Emanuele Bastianelli, Andrea Vanzo, Pawel Swietojanski, and Verena Rieser. 2020. SLURP: A spoken language understanding resource package. In *Proceedings of the 2020 Conference on Empirical Methods in Natural Language Processing (EMNLP)*, pages 7252–7262, Online. Association for Computational Linguistics.

Darshana Buddhika, Ranula Liyadipita, Sudeepa Nadeeshan, Hasini Witharana, Sanath Javasena, and Uthayasanker Thayasivam. 2018. Domain specific intent classification of sinhala speech data. In *2018 International Conference on Asian Language Processing (IALP)*, pages 197–202. IEEE.

Yuan-Ping Chen, Ryan Price, and Srinivas Bangalore. 2018. Spoken language understanding without speech recognition. In *2018 IEEE International Conference on Acoustics, Speech and Signal Processing (ICASSP)*, pages 6189–6193. IEEE.

Laurence Devillers, Hélène Maynard, Sophie Rosset, Patrick Paroubek, Kevin McTait, Djamel Mostefa, Khalid Choukri, Laurent Charnay, Caroline Bousquet, Nadine Vigouroux, et al. 2004. The french media/evalda project: the evaluation of the understanding capability of spoken language dialogue systems. In *LREC*. Citeseer.

Jacob Devlin, Ming-Wei Chang, Kenton Lee, and Kristina Toutanova. 2018. Bert: Pre-training of deep bidirectional transformers for language understanding. *arXiv preprint arXiv:1810.04805*.

Allen L Gorin, Giuseppe Riccardi, and Jeremy H Wright. 1997. How may i help you? *Speech communication*, 23(1-2):113–127.

Zhiyuan Guo, Yuexin Li, Guo Chen, Xingyu Chen, and Akshat Gupta. 2021. Word-free spoken language understanding for mandarin-chinese. *arXiv preprint arXiv:2107.00186*.

Akshat Gupta, Olivia Deng, Akruti Kushwaha, Saloni Mittal, William Zeng, Sai Krishna Rallabandi, and Alan W Black. 2021. Intent recognition and unsupervised slot identification for low resourced spoken dialog systems. *arXiv preprint arXiv:2104.01287*.

Akshat Gupta, Xinjian Li, Sai Krishna Rallabandi, and Alan W Black. 2020a. Acoustics based intent recognition using discovered phonetic units for low resource languages. *arXiv preprint arXiv:2011.03646*.

Akshat Gupta, Sai Krishna Rallabandi, and Alan W Black. 2020b. Mere account mein kitna balance hai?–on building voice enabled banking services for multilingual communities. *arXiv preprint arXiv:2010.16411*.

Charles T Hemphill, John J Godfrey, and George R Doddington. 1990. The atis spoken language systems pilot corpus. In *Speech and Natural Language: Proceedings of a Workshop Held at Hidden Valley, Pennsylvania, June 24-27, 1990*.

Sepp Hochreiter and Jürgen Schmidhuber. 1997. Long short-term memory. *Neural computation*, 9(8):1735–1780.

Sergey Ioffe and Christian Szegedy. 2015. Batch normalization: Accelerating deep network training by reducing internal covariate shift. In *International conference on machine learning*, pages 448–456. PMLR.

Yohan Karunanayake, Uthayasanker Thayasivam, and Surangika Ranathunga. 2019a. Sinhala and tamil speech intent identification from english phoneme based asr. In *2019 International Conference on Asian Language Processing (IALP)*, pages 234–239. IEEE.

Yohan Karunanayake, Uthayasanker Thayasivam, and Surangika Ranathunga. 2019b. Transfer learning based free-form speech command classification for low-resource languages. In *Proceedings of the 57th Annual Meeting of the Association for Computational Linguistics: Student Research Workshop*, pages 288–294.

Yann LeCun, Léon Bottou, Yoshua Bengio, and Patrick Haffner. 1998. Gradient-based learning applied to document recognition. *Proceedings of the IEEE*, 86(11):2278–2324.

Xinjian Li, Siddharth Dalmia, Juncheng Li, Matthew Lee, Patrick Littell, Jiali Yao, Antonios Anastasopoulos, David R Mortensen, Graham Neubig, Alan W Black, et al. 2020. Universal phone recognition with a multilingual allophone system. In *ICASSP 2020-2020 IEEE International Conference on Acoustics, Speech and Signal Processing (ICASSP)*, pages 8249–8253. IEEE.

Loren Lugosch, Mirco Ravanelli, Patrick Ignoto, Vikrant Singh Tomar, and Yoshua Bengio. 2019. Speech model pre-training for end-to-end spoken language understanding. *arXiv preprint arXiv:1904.03670*.

Grégoire Mesnil, Yann Dauphin, Kaisheng Yao, Yoshua Bengio, Li Deng, Dilek Hakkani-Tur, Xiaodong He, Larry Heck, Gokhan Tur, Dong Yu, et al. 2014. Using recurrent neural networks for slot filling in spoken language understanding. *IEEE/ACM Transactions on Audio, Speech, and Language Processing*, 23(3):530–539.

Bart Ons, Jort F Gemmeke, et al. 2014. The self-taught vocal interface. *EURASIP Journal on Audio, Speech, and Music Processing*, 2014(1):43.

Yao Qian, Rutuja Ubale, Vikram Ramanaryanan, Patrick Lange, David Suendermann-Oeft, Keelan Evanini, and Eugene Tsuprun. 2017. Exploring asr-free end-to-end modeling to improve spoken language understanding in a cloud-based dialog system. In *2017 IEEE Automatic Speech Recognition and Understanding Workshop (ASRU)*, pages 569–576. IEEE.

Vincent Renkens, Steven Janssens, Bart Ons, Jort F Gemmeke, et al. 2014. Acquisition of ordinal words using weakly supervised nmf. In *2014 IEEE Spoken Language Technology Workshop (SLT)*, pages 30–35. IEEE.

Alaa Saade, Alice Coucke, Alexandre Caulier, Joseph Dureau, Adrien Ball, Théodore Bluche, David Leroy, Clément Doumouro, Thibault Gisselbrecht, Francesco Caltagirone, et al. 2018. Spoken language understanding on the edge. *arXiv preprint arXiv:1810.12735*.

Steffen Schneider, Alexei Baevski, Ronan Collobert, and Michael Auli. 2019. wav2vec: Unsupervised pre-training for speech recognition. *arXiv preprint arXiv:1904.05862*.

Sebastian Schuster, Sonal Gupta, Rushin Shah, and Mike Lewis. 2019. Cross-lingual transfer learning for multilingual task oriented dialog. In *Proceedings of the 2019 Conference of the North American Chapter of the Association for Computational Linguistics: Human Language Technologies, Volume 1 (Long and Short Papers)*, pages 3795–3805, Minneapolis, Minnesota. Association for Computational Linguistics.

Dmitriy Serdyuk, Yongqiang Wang, Christian Fuegen, Anuj Kumar, Baiyang Liu, and Yoshua Bengio. 2018. Towards end-to-end spoken language understanding. In *2018 IEEE International Conference on Acoustics, Speech and Signal Processing (ICASSP)*, pages 5754–5758. IEEE.

Ian Tenney, Dipanjan Das, and Ellie Pavlick. 2019. BERT rediscovers the classical NLP pipeline. In *Proceedings of the 57th Annual Meeting of the Association for Computational Linguistics*, pages 4593–4601, Florence, Italy. Association for Computational Linguistics.

Netsanet Merawi Tessema, Bart Ons, Janneke van de Loo, Jort Gemmeke, Guy De Pauw, Walter Daelemans, et al. 2013. Metadata for corpora patcor and domotica-2. *Technical report KUL/ESAT/PSI/1303, KU Leuven, ESAT, Leuven, Belgium*.

Gokhan Tur and Renato De Mori. 2011. *Spoken language understanding: Systems for extracting semantic information from speech*. John Wiley & Sons.

Mike Wu, Jonathan Nafziger, Anthony Scodary, and Andrew Maas. 2020. Harpervalleybank: A domain-specific spoken dialog corpus. *arXiv preprint arXiv:2010.13929*.

Hemant Yadav, Akshat Gupta, Sai Krishna Rallabandi, Alan W Black, and Rajiv Ratn Shah. 2021. Intent classification using pre-trained embeddings for low resource languages. *arXiv preprint arXiv:2110.09264*.

Su Zhu, Zijian Zhao, Tiejun Zhao, Chengqing Zong, and Kai Yu. 2019. Catslu: The 1st chinese audio-textual spoken language understanding challenge. In *2019 International Conference on Multimodal Interaction*, pages 521–525.

A Implementation Details

All models are trained using the NVIDIA GeForce GTX 1070 GPU using python3.7. The training is very quick due to the small dataset sizes, with each epoch taking 1-2 seconds. For each experiment, a validation set identical to the test set was used. For the FSC dataset, the validation set had 10 speakers with no speaker overlap with the training or the test set. Similarly for the GRABO dataset, the validation set had 2 speakers that were not present in the training or the test set. Each experiment in Tables 2-9 was repeated 3 times with a different training set and the average accuracy has been reported.

As mentioned in section 4, we use a CNN+LSTM architecture, as proposed in (Gupta et al., 2020a). We performed a grid search over various parameters of the architecture. The best performing models varied slightly for each experiment. The exact model parameters for the results reported in Tables 2-9 are shown in Table 10. For larger amounts of utterances recorded per speaker, we found better results with 2 LSTM layers instead of one.

Model Parameters	**Value**
Embedding Size	256
CNN kernel size	3
No. of CNN filters	256
No. of LSTM layers	1 (or 2)
LSTM hidden size	256
Batch Normalization	False

Table 10: Model Parameters

Unsupervised morphological segmentation in a language with reduplication

Simon Todd and **Annie Huang**
Department of Linguistics
University of California, Santa Barbara
{sjtodd, anniehuang}@ucsb.edu

Jeremy Needle
jeremyneedle@gmail.com

Jennifer Hay and **Jeanette King**
New Zealand Institute of Language, Brain and Behaviour
University of Canterbury
{jen.hay, j.king}@canterbury.ac.nz

Abstract

We present an extension of the Morfessor Baseline model of unsupervised morphological segmentation (Creutz and Lagus, 2007) that incorporates abstract templates for reduplication, a typologically common but computationally underaddressed process. Through a detailed investigation that applies the model to Māori, the Indigenous language of Aotearoa New Zealand, we show that incorporating templates improves Morfessor's ability to identify instances of reduplication, and does so most when there are multiple minimally-overlapping templates. We present an error analysis that reveals important factors to consider when applying the extended model and suggests useful future directions.

1 Introduction

Unsupervised models that can learn to segment words into morphemes without requiring extensive hand-written rules have two important advantages (see Creutz and Lagus, 2007, for discussion). First, their unsupervised nature allows them to capture a key facet of human morphological learning: learning despite the lack of both direct and negative evidence. Second, their lack of hand-written rules makes them very flexible: they can be deployed in a range of applications, across diverse languages.

However, in order to learn effectively, unsupervised models must make general assumptions about underlying morphological processes, and their success in part reflects the appropriateness of these assumptions for the language(s) under investigation. This can cause the underlying assumptions to become tuned to the morphological processes of high-resource languages used in development and evaluation (Bender, 2009), leading models to overlook processes that do not occur in such languages, even if they are typologically common.

Recent work has highlighted the advantages to such models of incorporating expert linguistic knowledge, such as language-specific morphemes and/or abstract morphological templates (Butler, 2016; Eskander et al., 2016; Godard et al., 2018; Xu et al., 2020). We explore the value added to a standard baseline model, Morfessor (Creutz and Lagus, 2007; Virpioja et al., 2013), by incorporating templates for reduplication, a typologically common but computationally underaddressed process. We conduct a detailed analysis of the successes and challenges in using an enriched model to capture reduplication in Māori (Polynesian), the Indigenous language of Aotearoa New Zealand, which reveals a promising path for unsupervised morphological segmentation of languages with reduplication more broadly.

2 Background

2.1 Unsupervised morphological segmentation

Morphological segmentation aims to identify boundaries within words by splitting them into parts, as in *de + forest + ation*. In unsupervised approaches, the inventory of parts is inferred from the training data, by identifying the *morphs* – sequences of characters, phonemes, or larger 'atoms' – that recur across words with statistical regularity. There are several models for unsupervised morphological segmentation, many permitting fine-grained structural assumptions about underlying morphological processes (e.g. Goldsmith, 2001; Johnson and Griffiths, 2007; Eskander et al., 2016; Godard et al., 2018; Xu et al., 2018, 2020).

We focus on the Morfessor family of models (Creutz and Lagus, 2007), often used as a baseline due to its extremely simple assumptions. Morfessor uses a Minimum Description Length framework

19th SIGMORPHON Workshop on Computational Research in Phonetics, Phonology, and Morphology, pages 12 - 22
July 14, 2022 ©2022 Association for Computational Linguistics

(Rissanen, 1978): it aims to identify the smallest and simplest set of morphs (the *lexicon*) that generates the training data with highest probability. The lexicon is treated as a bag of morphs, where the cost of adding a given morph to the lexicon in training is based on the complexity of its form as well as the frequency with which it recurs across words. The training data are assumed to be generated from the lexicon by concatenating morphs that are drawn independently from it, with no consideration of contraints based on position, sequencing, or morphosyntactic category. Morfessor is particularly suited to languages that make heavy use of concatenative morphological processes with limited or no phonological alternations. We explore whether it can be expanded to account for reduplication, by extending the Python implementation of Morfessor 2.0 (Virpioja et al., 2013).

2.2 Reduplication and Morfessor

Reduplication is defined by Rubino (2005) as "the systematic repetition of phonological material within a word for semantic or grammatical purposes". Informally, it is often described as a process by which a *reduplicant* phonologically 'copies' part of a *base* to which it is morphologically attached. The reduplicant may copy the entire base, as in the Māori *pakipaki* 'to clap' (from *paki* 'to slap'), or only part of it, as in Māori *nunui* 'big.PL' (from *nui* 'big.SG'). In formal linguistic theory, the reduplicant is commonly treated as a morpheme, RED, which has little or no inherent phonological content, and copies content from the base in order to satisfy prosodic wellformedness templates (e.g. Marantz, 1982; McCarthy and Prince, 1996). In this view, the reduplicant attaches to the base in the same way as any other morpheme would. However, for clarity, we notate these kinds of morphological attachment differently, using ⊕ to represent a boundary between a reduplicant and its base, and + to represent all other boundaries.

Rubino (2013) reports that 85% of languages documented in the World Atlas of Language Structures include some productive form of reduplication. Yet, despite its prominence, reduplication is not typically given special treatment in unsupervised approaches to morphological segmentation. For Morfessor, we are only aware of one system incorporating reduplication (Butler, 2016); however, it identifies and rewrites potential instances of reduplication *outside* of Morfessor, following a heuristic, rather than *within* Morfessor, according to statistical evaluation. It treats reduplication as a feature of the data rather than of the probabilistic grammar of the language, limiting the ability to leverage knowledge of reduplication to navigate ambiguity or generalize beyond the training set.[1]

The lack of integrated special treatment of reduplication limits Morfessor's ability to consistently identify reduplicants, due to their variable form. In turn, the repeated failure to isolate reduplicants from their bases limits Morfessor's ability to identify these bases as independent morphs elsewhere, outside of reduplication. The incorporation of special treatment of reduplication into Morfessor thus stands to vastly improve its reliability, not only in reduplicated words but also in general.

2.3 The Māori language

Māori is an ideal test case for four reasons. First, its orthography maps to phonemes unambiguously[2], enabling morphological segmentation to be applied straightforwardly to written words. Second, it has clear atoms for morphological segmentation, as morpheme boundaries typically coincide with the boundaries of (C)V units (Bauer, 1993). Third, its morphology predominantly includes concatenative processes (Krupa, 1968) and makes heavy use of compounding, alongside a few highly productive affixes (Bauer, 1993; Harlow, 1993). Fourth, approximately 25% of its word types include reduplication (often alongside other morphological processes; Todd et al., 2019), implying that it stands to gain a lot from the incorporation of reduplication into morphological segmentation systems.

Māori has many kinds of reduplication (see Keegan, 1996), all requiring the base to contain at least 2 morae, where a syllable with a short vowel has 1 mora and a syllable with a long vowel has 2 (Harlow, 1991). We focus on the 5 most common kinds: *full*, in which the reduplicant copies the whole base; *left-1*, in which it copies the first mora from the base; *left-1L*, in which it copies the first mora and lengthens its vowel; *left-2*, in which it copies the first 2 morae from a base containing at least 3 morae; and *right*, in which it copies the last 2 morae from a base containing 4 morae, where the first syllable has a long vowel (see Table 1).

[1] A direct comparison between our extension to Morfessor and alternative models is left for future work.

[2] Each phoneme is represented by a single character, except for the digraphs ⟨wh⟩ (/f/) and ⟨ng⟩ (/ŋ/). Macrons ⟨ā, ē, ī, ō, ū⟩ designate long vowels.

Kind	Examples
full	*pakipaki, whiuwhiu, tōtō*
left-1	*nunui, hahana, huhū*
left-1L	*kākahu, mīmiro, rērere*
left-2	*huahuaki, kuikuia, māmāika*
right	*tākaikai, hāmamamama, ūkuikui*

Table 1: Common kinds of Māori reduplication.

3 Extending Morfessor to reduplication

3.1 General approach

Consistent with the common approach within linguistic theory, we treat all reduplicants as corresponding to one morph, RED, which has no phonological content. We add RED to the lexicon underlying the Morfessor training and testing algorithms, such that identifying a new instance of reduplication allows the algorithms to ignore the form-based component of the cost of the reduplicant, and to reduce its usage-based cost by pooling counts across all other reduplicants in already-identified instances of reduplication. Importantly, we do not assume that all potential instances of reduplication are actual instances of reduplication, either in training (Section 3.2) or in testing (Section 3.3).[3]

We use manually-defined templates to identify potential instances of reduplication, which are assessed by Morfessor for their statistical support as actual instances. The templates are loosely specified, to permit them to capture arbitrary copying in any language. Given the side of reduplicant attachment and the minimum size of the base, potential instances of reduplication are flagged by string comparison of adjacent sequences of atoms (phonemes, syllables, etc.). Additional specifications can be added on a language-by-language basis, leveraging expert knowledge for tighter control; these may include constraints on size or shape of the reduplicant or base, or even systematic alternations between correspondents in the reduplicant and base (e.g. Māori *left-1L* reduplication, *kākahu*).

For Māori, we define three mutually-exclusive templates as generalizations over the kinds and constraints described in Section 2.3. In all templates, the base must be at least bimoraic. In the full-reduplication template, the reduplicant and base must be the same size; in the left-reduplication template, the reduplicant may be any size smaller than the base, and, if monosyllabic, may consist of a single syllable that lengthens the vowel of its correspondent in the base; and in the right-reduplication template, the reduplicant must be at least bimoraic and shorter than the base, which must have a long vowel in the first syllable. Because the templates are mutually exclusive, each may be included in the model or excluded, independent of the others.[4]

We also make the (Māori-specific) assumption that the base must be morphologically simplex (following Krupa, 1968). Thus, when Morfessor commits to analyzing a word as an instance of reduplication (e.g. of analyzing *tākaikai* as tākai $\oplus$ RED), we block it from considering any future placement of boundaries within the minimal base (tākai).

3.2 Training models with reduplication

Training in Morfessor uses the recursive splitting algorithm (henceforth, RS; Creutz and Lagus, 2002). For a given input, RS evaluates all possible analyses that split the input into two parts, as well as the analysis that leaves it unsplit. It chooses the analysis for which the associated parameter update permits lowest-cost generation of the training data. If the chosen analysis splits the input into parts, the algorithm recurses to evaluate analyses of each part; otherwise, it moves on to evaluate the next input. It cycles through all words in a training set once per epoch, and repeats until the epoch-wise decrease in cost falls below a threshold.

We extend RS to consider reduplication. When the analysis under consideration splits a potential reduplicant at the edge of the input from its apparent base (e.g. nu $\oplus$ nui), we consider an analysis that replaces the reduplicant with RED (RED $\oplus$ nui). This analysis will be chosen if it is associated with lower cost than any alternative.

We do not automatically consider an analysis involving reduplication if the potential reduplicant is not at the edge of the input, as in many words involving compounding or affixation (e.g. *whārarahi*, whā + [RED $\oplus$ rahi]). If the compound component or affix (*whā*) is split off first, leaving the reduplicant at the edge of one part (*rarahi*), we consider reduplication as above. Otherwise, we only con-

[3]Code for our approach, consisting of a patch to Morfessor 2.0 (Virpioja et al., 2013), is available at `https://github.com/sjtodd/morfessoRED`. At the time of writing, detailed documentation is still under development.

[4]The full-reduplication template assumes that the 'default' side on which the reduplicant attaches is the left, unless the left-reduplication template is not included in the model and the right-reduplication template is, in which case it assumes attachment on the right for parsimony.

sider reduplication if RS finds no binary-splitting analysis that is better than leaving the input unsplit (whārarahi), in which case we evaluate whether the ternary-splitting analysis implied by reduplication is associated with lower cost than the unsplit analysis. This allows reduplication to be leveraged as a cue to the presence of compounding or affixation, but ensures that we do not overgeneralize by relying on this cue too strongly.

Finally, if it is ambiguous whether an edge-aligned reduplicant corresponds to full-reduplication or another kind of reduplication (e.g. whether *huahuaki* is [RED ⊕ hua] + ki or RED ⊕ huaki), we leave both options open by neither enforcing nor restricting a boundary placement after the apparent full-reduplication base (hua). If RS goes on to place a boundary here, we analyze it as full-reduplication; otherwise, we analyze it as the other kind of reduplication. This is consistent with the use of loosely-specified templates that allow arbitrary copying.

3.3 Applying models to seen and unseen data

In testing, Morfessor uses the segmentation obtained from RS if the word was observed in training. Otherwise, it uses the Viterbi algorithm (Viterbi, 1967) to find the optimal path through potential boundary sites (see Virpioja et al., 2013).

The standard Viterbi algorithm proceeds 'horizontally' through potential boundary sites in a word, identifying at each site the optimal previous site to have come from in left-to-right order (Figure 1(a)). We extend the algorithm by adding a 'vertical' dimension, which holds partial analyses matching different reduplication templates (Figure 1(b)). At each potential boundary site in the word, the set of 'horizontal' candidates for optimal previous site is augmented with a small number of directly neighboring 'vertical' sites representing partial analyses based on reduplication templates. As in RS, the reduplicant is replaced by RED in the evaluation of reduplication partial analyses.

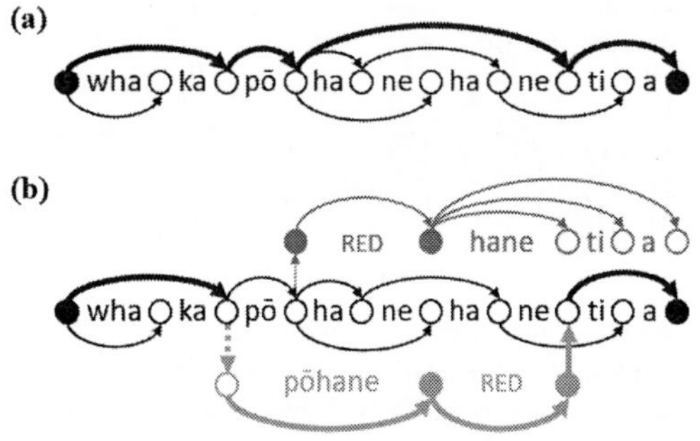

Figure 1: Segmentation traces for *whakapōhanehanetia* from the Viterbi algorithm. Solid circles indicate required boundaries. We extend the standard algorithm (a) by adding a dimension for reduplication paths (b).

Data	*full*	*left-1*	*left-1L*	*left-2*	*right*
Training	816	588	169	786	1191
Test	747	314	79	56	693

Table 2: Distribution of words across different kinds of reduplication. The training data also contains 16,045 other words, many of which combine reduplication with compounding and/or affixation.

4 Experiments

4.1 Data

The models were trained on a set of 19,595 word types from the Te Aka Dictionary (Moorfield, 2011), with all kinds of morphological structures (i.e. not just reduplication). To form this set, we took all headwords, together with their listed inflections. When a headword was composed of words separated by whitespace or hyphens, we split it into components. We then removed (capitalized) proper nouns, because they are likely to be place name borrowings, or are otherwise unlikely to follow the same morphological grammar as other words.

The models were tested on a set of 1,889 word types categorized by Keegan (1996, Appendices A–D) as clear instances of the kinds of reduplication under investigation. Based on Keegan's categorization, we inferred a gold standard segmentation for each word. We removed words where the apparent base was likely morphologically complex, as determined by consisting of more than 4 morae or more than 3 syllables (cf. Krupa, 1968; de Lacy, 2003), to allow us to focus on the ability to capture reduplication without influence of other morphological processes. We cross-referenced the final test items with the Te Aka Dictionary (Moorfield, 2011) in order to ensure consistency in the identification of long vowels. 83.5% of the test items were in the dictionary (i.e. the training data).

Table 2 shows the distribution of words across reduplication templates in the two datasets.

4.2 Metrics

We report four metrics: accuracy, recall, and two versions of precision. Each metric is macro-

Segmentation	*Acc.*	*Rec.*	*Prec.0*	*Prec.1*
tākai ⊕ kai	1	1	1	1
tā + kaikai	0	0	0	0
tā + kai ⊕ kai	0	1	0.5	0.5
tākaikai	0	0	0	1

Table 3: Example metrics for various segmentations of *tākaikai*, where + designates a boundary and ⊕ designates the gold boundary between reduplicant and base. This designation is for ease of reference only; all predicted boundaries are treated alike in calculations.

Model	Acc.	Rec.	Prec.0	Prec.1
original	0.23	0.34	0.28	0.59
extended	**0.83**	**0.98**	**0.91**	**0.91**

Table 4: Test metrics for original Morfessor (no reduplication templates) and extended model (all templates).

averaged, i.e. calculated on a per-word basis and then averaged across all words in the test set. All metrics are calculated based on the morph boundaries contained within the segmentation of a word. Since the words in the test set have morphologically simplex bases for reduplication, the gold standard segmentation contains only a single boundary.

For a given word, accuracy (*Acc.*) is 1 if the model predicts a single boundary matching the gold boundary, and 0 otherwise. Recall (*Rec.*) is 1 if the model's predicted boundaries include the gold boundary, and 0 otherwise. When the model predicts $n \geq 1$ boundaries, both versions of precision (*Prec.0* and *Prec.1*) are $1/n$ if one of those boundaries is the gold boundary, and 0 otherwise. When the model leaves a word unsplit, predicting no boundaries for it, *Prec.0* is 0, while *Prec.1* is 1.[5] The metrics are illustrated in Table 3.

4.3 Overall effects of reduplication templates

Our results show that incorporating reduplication templates leads to substantial improvements over the original Morfessor model (see Table 4). The original model has two main issues. First, it predicts no boundaries for a lot of test items (571 items / 30.2%). Second, the boundaries it does predict usually do not match the gold boundary; for example, it predicts a single boundary for 1,094 items (57.9%), but this only matches the gold boundary 39.9% of the time (437 items). Even when it (incorrectly) predicts multiple boundaries (224 items), the gold boundary is not among them 9.4% of the time (21 items). By contrast, the extended model predicts no boundaries for very few test cases (14 items / 0.7%) and a single boundary for most (1,579 items / 83.6%), matching the gold boundary 99.4% of the time (1,570 items). It (incorrectly) predicts multiple boundaries slightly more often than the original (296 items), but it is rarer for the gold boundary not to be among them (13 items / 4.4%).

[5] *Prec.1* is the version of precision in the Morfessor 2.0 Python implementation (Virpioja et al., 2013). It artificially rewards models that leave words unsplit; introducing *Prec.0* allows us to make comparisons that account for this. To avoid ambiguity of interpretation resulting from the presence of two versions of precision, we do not calculate an F-score.

n	Templates			*Acc.*	*Rec.*	*Prec.0*	*Prec.1*
0	-F	-L	-R	0.23	0.34	0.28	0.59
1	-F	+L	-R	0.34	0.44	0.39	0.67
1	-F	-L	+R	0.47	0.53	0.50	0.77
1	+F	-L	-R	0.48	0.83	0.65	0.72
2	+F	-L	+R	0.54	0.87	0.70	0.75
2	+F	+L	-R	0.59	0.97	0.78	0.79
2	-F	+L	+R	0.65	0.71	0.68	0.86
3	+F	+L	+R	**0.83**	**0.98**	**0.91**	**0.91**

Table 5: Test metrics for models with different numbers (n) and types of reduplication templates.

4.4 Effects of individual templates

Table 5 gives a comparison of models with different combinations of templates. It clearly shows that all templates are needed in order to attain best model performance. It also shows that performance generally increases with the number of templates included, especially if they cover a diverse and minimally-overlapping range of situations.

When the model contains only a single reduplication template, its performance is largely driven by the prevalence of that template in the test data. When the model contains two templates, performance is no longer driven entirely by prevalence, because the templates may interact: both may match the same test item and compete over it, while neither matches a large class of other items. For example, the two-template model containing right- and full-reduplication templates performs worse than the model containing left- and full-reduplication templates, despite there being more *right* test items than *left* test items.

The templates interact here for two main reasons. The full-reduplication template interacts with any other because it allows the reduplicant to attach on

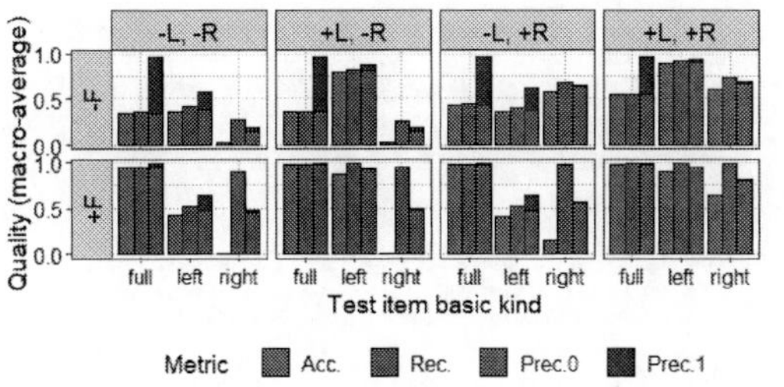

Figure 2: Performance metrics for models with different reduplication templates on test items with different basic kinds of reduplication.

a 'default' side set by the other template. Combining the left- and full-reduplication templates causes competition over *left-2* test items (e.g. RED ⊕ huaki vs. [RED ⊕ hua] + ki for *huahuaki*) and coercion of all *right* test items to the full-reduplication template (e.g. tā + [RED ⊕ kai] for *tākaikai*), and vice versa for combining the right- and full-reduplication templates. The full- and right-reduplication templates also interact because they both allow reduplicants of the same size. Combining them in a single model causes some *right* test items to be coerced to the full-reduplication template (e.g. tā + [RED ⊕ kai] for *tākaikai*), while *left-1* items (e.g. *nunui*) are left unmatched to any template.

Above and beyond such interactions, a consistent property of the full-reduplication template shines through: it consistently closes the gap between the two versions of precision. This suggests that, in the absence of relevant templates, *full* test items such as *pakipaki* are typically predicted not to contain a boundary. To a human, this failure to predict a boundary is remarkable, as full reduplication is a highly salient cue to morphological structure.

4.5 Kinds of reduplication captured

To confirm the idea that the model performs well with the addition of new templates because they allow more (and more diverse) test items to be matched to a template, we explored performance across items representing different kinds of reduplication. The results (Figure 2) confirm three key patterns noted earlier. First, the model containing all templates performs best because it can capture all kinds of reduplication well. Second, models generally perform better on a given kind of reduplication when they include the corresponding template; for example, *left* items are best captured if models contain the left-reduplication template. Third, interactions between templates can cause competition, reducing performance on certain kinds of items. For example, when the model contains the right-reduplication template but not the left-reduplication template, accuracy and precision for *right* items decrease with the inclusion of the full-reduplication template, as discussed in Section 4.4.

There is also a fourth pattern, which elaborates on the observation that performance generally increases with the number of templates included. In Figure 2, it is clear that the increase is not driven just by the diversification of templates, but also by the increased statistical support that more templates bring for the recognition of RED as a morph. Since the same RED morph is shared across all templates, increased ability to identify RED in test items matching one template may also increase the ability to identify it in test items matching a different template. This can be seen in the way that adding the right-reduplication template to a model already including the left-reduplication template causes an improvement on *left* test items.

The same patterns are revealed by detailed breakdowns within a given kind of reduplication, as shown for left-reduplication in Figure 3. This breakdown also shows that different subkinds exhibit the patterns to different extents. For example, *left-1* items benefit more from the inclusion of the left-reduplication template than *left-1L* items do, because the CV̄ reduplicant in *left-1L* cases typically has the same form as one of several (fossilized) prefixes that recur across a number of words (Krupa, 1968; Harlow, 2007), so it has sufficient statistical support to be segmented away from the base without recourse to reduplication. Similarly, *left-2* items are uniquely affected by an interaction that sees them coerced to a full-reduplication template (e.g. [RED ⊕ horo] + i instead of RED ⊕ horoi for *horohoroi*), because only they have a bimoraic reduplicant that is identical to its correspondent in the base.

These results show that careful thought is needed when adding reduplication templates to the model. If templates are attuned to distinct reduplication patterns in the language, they can allow the model to perform well both specifically, on items matching these templates, and generally, across all items containing reduplication. But, if the templates are too general or too numerous, they can interact with each other and endanger the ability to capture particular subsets of test items.

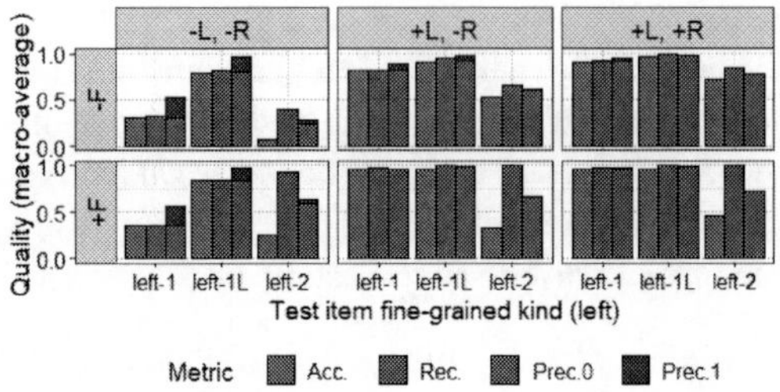

Figure 3: Performance metrics for models with different reduplication templates on test items with different kinds of left-reduplication.

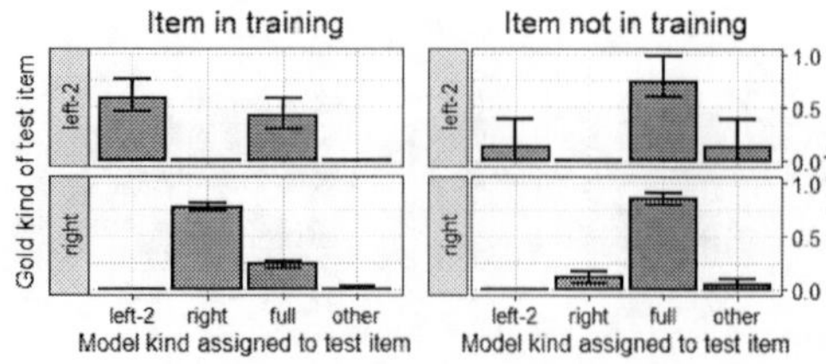

Figure 4: Partial confusion matrix for classification of *left-2* and *right* test items, based on whether the item was in the training data.

5 Error analysis and improvements

5.1 Coercion to full reduplication

As previously noted, different reduplication templates can interact (Section 4.4), affecting model performance on items with certain kinds of reduplication (Section 4.5). In particular, including the full-reduplication template can limit accuracy and precision on *left-2* and *right* test items, as these items are coerced to match the full template rather than their own. Since the best model includes all templates, it shows these interactions: coercion of *left-2* and *right* test items to the full-reduplication template accounts for 88.4% of errors (221 of 250). Nevertheless, because there are so many *full* items in the test set, and because the identification of RED in these highly salient items offers increased statistical support for the identification of RED elsewhere, it is still better to include the full-reduplication template than not, as shown in Table 5.

One strategy for reducing coercion of *left-2* items to the full-reduplication template might be to require that, when the left-reduplication template is matched, the base must be longer than the reduplicant. Currently, the base must contain at least 2 morae, but it is not required to be longer if the reduplicant is bimoraic. However, this would likely cause problems for items involving full reduplication alongside compounding or affixation, such as *tomotomokanga* ([RED ⊕ tomo] + kanga), which are omitted from the current test set but frequent in the language. These would only be able to be recognized as containing full reduplication if the part of the word that is not reduplicated is split off prior to the reduplication template being matched, which is unlikely as RED has more statistical support than any single affix or compound component.

This strategy would not apply to *right* items, as that template already requires that the base be longer than the reduplicant. These items are coerced to the full-reduplication template mainly because the initial CV̄ has the same form as one of several prefixes (cf. Section 4.5). A strategy for mitigating this might be to introduce a penalty for overzealous splitting off of monosyllabic morphs. The size of such a penalty would have to be tuned carefully so that an initial CV̄ syllable can still be split off outside of *right* items, where it has no better alternative analysis than as a prefix.

5.2 Coercion-blocking and Viterbi decoding

As described in Section 3.3, segmentations are obtained for test items in different ways. For items observed in training, the segmentation obtained from RS is used, while for items not observed in training, a segmentation is obtained from the Viterbi algorithm. As shown in Figure 4, it is test items that were not observed in training that show the most coercion to the full-reduplication template.[6]

RS blocks coercion to the full-reduplication template because it commits to boundaries one at a time. In RS, a *right* item such as *tākaikai* will usually have its first boundary placed in-between the reduplicant and base (tākai ⊕ RED), which commits the algorithm to a right-reduplication template and prevents any further boundaries from being placed within the base (tākai). The only way RS could end up coercing the item to the full-reduplication template (tā + [RED ⊕ kai]) is if it placed the first boundary after the initial CV̄ syllable (tā + kaikai) instead, but this is unlikely because the CV̄ syllable is much less common than RED and thus has less statistical support for being split off.

By contrast, the Viterbi algorithm does not

[6]The extended model still outperforms original Morfessor on items not observed in training, in spite of the large amount of coercion, through improved treatment of other kinds of reduplication. Metrics on untrained items (*Acc. / Rec. / Prec.0 / Prec.1*) for original: 0.29 / 0.49 / 0.38 / 0.41; for extended: 0.51 / 0.94 / 0.72 / 0.72.

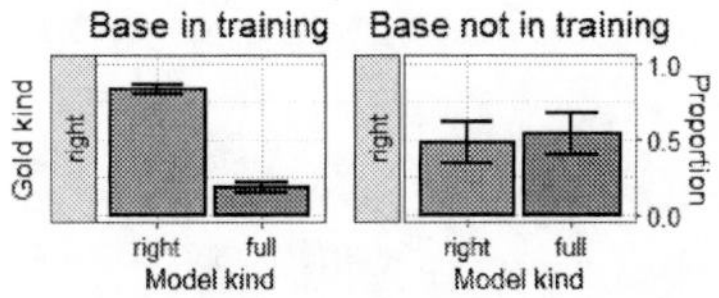

Figure 5: Partial confusion matrix for classification of *right* test items from the training data, based on whether the base was separately observed in training.

block coercion to the full-reduplication template because it does not commit to boundaries independent of each other. When evaluating the best segmentation for a *right* item such as *tākaikai*, it will typically end up comparing the complete full-reduplication segmentation (tā + [RED ⊕ kai]) with the complete right-reduplication segmentation (tākai ⊕ RED). Because the initial CV̄ syllable (tā) recurs across words much more than the actual base (tākai), the full-reduplication template will typically have more statistical support.

This difference suggests two possible strategies for improving model performance. One is to train the model on as many different word types as possible, increasing the chance that any given test item will have been observed in training and will therefore get its segmentation through RS. An alternative strategy is to develop a recursive segmentation algorithm that can be used in testing without triggering changes to trained model parameters.

5.3 Independence of the base

While *right* test items that were observed in training are coerced to the full-reduplication template much less often than those that were not observed, they are still coerced sometimes (see Figure 4). As shown in Figure 5, RS coerces *right* test items to the full-reduplication template more often when the base for reduplication was not separately observed in training. This is because it considers the statistical support for both word-parts created by the insertion of a boundary: the base and the reduplicant. When the base is listed independently in the training set, both parts have some support, and the segmentation is likely to be accepted. But when the base is not listed in the training set – for example, for the word *pānekeneke* – only RED has support, and the algorithm penalizes the right-reduplication segmentation for having to add the base to the lexicon. By contrast, the placement of a boundary after the initial CV̄ syllable (pā + nekeneke) can yield two word-parts that are already listed in the training set (*pā* and *nekeneke*), offering a penalty-free alternative segmentation. Because RS inherits its pre-identified substructure of word-parts, and because one of the parts in this case is likely to have been pre-identified as an instance of full reduplication (RED ⊕ neke), the alternative segmentation amounts to coercion to the full-reduplication template. Both the right-reduplication segmentation and the alternative segmentation therefore gain equally strong statistical support from RED, and the alternative segmentation typically wins because it does not enforce a new-morph penalty.

One strategy that might limit errors when the base for reduplication is not in the training set is to alter RS to block the inheritance of pre-identified substructure pertaining to a reduplication template. However, it is possible that this would limit the ability to use reduplication as a cue to the internal structure of a compound such as *pōpōroroa*.

6 Experiments on complex words

To see how incorporating reduplication templates affects segmentation of morphologically complex words, we now compare the extended model (all templates) with the original (no templates) on a broader subset of training data, examining their agreement with fluent-speaker segmentations.

Data. We analyze model segmentations of 4,213 words of 3+ morae on which two fluent speakers of Māori agreed. None of these words contain long vowels, since we have documented elsewhere that these speakers show an extreme sensitivity to long vowels (Todd et al., 2019; Panther et al., under review); for example, they segmented *hāro* (which is morphologically simplex) as hā + ro, and routinely split off the initial long-vowel syllable of *right* reduplication items, as in kā + witi ⊕ witi and hā + upaupa. As such, the dataset contains no instances of *right* or *left-1L* reduplication, which require a long vowel, and reduced instances of *left-2* reduplication, for which the reduplicant may contain a long vowel. It also contains no instances of *full* reduplication alone (e.g. *pakipaki*), as the original data collection purposes did not require segmentations for words with transparent structures.

Methods. We treat the fluent-speaker segmentations as a reference set, such that performance metrics describe *agreement* between models and speakers. This approach is imperfect; for example, the speakers failed to segment a number of instances of *left-1* reduplication (e.g. ririki instead of ri ⊕ riki) and missegmented others (e.g. hoho + rea instead of ho ⊕ hore + a). In particular, due to the concentration of speaker errors on reduplicated words and the omission of a large host of reduplicated words from the dataset, this approach under-rewards models that correctly handle reduplication. Nevertheless, it gives a sense of how the models perform in more complex settings than our previous test set.

Results. On this subset, the models have very similar accuracies (agreement with speakers): 0.68 for the original model, and 0.70 for the extended model. Thus, incorporating reduplication templates does not hurt model performance in general.

Figure 6 breaks down the results by morphological process for the 3,380 words judged by the speakers to involve affixation and/or compounding. The extended model performs much better than the original on complex reduplicated words, generalizing advantages seen previously for simple words. While it performs slightly worse than the original on complex non-reduplicated words, particularly affixed words, this decrease is small relative to the increased performance on reduplicated words, and does not decrease performance overall.

Error analysis. There are 228 words for which the extended model is discrepant with the speakers but the original is not. We could unambiguously infer a correct segmentation from Te Aka (Moorfield, 2011) for 191 words, highlighting three main reasons for discrepancies. First, the speakers failed to segment reduplicant in 39 reduplicated words. This reflects imperfections of the reference set, not failures of the model. Second, the model identifies reduplication in 31 non-reduplicated words (e.g. ni ⊕ nia instead of nini + a). False positives like these are to be expected, and can be tolerated because they are few in relation to the true positives. Third, the model undersegments in 102 words, including failing to segment out affixes in 71 words. This is not a major cause for concern, as the undersegmentation is not systematic: the missed affixes are correctly segmented in other words.

7 Conclusion

We have described a method to incorporate abstract reduplication templates into the Morfessor baseline model of unsupervised morphological segmentation (Creutz and Lagus, 2007; Virpioja et al., 2013). Our test on Māori shows three main results. First, incorporating templates allows Morfessor to better identify instances of reduplication. Second, the more distinct templates incorporated, the better the model performs. Third, the benefits of incorporating additional templates are strongest for items matching those templates, but also present for items matching other templates, due to the pooling of statistical support for the reduplicant morph, RED.

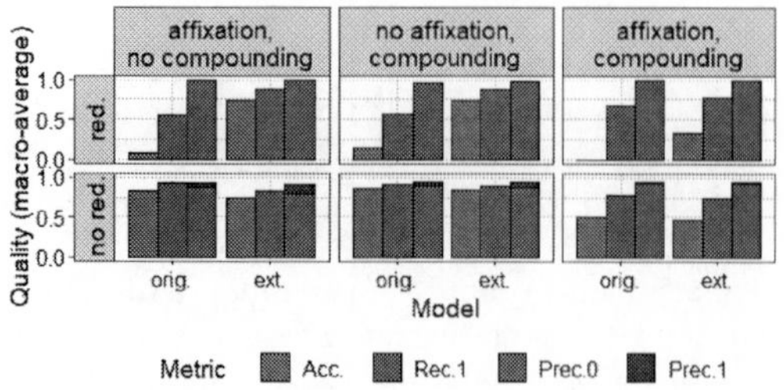

Figure 6: Performance metrics for original and extended Morfessor models against fluent-speaker segmentations of 3,380 words involving affixation and/or compounding, with (top) or without (bottom) reduplication.

We have also discussed factors that should be considered when applying the extended model. First, care should be taken to minimize interactions between templates, to avoid competition that coerces multiple kinds of reduplication to the same template. Second, the training set should be as large and as similar to the test set as possible, because coercion between templates is more prevalent in the Viterbi algorithm used for untrained items than it is in the recursive algorithm used for trained items. Third, the training set should include both reduplicated forms and their (apparent) bases of reduplication, as excluding the base can preclude it from being identified in the reduplicated form, which can in turn increase the risk of coercion to an incorrect reduplication template.

Our results clearly show the value of incorporating expert linguistic knowledge into unsupervised morphological segmentation. We have shown how this improves segmentation of reduplicated words in Māori, while still permitting accuracy on non-reduplicated words. While we have focused on Māori, we expect performance gains to transfer to other Polynesian languages with similar reduplication templates, and we expect the higher level modeling approach and insights to extend more broadly to any language that has productive reduplication processes. Given the high typological prominence of reduplication (Rubino, 2013), the incorporation of reduplication templates offers a promising avenue for improving the cross-linguistic adequacy of unsupervised morphological segmentation.

Acknowledgments

We thank the three anonymous reviewers for their feedback. We are grateful to Te Puawai Wilson-Leahy and Tamahou Thoms for providing fluent-speaker segmentations, and to John C. Moorfield for permission to use data from Te Aka. This work was supported by funding from Te Pūtea Rangahau a Marsden / The Marsden Fund (UOC1502).

References

Winifred Bauer. 1993. *Maori*. Routledge, London.

Emily M. Bender. 2009. Linguistically naïve != language independent: Why NLP needs linguistic typology. In *Proceedings of the EACL 2009 Workshop on the Interaction between Linguistics and Computational Linguistics: Virtuous, Vicious or Vacuous?*, pages 26–32.

Steven R. Butler. 2016. *Infixer: A Method for Segmenting Non-Concatenative Morphology in Tagalog*. Unpublished MA thesis, City University of New York.

Mathias Creutz and Krista Lagus. 2002. Unsupervised discovery of morphemes. In *Proceedings of the ACL-02 Workshop on Morphological and Phonological Learning*, pages 21–30. Association for Computational Linguistics.

Mathias Creutz and Krista Lagus. 2007. Unsupervised models for morpheme segmentation and morphology learning. *ACM Transactions on Speech and Language Processing*, 4(1):1–34.

Paul de Lacy. 2003. Maximal words and the Maori passive. In *Proceedings of AFLA VIII: The eighth meeting of the Austronesian Formal Linguistics Association*, volume 44, pages 20–39, Cambridge, MA. MIT Linguistics Department.

Ramy Eskander, Owen Rambow, and Tianchun Yang. 2016. Extending the use of adaptor grammars for unsupervised morphological segmentation of unseen languages. In *Proceedings of COLING 2016, the 26th International Conference on Computational Linguistics*, pages 900–910.

Pierre Godard, Laurent Besacier, François Yvon, Martine Adda-decker, Gilles Adda, Hélène Maynard, Annie Rialland, and Inria Grenoble. 2018. Adaptor grammars for the linguist: Word segmentation experiments for very low-resource languages. In *Proceedings of the 15th SIGMORPHON Workshop on Computational Research in Phonetics, Phonology, and Morphology*, pages 32–42.

John Goldsmith. 2001. Unsupervised learning of the morphology of a natural language. *Computational Linguistics*, 27(2):153–198.

Ray Harlow. 1991. Consonant dissimilation in Maori. In Robert Blust, editor, *Currents in Pacific Linguistics: Papers in Austronesian Languages and Ethnolinguistics in honour of George W. Grace*, pages 117–128. Australian National University, Canberra.

Ray Harlow. 1993. Lexical expansion in Maori. *Journal of the Polynesian Society*, 102(1):99–107.

Ray Harlow. 2007. *Māori: A Linguistic Introduction*. Cambridge University Press, Cambridge.

Mark Johnson and Thomas L. Griffiths. 2007. Adaptor grammars: A framework for specifying compositional nonparametric Bayesian models. In *Advances in Neural Information Processing Systems 19*, pages 641–648.

Peter Julian Keegan. 1996. *Reduplication in Maori*. Unpublished MA thesis, University of Waikato.

Victor Krupa. 1968. *The Maori Language*. Nauka, Moscow.

Alec Marantz. 1982. Re reduplication. *Linguistic Inquiry*, 13(3):435–482.

John J. McCarthy and Alan S. Prince. 1996. Prosodic morphology. In John A. Goldsmith, editor, *The Handbook of Phonological Theory*, chapter 9, pages 283–305. Blackwell, Malden, MA.

John C. Moorfield. 2011. *Te Aka: Māori-English, English-Māori Dictionary*, 3rd edition. Pearson, Auckland.

Forrest Panther, Wakayo Mattingley, Jennifer Hay, Simon Todd, Jeanette King, and Peter Keegan. under review. Morphological segmentations of non-Māori speaking New Zealanders match proficient speakers.

Jorma Rissanen. 1978. Modelling by shortest data description. *Automatica*, 14:465–471.

Carl Rubino. 2005. Reduplication: Form, function and distribution. In Bernhard Hurch, editor, *Studies on Reduplication*, pages 11–30. Mouton de Gruyter, Berlin.

Carl Rubino. 2013. Reduplication. In Matthew S. Dryer and Martin Haspelmath, editors, *The World Atlas on Language Structures Online*, chapter 27. Max Planck Institute for Evolutionary Anthropology, Leipzig.

Simon Todd, Jeremy Needle, Jeanette King, and Jennifer Hay. 2019. Quantitative insights into Māori word structure. Paper presented at the Annual Meeting of the Linguistic Society of New Zealand.

Sami Virpioja, Peter Smit, Stig-Arne Grönroos, and Mikko Kurimo. 2013. Morfessor 2.0: Python implementation and extensions for Morfessor Baseline. Technical report, Department of Signal Processing and Acoustics, Aalto University, Helsinki.

Andrew J. Viterbi. 1967. Error bounds for convolutional codes and an asymptotically optimum decoding algorithm. *IEEE Transactions on Information Theory*, 13(2):260–269.

Hongzhi Xu, Jordan Kodner, Mitchell Marcus, and Charles Yang. 2020. Modeling morphological typology for unsupervised learning of language morphology. In *Proceedings of the 58th Annual Meeting of the Association for Computational Linguistics*, pages 6672–6681.

Hongzhi Xu, Mitchell Marcus, Charles Yang, and Lyle Ungar. 2018. Unsupervised morphology learning with statistical paradigms. In *Proceedings of COLING 2018, the 27th International Conference on Computational Linguistics*, pages 44–54.

Investigating phonological theories with crowd-sourced data: The Inventory Size Hypothesis in the light of Lingua Libre

Mathilde Hutin
Université Paris-Saclay
LISN-CNRS (UMR 9015)
Bât 507, 91405 Orsay, France
mathilde.hutin@lisn.fr

Marc Allassonnière-Tang
Muséum national d'Histoire naturelle
Laboratoire Eco-Anthropologie (UMR 7206)
17, place du Trocadéro, 75016 Paris, France
marc.allassonniere-tang@mnhn.fr

Abstract

Data-driven research in phonetics and phonology relies massively on oral resources, and access thereto. We propose to explore a question in comparative linguistics using an open-source crowd-sourced corpus, Lingua Libre, Wikimedia's participatory linguistic library, to show that such corpora may offer a solution to typologists wishing to explore numerous languages at once. For the present proof of concept, we compare the realizations of Italian and Spanish vowels (sample size = 5000) to investigate whether vowel production is influenced by the size of the phonemic inventory (the Inventory Size Hypothesis), by the exact shape of the inventory (the Vowel Quality Hypothesis) or by none of the above. Results show that the size of the inventory does not seem to influence vowel production, thus supporting previous research, but also that the shape of the inventory may well be a factor determining the extent of variation in vowel production. Most of all, these results show that Lingua Libre has the potential to provide valuable data for linguistic inquiry.

1 Introduction

One of the main challenges in data-driven research on the phonetics-phonology interface is the access to reliable, exploitable oral resources in sufficient amounts. While linguists working on other linguistic levels such as semantics or syntax can use written data as a proxy for language production, phoneticians and phonologists are limited to oral data, thus relying on audio recordings for vocal languages or video recordings for signed languages. Accessing massive amounts of such data is difficult enough, especially for studies in language comparison, that require such amounts in not one, but at the very least two languages.

To overcome this challenge, researchers developed two strategies. On the one hand, they can collect their own corpora, e.g., the CMU Wilderness Corpus (Black, 2019) or its emanation, the VoxClamantis corpus (Salesky et al., 2020), or other types of language-specific laboratory recordings such as the TIMIT database for English (Garofolo et al., 1993) or NCCFr for French (Torreira et al., 2010). On the other hand, they can gather audio recordings from other sources such as TV or radio shows, as was done for instance in the framework of the international project OSEO Quaero (`www.quaero.org/`), or from audio books, as exemplified by the LibriSpeech corpus for English (Panayotov et al., 2015, `www.openslr.org/12`). Both options have the disadvantage of being overly costly, both in money and human resources, and sometimes not freely accessible to the community. A third path has been recently explored: crowd-sourced data, recorded by volunteers and therefore much less costly in time and money and generally open-source. The project Common Voice (Ardila et al., 2020, `https://commonvoice.mozilla.org`) for instance was launched in 2017 by Mozilla for the intended purpose of creating a free database for the development of speech recognition software. In March 2022, it contains ∼18,000 hours of speech, 14,000 of which have been validated by other speakers, in 87 languages.

In the present paper, we explore a similar project: Lingua Libre, a participatory linguistic media library developed by Wikimedia France (`https://lingualibre.org`). It was launched in 2015, and, in March 2022, it counts ∼700,000 recordings in 148 languages across 775 speakers. This database is interesting to explore because it differs from Common Voice in the fact that its aim is not primarily the development of new technologies, or even linguistic inquiry in general, but patrimonial conservation of languages. Lingua Libre was used only once for academic purposes, i.e., to automatically estimate the transparency of orthographies in 17 languages (Marjou, 2021). With this study,

19th SIGMORPHON Workshop on Computational Research in Phonetics, Phonology, and Morphology, pages 23 - 28
July 14, 2022 ©2022 Association for Computational Linguistics

we aim to show that such data can be easily processed and useful to answer phonological questions in linguistic typology. In this proof of concept, we explore the realization of vowels by comparing two Romance languages: Italian and Spanish.

The outline of the paper is as follows. In Section 2, we describe our research question to justify our choice of languages. In Section 3, we present our corpus and methodology. In Section 4, we provide an analysis of the vowels in Italian and Spanish. Section 5 concludes and discusses the results.

2 The Inventory Size Hypothesis *vs* the Vowel Quality Hypothesis

In this paper, we offer to use Lingua Libre to tackle the question of vowel production with regards to vowel inventory. Our research question stems from various theories regarding the shape of vowel inventories in the world's languages. Our study however focuses on synchronic phonetic variation with regards to phonological systems (on the phylogeny of vowel systems in the languages of the world, see Zhang and Gong (2022) and references therein).

The original Vowel Dispersion Theory (Liljencrants and Lindblom, 1972; Lindblom, 1986) and a few years later the Adaptive Dispersion Theory (Lindblom, 1990), stem from the H&H ("Hypo- and Hyperspeech") model of communication, that assumes that speakers tend toward minimal and sufficient perceptual contrast, i.e., operate a trade-off between articulatory economy (hypospeech) and perceptual distinctiveness (hyperspeech). In the original works, these theories are the foundation for phylogenetic research on the distribution of vocalic categories in the languages of the world, for instance to explain why three-vowel systems usually display /a, i, u/ and not, say, /a, y, u/. Phoneticians however have particularly focused on one hypothesis that emerges from this model: The more vocalic categories the language has in its phonemic inventory, the less phonetic variation the corresponding vowel realizations will display. This is the hypothesis we ourselves focus on in the present paper, to which we will refer as the Inventory Size Hypothesis, henceforth ISH.

This hypothesis has been tested in a number of studies, with contradictory results. Jongman et al. (1989) on American English, Greek and German, Al-Tamimi and Ferragne (2005) on French and two dialects of Arabic and Larouche and Steffann (2018) on Quebec French and Inuktitut support the ISH while Bradlow (1995) on English and Spanish, Meunier et al. (2003) on English, Spanish and French, Recasens and Espinosa (2009) on 5 dialects of Catalan, Lee (2012) on 5 dialects of Chinese and Heeringa et al. (2015) on 3 German languages, do not provide evidence in favor of the ISH, which can be due, for the last three at least, to the genetic and geographical closeness of the languages and possible bilingualism of the speakers. Studies on larger sets of languages however tend to invalidate the hypothesis: Engstrand and Krull (1991) found inconclusive results on 7 languages across 6 language families; Livijn (2000) on 28 languages, Gendrot and Adda-Decker (2007) on 8 languages across 4 families, and Salesky et al. (2020) on 38 languages across 11 families, found no evidence for an effect of inventory size on the global acoustic space.

Building on these negative results, we suggest that it may not so much be the number of categories but their actual quality that influences the vowel's realizations. For instance, between two imaginary languages A and B displaying /a, e, i, o, u/ *vs* /a, e, i, y, o, u/ respectively, it is also possible that not all the categories in language B will display less variation than those in language A: Only [i] and possibly [u], which compete with /y/ in B but not in A, would show less variation in B than in A. We propose to refer to this restatement of the original hypothesis, as the Vowel Quality Hypothesis, henceforth VQH.

In this paper, we aim to test this alternative: Either the ISH is valid, and all the vowels of the system will be affected by the size of the inventory, or the VQH is more accurate, and only some vowels or some acoustic parameters will be affected depending on the other vowels comprised in the system. The third possible outcome is that neither the ISH nor the VQH is accurate.

To test our hypothesis, we focus on the F1 and F2 values of the vowels in two Romance languages: Spanish and Italian. Spanish has a limited vowel inventory, with only 5 categories /a, e, i, o, u/ while Italian has 7: /a, ɛ, e, i, o, ɔ, u/. Their inventories differ only in the number of degrees of aperture (Spanish has open, mid and closed vowels while Italian has open, mid-open, mid-closed and closed vowels), which manifest as variation on the first frequency, F1. If the ISH is valid, we expect vowel productions from each language to differ in both F1 and F2, while if the VQH is valid, we expect Spanish and Italian vowels to differ only in F1.

3 Materials and Methodology

As a crowd-sourcing tool, Lingua Libre allows any speaker to log in, fill in a profile with basic metadata for themselves of for other speakers, and record themselves or their guests reading lists of words in their language. The device detects pauses, which allows for the recording to end when the word has been read and the next recording to start automatically after, therefore effortlessly generating relatively short audio files for each word. Each audio file is supposed to be titled on the same template of 'Language - Speaker - Item'. For example, for the recording 'spa.-Marreromarco-solucionar.wav', the language is Spanish ('spa'), the speaker ID is 'Marreromarco', and the recorded item is 'solucionar', 'solve'. All audio files are under a Creative Commons licence, i.e., open-source.

First, the recordings are scrapped from the Lingua Libre database. In the present study, we extract a subsample of 500 items for /a, e, i, o, u/ in each language, to counter the fact that both languages have different amounts of data points and to also control for number of speakers (5) in each language. In total, we have 500 occurrences for each of the 5 vowels in both Italian and Spanish, which results in 5000 tokens. To avoid a potential sample bias, the sampling of tokens is conducted 10 times. We also took care to limit our investigation to the European variety of Spanish, to avoid any mismatch with the more limited geographical expansion of Italian.

Second, the recordings are segmented and aligned using WebMAUS (Kisler et al., 2017), the online open-access version of the MAUS software (Schiel, 2004). MAUS creates a pronunciation hypothesis graph based on the orthographic transcript of the recording (extracted from the name of the audio file) using a grapheme-to-phoneme converter. During this process, the orthographic transcription is converted to the Speech Assessment Methods Phonetic Alphabet (SAMPA). The signal is then aligned with the hypothesis graph and the alignment with the highest probability is chosen. Experiments have shown that the MAUS-based alignment is 95% accurate compared to human-based alignments (Kipp et al., 1997).

Third, the selected vowels are extracted from the recordings and analyzed in terms of formants. For each recording of each vowel, the mean F1 and F2 of the entire sound are calculated. The mean formants are considered to attenuate the effect of co-articulation with the left and right contexts.

Vowel	a	i	o
ID	9309	4238	48269
iso	ita	ita	spa
F1	664	315	628
F2	1451	2494	1153
Speaker	LangPao	LangPao	Rodelar
Item	rosa	chimica	todo

Table 1: Example of the data extracted and compiled from Lingua Libre. Each column represents one data point.

Table 1 shows an example of the extracted and compiled data used in this study. Each occurrence of vowel is given a unique identifier to allow tracking it within a word that has several vowels. The language iso code is provided along with the values of F1 and F2. Finally, the recorded word and its contributor are also noted. For the whole process, the following R packages are used: `emuR` (Winkelmann et al., 2021), `PraatR` (Albin, 2014), and `tidyverse` (Wickham, 2017).

4 Results: Shape of the inventory, more than size, influences vowel production

We focus on the F1 and F2 values for the 5 vowels that Spanish and Italian have in common, /a, e, i, o, u/. Our hypothesis is that, if the ISH is valid, we will find variation in both F1 and F2 for all vowels, while if the VQH is valid, we will find variation only in F1, especially in /a/, /e/ and /o/, which are in direct competition with /ɛ/ and /ɔ/.

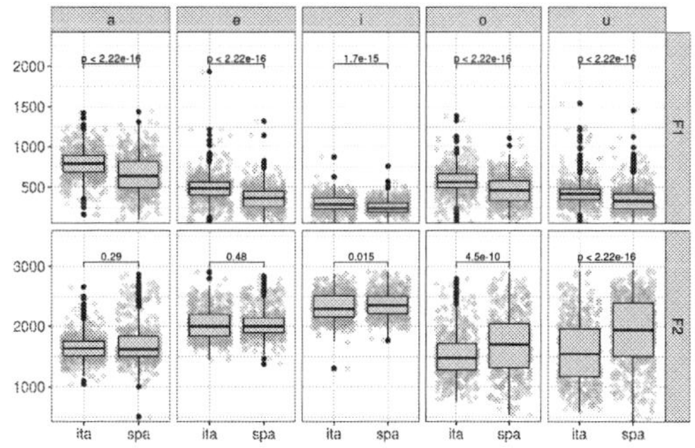

Figure 1: Distribution of formants for each of the 500 [a], [e], [i], [o], and [u] across the Italian and Spanish data extracted from Lingua Libre. The significance labels indicate the output of a wilcoxon test with bonferroni correction.

As general information, Figure 1 provides the mean values for F1 (top tier) and F2 (bottom tier) in Italian (left brackets) and Spanish (right brackets) for all 5 vowels of interest. It shows that F1 is significantly lower in Spanish for all 5 vowels, while F2 is statistically higher only for back vowels.

To test our hypotheses, however, we are less interested in F1 and F2 values in general than in their variation. Figure 2 shows the variation coefficient (standard deviation divided by the mean) of F1 (top tier) and F2 (bottom tier) for each replication of each vowel category in Italian (left brackets) and Spanish (right brackets). Each point represents the variation coefficient of a formant and a vowel for a replication. These results show that there is significantly less variation in F1 in Italian /a/, /e/, /o/ and /u/ than in Spanish, thus supporting the VQH. The difference between F2 variation coefficients is also significant but inverted for /e/, /i/, and /u/ where we observe more variation for Italian than for Spanish, thus invalidating the ISH.

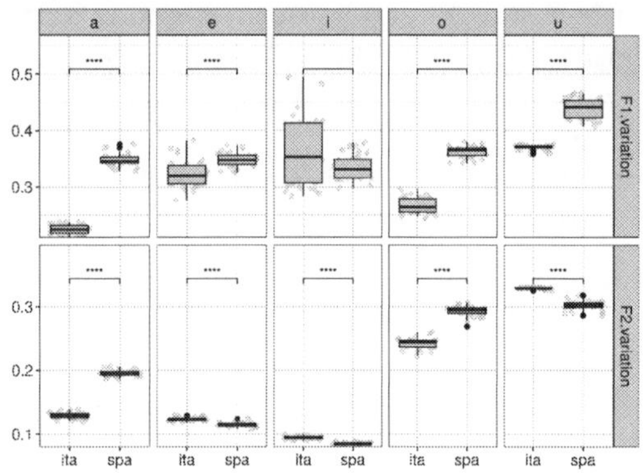

Figure 2: The distribution of the variation coefficient for each of the 500 [a], [e], [i], [o], and [u] across the Italian and Spanish data extracted from Lingua Libre in each of the replications. The significance labels indicate the output of a wilcoxon test with bonferroni correction.

These results are also supported by the linear mixed models we conducted (in both Bayesian and non-Bayesian versions) based on the 500 data points from each of the 10 replications. First, Table 2 shows that the estimate for the variation of Spanish for F1 is five times larger than the one for F2. Furthermore, we also observe that the variation is generally larger for most of the vowels in F1 (except for /a/), while the variation varies for F2, in which the estimates are negative for /e/ and /i/. The same observation is found when comparing the overall areas covered by the polygons formed by the contours of F1 and F2. We conduct a 2D kernel density estimation (Venables and Ripley, 2002) to extract the contours of the area covered by the

Dep.Var	Pred	Est	t value	p value
CV F1	spa	0.05	6.97	***
CV F1	/e/	0.06	5.79	***
CV F1	/i/	0.07	6.36	***
CV F1	/o/	0.04	3.41	***
CV F1	/u/	0.12	11.19	***
CV F2	spa	0.01	3.35	**
CV F2	/e/	-0.04	-6.87	***
CV F2	/i/	-0.07	-11.64	***
CV F2	/o/	0.11	16.56	***
CV F2	/u/	0.15	23.45	***
Area	spa	212	8.981	***
Area	/e/	-88	-2.35	*
Area	/i/	-210	-5.63	***
Area	/o/	230	6.16	***
Area	/u/	196	5.25	***

Table 2: The output of linear mixed models based on the output of 10 vowel samplings with 500 tokens for each vowel in Italian and Spanish. The areas are counted as units of thousands. The abbreviations are read as follows: Pred = predictor, Est = estimate, CV = coefficient of variation, Dep.Var = Dependent variable.

occurrences of each vowel in the two-dimensional space from F1 and F2. While there is generally more variation in Spanish than in Italian, this varies across vowels, as /e/ and /i/ tend to have a smaller formant space in general.

5 Conclusion and discussion

We used crowd-sourced data to test two competing hypotheses in language typology: The production of vowels is influenced either by the size of the inventory, or by its shape. Our proof-of-concept on Italian and Spanish shows that the size of the inventory does not influence the realization of vowels, but the exact quality of the vowels at hand does.

Our study also points to several caveats. First, all audio files were not properly labeled and were thus unusable. Moreover, from a human point of view, it should be noted that crowd-sourced data heavily rely on the participants' good will and that researchers have no choice but to trust the provided metadata. One possible solution to that last problem would be for Lingua Libre to propose a verification tool, as does Common Voice, to improve the reliability of the data and metadata. However, crowd-sourced data proved to be a promising tool for linguistic inquiry, especially to investigate language universals, and could thus be tested on more substantial sets of languages.

Acknowledgments

This research was partially supported by Institut DATAIA and the MSH Paris-Saclay in the framework of the Excellency Award for the project OTELO - OnTologies pour l'Enrichissement de l'analyse Linguistique de l'Oral (PI Ioana Vasilescu and Fabian Suchanek), and by the French National Research Agency in the framework of the grant EVOGRAM: The role of linguistic and non-linguistic factors in the evolution of nominal classification systems, ANR-20-CE27-0021 (PI Marc Allassonnière-Tang). The authors would also like to thank the Wikimedia community for their interest in the project, and in particular Lucas Lévêque for his help on the Lingua Libre tool.

References

Jalal-Eddin Al-Tamimi and Emmanuel Ferragne. 2005. Does vowel space size depend on language vowel inventories? Evidence from two Arabic dialects and French. In *INTERSPEECH EUROSPEECH 2005*, pages pp.2465–2468, Lisbonne, Portugal.

Aaron Albin. 2014. Praatr: An architecture for controlling the phonetics software "praat" with the r programming language. *Journal of the Acoustical Society of America*, 135(4):2198.

Rosana Ardila, Megan Branson, Kelly Davis, Michael Henretty, Michael Kohler, Josh Meyer, Reuben Morais, Lindsay Saunders, Francis M. Tyers, and Gregor Weber. 2020. Common voice: A massively-multilingual speech corpus. In *Proceedings of LREC*.

Alan W Black. 2019. Cmu wilderness multilingual speech dataset. In *ICASSP 2019 - 2019 IEEE International Conference on Acoustics, Speech and Signal Processing (ICASSP)*, pages 5971–5975.

Ann R. Bradlow. 1995. A comparative acoustic study of english and spanish vowels. *The Journal of the Acoustical Society of America*, 97:1916–1924.

Olle Engstrand and D. Krull. 1991. Effects of inventory size on the distribution of vowels in the formant space: preliminary data from seven languages. *PERILUS*, pages 15–18.

John S Garofolo, Lori F Lamel, William M Fisher, Jonathan G Fiscus, David S Pallett, Nancy L Dahlgren, and Victor Zue. 1993. Timit acoustic-phonetic continuous speech corpus. *Linguistic Data Consortium*.

Cédric Gendrot and Martine Adda-Decker. 2007. Impact of duration and vowel inventory on formant values of oral vowels: An automated formant analysis from eight languages. In *International Conference on Phonetics Sciences*, pages 1417–1420, Saarbrücken, Germany.

Wilbert Heeringa, Heike Schoormann, and Jörg Peters. 2015. Cross-linguistic vowel variation in saterland: Saterland frisian, low german, and high german. *The Journal of the Acoustical Society of America*, pages 25–29.

Allard Jongman, Marios Fourakis, and Joan A. Sereno. 1989. The Acoustic Vowel Space of Modern Greek and German. *Language and Speech*, 32(3):221–248.

Andreas Kipp, Maria-Barbara WesenickM, and Florian Schiel. 1997. 2004): Maus goes iterative. In *Proceedings of the Fifth European Conference on Speech Communication and Technology EUROSPEECH 1997*.

Thomas Kisler, Uwe Reichel, and Florian Schiel. 2017. Multilingual processing of speech via web services. *Computer Speech & Language*, 45:326–347.

Chloé Larouche and François Steffann. 2018. Vowel space of french and inuktitut: An exploratory study of the effect of vowel density on vowel dispersion. In *Proceedings of the Workshop on the Structure and Constituency of Languages of the Americas*, volume 21.

Wai-Sum Lee. 2012. A cross-dialect comparison of vowel dispersion and vowel variability. *2012 8th International Symposium on Chinese Spoken Language Processing*, pages 25–29.

Johan Liljencrants and Björn Lindblom. 1972. Numerical simulation of vowel quality systems: The role of perceptual contrast. *Language*, 48(4):839–862.

Björn Lindblom. 1986. Phonetic universals in vowel systems. *Experimental Phonology*, pages 13–44.

Björn Lindblom. 1990. Explaining phonetic variation: A sketch of the h&h theory. In William J. Hardcastle and Alain Marchal, editors, *Speech Production and Speech Modelling*, pages 403–439. Springer Netherlands, Dordrecht.

Peter Livijn. 2000. Acoustic distribution of vowels in differently sized inventories - hot spots or adaptive dispersion? *PERILUS*, pages 93–96.

Xavier Marjou. 2021. Oteann: Estimating the transparency of orthographies with an artificial neural network. In *Proceedings of the Third Workshop on Computational Typology and Multilingual NLP*, pages 1–9. Association for Computational Linguistics.

Christine Meunier, Cheryl Frenck-Mestre, Taissia Lelekov-Boissard, and Martine Le Besnerais. 2003. Production and perception of vowels: does the density of the system play a role? In *hal archives ouvertes*, pages 723–726. Université Autonome de Barcelone.

Vassil Panayotov, Guoguo Chen, Daniel Povey, and Sanjeev Khudanpur. 2015. Librispeech: An asr corpus based on public domain audio books. In *2015 IEEE International Conference on Acoustics, Speech and Signal Processing (ICASSP)*, pages 5206–5210.

Daniel Recasens and Aina Espinosa. 2009. Dispersion and variability in catalan five and six peripheral vowel systems. *Speech Communication*, 51:240–258.

Elizabeth Salesky, Eleanor Chodroff, Tiago Pimentel, Matthew Wiesner, Ryan Cotterell, Alan W Black, and Jason Eisner. 2020. A corpus for large-scale phonetic typology. In *Proceedings of the 58th Annual Meeting of the Association for Computational Linguistics*, pages 4526–4546, Online. Association for Computational Linguistics.

Florian Schiel. 2004. 2004): Maus goes iterative. In *Proceedings of the LREC 2004*, pages 1015–1018.

Francisco Torreira, Martine Adda-Decker, and Mirjam Ernestus. 2010. The nijmegen corpus of casual french. *Speech Communication*, 52:201–212.

W. N. Venables and Brian D. Ripley. 2002. *Modern applied statistics with S*, 4th ed edition. Statistics and computing. Springer, New York. OCLC: ocm49312402.

Hadley Wickham. 2017. tidyverse: Easily install and load the Tidyverse. *R package version*, 1.2.1.

Raphael Winkelmann, Klaus Jaensch, Steve Cassidy, and Jonathan Harrington. 2021. *emuR: Main Package of the EMU Speech Database Management System.* R package version 2.3.0.

Menghan Zhang and Tao Gong. 2022. Structural variability shows power-law based organization of vowel systems. *Frontiers in Psychology*, 13.

Logical Transductions for the Typology of Ditransitive Prosody

Mai Ha Vu
Dept. of Linguistics
and Scandinavian Studies
University of Oslo, Oslo, Norway
m.h.vu@iln.uio.no

Aniello De Santo
Department of Linguistics
University of Utah
Salt Lake City, Utah, USA
aniello.desanto@utah.edu

Hossep Dolatian
Department of Linguistics
Stony Brook University
Stony Brook, NY, USA
hossep.dolatian@alumni.stonybrook.edu

Abstract

Given the empirical landscape of possible prosodic parses, this paper examines the computations required to formalize the mapping from syntactic structure to prosodic structure. In particular, we use logical tree transductions to define the prosodic mapping of ditransitive verb phrases in SVO languages, building off of the typology described in Kalivoda (2018). Explicit formalization of syntax-prosody mapping revealed a number of unanswered questions relating to the fine details of theoretical assumptions behind prosodic mapping.

1 Introduction

Within computational and mathematical phonology, there is ample work on formalizing segmental and suprasegmental phonological processes that are word-bounded, such as by using finite state acceptors (FSAs) and transducers (FSTs) (Kaplan and Kay, 1994; Roche and Schabes, 1997; Hulden, 2009; Chandlee, 2014; Heinz, 2018), or using equivalent logical transductions (Potts and Pullum, 2002; Jardine, 2016; Strother-Garcia, 2019; Dolatian, 2020; Dolatian et al., 2021b).

Until recently however, there was little work on the computational machinery required by sentence-level or phrase-level phonology (prosodic phonology). This gap may be because early work on prosodic phonology found that some common aspects of prosody were computationally regular over strings, and can be formalized with FSAs (Pierrehumbert, 1980). However, the abstract representations that are the target of prosodic processes are subject to extensive debates in the linguistic literature, and they play a crucial role for questions about the nature of the linguistic phenomena at the phonology-syntax interface (Nespor and Vogel, 1986; Selkirk, 1982, 2011; Yu, 2021).

It is an established fact that phonological processes can refer to domains larger than a word. These domains form hierarchical layers: the prosodic word (w or PW), the prosodic phrase (p or PPh)[1], and the intonational phrase (i or iP). These prosodic constituents show systemic relations with syntactic constituents. However, such relations have been argued not to be strictly isomorphic — that is, prosodic constituency cannot be read directly from syntactic constituency. The characteristics of the *mapping* between syntactic structure and prosodic structure are important to theoretical approaches that consider prosodic constituency to be relevant for phonological generalizations. In this sense, distransitive constructions — verbs with multiple *internal arguments* (e.g. *gave Mary books*) — are a core example of prosodic-syntax mismatches cross-linguistically.

Building on the systematic report of such mismatches in SVO languages provided by Kalivoda (2018), this paper works out a formalization of the typology of attested syntax-prosodic mappings for ditransitive constructions in terms logical transductions (Courcelle, 1994; Courcelle and Engelfriet, 2012). In other linguistic domains, the rigor provided by computational/mathematical formalization has helped researchers commit to details of their theoretical assumptions, and fully understand the impact of particular representational choices. In line with this observation, this paper contributes to recent work laying the ground for mathematical investigations of the syntax-prosody interface (Yu, 2017, 2022, 2021; Dolatian et al., 2021a). These first steps already shed light on how a variety of theoretical details often unspecified in the literature need further clarification before extensive logical formalization of the syntax-prosody interface can be achieved.

The paper is organized as follows. Section 2 goes over the basic empirical typology of ditransitive prosody. Section 3 presents the formal preliminaries for the logical notation. Section 4 formally defines the

[1] Although a prosodic phrase is traditionally marked as ϕ, in what follows we will use p. We will instead use ϕ to indicate logical predicates.

19th SIGMORPHON Workshop on Computational Research in Phonetics, Phonology, and Morphology, pages 29 - 38
July 14, 2022

bulk of syntactic information relevant for ditransitive prosody. Section 5 shows how such information can be used to formally define the mapping from syntax to prosody. We then discuss (§6) and conclude (§7).

2 Typology of ditransitive prosody

In prosodic phonology, syntactic constituents (e.g. XP's) are said to map onto prosodic constituents (e.g. prosodic phrases). These two types of constituents are often mis-aligned, meaning that an XP can be larger or smaller than its corresponding prosodic phrase. Unsurprisingly, different languages have different rules for how XPs are mapped. In this paper, we focus on a formal exploration of the prosody of ditransitive sentences in SVO languages, given that there is data available on their typology (Dobashi, 2003; Kalivoda, 2018).

2.1 What is prosodic structure

In a ditransitive sentence, the verb phrase includes two internal arguments: colloquially, the direct object and the indirect object. Cross-linguistically, ditransitive sentences can have different types of prosodic phrasings (Dobashi, 2003). In some SVO languages like English, a typical phrasing is to make the verb be in the same prosodic phrase p as the first object, while the second object is a separate prosodic phrase (Kalivoda 2018, 46 citing Selkirk (2000); examples are our own).

1. ($_p$ she gave a book) ($_p$ to Mary)

   ($_p$ she gave Mary) ($_p$ books)

Note that throughout the paper, we only focus on the mapping of syntactic constituents to prosodic constituents (= prosodic phrases). Within a given language, the edges of these prosodic constituents should be retrievable from the acoustic signal, such as via some language-specific phonological or phonetic rule that references these edges.

2.2 Types of ditransitive phrasings

For a language like English, ditransitive verb phrases are phrased as two separate prosodic phrases: (VN)(N). In a survey of work on ditransitive prosody, Kalivoda (2018, 38) finds that SVO languages can prosodically parse ditransitive phrases in one of four ways.[2] The names of the distinct 'prosodic types' we refer to throughout the paper are our own (see Table 1).

[2]For SOV languages like Korean, Kalivoda (2018) finds only one possible phrasing: (N)(NV). They acknowledge though that the SOV gaps may be accidental gaps that are due to the smaller number of studied SOV languages. We set aside SOV languages from our current formalization.

Table 1: Kalivoda (2018)'s typology of prosodic phrasing in ditransitives

Syntax	Prosodic Type	Phrasing	Language
SVO	separated	(V) (N) (N)	Ewe
SVO	closest-merged	(V N) (N)	Chimwiini
SVO	recursive	((V N) N)	Kimatuumbi
SVO	all-merged	(V N N)	Zulu

In a language like Ewe, the verb and two objects are each phrased separately: (V)(N)(N). In Chimwini, the verb and closest noun are phrased together, while the second object is phrased separately, like English: (VN)(N). In Kimatuumbi, the VOO sequence is phrased recursively: ((VN)N). In Zulu, all three items are phrased together: (VNN).

2.3 Syntactic structure of ditransitives

For the input syntactic structure of the verbal cluster that we want to map to the output prosodic structure, we follow (Kalivoda, 2018). As consistent with most modern generative work, we assume that a surface VOO sequence is made up of two VP-like layers (*VP shell*, Larson, 1988; Aoun and Li, 1989; Harley, 2002, a.o.). The lower VP layer consists of the two objects: the first object in spec-VP and the second object in the complement of VP. The verb undergoes head-movement from its base position within VP to adjoin to v in the higher layer. We illustrate this in Figure 1.

For illustration, assume that the subject is in a higher position in the clause (TP or CP). The CP is mapped to an intonational phrase, while intermediate functional levels are ignored (Dobashi, 2003). The intonational phrase dominates the prosodic phrases of the VP. We omit the subject's prosodic phrase because it is irrelevant to the issue of correctly mapping the verb + objects cluster into prosodic constituents.

2.4 Formal relationship between syntax and prosody

Given this set of relations between the input syntax and the output prosodic representation (Figure 1), different analyses can be given for the correspondence of individual syntactic phrases with specific prosodic phrases. Indexes on each tree in Figure 1 illustrate these possible associations. These indexes can be thought of as numeral shorthand for the Gorn addresses of nodes in the syntactic tree. For instance, the CP node at index 9 is mapped to the intonational phrase at index $9'$. Overt terminal nodes (1,2,4) each get mapped to a prosodic word ($1'$,$2'$,$4'$).

Crucially, there is ambiguity in the literature about

Figure 1: Syntactic and prosodic structure of a ditransitive phrase in an SVO language

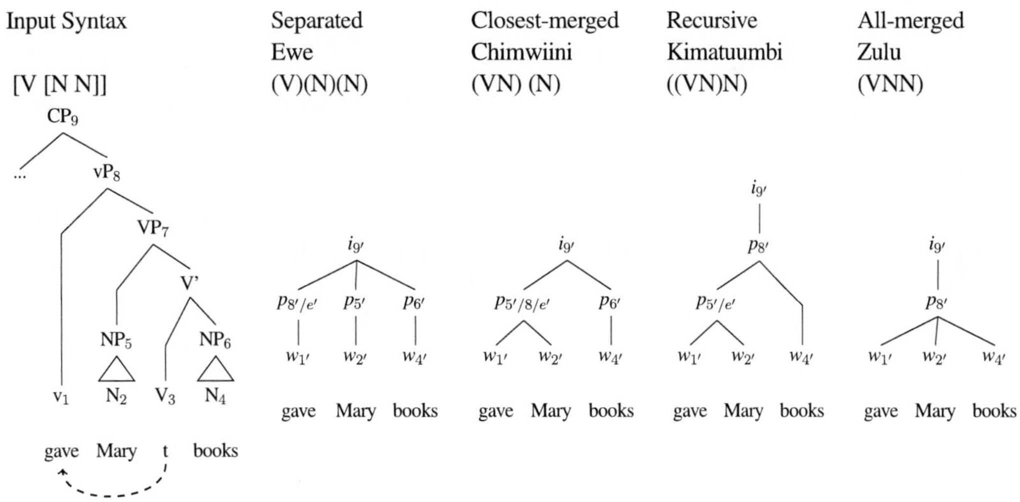

the exact input-output correspondences for prosodic phrases. In the Ewe (V)(N)(N) system, for example, the two noun phrases $(5,6)$ each get mapped to a prosodic phrase $(5',6')$. As for the verb, its surface prosodic phrase can be argued to either be a) epenthesized/inserted or created from no existing syntactic phrase (e'), or b) derived from the vP (index 12). In the latter case, the vP is phrased to a small prosodic phrase that excludes its arguments; such mismatches in the size of an XP and its prosodic phrase have been called underparsing or undermatch in the literature (Elfner, 2015; Guekguezian, 2017, 2021).

3 Logical Tree Transductions

In this section, we illustrate the use of Monadic Second Order (MSO) logic to define tree-to-tree transductions. MSO transductions are equivalent to regular functions (Filiot, 2015), and have been commonly employed to model both segmental and autosegmental phonological processes (Jardine, 2016; Chandlee and Jardine, 2019a; Strother-Garcia, 2018). For the current discussion, we assume familiarity with logic (boolean connectives, first-order quantification, etc.) and set notation on the reader's part.

With logical transductions, the input tree model is defined in terms of a signature $\langle D,R\rangle$. The segments are defined in terms of a set of domain elements D taken from the set of positive integers. For tree models, the common practice is to use Gorn-addresses. The domain elements satisfy a set of relations R which can be unary or binary. Unary relations designate the labels L of these domain elements, e.g. the label $\mathsf{V}(x)$ designates domain elements which are nodes labeled V (for verb). Domain elements are connected via

Figure 2: Example tree transduction

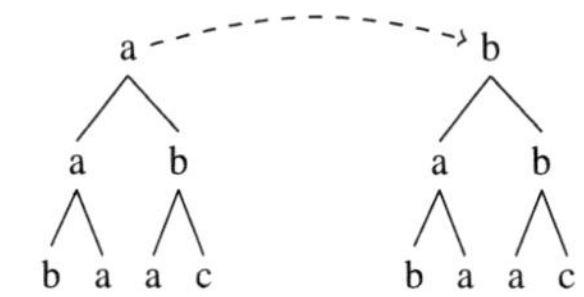

binary relations. Two binary relations are standardly considered to be relevant for trees, immediate dominance $\triangleleft(x,y)$ and left-of $\prec(x,y)$. In our current discussion, only immediate dominance will be used.

As a toy example, take a tree transduction that changes root nodes that are labeled a into root nodes that are labeled b (Figure 2). We first illustrate the logical definition of a tree for the input tree in this example transduction, with more extended illustration of each logical statement in Equation 2 in Figure 3. The model definition first establishes the domain of the structure, here using Gorn addresses. Each unary relation corresponds to labels and is the set of nodes for whom that label applies. For instance, the set for a(x) are the nodes which are labeled a: these are the nodes with Gorn addreses ε,0,1,00,01,10,11, as can also be seen in Figure 3. Each binary relation is a set of pairs for which the binary relation holds: Equation 2 thus states that the dominance relation $\triangleleft$ holds for nodes ϵ and 0, meaning that the node with addres ϵ dominates the node with address 0, and so on. Proper dominance ($\triangleleft^+$) is defined as the transitive closure of immediate dominance ($\triangleleft$).

2. Tree model for input tree in Figure 2
   Domain $D=\{\varepsilon,0,1,00,01,10,11\}$
   Unary relations $L\subset R$:

Figure 3: Illustration of the tree model for the input tree in Figure 2

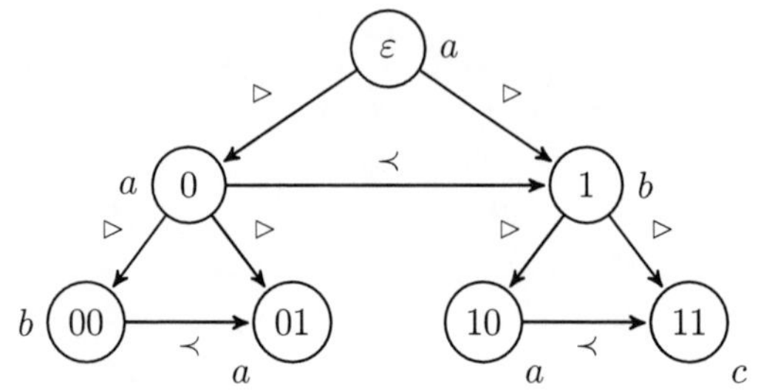

- $\mathsf{a}(x) = \{\varepsilon,0,01,12\}$
- $\mathsf{b}(x) = \{1,00\}$
- $\mathsf{c}(x) = \{11\}$

Binary relations in R:

- $\lhd(x,y) = \{\langle\epsilon,0\rangle,\langle\epsilon,1\rangle,\langle 0,00\rangle,\langle 0,01\rangle,\langle 1,10\rangle,\langle 1,11\rangle\}$
- $\prec(x,y) = \{\langle 0,1\rangle,\langle 00,01\rangle,\langle 10,11\rangle\}$

In order to transform input trees into output trees, MSO logical transductions define a *copy set* C of some fixed size k. The k members of the copy set act as indexes for copies of the input. If the output structure needs less than or equal nodes as the input, then a copy set of size 1 is sufficient: $|C|=1$. If the output has a larger number of nodes than the input, then a larger copy set is needed.

Output functions define segments in the output copies in terms of the input segments. The apostrophe marks output elements. We mark these functions using ϕ`this font`. For example, to change a root node *a* to *b*, we need a transduction with a copy set of size 1, since the output tree has the same number of nodes as the input tree. In order to make the transduction easier to read, we define the root *a* segment with the predicate in (1) as a shorthand, using **this font**. Crucially, every pair of segments has the same dominance relation in the output as in the input (2). Nodes in the output are labeled *a* if they are labeled *a* in the input and they are not the root (3). The label *b* is generated for all underlying *b*'s and for underlying root *a*'s (4). Nodes labeled *c* in the input stay *c* in the output (5). We visualize an example of this transduction in Figure 2.

$$\mathbf{root\_a}(x) \overset{\text{def}}{=} \mathsf{a}\wedge\neg\exists y[\lhd(y,x)] \quad (1)$$

$$\lhd(x',y') \overset{\text{def}}{=} \lhd(x,y) \quad (2)$$

$$\phi\mathsf{a}(x') \overset{\text{def}}{=} \mathsf{a}(x)\wedge\neg\mathbf{root\_a}(x) \quad (3)$$

$$\phi\mathsf{b}(x') \overset{\text{def}}{=} \mathsf{b}(x)\vee\mathbf{root\_a}(x) \quad (4)$$

$$\phi\mathsf{c}(x') \overset{\text{def}}{=} \mathsf{c}(x) \quad (5)$$

For representational ease, in what follows we use simple integers like $\{1,2,3,...\}$ as numeral shorthands for Gorn addresses.

4 Formalizing core syntactic information

In ditransitives, prosodic phrasing is sensitive to some but not all aspects of the syntactic structure (Nespor and Vogel, 1986; Selkirk, 1986, 2011; Inkelas and Zec, pages; Truckenbrodt, 1995, 1999, 2007; Elfner, 2015; Bennett and Elfner, 2019). These aspects are overtness, headedness, tree geometry, arguments, and linearity. It ignores category labels.

In this section, we define predicates that pick out these aspects of syntactic structure. These predicates will be later used to define the logical mappings from syntax to prosody.

Note that existent prosodic mapping studies have not directly addressed adjunction, namely the nature of the prosodic mapping when an unbounded number of adjoining phrases are added to the sentence. Additionally, unbounded adjunction introduces non-locality between a head and its argument. Because of the lack of data and these non-trivial open issues related to adjunction, we set it aside in our preliminary formalization.

4.1 Overt material

Prosody works over overt or pronounced terminal items. Predicate $\mathbf{Trm}(x)$ defines terminal syntactic items (N, V, v). $\mathbf{oTrm}(x)$ defines the overt items (thus excluding the trace of the verb once it moves to v, assuming V-to-v movement in all cases).

$$\mathbf{Trm}(x) \overset{\text{def}}{=} \mathsf{N}(x)\vee\mathsf{V}(x)\vee\mathsf{v}(x) \quad (6)$$

$$\mathbf{oTrm}(x) \overset{\text{def}}{=} \mathsf{N}(x)\vee\mathsf{v}(x) \quad (7)$$

4.2 Headedness

For headedness, we assume that we can reconstruct which terminal node x is the head of a maximal projection y based on the local geometry of the tree (hence, on their indexes).[3]

$$\mathbf{mxPrj}(x) \overset{\text{def}}{=} \mathsf{NP}(x)\vee\mathsf{VP}(x)\vee \mathsf{vP}(x) \quad (8)$$

$$\mathbf{hdOf}(x,y) \;\; is \;\; \text{TRUE if } (x,y)\in \{(1,8),(2,5),(3,7),(4,6)\} \quad (9)$$

[3]Though it is possible to define a predicate $\mathbf{hdOf}$(x,y) with MSO logic, such definition requires an explicit list of the syntactic features on each lexical item, which is outside the scope of this paper. In lay terms, terminal node x is the head of the phrase represented by node y, if y is the result of the Merge operation that checks off the last selector feature on x during the derivation.

A maximal projection is then headed if it contains an overt head.

$$\mathbf{hdedPhr}(x) \overset{\text{def}}{=} \mathbf{mxPrj}(x) \wedge \exists y [\mathbf{hdOf}(y,x) \wedge \mathbf{oTrm}(y)] \tag{10}$$

$$\mathbf{unhdedPhr}(x) \overset{\text{def}}{=} \mathbf{mxPrj}(x) \wedge \exists y [\mathbf{hdOf}(y,x) \wedge \neg \mathbf{oTrm}(y)] \tag{11}$$

4.3 Tree geometry

For tree geometry, phrasing is sensitive to whether a pair of nodes x,y are structurally sisters, and arguably to c-command.

$$\mathbf{sisOf}(x,y) \overset{\text{def}}{=} x \neq y \wedge \forall z [z \lhd x \leftrightarrow z \lhd y] \tag{12}$$

$$\mathbf{ccom}(x,y) \overset{\text{def}}{=} x \neq y \wedge \forall z [\lhd^{+}(z,x) \rightarrow \lhd^{+}(z,y)] \tag{13}$$

4.4 Argument structure and head movement

For argument structure, we distinguish two types of configurations: with and without head-movement. Without head-movement, a maximal projection XP has at most two arguments: a complement and a specifier. Thus the VP_7 has the two noun phrases NP_5 and NP_6 as arguments. The head X of XP (the covert V_3) can then claim the arguments of its maximal projection.

$$\mathbf{cmpOf}(x,y) \overset{\text{def}}{=} \mathbf{mxPrj}(x) \wedge \mathbf{mxPrj}(y) \wedge \exists z [\mathbf{hdOf}(z,y) \wedge \mathbf{sisOf}(x,z)] \tag{14}$$

$$\mathbf{spcOf}(x,y) \overset{\text{def}}{=} \mathbf{mxPrj}(x) \wedge \mathbf{mxPrj}(y) \wedge y \lhd x \tag{15}$$

$$\mathbf{argOf}(x,y) \overset{\text{def}}{=} \exists z [(\mathbf{cmpOf}(x,z) \vee \mathbf{spcOf}(x,z)) \wedge \mathbf{hdOf}(y,z)] \tag{16}$$

The above predicates capture the fact that the covert V_3 has two arguments. However, this V is covert because its lexical item *gave* underwent head movement to v_1. Based on observations made in the prosodic literature Kalivoda (2018), we make the (syntactically anomalous) assumption that when some item undergoes head-movement, its final landing slot inherits the arguments of its base position. Thus the verb '*gave*' as v_1 inherits the arguments of the covert V_3.

For simplicity, we assume that the movement path of head movement is defined a priori in terms of indexes or Gorn addresses. V_3 is the base position, while v_1 is the target or landing position. This is not a problem given that the head-movement relations observed in the typology work we rely on are always local, but we will come back to this point in Section 6.

$$\mathbf{mvPth}(x,y) \ \ is \ \ \text{TRUE if } (x,y) = (1,3) \tag{17}$$

$$\mathbf{mvBase}(x) \overset{\text{def}}{=} \neg \mathbf{oTrm}(x) \tag{18}$$

$$\mathbf{mvLand}(x) \overset{\text{def}}{=} \exists (y) [\mathbf{mvBase}(y) \wedge \mathbf{mvPth}(x,y)] \tag{19}$$

Thus, the argument x of some terminal node y is either a) the direct argument of y, if y did not move, or b) the argument that y inherited via head-movement from a node z moved into y from its base position.

$$\mathbf{genArg}(x,y) \overset{\text{def}}{=} \mathbf{argOf}(x,y) \vee [\mathbf{mvLand}(y) \wedge \exists z (\mathbf{mvPth}(y,z) \wedge \mathbf{mvBase}(z) \wedge \mathbf{argOf}(x,z))] \tag{20}$$

4.5 Linearity

The final syntactic property that prosody is sensitive to is linearity. In a ditransitive phrase, the verb can be phrased with its closest argument. We define 'closeness' in terms of c-command. We assume that if a node underwent head movement, then it c-commands all its arguments from its landing position.[4] Using c-command, we can define the first and second argument of a ditransitive verb.

$$\mathbf{arg1}(x,y) \overset{\text{def}}{=} \mathbf{genArg}(x,y) \wedge \mathbf{ccom}(y,x) \wedge \neg \exists z [\mathbf{ccom}(y,z) \wedge \mathbf{ccom}(z,x) \wedge \mathbf{genArg}(z,y)] \tag{21}$$

$$\mathbf{arg2}(x,y) \overset{\text{def}}{=} \mathbf{genArg}(x,y) \wedge \neg \mathbf{arg1}(x,y) \tag{22}$$

4.6 Avoiding category labels

As observed during our earlier discussion of the prosodic typology of ditransitives, in the SVO languages under analysis, vPs and NPs behave differently with respect to what kind of nodes they are mapped into in the output prosodic trees. However, syntax-prosody mappings are generally taken to be blind to category labels (except for CP). Thus, the prosody should not be able to distinguish between vPs and

[4] We define the first argument of a head as the the one that follows the head after linearization. That is, the first argument of the verb head is the direct object, not the subject.

NPs based on the labels of their heads, but possibly only in terms of argument structure and linearity.

While from a modern syntactic perspective it is debatable that the verbal and nominal domain actually differ in terms of the geometry of their argument structure, the examples reported by Kalivoda (2018) are of NPs without arguments. We thus do not know how more complex NPs (e.g. NPs with a complement prepositional phrase) would be mapped into prosodic constituents. Given the preliminary nature of our formalization attempt and our reliance on existing work on prosodic parsing, in what follows we define predicates that pick out headed phrases that have arguments (the vP) and headed phrases that lack arguments (NPs).

$$\mathbf{hasArg}(x) \overset{\text{def}}{=} \exists y[\mathbf{genArg}(y,x)] \quad (23)$$

$$\mathbf{hdedWArg}(x) \overset{\text{def}}{=} \mathbf{hdedPhr}(x) \land \mathbf{hasArg}(x) \quad (24)$$

$$\mathbf{hdedWoArg}(x) \overset{\text{def}}{=} \mathbf{hdedPhr}(x) \land \neg \mathbf{hasArg}(x) \quad (25)$$

5 Logical transductions for the syntax-to-prosofy typology

With all the preliminary predicates in place, in this section we define tree-to-tree logical transductions for each type of prosodic mapping laid out in Section 2 As discussed before, for each case there are multiple possible choices for the exact node-to-node maps. For reasons of space, here we only showcase predicates for one option per language, and focus on highlighting the necessary formal mechanisms that arise due to differences in the typology of the mappings.

5.1 Commonalities

Some node-to-node relations are common across all the typological examples. In particular, the iP node is mapped from the CP node at index 9.

$$\phi\texttt{iP}(x') \overset{\text{def}}{=} \texttt{CP}(x) \quad (26)$$

Additionally, all the overt terminal items (N and V) map to prosodic words (PW).

$$\phi\texttt{PW}(x') \overset{\text{def}}{=} \mathbf{oTrm}(x) \quad (27)$$

5.2 Ewe: (V)(N)(N)

For Ewe-type languages, the NPs each map to a prosodic phrase. The V is also part of a separate prosodic phrase. Let us assume that the V is phrased in a prosodic phrase $\text{PPh}_{8'}$, mapped from the $v\text{P}_8$.

Figure 4: Structure of Ewe: (V)(N)(N)

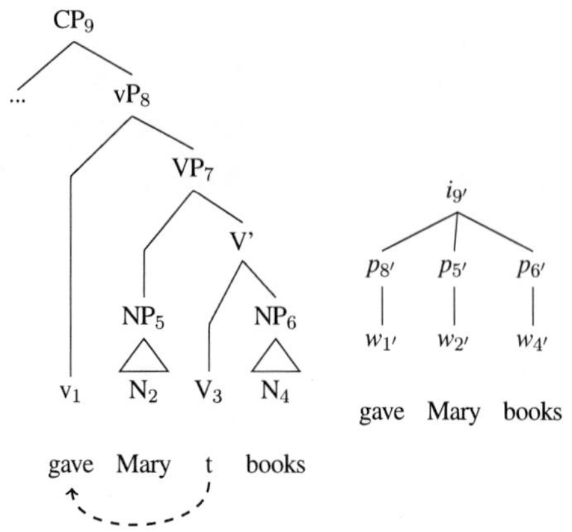

Thus, each overtly headed phrase (vP and NP) is mapped to a prosodic phrase.

$$\phi\texttt{PPh}(x') \overset{\text{def}}{=} \mathbf{hdedPhr}(x) \quad (28)$$

In terms of dominance relations, each PPh (p, mapped from an overt headed phrase) dominates its overt head (mapped into a w). The iP then dominates every p.

$$\phi\triangleleft(x',y') \overset{\text{def}}{=} [\phi\texttt{PW}(x')\land\triangleleft(y,x)]\lor [\phi\texttt{PPh}(x')\land\mathbf{hdOf}(y,x)]\lor [\phi\texttt{iP}(x')\land\phi\texttt{PPh}(y')] \quad (29)$$

5.3 Zulu: (VNN)

Figure 5: Structure of Zulu (VNN)

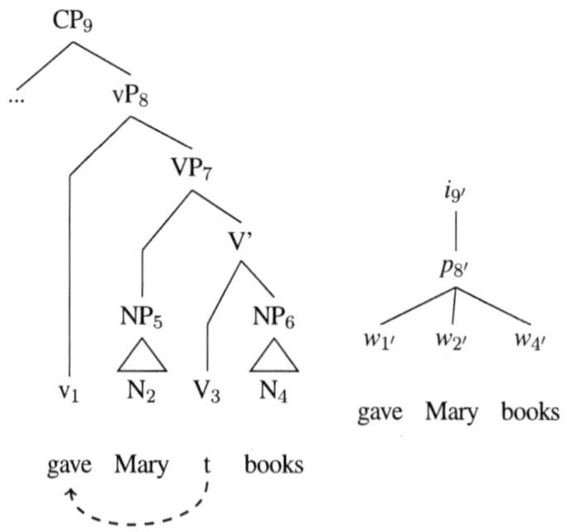

For Zulu-type languages, only one prosodic phrase is created. Assume this phrase is mapped from the vP at index 8. The vP is the only headed phrase that has arguments. Only this XP gets its own PPh.

$$\phi\texttt{PPh}(x') \overset{\text{def}}{=} \mathbf{hdedWArg}(x) \quad (30)$$

In terms of dominance, the sole PPh dominates every PWord.

$$\phi\lhd(x',y') \stackrel{\text{def}}{=} [\phi\texttt{PW}(x')\wedge\lhd(y,x)]\vee [\phi\texttt{PPh}(x')\wedge\phi\texttt{PW}(y')]\vee [\phi\texttt{iP}(x')\wedge\phi\texttt{PPh}(y')] \quad (31)$$

5.4 Chimwiini: (VN)(N)

Figure 6: Structure of Chimwiini (VN) (N)

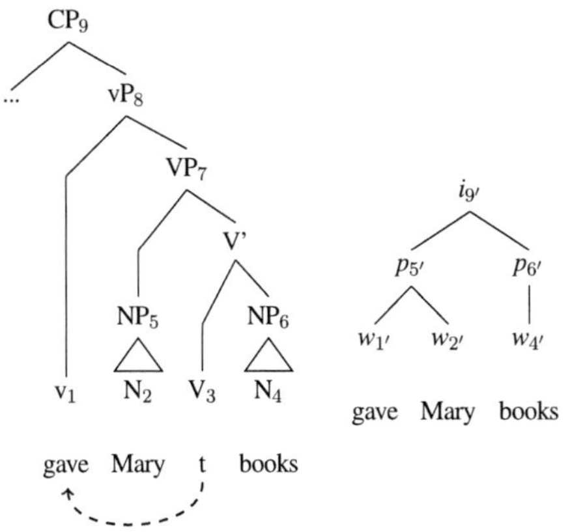

For the Chimwiini system, there is an ambiguity in the syntactic origins of the first PPh. This PPh can map either from the vP, the first NP, or be epenthetic. To make it easier to contrast this system with the one for Kimatuumbi (in the following section), we here only illustrate how this PPh can be mapped from the NP.

In this system, the two PPhrases originate from NPs, thus from XPs that have overt heads but no arguments.

$$\phi\texttt{PPh}(x') \stackrel{\text{def}}{=} \mathbf{hdedWoArg}(x) \quad (32)$$

In terms of prosodic dominance: PPhrases dominate the PWords that are the heads of the PPhrase's XP (second disjunct). Additionally (third disjunct), the PPhrase of the first NP (the first argument) dominates the PW of the vP (the argument-taking XP).

$$\phi\lhd(x',y') \stackrel{\text{def}}{=} [\phi\texttt{PW}(x')\wedge\lhd(y,x)]\vee [\phi\texttt{PPh}(x')\wedge\mathbf{hdOf}(y,x)]\vee \exists z[\mathbf{hdedWArg}(z)\wedge \mathbf{hdOf}(y,z)\wedge\mathbf{arg1}(x,z)]\vee [\phi\texttt{iP}(x')\wedge\phi\texttt{PPh}(y')] \quad (33)$$

5.5 Kimatuumbi: ((VN)N)

Figure 7: Structure of Kimatuumbi ((VN)N)

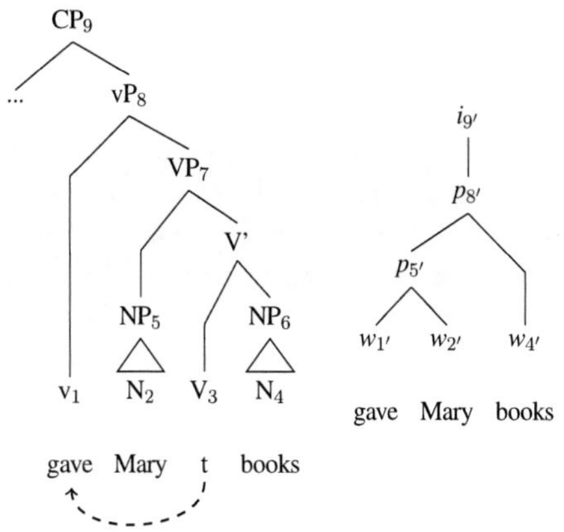

In the Kimatuumbi system, we need to allow for prosodic recursion. The highest PPhrase is mapped from the vP. The bottom PPhrase must be mapped either from the first NP or be epenthetic. We assume it is mapped from the first NP: the first argument of the headed phrase.

$$\phi\texttt{PPh}(x') \stackrel{\text{def}}{=} \mathbf{hdedWArg}(x)\vee\exists y [\mathbf{hdedWArg}(y)\wedge\mathbf{arg1}(x,y)] \quad (34)$$

Even in this bounded context, the use of recursion requires more convoluted contexts for prosodic dominance. The bottom PPhrase is mapped from the NP, the PPhrase dominates the head of the vP (second disjunct) and the head of the first NP (third disjunct). The top PPh is mapped from vP: it dominates the lower PPhrase and the head of the second argument (fourth disjunct).

$$\phi\lhd(x',y') \stackrel{\text{def}}{=} [\phi\texttt{PW}(x')\wedge\lhd(y,x)]\vee [\exists z[\mathbf{hdedWArg}(z)\wedge \mathbf{hdOf}(y,z)]\vee [\exists z[\mathbf{hdedWArg}(z)\wedge \mathbf{arg1}(x,z)\wedge\mathbf{hdOf}(y,x)]\vee [\exists z[\mathbf{hdedWArg}(x)\wedge \mathbf{arg2}(z,x)\wedge\mathbf{hdOf}(y,z)]\vee [\phi\texttt{iP}(x')\wedge\phi\texttt{PPh}(y')] \quad (35)$$

The logical formulation of prosodic dominance relations in this system would likely be more straightforward if we defined *both* of the two surface prosodic phrases as mapped from the same vP. This would require one-to-many associations for prosodic mappings, such that an input XP can correspond to two output PPhrases — however, such one-to-many associations are usually avoided in prosodic theory (Ito and Mester, 2019).

6 Discussion

In this paper, we used logical tree transductions to characterize mappings between syntactic and prosodic structure in ditransitive constructions. Based on the cross-linguistic typology of prosodic mappings reported in Kalivoda (2018), we showed that logical transductions seem appropriate to derive the alignment mismatches between syntactic and prosodic constituents. In doing so, we highlighted how details of prosodic and syntactic structures often left unspecified in the linguistic literature become fundamental in deciding the linguistic naturalness of such mappings. These results then provide a baseline for future, extensive formalization of syntax-prosody mismatches and open the way for a vast array of computationally informed questions and computationally-driven empirical predictions.

6.1 Head-movement and locality

In this paper we relied on Gorn addresses (node indexes) to handle the discontinuity created by head movement of V into v. While seemingly ad-hoc, this move was justified by the assumption that the observed head-movement dependency is — in the examples provided in the prosodic literature — always bounded within the vP domain. Hence, the information relevant to that a particular syntax-prosodic relation could be deterministically inferred from the geometry of the trees, and Gorn addresses were just a convenient shorthand. Theoretically, if we adopt a fully explicit syntactic formalism (e.g. Minimalist Grammars, Stabler, 1996), then it should be possible to extend our predicates to account for unbounded head-movement paths explicitly, for example by relying on feature chains (Kobele et al., 2007; Graf, 2012).

However, the open linguistic question is whether we can find cases where unbounded head-movement of the verb is relevant for prosodic structure, and what exactly would the resulting prosodic constituents be. Similarly, it is unclear whether the approach we adopted for the "recursive" structure in Kimatuumbi would work as straightforwardly for additional levels of embedding. Potential issues related to unbounded prosodic recursion that are not tied to local contexts have been pointed out by other work on prosodic transductions (Yu, 2021; Dolatian et al., 2021a).

6.2 Category Blindness

Throughout the paper, we had to make assumptions about properties of the syntactic/prosodic representations based on what had been observed/assumed in the existing literature on prosodic constituency. Among these, a non-trivial issue was the hypothesis that prosody is blind to category information — and thus, that mappings can only rely on tree geometry. For instance, based on this hypothesis we defined mappings that differentiated vPs from NPs based on the number of arguments they have in the trees. This allowed us to be faithful to the observation that, in the examples studied by Kalivoda (2018), vPs and NPs behaved strikingly differently with respect to prosodic mappings. Crucially though, such examples only reported bare NPs without complements nor specifiers — and it is thus possible that what we are observing is a prosodic sensitivity to syntactic phrases with and without complements.

Additionally, modern linguistic theory tends to assume that the verbal and nominal domain are similar in terms of domain-internal syntactic relations, and we would not predict a difference in behavior with respect to systems that are blind to category information. We can thus ask whether "*category-blindness*" is actually a real property of prosodic mappings, or whether it is just an epiphenomenon arising from the particular type of observations collected in the literature. If category blindness is indeed a core property, and if syntax-prosody mappings are tied to tree geometry, we would predict that complex nominal domains (e.g. NPs with prepositional complements) should be parsed the same way as vP.

6.3 Broad complexity considerations

From a formal perspective, this paper looks at the computational requirements of prosodic transductions via logical transductions (cf. logical formalizations in Dolatian, 2020). Following a rich tradition in model-theoretic syntax and phonology, we started out with the intent of using MSO to express the syntax-prosody relations. However, if we go back and look at the predicates we defined, we will note that we only make use of quantification to scope over individual variables. Thus, our mappings are essentially just first-order logic predicates. In this respect, recent work on phonological transformations has shown that they can be handled with Quantifier-Free string transductions (Chandlee and Lindell, in in review; Strother-Garcia, 2019; Chandlee and Jardine, 2019b), and in the future it would be interesting to see if our mappings could be further refined to work in terms of Quantifier-Free tree transductions (Ikawa et al., 2020; Dolatian, 2020).

Similarly, it is important to note that while logical transductions allow us to focus on the global properties of the representations we cast our mappings onto, existing computational work on prosody has made use of tree transducers (in particular, multi-bottom up tree transducers, Dolatian et al., 2021a; Yu, 2022). Multi-bottom up tree transducers have been shown to be relevant to syntactic processes (specifically involving copying, Kobele et al., 2007) and their computational properties are relatively well-understood. Moreover, tree transducers can be incorporated within a variety of parsing algorithms, and therefore offer a way to more deeply integrate prosodic and syntactic parsing (Yu and Stabler, 2017; Graf and De Santo, 2019; Yu, 2019). On the other side, the specification of tree transducers is more focused on the procedural requirements of the transformations and might, for instance, put stricter constraints on the relation between constituent rewriting and unboundedness (Yu, 2021).

7 Conclusion

This paper offers a contribution to the scarce existing literature on the formal characterization of prosodic processes, and their relation to syntactic representations. While much work remains to be done, our results further show how careful mathematical formalization can help up refine long-standing theoretical questions, suggest the need for more and different types of data, and make us more critical of theoretical assumptions about linguistic representations across subdomains.

References

Joseph Aoun and Yen-hui Audrey Li. 1989. Scope and constituency. *Linguistic inquiry*, 20(2):141–172.

Ryan Bennett and Emily Elfner. 2019. The syntax-prosody interface. *Annual Review of Linguistics*, 5:151–171.

Jane Chandlee. 2014. *Strictly Local Phonological Processes*. Ph.D. thesis, University of Delaware, Newark, DE.

Jane Chandlee and Adam Jardine. 2019a. Autosegmental input strictly local functions. *Transactions of the Association for Computational Linguistics*, 7:157–168.

Jane Chandlee and Adam Jardine. 2019b. Quantifier-free least fixed point functions for phonology. In *Proceedings of the 16th Meeting on the Mathematics of Language*, pages 50–62, Toronto, Canada. Association for Computational Linguistics.

Jane Chandlee and Steven Lindell. in in review. A logical characterization of input strictly local functions. In Hossep Dolatian, Jeffrey Heinz, and Kristina Strother-Garcia, editors, *Doing Computational Phonology*. Oxford University Press, Oxford.

Bruno Courcelle. 1994. Monadic second-order definable graph transductions: A survey. *Theoretical Computer Science*, 126(1):53–75.

Bruno Courcelle and Joost Engelfriet. 2012. *Graph Structure and Monadic Second-Order Logic, a Language Theoretic Approach*. Cambridge University Press, Cambridge.

Yoshihito Dobashi. 2003. *Phonological phrasing and syntactic derivation*. Ph.D. thesis, Cornell University.

Hossep Dolatian. 2020. *Computational locality of cyclic phonology in Armenian*. Ph.D. thesis, Stony Brook University.

Hossep Dolatian, Aniello De Santo, and Thomas Graf. 2021a. Recursive prosody is not finite-state. In *Proceedings of the 18th SIGMORPHON Workshop on Computational Research in Phonetics, Phonology, and Morphology*, pages 11–22, Online. Association for Computational Linguistics.

Hossep Dolatian, Jonathan Rawski, and Jeffrey Heinz. 2021b. Strong generative capacity of morphological processes. *Proceedings of the Society for Computation in Linguistics*, 4(1):228–243.

Emily Elfner. 2015. Recursion in prosodic phrasing: Evidence from Connemara Irish. *Natural Language & Linguistic Theory*, 33(4):1169–1208.

Emmanuel Filiot. 2015. Logic-automata connections for transformations. In *Logic and Its Applications*, pages 30–57, Berlin, Heidelberg. Springer Berlin Heidelberg.

Thomas Graf. 2012. Movement-generalized minimalist grammars. In *International Conference on Logical Aspects of Computational Linguistics*, pages 58–73. Springer.

Thomas Graf and Aniello De Santo. 2019. Sensing tree automata as a model of syntactic dependencies. In *Proceedings of the 16th Meeting on the Mathematics of Language*, pages 12–26, Toronto, Canada. Association for Computational Linguistics.

Peter Ara Guekguezian. 2017. *Prosodic recursion and syntactic cyclicity inside the word*. Ph.D. thesis, University of Southern California.

Peter Ara Guekguezian. 2021. Morphosyntax–phonology mismatches in Muskogee. *Phonology*, 38(2):277–316.

Heidi Harley. 2002. Possession and the double object construction. *Linguistic variation yearbook*, 2(1):31–70.

Jeffrey Heinz. 2018. The computational nature of phonological generalizations. In Larry Hyman and Frans Plank, editors, *Phonological Typology*, Phonetics and Phonology, chapter 5, pages 126–195. Mouton de Gruyter, Berlin.

Mans Hulden. 2009. *Finite-state machine construction methods and algorithms for phonology and morphology*. Ph.D. thesis, University of Arizona.

Shiori Ikawa, Akane Ohtaka, and Adam Jardine. 2020. Quantifier-free tree transductions. In *Proceedings of the Society for Computation in Linguistics*, volume 3, pages 145–153.

Sharon Inkelas and Draga Zec. pages. The phonology-syntax interface. In John Goldsmith, editor, *The Handbook of Phonological Theory*, 1 edition, pages 535–549. Blackwell Publishers, Cambridge, MA.

Junko Ito and Armin Mester. 2019. Match as syntax-prosody MAX/DEP: Prosodic enclisis in English. *English linguistics*, 36(1).

Adam Jardine. 2016. *Locality and non-linear representations in tonal phonology*. Ph.D. thesis, University of Delaware, Newark, DE.

Nicholas Kalivoda. 2018. *Syntax-prosody mismatches in Optimality Theory*. Ph.D. thesis, University of California, Santa Cruz.

Ronald M Kaplan and Martin Kay. 1994. Regular models of phonological rule systems. *Computational linguistics*, 20(3):331–378.

Gregory M. Kobele, Christian Retoré, and Sylvain Salvati. 2007. An automata-theoretic approach to minimalism. *Model theoretic syntax at 10*, pages 71–80.

Richard K Larson. 1988. On the double object construction. *Linguistic inquiry*, 19(3):335–391.

Marina Nespor and Irene Vogel. 1986. *Prosodic phonology*. Foris, Dordrecht.

Janet Breckenridge Pierrehumbert. 1980. *The phonology and phonetics of English intonation*. Ph.D. thesis, Massachusetts Institute of Technology.

Christopher Potts and Geoffrey K Pullum. 2002. Model theory and the content of OT constraints. *Phonology*, 19(3):361–393.

Emmanuel Roche and Yves Schabes, editors. 1997. *Finite-state language processing*. MIT press, Cambridge.

Elisabeth Selkirk. 1982. *The syntax of words*. Number 7 in Linguistic Inquiry Monographs. MIT Press, Cambridge, Mass.

Elisabeth Selkirk. 1986. On derived domains in sentence phonology. *Phonology Yearbook*, 3(1):371–405.

Elisabeth Selkirk. 2000. The interaction of constraints on prosodic phrasing. In Merle Horne, editor, *Prosody: Theory and experiment*, pages 231–261. Springer.

Elisabeth Selkirk. 2011. The syntax-phonology interface. In John Goldsmith, Jason Riggle, and Alan C. L. Yu, editors, *The Handbook of Phonological Theory*, 2 edition, pages 435–483. Blackwell, Oxford.

Edward Stabler. 1996. Derivational minimalism. In *International Conference on Logical Aspects of Computational Linguistics*, pages 68–95. Springer.

Kristina Strother-Garcia. 2018. Imdlawn Tashlhiyt Berber syllabification is quantifier-free. In *Proceedings of the Society for Computation in Linguistics*, volume 1, pages 145–153.

Kristina Strother-Garcia. 2019. *Using model theory in phonology: a novel characterization of syllable structure and syllabification*. Ph.D. thesis, University of Delaware.

Hubert Truckenbrodt. 1995. *Phonological phrases–their relation to syntax, focus, and prominance*. Ph.D. thesis, Massachusetts Institute of Technology.

Hubert Truckenbrodt. 1999. On the relation between syntactic phrases and phonological phrases. *Linguistic Inquiry*, 30(2):219–255.

Hubert Truckenbrodt. 2007. The syntax-phonology interface. In Paul de Lacy, editor, *The Cambridge Handbook of Phonology*, page 435–456. Cambridge University Press, Cambridge.

Kristine M Yu. 2017. Advantages of constituency: Computational perspectives on Samoan word prosody. In *International Conference on Formal Grammar 2017*, pages 105–124, Berlin. Spring.

Kristine M Yu. 2019. Parsing with minimalist grammars and prosodic trees. In Robert C. Berwick and Edward P. Stabler, editors, *Minimalist Parsing*, pages 69–109. Oxford University Press, London.

Kristine M Yu. 2021. Computational perspectives on phonological constituency and recursion. *Catalan journal of linguistics*, 20:77–114.

Kristine M Yu. 2022. Representing multiple dependencies in prosodic structures. *Proceedings of the Society for Computation in Linguistics*, 5(1):171–183.

Kristine M Yu and Edward P Stabler. 2017. (in) variability in the Samoan syntax/prosody interface and consequences for syntactic parsing. *Laboratory Phonology: Journal of the Association for Laboratory Phonology*, 8(1):1–44.

A Masked Segmental Language Model for Unsupervised Natural Language Segmentation

C.M. Downey Fei Xia Gina-Anne Levow Shane Steinert-Threlkeld
Department of Linguistics, University of Washington
{cmdowney, fxia, levow, shanest}@uw.edu

Abstract

We introduce a Masked Segmental Language Model (MSLM) for joint language modeling and unsupervised segmentation. While near-perfect supervised methods have been developed for segmenting human-like linguistic units in resource-rich languages such as Chinese, many of the world's languages are both morphologically complex, and have no large dataset of "gold" segmentations for supervised training. Segmental Language Models offer a unique approach by conducting unsupervised segmentation as the byproduct of a neural language modeling objective. However, current SLMs are limited in their scalability due to their recurrent architecture. We propose a new type of SLM for use in both unsupervised and lightly supervised segmentation tasks. The MSLM is built on a span-masking transformer architecture, harnessing a masked bidirectional modeling context and attention, as well as adding the potential for model scalability. In a series of experiments, our model outperforms the segmentation quality of recurrent SLMs on Chinese, and performs similarly to the recurrent model on English.

1 Introduction

Outside of the orthography of English and languages with similar writing systems, natural language is rarely overtly segmented into meaningful units. Languages such as Chinese, are written with no spaces in between characters, and Chinese Word Segmentation remains an active field of study (e.g. Tian et al., 2020). Running speech is also highly fluent with no meaningful pauses existing between "words" like in orthography.

Tokenization schemes for large modern language models are now largely passed off to greedy information-theoretic algorithms like Byte-Pair Encoding (Sennrich et al., 2016) and the subsequent SentencePiece (Kudo and Richardson, 2018), which create subword vocabularies of a desired size by iteratively joining commonly co-occuring units. However, these segmentations are usually not sensical to human readers (Park et al., 2021). Given the current performance of models using BPE-type tokenization, the nonsensical nature of these segmentations does not necessarily seem to inhibit the success of neural models.

Nevertheless, BPE does not necessarily help in situations where knowing a sensical segmentation of linguistic-like units is important, such as attempting to model the ways in which children acquire language (Goldwater et al., 2009), segmenting free-flowing speech (Kamper et al., 2016; Rasanen and Blandon, 2020), creating linguistic tools for morphologically complex languages (Moeng et al., 2021), or studying the structure of an endangered language with few or no current speakers (Dunbar et al., 2020).

While near-perfect supervised models have been developed for resource-rich languages like Chinese, most of the world's languages do not have large corpora of training data (Joshi et al., 2020). Especially for morphologically complex languages, large datasets containing "gold" segmentations into units like morphemes are very rare.

To help mitigate this problem, we propose a novel variant of the unsupervised Segmental Language Model (Sun and Deng, 2018; Kawakami et al., 2019). Segmental Language Models (SLMs) function as neural LMs that can also be used for unsupervised segmentation correlating with units like words and morphemes (Kawakami et al., 2019).

Traditional (recurrent) SLMs provide a good tradeoff between language-modeling performance and segmentation quality. However, in order to embrace a fully bidirectional modeling context, attention, and the scalability afforded by parallelization, we present a Masked Segmental Language Model (MSLM), built on a span-masking transformer architecture (Vaswani et al., 2017). As far as we are aware, we are the first to introduce a non-recurrent

19th SIGMORPHON Workshop on Computational Research in Phonetics, Phonology, and Morphology, pages 39 - 50

architecture for segmental modeling.

In this paper, we seek to compare our model to recurrent baselines across two standard word-segmentation datasets in Chinese and English, with the hope of expanding to more languages and domains (such as speech) in future work. We constrain the scope of our work to comparison with recurrent SLMs both because standard Bayesian models have been compared to SLMs elsewhere (Kawakami et al., 2019, Section 2), and because SLMs have different use cases from Bayesian algorithms, which tend to be weaker language models and lack continuous character representations that are invaluable in settings such as transfer learning.

In what follows, we overview baselines in unsupervised segmentation as well as other precursors to SLMs (Section 2), provide a formal characterization of SLMs in general, as well as the architecture and modeling assumptions that make the MSLM distinct (Section 3), present our experimental method comparing recurrent and masked SLMs (Section 4), and finally show that the MSLM outperforms its recurrent counterpart on Chinese segmentation, and performs similarly to the recurrent model on English (Sections 5-6). Section 7 lays out directions for future work.

2 Related Work

Segmentation Techniques and SLM Precursors An early application of machine learning to unsupervised segmentation is Elman (1990), who shows that temporal surprisal peaks in RNNs provide a heuristic for inferring word boundaries. Subsequently, Minimum Description Length (MDL) (Rissanen, 1989) was widely used. The MDL model family underlies well-known segmentation tools such as *Morfessor* (Creutz and Lagus, 2002) and other notable works (de Marcken, 1996; Goldsmith, 2001).

More recently, Bayesian models have proved some of the most accurate in their ability to model word boundaries. Some of the best examples are Hierarchical Dirichlet Processes (Teh et al., 2006), e.g. those applied to natural language by Goldwater et al. (2009), as well as Nested Pitman-Yor (Mochihashi et al., 2009; Uchiumi et al., 2015). However, Kawakami et al. (2019) notes most of these do not adequately account for long-range dependencies in the same capacity as modern neural LMs.

Segmental Language Models follow a variety of recurrent models proposed for finding hierarchical structure in sequential data. Influential among these are Connectionist Temporal Classification (Graves et al., 2006), Sleep-Wake Networks (Wang et al., 2017), Segmental RNNs (Kong et al., 2016), and Hierarchical Multiscale Recurrent Neural Networks (Chung et al., 2017).

In addition, SLMs draw heavily from character and open-vocabulary language models. For example, Kawakami et al. (2017) and Mielke and Eisner (2019) present open-vocabulary language models in which words are represented either as atomic lexical units, or built out of characters. While the hierarchical nature and dual-generation strategy of these models did influence SLMs (Kawakami et al., 2019), both assume that word boundaries are available during training, and use them to form word embeddings from characters on-line. In contrast, SLMs usually assume no word boundary information is available in training.

Segmental Language Models The next section has a more technical description of SLMs; here we give a short overview of related work. The term Segmental Language Model seems to be jointly due to Sun and Deng (2018) and Kawakami et al. (2019). Sun and Deng (2018) demonstrate strong results for Chinese Word Segmentation using an LSTM-based SLM and greedy decoding, competitive with and sometimes exceeding state of the art for the time. This study tunes the model for segmentation quality on a validation set, which we will call a "lightly supervised" setting (Section 4.3).

Kawakami et al. (2019) use LSTM-based SLMs in a strictly unsupervised setting in which the model is only trained to optimize language-modeling performance on the validation set, and is not tuned on segmentation quality. Here they report that "vanilla" SLMs give sub-par segmentations unless combined with one or more regularization techniques, including a character n-gram "lexicon" and length regularization.

Finally, Wang et al. (2021) very recently introduce a bidirectional SLM based on a Bi-LSTM. They show improved results over the unidirectional SLM of Sun and Deng (2018), test over more supervision settings, and include novel methods for combining decoding decisions over the forward and backward directions. This study is most similar to our own work, though our transformer-based SLMs utilize a bidirectional context in a qualitatively different way, and do not require an additional layer to capture the reverse context.

3 Model

3.1 Recurrent SLMs

A schematic of the original Recurrent SLM can be found in Figure 1. Within an SLM, a sequence of symbols or time-steps **x** can further be modeled as a sequence of segments $\underline{\mathbf{y}}$, which are themselves sequences of the input time-steps, such that the concatenation of segments $\pi(\underline{\mathbf{y}}) = \mathbf{x}$.

SLMs are broken into two levels: a Context Encoder and a Segment Decoder. The Segment Decoder estimates the probability of the jth character in the segment starting at index i, y^i_j, as:

$$p(y^i_j | y^i_{0:j}, x_{0:i}) = Decoder(h^i_{j-1}, y^i_{j-1})$$

where the indices for $x_{i:j}$ are $[i, j)$. The Context Encoder encodes information about the input sequence up to index i. The hidden encoding h_i is

$$h_i = Encoder(h_{i-1}, x_i)$$

Finally, the Context Encoder "feeds" the Segment Decoder: the initial character of a segment beginning at i is decoded using (transformations of) the encoded context as initial states ($g_h(x)$ and $g_{start}(x)$ are single feed-forward layers):

$$\begin{aligned} p(y^i_0 | x_{0:i}) &= Decoder(h^i_\emptyset, start^i) \\ h^i_\emptyset &= g_h(h_{i-1}) \\ start^i &= g_{start}(h_{i-1}) \end{aligned}$$

For inference, the probability of a segment $\mathbf{y}_{i:i+k}$ (starting at index i and of length k) is modeled as the log probability of generating $\mathbf{y}_{i:i+k}$ with the Segment Decoder given the left context $\pi(\underline{\mathbf{y}}_{0:i}) = x_{0:i}$. Note that the probability of a segment is **not** conditioned on other segments / segmentation choice, but only on the unsegmented input time-series. Thus, the probability of the segment is

$$p(y^i_0 | h^i_\emptyset, start^i) \prod_{j=1}^{k} p(y^i_j | h^i_{j-1}, y^i_{j-1})$$

where y^i_k is the end-of-segment symbol.

The probability of a sentence is thus modeled as the marginal probability over all possible segmentations of the input, as in equation (1) below (where $Z(|\mathbf{x}|)$ is the set of all possible segmentations of an input **x**). However, since there are $2^{|\mathbf{x}|-1}$ possible segmentations, directly marginalizing is intractable. Instead, dynamic programming over a forward-pass lattice can be used to recursively compute the marginal as in (2) given the base condition that $\alpha_0 = 1$. The maximum-probability segmentation can then be read off of the backpointer-augmented lattice through Viterbi decoding.

$$p(\mathbf{x}) = \sum_{\mathbf{z} \in Z(|\mathbf{x}|)} \prod_i p(\mathbf{y}_{i:i+z_i}) \quad (1)$$

$$p(\mathbf{x}_{0:i}) = \alpha_i = \sum_{k=1}^{L} p(\mathbf{y}_{i-k:i} | \mathbf{x}_{0:i-k}) \alpha_{i-k} \quad (2)$$

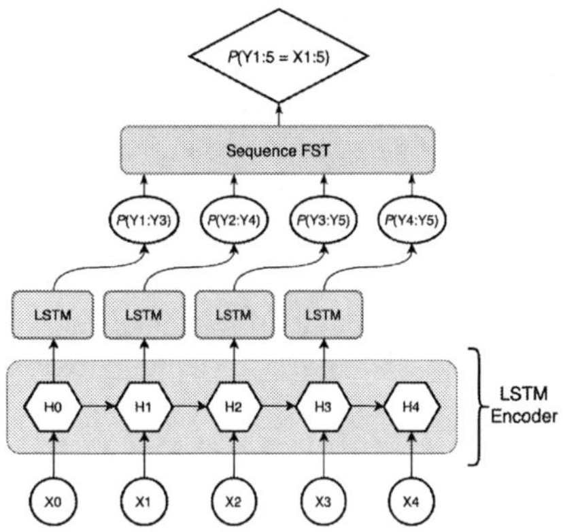

Figure 1: Recurrent Segmental Language Model

3.2 New Model: Masked SLM

We present a Masked Segmental Language Model, which leverages a non-directional transformer as the Context Encoder. This reflects recent advances in bidirectional (Schuster and Paliwal, 1997; Graves and Schmidhuber, 2005; Peters et al., 2018) and adirectional language modeling (Devlin et al., 2019). Such modeling contexts are also psychologically plausible: Luce (1986) shows that in acoustic perception, most words need some following context to be recognizable.

A key difference between our model and standard Masked LMs like BERT is that the latter predict single tokens based on the rest, while for SLMs we must predict a *segment* of tokens based on all other tokens *outside the segment*. For instance, to predict the three-character segment starting at x_t, the modeled distribution is $p(\mathbf{x}_{t:t+3} | \mathbf{x}_{<t}, \mathbf{x}_{\geq t+3})$.

Some recent pre-training techniques for transformers, such as MASS (Song et al., 2019) and

BART (Lewis et al., 2020) mask out spans to be predicted. A key difference between our model and these approaches is that the pre-training data for large transformer models is usually large enough that only about 15% of training tokens are masked, while we need to estimate the generation probability for *every* possible segment of $\mathbf{x}$. Since the usual method for masking is to replace the masked token(s) with a special symbol, only one span can be predicted with each forward pass. However, each sequence contains $O(|\mathbf{x}|)$ possible segments, so replacing each one with a mask token and recovering it would require as many forward passes.

These design considerations motivate our **Segmental Transformer Encoder**, and the **Segmental Attention Mask** around which it is based. Each forward pass of the encoder generates an encoding for every possible start-position in $\mathbf{x}$, for a segment of up to length k. The encoding at timestep $t-1$ corresponds to every possible segment whose first timestep is at index t. Thus with maximum segment length of k and total sequence length n, the encoding at each index $t-1$ will approximate

$$p(\mathbf{x}_{t:t+1}, \mathbf{x}_{t:t+2}, ...\mathbf{x}_{t:t+k}|\mathbf{x}_{<t}, \mathbf{x}_{\geq t+k})$$

This encoder leverages an attention mask that conditions predictions only on indices outside the predicted segment. An example of this mask with $k = 3$ is shown in Figure 2. For max segment length k, the mask is given by:

$$\alpha_{i,j} = \begin{cases} -\infty & \text{if } 0 < j - i \leq k \\ 0 & \text{else} \end{cases}$$

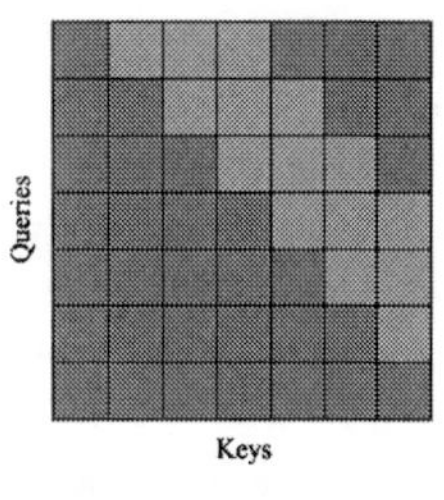

Figure 2: Segmental Attention Mask with segment-length (k) of 3. Blue squares are equal to 0, orange squares are equal to $-\infty$. This mask blocks the position encoding the segment in the Queries from attending to segment-internal positions in the Keys.

This solution is similar to that of Shin et al. (2020), developed independently and concurrently with our work, which uses a custom attention mask to "autoencode" each position without needing a special mask token. One key difference is that their masking scheme is used to predict single tokens, rather than spans. In addition, their mask runs directly along the diagonal of the attention matrix, rather than being offset. This means that to preserve self-masking in the first layer, the Queries are the "pure" positional embeddings.

To prevent information leaking "from under the mask", our encoder uses a different configuration in its first layer than in subsequent layers. In the first layer, Queries, Keys, and Values are all learned from the original input embeddings. In subsequent layers, the Queries come from the hidden encodings output by the previous layer, while Keys and Values are learned directly from the original embeddings. If Queries and either Keys or Values both come from the previous layer, information can leak from positions that are supposed to be masked for a particular query position. Shin et al. (2020) come to a similar solution to preserve their auto-encoder masking.

The encodings learned by the segmental encoder are then input to an SLM decoder in exactly the same way as previous models (Figure 3).

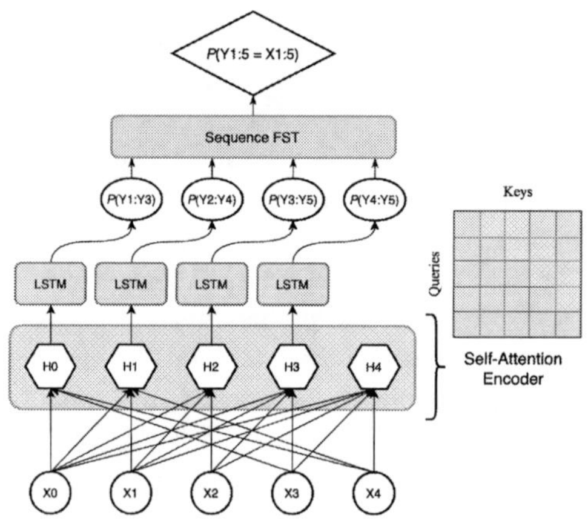

Figure 3: Masked Segmental Language Model, $k = 2$.

To tease apart the role of an adirectional modeling assumption itself, vs the role of attention, we additionally define a Directional MSLM, which uses a directional ("causal") mask instead of the span masking type. Using the directional mask, the encoder is still attention-based, but the language modeling context is strictly "directional", in that positions are only allowed to attend over a monotonic "leftward" context (Figure 4).

Finally, to add positional information to the encoder, we use static sinusoidal encodings (Vaswani et al., 2017) and additionally employ a linear mapping f to the concatenation of the original and positional embeddings to learn the ratio at which to add the two together.

$$g = 1.0 + ReLU(f([embedding, position]))$$
$$embedding \leftarrow g * embedding + position$$

4 Experiments

Our experiments assess SLMs across three dimensions: (1) network architecture and language modeling assumptions, (2) evaluation metrics, specifically segmentation quality and language-modeling performance, and (3) supervision setting (if and where gold segmentation data is available).

4.1 Architecture and Modeling

To analyze the importance of the self-attention architecture versus the bidirectional conditioning context, we test SLMs with three different encoders: the standard R(ecurrent)SLM based on an LSTM, the M(asked)SLM introduced in 3.2 with a segmental or "cloze" mask, and a D(irectional)MSLM, with a "causal" or directional mask. The RSLM is thus (+recurrent context, +directional), the DM-SLM is (-recurrent context, +directional), and the MSLM is (-recurrent context, -directional).

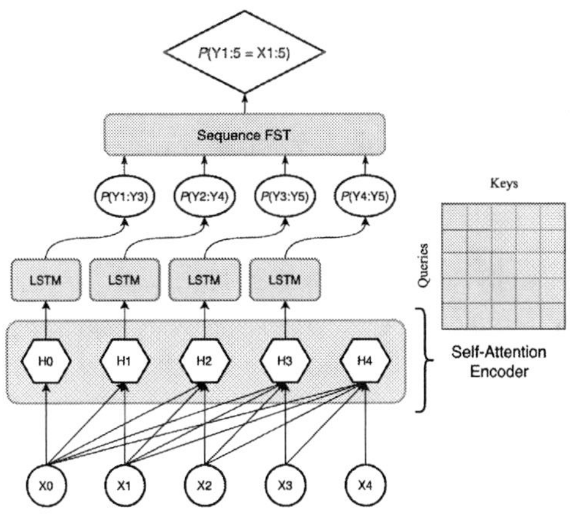

Figure 4: Directional MSLM

For all models, we use an LSTM for the segment decoder, as a control and because the decoded sequences are relatively short and may not benefit as much from an attention model. See also Chen et al. (2018) for hybrid models with transformer encoders and recurrent decoders.

4.2 Evaluation Metrics

Part of the motivation for SLMs is to create strong language models that can also be used for segmentation (Kawakami et al., 2019). Because of this, we report both segmentation quality and language modeling performance.

For segmentation quality, we get the word-F1 score for each corpus using the script from the SIGHAN Bakeoff (Emerson, 2005). Following Kawakami et al. (2019), we report this measure over the entire corpus. For language modeling performance, we report the average Bits Per Character (bpc) loss over the test set.

4.3 Supervision Setting

Because previous studies have used SLMs both in "lightly supervised" settings (Sun and Deng, 2018) and totally unsupervised ones (Kawakami et al., 2019), and because we expect SLMs to be deployed in either use case, we test both. For all model types, we conduct a hyperparameter sweep and select both the configuration that maximizes the validation segmentation quality (light supervision) and the one that minimizes the validation bpc (unsupervised).

4.4 Datasets

We evaluate our SLMs on two datasets used in Kawakami et al. (2019). For each, we use the same training, validation, and test split. The sets were chosen to represent two relatively different writing systems: Chinese (PKU) and English (PTB). Statistics for each are in Table 1. One striking difference between the two writing systems can be seen in the character vocabulary size: phonemic-type writing systems like English have a much smaller vocabulary of tokens, with words being built out of longer sequences of characters that are not meaningful on their own.

Corpus	PKU	PTB
Tokens/Characters	1.93M	4.60M
Words	1.21M	1.04M
Lines	20.78k	49.20k
Avg. Characters per Word	1.59	4.44
Character Vocabulary Size	4508	46

Table 1: Statistics for the datasets

Peking University Corpus (PKU) PKU has been used as a Chinese Word Segmentation benchmark since the International Chinese Word Segmentation Bakeoff (Emerson, 2005). One minor change we make to this dataset is to tokenize English, number, and punctuation tokens using the module from Sun and Deng (2018), to make our results more comparable to theirs. Unlike them, we do not pre-split sequences on punctuation.

Penn Treebank (PTB) For English, we use the version of the Penn Treebank corpus from (Kawakami et al., 2019; Mikolov et al., 2010).

4.5 Parameters and Trials

For all models, we tune among six learning rates on a single random seed. After the parameter sweep, the configuration that maximizes validation segmentation quality and the one that minimizes validation bpc are run over an additional four random seeds. All models are trained using Adam (Kingma and Ba, 2015) for 8192 steps.

All models have one encoder layer and one decoder layer, as well as an embedding and hidden size of 256. The transformer-based encoder has a number of trainable parameters less than or equal to the number in the LSTM-based encoder.[1]

One important parameter for SLMs is the maximum segment length k. Sun and Deng (2018) tune this as a hyperparameter, with different values for k fitting different CWS standards more or less well. In practice, this parameter can be chosen empirically to be an upper bound on the maximum segment length one expects to find, so as to not rule out long segments. We follow Kawakami et al. (2019) in choosing $k = 5$ for Chinese and $k = 10$ for English. For a more complete characterization of our training procedure, see Appendix A.[2]

5 Results

5.1 Chinese

For PKU (Table 2), Masked SLMs yield better segmentation quality in both the lightly-supervised and unsupervised settings, though the advantage in the former setting is much larger (+12.4 median F1). The Directional MSLM produces similar quality segmentations to the MSLM, but it has worse language modeling performance in both settings (+0.23 bpc for lightly supervised and +0.11 bpc for unsupervised); the RSLM produced the second-best bpc in the unsupervised setting.

The RSLM gives the best bpc in the lightly-supervised setting. However for this setting, the strict division of the models that maximize segmentation quality and those that minimize bpc can be misleading. In between these two configurations, many have both good segmentation quality and low bpc, and if the practitioner has gold validation data, they will be able to pick a configuration with the desired tradeoff.

In addition, there is some evidence that "undershooting" the objective in the unsupervised case with a slightly lower learning rate may lead to more stable segmentation quality. The unsupervised MSLM in the table was trained at rate 2e-3, and achieved 5.625 bpc (validation). An MSLM trained at rate 1e-3 achieved only a slightly worse bpc (5.631) and resulted in better and more stable segmentation quality (69.4 $\pm$ 2.0 / 70.4).

5.2 English

Results for English (PTB) can also be found in Table 2. By median, results remain comparable between the recurrent and transformer-based models, but the RSLM yields better segmentation performance in both settings (+4.0 and +4.7 F1). However, both types of MSLM are slightly more susceptible to random seed variation, causing those means to be skewed slightly lower. The DMSLM seems more susceptible than the MSLM to outlier performance based on random seeds, as evidenced by its large standard deviation. Finally, the RSLM gives considerably better bpc performance in both settings (-0.29 and -0.31 bpc).

6 Analysis and Discussion

6.1 Error Analysis

We conduct an error analysis for our models based on the overall Precision and Recall scores for each (using the character-wise binary classification task, i.e. word-boundary vs no word-boundary).

As can be seen in Table 3, all model types trained on Chinese have a Precision that approaches 100%, meaning almost all boundaries that are inserted are true boundaries. On first glance the main difference in the unsupervised case seems to be the RSLM's relatively higher Recall. However, the higher Precision of both MSLM types seems to be more important for the overall segmentation

[1] 592,381 trainable parameters in the former, 592,640 in the latter

[2] The code used to build SLMs and conduct these experiments can be found at (url redacted)

Dataset	Model	Tuned on Gold		Unsupervised	
		F1 Mean / Median	BPC	F1 Mean / Median	BPC
PKU	RSLM	61.2 ± 3.6 / 60.2	**5.67 ± 0.01**	59.4 ± 1.9 / 58.7	5.63 ± 0.01
	DMSLM	72.2 ± 2.0 / 72.7	6.08 ± 0.31	62.9 ± 2.6 / 63.4	5.67 ± 0.03
	MSLM	**72.3 ± 0.7 / 72.6**	5.85 ± 0.12	**62.9 ± 2.8 / 64.1**	**5.56 ± 0.01**
PTB	RSLM	**77.4 ± 0.7 / 77.6**	**2.10 ± 0.04**	**75.7 ± 2.6 / 76.2**	**1.96 ± 0.00**
	DMSLM	70.6 ± 6.4 / 73.3	2.36 ± 0.07	67.9 ± 10.6 / 73.8	2.27 ± 0.04
	MSLM	71.1 ± 5.6 / 73.6	2.39 ± 0.06	69.3 ± 5.6 / 71.5	2.27 ± 0.01

Table 2: Results on the Peking University Corpus and English Penn Treebank (over 5 random seeds)

performance.[3] In the lightly-supervised case, the MSLM variants learn to trade off a small amount of Precision for a large gain in Recall, allowing them to capture more of the true word boundaries in the data. Given different corpora have different standards for the coarseness of Chinese segmentation, this reinforces the need for studies on a wider selection of datasets.

Because the English results (also in Table 3) are similar between supervision settings, we only show the unsupervised variants. Here, the RSLM shows a definitive advantage in Recall, leading to overall better performance. The transformer-based models show equal or higher Precision, but tend to under-segment, i.e. produce longer words. Example model segmentations for PTB can be found in Table 4. Some intuitions from our error analysis can be seen here: the moderate Precision of these models yields some false splits like `be + fore` and `quest + ion`, but all models also seem to pick up some valid morphological splits not present in the gold standard (e.g. `+able` in *questionable*). Predictably, rare words with uncommon structure remain difficult to segment (e.g. *asbestos*).

6.2 Discussion

For Chinese, the transformer-based SLM exceeds the recurrent baseline for segmentation quality, by a moderate amount for the unsupervised setting, and by a large amount when tuned on gold validation segmentations. The MSLM also gives stronger language modeling. Given the large vocabulary size for Chinese, it is intuitive that the powerful transformer architecture may make a difference in this difficult language-modeling task. Further, though the DMSLM achieves similar segmentation quality, the bidirectional context of the MSLM does seem to be the source of the best bpc modeling performance.

In English, on the other hand, recurrent SLMs seem to retain a slight edge. By median, segmentation quality remains fairly similar between the three model types, but the RSLM holds a major language-modeling advantage in our experiments. Our main hypothesis for the disparity in modeling performance between Chinese and English comes down to the nature of the orthography for each. As noted before, Chinese has a much larger character vocabulary. This is because in Chinese, almost every character is a morpheme itself (i.e. it has some meaning). English, on the other hand, has a roughly phonemic writing system, e.g. the letter *c* has no inherent meaning outside of a context like *cat*.

Intuitively, one can see why this might pose a limitation on transformers. Without additive or learned positional encodings, they are essentially adirectional. In English, *cat* is completely different from *act*, but this might be difficult to model for an attention model without robust positional information. To try to counteract this, we added dynamic scaling to our static positional encodings, but without deeper networks or more robust positional information, the discrepancy in character-based modeling for phonemic systems may remain.

7 Conclusion

This study provides strong proof-of-concept for the viability of transfomer-based Masked Segmental Language Models as an alternative to recurrent SLMs in their ability to perform joint language modeling and unsupervised segmentation. MSLMs

[3]This table also shows that though character-wise segmentation quality (i.e. classifying whether a certain character has a boundary after it) is a useful heuristic, it does not always scale straightforwardly to word-wise F1 like is traditionally used (e.g. by the SIGHAN script).

Dataset	Model	Avg. Word Length	Precision	Recall
PKU	Gold	1.59	-	-
	RSLM (*unsup.*)	1.93 ± 0.02	98.2 ± 0.1	80.8 ± 0.6
	DMSLM (*unsup.*)	1.99 ± 0.04	98.6 ± 0.1	78.5 ± 1.8
	MSLM (*unsup.*)	2.00 ± 0.05	98.5 ± 0.1	78.1 ± 1.9
	RSLM (*sup.*)	1.92 ± 0.02	98.2 ± 0.1	81.3 ± 0.7
	DMSLM (*sup.*)	1.83 ± 0.04	97.5 ± 0.5	84.6 ± 1.5
	MSLM (*sup.*)	1.83 ± 0.01	97.6 ± 0.1	84.5 ± 0.4
PTB	Gold	4.44	-	-
	RSLM (*unsup.*)	4.02 ± 0.08	86.1 ± 1.9	95.5 ± 0.1
	DMSLM (*unsup.*)	4.27 ± 0.17	85.4 ± 5.4	88.9 ± 4.6
	MSLM (*unsup.*)	4.29 ± 0.12	86.2 ± 1.5	89.5 ± 3.5

Table 3: Error analysis statistics (over 5 random seeds)

	Examples
Gold	we 're talking about years ago before anyone heard of asbestos having any questionable...
RSLM Median	**we're** talking about years ago **be fore any one** heard of **as best os** having any **question able**
DMSLM Median	**we're** talking about years ago **be fore any one** heard of **as bestos** having any **quest ion able**
MSLM Median	**we're** talking about years ago **be fore any one** heard of **as bestos** having any **quest ion able**

Table 4: Example model segmentations from the Penn Treebank

provide the advantage of a parallelizable architecture, and have several open avenues for extending their utility. To close, we lay out directions for future work.

The most obvious next step is evaluating MSLMs on additional segmentation datasets. As mentioned, the criteria for "wordhood" in Chinese are not agreed upon, thus more experiments are warranted using corpora with different standards. Prime candidates include the Chinese Penn Treebank (Xue et al., 2005), as well as those included in the SIGHAN segmentation bakeoff: Microsoft Research, City University of Hong Kong, and Academia Sinicia (Emerson, 2005).

The sets used here are also relatively formal orthographic datasets. An eventual use of SLMs may be in speech segmentation, but a smaller step in that direction could be using phonemic transcript datasets like the Brent Corpus, also used in Kawakami et al. (2019). This set consists of phonemic transcripts of child-directed English speech (Brent, 1999). SLMs could also be applied to the orthographies of more typologically diverse languages, especially ones with complicated systems of morphology (e.g. Swahili, Turkish, Hungarian, Finnish).

Further, though we only test shallow models here, one of the main advantages of transformers is their ability to scale to deep architectures due to their short derivational chains. Thus, extending segmental models to "deep" settings would be more feasible using MSLMs than RSLMs.

Lastly, Kawakami et al. (2019) propose regularization techniques for SLMs due to low segmentation quality from their "vanilla" models. They report good findings using a character n-gram "lexicon" jointly with expected segment length regularization based on Eisner (2002) and Liang and Klein (2009). Both techniques are implemented in our codebase, and we have tested them in pilot settings. Oddly, neither has given us any gain in performance over our "vanilla" models. A more exhaustive hyperparameter search with these methods may produce a future benefits as well.

In conclusion, the present study shows strong potential for the use of MSLMs. They show particular promise for writing systems with a large inventory of semantic characters (e.g. Chinese), and we believe that they could be stable competitors of recurrent models in phonemic-type writing systems given some mitigation of the relative weakness of the positional information available in transformers.

References

Michael R. Brent. 1999. An Efficient, Probabilistically Sound Algorithm for Segmentation and Word Discovery. *Machine Learning*, 34:71–105.

Mia Xu Chen, Orhan Firat, Ankur Bapna, Melvin Johnson, Wolfgang Macherey, George Foster, Llion Jones, Mike Schuster, Noam Shazeer, Niki Parmar, Ashish Vaswani, Jakob Uszkoreit, Lukasz Kaiser, Zhifeng Chen, Yonghui Wu, and Macduff Hughes. 2018. The Best of Both Worlds: Combining Recent Advances in Neural Machine Translation. In *Proceedings of the 56th Annual Meeting of the Association for Computational Linguistics (Volume 1: Long Papers)*, pages 76–86, Melbourne, Australia. Association for Computational Linguistics.

J. Chung, Sungjin Ahn, and Yoshua Bengio. 2017. Hierarchical Multiscale Recurrent Neural Networks. In *5th International Conference on Learning Representations, ICLR 2017, Conference Track Proceedings*, Toulon, France.

Mathias Creutz and Krista Lagus. 2002. Unsupervised Discovery of Morphemes. In *Proceedings of the ACL-02 Workshop on Morphological and Phonological Learning*, pages 21–30. Association for Computational Linguistics.

Carl de Marcken. 1996. Linguistic Structure as Composition and Perturbation. In *34th Annual Meeting of the Association for Computational Linguistics*, pages 335–341, Santa Cruz, California, USA. Association for Computational Linguistics.

Jacob Devlin, Ming-Wei Chang, Kenton Lee, and Kristina Toutanova. 2019. BERT: Pre-training of Deep Bidirectional Transformers for Language Understanding. In *Proceedings of the 2019 Conference of the North American Chapter of the Association for Computational Linguistics: Human Language Technologies, Volume 1 (Long and Short Papers)*, pages 4171–4186, Minneapolis, Minnesota. Association for Computational Linguistics.

Ewan Dunbar, Julien Karadayi, Mathieu Bernard, Xuan-Nga Cao, Robin Algayres, Lucas Ondel, Laurent Besacier, Sakriani Sakti, and Emmanuel Dupoux. 2020. The Zero Resource Speech Challenge 2020: Discovering discrete subword and word units. In *Proceedings of INTERSPEECH 2020*.

Jason Eisner. 2002. Parameter Estimation for Probabilistic Finite-State Transducers. In *Proceedings of the 40th Annual Meeting of the Association for Computational Linguistics*, pages 1–8, Philadelphia, Pennsylvania, USA. Association for Computational Linguistics.

Jeffrey L. Elman. 1990. Finding structure in time. *Cognitive Science*, 14(2):179–211.

Thomas Emerson. 2005. The Second International Chinese Word Segmentation Bakeoff. In *Proceedings of the Fourth SIGHAN Workshop on Chinese Language Processing*.

John Goldsmith. 2001. Unsupervised Learning of the Morphology of a Natural Language. *Computational Linguistics*, 27(2):153–198.

Sharon Goldwater, Thomas L. Griffiths, and Mark Johnson. 2009. A Bayesian framework for word segmentation: Exploring the effects of context. *Cognition*, 112(1):21–54.

Alex Graves, Fernández Santiago, Faustino Gomez, and Jürgen Schmidhuber. 2006. Connectionist Temporal Classification: Labelling Unsegmented Sequence Data with Recurrent Neural Networks. In *Proceedings of the 23rd International Conference on Machine Learning*, Pittsburgh, PA.

Alex Graves and Jürgen Schmidhuber. 2005. Framewise phoneme classification with bidirectional LSTM and other neural network architectures. In *Neural Networks*, volume 18, pages 602–610. Pergamon.

Pratik Joshi, Sebastin Santy, Amar Budhiraja, Kalika Bali, and Monojit Choudhury. 2020. The State and Fate of Linguistic Diversity and Inclusion in the NLP World. In *Proceedings of the 58th Annual Meeting of the Association for Computational Linguistics*, pages 6282–6293, Online. Association for Computational Linguistics.

Herman Kamper, Aren Jansen, and Sharon Goldwater. 2016. Unsupervised word segmentation and lexicon discovery using acoustic word embeddings. *IEEE/ACM Transactions on Audio, Speech and Language Processing*, 24(4):669–679.

Kazuya Kawakami, Chris Dyer, and Phil Blunsom. 2017. Learning to Create and Reuse Words in Open-Vocabulary Neural Language Modeling. In *Proceedings of the 55th Annual Meeting of the Association for Computational Linguistics (Volume 1: Long Papers)*, pages 1492–1502, Vancouver, Canada. Association for Computational Linguistics.

Kazuya Kawakami, Chris Dyer, and Phil Blunsom. 2019. Learning to Discover, Ground and Use Words with Segmental Neural Language Models. In *Proceedings of the 57th Annual Meeting of the Association for Computational Linguistics*, pages 6429–6441, Florence, Italy. Association for Computational Linguistics.

Diederik Kingma and Jimmy Ba. 2015. Adam: A Method for Stochastic Optimization. In *3rd International Conference on Learning Representations, ICLR 2015, Conference Track Proceedings*, San Diego, CA, USA.

Lingpeng Kong, Chris Dyer, and Noah A Smith. 2016. Segmental Recurrent Neural Networks. In *4th International Conference on Learning Representations, ICLR 2016, Conference Track Proceedings*, San Juan, Puerto Rico.

Taku Kudo and John Richardson. 2018. SentencePiece: A simple and language independent subword tokenizer and detokenizer for Neural Text Processing. In *Proceedings of the 2018 Conference on Empirical Methods in Natural Language Processing: System Demonstrations*, pages 66–71, Brussels, Belgium. Association for Computational Linguistics.

Mike Lewis, Yinhan Liu, Naman Goyal, Marjan Ghazvininejad, Abdelrahman Mohamed, Omer Levy, Veselin Stoyanov, and Luke Zettlemoyer. 2020. BART: Denoising Sequence-to-Sequence Pretraining for Natural Language Generation, Translation, and Comprehension. In *Proceedings of the 58th Annual Meeting of the Association for Computational Linguistics*, pages 7871–7880, Online. Association for Computational Linguistics.

Percy Liang and Dan Klein. 2009. Online EM for Unsupervised Models. In *Proceedings of Human Language Technologies: The 2009 Annual Conference of the North American Chapter of the Association for Computational Linguistics*, pages 611–619, Boulder, Colorado. Association for Computational Linguistics.

Paul A. Luce. 1986. A computational analysis of uniqueness points in auditory word recognition. *Perception & Psychophysics*, 39(3):155–158.

Sabrina Mielke and Jason Eisner. 2019. Spell Once, Summon Anywhere: A Two-Level Open-Vocabulary Language Model. *Proceedings of the AAAI Conference on Artificial Intelligence*, 33(01):6843–6850. Number: 01.

Tomas Mikolov, Kai Chen, G. Corrado, and J. Dean. 2013. Efficient Estimation of Word Representations in Vector Space. In *1st International Conference on Learning Representations, ICLR 2013, Workshop Track Proceedings*, Scottsdale, AR, USA.

Tomas Mikolov, Martin Karafiát, Lukas Burget, Jan Cernocký, and Sanjeev Khudanpur. 2010. Recurrent neural network based language model. volume 2, pages 1045–1048.

Daichi Mochihashi, Takeshi Yamada, and Naonori Ueda. 2009. Bayesian Unsupervised Word Segmentation with Nested Pitman-Yor Language Modeling. In *Proceedings of the Joint Conference of the 47th Annual Meeting of the ACL and the 4th International Joint Conference on Natural Language Processing of the AFNLP*, pages 100–108, Suntec, Singapore. Association for Computational Linguistics.

Tumi Moeng, Sheldon Reay, Aaron Daniels, and Jan Buys. 2021. Canonical and Surface Morphological Segmentation for Nguni Languages. *ArXiv*.

Hyunji Hayley Park, Katherine J. Zhang, Coleman Haley, Kenneth Steimel, Han Liu, and Lane Schwartz. 2021. Morphology Matters: A Multilingual Language Modeling Analysis. *Transactions of the Association for Computational Linguistics*, 9:261–276. _eprint: https://direct.mit.edu/tacl/article-pdf/doi/10.1162/tacl_a_00365/1924158/tacl_a_00365.pdf.

Matthew Peters, Mark Neumann, Mohit Iyyer, Matt Gardner, Christopher Clark, Kenton Lee, and Luke Zettlemoyer. 2018. Deep Contextualized Word Representations. In *Proceedings of the 2018 Conference of the North American Chapter of the Association for Computational Linguistics: Human Language Technologies, Volume 1 (Long Papers)*, pages 2227–2237, New Orleans, Louisiana. Association for Computational Linguistics.

O. Rasanen and M. A. Cruz Blandon. 2020. Unsupervised Discovery of Recurring Speech Patterns using Probabilistic Adaptive Metrics. In *Proceedings of INTERSPEECH 2020*.

Jorma Rissanen. 1989. *Stochastic Complexity in Statistical Inquiry*, volume 15 of *Series in Computer Science*. World Scientific, Singapore.

Mike Schuster and Kuldip K. Paliwal. 1997. Bidirectional recurrent neural networks. *IEEE Transactions on Signal Processing*, 45(11):2673–2681.

Rico Sennrich, Barry Haddow, and Alexandra Birch. 2016. Neural Machine Translation of Rare Words with Subword Units. In *Proceedings of the 54th Annual Meeting of the Association for Computational Linguistics (Volume 1: Long Papers)*, pages 1715–1725, Berlin, Germany. Association for Computational Linguistics.

Joongbo Shin, Yoonhyung Lee, Seunghyun Yoon, and Kyomin Jung. 2020. Fast and Accurate Deep Bidirectional Language Representations for Unsupervised Learning. In *Proceedings of the 58th Annual Meeting of the Association for Computational Linguistics*, pages 823–835, Online. Association for Computational Linguistics.

K. Song, X. Tan, Tao Qin, Jianfeng Lu, and T. Liu. 2019. MASS: Masked Sequence to Sequence Pretraining for Language Generation. In *Proceedings of the 36th International Conference on Machine Learning*, Long Beach, CA.

Zhiqing Sun and Zhi-Hong Deng. 2018. Unsupervised Neural Word Segmentation for Chinese via Segmental Language Modeling. In *Proceedings of the 2018 Conference on Empirical Methods in Natural Language Processing*, pages 4915–4920, Brussels, Belgium. Association for Computational Linguistics.

Yee Whye Teh, Michael I. Jordan, Matthew J. Beal, and David M. Blei. 2006. Hierarchical Dirichlet Processes. *Journal of the American Statistical Association*, 101(476):1566–1581.

Yuanhe Tian, Yan Song, Fei Xia, Tong Zhang, and Yonggang Wang. 2020. Improving Chinese Word Segmentation with Wordhood Memory Networks. In *Proceedings of the 58th Annual Meeting of the Association for Computational Linguistics*, pages

8274–8285, Online. Association for Computational Linguistics.

Kei Uchiumi, Hiroshi Tsukahara, and Daichi Mochihashi. 2015. Inducing Word and Part-of-Speech with Pitman-Yor Hidden Semi-Markov Models. In *Proceedings of the 53rd Annual Meeting of the Association for Computational Linguistics and the 7th International Joint Conference on Natural Language Processing (Volume 1: Long Papers)*, pages 1774–1782, Beijing, China. Association for Computational Linguistics.

Ashish Vaswani, Noam Shazeer, Niki Parmar, Jakob Uszkoreit, Llion Jones, Aidan N Gomez, Lukasz Kaiser, and Ilia Polosukhin. 2017. Attention is All You Need. In *Proceedings of the 31st Conference on Neural Information Processing Systems*, Long Beach, CA. Neural Information Processing Systems Foundation.

Chong Wang, Yining Wang, Po-Sen Huang, Abdelrahman Mohamed, Dengyong Zhou, and Li Deng. 2017. Sequence Modeling via Segmentations. In *Proceedings of the 34th International Conference on Machine Learning*, volume 70 of *Proceedings of Machine Learning Research*, pages 3674–3683, International Convention Centre, Sydney, Australia. PMLR.

L. Wang, Zongyi Li, and Xiaoqing Zheng. 2021. Unsupervised Word Segmentation with Bi-directional Neural Language Model. *ArXiv*.

Nianwen Xue, Fei Xia, Fu-Dong Chiou, and Martha Palmer. 2005. The Penn Chinese TreeBank: Phrase Structure Annotation of a Large Corpus. *Natural Language Engineering*, 11(2):207–238.

A Training Details

A.1 Data

The datasets used here are sourced from Kawakami et al. (2019), and can be downloaded at `https://s3.eu-west-2.amazonaws.com/k-kawakami/seg.zip`. Our PKU data is tokenized slightly differently, and all data used in our experiments can be found in our project repository (url redacted).

A.2 Architecture

A dropout rate of 0.1 is applied leading into both the encoder and the decoder. Transformers use 4 attention heads and a feedforward size of 509 (chosen to come out less than or equal to the number of parameters in the standard LSTM). This also includes a 512-parameter linear mapping to learn the combination proportion of the word and sinusoidal positional embeddings. The dropout within transformer layers is 0.15.

A.3 Initialization

Character embeddings are initialized using CBOW (Mikolov et al., 2013) on the given training set for 32 epochs, with a window size of 5 for Chinese and 10 for English. Special tokens like <eoseg> that do not appear in the training corpus are randomly initialized. These pre-trained embeddings are not frozen during training.

A.4 Training

For PKU, the learning rates swept are {6e-4, 7e-4, 8e-4, 9e-4, 1e-3, 2e-3}, and for PTB we use {6e-4, 8e-4, 1e-3, 3e-3, 5e-3, 7e-3}. For Chinese, we found a linear warmup for 1024 steps was useful, followed by a linear decay. For English, we apply simple linear decay from the beginning. Checkpoints are taken every 128 steps. A gradient norm clip threshold of 1.0 is used. Mini-batches are sized by number of characters rather than number of sequences, with a size of 8192 (though this is not always exact since we do not split up sequences). The five random seeds used are {2, 3, 5, 8, 13}.

Each model is trained on an Nvidia Tesla M10 GPU with 8GB memory, with the average per-batch runtime of each model type listed in Table 5.

Model	s / step	
	PKU	PTB
RSLM	2.942	2.177
DMSLM	2.987	2.190
MSLM	2.988	2.200

Table 5: Average runtime per batch in seconds

A.5 Optimal Hyperparameters

The optimal learning rate for each model type, dataset, and supervision setting are listed in the Table 6. Parameters are listed by the validation objective they optimize: segmentation MCC or language-modeling BPC.

Dataset	Model	by MCC	by BPC
PKU	RSLM	6e-4	9e-4
	DMSLM	6e-4	2e-3
	MSLM	6e-4	2e-3
PTB	RSLM	7e-3	3e-3
	DMSLM	1e-3	8e-4
	MSLM	1e-3	6e-4

Table 6: Optimum learning rates

Trees probe deeper than strings: an argument from allomorphy

Hossep Dolatian
Department of Linguistics
Stony Brook University
Stony Brook, NY, USA
hossep.dolatian@alumni.stonybrook.edu

Shiori Ikawa
Department of English Language and Culture,
Fuji Women's University, Japan
shiori.ikawa@fujijoshi.ac.jp

Thomas Graf
Department of Linguistics
Stony Brook University
Stony Brook, NY, USA
mail@thomasgraf.net

Abstract

Linguists disagree on whether morphological representations should be strings or trees. We argue that tree-based views of morphology can provide new insights into morphological complexity even in cases where the posited tree structure closely matches the surface string. Our argument is based on a subregular case study of morphologically conditioned allomorphy, where the phonological form of some morpheme (the target) is conditioned by the presence of some other morpheme (the trigger) somewhere within the morphosyntactic context. The trigger and target can either be linearly adjacent or non-adjacent, and either the trigger precedes the target (inwardly sensitive) or the target precedes the trigger (outwardly sensitive). When formalized as string transductions, the only complexity difference is between local and non-local allomorphy. Over trees, on the other hand, we also see a complexity difference between inwardly sensitive and outwardly sensitive allomorphy. Just as unboundedness assumptions can sometimes tease apart patterns that are equally complex in the finitely bounded case, tree-based representations can reveal differences that disappear over strings.

1 Introduction

Morphology can be taken to operate over either strings or trees. Consider the simple case of English *undoable*, which is ambiguous between *not doable* with *un-* scoping over *doable*, and *can be undone* with *-able* scoping over *undo*. If one's primary concern is morphotactics, i.e. how morphemes can be arranged to obtain a well-formed word, then it is sufficient to represent *undoable* as a string *un+do+able*, consisting of three morphemes in a particular order. But this representation does not encode the scopal relations between the affixes *un-* and *-able*. Linguists instead use trees to encode the scopal relations between the affixes *un-* and *-able*, giving us *[un[do able]]* and *[[un do]able]* for each respective interpretation of *undoable*. But strings and trees are vastly different data structures that greatly affect computational complexity. For instance, every dependency that is context-free over strings is only regular over trees. This paper explores the typology of allomorphy to probe how the choice between strings and trees can affect morphological complexity. Our key insight is that even in cases where trees seem to add little over strings, trees can reveal complexity differences between empirical phenomena that are opaque at the string level.

Tree-based models are still rare in computational morphology, where morphological phenomena are usually modeled with finite-state machinery (Koskenniemi, 1983; Beesley and Karttunen, 2003; Roark and Sproat, 2007). From this perspective, morphological dependencies form regular string languages, and morphological processes can be computed by 1-way finite-state transducers.[1] In fact, many aspects of morphology are *subregular* over strings and fall within remarkably simple subclasses of regular string languages and finite-state transductions (Chandlee, 2014, 2017; Aksënova et al., 2016; Dolatian et al., 2021).

There is little formal work on evaluating the expressivity of morphological dependencies and processes over tree-based representations. In particular, the fine-grained notions of subregular complexity have not been applied to tree-based views of morphology even though many subregular classes can easily be generalized from strings to trees. Previous analyses of morphology that implicitly posit tree structure (Selkirk, 1982, Trost, 1991, a.o.), do not explore the implications of tree structure for complexity, either. This paper seeks to demonstrate

[1]The only major exception is total reduplication (Culy, 1985), which we set aside throughout this paper; see Dolatian and Heinz (2020) for detailed discussion.

19th SIGMORPHON Workshop on Computational Research in Phonetics, Phonology, and Morphology, pages 51 - 60
July 14, 2022

that this focus on string representations to the exclusion of tree structure means that subtle complexity differences between phenomena may be missed. It is not just cases like *undoable* where trees are useful, but even phenomena where the tree structure provides seemingly no additional information over the string representation.

To this end, we contrast string-based and tree-based views of morphologically conditioned allomorphy in terms of their subregular complexity. Morphologically conditioned allomorphy covers phenomena where some morpheme (the target) has multiple possible realizations, the choice of which is conditioned by the presence of another morpheme (the trigger) within the word. Cross-linguistically, morphologically-conditioned allomorphy can be parameterized in terms of directionality and the degree of locality between the target and trigger morpheme (Carstairs, 1987; Bobaljik, 2000, 2012; Bonet and Harbour, 2012; Embick, 2015).[2]

Table 1: Parameters for morphologically-conditioned allomorphy between trigger x and target y

Adjacency \ Direction	Inward	Outward
Local	$x < y$	$y < x$
Non-adjacent	$x < \ldots < y$	$y < \ldots < x$

If the trigger x is structurally lower than the target y, then allomorphy is *inwardly-sensitive*. If the trigger x is structurally higher than the target y, then allomorphy is *outwardly-sensitive*. If the target and trigger are structurally adjacent, then allomorphy is *locally computed*. If the target and trigger are non-adjacent, and if there can be one or more intervening morphemes, then the process is long-distance or *non-local*. Typologically, local allomorphy is the most common in both directions. Non-adjacent allomorphy is significantly less common, but attested (Božič, 2019).

We find that these four types do not pattern the same way depending on whether one models them over strings or trees (see Table 6). When modeled over strings, there is no complexity difference between inwardly and outwardly sensitive allomorphy. The only relevant split is whether the trigger and target are in a local configuration, which corresponds to a difference between input strictly local (ISL) transductions and sequential transductions. Over trees, we find the same split. But in addition we also see a difference between non-local inwardly sensitive allomorphy and non-local outwardly sensitive allomorphy, with the former but not the latter constituting a sequential tree transduction.

The paper is organized as follows. Section 2 defines relevant families of string and tree transducers, including the (to the best of our knowledge) novel classes of bottom-up and top-down sequential tree transductions. In §3 and §4, we illustrate the typological parameters of allomorphy with attested examples from natural languages. In each section we formalize the respective type of allomorphy over strings as well as trees and contrast their complexity. We then synthesize the main insights in §5. We conclude in §6.

2 Mathematical preliminaries

We cover several classes of subregular string and tree transductions in this paper. Due to space constraints, we cannot give full definitions of each class, but the discussion in the subsequent sections is sufficiently straightforward on a formal level that the reduced rigor should not impact clarity.

2.1 Subregular string transductions

Subregular string transductions are computed by finite-state transducers (FSTs) that obey additional restrictions. One well-known class is the class of *subsequential* transductions, but for our purposes the even more restrictive class of *sequential* transductions will do.[3]

Definition 1 (Sequential) *An FST $\mathcal{T}$ is* left-to-right sequential *iff $\mathcal{T}$ is deterministic and all states are final. We use $\tau(\mathcal{T})$ to denote the transduction computed by $\mathcal{T}$. An FST $\mathcal{T}$ is* right-to-left sequential *iff there is a left-to-right sequential FST $\mathcal{T}'$ such that $\tau(\mathcal{T}) = \{\langle i, o\rangle \mid \langle i^{-1}, o^{-1}\rangle \in \tau(\mathcal{T}')\}$, where s^{-1} is the mirror image of string s. We say that $\mathcal{T}$ (or $\tau(\mathcal{T})$) is* sequential *iff it is left-to-right sequential or right-to-left sequential.*

[2] Bobaljik (2000) suggest that the directionality difference correlates with the distinction between phonologically conditioned and morphologically conditioned allomorphy. Following Paster (2006), we take these two splits to form two separate axes of variation and consider only directionality. The phonological nature of the trigger should be examined independently from the formal characteristics of the computation involved.

[3] Our definition of sequential is derived from the non-standard definition of subsequential transducers in Chandlee (2014), which requires all states to be final.

If one further limits the state space of a sequential transducer so that it consists of all and only those states that record the previous k symbols in the input string, one obtains an *input strictly k-local* (ISL-k) transducer. As pointed out in Chandlee et al. (2018), a transduction is guaranteed to be ISL-k if it can be described by a finite set of rewrite rules of the form $a \to b \mid u\_v$ such that $a, b \in \Sigma$, $u, v \in \Sigma^*$, and the combined length of u and v is at most $k - 1$. Crucially, the output of one rewrite rule cannot serve as the input for another rewrite rule. All the rules apply in parallel. We say that a transduction is ISL iff it is ISL-k for some $k \geq 1$.

2.2 Subregular tree transductions

Since the tree transductions encountered in this paper are exceedingly simple, we introduce bottom-up and top-down tree transductions via examples. Our generalizations of sequential transductions from strings to trees then are easily defined as special cases of these two well-known types of tree transducers, full definitions of which can be found in Comon et al. (2008) and Gécseg and Steinby (1984), among others.

Suppose our input trees are strictly binary branching and all nodes are either labeled a, b, or c. Now consider a transduction that leaves almost all nodes the same, except that something special happens to the root of each subtree that contains an even number of as (not counting the root itself). If the label of the subtree's root is b, then it should be relabeled d. If the label is a, then the left subtree will be deleted. In addition, every leaf node c in the input tree is rewritten as $v(w, w)$. Hence the input tree on the left would become the output tree on the right.

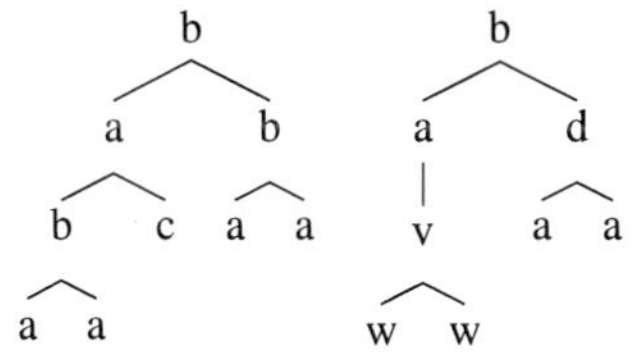

This transduction can be computed by a bottom-up tree automaton. We use two states, q_o and q_e, which keep track of whether a subtree contains an odd or an even number of as. Next, we define transition rules for the leafs: $a() \to q_o(a)$, $b() \to q_e(b)$, and $c() \to q_e(v(w, w))$. Let us also add a rewrite rule for interior node b: $b(q_o(x), q_o(y)) \to q_e(d(x, y))$ expresses that when we encounter a node labeled b such that the left subtree and the right subtree both contain an odd number of as (and thus the whole subtree contains an even number of as), b should be replaced with a d while keeping the left subtree x and the right subtree y in the same position. With these rules, we can already begin to rewrite the input tree.

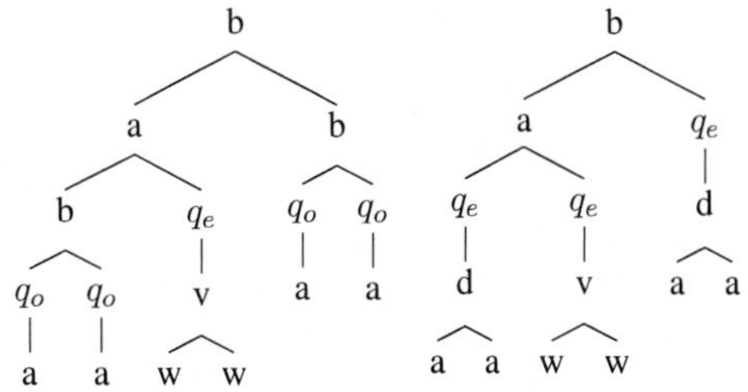

We also need rewrite rules for a as an interior node. For the concrete case at hand, the relevant transition rule is $a(q_e(x), q_e(y)) \to q_o(a(y))$, which removes the left subtree x. We then add a few more rules to handle the remaining cases. For example, $b(q_o(x), q_e(y)) \to q_o(b(x, y))$ ensures that nothing is changed when a subtree rooted in b does not contain an even number of as.

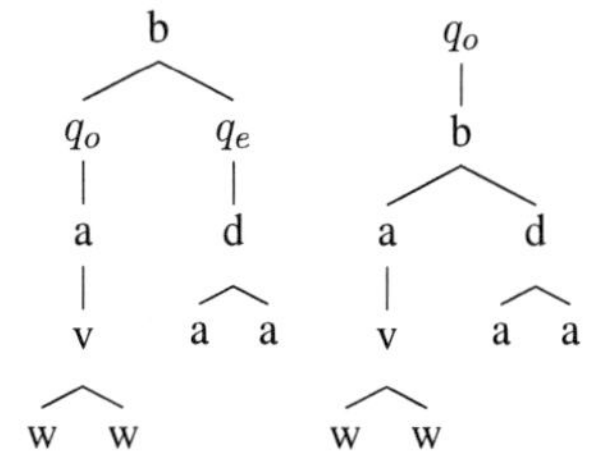

If q_o is a final state, then the subtree beneath it is chosen as the output of the transformation, otherwise it is rejected.

Now consider instead the case of a top-down transducer, which rewrites the input tree from the root towards the leafs. Assume the same input tree as before, but this time something special happens when the root of a subtree is dominated by an odd number of bs (not counting the root itself). In this case, b is rewritten as d, and c is replaced with $v(w, w)$. In addition, a with two daughters has the left one deleted. This will produce the very same output tree as before, but it does so in a different manner. First, we always start with an initial state q_e, and we set $q_e(b(x, y)) \to b(q_o(x), q_o(y))$.

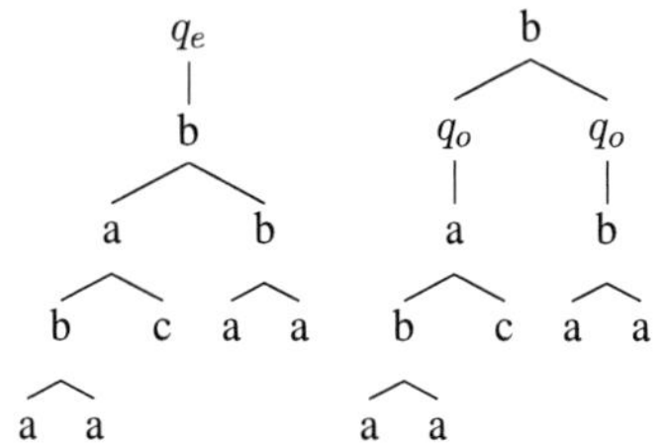

Next we add one rule for a and one for b: $q_o(a(x, y)) \rightarrow a(q_o(y))$ and $q_o(b(x, y)) \rightarrow d(q_e(x), q_e(y))$. This leaves us will only leaf nodes to rewrite, which is handled by the rules $q_o(c()) \rightarrow v(w, w)$ and $q_o(a()) \rightarrow a$.

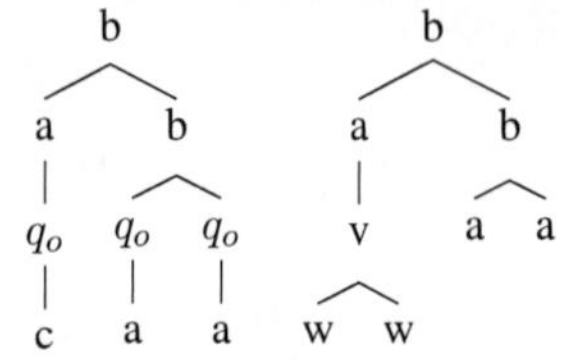

The tree is a valid output for the input because we were able to process the whole tree from the root to all its leaves.

Of course we would have to add more rules to both transducers to also cover the configurations that do not arise in our toy examples. But even then the transducers would still be *deterministic*: given two transitions rules of the form $a \rightarrow u$ and $b \rightarrow v$, $u \neq v$ implies $a \neq b$ (and in addition, the top-down tree automaton has exactly one initial state). In fact, our two example transductions satisfy additional properties that make them natural analogs of sequential string transductions.

Definition 2 (Tree sequential) *A deterministic bottom-up tree transducer is* bottom-up sequential *iff all its states are final. A deterministic top-down tree transducer is* top-down sequential *iff it holds for every state q and every leaf symbol σ that the transducer has a transition rule $q(\sigma()) \rightarrow t$, where t is some tree not containing any states.*

Finally, we also need a tree analogue of ISL string transductions. We adopt the definition in Graf (2020), but since it spans multiple pages, we only convey the intuition here. An ISL tree transduction is state-free in the sense that what a given node should be rewritten as is fully determined by its label and the local context. For the purposes of this paper, we can limit this even further to just the class of ISL tree transductions that only relabel nodes but do not change the structure of the input tree. As a concrete example, consider this rewrite rule:

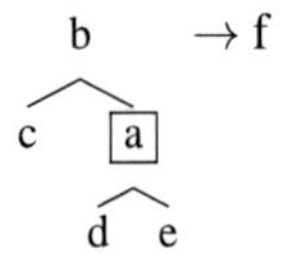

This says that a node that is labeled a is relabeled as f if the node has b as its mother, c as its left sister, d as its left daughter, e as its right daughter, and the node has no other sisters or daughters.

3 Inwardly-sensitive allomorphy

We now turn to local (§3.1) and non-local (§3.2) inwardly-sensitive allomorphy, followed by outwardly-sensitive allomorphy in §4. Local inwardly-sensitive allomorphy can be modeled with ISL FSTs and by ISL tree-transducers, suggesting that the choice between strings and trees is innocuous here. Non-local inwardly-sensitive allomorphy only falls within those classes if one assumes a finite upper bound. Otherwise, if no finite bound is assumed, then ISL is insufficient, but the allomorphy phenomena can still be captured by left-to-right sequential string transducers or bottom-up sequential tree transducers.

3.1 Local and inwardly-sensitive

As previously indicated in Table 1, an allomorphic pattern is local and inwardly-sensitive iff the conditioning morpheme (the trigger x) is structurally below the alternating morpheme (the target y) and x is structurally adjacent to y. Table 2 illustrates this with the past suffix alternation in Latin.

Table 2: Local inwardly-sensitive allomorphy from Latin (Embick, 2015, ch4.6)

imperfect	pluperfect
laud-ā-**ba**-m	laud-ā-**ve**-**ra**-m
praise-*v*-**PST**$_\mathrm{y}$-1SG	praise-*v*-**ASP**$_\mathrm{x}$-**PST**$_\mathrm{y}$-1SG
T[+past]→-*ba*	T[+past]→-*ra* / ASP[perf]_

Following Embick (2015), the Latin past suffix is by default *-ba*. After the aspect suffix *-ve*, it is instead realized as *-ra*. In terms of rewrite rules, we have the following:

1. (a) PST $\Rightarrow$ *-ra* | ASP _
   (b) PST $\Rightarrow$ *-ba* | W _

Here, and throughout the rest of the paper, we use W to denote any morpheme that is irrelevant to the alternation, e.g. any morphemes that are not ASP or PST in this example. Since the alternation can be described by finitely many rewrite rules with a context of size 1, it is an ISL-2 string transduction.

The allomorphy is also ISL over trees, but the size of the window increases slightly to ISL-3. Suppose that the two forms in Table 2 have the underlying tree structures below.

2. (a) (b)

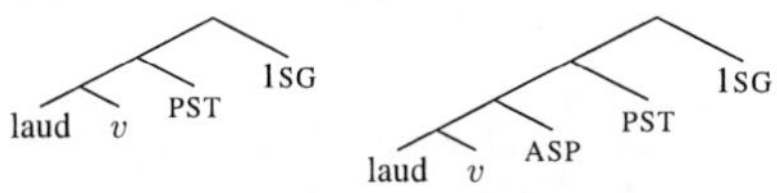

In order to derive the pattern in Table 2 given this tree structure, an ISL tree transducer has to include the rewrite rules below. They are ISL-3 rewrite rules because the depth of the tree on the left-hand side is 3.

3. ISL-3 rewrite rules for Latin Past

(a) 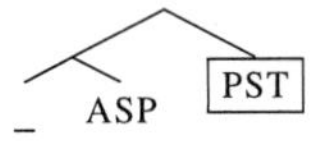 ↦ ra

(b)  ↦ ba

3.2 Non-adjacent and inwardly-sensitive

We now turn to non-adjacent inwardly-sensitive allomorphy. Recall that in these cases, the trigger x and target y are not adjacent, and x is structurally above y. We illustrate this with an example from Kiowa.

Table 3: Non-adjacent inwardly-sensitive allomorphy from Kiowa (Bonet and Harbour, 2012, 231)

héib-e-gų̀ų̀-mɔɔ-**tɔɔ** enter-**TR**$_x$-DISTR-NEG-**MOD**$_y$	héib-**é**-gų̀ų̀-mɔɔ-**t!ɔɔ** enter-**INTR**$_x$-DISTR-NEG-**MOD**$_y$
MOD→-*tɔɔ* / TR . . . _	MOD→-*t!ɔɔ* / INTR . . . _

The modality suffix (target y) surfaces as -*tɔɔ* (-*t!ɔɔ*) if the verb is transitive (intransitive). Transitivity is marked on the post-root suffix (trigger x). The trigger and target are not adjacent.

Over strings, the alternation for the attested Kiowa examples would be ISL-4. The context must span at least four 4 morphemes because the target and trigger are separated by at most 2 interveners. Similarly, over a tree, this function can be captured by an ISL-5 transduction. The crucial rewrite rules are shown below. These rules indicate that MOD is rewritten as *tɔɔ* if there is a TR with (i) no intervener, or (ii) one intervener or (iii) two interveners. In all other cases, MOD is rewritten as *tɔɔ*.

4. (a)  ↦ -tɔɔ

(b)  ↦ -tɔɔ

(c) 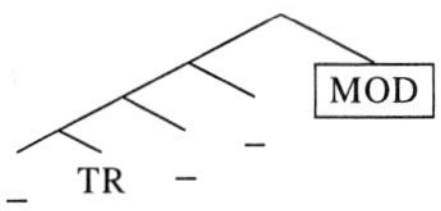 ↦ -tɔɔ

(d) 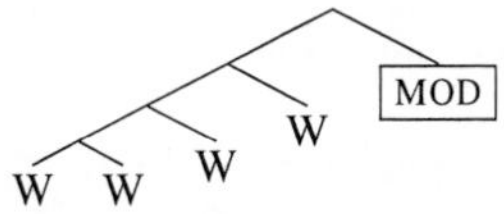 ↦ -t!ɔɔ

This treatment works for the observed cases as there is necessarily an upper bound on how far the trigger and the target can be apart. But it fails to capture the fact that the interveners do not affect the allomorphy at all. Instead, we may assume that there is no upper bound on the number of intervening morphemes. In that case, Kiowa allomorphy is no longer ISL, neither over strings nor over trees.

That said, over strings the Kiowa allomorphy pattern still falls within the class of left-to-right sequential transductions. The corresponding transducer is shown in Figure 1.

Figure 1: Sequential FST (left-to-right) for Kiowa

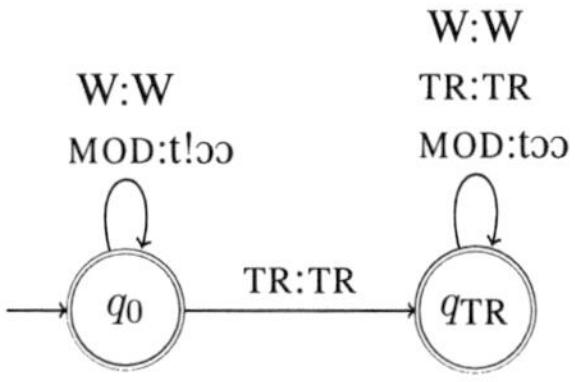

Over trees, it is also a fairly simple transduction and is, in fact, bottom-up sequential. In order to capture the allomorphy conditioned by TR, the transducer has to distinguish between a state q_{TR} where it has already processed TR and a state q_W where it has not. If the transducer sees MOD in state q_{TR}, MOD is rewritten as *tɔɔ*. Whereas if it sees MOD in state q_W, MOD is transformed into *t!ɔɔ*.

Note, however, that the crucial morphemes, MOD and TR, do not stand in a dominance relation if one assumes a phrase structure tree as depicted in Figure 2.

Figure 2: The phrase structure tree for the Kiowa modality suffixes

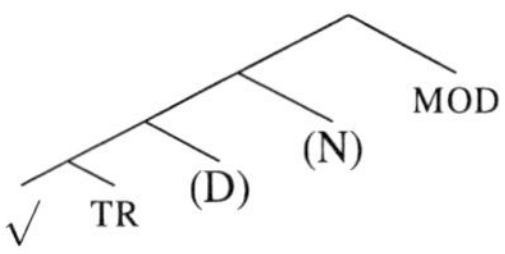

Thus, even if a bottom-up sequential transducer processes TR and moves to the state q_{TR}, the transducer reads MOD separately from that state transition. The transducer thus needs to delay its output when it reads MOD: instead of immediately choosing an output for MOD, it switches to a state q_{MOD}

without outputting anything. Then, at the next node, if the state from the left branch is q_{TR}, the transducer outputs a tree such that its right branch is *tɔɔ*. If the state from the left branch is not q_{TR}, on the other hand, then the transducer outputs a tree with the right branch *t!ɔɔ*. The relevant transition rules are shown below, with $\cdot$ as the label of interior nodes.

5. (a) $\text{MOD}() \rightarrow q_{\text{MOD}}()$
   (b) $\text{TR}() \rightarrow q_{\text{TR}}(\text{TR})$
   (c) $W() \rightarrow q_W(W)$
   (d) $\cdot(q_{\text{TR}}(x), q_{\text{MOD}}(y))$
   $\rightarrow q_{\text{TR}}(\cdot(x, \text{-}t\text{ɔɔ}))$
   (e) $\cdot(q_W(x), q_{\text{MOD}}(y))$
   $\rightarrow q_W(\cdot(x, \text{-}t!\text{ɔɔ}))$

In sum, the move from a local to a non-local phenomenon continues the parallelism already observed in the local case. Local inwardly-sensitive allomorphy is ISL over strings as well as trees, and its non-local counterpart is left-to-right sequential over strings or bottom-up sequential over trees. The only noteworthy difference is that the bottom-up sequential transducer has to make use of a *delayed output* strategy. While this may seem innocuous, this will be the decisive reason in §4.2 why non-local outwardly-sensitive allomorphy over trees is more complex.

4 Outwardly-sensitive allomorphy

Mirroring inwardly-sensitive allomorphy, outwardly-sensitive allomorphy is either local (§4.1) or non-local (§4.2). As we will see, local patterns are once again ISL over strings as well as trees. If we model non-local patterns as involving potentially unbounded distances between the target and trigger, then these patterns are sequential over strings, but not necessarily over trees.

4.1 Local and outwardly-sensitive

An allomorphic pattern is local and outwardly-sensitive iff the conditioning morpheme (the trigger x) is structurally above the alternating morpheme (the target y), and x is structurally adjacent to y. Table 4 gives an example from Hungarian: the plural suffix surfaces as *-k* by default but must be *-ai* before the 1SG possessive suffix *-m*.

Table 4: Local outwardly-sensitive allomorphy from Hungarian (Carstairs 1987, 165; Embick 2010, 62)

ruhá-**m**	ruhá-**k**	ruha-**ái-m**
dress-**POSS**$_{\text{x}}$	dress-**PL**$_{\text{y}}$	dress-**PL**$_{\text{y}}$-**POSS**$_{\text{x}}$

Over strings, the above phenomenon is ISL-2 as it can be described by the following rewrite rules:

6. (a) PL $\rightarrow$ *ai* | _POSS1SG
   (b) PL $\rightarrow$ *k* | _W (where W may also denote the end of the string).

Over trees, the Hungarian plural suffix alternation is ISL-3. Assume once again a right-linear structure where each affix is the right sibling of a subtree containing all the material to its left. The possessive affix is the right sibling of the interior node that immediately dominates the plural suffix. Hence an ISL tree transduction for the pattern in Table 4 must include the plural alternation rules shown in 7 (⋊ indicates that the node is the root). The depth of the context specified in the left-hand side of these rules is at most 3, and hence the plural alternation is ISL-3.

7. (a) (b) (c)

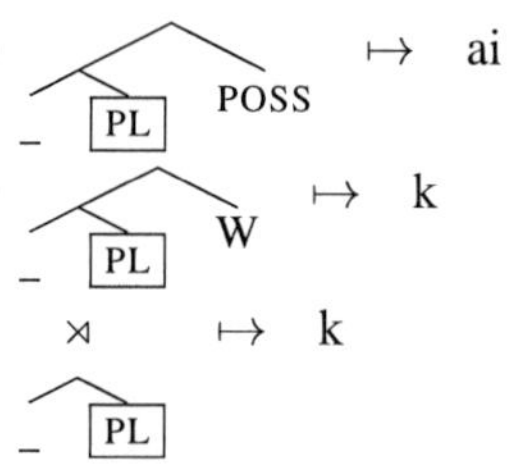

4.2 Non-adjacent and outwardly-sensitive

We now consider the case of outwardly-sensitive allomorphy where the trigger x is still above the target y, but no longer string-adjacent to it. We illustrate with Slovenian.

Table 5: Non-adjacent outwardly-sensitive allomorphy from Slovenian (Božič, 2016, 2019, 501)

žanj-e-∅-m	**ž**-e-**l**-a
reap$_{\text{y}}$-ASP-PRES-2P.SG	**reap**$_{\text{y}}$-ASP-**PTC**$_{\text{x}}$-F.SG
$\sqrt{reap}$ →*žanj*	$\sqrt{reap}$ →*ž* / _ . . . PTC

The root 'reap' surfaces as *žanj* by default. It surfaces as *ž* when the participle suffix *-l* is present. The root and suffix are not adjacent but are separated by an aspect suffix.

As with Kiowa's inwardly-conditioned non-adjacent allomorphy in §3.2, the above case can be analyzed as ISL-k with a larger value for k. Over strings, it would be ISL-3, with the central rewrite rule being $\sqrt{reap} \to \_W\text{PTC}$. Over trees, the alternation is also ISL-3, as is evidenced by the relevant rewrite rules below.

8. (a) 

$\mapsto$ ž

   (b) 

$\mapsto$ žanj

If, for the sake of argument, we treat this allomorphy as truly long-distance, then ISL is no longer sufficient. But as in the case of inwardly-sensitive non-local allomorphy, the parallel between strings and trees remains as we are dealing with a sequential transduction in both cases. The sequential string transducer is shown in Figure 3. Note that this transducer operates right-to-left, whereas inwardly-sensitive non-local allomorphy is left-to-right sequential.

Figure 3: Sequential transducer (right-to-left) for Slovenian root allomorphy

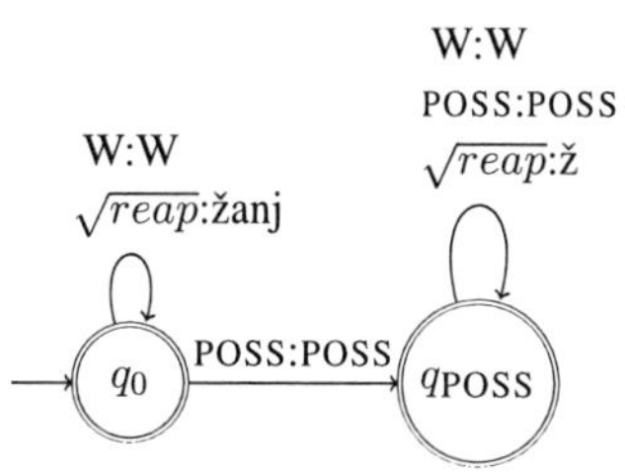

When operating with trees, we observe a curious split: sequentiality hinges on whether interior nodes are labeled with projections of affixes. Suppose that trees are labeled in the manner shown in Figure 4, where the the tree's root has the label PTCP and the suffix has PTC.

Figure 4: A phrase structure tree for Slovenian root allomorphy

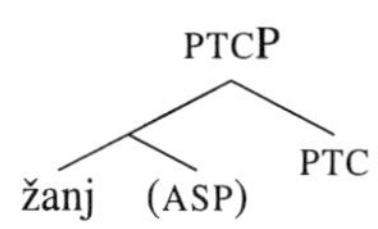

In this case, it is easy to provide a top-down sequential tree transducer for the Slovenian root allomorphy. By default, the transducer is in state q_W. When encountering the node PTCP, the transducer changes to a new state q_{PTC}, which then gets passed down into the subtrees along both branches. We then have two distinct rewrite rules such that $q_W(\sqrt{reap})$ is rewritten as *žanj*, whereas $q_{\text{PTC}}(\sqrt{reap})$ results in *ž*. If PTCP is present in the tree, then the transducer, by virtue of moving from the tree root towards the leaves, must have encountered it before reaching the morphological root $\sqrt{reap}$. The transducer will thus correctly rewrite it as *ž* in these cases, and only these cases. The key transition rules are explicitly listed in 9a–9c.

9. (a) $q_W(\text{PTC}P(x, y))$
   $\to \text{PTC}P[q_{\text{PTC}}(x), q_{\text{PTC}}(y)]$
   (b) $q_W(\sqrt{reap}) \to$ žanj
   (c) $q_{\text{PTC}}(\sqrt{reap}) \to$ ž

But on the other hand, without labels like PTCP, the alternation is not top-down sequential. In fact, it is not even top-down deterministic. The problem is that top-down transition rules are of the form $q(\sigma(x_1, \ldots, x_n)) \to \omega(q_1(x_1), \ldots, q_2(x_2))$. This means that the state assigned to a daughter x_i depends only on the label of its mother, and the state assigned to the mother. Neither the label of x_i itself, nor the labels of any of its siblings are taken into consideration. But this is exactly what is needed in the case of Slovenian. Without interior labels like PTCP, the rewrite rules would have to be $q_W(\cdot(x, W) \to \cdot(q_W(x), W)$ and $q_W(\cdot(x, \text{PTC})) \to \cdot(q_{\text{PTC}}(x), \text{PTC})$. The state that controls the processing of the subtree x must be contingent on the label of the right daughter (like PTC), and this is not possible with deterministic top-down transducers, which top-down sequential transducers are a proper subclass of.

However, one could equip the transducer with a finite look-ahead of depth 1, which would allow it to inspect the labels of daughters, too, before assigning states. This would be a *sensing tree transducer* as defined in Graf and De Santo (2019). Note that the need for look-ahead does not arise with sequential string transductions because they can emulate finite look-ahead by delaying their output; and to a more limited extent, this is also an option for the sequential bottom-up transducer. Inwardly-sensitive and outwardly-sensitive allomorphy thus seem to exhibit exactly the same complexity in the string case, but diverge at least for non-local phenomena if one switches from strings to trees. The additional complexity of trees brings to light an additional challenge that is not readily apparent in the string case.

Table 6: Summary of formal results for directionality and locality of allomorphy types; patterns marked with $*$ are ISL if one does not assume unboundedness

Pattern	String-based computation	Tree-based computation
Inward & local	ISL	ISL
Inward & non-local	Left-to-right sequential$*$	bottom-up sequential$*$
Outward & local	ISL	ISL
Outward & non-local	Right-to-left sequential$*$	top-down sequential or STFTT$*$ (sensing)

5 Discussion

This paper surveyed the attested categories of local and non-local allomorphy, with the key findings summarized in Table 6. Our central insight is that even though the choice between strings and trees seems innocuous given how closely our right-linear tree structures mirror the strings, it does reveal a difference in complexity between inwardly-sensitive and outwardly-sensitive allomorphy. Hence the use of trees can be motivated on the same grounds as unboundedness assumptions, namely that it reveals complexity differences that would be missed otherwise.

The relevant complexity difference may seem minor compared to, say, the difference between regular and context-free dependencies, which greatly matters for practical purposes such as parsing. However, this is true for most subregular complexity differences. Since all subregular dependencies and transductions can be handled with finite-state machinery, subregular distinctions do not impact efficiency. That does not mean, though, that the distinctions are irrelevant. They affect learnability, and they make different typological predictions about what kind of patterns we should expect to find across languages. One way to construe our finding, then, is that it urges us to look for empirical differences between inward non-local and outward non-local allomorphy that can be traced back to the gap in computational complexity.

Of course this argument hinges on the assumption that these phenomena are indeed unbounded and operate over trees. Unboundedness is far from a given because inflectional morphology in natural language morphology usually exhibits limits on the linear distance between the targets and triggers of allomorphy. What is unclear is whether this is an intrinsic limitation of allomorphy itself or an accidental confluence of multiple independent factors.

Our findings provide a *modus tollens* argument to address this: if we do find differences between inwardly-sensitive and outwardly-sensitive allomorphy that can be explained in terms of the subregular complexity split, then that argues in favor of underlying unboundedness and morphological tree structures because that is the only case where we find a difference in subregular complexity. If there are no discernible differences, then either unboundedness or tree structure should be jettisoned for inflectional morphology.

If there is evidence for both unboundedness and tree structure, that would be an interesting parallel to syntax. In fact, the split between inwardly-sensitive and outwardly-sensitive allomorphy already has a connection to syntax. The sensing tree transducers of Graf and De Santo (2019) were motivated by the desire to address shortcomings of deterministic top-down transducers for syntax, so it is interesting that they are also needed for tree-based morphology with the unboundedness assumption.

While the argument we present can be made with the coarse split between ISL and sequential transductions, it would be interesting to explore a possible middle-ground between the two. Tier-based strict locality has been explored in various areas — including phonology, morphology, and syntax — as an extension of the strict locality underpinning ISL (Heinz et al., 2011; Aksënova et al., 2016; Graf, 2018; Burness et al., 2021; Dolatian and Guekguezian, 2021). The non-local case of allomorphy discussed in this paper may be describable along those lines. So far, no counterpart has been defined for tree transductions, but once this happens, the issues explored in this paper should be revisited from the perspective of tier-based strict locality.

6 Conclusion

We have investigated four types of allmorphy from the perspective of strings and trees: local and non-local inwardly-sensitive allomorphy, and local and non-local outwardly-sensitive allomorphy. Even though our tree structures closely track the surface strings, our findings are not the same over the two types of representations. While the split between local and non-local allomorphy always leads to a complexity difference if one assumes unboundedness, inwardly- and outwardly-sensitive allomorphy are equally complex over strings but not over trees. If there are empirical differences between these allomorphy types that can be derived from the split in complexity, that would provide evidence for both unboundedness and tree structure in inflectional morphology. Our study thus highlights the importance of representations even in cases where the difference of representations seems innocuous at a first glance. An approach firmly rooted in trees and unboundendess may reveal subtle computational differences that would be missed otherwise.

Acknowledgments

Thomas Graf's work on this project was supported by the National Science Foundation under Grant No. BCS-1845344.

References

Alëna Aksënova, Thomas Graf, and Sedigheh Moradi. 2016. Morphotactics as tier-based strictly local dependencies. In *Proceedings of the 14th sigmorphon workshop on computational research in phonetics, phonology, and morphology*, pages 121–130.

Kenneth Beesley and Lauri Karttunen. 2003. *Finite-state morphology: Xerox tools and techniques*. CSLI Publications, Stanford, CA.

Jonathan David Bobaljik. 2000. The ins and outs of contextual allomorphy. In Kleanthes K. Grohmann and Caro Struijke, editors, *University of Maryland working papers in linguistics*, volume 10, pages 35–71. University of Maryland, College Park.

Jonathan David Bobaljik. 2012. *Universals in comparative morphology: Suppletion, superlatives, and the structure of words*. Number 50 in Current Studies in Linguistics. MIT Press, Cambridge, MA.

Eulàlia Bonet and Daniel Harbour. 2012. Contextual allomorphy. In *The morphology and phonology of exponence*, number 41 in Oxford Studies in Theoretical Linguistics, pages 195–235. Oxford University Press, Oxford.

Jurij Božič. 2016. Locality of exponence in distributed morphology: Root suppletion in Slovenian. In *North East Linguistic Society (NELS)*, volume 46, pages 137–146, Amherst. GLSA.

Jurij Božič. 2019. Constraining long-distance allomorphy. *The Linguistic Review*, 36(3):485–505.

Phillip Alexander Burness, Kevin James McMullin, and Jane Chandlee. 2021. Long-distance phonological processes as tier-based strictly local functions. *Glossa: a journal of general linguistics*, 6(1).

Andrew Carstairs. 1987. *Allomorphy in inflexion*. Croom Helm, London.

Jane Chandlee. 2014. *Strictly Local Phonological Processes*. Ph.D. thesis, University of Delaware, Newark, DE.

Jane Chandlee. 2017. Computational locality in morphological maps. *Morphology*, 27(4):1–43.

Jane Chandlee, Jeffrey Heinz, and Adam Jardine. 2018. Input strictly local opaque maps. *Phonology*, 35(2):171–205.

H. Comon, M. Dauchet, R. Gilleron, C. Löding, F. Jacquemard, D. Lugiez, S. Tison, and M. TommasiK. 2008. Tree automata: Techniques and applications. Published online: `http://www.grappa.univ-lille3.fr/tata`. Release from November 18, 2008.

Christopher Culy. 1985. The complexity of the vocabulary of Bambara. *Linguistics and Philosophy*, 8:345–351.

Hossep Dolatian and Peter Ara Guekguezian. 2021. Relativized locality: Phases and tiers in long-distance allomorphy in Armenian. *Linguistic Inquiry*.

Hossep Dolatian and Jeffrey Heinz. 2020. Computing and classifying reduplication with 2-way finite-state transducers. *Journal of Language Modeling*, 8:79–250.

Hossep Dolatian, Jonathan Rawski, and Jeffrey Heinz. 2021. Strong generative capacity of morphological processes. *Proceedings of the Society for Computation in Linguistics*, 4(1):228–243.

David Embick. 2010. *Localism versus globalism in morphology and phonology*, volume 60 of *Linguistic Inquiry Monographs*. MIT Press, Cambridge, MA.

David Embick. 2015. *The morpheme: A theoretical introduction*, volume 31. Walter de Gruyter, Boston and Berlin.

Thomas Graf. 2018. Why movement comes for free once you have adjunction. In *Proceedings of CLS 53*, pages 117–136.

Thomas Graf. 2020. Curbing feature coding: Strictly local feature assignment. In *Proceedings of the Society for Computation in Linguistics 2020*, pages 224–233, New York, New York. Association for Computational Linguistics.

Thomas Graf and Aniello De Santo. 2019. Sensing tree automata as a model of syntactic dependencies. In *Proceedings of the 16th Meeting on the Mathematics of Language*, pages 12–26, Toronto, Canada. Association for Computational Linguistics.

Ferenc Gécseg and Magnus Steinby. 1984. *Tree Automata*. Academei Kaido, Budapest.

Jeffrey Heinz, Chetan Rawal, and Herbert G Tanner. 2011. Tier-based strictly local constraints for phonology. In *Proceedings of the 49th Annual Meeting of the Association for Computational Linguistics: Human Language Technologies: Short papers-Volume 2*, pages 58–64. Association for Computational Linguistics.

Kimmo Koskenniemi. 1983. *Two-level morphology: A General Computational Model for Word-Form Recognition and Production*. Ph.D. thesis, University of Helsinki.

Mary Paster. 2006. *Phonological conditions on affixation*. Ph.D. thesis, University of California, Berkeley, Berkeley, CA.

Brian Roark and Richard Sproat. 2007. *Computational Approaches to Morphology and Syntax*. Oxford University Press, Oxford.

Elisabeth Selkirk. 1982. *The syntax of words*. Number 7 in Linguistic Inquiry Monographs. MIT Press, Cambridge, Mass.

Harald Trost. 1991. Recognition and generation of word forms in natural language understanding systems: Integrating two-level morphology and feature unification. *Applied Artificial Intelligence*, 4:411–457.

Subword-based Cross-lingual Transfer of Embeddings from Hindi to Marathi and Nepali

Niyati Bafna and Zdeněk Žabokrtský,
Charles University, Faculty of Mathematics and Physics,
Institute of Formal and Applied Linguistics
niyatibafna13@gmail.com, zabokrtsky@ufal.mff.cuni.cz

Abstract

Word embeddings are growing to be a crucial resource in the field of NLP for any language. This work introduces a novel technique for static subword embeddings transfer for Indic languages from a relatively higher resource language to a genealogically related low resource language. We primarily work with Hindi-Marathi, simulating a low-resource scenario for Marathi, and confirm observed trends on Nepali. We demonstrate the consistent benefits of unsupervised morphemic segmentation on both source and target sides over the treatment performed by fastText. Our best-performing approach uses an EM-style approach to learning bilingual subword embeddings; we also show, for the first time, that a trivial "copy-and-paste" embeddings transfer based on even perfect bilingual lexicons is inadequate in capturing language-specific relationships. We find that our approach substantially outperforms the fastText baselines for both Marathi and Nepali on the Word Similarity task as well as WordNet-Based Synonymy Tests; on the former task, its performance for Marathi is close to that of pretrained fastText embeddings that use three orders of magnitude more Marathi data.

1 Introduction

Subword-level embeddings are useful for many tasks, but require large amounts of monolingual data to train. While about 15 Indian languages such as Hindi, Bengali, and Marathi have the required magnitudes of data, most Indian languages are highly under-resourced; they have very little monolingual data and almost no parallel data, and not much digitization. For example, to the best of our knowledge, Marwadi, spoken by 14M people, has no available monolingual corpus; Konkani, spoken by about 3M people, has a monolingual corpus containing 3M tokens, and no parallel data.[1] However, many of these languages have very close syntactic, morphological, and lexical connections to surrounding languages including the mentioned high-resource languages. Our approach aims to leverage these connections in order to build embeddings for these low-resource languages, in the hope that this will aid further development of other NLP tools for these languages.[2]

While there is a growing interest in shifting towards contextual embeddings with BERT (Devlin et al., 2018), as well as extending them to low-resource languages, static embeddings retain value in being lightweight and less computationally expensive, especially as studies show that they can perform comparably to contextual embeddings in certain settings (Arora et al., 2020) and encode similar linguistic information (Miaschi and Dell'Orletta, 2020). Thus, an efficient method to develop static embeddings for languages with minimal or no NLP research remains a relevant step to building a basic range of resources in these languages. In this study, we primarily work with Hindi-Marathi as our genealogically and culturally related language pair, and use asymmetric resources (large data for Hindi, artificially small monolingual data for Marathi), confirming our final results for Nepali.

Most languages of the Indic/Indo-Aryan family, spoken over most parts of North India, are morphologically rich, including Hindi, Marathi, and Nepali. This means that while related language pairs may have a high number of cognates, these may be "disguised" by surrounding inflectional or derivational morphemes. Therefore, even with an identical underlying syntactic structure, lexical correspondences between languages may be obscured or rendered incongruent. Further, when working with small data, the corpus frequencies of

[1]The Opus Corpus (Tiedemann, 2012), one of the most popular collection of parallel texts, contains no parallel data for languages such as Konkani or Bundeli.

[2]While some languages may have a little parallel data, we assume none, so as to cater to languages that are just undergoing digitization.

19th SIGMORPHON Workshop on Computational Research in Phonetics, Phonology, and Morphology, pages 61 - 71

fully inflected surface forms would be much less reliable than those of stem and affix morphemes, intuitively resulting in a less robust embeddings transfer. These factors add weight to the intuition that many Indic languages share morpheme-level correspondences with each other. This motivated us to apply unsupervised morphemic segmentation on both the source and target language data; we demonstrate the benefits of doing so in our evaluations. Note that this also makes it natural to work with subword-level embeddings rather than word embeddings; studies show that the former have an advantage over word embeddings especially for morphologically rich languages. (Chaudhary et al., 2018; Zhu et al., 2019b; Li et al., 2018).

The idea of the transfer is to project the low-resource language (LRL) subwords into a shared bilingual space with the high-resource language (HRL). We first attempt a trivial transfer that simply finds the "closest" HRL subword for each LRL subword, and copies its embedding. We demonstrate that this approach, while tempting, is not enough to capture the relationships between even identical words in both languages; embeddings spaces appear to encode more complex information that this approach would suggest. For our best performing approach, we adapt the EM-style algorithm described in Artetxe et al. (2017) to a subword-setting; the algorithm alternately optimizes the distance between pairs belonging to a bilingual mapping, and generates a bilingual mapping between words from the resulting bilingual embeddings. As far as we know, our work is the first to apply this algorithm in the context of embeddings transfer. We compare the resulting bilingual embeddings to data-intensive fastText models using the Word Similarity and WordNet-Based Synonymy Tests for Marathi; for Nepali, we evaluate on the latter task due to the lack of a Word Similiarity dataset.

2 Previous Work

2.1 Subwords in Embedding Spaces

In a seminal work, Bojanowski et al. (2017) present fastText embeddings, that work at a subword level by representing words as bags of chargrams. Kudo and Richardson (2018) present a subword tokenizer for neural text processing, and Kudo (2018) shows the benefits of using multiple subword segmentations in neural machine translation, especially in low-resource settings. Zhu et al. (2019b) look at the segmentation of a word, such as using chargrams, Byte Pair Encoding (BPE) (Gage, 1994; Sennrich et al., 2016), Morfessor, as well as the composition of the subword embeddings (addition, averaging, etc.) to construct the final word vector, and conclude that the best performing configuration is highly language and task dependent. A subsequent work (Zhu et al., 2019a) focuses on LRLs and finds the combination of BPE and addition largely robust, although they once again note language-dependent variability. They also find that encoding "affix" information with positional embeddings is beneficial, hinting that the embedding space may distinguish the importance of different kinds of subwords.

2.2 Cross-lingual embeddings

The problem of learning bilingual embeddings has usually been studied in a symmetric resources scenario. Xu et al. (2018) propose an unsupervised method of mapping two sets of monolingual static embeddings into a shared space; they present results for English paired with Spanish, Chinese, and French, evaluated on the bilingual lexicon induction and Word Similarity tasks. Chaudhary et al. (2018) experiment with joint and transfer learning for training bilingual subword embeddings for pairs of Indic LRLs from scratch, by projecting different scripts into the International Phonetic Alphabet (IPA). Kayi et al. (2020) present an extension of the BiSkip cross-lingual learning objective that leverages subword information to train English-paired bilingual embeddings for LRLs, using around 30K parallel sentences. We describe Artetxe et al. (2017) in some detail below, since we use this algorithm in our approach. There is also growing interest in multilingual contextual embeddings (Devlin et al., 2018; Kakwani et al., 2020; Ruder et al., 2019) such as multilingual BERT; Wang et al. (2020) propose an approach to extend multilingual BERT to low-resource languages without retraining it, Pfeiffer et al. (2020) suggest an approach towards incorporating previously unseen scripts into a multilingual BERT model.

2.3 Bilingual Lexicon Induction

This task is closely related to that of embeddings transfer; we see that these two tasks leverage each other in the literature. Older works such as Koehn and Knight (2002) and Haghighi et al. (2008) use monolingual features such as frequency heuristics, orthographic features, tags, and context vectors in order to find bilingual mappings for mainly European language pairs. Hauer et al. (2017) use word2vec embeddings (Mikolov et al., 2013) in order to iteratively train a translation matrix.

2.4 Summarizing Artetxe et al. (2017)

Artetxe et al. (2017) present an EM-style approach to training bilingual embeddings from monolingual embeddings without parallel data; however, it assumes high quality monolingual embeddings for both languages trained on at least 1 billion word corpora each. Given the two sets of word embeddings, they find a bilingual dictionary D by choosing the closest target word for each source word with respect to the cosine distance between source and target word embeddings. In the next step, they use the dictionary D to calculate a linear transformation matrix that minimizes the sum of cosine distances of the embeddings of all word pairs in D. They apply an orthogonality constraint on the transformation matrix in order to preserve monolingual invariance i.e. to prevent the degradation of the monolingual relationships in the resulting embedding space. These steps are repeated until convergence.

3 Note on languages

Hindi, spoken by about 340M people, is related to other large Indic languages such as Marathi, Punjabi, and Bangla, and has 48 recognized "dialects" over India, which makes it a good choice for the HRL in this project. Hindi is written in the Devanagari script, which is also used for over 120 other (often related) languages, including Marathi and Nepali. Hindi, Marathi, and Nepali share morpho-syntactic properties common within the Indic language family, such as (split) ergativity and primarily SOV structure with reordering allowed under constraints. For all three languages, (some) nouns inflect for case and number, verbs inflects for tense, number, gender, and person, and adjectives inflect for gender and number, and case in Hindi and Marathi. Some differences are that Marathi and Nepali exhibit more agglutinative tendencies than Hindi, both allowing suffix stacking with certain boundary changes. For example, a Marathi token may be a sequence of verb+nominalizing-morpheme+case-marker or noun+postposition+genitive, whereas Hindi separates these morphemes into tokens in many cases (while still exhibiting inflectional and some derivational morphology). See Figure 1.

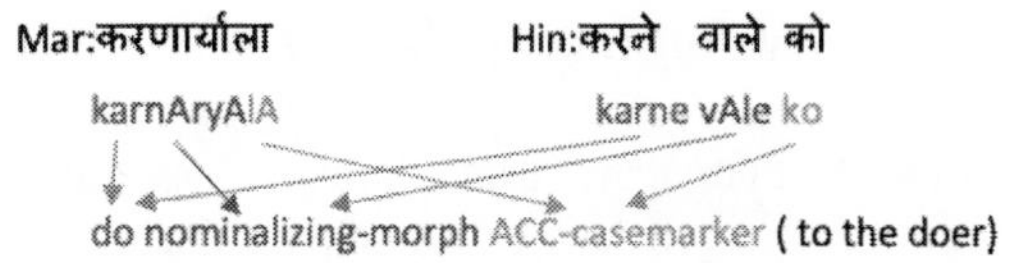

Figure 1: Tokens in Marathi and Hindi. The stem for "do" is the same (i.e. "kar") in both languages; Marathi uses one token whereas Hindi uses three.

4 Data and Resources

4.1 Training Data

For Hindi, we used 1M sentences containing roughly 18M tokens from the HindMonoCorp 0.5 (Bojar et al., 2014). For Marathi, we used 50K sentences containing 0.8M tokens from the IndicCorp Marathi monolingual dataset (Kakwani et al., 2020)[3], and for Nepali, we use 1.4M tokens from the Wortschatz corpus (Goldhahn et al., 2012). We choose these numbers for Marathi and Nepali because it seems to be the ballpark of the amount of monolingual data collected for newly digitized Indic languages.[4] All the above corpora, as well as following resources, are in the Devanagari script.

4.2 Pretrained Embeddings

We use pretrained fastText embeddings for Hindi, presented by Grave et al. (2018), in line with the assumption that we have good quality resources for the HRL. These embeddings (HIN-PRETR-2G[5]) are trained on the *Wikipedia* corpus as well as *Common Crawl*, containing a total of about 2G tokens. We also use the pretrained fastText embeddings (MAR-PRETR-334M, NEP-PRETR-393M) presented in the same work, solely for the purpose of evaluation; these embeddings are trained on 334M tokens (Marathi) and 393M tokens (Nepali).

4.3 Evaluation datasets

4.3.1 Word Similarity Dataset

A Word Similarity dataset is a set of word pairs, each annotated by humans according to the de-

[3]Note that we do not lemmatize our data; good-quality lemmatizers are a scarce resource that we cannot assume for the LRL.

[4]See `https://www.ldcil.org/resourcesTextCorp.aspx` for efforts on collecting data on under-resourced languages such as Bodo, Dogri, Santhali, etc.

[5]We use the following shorthand to refer to our models unless otherwise specified: <language>-<method_label>-<tokens_of_training_data>. There may be two data slots in the case of bilinugal embeddings, containing amount of Marathi/Nepali and Hindi data respectively.

gree of similarity (integers ranging from 1 to 10) between the two words. Evaluation is usually performed by finding the cosine similarity between the two words vectors, and calculating the Spearman's Rank Correlation between the human and model "similarity" judgments for all word pairs. We report this correlation multiplied by 100.

We present results on the Marathi Word Similarity dataset presented by Akhtar et al. (2017), containing 104 word pairs. This dataset is created by translating a subset of the WordSimilarity-353 English dataset into Marathi by native Marathi speakers, and re-evaluating the similarity scores by 8 native speaker annotators.[6]

4.3.2 WordNet-Based Synonymy Tests

We also perform WordNet-Based Synonymy Tests (WBST) (Piasecki et al., 2018) for Marathi and Nepali. A WBST consists of a set of "questions" consisting of one "query word", and N options, all of which occur MIN times in the corpus. One of the options is a synonym or closely related to the query word, while the rest are "distracters", or randomly selected words. The task is to identify the synonym; we do this by calculating the cosine distances between the query word vector and each of the options and selecting the closest. The reported score is the percentage of correctly answered questions. We use the IndoWordNet,[7] built by Sinha et al. (2006); Debasri et al. (2002), for generating the WBST.

5 Segmentation

5.1 Motivation

Due to the fusional/agglutinative nature of the languages, as well as the morphological and tokenization differences as discussed in Section 3, we apply unsupervised morphemic segmentation to both source and target side data. This is motivated by the need to handle data scarcity on the LRL side, since fully inflected tokens are much rarer than their constituent subwords; we see that the unsegmented Marathi and Nepali data have 100K and 140K distinct tokens respectively, but only 20K and 40K distinct "morphemes", respectively, post-segmentation.

The morphemic segmentation is also an attempt to isolate the morphs in the language data since,

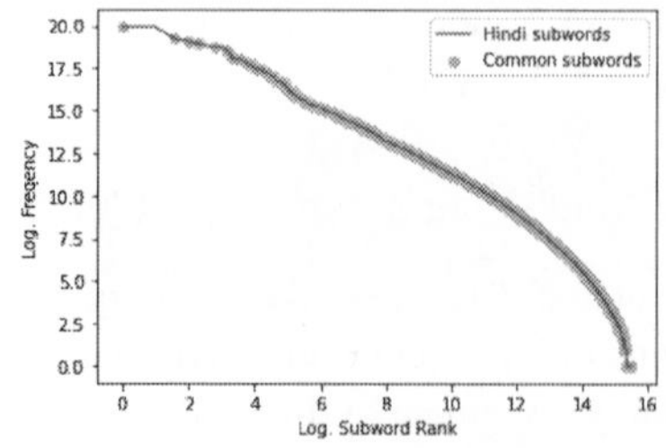

Figure 2: Shared subwords in Hindi and Marathi corpora; numbering up to 17.23% of the total # of subwords in the Hindi corpus. Common subwords are well-distributed over the range.

according to our hypothesis, it is easier to find correspondences between the two languages at this level rather than at the token level. This is clear in the fact that 50% of the subwords in the Marathi segmented data also occur in the Hindi corpus, whereas for the unsegmented data, this is only 20% of tokens. For Nepali, the difference is lower, in particular, 40% and 20% respectively. See Figures 2 and 3 for a visualisation of the frequency range of the common subwords over that of all subwords in the Hindi and Marathi corpora respectively. Finally, we see that while the mean length of subwords in the Marathi and Hindi corpora are 5.02 and 4.72 respectively, the mean length of common subwords is 3.95; this indicates that shorter subwords are (naturally) more likely to be common than longer counterparts. We see similar numbers for Nepali.

The most obvious fallout to attempting static embedding transfer at the subword level is morphological homonymy i.e. morphs that may have more than one "meaning", and therefore deserve more than one static embedding.[8] There are many examples of such morphs, e.g. /te/ is both the (free) third person plural pronoun, as well as the (bound) first person female present tense morph in Marathi.

5.2 Tools and evaluation

We experimented with BPE and Morfessor and decided to use the latter, since BPE seemed unable to preserve longer morphs regardless of parameter settings. However, this decision may vary according to language type. We perform a manual evaluation

[6] not available for Nepali.

[7] See `http://www.cfilt.iitb.ac.in/WordNet/webmwn/`

[8] This is of course a general problem with static embeddings; however, it is exacerbated at the level of subwords, especially imperfectly segmented, since they are shorter and more multifunctional, as it were, than longer lexemes.

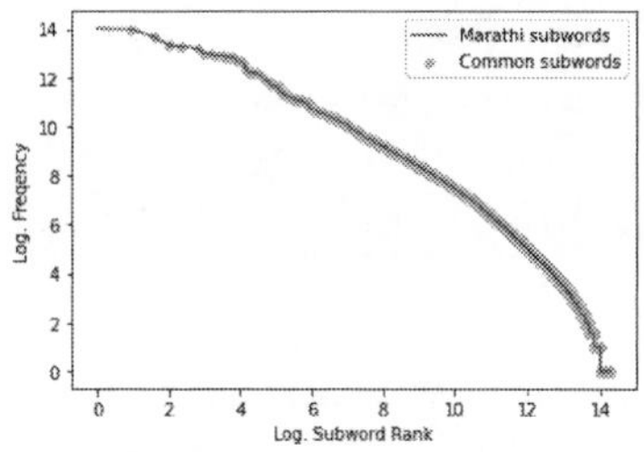

Figure 3: Shared Hindi-Marathi subwords, numbering up to 40.39% of the total # of subwords in the Marathi corpus. As in Figure 2, we see a distribution over the frequency range with the bulk in the mid-to-low frequency range.

of the resulting Marathi segmentation[9] over 100 words sampled by frequency, which shows 72.6% precision and 64.9% recall. True and false positives are counted with respect to morph boundaries rather than at the word level, and each boundary prediction contributes equally to precision/recall. 61% of words are segmented completely correctly.

6 Approach

As baseline, we train fastText models on the available tokenized data (MAR-BASE-0.8M, NEP-BASE-1.4M) for both languages. We work with 300-dimensional embeddings for all experiments.[10]

6.1 Normalized Edit Distance (NED) Approach (Marathi)

Our initial experiments were performed on Hindi-Marathi. The NED approach is based on finding a bilingual subword-level mapping; it takes advantage of the high number of cognates and borrowings between related languages as well as the common script. Its primary intuition is that since the languages share not only lexical items but also syntactic and morphological properties, embedding vectors can essentially be "copied" over to the LRL from the HRL.

For each Marathi morph, we choose the Hindi subword with the minimum NED from it. NED is calculated in the following way:

$$NED(l,h) = \frac{edit\_distance(l,h)}{max(length(l), length(h))}$$

To obtain the embedding of any Marathi word, we first segment it. For each subword, we look for the closest Hindi subword by NED, and retrieve the corresponding Hindi subword embedding. Finally, we compose the subword embeddings, using addition, to give the word embedding. See Algorithm 1 for a depiction.[11]

Algorithm 1: NED Approach

```
l_word ← LRL word;
H_EMB ← HRL embeddings;
l_morphs ← segment_lrl(l_word);
  l_subwords_emb ← empty list;
for l_morph in l_morphs do
  | h_closest ← closest_HRL_morph(l_word);
  | append(l_subwords_emb, H_EMB(h_closest));
end
l_emb ← compose_subwords(l_subwords_emb);
return l_emb ;
```

6.2 Iterative approach (Marathi, Nepali)

Although the approach presented in Artetxe et al. (2017) is intended to generate bilingual *word* embeddings for equally well-resourced languages (See Section 2.4), we hypothesize that the algorithm will maintain its quality at the subword level for morphologically rich languages; further, that in our data-asymmetry situation, this approach will serve to "transfer" some of the higher quality of the HRL embedding space to the LRL embeddings, by leveraging a bilingual mapping to induce the relationships already encoded in the HRL embeddings.

We apply this approach to both Marathi and Nepali. As the initial set of LRL embeddings, we use fastText vectors trained on available segmented data (MAR-SEGM-0.8M, NEP-SEGM-1.4M). For the HRL, we can use any available resource. We try using pretrained fastText vectors (HIN-PRETR-2G); we also retrain fastText on the segmented Hindi data (HIN-SEGM-18M). For all runs, we set the initial seed dictionary as identical words[12] in the source and target corpora.[13] See Algorithm 2 for a depiction of OOV handling for this approach. For composing the subword embeddings of a word, we tried

[9]The authors do not speak Nepali and are therefore unable to provide a manual evaluation.

[10]Repeating some experiments for 100 dimensional embeddings spaces, we observe similar trends, with a generally lower performance.

[11]Of course, an NED-based approach is highly limited to related words in the language. However, testing it out gives us an interesting insight about cognates and identical words (see Section 9.1)

[12]This is only possible because the languages share a script.

[13]Note that this approach does not use any parallel data or bilingual lexicons; this aligns with our assumptions about parallel data. However, in the case that parallel data does exist, it can be used to find a good quality bilingual seed lexicon in lieu of using identical words; this has been shown to improve the quality of the resulting bilingual embeddings.

Algorithm 2: Bilingual embeddings with MAR-SEGM-0.8M/NEP-SEGM-1.4M as backoff

```
l_word ← LRL word;
L_EMB ← Bilinual LRL embeddings;
L_EMB_backoff ← Monolingual LRL embeddings;
l_morphs ← segment_lrl(l_word);
l_subwords_emb ← empty list;
for l_morph in l_morphs do
    l_morph_emb ← empty list ;
    if l_morph in L_EMB then
        l_morph_emb ← L_EMB(l_word);
    end
    else
        l_morph_emb←L_EMB_backoff(l_morph);
    end
    append(l_subwords_emb, l_morph_emb);
end
l_emb← compose_subwords(l_subwords_emb);
return l_emb ;
```

Approach	Score
MAR-BASE-0.8M	24.64
MAR-SEGM-0.8M	**43.23**
BI-MAR-JOINT-0.8M-18M	35.48

Table 1: Marathi monolingual and Marathi-Hindi Joint results on Marathi WordSim task. Notation of models explained in Section 4.2.

addition, averaging, and picking the first subword embedding while discarding the rest. The idea behind the last method is that this approximates the word stem, and also reduces the noise created by summing different subword embeddings.

7 Results: Word Similarity (Marathi)

7.1 Baseline and Comparison Models

In Table 1, we show the performance of MAR-BASE-0.8M and MAR-SEGM-0.8M. taking motivation from Chaudhary et al. (2018), we also try a joint approach i.e. we train bilingual embeddings jointly on the segmented Hindi and Marathi data (BI-MAR-JOINT-0.8M-18M). We observe that simple segmentation of the data causes an improvement of over 20 points, outdoing not only MAR-BASE-0.8M but MAR-SKIPGR-27M (See Table 2). Surprisingly, the joint model BI-MAR-JOINT-0.8M-18M dips in performance in comparison to the MAR-SEGM-0.8M. We discuss this effect of the Hindi data on the bilingual embeddings in Section 9.1.

In Table 2, we show the performance of pretrained fastText Marathi embeddings mentioned in Section 4.2 (MAR-PRETR-334M), as well as the best performing model score from Akhtar et al. (2017) on this evaluation dataset. Akhtar et al. (2017) test

Embeddings	Score
MAR-PRETR-334M	**54.89**
MAR-SKIPGR-27M	41.12
HIN-PRETR-2G	39.94

Table 2: Scores of high-resource Marathi and Hindi models on Marathi WordSim task for comparison.

Embeddings	Identical Word Score
HIN-PRETR-2G	41.17
MAR-PRETR-334M	**50.38**

Table 3: Scores of pretrained embeddings on word pairs from the Marathi WordSim dataset that are identical in both languages

different sets of embeddings including Skip-gram, CBOW (Mikolov et al., 2013) and fastText (Bojanowski et al., 2017) algorithms, all trained on a corpus with 27M tokens, of which the Skip-Gram (MAR-SKIPGR-27M) performed best.

Finally, Table 3 shows the performance of the MAR-PRETR-334M and HIN-PRETR-2G on certain word pairs in the Marathi WordSim dataset such that both words are also used identically in Hindi.[14] These word pairs were manually identified from the Marathi evaluation dataset; we found that there were 64 such word pairs.[15] Surprisingly, we see a significant dip in the performance of HIN-PRETR-2G on these word pairs as compared to MAR-PRETR-334M, indicating that while the word pairs appear identical in both languages to a native speaker, their usage in the corpora or interaction with other words from the language is different.[16]

7.2 Normalized Edit Distance (NED)

Our NED models use only Hindi embeddings, and project Marathi morphs onto Hindi morphs as shown in Algorithm 1. For further simplicity, we also tried a self-mapping; i.e. we simply calculate the (Hindi) embeddings of the Marathi morphs obtained by segmentation, as they are. Note that this

[14] That is, both of the words in the word pair must be both Hindi and Marathi words with the same spelling, and near-identical senses.

[15] Many of these are transliterations of English words. 24 of the total 135 unique words are transliterations, and they occur 40 times i.e. 19.6% times in the 104 word pairs.

[16] Note that HIN-PRETR-2G performs very well on the Hindi WordSim dataset; its monolingual quality is not the problem.

Approach	Score
Bi-Mar-Self-Segm-0.8M-18M	**43.62**
Bi-Mar-Self-Pretr-0.8M-2G	42.72
Bi-Mar-NED-Pretr-0.8M-2G	41.85
Bi-Mar-NED-Segm-0.8M-18M	39.37

Table 4: Scores on Marathi WordSim for self-mapping and NED strategies, using different Hindi embeddings. Notation: Bi-<lrl>-<mapping_method>-<hin_embs>-<lrl_tokens>-<hin_tokens>.

is only possible because Marathi and Hindi share a common script. The resulting embeddings are composed by addition unless otherwise mentioned. See Table 4 for the results on different combinations of embeddings and mappings.

Firstly, we observe that the self-mapping performs better than NED in general.[17] This is unsurprising; NED would only perform better for Marathi words that are cognates with Hindi words and show a slight difference in spelling; it will perform competitively with self-mapping for identical words in Hindi and Marathi. As we discuss in Section 7.1, such words form a large part of the evaluation dataset. As for the remaining words, it seems that the Hindi embeddings are able to capture the meaning of the unknown Marathi morphs, perhaps due to similarities at a subword level. Applying the NED mapping, however, can result in Marathi words being mapped to arbitrary Hindi words that may share no semantics with the Marathi word.

Another interesting observation is that the Bi-Mar-Self-Segm-0.8M-18M performs a little better than Bi-Mar-Self-Pretr-0.8M-2G. This affirms our intuition in Section 5 that segmentation on the Hindi side may facilitate the correspondence between commmon subwords, leading to better performance on a Marathi evaluation set despite orders of magnitude less (Hindi) data.

7.3 Iterative Approach

There are several points of interest in the results, given in Table 5. Firstly, we see that the Bi-Mar-Iter-Segm-0.8M-18M outperforms Bi-Mar-Iter-Pretr-0.8M-2G; i.e. once again, we find that it is better to use embeddings trained on segmented Hindi data for the transfer, even though Hin-Segm-18M is trained on two orders of magnitude fewer data than Hin-Pretr-2G. Since this approach is explicitly bilingual and attempts to project the Marathi and Hindi embeddings into a shared space, this is a much more direct affirmation that the similarities between Hindi and Marathi are best exploited at the subword level from *both* sides. Secondly, we see that the "first-morph" manner of composition does slightly better than summing or averaging[18] the subword embeddings.[19] Finally, note that doubling the amount of Hindi data used to train the initial Hindi embeddings does not help. This indicates that the Hindi data is only useful up to a point.

Approach	Comp.	Score
(Mar-Base-0.8M	-	24.64)
Bi-Mar-Iter-Pretr-0.8M-2G	Sum	44.28
Bi-Mar-Iter-Segm-0.8M-9M	Sum	49.49
Bi-Mar-Iter-Segm-0.8M-18M	Sum	49.21
Bi-Mar-Iter-Segm-0.8M-18M	FM	50.06
Bi-Mar-Iter-Segm-0.8M-36M	FM	**50.10**

Table 5: Iterative approach results on Marathi WordSim task using different sets of Hindi embeddings for the crosslingual transfer. Format of the approach name: Bi-<lrl>-Iter-<hin_embs>-<lrl_tokens>-<hin_tokens>. **Comp.**: Composition function. FM (first morph) refers to the strategy of simply using the embedding of the first morph

8 Results: WordNet-Based Synonymy Tests (Marathi, Nepali)

See Table 6 and Table 7 for the Marathi and Nepali scores respectively. These results confirm some of the findings from the WordSim results for Marathi, while showing similar trends for Nepali. We see once more that segmentation helps: Mar-Segm-0.8M and Nep-Segm-1.4M consistently outperform the baselines; further, the iterative method is the best among the low-resource embeddings. We also note that doubling the Hindi data for the iterative approach (e.g. with Bi-Mar-Iter-0.8M-36M) seems not to have much effect on the resulting embeddings for both Marathi and Nepali. It is interesting to observe that Nepali is slightly less respon-

[17]Note that there is a difference between the self-mapping model and directly applying Hin-Pretr-2G as in Table 2 In the former, we segment the Marathi word ourselves and apply Hindi embeddings to the resulting subwords; in the latter, we leave it up to fastText. We note that the former does better.

[18]We do not report averaging scores since they are almost identical to the summing scores.

[19]This could be for several reasons; for example, if the first subword approximates the root of the word, then it may capture most of the meaning, whereas the remaining information may be irrelevant or add noise.

(MIN, N)	Test size	MAR-BASE -0.8M	MAR-SEGM -0.8M	BI-MAR-ITER -SEGM-0.8M-18M	BI-MAR-ITER -SEGM-0.8M-36M	MAR-PRETR -334M
(10,6)	1183	51.23	58.92	**61.62**	57.06	**84.70**
(10,5)	1183	51.90	54.78	58.66	**61.54**	**84.87**
(20,6)	684	48.98	53.65	**59.94**	58.19	**84.50**
(20,5)	684	57.89	59.94	**64.47**	64.33	**87.57**
(50,5)	293	58.02	63.14	67.24	**68.94**	**81.23**

Table 6: WBST Results. MIN: min. freq. of the question and options in the corpus, N: number of total options, Test size: number of questions. The two best-performing models have been bolded.

(MIN, N)	Test size	NEP-BASE -1.4M	NEP-SEGM -1.4M	BI-NEP-ITER -SEGM-1.4M-18M	BI-NEP-ITER -SEGM-1.4M-36M	NEP-PRETR -393M
(10,6)	1414	58.20	63.93	**65.28**	65.06	**74.11**
(10,5)	1414	61.10	67.75	**69.17**	69.10	**76.37**
(20,6)	974	62.32	69.30	**69.71**	69.10	**76.38**
(20,5)	974	63.86	69.51	**70.74**	70.12	**78.23**
(50,5)	451	66.29	70.29	71.62	**71.84**	**77.16**

Table 7: WBST Results for Nepali. Formatted similarly to Table 6.

sive to the iterative approach than Marathi; this can perhaps be explained by its lower shared subword vocabulary with Hindi (approximately 40% as compared to 50% for Marathi-Hindi). Finally, as MIN increases, the performance of the low-resource methods generally increases; they naturally perform better on words seen more frequently in the corpus.

9 Discussion

Some of the clearer findings of our experiments are as regards segmentation and the benefits of a non-trivial bilingual embeddings transfer.

We see repeatedly that segmentation on both sides of the transfer helps the quality of the LRL embeddings. Segmenting the Marathi data causes a large boost in monolingual performance (Table 1); furthermore, when transferring from Hindi embeddings, BI-MAR-ITER-SEGM-0.8M-18M outperforms BI-MAR-ITER-PRETR-0.8M-2G (Table 5); the Hindi embeddings used in the latter are trained on 2 orders of magnitude higher (unsegmented) data.[20] This suggests that the interaction between the two languages is indeed facilitated at a subword level, validating our bilingual native speaker intuition about the same. We also see that the iterative approach consistently outperforms both monolingual models MAR-BASE-0.8M and MAR-SEGM-0.8M, indicating that bilingual interaction between the related languages is indeed beneficial. In general, this is a good sign for the project of building NLP tools for low-resource languages, although it invites exploration of the impact of different typologies on the observed bilingual effect.

Finally, we find that, in agreement with the findings of the papers that investigate subword composition functions (Zhu et al., 2019a,b), the best-performing composition function for subword embeddings seems to be task and data dependent; even discarding everything except the first subword seems to work better sometimes than aggregating all subword embeddings.

9.1 Using Hindi data

To the best of our knowledge, this is the first work that clearly demonstrates that a trivial "copy-and-paste" transfer approach, such as our NED models, is not adequate, even when working with two culturally related languages that share a very high percentage of vocabulary as well as morphosyntactic properties. Our experiments with identical words pairs in Table 3 especially show that even identical words that are not false friends may behave dif-

[20] Note that we are talking about performance in terms of the resultant Marathi bilingual embeddings rather than the direct evaluation of the Hindi embeddings.

ferently depending on the language;[21] using Hindi embeddings *directly*, even for identical words, is problematic. We believe that this is an important insight into embeddings transfer that rejects relying on trivial or simplistic approaches.

Many of our experiments are intended to indicate how useful the Hindi data and embeddings are to the LRL; e.g. we evaluate HIN-PRETR-2G directly on the Marathi WordSim task (Table 2), we experiment with different amounts of Hindi data for both tasks (Tables 5 and 6), and we try a self-mapping with the NED model (see Table 4). We see that doubling the amount of Hindi data sometimes even harms performance;[22] we also see that BI-MAR-JOINT-0.8M-18M performs worse than MAR-SEGM-0.8M (see Table 1). In conjunction, these results imply that under the current transfer paradigm, adding more Hindi data may sometimes hurt rather than benefit; too much Hindi data for the purpose of training bilingual embeddings may actually "conceal" Marathi word interactions. We also applied the iterative approach on Konkani-Hindi, with a mere 100K tokens of Konkani data and 18M tokens of Hindi data as before; however, the bilingual effect was less clearly visible with this setup, supporting the need for investigation into the optimal balance of LRL-HRL data. We invite further investigation of this effect.

10 Future Work

This work is intended to be the pilot in a series of similar studies. We hypothesize that we can obtain similar results for other genealogically related LRL-HRL pairs. We intend to repeat these experiments for language pairs (simulating LRL environments) such as Punjabi-Hindi, Assamese-Bengali, Konkani-Marathi, and others. Some of the issues we will be working against are different scripts, morphemic segmentation of typologically different languages, and the lack of evaluation data. We would also like to experiment with the integration of parallel data into this approach. Finally, we also think it would be interesting to extend our solution from a bilingual to a multilingual one, with multiple sources for a target language. This would be highly pertinent in the case of Indic languages, where even major Indic languages may be interconnected, and regional languages may benefit from the resources of more than one HRL.

11 Conclusion

Embeddings transfer from a high-resource language to a low-resource related language is an important task in today's scenario of data inequality across languages. We target a family of geographically and genealogically related languages, including some high-resource languages and other low-resource languages, possibly undergoing digitization and data collection. We take two Indic language pairs, Hindi-Marathi/Nepali, simulating a low-resource scenario for Marathi and Nepali, and present an approach to embeddings transfer that uses very little monolingual data on the LRL side, and no parallel data. We demonstrate the benefits of unsupervised morphemic segmentation on both source and target sides for subword-level embeddings transfer. Our final approach improves substantially over monolingual fastText baselines for the Marathi WordSim task, and the WBST task for Marathi and Nepali. Further, we show that a "copy-and-paste" embeddings transfer fails even with a perfect bilingual dictionary for a closely related language pair, establishing the need for more sophisticated methods of low-resource bilingual transfer.

Acknowledgements

This work has been using data, tools and services provided by the LINDAT/CLARIAH-CZ Research Infrastructure (`https://lindat.cz`), supported by the Ministry of Education, Youth and Sports of the Czech Republic (Project No. LM2018101).

[21]This is to say even if words a and b occur identically and with the same senses in both languages, the word pair (a, b) may have a different relationship depending on the language.

[22]Our particular "doubled" dataset actually shows roughly the percentage of shared subwords as before doubling; it is possible that data introducing new subwords will perform better. However, in any case, it is interesting to note that the transfer is not improved by having more HRL data for the same subwords which we might intuitively hope would help the quality of the HRL embeddings and therefore the transfer.

References

Syed Sarfaraz Akhtar, Arihant Gupta, Avijit Vajpayee, Arjit Srivastava, and Manish Shrivastava. 2017. Word similarity datasets for Indian languages: Annotation and baseline systems. In *Proceedings of the 11th Linguistic Annotation Workshop*, pages 91–94, Valencia, Spain. Association for Computational Linguistics.

Simran Arora, Avner May, Jian Zhang, and Christopher

Ré. 2020. Contextual embeddings: When are they worth it? *CoRR*, abs/2005.09117.

Mikel Artetxe, Gorka Labaka, and Eneko Agirre. 2017. Learning bilingual word embeddings with (almost) no bilingual data. In *Proceedings of the 55th Annual Meeting of the Association for Computational Linguistics (Volume 1: Long Papers)*, pages 451–462.

Piotr Bojanowski, Edouard Grave, Armand Joulin, and Tomas Mikolov. 2017. Enriching word vectors with subword information. *Transactions of the Association for Computational Linguistics*, 5:135–146.

Ondřej Bojar, Vojtěch Diatka, Pavel Rychlý, Pavel Straňák, Vít Suchomel, Aleš Tamchyna, and Daniel Zeman. 2014. HindMonoCorp 0.5. LINDAT/CLARIAH-CZ digital library at the Institute of Formal and Applied Linguistics (ÚFAL), Faculty of Mathematics and Physics, Charles University.

Aditi Chaudhary, Chunting Zhou, Lori Levin, Graham Neubig, David R Mortensen, and Jaime G Carbonell. 2018. Adapting word embeddings to new languages with morphological and phonological subword representations. *arXiv preprint arXiv:1808.09500*.

Chakrabarti Debasri, Narayan Dipak Kumar, Pandey Prabhakar, and Bhattacharyya Pushpak. 2002. Experiences in building the Indo-Wordnet: A Wordnet for Hindi. In *Proceedings of the First Global WordNet Conference*.

Jacob Devlin, Ming-Wei Chang, Kenton Lee, and Kristina Toutanova. 2018. Bert: Pre-training of deep bidirectional transformers for language understanding. *arXiv preprint arXiv:1810.04805*.

Philip Gage. 1994. A new algorithm for data compression. *C Users Journal*, 12(2):23–38.

Dirk Goldhahn, Thomas Eckart, and Uwe Quasthoff. 2012. Building large monolingual dictionaries at the leipzig corpora collection: From 100 to 200 languages. In *Proceedings of the Eighth International Conference on Language Resources and Evaluation (LREC'12)*, pages 759–765.

Edouard Grave, Piotr Bojanowski, Prakhar Gupta, Armand Joulin, and Tomas Mikolov. 2018. Learning word vectors for 157 languages. *arXiv preprint arXiv:1802.06893*.

Aria Haghighi, Percy Liang, Taylor Berg-Kirkpatrick, and Dan Klein. 2008. Learning bilingual lexicons from monolingual corpora. In *Proceedings of ACL-08: Hlt*, pages 771–779.

Bradley Hauer, Garrett Nicolai, and Grzegorz Kondrak. 2017. Bootstrapping unsupervised bilingual lexicon induction. In *Proceedings of the 15th Conference of the European Chapter of the Association for Computational Linguistics: Volume 2, Short Papers*, pages 619–624.

Divyanshu Kakwani, Anoop Kunchukuttan, Satish Golla, NC Gokul, Avik Bhattacharyya, Mitesh M Khapra, and Pratyush Kumar. 2020. inlpsuite: Monolingual corpora, evaluation benchmarks and pre-trained multilingual language models for Indian languages. In *Proceedings of the 2020 Conference on Empirical Methods in Natural Language Processing: Findings*, pages 4948–4961.

Efsun Sarioglu Kayi, Vishal Anand, and Smaranda Muresan. 2020. Multiseg: Parallel data and subword information for learning bilingual embeddings in low resource scenarios. In *Proceedings of the 1st Joint Workshop on Spoken Language Technologies for Under-resourced languages (SLTU) and Collaboration and Computing for Under-Resourced Languages (CCURL)*, pages 97–105.

Philipp Koehn and Kevin Knight. 2002. Learning a translation lexicon from monolingual corpora. In *Proceedings of the ACL-02 workshop on Unsupervised lexical acquisition*, pages 9–16.

Taku Kudo. 2018. Subword regularization: Improving neural network translation models with multiple subword candidates. In *Proceedings of the 56th Annual Meeting of the Association for Computational Linguistics (Volume 1: Long Papers)*, pages 66–75, Melbourne, Australia. Association for Computational Linguistics.

Taku Kudo and John Richardson. 2018. SentencePiece: A simple and language independent subword tokenizer and detokenizer for neural text processing. In *Proceedings of the 2018 Conference on Empirical Methods in Natural Language Processing: System Demonstrations*, pages 66–71, Brussels, Belgium. Association for Computational Linguistics.

Bofang Li, Aleksandr Drozd, Tao Liu, and Xiaoyong Du. 2018. Subword-level composition functions for learning word embeddings. In *Proceedings of the Second Workshop on Subword/Character LEvel Models*, pages 38–48, New Orleans. Association for Computational Linguistics.

Alessio Miaschi and Felice Dell'Orletta. 2020. Contextual and non-contextual word embeddings: an in-depth linguistic investigation. In *Proceedings of the 5th Workshop on Representation Learning for NLP*, pages 110–119, Online. Association for Computational Linguistics.

Tomas Mikolov, Kai Chen, Greg Corrado, and Jeffrey Dean. 2013. Efficient estimation of word representations in vector space. *arXiv preprint arXiv:1301.3781*.

Jonas Pfeiffer, Ivan Vulić, Iryna Gurevych, and Sebastian Ruder. 2020. Unks everywhere: Adapting multilingual language models to new scripts. *arXiv preprint arXiv:2012.15562*.

Maciej Piasecki, Gabriela Czachor, Arkadiusz Janz, Dominik Kaszewski, and Paweł Kędzia. 2018. Wordnet-based evaluation of large distributional models for

Polish. In *Proceedings of the 9th Global Wordnet Conference*, pages 229–238, Nanyang Technological University (NTU), Singapore. Global Wordnet Association.

Sebastian Ruder, Ivan Vulić, and Anders Søgaard. 2019. A survey of cross-lingual word embedding models. *Journal of Artificial Intelligence Research*, 65:569–631.

Rico Sennrich, Barry Haddow, and Alexandra Birch. 2016. Neural machine translation of rare words with subword units. In *Proceedings of the 54th Annual Meeting of the Association for Computational Linguistics (Volume 1: Long Papers)*, pages 1715–1725.

Manish Sinha, Mahesh Reddy, and Pushpak Bhattacharyya. 2006. An approach towards construction and application of multilingual Indo-Wordnet. In *3rd Global Wordnet Conference (GWC 06), Jeju Island, Korea*. Citeseer.

Jörg Tiedemann. 2012. Parallel Data, Tools and Interfaces in OPUS. In *Proceedings of the Eight International Conference on Language Resources and Evaluation (LREC'12)*, Istanbul, Turkey. European Language Resources Association (ELRA).

Zihan Wang, Stephen Mayhew, Dan Roth, et al. 2020. Extending multilingual BERT to low-resource languages. *arXiv preprint arXiv:2004.13640*.

Ruochen Xu, Yiming Yang, Naoki Otani, and Yuexin Wu. 2018. Unsupervised cross-lingual transfer of word embedding spaces. In *Proceedings of the 2018 Conference on Empirical Methods in Natural Language Processing*, pages 2465–2474.

Yi Zhu, Benjamin Heinzerling, Ivan Vulić, Michael Strube, Roi Reichart, and Anna Korhonen. 2019a. On the importance of subword information for morphological tasks in truly low-resource languages. In *Proceedings of the 23rd Conference on Computational Natural Language Learning (CoNLL)*, pages 216–226.

Yi Zhu, Ivan Vulić, and Anna Korhonen. 2019b. A systematic study of leveraging subword information for learning word representations. In *Proceedings of the 2019 Conference of the North American Chapter of the Association for Computational Linguistics: Human Language Technologies, Volume 1 (Long and Short Papers)*, pages 912–932.

Multidimensional acoustic variation in vowels across English dialects

James Tanner[a] **Morgan Sonderegger**[a] **Jane Stuart-Smith**[b]
[a]McGill University [b]University of Glasgow
james.tanner@mail.mcgill.ca
morgan.sonderegger@mcgill.ca
Jane.Stuart-Smith@glasgow.ac.uk

Abstract

Vowels are typically characterized in terms of their static position in formant space, though vowels have also been long-known to undergo dynamic formant change over their timecourse. Recent studies have demonstrated that this change is highly informative for distinguishing vowels within a system, as well as providing additional resolution in characterizing differences between dialects. It remains unclear, however, how both static and dynamic representations capture the main dimensions of vowel variation across a large number of dialects. This study examines the role of static, dynamic, and duration information for 5 vowels across 21 British and North American English dialects, and observes that vowels exhibit highly structured variation across dialects, with dialects displaying similar patterns within a given vowel, broadly corresponding to a spectrum between traditional 'monophthong' and 'diphthong' characterizations. These findings highlight the importance of dynamic and duration information in capturing how vowels can systematically vary across a large number of dialects, and provide the first large-scale description of formant dynamics across many dialects of a single language.

1 Introduction

Both the classification and measurement of vowels have long been central, intersecting, issues for phonetic research. Vowels are dynamic in production, yet language-specific vowel descriptions typically use broad categories referring to more or less general 'movement' of a vowel, such as distinguishing between *monophthongal* and *diphthongal* vowel realizations. At the same time, it is still unclear in what low-dimensional space vowels themselves vary: which acoustic properties best capture differences between vowels, and how securely categories like 'monophthong' and 'diphthong' can be established empirically within and across languages. Do these discrete categories reflect the ways in which vowels vary, or are vowel distinctions better characterized by a spectrum, reflecting various degrees of 'movement'? This study addresses this question by examining vowel variation *within* a language – across dialects – to consider how both *static* and *dynamic* properties of vowels capture dialectal variation across English.

Static measurements of formants, taken at a single time-point within the vowel, have long provided useful approximations for cues to vowel properties such as height and backness (e.g. Peterson and Barney, 1952; Hillenbrand and Gayvert, 1993), and have been central to previous descriptions of how vowels vary across dialects (e.g., Hagiwara, 1997; Clopper et al., 2005; Labov et al., 2006). Beyond single-point measurements of vowels, however, the importance of time-dependent *dynamic* information – such as spectral change and duration – has also been recognized since the earliest phonetic studies of vowel production and perception (e.g. Peterson and Barney, 1952; House, 1961; Gay, 1968).

Research on English has shown that this dynamic information may be utilized for better distinguishing vowels within a language (Harrington and Cassidy, 1994; Watson and Harrington, 1999; Williams and Escudero, 2014; Docherty et al., 2015), can reflect detailed dialectal and sociolinguistic meaning (Risdal and Kohn, 2014; Farrington et al., 2018; Williams et al., 2019), play a role in the development of dialect-specific vowel shifts (Evans, 1935; Labov, 1991; Clopper et al., 2005; Labov et al., 2006; Fox and Jacewicz, 2017), and constitute a robust source of variation across speakers (e.g. MacDougall, 2006; Morrison, 2009). Studies on single dialects have demonstrated that vowels vary in their average duration (House and Fairbanks, 1953; Peterson and Lehiste, 1960; Crystal and House, 1982), though our understanding of how vowel durations systematically vary across dialects is relatively limited (e.g., Bailey, 1968; Wetzell, 2000; Fridland et al., 2014; Tauberer and Evanini, 2009).

19th SIGMORPHON Workshop on Computational Research in Phonetics, Phonology, and Morphology, pages 72 - 82
July 14, 2022

Looking across *many* English dialects, however, it still remains unclear how best to characterize, on one hand, vowel variability across multiple acoustic dimensions (including how robustly monophthong/diphthong categories hold up across dialects), and on the other hand, the extent to which dynamic representations compare with static measures for characterizing differences between dialects on the basis of vowel realization. This study takes a computational and exploratory approach to addressing these issues, by considering the following research question: *to what extent do dynamic representations of vowels (formant trajectories, duration) capture additional information (over static F1/F2 position) in describing vowel variation across English dialects?* Concretely, answers to this question are addressed in two ways: 1. through an exploratory analysis of English vowel variability (Section 3.1), which enables inspection of the 'same' vowel across different dialects, including the evidence for monophthong/diphthong classification; 2. through a dialect classification experiment, where different combinations of formant position, trajectory shape, and duration are compared in their ability to correctly classify the dialect of a given vowel (Section 3.2). The exploratory analysis is motivated by the phonetic literature discussed above, which uses formant dynamics to characterize the vowel space of a given dialect, while the classification experiment is inspired by by the computational literature on dialect classification, where different kinds of acoustic information have been found to independently help differentiate dialects (e.g. Woehrling et al., 2009; Hanani et al., 2013; Chittaragi and Koolagudi, 2019).

The study takes a 'large-scale' approach, through the consistent extraction of the same measures for a large amount of data collected from speech corpora of 21 English dialects. Scaling up the analysis across multiple dialects is made possible by tools for automatic annotation (e.g. Schiel, 1999; Fromont and Hay, 2012; McAuliffe et al., 2017a), acoustic analysis (Rosenfelder et al., 2014; Mielke et al., 2019), and integrating information across idiosyncratic data formats (McAuliffe et al., 2017b, 2019). To our knowledge, this is the largest cross-dialect study to date of formant dynamics.

Vowels for the study were selected to provide a spectrum of qualities which are described in the English dialectological literature as ranging from largely monophthongal through to usually diphthongal, varying dialectally by the presence of a glide (Ladefoged and Maddieson, 1993), reflected in the degree of formant change over their time-course. Specifically, the vowels were the following, as represented in terms of lexical sets (a characteristic word of a particular vowel) (Wells, 1982): FLEECE, FACE, PRICE, MOUTH, and CHOICE. FLEECE is expected to be monophthongal across dialects; MOUTH, PRICE, and CHOICE are expected to be diphthongs, which vary across dialects in both the degree of dynamic change and overall position (e.g. 'monophthongization' of PRICE in Southern US varieties, 'Canadian raising' of MOUTH in some Canadian/US varieties: Thomas, 2001; Labov et al., 2006; Boberg, 2010). FACE is expected to be intermediate between monophthongs and diphthongs, dependent on the specific dialect (e.g. Trudgill, 1999; Labov et al., 2006; Haddican et al., 2013).

2 Data

This study examines variation in stressed vowels from 21 British and North American English dialects, using corpus data collated as part of the SPeech Across Dialects of English (SPADE) project (Sonderegger et al., 2022, https://spade.glasgow.ac.uk/), including multi-dialect corpora from the United Kingdom (Coleman et al., 2012; Grabe, 2004; Anderson et al., 2007) and North America (Godfrey et al., 1992; Greenbaum and Nelson, 1996), as well as multiple individual English dialect corpora (Pitt et al., 2007; Dodsworth and Kohn, 2012; Stuart-Smith et al., 2017; Rosen and Skriver, 2015; Fabricius, 2000; Holmes-Elliott, 2015). Here, North American dialects refers to dialects in Canada and the United States as outlined in *The Atlas of North American English* (Labov et al., 2006). Due to the relative sparsity of Canadian data compared with United States and British dialects, Canadian dialects were distinguished along rural and urban dimensions instead of geographical location (Greenbaum and Nelson, 1996; Rosen and Skriver, 2015). Dialectal distinctions for British English used Trudgill's (1999) modern dialectal groupings, based on both phonological and lexical distinctions. Speakers for Scottish dialects were grouped based on information from *The Scottish National Dictionary* (Skretkowicz and Rennie, 2005).

Tokens with a duration shorter than 50 milliseconds were not extracted, in line with previous studies of vowel formants (Dodsworth, 2013; Frue-

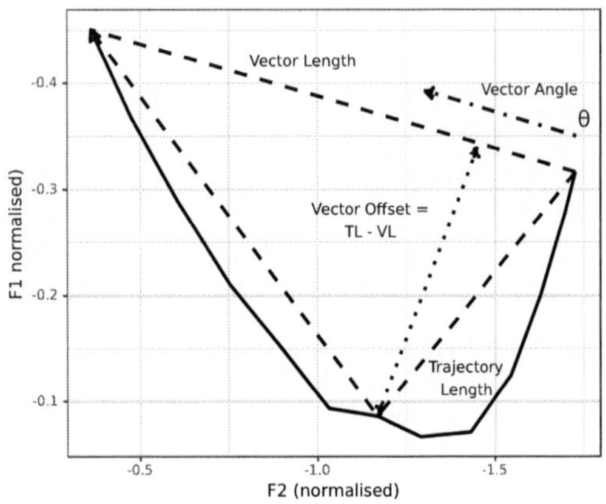

Figure 1: Schematic of all dynamic measures (dashed lines) used in the study mapped to a hypothetical CHOICE vowel trajectory (solid line).

hwald, 2013). Vowels with a duration longer than 500 milliseconds were also excluded. Formants were extracted in Hertz at 21 equally-spaced points, and were automatically measured with PolyglotDB (McAuliffe et al., 2017b) using the measurement scheme described in Mielke et al. (2019). The first and last 20% of the vowel was excluded to minimise the influence of surrounding segments (Fox and Jacewicz, 2009; Williams and Escudero, 2014; Williams et al., 2019). The remaining middle 60% of the vowel (13 points) was then z-score normalized against all vowels produced by the speaker ('Lobanov normalization', Lobanov, 1971).

In order to inspect spectral change across dialects more easily, and to allow comparison of our exploratory formant-based analyses with existing cross-dialect research (Section 3.1), we calculated a set of measures which are based on calculations of 'vowel section length' (VSL): the Euclidean distance between two formant points (n, m):

$$VSL_{n,m} = \sqrt{(F1_n - F1_m)^2 + (F2_n - F2_m)^2}$$

A measure of the overall spectral change (called 'Vector Length') is derived from calculating the VSL of the vowel onset and offset, whilst more complex representations of the trajectory can be derived from the summation of VSLs calculated from subsets of the points, such as onset to midpoint + midpoint to offset (Fox and Jacewicz, 2009). Figure 1 illustrates these measures on a hypothetical formant trajectory. A wide range of measures have been utilized within the vowel dynamic literature for capturing the dynamic properties of a formant trajectory, such as polynomial functions (MacDougall and Nolan, 2007; Van der Harst et al., 2014; Themistocleous, 2017), discrete cosine transforms (Watson and Harrington, 1999; Williams and Escudero, 2014), target-locus scaling (Broad and Clermont, 2017), and additive models (Kirkham et al., 2019; Renwick and Stanley, 2020) – the choice to use vector-based measurements of formant trajectories was motivated by their use in numerous studies of dialectal variation in English (Fox and Jacewicz, 2009; Cardoso, 2015; Farrington et al., 2018) and other languages (Mayr and Davies, 2011; Schoorman et al., 2015). Whilst these methods have not been explicitly compared, the decision to make use of the vector-based measurements in this study is based around the relative comparability with the previous cross-dialectal work using this measure, as well as its relative interpretability as a representation of spectral change. More information about the data, vowel formant extraction, and measurement calculation methods used in this study can be found in Tanner (2020). In total, 323,060 tokens (6259 types), corresponding to 1245 speakers from 21 dialects of North American and British English, were analyzed (Table 1).

3 Results

Figure 2 shows the vowel plot for each dialect included in the study, with arrows reflecting the vowel trajectories for each of the five vowels. Even from the empirical data, two findings are immediately clear: dialects are variable in their phonetic implementation of a given vowel, but there are also consistent patterns for the same vowel across dialects, including the anticipated monophthong-diphthong spectrum: from least movement for FLEECE to visible trajectories for CHOICE, PRICE, and MOUTH, with FACE showing dialect-specific variation consistent with monophthongal realization in Scottish dialects (Central Scotland, Edinburgh, Glasgow, N. Scotland & I) to diphthongs in other regions (East England, Midwest US). Again, the Scottish dialects show a distinct fronting pattern for MOUTH (shown as a reduction in normalized F2) compared with other dialects where MOUTH typically shows a backing pattern as it raises.

3.1 Exploratory analysis

To capture the formant position, the speaker-normalized F1 and F2 values were taken from the 20% and 80% points, corresponding to the vowel **Onset** and **Offset** respectively. Figure 3 (top) illus-

Continent	Dialect	Corpus	Speakers	Tokens
North America	Canada (rural)	Canadian-Prairies	44	20042
	Canada (rural)	ICE-Canada	8	2764
	Canada (urban)	Canadian-Prairies	67	38021
	Canada (urban)	ICE-Canada	8	877
	Midwest US	Buckeye	40	17669
	New England	Switchboard	18	2868
	North Midland US	Switchboard	44	7126
	Northern US	Switchboard	53	7494
	NYC	Switchboard	19	3183
	Raleigh US	Raleigh	100	64659
	South Midland US	Switchboard	106	20327
	Southern US	Switchboard	37	5595
	Western US	Switchboard	45	6376
United Kingdom	Central Scotland	SCOTS	23	5237
	East Central England	Audio BNC	30	3877
	East England	Audio BNC	100	13429
	East England	Hastings	49	25477
	East England	IViE	12	972
	East England	IViE	11	992
	East England	ModernRP	48	2811
	Edinburgh	SCOTS	18	2361
	Glasgow	SCOTS	26	4432
	Glasgow	SOTC	155	45487
	Lower North England	Audio BNC	41	5445
	Lower North England	IViE	11	891
	Lower North England	IViE	10	760
	North East England	Audio BNC	10	917
	North East England	IViE	12	1018
	Northern Scotland & Islands	SCOTS	31	3998
	South West England	Audio BNC	37	3458
	West Central England	Audio BNC	32	4497
Total	**21**	**11**	**1245**	**323060**

Table 1: Speaker and token count for each dialect used in this study, separated by the corpus from which the data was originally sourced.

trates the position of the onset and offset of each dialect, for each of the five vowels. This figure again captures overall consistency in the broad realization of a given vowel across dialects, but also the substantial differences between dialects in occupying the formant space for each vowel. The degree of this difference, however, varies by vowel. For example, dialects are somewhat diffused for CHOICE (outer left) FACE, (inner left), and PRICE (outer right), whilst maintaining some similarity in the difference between the onset and offset (reflected in the direction of the arrow) across dialects.

Three measures were calculated to capture properties of a vowel's formant trajectory independent of its position in formant space. The first, **Vector Length** (calculated from VSL, Equation 2), was calculated between the onset and offset value, reflecting the overall degree of linear spectral change over the vowel's timecourse. One measurement commonly used in studies of trajectory shape, trajectory length (Fox and Jacewicz, 2009; Mayr and Davies, 2011; Farrington et al., 2018) is calculated as the summation of two VSLs: one measuring the distance from the vowel onset to midpoint, and another measuring the distance from the midpoint to the vowel offset. As trajectory length is highly correlated with Vector Length ($r = 0.99$, $p < 0.001$ for this data), we derived our second measure, **Vec-**

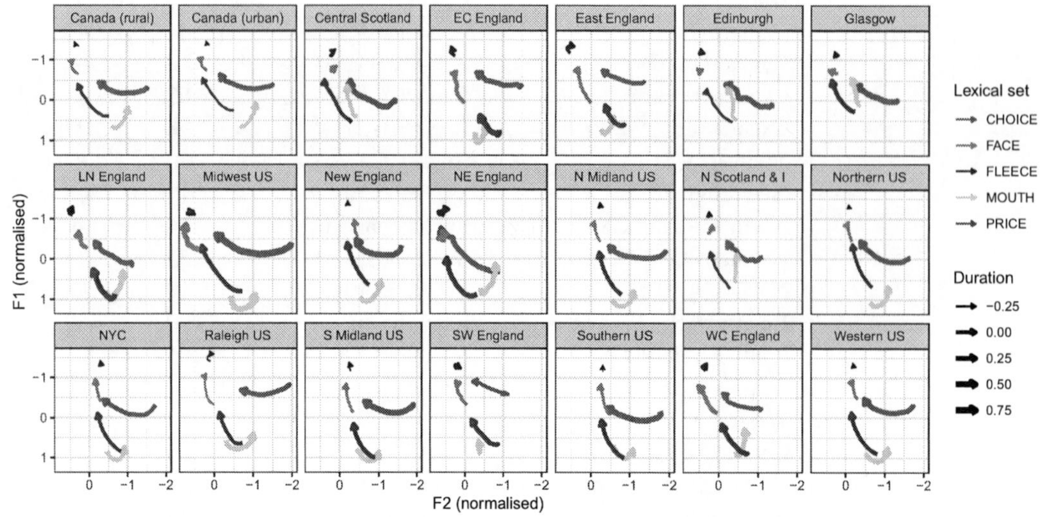

Figure 2: normalized by-dialect vowel trajectories for the central 60% of the five vowels analyzed, averaged over all tokens for that dialect. Duration corresponds to the within-speaker z-score normalization.

tor Offset, as trajectory length subtracted from Vector Length, reflecting the residual difference between the two measures. Finally, **Vector Angle**, the measure of a vowel's *direction* of change, was derived from the onset and offset position, on a $180/-180°$ scale (e.g., $\uparrow$ = 0 °, $\leftarrow$ = 90 °). Figure 3 (bottom) illustrates the dialectal variation in both Vector Length (a dialect's distance from the centre of the compass) and Vector Angle (the orientation around the compass). This figure demonstrates that, as with formant position (Fig. 3 top), the degree of dialectal variation for these dimensions differs between vowels, while showing some consistency within-vowel. FACE and PRICE show little dialectal variation in Vector Angle; instead, dialects differ in Vector Length. CHOICE and MOUTH show dialectal variation in both Vector Angle and Vector Length, within a clear range. (For example, CHOICE always points between $-90°$ and $0°$.) FLEECE shows very little overall spectral change, reflected in all dialects clustered around the centre of the compass.

Vowel **Duration** was calculated by z-score normalizing the vowel's force-aligned duration against all of the speaker's vowels (including vowels not analyzed in this study). As with previous measures, duration exhibits a wide range of variability across dialects, but this variability is somewhat structured within-vowel, roughly along the anticipated monophthong–diphthong axis: FLEECE shows the lowest average duration across dialects, with the least variability, followed by FACE (higher average, more variability), followed by PRICE/MOUTH/CHOICE.

Overall, the exploratory analysis shows that dialects tend to vary in how they produce the 'same' vowel, in fairly constrained ways, across both formant position and dynamics, consistent with the intuitive axis of degree of 'movement': FLEECE < FACE < PRICE, MOUTH, CHOICE in terms of how much dialectal variation there is in both spectral change and duration.

3.2 Dialect classification experiment

We now turn to quantitative characterization of the extent to which dynamics (trajectory shape, duration) provide additional information about dialectal variability on top of static measures (F1/F2 position). In this experiment, different combinations of measures are used to train a supervised learning model to predict the dialect label associated with data from a single vowel/speaker pair. Support vector machines (SVMs) were trained on each vowel using the `e1071` package (Meyer et al., 2019) in R (R Core Team, 2019). SVMs are a class of supervised learning model, which can be trained to assign ('classify') a label (such as dialect, e.g., Southern US, Glasgow) to a datapoint based on predictor values such as formant, trajectory, and duration measurements. The radial basis function kernel was used for SVMs in this study, which allows for fitting non-linear decision boundaries, since we do not a priori expect boundaries between dialects to

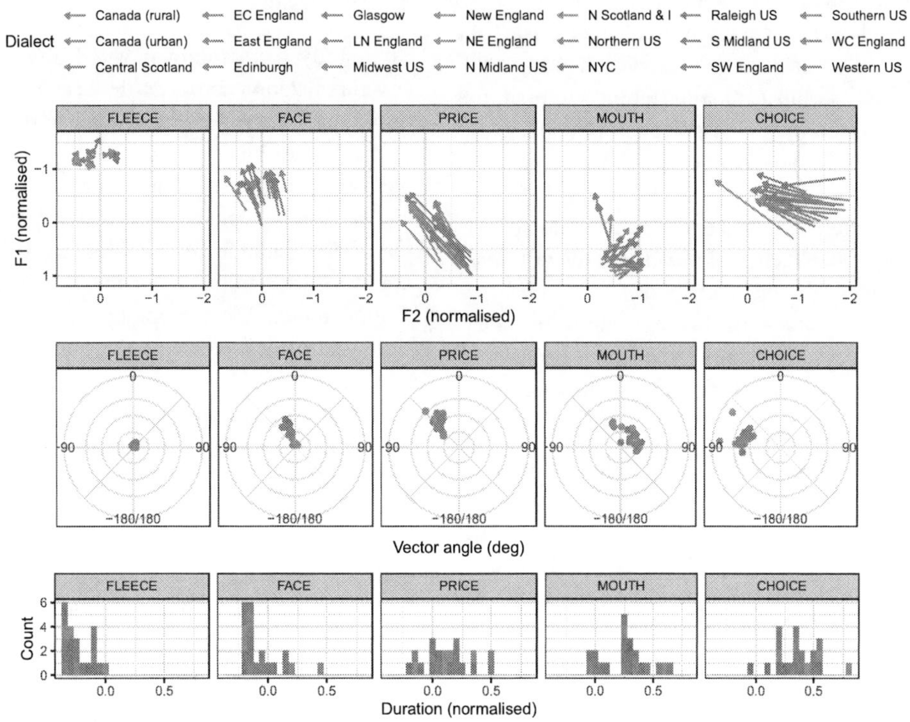

Figure 3: Top: Mean dialect F1 and F2 values for the 5 vowels (CHOICE, FACE, FLEECE, MOUTH, PRICE). One point per dialect. Onset value represented by the start point of the arrow; offset represented by position of arrowhead. Middle: Mean dialect values for Vector Angle (direction on compass) and Vector Length (distance from centre), for each of the five vowels in the study. Bottom: Mean z-normalized duration values per dialect.

be linear. We use a multiclass version of SVMs, to predict one of N-many possible dialect labels given prototypical formant position, trajectory shape, and duration values.

The data was prepared for SVM training by averaging formant, trajectory shape, and duration values for each speaker across each vowel, and separate SVMs were trained for each of the 5 vowels analyzed in this study. The choice to use one observation per speaker (compared to one value for each observation in the dataset) was motivated by the desire to abstract away from variability due to phonological environment, and instead achieve an 'average' value for a vowel for a speaker by averaging over all observations of that vowel by that speaker. To examine how different combinations of measures best contribute to accurately predicting the dialect, 7 SVMs were trained for each vowel on a different set of measurements (for a total of 35 SVMs):

1. Formant values (F1/F2 onset + offset)
2. Trajectory shape (Vec. Length, Offset, Angle)
3. Duration
4. Formants + duration
5. Trajectory + duration
6. Formants + trajectory
7. Formants + trajectory + duration

Each SVM was trained on a 80% subset of the data, and tuned to derive the best parameters (margin parameter C, kernel parameter γ) via 10-fold cross validation. A 'dummy classifier' model which returns the most common dialect label from the test set was also included as a baseline model. The performance on the 20% test set is evaluated using a metric that appropriately accounts for class imbalance. This measure, balanced accuracy, is the average of a model's sensitivity and specificity, and accounts for class imbalance by normalizing the true positive and negative rates by the relative number of samples (Kelleher et al., 2015).

(Note that balanced accuracy is 0.5 for the baseline.) Balanced accuracy was calculated using the `yardstick` package (Kuhn and Vaughan, 2020). To directly compare how different combinations of metrics aid in the classification of dialects, the differences in balanced accuracy for each vowel was calculated, and significance of the difference was evaluated through a one-sided permutation test, comparing the likelihood of whether the difference was greater than the average difference observed for 1000 permutations (Table 3), and were subject to within-vowel Benjamini-Hochberg False Discovery Rate (FDR) adjustment for multiple comparisons.

Table 2 shows the classification performance for each SVM, which demonstrates that using all SVMs improve over the naive baseline model (row 1), and the best-performing SVM includes dynamic information (trajectory or duration), for every vowel. Table 3 shows the performance differences between SVMs trained with different combinations of measurements, specifically comparing how dynamic measurements aid in distinguishing dialects relative to formant-only models (rows 1-2), as well as how utilizing *all* measurements compare with removing either trajectory measurements (row 3) or duration (row 4).

Comparing how dynamic (trajectory and duration) information provides additional resolution for distingiushing between dialects, the use of duration as a cue alongside formant information provides a large and significant increase in accuracy across all vowels (Table 3 row 1); alongside the observation that duration in isolation largely returns the lowest accuracy of all model sets (Table 2 row 4), this suggests English dialects do not sufficiently vary in duration for duration to uniquely distinguish dialects, but instead is a meaningful cue alongside a vowel's formant position. The additional effect of duration is mitigated when all measurements are included (Table 3 row 4), though including duration still results in significantly better classification accuracy for FLEECE, MOUTH, and PRICE. The additional role of trajectory information relative to formant position, in contrast, is much more variable across vowels (Table 3 row 2). Trajectory information plays the largest role for distinguishing MOUTH vowels across dialects, reflecting the fact that both Vector Length and Vector Angle vary substantially across dialects (Figure 3), with MOUTH in Scottish dialects fronting over its timecourse.

4 Discussion

This study has examined variability in English vowel realization across 21 dialects, to address the broad question of how to characterize variability in the 'same' vowel, across multiple acoustic dimensions, considering both static formant position and time-dependent dynamic information (trajectory shape, duration). What low-dimensional space does vowel variability lie in, does it line up with traditional notions of 'monophthong' vs. 'diphthong', and what role do static versus dynamic information play?

Our exploratory analysis (Section 3.1) found that while dialects vary in the static and dynamic realization of vowels, this cross-dialectal variation is clearly structured: the 'same' vowel patterns similarly with respect to dynamic realization, across dialects. As a first approximation, the patterns of dynamic variation within vowels seems to broadly correspond to the general monophthong/diphthong characterization, related to varying degrees of formant 'movement' during the vowel timecourse: FLEECE exhibits the least change, followed by FACE, with PRICE, MOUTH, CHOICE showing the most change; duration patterns similarly. Future work should incorporate more vowels into the analysis, to fully map out the structure of variability within and between dialects, and assess its possible sources.

The dialect classification experiment (Section 3.2) showed that whilst both formant position and trajectory shape can separately inform the prediction of a given dialect, accuracy is improved with both types of measures are used together. While previous work has shown that trajectory information is informative *within* a given dialect, these results demonstrate that characterizations of the formant trajectory also provide additional resolution as to the ways vowels can systematically differ across individual dialects. This study utilized one particular representation of trajectory shape: Vector Length/Offset/Angle. Testing other representations of trajectory shape, such as DCTs (Watson and Harrington, 1999; Williams and Escudero, 2014; Williams et al., 2019), would be a useful avenue for future research, especially if these improve on dialect classification accuracy, which is fairly low when using Vector Length/Offset/Angle.

Our understanding of cross-dialectal variation in vowel duration has been largely limited to studies of North American dialects, especially in the

Measures	FLEECE	FACE	PRICE	MOUTH	CHOICE
Baseline (most common dialect label)	50	50	50	50	50
Formants (F1, F2 onset + offset)	58	61.3	62.2	61.4	56.7
Trajectory (Vector Length, Offset, Angle)	54.5	62.1	56	63.6	56
Duration	55	52.9	57.4	52.7	51.9
{Formants, duration}	62.5	**65.3**	66.2	66.4	**60.3**
{Trajectory, duration}	56.7	65.1	60.6	65.4	55.9
{Formants, trajectory}	60.8	62.7	65	67.4	57.6
{Formants, trajectory, duration}	**63.4**	**64.2**	**69.4**	**70**	**59.2**

Table 2: Balanced accuracy (%) for each SVM, trained with different configurations of formant position, trajectory shape, and duration measures.

	FLEECE		FACE		PRICE		MOUTH		CHOICE	
Comparisons	**ΔBa.**	p	**ΔBa.**	p	**ΔBa.**	p	**ΔBa.**	p	**ΔBa.**	p
{F, D} vs F	4.5	**0.004**	4	**0.004**	4	**0.006**	5	**0**	3.6	**0.046**
{F, T} vs F	2.8	**0.034**	1.4	0.122	2.8	**0.018**	6	**0**	0.9	0.231
{F, T, D} vs {F, D}	0.9	0.148	−1.1	0.39	3.2	**0.009**	3.6	**0.008**	−1.1	0.364
{F, T, D} vs {F, T}	2.6	**0.034**	1.5	0.122	4.4	**0.002**	2.6	**0.021**	1.6	0.181

Table 3: Differences in balanced accuracy (ΔBa., %) between different combinations of measurements, with within-vowel FDR-adjusted p-values calculated using a one-sided permutation test with 1000 permutations (bold indicates $p < 0.05$). *F* = Formants, *T* = Trajectory, *D* = Duration.

US South (e.g. Jacewicz et al., 2007; Tauberer and Evanini, 2009; Fridland et al., 2014), leaving open the question of how duration varies across English dialects more generally. Results of the dialect classification experiment suggest that duration does contribute unique information over formant position and trajectory shape, but it is the least informative feature. However, this study only included vowels which are 'tense' in most dialects, which tend to be longer (than 'lax' vowels). Future work incorporating more vowels into the analysis would allow for better assessment of the role of duration, and would provide additional information about about dialectal differences in duration across English vowels in general.

To our knowledge, this is the largest study to date of formant dynamics (in terms of number of dialects, and tokens), for any language. Analyzing data at this scale was made possible due to access to a large number of corpora and tools for automated acoustic measurement. Previous large cross-dialectal analyses (e.g. Wells, 1982; Thomas, 2001; Labov et al., 2006) were multi-year enterprises requiring substantial time and labor-intensive manual annotation, making only simple characterizations of vowel dynamics (e.g. onset + offset) possible. Access to force-aligned speech corpora and the automatic measurement of formants allows the analysis to be 'scaled-up' easily relative to many other dialectal studies of vowel quality, but also requires recognition of a number of limitations for studies of this kind. Whilst this method has been shown to generate accurate formant values and procedures are taken to avoid tracking 'false formants' (Mielke et al., 2019), it is simply not possible with data at this scale to be manually validated. Similarly forced aligned segments have a minimum time duration (often 30ms) and a minimum time resolution (often 10ms), particularly for vowels which may have undergone substantial reduction. We attempted to account for this by applying lower and upper-limits for vowel durations to be included in the study; it remains possible that biases or inaccuracies in vowel duration exist within the dataset.

Acknowledgements

We acknowledge the crucial contribution of The SPADE Consortium, which comprises the Data Guardians who generously shared their datasets which are reported in this paper, and/or whose datasets were used in the development of the Integrated Speech Corpus Analysis tool. No SPADE research would have been possible without The SPADE Consortium (https://spade.glasgow.ac.uk/the-spade-consortium/). Additional thanks to Jeff

Mielke, Rachel Macdonald, Vanna Willerton, and SPADE research assistants. This research was supported by SPeech Across Dialects of English (SPADE): Large-scale digital analysis of a spoken language across space and time (2017-2020), ESRC Grant ES/R003963/1, NSERC/CRSNG Grant RGPDD 501771-16, SSHRC/CRSH Grant 869-2016-0006, NSF Grant SMA-1730479 (Digging into Data/Trans-Atlantic Platform), and SSHRC #435-2017-0925.

References

Jean Anderson, Dave Beavan, and Christian Kay. 2007. The Scottish corpus of texts and speech. In J. C. Beal, K. P. Corrigan, and H. L. Moisl, editors, *Creating and Digitizing Language Corpora*, pages 17–34. Palgrave, New York.

Charles-James Bailey. 1968. Segmental length in Southern States English: an instrumental phonetic representation of a standard dialect in South Carolina. In *PEGS Paper No. 20*. Center for Applied Linguistics, Washington DC.

Charles Boberg. 2010. *The English Language in Canada: Status, History and Comparative Analysis*. Cambridge University Press, Cambridge.

David J. Broad and Frantz Clermont. 2017. Target-locus scaling for modeling formant transitions in vowel + consonant + vowel utterances. *Journal of the Acoustical Society of America*, 141:EL192–EL198.

Amanda Beth Cardoso. 2015. *Dialectology, phonology, diachrony: Liverpool English realisations of price and mouth*. Ph.D. thesis, University of Edinburgh.

Nagaratna B Chittaragi and Shashidhar G Koolagudi. 2019. Acoustic-phonetic feature based kannada dialect identification from vowel sounds. *International Journal of Speech Technology*, 22(4):1099–1113.

Cynthia G. Clopper, David B. Pisoni, and Kenneth de Jong. 2005. Acoustic characteristics of the vowel systems of six regional varieties of American English. *Journal of the Acoustical Society of America*, 118:1661–1676.

John Coleman, Ladan Baghai-Ravary, John Pybus, and Sergio Grau. 2012. Audio BNC: the audio edition of the Spoken British National Corpus. Technical report, Oxford. Http://www.phon.ox.ac.uk/AudioBNC.

Thomas H. Crystal and Arthur S. House. 1982. Segmental durations in connected speech signals: preliminary results. *Journal of the Acoustical Society of America*, 72:705–716.

Gerry Docherty, Simon Gonzalez, and Nathaniel Mitchell. 2015. Static vs dynamic perspectives on the realization of vowel nucleii in West Australian English. In *Proceedings of the 18th International Congress of Phonetic Sciences*.

Robin Dodsworth. 2013. Retreat from the Southern Vowel Shift in Raleigh, NC: social factors. *University of Pennsylvania Working Papers in Linguistics*, 19:31–40.

Robin Dodsworth and Mary Kohn. 2012. Urban rejection of the vernacular: The SVS undone. *Language Variation and Change*, 24:221–245.

Medford Evans. 1935. Southern 'long i'. *American Speech*, 10:188–190.

A. H. Fabricius. 2000. *T-glottalling between stigma and prestige: a sociolinguistic study of Modern RP*. Ph.D. thesis, Copenhagen Business School, Copenhagen, Denmark.

Charlie Farrington, Tyler Kendall, and Valerie Fridland. 2018. Vowel dynamics in the southern vowel shift. *American Speech*, 93:186–222.

Robert Allen Fox and Ewa Jacewicz. 2009. Cross-dialectal variation in formant dynamics of American English. *Journal of the Acoustical Society of America*, 126:2603–2618.

Robert Allen Fox and Ewa Jacewicz. 2017. Reconceptualizing the vowel space in analyzing regional dialect variation and sound change in American English. *Journal of the Acoustical Society of America*, 142:444–459.

Valerie Fridland, Tyler Kendall, and Charlie Farrington. 2014. Durational and spectral differences in American English vowels: dialect variation within and across groups. *Journal of the Acoustical Society of America*, 136:341–349.

R. Fromont and J. Hay. 2012. LaBB-CAT: an annotation store. In *Australasian Language Technology Workshop 2012*, volume 113, pages 113–117.

Josef Fruehwald. 2013. *The Phonological Influence on Phonetic Change*. Ph.D. thesis, University of Pennsylvania.

T. Gay. 1968. Effects of speaking rate on dipthong formant movements. *Journal of the Acoustical Society of America*, 44:1570–1573.

John J. Godfrey, Edward C. Holliman, and Jane McDaniel. 1992. SWITCHBOARD: telephone speech corpus for research and development. In *Proceedings of the 1992 IEEE international conference on Acoustics, speech and signal processing - Volume 1*, pages 517–520.

E. Grabe. 2004. Intonational variation in English. In P. Gilles and J. Peters, editors, *Regional Variation in Intonation*, pages 9–31. Niemeyer, Tubingen.

S. Greenbaum and G. Nelson. 1996. The International Corpus of English (ICE project). *World Englishes*, 15:3–15.

Bill Haddican, Paul Foulkes, Vincent Hughes, and Hazel Richards. 2013. Interaction of social and linguistic constraints on two vowel changes in northern England. *Language Variation and Change*, 25:371–403.

Robert Hagiwara. 1997. Dialect variation and formant frequency: The American English vowels revisited. *Journal of the Acoustical Society of America*, 102.

Abualsoud Hanani, Martin J Russell, and Michael J Carey. 2013. Human and computer recognition of regional accents and ethnic groups from british english speech. *Computer Speech & Language*, 27(1):59–74.

Jonathon Harrington and Stephan Cassidy. 1994. Dynamic and target theories of vowel classification: evidence from monophthongs and diphthongs in Australian English. *Language and Speech*, 37:357–373.

James Hillenbrand and R. T. Gayvert. 1993. Vowel classification based on fundamental frequency and formant frequencies. *Journal of Speech, Language, and Hearing Research*, 36:694–700.

Sophie Holmes-Elliott. 2015. *London calling: assessing the spread of metropolitan features in the southeast.* Ph.D. thesis, University of Glasgow.

A. S. House and G. Fairbanks. 1953. The influence of consonant environment upon the secondary acoustical characteristics of vowels. *Journal of the Acoustical Society of America*, 25:105–113.

Arthur S. House. 1961. On vowel duration in English. *Journal of the Acoustical Society of America*, 33:1174–1178.

Ewa Jacewicz, Robert Allen Fox, and J. Salmons. 2007. Vowel duration in three American English dialects. *American Speech*, 82:367–385.

John D. Kelleher, Brian Mac Namee, and Aoife D'Arcy. 2015. *Fundamental of Machine Learning for Predictive Data Analytics*. MIT Press, Cambridge MA.

Sam Kirkham, Claire Nance, Bethany Littlewood, Kate Lightfoot, and Eve Groake. 2019. Dialect variation in formant dynamics: the acoustics of lateral and vowel sequences in Manchester and Liverpool English. *Journal of the Acoustical Society of America*, 145:784–794.

Max Kuhn and Davis Vaughan. 2020. *yardstick: Tidy Characterizations of Model Performance*. R package version 0.0.6.

William Labov. 1991. Three dialects of English. In Penelope Eckert, editor, *New ways of analyzing variation in English*, pages 1–45. Academic, New York.

William Labov, Sharon Ash, and Charles Boberg. 2006. *The Atlas of North American English: Phonetics, Phonology, and Sound Change*. Mouton de Gruyter, Berlin.

Peter Ladefoged and Ian Maddieson. 1993. *The Sounds of the World's Languages*. Wiley, Oxford.

B. M. Lobanov. 1971. Classification of Russian vowels spoken by different speakers. *Journal of the Acoustical Society of America*, 49:606–608.

Kirsty MacDougall. 2006. Dynamic features of speech and the characterization of speakers: Toward a new approach using formant frequencies. *The International Journal of Speech, Language and the Law*, 13:89–126.

Kirsty MacDougall and Francis Nolan. 2007. Discrimination of speakers using the formant dynamics of /u:/ in British English. In *Proceedings of the 16th International Congress of Phonetic Sciences*, pages 1825–1828. Saarbrucken.

Robert Mayr and Hannah Davies. 2011. A cross-dialectal acoustic study of the monophthongs and diphthongs of Welsh. *Journal of the International Phonetic Association*, 41:1–25.

Michael McAuliffe, Arlie Coles, Michael Goodale, Sarah Mihuc, Michael Wagner, Jane Stuart-Smith, and Morgan Sonderegger. 2019. ISCAN: A system for integrated phonetic analyses across speech corpora. In *Proceedings of the 19th International Congress of Phonetic Sciences*, Melbourne.

Michael McAuliffe, Michaela Scolof, S. Mihuc, Michael Wagner, and Morgan Sonderegger. 2017a. Montreal forced aligner [computer program]. Https://montrealcorpustools.github.io/Montreal-Forced-Aligner/.

Michael McAuliffe, Elias Stengel-Eskin, Michaela Socolof, and Morgan Sonderegger. 2017b. Polyglot and Speech Corpus Tools: a system for representing, integrating, and querying speech corpora. In *Proceedings of Interspeech 2017*.

David Meyer, Evgenia Dimitriadou, Kurt Hornik, Andreas Weingessel, and Friedrich Leisch. 2019. *e1071: Misc Functions of the Department of Statistics, Probability Theory Group (Formerly: E1071), TU Wien*. R package version 1.7-3.

Jeff Mielke, Erik R. Thomas, Josef Fruehwald, Michael McAuliffe, Morgan Sonderegger, Jane Stuart-Smith, and Robin Dodsworth. 2019. Age vectors vs. axes of intraspeaker variation in vowel formants measured automatically from several English speech corpora. In *Proceedings of the 19th International Congress of Phonetic Sciences*, Melbourne, Australia.

Geoffrey Stewart Morrison. 2009. Likelihood-ratio forensic voice comparison using parametric representations of the formant trajectories of diphthongs. *Journal of the Acoustical Society of America*, 125:2387–2397.

G. E. Peterson and H. L. Barney. 1952. Control methods used in a study of the vowels. *Journal of the Acoustical Society of America*, 24:175–184.

Gordon E. Peterson and Ilse Lehiste. 1960. Duration of syllable nuclei in English. *Journal of the Acoustical Society of America*, 32:693–703.

M. A. Pitt, L. Dilley, K. Johnson, S. Kiesling, W. Raymond, E. Hume, and E. Fosler-Lussier. 2007. *Buckeye Corpus of Spontaneous Speech*, 2 edition. Ohio State University, Columbus.

R Core Team. 2019. *R: A Language and Environment for Statistical Computing*. R Foundation for Statistical Computing, Vienna, Austria.

Margret E. L. Renwick and Joseph A. Stanley. 2020. Modeling dynamic trajectories of front vowels in the American South. *Journal of the Acoustical Society of America*, 147:579–595.

Megan L. Risdal and Mary E. Kohn. 2014. Ethnolectal and generational differences in vowel trajectories: Evidence from African American English and the Southern vowel system. In *Selected papers from NWAV 42*, pages 139–148, Philadelphia. University of Pennsylvania.

Nicole Rosen and Crystal Skriver. 2015. Vowel patterning of Mormons in Southern Alberta, Canada. *Language & Communication*, 42:104–115.

Ingrid Rosenfelder, Josef Fruehwald, Keelan Evanini, Scott Seyfarth, Kyle Gorman, Hilary Prichard, and Jiahong Yuan. 2014. FAVE (Forced Alignment and Vowel Extraction) program suite v1.2.2 10.5281/zenodo.22281.

F. Schiel. 1999. Automatic Phonetic Transcription of Non-Prompted Speech. In *Proc. of the ICPhS*, pages 607–610, San Francisco.

Heike Schoorman, Wilbert Heeringa, and J *o*rg Peters. 2015. Regional variation of Saterland Frisian vowels. In *Proceedings of the 18th International Congress of Phonetic Sciences*. University of Glasgow.

Victor Skretkowicz and Susan Rennie. 2005. *Scottish National Dictionary*. Dictionaries of the Scottish Language.

Morgan Sonderegger, Jane Stuart-Smith, Michael McAuliffe, Rachel Macdonald, and Tyler Kendall. 2022. Managing data for integrated speech corpus analysis in SPeech Across Dialects of English (SPADE). In *Open Handbook of Linguistic Data Management*, pages 195–207. MIT Press, Cambridge.

Jane Stuart-Smith, B. Jose, Tamara Rathcke, Rachel MacDonald, and E. Lawson. 2017. Changing sounds in a changing city: An acoustic phonetic investigation of real-time change over a century of Glaswegian. In C. Montgomery and E. Moore, editors, *Language and a Sense of Place: Studies in Language and Region*, pages 38–65. Cambridge University Press, Cambridge.

James Tanner. 2020. *Structured phonetic variation across dialects and speakers of English and Japanese*. Ph.D. thesis, McGill University.

Joshua Tauberer and Keelan Evanini. 2009. Intrinsic vowel duration and the post-vocalic voicing effect: some evidence from dialects of North American English. In *Proceedings of Interspeech*.

Charalambos Themistocleous. 2017. Dialect classification using vowel acoustic parameters. *Speech Communication*, 92:13–22.

Erik R. Thomas. 2001. *An acoustic analysis of vowel variation in New World English*. American Dialect Society.

Peter Trudgill. 1999. *The Dialects of England*. Blackwell, Oxford.

Sander Van der Harst, Hans Van de Velde, and Roeland Van Hout. 2014. Variation in standard dutch vowels: The impact of formant measurement methods on identifying the speaker's regional origin. *Language Variation and Change*, 26(2):247–272.

Catherine I. Watson and Jonathon Harrington. 1999. Acoustic evidence for dynamic formant trajectories in Australian English vowels. *Journal of the Acoustical Society of America*, 106:458–468.

John C. Wells. 1982. *Accents of English*. Cambridge University Press, New York.

Brett Wetzell. 2000. Rhythm, dialects, and the Southern Drawl. Master's thesis, North Carolina State University.

Daniel Williams, Jaydene Elvin, Paola Escudero, and Adamanitos Gafos. 2019. Multidimensional variation in English diphthongs. In *Proceedings of the 19th International Congress of Phonetic Sciences*, Melbourne, Australia.

Daniel Williams and Paola Escudero. 2014. A cross-dialectal acoustic comparison of vowels in Northern and Southern British English. *Journal of the Acoustical Society of America*, 136:2751–2761.

Cécile Woehrling, Philippe Boula de Mareüil, and Martine Adda-Decker. 2009. Linguistically-motivated automatic classification of regional french varieties. In *Tenth Annual Conference of the International Speech Communication Association*.

Domain-Informed Probing of wav2vec 2.0 Embeddings for Phonetic Features

Patrick Cormac English[1], **John D. Kelleher**[2], **Julie Carson-Berndsen**[1]
SFI Centre for Research Training in Digitally-Enhanced Reality (d-real),
[1]ADAPT Research Centre, School of Computer Science, University College Dublin, Ireland
[2]ADAPT Research Centre, Technological University Dublin, Ireland

Abstract

In recent years large transformer model architectures have become available which provide a novel means of generating high-quality vector representations of speech audio. These transformers make use of an attention mechanism to generate representations enhanced with contextual and positional information from the input sequence. Previous works have explored the capabilities of these models with regard to performance in tasks such as speech recognition and speaker verification, but there has not been a significant inquiry as to the manner in which the contextual information provided by the transformer architecture impacts the representation of phonetic information within these models. In this paper, we report the results of a number of probing experiments on the representations generated by the wav2vec 2.0 model's transformer component, with regard to the encoding of phonetic categorization information within the generated embeddings. We find that the contextual information generated by the transformer's operation results in enhanced capture of phonetic detail by the model, and allows for distinctions to emerge in acoustic data that are otherwise difficult to separate.

1 Introduction

In recent years large transformer models have become available which provide a novel means of generating high-quality vector representations of input speech audio sequences. These transformers aim to exploit feature learning on large unlabelled datasets to perform sequence-to-sequence transformations on audio that capture and preserve salient features from the input sequence in a quantised and contextual output representation. While most work on transformer models in automatic speech recognition focus on performance improvements and applications in down-stream tasks, this paper focuses on whether the internal layers of a transformer model provide any information as to the emergence of phonetic and phonological properties of speech. Specifically we interrogate the wav2vec 2.0 model (Baevski et al., 2020) by probing the internal layers of the transformer using domain-informed features. The structure of this paper is as follows. Firstly, in section 2 we present some existing research related to our approach followed by a discussion of transformer-based models in section 3. Section 4 presents the resources used, and the experimental methodology is described in section 5. In section 6 we present our results, followed by conclusions and future work in section 7.

2 Related Work

There has been considerable work in recent years as to the extent and nature of phonetic information captured in the embeddings used by deep learning models. The word2vec model (Mikolov et al., 2013) has been applied below the level of the word to investigate phonological analogies and similarities. Silfverberg et al. (2018) have explored the sound analogies generated by phoneme embeddings. Kolachina and Magyar (2019) detailed the ability of embeddings to capture phonemic and allophonic relationships within an artificial language, noting that contrastive elements within the embedding space correlated with articulatory features. O'Neill and Carson-Berndsen (2019) demonstrate that embeddings derived purely from text using a grapheme-to-phoneme mapping and applying a word2vec approach exhibit similarity between phoneme classes. These phoneme embeddings were subsequently integrated with the data-driven acoustic similarities of Kane and Carson-Berndsen (2016) to generate a similarity matrix for use in phonemically driven spell checking (O'Neill et al., 2021).

19th SIGMORPHON Workshop on Computational Research in Phonetics, Phonology, and Morphology, pages 83 - 91

Specifically with respect to the capture of phonetic information in the embeddings of automatic speech recognition, Belinkov and Glass (2017) have investigated the internal layers of end-to-end recognition systems using a connectionist temporal classification (CTC) approach with DeepSpeech2 (Amodei et al., 2016). They found significant differences across layers in their architecture with respect to predictive performance of phoneme categories. Their work also demonstrated that certain categories became represented in the embedding space of their chosen model such that intra-category separation was significantly more difficult than for other categories. They noted that these categories saw better performance in later layers, at the expense of degraded performance in more easily separable categories. Scharenborg et al. (2019) have investigated the representation of speech in deep neural networks using a 3-layer model trained to distinguish consonants and vowels. They performed a wide-ranging comparison of PCA-transformed embedding spaces, and their work saw strong clustering on the basis of the vowel/consonant categorisation and manner of articulation. Most recently, Ma et al. (2021) investigated the extent to which phonetic properties emerge from the acoustic representations of transformer-based speech recognition architectures. Using four pre-trained acoustic representations from transformer-based speech recognition architectures, they designed probing tasks using linear regression, a support vector machine and a feedforward neural network consisting of two fully-connected layers. Their embeddings are associated with high-level categorisations derived from the TIMIT dataset (Garofolo et al., 1992), perform at a high level and see significant improvements across layers when considering less-separable classes such as fricatives.

Conneau et al. (2018) proposed a methodology known as probing as a way to examine what information is present in an embedding. In Conneau et al.'s framing a probing task involves training a classification model to predict properties (e.g., length, tense, parse tree depth, and so on) of a sentence based on the embedding of the sentence. Probing assumes that the accuracy of the classification model (i.e., a probe) on the task indicates whether the embeddings encode information relevant to task target. There is a growing body of work using probing to examine what types of information are encoded in the embeddings created by Transformer models (Hewitt and Manning, 2019; Liu et al., 2019; Tenney et al., 2019; Nedumpozhimana and Kelleher, 2021), and also exploring what layer in the Transformer architecture different types of information are encoded in (Jawahar et al., 2019). In this work, we adapt the probing methodology to speech embeddings, and use it to understand and compare the phonetic information encoded in different layers of a Transformer model. Through this comparision of probing performance across layers on phonetic tasks we hope to better understand whether the information encoded in these speech embeddings, and the sequencing of this encoding across layers, accords with domain-knowledge expectations regarding phonetics.

The work presented in this paper focuses specifically on the transformer module of the wav2vec2.0 model (Baevski et al., 2020) and the representations generated at each layer of the transformer. It will not probe the attention mechanism itself, which is outside the scope of this paper. The primary goal of this investigation is not to deliver an explanation of the operations undertaken by the transformer architecture in generating these representations, but instead to probe the representations generated at different layers across the architecture in order to examine the development of the architecture's ability to delineate between phonetic categories.

3 Transformer-Based Models

In recent years transformer-based models have reported state-of-the-art results on a range of speech processing tasks, and today pre-trained models are available for a variety of high-demand tasks such as automatic speech recognition (ASR). These models leverage the availability of large unlabelled acoustic datasets, in parallel with enhanced architectural features such as attention mechanisms, to produce information-dense distributed vector representations (embeddings) of input audio signals. In the architecture examined herein, embeddings are of a N*T dimensionality, with width N dependent upon input length, and each instance of T representing the dimensionality of the encoded information within a specific time-frame, and specific variance within that dimensionality relating to differences in the acoustic feature space for that frame.

The excellent performance of transformer based models on speech processing tasks suggests that these models have the ability to encode within the embeddings they generate aspects of the input signal relating to speech phenomena, while discarding low-information aspects of the input signal such as background noise and variation deemed to be unimportant during the training cycle. Furthermore, some architectures such as wav2vec 2.0 have been designed to exploit the high-quality of embeddings generated from unlabelled data by allowing for very small quantities of labelled data to be provided as fine-tuning information during a separate training stage while still achieving high levels of transcription performance.

However, while there has been significant inquiry as to the final-level performance of these models, relatively little is known as to the specific information captured within the embedding space, and whether that encoded information accords with domain-knowledge expectations. Previous works have explored the use of these embeddings as the basis for higher-order operations, such as accent-resilient ASR (Li et al., 2021), identification of speaker emotional state (Pepino et al., 2021), and modelling of prosody in speaker input (Gan et al., 2022).

For the probing task detailed in section 5, the phoneme embeddings (calculated by averaging the embeddings for the frames within the phoneme interval) for each layer in the multi-layer wav2vec2.0 transformer stack are used as inputs for the training of a multi-layer perceptron (MLP) on the task of identifying an associated TIMIT phonetic label. The performance of this model is taken as indicative of the relative richness of specific phonetic data within the output embeddings from wav2vec 2.0.

4 Resources

4.1 TIMIT

The TIMIT read-speech corpus (Garofolo et al., 1992) was used due to the high-quality metadata present in the dataset. The dataset is comprised of 5.4 hours of spoken English audio sampled at 16kHz in *wav* format. The audio is American-accented, with 8 major US English dialects represented, with each speaker recorded uttering ten high acoustic-information sentences. Each utterance is a single sentence of spoken audio, with manual character, phonetic, and orthographic transcriptions, in time-aligned format, provided for each recording.

4.2 wav2vec 2.0

This work uses wav2vec 2.0 (Baevski et al., 2020). This section outlines the pre-training task, training task, and architecture of the pre-trained wav2vec 2.0 model "base_960" [1] used at the pre-experimental stage. It then proceeds to the application of the model to the production of the ASR data used in the primary task.

4.2.1 Architecture

wav2vec 2.0 makes use of a transformer architecture for the purposes of transforming raw audio input W into a vector context representation C. A 1D ConvNet feature encoder first parses the waveform into a latent speech representation which is passed to the transformer. The transformer component is composed of a stack of 12 transformer layers each with an internal dimension of 768, a feed-forward dimension of 3072, and 8 attention heads. The component takes the output of the feature encoder, applies relative positional encoding and a GELU activation to the inputs, before a layer normalisation. This outputs context representation C.

The "base_960" model used can be loaded in a headless or LM-head configuration, the latter of which includes a language modelling head applied on top of the transformer architecture which divides output into a vocabulary of 32 characters including alphabetical characters and separators. This outputs character representations of C, which is the ASR transcription of W.

4.2.2 Training Task and Dataset

The wav2vec 2.0 model was pre-trained on the unlabelled Librispeech corpus containing 960 hours of audio. The wav2vec 2.0 model features both a pre-training and fine-tuning objective. The fine-tuning task is not relevant for this work, as it pertains to the language-modelling head which was not used in our experiments. The pre-training task requires the transformer module to correctly identify the "true" latent quantised speech representation, provided by the pre-transformer quantisation CNN module, for a masked time-step. A certain proportion of the inputs (representing quantisations of a particular time-step) to the transformer module are masked, and the transformer must identify them from a set of distractors sampled from the overall set of masked time-steps.

[1] https://huggingface.co/facebook/wav2vec2-base-960h

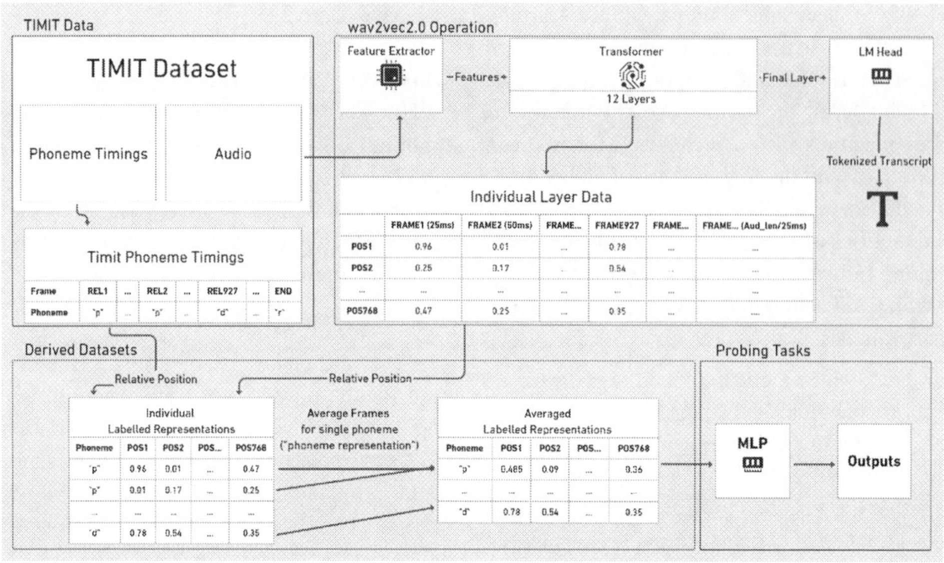

Figure 1: Overview of Experimental Methodology

5 Methodology

This section sets out the experimental methodology employed in this paper, outlining specifically how the relevant data was generated and the description of the probing task. Figure 1 provides an overview of the steps involved.

5.1 Data Generation

Firstly, utterance embeddings are generated using wav2vec 2.0. For each utterance in the full TIMIT training dataset (4620 separate 16kHz wav-formatted files), 12 sets of embeddings were generated, one per transformer layer. This was performed by operating the model without its language modelling head, and specifying the return of hidden-layer representations, where each transformer block is a single hidden-layer. Each audio file input generates an output of format [N*768] (N being the number of 25ms frames, proportional to the duration of the input audio); this results in the *Individual Layer Data* in figure 1. In contrast to the representations explored by Belinkov and Glass (2017), the representations here retain a constant dimensionality throughout each layer of the transformer, in distinction to the variety of layer architectures employed in DeepSpeech2.

The next step is to generate a frame-based dataset for the probing tasks. Since the TIMIT dataset provides frame-aligned annotations, marking the beginning and end of a given phoneme in the associated audio file, this data can be used to calculate phoneme-averaged durations. Taking the proportion between the maximum number of TIMIT frames in a given audio sequence and the number of wav2vec 2.0 frames N generated for that sequence, a relative positional mapping is generated for each [N*768] embedding, whereby a given frame of shape [1*768] is labelled with the phoneme[2] occurring at that position in the audio sequence, as according to the TIMIT labels. In this way a vector of shape [1*767] is generated, containing the vector representation of a given wav2vec 2.0 frame and the TIMIT-derived phoneme annotation. This process is depicted in figure 1 under *Derived Datasets*. 12 of these frame datasets were generated from the TIMIT dataset, to be used in the next section as the basis for deriving the phoneme-averaged representations used in the probing task.

Employing a variant of the method used in (Shah et al., 2021), the vector values of individual frames occurring during a specific phoneme interval are averaged, to create a representation in the embedding space of a given instantiation of a phoneme. This generated a dataset of 175,232 individual phoneme representations in the format [1*767], where the first field contains the phoneme label and the remaining 768 fields contain the column-wise average of all frames generated during a given phoneme

[2] We use the term phoneme here for labels that align with the English phoneme set. TIMIT also separates out the stop closures e.g. with the label "bcl". We retain these labels.

occurrence in the input audio. Figure 1 depicts this process for a simplified two-frame phoneme example. Twelve such datasets were derived, one per chosen layer. These datasets are then used as inputs to the probing task.

5.2 Probing Task

For the probing task, 12 multi-layer perceptron models were trained to predict TIMIT phoneme labels from the phoneme-averaged wav2vec 2.0 embeddings. A scikit-learn (Pedregosa et al., 2011) implementation of the multi-layer perceptron (MLP) was used, comprised of a single hidden layer of 200 neurons with ReLu activation, and an output layer of a single neuron with a logistic activation function. The models used the default hyper-parameters implemented in scikit-learn, with the exception of the hidden layer size which was expanded to 200 neurons.

To train the model, each multi-layer perceptron was provided with the phoneme-averaged dataset for a given layer as training material, with 43,808 samples reserved for testing. During training, the averaged vector representations of shape [1*768] were the input data with the [1*1] TIMIT phoneme label as the target category. The division of each layer's embeddings was static, with each model provided with its respective layer's wav2vec 2.0 outputs for the same audio files.

To generate the outputs described in section 6, the model was provided with the reserved rows, containing only the [1*768] vector information. The [1*1] phoneme label was removed and stored separately as the ground truth for each vector representation. The model then generated a predicted phoneme label per vector representation, which was stored with the ground truth in a collection of [1*2] ground-truth/predicted-label pairs.

Following best practice (Belinkov, 2021), we created a separate sub-experiment to assess the potential effects of chance correlation on our results. The primary probing task was re-conducted with an artificial dataset of the same dimensions as the phoneme-averaged dataset. This new dataset was comprised of values randomly sampled from the range of each feature column in the phoneme-averaged dataset, with the labels left unchanged. The performance of the probe on this task was very low (<2% accuracy per phone across layers). This result is substantially lower than the performance observed with the real embedding data, and we took this difference to indicate that the performance of our primary probing results reflect actual information relevant to the task, rather than chance correlation. Future work will seek to investigate the dataset in more detail, and incorporate any findings into a more robust probing task.

From the primary probing task, the following outputs were generated for each layer of the wav2vec 2.0 base model:

- Ground-truth/predicted-label pairs
- Average accuracy scores for each phoneme label, manner and place of articulation for each layer
- Phone label confusion matrices for each layer
- Dendrograms depicting sections of the confusion matrices for domain-informed categories

6 Results

This section presents a discussion of the results of the probing task. Firstly, categorisation accuracies for each predicted category per layer were considered. Then, heatmap representations of all phoneme confusions for layers of interest were considered in order to focus on the emergence of specific domain-informed categories, in this case a grouping of the consonants categorised with respect to manner of articulation based on hierarchical clustering.

6.1 Categorisation Accuracies

The accuracy scores for phoneme labels, manner of articulation (MOA) and place of articulation (POA) are presented in figures 2, 3 and 4 respectively. The accuracy scores here were derived by first obtaining a list of phoneme label predictions from the model, and then evaluating the number of correct labels with regard to the total number of predictions. Average accuracies for MOA and POA were derived by applying a category mapping to the original phoneme label predictions.

Of interest in figures 3 and 4 is that robust results are achieved around layer 7 which provides an indicator as to where to focus further investigation. This tallies with results from other work which have demonstrated a similar drop-off in performance in later layers (Belinkov and Glass, 2017).

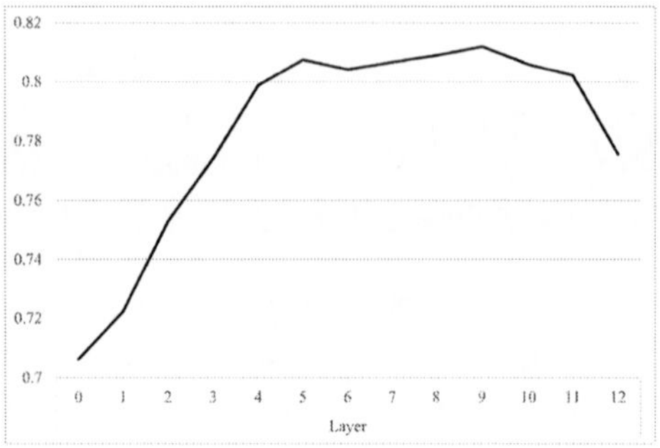

Figure 2: Average phoneme label accuracies per layer

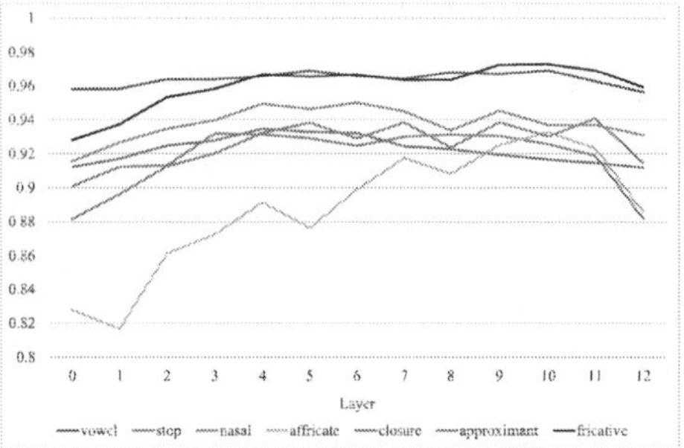

Figure 3: Accuracy per layer for MOA categorisation

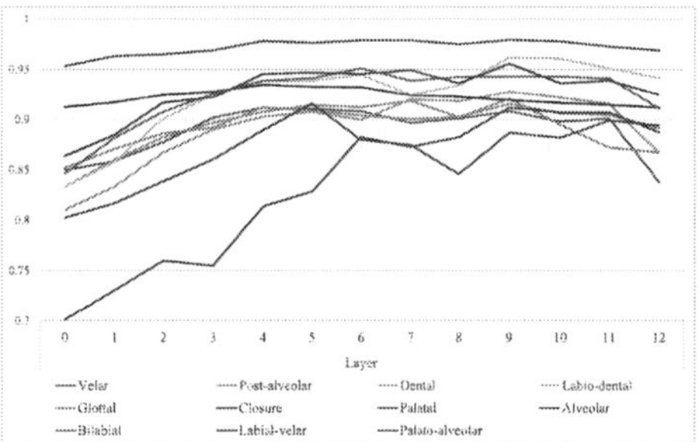

Figure 4: Accuracy per layer for POA categorisation

6.2 Confusion Heatmaps

To better understand the specific intra-categorical relationships captured in the MLP predictions, a confusion matrix was generated for each layer that detailed the confusions between ground-truth phoneme labels and the predicted label. This was done for each layer, with the labels arranged such that phonemes in the same manner-of-articulation category were adjacent. From this, a heatmap visualisation was generated for each matrix such that intra-MOA confusions occupy a contiguous subsection of the overall figure. Figure 5 depicts the overall confusions across all phoneme labels at layers 0, 7, and 12, whereby the bottom right represents vowels and the top left stops, closures, fricatives and affricates. Although the resolution in this figure is low, changes in patterns can be seen in the top left of the heatmap for each layer. For this reason, we have focused on those classes occupying that area in the next section.

6.3 Hierarchical Clustering

To allow assessment of changes in the MLP model's predictive certainty, dendrogram visualisations were created using hierarchical clustering with Ward linkage (Ward, 1963) for sounds with the manner of articulation stop, closure, fricative and affricate. This was done by first applying a transformation to the confusion matrix for all phonemes detailed above such that each cell now represented the probability of confusion at a given ground-truth/prediction intersection in the matrix. As this was a probability distribution, each row, representing the confusions for a given ground-truth label, sums to 1. The relevant rows and columns were then extracted as input to the clustering in no particular order. Figures 6, 7 and 8 show the dendrograms for these classes at layers 0, 7 and 12 respectively.

The hierarchical view in this context represents the clusters found by Ward's method in the probabilistic confusion matrices, and proximity in the hierarchy can be understood as representing "similarity", as the clustering method used seeks to minimise the loss of information incurred by merging nodes. Nodes adjacent to each other are minimally variant, with each sub-tree representing a grouping of less-variant nodes. As the data being clustered is the probability outputs from the model's confusion matrix, we can interpret proximity in the dendrogram images as indicating items that the model frequently confuses and hence with proximity within the model's representation of a given phoneme.

There are several patterns of interest captured in the hierarchical view, particularly with respect to the model's apparent enhanced understanding of phonetic structures and positional context. Viewing figures 7 and 8, it can be seen that the model has developed a representation of the various phoneme relationships within the category that better aligns with domain-informed expectations, with e.g. the closure/stop pairs for various stops having con-

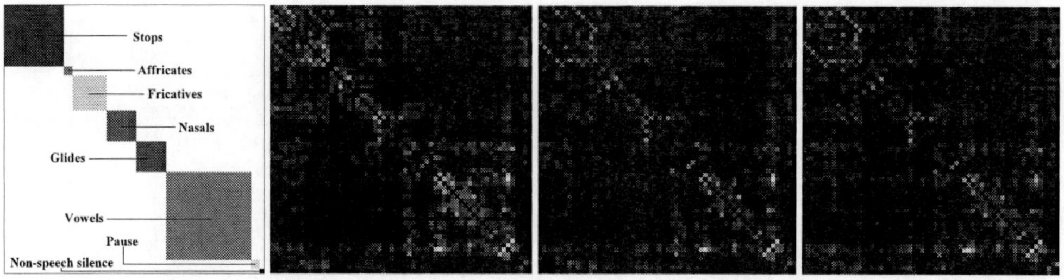

Figure 5: Heatmaps of confusions across all phoneme labels at layers 0, 7, and 12 with vowels in the bottom left quadrant and consonants in the top right quadrant. The leftmost grid describes layout of features within the matrix.

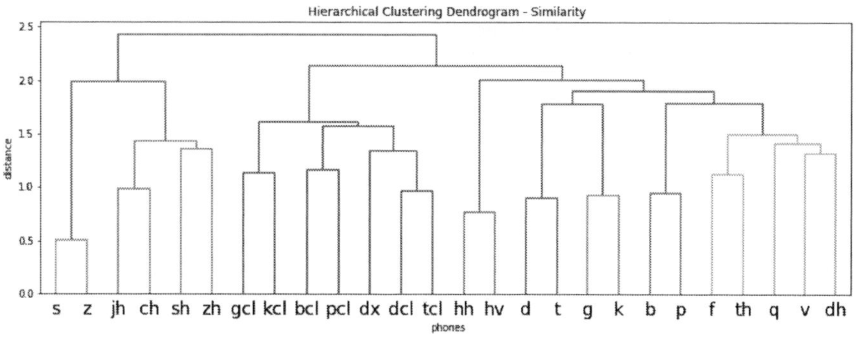

Figure 6: Obstruents at layer 0

verged. The labels /k/ and "kcl"[3], which were significantly detached in layer 0 have repositioned to be adjacent. Similarly, within the fricative region on the right hand side of the figure, the labio-dental fricatives (/f/, /v/) have become separated from the dental fricatives (/th/, /dh/).

Similarly certain acoustically-similar adjacent phonemes in layer 0, such as /d/ and /t/, see significant transformation within the clustering tree. The /d/ and /t/ labels occupy a separated sub-tree within the dendrogram produced for layer 0, but by layer 12 they have transitioned to become proximate to both their closures ("dcl" and "tcl") and their variants, such as /d-/dx/ and /t/-/q/. We can observe further development in this transition in the layer 7 representation (see figure 7) where certain proximate relationships have been established (as between the variants of /t/, /q/, and the closure "tcl") while other positionings remain (as with the inclusion of /t/ in the /d/-/dx/-"dcl" sub-tree).

The positioning of closures ("gcl", "kcl" etc.) is also of interest with regard to the apparent transition from acoustic to positional relations. Initially, given their strong acoustic similarity (representing a lack of sound production) it is intuitive that they should form a distinctive sub-group within the dendrogram, as they do in figure 6. At layer 7 this cluster has already separated significantly into several sub-trees of closure/stop pairs, such as /k/-"kcl". By layer 12, all closures have become proximate to their respective stop label.

[3]We do not describe these labels as phonemes.

7 Conclusions and Future Work

While the specific nature of the phonetic information captured by modern large transformer models will require significant further work to adduce, this paper has demonstrated that there is significant evidence to suggest that transformer architectures are capable of capturing significant levels of phonetic detail that accords with domain-informed understandings of phoneme relationships, and that permit distinction between less separable phonemes. Future work will look to establish more concretely the nature and effective mechanism of the layer-wise changes to these characteristics and the emergence of phonological generalisations, as well as looking to explore other aspects of the mechanisms asso-

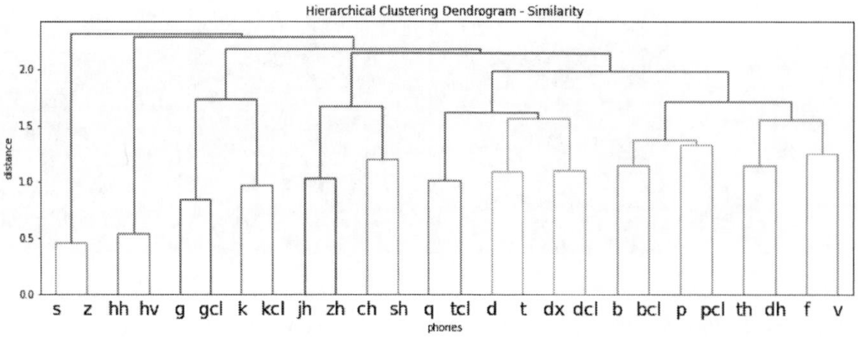

Figure 7: Obstruents at layer 7

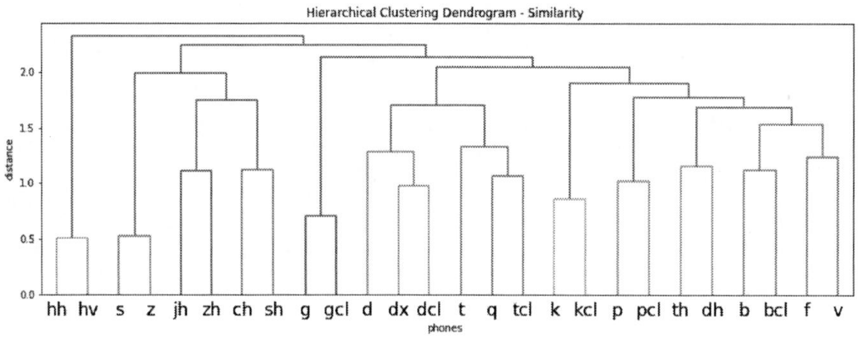

Figure 8: Obstruents at layer 12

ciated with these networks, such as the operation of their feature extractor modules and the attention matrices associated with each layer. While a chance-correlation experiment was conducted for this work, label imbalance in the TIMIT dataset was not specifically accounted for in the probing task; this will be assessed as a next step. Another focus of future work will be the investigation of the relationship of the emerging phonetic categories to infant language acquisition.

Acknowledgements

This work was conducted with the financial support of the Science Foundation Ireland Centre for Research Training in Digitally-Enhanced Reality (d-real) under Grant No. 18/CRT/6224. The ADAPT Centre for Digital Content Technology is funded under the SFI Research Centres Programme (Grant 13/RC/2106_P2) and is co-funded under the European Regional Development Fund. For the purpose of Open Access, the author has applied a CC BY public copyright licence to any Author Accepted Manuscript version arising from this submission.

References

Dario Amodei, Sundaram Ananthanarayanan, Rishita Anubhai, Jin Bai, Eric Battenberg, Carl Case, Jared Casper, Bryan Catanzaro, Jingdong Chen, Mike Chrzanowski, Adam Coates, Gregory Frederick Diamos, Erich Elsen, Jesse Engel, Linxi (Jim) Fan, Christopher Fougner, Awni Y. Hannun, Billy Jun, Tony Han, Patrick LeGresley, Xiangang Li, Libby Lin, Sharan Narang, A. Ng, Sherjil Ozair, Ryan J. Prenger, Sheng Qian, Jonathan Raiman, Sanjeev Satheesh, David Seetapun, Shubho Sengupta, Anuroop Sriram, Chong-Jun Wang, Yi Wang, Zhiqian Wang, Bo Xiao, Yan Xie, Dani Yogatama, Junni Zhan, and Zhenyao Zhu. 2016. Deep speech 2 : End-to-end speech recognition in english and mandarin. *ArXiv*, abs/1512.02595.

Alexei Baevski, Yuhao Zhou, Abdelrahman Mohamed, and Michael Aul. 2020. wav2vec 2.0: A framework for self-supervised learning of speech representations. *Neural Information Processing Systems (NeurIPS)*.

Yonatan Belinkov. 2021. Probing classifiers: Promises, shortcomings, and advances. *Association for Computational Linguistics*, 48:207–219.

Yonatan Belinkov and James R. Glass. 2017. Analyzing hidden representations in end-to-end automatic speech recognition systems. In *NIPS*.

Alexis Conneau, German Kruszewski, Guillaume Lample, Loïc Barrault, and Marco Baroni. 2018. What you can cram into a single $&!#* vector: Probing sentence embeddings for linguistic properties. In *Proceedings of the 56th Annual Meeting of the Association for Computational Linguistics (Volume 1: Long Papers)*, Melbourne, Australia. Association for Computational Linguistics.

Wendong Gan, Bolong Wen, Yin Yan, Haitao Chen, Zhichao Wang, Hongqiang Du, Lei Xie, Kaixuan Guo, and Hai Li. 2022. Iqdubbing: Prosody modeling based on discrete self-supervised speech representation for expressive voice conversion.

J. Garofolo, Lori Lamel, W. Fisher, Jonathan Fiscus, D. Pallett, N. Dahlgren, and V. Zue. 1992. Timit acoustic-phonetic continuous speech corpus. *Linguistic Data Consortium*.

John Hewitt and Christopher D. Manning. 2019. A structural probe for finding syntax in word representations. In *Proceedings of the 2019 Conference of the North American Chapter of the Association for Computational Linguistics: Human Language Technologies, Volume 1 (Long and Short Papers)*, Minneapolis, Minnesota. Association for Computational Linguistics.

Ganesh Jawahar, Benoît Sagot, and Djamé Seddah. 2019. What does BERT learn about the structure of language? In *Proceedings of the 57th Conference of the Association for Computational Linguistics, ACL 2019, Florence, Italy, July 28- August 2, 2019, Volume 1: Long Papers*, pages 3651–3657. Association for Computational Linguistics.

Mark Kane and Julie Carson-Berndsen. 2016. Enhancing data-driven phone confusions using restricted recognition. In *INTERSPEECH*, pages 3693–3697.

Sudheer Kolachina and Lilla Magyar. 2019. What do phone embeddings learn about phonology? *Proceedings of the 16th Workshop on Computational Research in Phonetics, Phonology, and Morphology*.

Jialu Li, Vimal Manohar, Pooja Chitkara, Andros Tjandra, Michael Picheny, Frank Zhang, Xiaohui Zhang, and Yatharth Saraf. 2021. Accent-robust automatic speech recognition using supervised and unsupervised wav2vec embeddings.

Nelson F. Liu, Matt Gardner, Yonatan Belinkov, Matthew E. Peters, and Noah A. Smith. 2019. Linguistic knowledge and transferability of contextual representations. *CoRR*, abs/1903.08855.

Danni Ma, Neville Ryant, and Mark Liberman. 2021. Probing acoustic representations for phonetic properties. In *ICASSP 2021 - 2021 IEEE International Conference on Acoustics, Speech and Signal Processing (ICASSP)*, pages 311–315.

Tomas Mikolov, Kai Chen, Greg Corrado, and Jeffrey Dean. 2013. Efficient estimation of word representations in vector space. corr abs/1301.3781 (2013). *arXiv preprint arXiv:1301.3781*.

Vasudevan Nedumpozhimana and John Kelleher. 2021. Finding bert's idiomatic key. In *Proceedings of the 17th Workshop on Multiword Expressions (MWE 2021)*, pages 57–62.

Emma O'Neill and Julie Carson-Berndsen. 2019. The effect of phoneme distribution on perceptual similarity in English. *Proc. Interspeech 2019*, pages 1941–1945.

Emma O'Neill, Joe Kenny, Anthony Ventresque, and Julie Carson-Berndsen. 2021. The influence of regional pronunciation variation on children's spelling and the potential benefits of accent adapted spellcheckers. In *Proceedings of the 25th Conference on Computational Natural Language Learning*, Online. Association for Computational Linguistics.

Fabian Pedregosa, Gaël Varoquaux, Alexandre Gramfort, Vincent Michel, Bertrand Thirion, Olivier Grisel, Mathieu Blondel, Peter Prettenhofer, Ron Weiss, Vincent Dubourg, et al. 2011. Scikit-learn: Machine learning in python. *the Journal of machine Learning research*, 12:2825–2830.

Leonardo Pepino, Pablo Ernesto Riera, and Luciana Ferrer. 2021. Emotion recognition from speech using wav2vec 2.0 embeddings. In *Interspeech*.

O. E. Scharenborg, Nikki van der Gouw, M. A. Larson, Elena Marchiori, Ioannis Kompatsiaris, Benoit Huet, Vasileios Mezaris, Cathal Gurrin, Wen-Huang Cheng, and Stefanos Vrochidis. 2019. The representation of speech in deep neural networks. *Lecture notes in computer science*, (Part II).

Jui Shah, Yaman Kumar Singla, Changyou Chen, and Rajiv Ratn Shah. 2021. What all do audio transformer models hear? probing acoustic representations for language delivery and its structure. *ArXiv*, abs/2101.00387.

Miikka P Silfverberg, Lingshuang Mao, and Mans Hulden. 2018. Sound analogies with phoneme embeddings. *Proceedings of the Society for Computation in Linguistics (SCiL) 2018*, pages 136–144.

Ian Tenney, Patrick Xia, Berlin Chen, Alex Wang, Adam Poliak, R. Thomas McCoy, Najoung Kim, Benjamin Van Durme, Samuel R. Bowman, Dipanjan Das, and Ellie Pavlick. 2019. What do you learn from context? probing for sentence structure in contextualized word representations. *CoRR*, abs/1905.06316.

Joe H Ward. 1963. Hierarchical grouping to optimize an objective function. *Journal of the American statistical association*, 58(301):236–244.

Morphotactic Modeling in an Open-source Multi-dialectal Arabic Morphological Analyzer and Generator

Nizar Habash,[†] **Reham Marzouk,**[†,††] **Christian Khairallah,**[†] **Salam Khalifa**[†,‡]
Computational Approaches to Modeling Language (CAMeL) Lab
[†]New York University Abu Dhabi
[††]Alexandria University, [‡]Stony Brook University
nizar.habash@nyu.edu, igsr.r.marzouk@alexu.edu.eg
christian.khairallah@nyu.edu, salam.khalifa@stonybrook.edu

Abstract

Arabic is a morphologically rich and complex language, with numerous dialectal variants. Previous efforts on Arabic morphology modeling focused on specific variants and specific domains using a range of techniques with different degrees of linguistic modeling transparency. In this paper we propose a new approach to modeling Arabic morphology with an eye towards multi-dialectness, resource openness, and easy extensibility and use. We demonstrate our approach by modeling verbs from Standard Arabic and Egyptian Arabic, within a common framework, and with high coverage.

1 Introduction

There has been a lot of work on Arabic computational morphology in the last three decades (Beesley et al., 1989; Kiraz, 1994; Al-Sughaiyer and Al-Kharashi, 2004; Graff et al., 2009; Boudchiche et al., 2017; Taji et al., 2018). These efforts were motivated by Arabic's many challenges, namely, its morphological richness and complexity, its orthographic ambiguity and noise, and its numerous dialectal variants. The work on Arabic computational morphology has led to the development of many resources that directly model morphology (e.g., analyzers, generators) and also resources and tools that use them (Maamouri et al., 2004; Pasha et al., 2014). Morphological analyzers have consistently shown that they are still valuable components in the NLP toolbox, even as the latter increasingly shifts toward the neural modeling space, and especially in low-resource and dialectal settings (Zalmout and Habash, 2017; Baly et al., 2017; Inoue et al., 2022).

The range of techniques explored for morphological modeling has been quite large, from finite-state machines to procedural and functional programming languages, covering different degrees of depth in different linguistic representations, different variants, and different domains and genres. However, a common challenge among these approaches is the inconsistent coverage of different linguistic features. For example, the Standard Arabic Morphological Analyzer (SAMA, v3.1) (Graff et al., 2009), which was developed in conjunction with work on Modern Standard Arabic (MSA) newswire text in the Penn Arabic Treebank (PATB) (Maamouri et al., 2004), has only 65 imperative verb forms, while it has over 13 thousand perfective verb forms. SAMA also has only 15 instances of the interrogative proclitic أ *Âa*[1] which in principle can attach to any word. Another example is the Calima-ARZ system for Egyptian Arabic (EGY) (Habash et al., 2012), which used automatically generated stem classes making it very hard to linguistically generalize and extend. Many of the Arabic morphology resources are not freely available, easy to augment, or ready to plug-and-play in open-source public libraries.

The work presented in this paper is part of a larger effort on the CAMELMORPH Project.[2] CAMELMORPH's goal is to build large open-source morphological models for Arabic and its dialects across many genres and domains. The focus in this paper is on the core components that define lexical and morphological information and the tools to convert them into models that are readily usable within an existing Python open-source suite for Arabic NLP, Camel Tools (Obeid et al., 2020). We demonstrate the effectiveness of our approach by modeling MSA and EGY verbs using a shared representation, and showing improved coverage compared to publicly available analyzers. Our data and code are publicly available.[2]

Next we present some related work (§2), a discussion of Arabic linguistic background (§3), and our approach (§4). We then present the MSA and EGY verbal models (§5) and evaluate them (§6).

[1]HSB Arabic transliteration (Habash et al., 2007).
[2]http://morph.camel-lab.com

19th SIGMORPHON Workshop on Computational Research in Phonetics, Phonology, and Morphology, pages 92 - 102

2 Related Work

There has been a considerable amount of work on Arabic morphological analysis (Al-Sughaiyer and Al-Kharashi, 2004; Habash, 2010). Altantawy et al. (2011) organized the various Arabic morphology processing efforts along a continuum of approaches that is characterized by two poles: on one end, very abstract and linguistically rich representations and rules are used to derive surface forms; while on the other end, simple and shallow techniques focus on efficient search in a space of pre-compiled (tabulated) solutions. The first type is typically but not strictly implemented using finite-state technology, and was one of the earliest efforts undertaken (Beesley et al., 1989; Kiraz, 1994; Beesley, 1996; Habash and Rambow, 2006; Smrž, 2007). These models can be rather complex and have many internal dependencies among the rules used for modeling sub-word structure and morphotactic and orthographic forms. The second type is typically not implemented in finite-state technology. Examples include the Buckwalter Arabic Morphological Analyzer (BAMA) (Buckwalter, 2004) and extensions of it (Graff et al., 2009; Taji et al., 2018). These systems do not represent the morphemic, phonological and orthographic rules directly, and instead compile their effect into the lexicon itself. Hulden and Samih (2012) demonstrated a method of mapping from the pre-compiled tabulated approaches to finite-state representation; and Altantawy et al. (2011) demonstrated the reverse process of going from finite-state to the tabulated representation.

In this paper we present an approach that is a middle ground between these two poles. In lieu of generative solutions employing rewrite rules to map from underlying forms (morphemes) to surface forms (allomorphs), we enumerate, in a limited pre-compiled manner, the various allomorphic forms, and indicate the different context conditions that select for their realization. Our morphological specifications also include information about how to order these different morphemes. Then, in an offline process, we convert our morphological specifications into a full pre-compiled tabulated format in the style of BAMA (Buckwalter, 2004) and CALIMA$_{Star}$ (Taji et al., 2018) databases (DBs) used in the open-source Python toolkit Camel Tools (Obeid et al., 2020). Camel Tools's morphological engines enable the use of the same morphological DB for analysis, generation, and reinflection.

Our approach is closest to Hockett (1954)'s Item-and-Arrangement approach, linguistically speaking; however, we do make use of post-processing transformations (a la Item-and-Process) in a limited way for phonological and orthographic phenomena that do not change the basic letter spelling of the Arabic word, but can change its diacritics. Also, to maximize the utility of our models, we use lemmas and features that allow us to relate our output to Word and Paradigm approaches (Bram, 2012).

Finally, while we do not explicitly rely on roots and patterns to derive our forms, as was done by Beesley (1996), and Habash and Rambow (2006), we plan, in future efforts, to abstract from existing entries templatic patterns that allow us to back off intelligently to unseen words if needed.

3 Arabic Linguistic Background

3.1 General Challenges

Arabic orthography, morphology, and dialectal variation pose a number of challenges for NLP.

Orthographic Ambiguity Arabic is typically written without the optional diacritical marks that are used for short vowels and consonantal gemination, leading to a high degree of ambiguity. MSA has upwards of 12 analyses per word (Pasha et al., 2014). A subtask of morphological analysis is producing the correct diacritization for each analysis.

Morphological Richness Arabic inflects for gender, number, person, aspect, mood, case, state and voice. In addition, Arabic orthography cliticizes a number of pronouns (direct object, possessive) and particles (conjunctions, prepositions, definite article, etc.). This results in thousands of forms for each verbal lemma. Because of orthographic ambiguity, words with analyses that differ in the presence of clitics are not uncommon, e.g., وحد *wHd* can be analyzed as *wa+Had∼a* 'and he limited' or *waH∼ada* 'he united', among other readings.

Morphological Complexity Arabic uses a combination of templatic morphemes (roots and patterns) and concatenative affixes and clitics. There are also many complex morphotactic rewriting operations that cause these morphemes to surface in different ways (allomorphs) in different contexts. We present a more detailed set of examples in Section 3.2 to motivate the approach in this paper.

Dialectal Variation In addition to MSA, the de facto official language in the Arab World, there is a number of different local dialects (e.g., Egyptian,

	(a)	(b)	(c)	(d)	(e)	(f)	(g)	(h)	(i)
	Modern Standard Arabic (MSA)								
(1)	**Root + Pattern**	**Lemma**	**Suff.P3MS**	**Suff.P3FS**	**Suff.P3MP**	**Suff.P2MS**	**Suff.P2FS**	**Suff.P2MP**	**Pron.3MS**
(2)			**+a**	**+at**	**+uwA**	**+ta**	**+ti**	**+tum**	**+hu**
(3)	**k.t.b + 1a2a3**	**katab**	katab+a	katab+at	katab+uwA	katab+ta	katab+ti	katab+tum	
(4)		*write*	katab+a+hu	katab+at+hu	katab+**uw**+hu	katab+ta+hu	katab+ti+**hi**	katab+**tumuw**+hu	✓
(5)	**n.H.t + 1a2a3**	**naHat**	naHat+a	naHat+at	naHat+uwA	naHat+**~a**	naHat+**~i**	naHat+**~um**	
(6)		*sculpt*	naHat+a+hu	naHat+at+hu	naHat+**uw**+hu	naHat+**~a**+hu	naHat+**~i**+**hi**	naHat+**~umuw**+hu	✓
(7)	**r.n.n + 1a2a3**	**ran~**	**ran~**+a	**ran~**+at	**ran~**+uwA	ranan+ta	ranan+ti	ranan+tum	
(8)		*ring*	**ran~**+a+hu	**ran~**+at+hu	**ran~**+**uw**+hu	ranan+ta+hu	ranan+ti+**hi**	ranan+**tumuw**+hu	✓
(9)	**r.m.y + 1a2a3**	**ramaY**	**ramaY**	**ram**+at	**ram**+**awA**	ramay+ta	ramay+ti	ramay+tum	
(10)		*throw*	**ramA**+hu	**ram**+at+hu	**ram**+**aw**+hu	ramay+ta+hu	ramay+ti+**hi**	ramay+**tumuw**+hu	✓
(11)	**k.t.b + 1A2a3**	**kAtab**	kAtab+a	kAtab+at	kAtab+uwA	kAtab+ta	kAtab+ti	kAtab+tum	
(12)		*correspond with*	kAtab+a+hu	kAtab+at+hu	kAtab+**uw**+hu	kAtab+ta+hu	kAtab+ti+**hi**	kAtab+**tumuw**+hu	✓
	Egyptian Arabic (EGY)								
(13)	**Root + Pattern**	**Lemma**	**Suff.P3MS**	**Suff.P3FS**	**Suff.P3MP**	**Suff.P2MS**	**Suff.P2FS**	**Suff.P2MP**	**Pron.3MS**
(14)			**+**	**+it**	**+uwA**	**+t**	**+tiy**	**+tuwA**	**+uh**
(15)	**k.t.b + 1a2a3**	**katab**	katab	katab+it	katab+uwA	katab+t	katab+tiy	katab+tuwA	
(16)		*write*	katab+uh	katab+it+uh	katab+**uw**+**h**	katab+t+uh	katab+tiy+**h**	katab+**tuw**+**h**	✓
(17)	**n.H.t + 1a2a3**	**naHat**	naHat	naHat+it	naHat+uwA	naHat+**~**	naHat+**~iy**	naHat+**~uwA**	
(18)		*sculpt*	naHat+uh	naHat+it+uh	naHat+**uw**+**h**	naHat+**~**+uh	naHat+**~iy**+**h**	naHat+**~uw**+**h**	✓
(19)	**r.n.n + 1a2a3**	**ran~**	**ran~**	**ran~**+it	**ran~**+uwA	**ran~ay**+t	**ran~ay**+tiy	**ran~ay**+tuwA	
(20)		*ring*	**ran~**+uh	**ran~**+it+uh	**ran~**+**uw**+**h**	**ran~ay**+t+uh	**ran~ay**+tiy+**h**	**ran~ay**+**tuw**+**h**	✓
(21)	**r.m.y + 1a2a3**	**ramaY**	**ramaY**	**ram**+it	**ram**+uwA	ramay+t	ramay+tiy	ramay+tuwA	
(22)		*throw*	**ramA**+**h**	**ram**+it+uh	**ram**+**uw**+**h**	ramay+t+uh	ramay+tiy+**h**	ramay+**tuw**+**h**	✓
(23)	**k.t.b + 1A2i3**	**kAtib**	kAtib	**kAtb**+it	**kAtb**+uwA	kAtib+t	kAtib+tiy	kAtib+tuwA	
(24)		*correspond with*	**kAtb**+uh	**kAtb**+it+uh	**kAtb**+**uw**+**h**	kAtib+t+uh	kAtib+tiy+**h**	kAtib+**tuw**+**h**	✓

Table 1: Segments of the verbal paradigms of four verbs illustrating complex morphotactics in MSA and EGY.

Levantine, and Gulf) that are commonly used on a daily basis. These dialects differ significantly from each other and from MSA in terms of phonology, morphology and lexicon although they share many similar aspects that support joint modeling. In Section 3.2, we present a more detailed example for MSA and EGY and compare them with each other.

Orthographic Inconsistency There is a high degree of orthographic inconsistency and variety in both MSA and dialectal Arabic (Zaghouani et al., 2014; Habash et al., 2018). For MSA there are standard guidelines with some minor regional differences; but dialectal Arabic has no official spelling rules. Habash et al. (2018) put forth a system for conventional orthography for dialectal Arabic (CODA), which has been used in some Arabic NLP resources. We consider CODA for EGY as our 'reference spelling,' but recognize its limitations.[3] We do not target modeling spelling variations in this work; and follow the philosophy that spelling errors need to be handled in components outside of the morphological analyzer. This is an important future research direction we plan to pursue.

[3]To allow comparing with previous work on Egyptian Arabic, we include a limited number of non-CODA-compliant phenomena, namely the negation and indirect object clitics, which CODA separates. This is simply a modeling decision that is independent of the framework.

3.2 Motivating Linguistic Phenomena

We describe in this section the linguistic facts relevant to this paper and approach. Arabic morphology includes a combination of templatic and concatenative morphemes, both with many allomorphic variants.[4] Table 1 (MSA) contrasts parts of the verbal paradigm for five verbs, all of which have triliteral roots, but four are in Form I (1a2a3); and one is in Form III (1A2a3 in MSA, 1A2i3 in EGY). We consider a few subject suffixes and one pronominal clitic; and we indicate the verbal citation form (or Lemma).[5] The table marks all *default* morpheme realizations in gray, and indicates in underlined black font allomorph changes. For example the word كَتَبَتْهُ *katab+at+hu* (cell Table 1.(4d)) simply composes the morphemic forms of the templatic root *k.t.b.* and pattern *1a2a3* with the suffix *+at* (P3FS, perfective 3rd person feminine singular) and the enclitic pronoun *+hu* (direct object 3rd person masculine singular). However, only in 29 out of 60 cells in the MSA examples, and 38 out of 60 in the EGY examples, is an allomorph

[4]We limit our discussion in this paper to the fully diacritized orthographic forms of the allomorphs in Arabic. We do not model phonological representations and only discuss them where necessary.

[5]Arabic Lemmas are based on the perfective 3rd person masculine singular form without the final diacritic vowel.

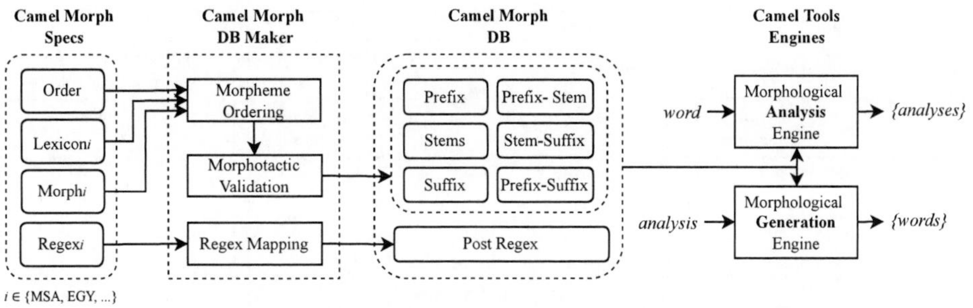

Figure 1: A high-level diagram of the CAMELMORPH approach.

of the root, pattern, suffix, or enclitic realized. It should be noted that although the five verbs happen to exist in both MSA and EGY, only 4 out of 60 forms in this example table match exactly. That said, the differences are regular and consistent, involving different suffix forms and different morphotactics. If we ignore the diacritics, 38 out of 60 forms match, an order of magnitude increase.

The following set of linguistic morphotactics can be observed in the examples in Table 1.

Geminate Verbs Verbs with geminate roots (equal second and third radicals) have an allomorph stem with an elided vowel in the context of vowel-initial suffixes (**v-suff**) in MSA, e.g. Table 1.(7c-8h) shows two variants: *ranan* (morpheme) and *ran* . The same phenomenon happens in EGY, but stems before consonant-initial suffixes (**c-suff**) also have a form different from the default interdigitation of root and pattern: a stem buffer vowel is inserted before the suffix, see Table 1.(19c-20h).

Defective Verbs Verbs with defective roots (third radical is *w* or *y*) have three allomorph stems that depend on the nature of the suffix in both MSA and EGY: vowel-initial, orthographically represented with a diacritic only (zero-letter suffix or **z-suff**), or being followed by an enclitic, e.g. Table 1.(9c-10h;21c-22h) shows four variants: *ramay* (morpheme), *ramaY*, *ramA*, and *ram*.

***t*-ending Verbs** Suffixes starting with the letter *t* in both MSA and EGY have orthographic allomorphs that replace the initial *t* with a letter gemination diacritic, Shadda ~, when following verbs ending with the letter *t* (#t), e.g. Table 1.(5f-6h).

Masculine Plural Suffixes The masculine plural suffixes (*+uwA*, *+tum* and *+tuwA* in Table 1.(e;h) also have multiple forms that depend on the presence of enclitics and the verbal stem ending.

***hu* Enclitic** The MSA clitic *+hu* has an allomorphic variant *+hi* that harmonizes with suffixes ending with the high front vowel *i*, e.g. Table 1.(g4).

Short Vowel Elision The short vowel in EGY verb stem *kAt[i]b* (in brackets) is elided when the stem is followed by a vowel, whether from a suffix or an enclitic, e.g. Table 1.(23;24). Similarly, the vowel of the EGY enclitic *+[u]h* is elided after vowel-ending base words (stem+suffix), e.g. Table 1.(22c;22e;22g-h). Such transformations which only change word diacritics are ideally modeled as orthographic rewrites (reflecting phonological and morpho-phonological adjustments).

It should be noted that words can be composed completely of allomorphs of the underlying morphemes, e.g. EGY word *ran~ay+tuw+h* in Table 1.(20h). These phenomena are only part of the complete list of phenomena we model, but are typical in terms of complexity. In the next section we will refer specifically to all of these phenomena and how we model them and their interactions.

4 The CAMELMORPH Approach

Figure 1 presents the overall approach we take in the CAMELMORPH project. The leftmost three boxes (CAMELMORPH **Specs**, **DB Maker** and DB) represent the offline process to create a Camel Tools-compatible morphological database (CAMELMORPH DB) from CAMELMORPH Specifications (**Specs**). The rightmost part of the figure represents the online process of using the DB in the Camel Tools morphological analysis and generation engines, where an input word results in a number of possible analyses, and an analysis can result in one or more words.

While we focus in this paper on the process of creating Camel Tools-compatible DBs, the overall approach can be used to generate other repre-

MO	Morph Order	DBPrefix	DBStem	DBSuffix
		[CONJ]	[PVStem] [PVBuff]	[PVSuff] [Pron]

		Class	Lemma/ Morpheme	Form	Gloss	Set Conds	Required Conds	katab+ti+hi	naHat+~umuw+hu	ran~+uw+hu	ranan+ta	ram+A+hu
Lexicon	L1	[PVStem]	katab	katab	write	trans		✓				
	L2	[PVStem]	naHat	naHat	sculpt	#t trans			✓			
	L3a	[PVStem]	ran~	ran~	ring	trans	v-suff			✓		
	L3b	[PVStem]	ran~	ranan	ring	trans	c-suff				✓	
	L4	[PVStem]	ramaY	ram	throw	#-ay trans						✓
Buffers	B1	[PVBuff]					else	✓			✓	
	B2a	[PVBuff]		aY			#-ay z-suff else					
	B2b	[PVBuff]		A			#-ay z-suff obj					✓
	B2c	[PVBuff]		ay			#-ay c-suff					
	B2d	[PVBuff]					#-ay v-suff					
Affixes	A1a	[PVSuff]	Suff.P3MS	a	he	v-suff	else					
	A1b	[PVSuff]	Suff.P3MS		he	z-suff	#-ay					✓
	A2	[PVSuff]	Suff.P3FS	at	she	v-suff						
	A3a	[PVSuff]	Suff.P3MP	uwA	they [mp]	v-suff	else else					
	A3b	[PVSuff]	Suff.P3MP	uw	they [mp]	v-suff	else obj			✓		
	A3c	[PVSuff]	Suff.P3MP	awA	they [mp]	v-suff	#-ay else					
	A3d	[PVSuff]	Suff.P3MP	aw	they [mp]	v-suff	#-ay obj					
	A4a	[PVSuff]	Suff.P2MS	ta	you [ms]	c-suff	else				✓	
	A4b	[PVSuff]	Suff.P2MS	~a	you [ms]	c-suff	#t					
	A5a	[PVSuff]	Suff.P2FS	ti	you [fs]	c-suff suff-i	else	✓				
	A5b	[PVSuff]	Suff.P2FS	~i	you [fs]	c-suff suff-i	#t					
	A6a	[PVSuff]	Suff.P2MP	tum	you [mp]	c-suff	else else					
	A6b	[PVSuff]	Suff.P2MP	tumuw	you [mp]	c-suff	else obj					
	A6c	[PVSuff]	Suff.P2MP	~um	you [mp]	c-suff	#t else					
	A6d	[PVSuff]	Suff.P2MP	~umuw	you [mp]	c-suff	#t obj		✓			
Clitics	C1	[Pron]									✓	
	C2a	[Pron]	Pron.3MS	hu	him	obj	trans else		✓	✓		✓
	C2b	[Pron]	Pron.3MS	hi	him	obj	trans suff-i	✓				

Figure 2: Sample Morphological Specifications for MSA perfective verbs, with examples.

sentations, e.g., finite-state machinery (directly or indirectly as Hulden and Samih (2012) has previously demonstrated). We chose to work with Camel Tools because it is a Python toolkit with growing popularity, and its morphological engine is relatively efficient.

Next, we describe the various components of the CAMELMORPH DB making process.

4.1 The CAMELMORPH Specifications

The morphological specifications (**Specs**) are the core of the CAMELMORPH project. There are four types of **Specs**: **Order**, **Lexicon**, various morphological units (**Morph**) – **Affixes**, **Clitics**, and **Buffers**, and Regular Expression Substitutions (**Regex**). An example of the set of **Order**, **Lexicon** and **Morph Specs** needed to model the MSA verbs in Table 1 is presented in Figure 2. We also present a **Regex** example to handle EGY verbs in Figure 2.

Morph Order The **Morph Order** specifies the arrangement of all the morphemes that can appear in a word. It only indicates the order of the morphemes, but not their morphotactic interactions. In Figure 2.(MO) (at the top of the figure), a minimal order is specified to form a perfective verb stem with a stem buffer, suffix, and pronominal clitic. The Prefix conjunction is allowed, but is not included in this example. Inside the **Morph Order**, the morphemes are specified by their class, e.g., **[PVStem]** refers to all the perfective verb stems.

The **Morph Order** also specifies which morpheme classes fall together to make the CAMELMORPH DB stem, and DB complex prefix and complex suffix sequences (sets of prefixes or suffixes that precede or follow the stem, respectively). In this example, a complex suffix sequence would include the resulting concatenation and rewriting of the perfective verb suffix and enclitic. The DB stem is created by concatenating the perfective verb stem and its buffer.

Different **Morph Order** lines are needed for the specifications of imperfect and command verb aspects. The number of specific **Morph Order** lines can vary depending on the choices of the linguist designing it.

Finally, since Arabic dialects and MSA all share the same morpheme order (with minor exceptions), we can use a common **Morph Order** for them all. This paves the way toward models of intra-word code-switching, which we leave for future work.

Lexicon, Buffers, Affixes, and Clitics All the morphemes used in the model are specified in a common style regardless of their type as lexical stem, inflectional affix, or attached clitic (syntactically independent, by phonological or orthographically dependent morpheme). The specification of any morphemes includes six elements.

(1) Class specifies the set of morphemes that the morpheme in question belongs to. The **Class** is the link between the Morph Order and the specific morphemes. It determines the position of the morpheme in the word.

(2) Lemma (in **Lexicon**) or **Morpheme** (in **Affixes and Clitics**) specifies the morpheme. For the **Lexicon**, the lemma is an abstraction over all the inflectional forms of a word's morphological inflection family. For the affixes and clitics, we use a functional specification. For example, *Suff.P3MP* refers to the perfective 3rd person masculine plural suffix. **Stem Buffers**, as in the class **[PVBuffer]**, are not morphemes per se, but rather fragments of stems that vary highly in different contexts. As such **Stem Buffers** have no proper *morpheme* form defined; but their class specifies their position in the word. This concept is an innovation that allows us to refer to specific parts of the word form where complex morphotactic interactions happen and isolate it from the rest of the verbal patterns. There are two advantages to this approach. First, it reduces the total number of stems needed to be specified. So, for the defective verb in Table 1.(9-10;21-22), instead of listing four stems, *ramaY, ramA, ram,* and *ramay*, we only specify *ram* with a condition term (see below) marking its class as **#-ay**, i.e. defective. A second advantage of the buffer concept is that it allows us to relate dialect and MSA stems to each other, e.g. by treating the stems of geminate EGY verbs *ran∼* and *ran∼ay* as the same (*ran∼*) with different conditioned buffer values. Obviously, more complex non-suffixing or prefixing stem changes cannot be handled meaningfully using the buffer concept. Nevertheless, the current method is able to handle all Arabic-related concatenative phenomena perfectly.

(3) Form specifies the actual realized form of the morpheme. Each of the allomorphs of a morpheme gets a different **Form** line. For example, the two forms of the clitic Pron.3MS (*hu* and *hi*) share the same **Morpheme** and **Class** but have different forms. When multiple forms appear for the same morpheme, they need to be distinguished through different **Required** Conditions (**Conds**), which specify their complementary distribution.

(4) Gloss specifies the English meaning of the morpheme. It is not an essential feature of the model, but still useful to distinguish and explain any semantic differences.

(5) Set Conds and **(6) Required Conds** are a collection of terms that allow us to specify which allomorphs are compatible. Each form (allomorph) both *sets* and *requires* zero or more conditions to be true to be validated for use. Effectively, these conditions define the various contexts of co-occurrence and control the complementary distribution of the allomoprhs. In the example in Figure 2, there are nine condition terms:

(1-2) **trans** (transitive) and **obj** (object pronoun) license the use of pronominal clitics with transitive verbs. The **obj** condition also interacts with some suffix and verb buffer forms, e.g., Figure 2.(B2b;A6b;A6d).

(3-5) **v-suff**, **c-suff**, and **z-suff** specify the form of the suffixes: vowel-initial, consonant-initial or zero letter suffixes. They interact with verb stems and buffer forms.

(6-7) **#-ay** and **#t** specify the type of the verb as defective or t-ending, respectively.

(8) **suff-i** specifies the context of a suffixes ending with a *i*, e.g. Figure 2.(A5a;A5b).

(9) Finally, the term **else** is not a condition in itself, but it allows specifying the negation of a condition or set of conditions to model complementary distributions. The scope of an **else** is the column it appears in the **Required Conds** field. For example, in Figure 2.(C2a), the **else** indicates the negation of the **suff-i** in Figure 2.(C2b).

The right-hand side of Figure 2 presents five word examples from Table 1 and highlights the specific allomorphs which are selected to form them. Here, the order of the allomorphs is determined by

(Input)	(R1)	(R2)	(Clean up)
	V! → ø / V C _ C V	**V! → ø / V: _**	**! → ø**
kAti!b	kAti!b	kAti!b	**kAtib**
kAti!b+it	**kAtb**+it	kAtb+it	kAtb+it
kAti!b+uwA	**kAtb**+uwA	kAtb+uwA	kAtb+uwA
kAti!b+t	kAti!b+t	kAti!b+t	**kAtib**+t
kAti!b+tiy	kAti!b+tiy	kAti!b+tiy	**kAtib**+tiy
kAti!b+tuwA	kAti!b+tuwA	kAti!b+tuwA	**kAtib**+tuwA
kAti!b+u!h	**kAtb**+u!h	kAtb+u!h	kAtb+**uh**
kAti!b+it+u!h	**kAtb**+it+u!h	kAtb+it+u!h	kAtb+it+**uh**
kAti!b+uw+u!h	**kAtb**+uw+u!h	kAtb+uw+**h**	kAtb+uw+h
kAti!b+t+u!h	kAti!b+t+u!h	kAti!b+t+u!h	**kAtib**+t+**uh**
kAti!b+tiy+u!h	kAti!b+tiy+u!h	kAti!b+tiy+**h**	**kAtib**+tiy+h
kAti!b+tuw+u!h	kAti!b+tuw+u!h	kAti!b+tuw+**h**	**kAtib**+tuw+h

Table 2: Example of the application of rewrite rules to model the EGY verbs in Table 1.(23;24).

the **Morph Order**, and their compatibility through the set and required condition terms. For instance, in the second example, *naHat+∼umuw+hu*, the selected stem sets the conditions **#t** and **trans**. The *Suff.P2MP* has four allomorphs, and the *Pron.3MS* enclitic has two. Two of the *Suff.P2MP* allomophs are compatible with the stem's **#t**; and only one of these two (requiring **#t** and **obj**) is compatible with one of the *Pron.3MS* allomorphs (setting **obj** and requiring **trans** and *not* **suff-i**).

Regex Substitution Rules The last component of the CAMELMORPH **Specs** is the regex substitution rules. These rules can be used to model orthographic and phonological rewrite phenomena that involve morpheme diacritics. Table 2 illustrates how three rules can be used to model the vowel elision phenomena in EGY verbs in Table 1.(23;24). While the rules are implemented in the system with regex substitutions over orthographic forms, we represent them in the headers of Table 2 in SPE-type rule form (Chomsky and Halle, 1968) for readability.[6] To control the scope of the rules, we also extend the EGY verb stem and enclitic entries by marking elision candidates in the morphemes directly using a ! character. Only marked vowel diacritics in elision contexts are deleted. In Table 2, we use two rules (R1) and (R2), applied in sequence, followed by a final cleanup step to remove the ! marker for vowels that were not deleted. The morpheme boundary (+) is maintained for illustrative purposes. The grayed out cells indicate where a rule is applied, and the bolding indicates the affected morpheme.

[6]V represents any vowel, which corresponds to short vowels (diacritical marks [aiu]) and long vowels represented as (aAliyluw). The symbol V: represents long vowels only.

To allow us to use regex substitution rules within Camel Tools, we needed to make some extensions, which we plan on releasing in future Camel Tools releases.

4.2 The CAMELMORPH DB

We describe next the format of the CAMELMORPH DB, which we want to generate from the CAMELMORPH **Specs**. The CAMELMORPH DB has the same basic structure as the Buckwalter Arabic Morphological Analyzer (BAMA) (Buckwalter, 2004): it consists of (a) three lexical tables for complex prefixes (sequences of all possible co-occurring proclitics and prefixes), complex suffixes (sequences of all possible co-occurring suffixes and enclitics), and stems, and (b) three compatibility tables that specify allowed co-occurrences of complex prefixes with stems, stems with complex suffixes, and complex prefixes with complex suffixes (see Figure 1). During the analysis of a word, all combinations of allowable prefixes, stems, and suffixes matching the input in undiacritized space are considered and checked for existence in the lexical tables, and if so, their lexical categories are checked for compatibility in compatibility tables. Only valid and compatible combinations are output. This representation, which was pioneered by Buckwalter (2002) has been used by many other systems since then (Habash, 2004; Taji et al., 2018; Obeid et al., 2020) with numerous extensions. Habash (2004) demonstrated how to extend the algorithm with the same DB to perform generation. And Taji et al. (2018) demonstrated its use for reinflection and more complex gender/number modeling.

In our work, we extend Obeid et al. (2020)'s version by factoring out some hard-coded components to handle regex-based post-processing, and include them in the DB files. Our extensions will be integrated in Camel Tools once the full morphological models are finalized for all parts-of-speech.

4.3 The CAMELMORPH DB Maker

The CAMELMORPH **DB Maker** takes the CAMELMORPH **Morph Specs** as input and generates a BAMA-like CAMELMORPH DB. The basic algorithm behind this conversion is to identify all the unique condition terms set and required from all the instances of the classes ordered in the **Morph Order**. Each such combination is checked for compatibility (i.e., morphotactic validation) and incompatible combinations are discarded. Surface strings and features associated with compatible combina-

		MSA			EGY		
		CAMELMORPH Specs	CAMELMORPH DB	Calima MSA	CAMELMORPH Specs	CAMELMORPH DB	Calima EGY
(a)	Lemmas	9,331	9,331	9,112	8,404	8,404	10,661
(b)	Prefix & Proclitic Morphemes (Allomorphs)	34 (35)			23 (24)		
	Suffix & Enclitic Morphemes (Allomorphs)	119 (231)			39 (56)		
	Stem Buffers (Pre-stem/Post-stem)	6 / 71			4 / 47		
	Unique Condition Terms	35			30		
	Morph Order	69			11		
(c)	Compatibility Tables		48,798	2,733		13,734	6,649
	Complex Prefix Sequence		2,440	1,127		896	5,499
	Complex Suffix Sequence		12,902	574		2,619	1,237
(d)	PV-Active Stems	10,514	13,329	13,299	8,718	11,421	10,487
	PV-Passive Stems	10,509	11,483	303	n/a	n/a	3,558
	IV-Active Stems	10,486	14,305	13,382	8,406	18,052	4,264
	IV-Passive Stems	10,486	14,246	2,825	n/a	n/a	707
	CV Stems	10,486	12,785	66	8,406	9,402	6,054
(e)	All Unique Diacritized Forms		93,212,172	37,017,732		192,427,668	9,795,021
	All Unique Full Analyses		254,312,696	87,968,972		515,194,392	95,795,018
	All Unique Full Analyses without Clitics		1,602,403	321,323		159,697	52,190

Table 3: Statistics of the MSA and EGY verbal morphology models in CAMELMORPH.

tions are split into complex prefix, complex suffix and stem sequences and added into the lexical tables. Also, compatibility categories are created for the complex morpheme sequences, and are added to the compatibility tables. Memoization is used to speed up this process and make it efficient. As for the **Regex** substitution rules, they are simply copied into the DB with minimal processing.

5 Modeling Arabic Verbs

We developed two morphological models for MSA and EGY verbs. This effort made use of publicly available resources and tools, together with extensive reformulation, quality assessment, and reference cross-checking by a team of linguists and computer scientists.

For MSA in particular, we filled many known gaps in previous models, namely, adding passive and imperative forms, and the interrogative proclitic. We also added some admittedly archaic forms from Classical Arabic: energetic and extra energetic moods and indirect object pronominal clitics used with ditransitive verbs. For EGY, we paid special attention to completing verbal paradigms and modeling phono-orthographic phenomena.

Table 3 presents some of the statistics about these two models. For each variant (MSA and EGY), we present three sets of contrasting numbers: The CAMELMORPH **Specs**, the CAMELMORPH DB, and two pre-existing Camel Tools MSA and EGY databases for reference: **Calima MSA** and **Calima EGY**, respectively.[7]

The total number of lemmas in CAMELMORPH, and in **Calima MSA** and **Calima EGY** is generally comparable, although **Calima EGY** has more lemmas, presumably because automatic methods of lexicographic population were used in that effort. However, the number of lemmas does not indicate the modeling of their full paradigm.

The total number of morphological specifications outside the lexicon (Table 3.(b)) is two orders of magnitude smaller than the forms compiled into CAMELMORPH DB (Table 3.(c)). MSA **Specs** are 2.6 times the number of those in EGY (Table 3.(b)), which is expected given MSA's richer inflectional features space.

Looking at the stem counts in both MSA and EGY (Table 3.(d)), we notice that the number of forms in CAMELMORPH DB is higher than those in **Specs** by 26% and 52% for MSA and EGY, respectively. This increase is because of the pre- and post-buffer merging with the stems. Additionally, MSA Passive and CV (Command) forms were enriched to match the size of other verb forms. This is a major coverage increase resulting in more complete verbal paradigms. EGY on the other hand has no passive stems in CAMELMORPH, as by design, we consider them to be unaccusative derivational forms and not inflectional passives. This is a de-

[7]For MSA, we compared with the `calima-msa-s31_0.4.2.utf8.db` version (Taji et al., 2018) based on SAMA (Graff et al., 2009). For EGY we only compared to the `calima-egy-c044_0.2.0.utf8.db` entries (no MSA extensions) based on Habash et al. (2012).

sign choice of our **Specs** and not a limitation of the framework. We also note the large increase in EGY IV stems which is due to pre-stem buffers that interact with some of the person and number prefixes. One advantage of the CAMELMORPH framework is the ease of configuring the specifications of the DB being generated while considering tradeoffs in efficiency.

In terms of the total number of analyses (Table 3.(e)), CAMELMORPH has 2.9 times and 5.4 times the number of analyses in **Calima MSA** and **Calima EGY**, respectively. The total number of unique CAMELMORPH EGY full analyses is remarkably twice that of MSA, while the respective number of analyses without clitics is one-tenth. This is consistent with MSA having a richer inflection space; while EGY has a richer enclitic space, which includes negation clitics and indirect and benefactive object pronouns.

6 Evaluation

We present two recall-based evaluations to measure the quality of the new verb morphological models we developed.

MSA Recall Evaluation and Error Analysis To evaluate the quality of our CAMELMORPH MSA verb model in terms of recall of correct morphological analyses, we used manually annotated verbal entries in the training portion of the PATB (latest versions of parts 1,2,3) (Maamouri et al., 2004) as defined by Diab et al. (2013). There are 47,691 verb tokens (14,786 unique analyses). Out of all verb tokens, 98.4% of their full analyses were recalled successfully, and 0.3% were out-of-vocabulary. Of the remainder 1.4% with no perfect matches, we randomly selected 100 unique verb analysis examples and manually analyzed the results. In 93% of the cases, the PATB annotation was suboptimal or incorrect: 64% (absolute) of the cases come from the use of a li/PREP clitic with verbs instead of li/CONJ_SUB, which seems like a consistent annotation choice, albeit odd for verbs. In 29% of the cases, the PATB annotation did not specify a lemma or diacritization (13%), or had an incorrect lemma or diacritization (16%). In 6% (absolute) of the latter, the lemma was incorrectly specified in the passive voice. Our CAMELMORPH MSA system failed to produce matches in 7% of the sample. Most of the cases were missing lexical entries or alternative spellings of some clitic combinations, e.g., *fa+li* as *fa+l*.

EGY Recall Evaluation and Error Analysis Similar to our MSA recall evaluation, we conducted a recall evaluation for EGY using the verbal entries in the training portion of the LDC's ARZATB (Maamouri et al., 2012) as defined by Diab et al. (2013). Given the inconsistencies in some of the ARZATB entries, we used a version of ARZATB that was automatically synchronized with a combination of EGY and MSA analyzers as our reference. This version was reported on in previous publications (Pasha et al., 2014; Zalmout and Habash, 2019; Inoue et al., 2022). For recall evaluation, we also use CAMELMORPH EGY and MSA together in a similar manner, with preference towards EGY if an imperfect (i.e., not all analysis features match) tie is reached. To deal with the common spelling variations in the input words, we use the a dediacritized version of the correct answer, which is intended to mimic a more CODA-compliant spelling. Of the original token count of 20,339 verbs, 69.9% of the full analyses are recalled successfully. In 1.4%, no analysis is generated, and in 24.2%, no single analysis matches the reference analysis perfectly. 4.5% of the reference analyses were not usable due to synchronization issues. We took a sample of 100 unique verb analyses from the set with no matches, and analyzed them manually. Almost half of the sample (47%) was due to reference errors. Another third (37%) involved valid alternative diacritizations reflecting different pronunciations (e.g. مسك *misik* vs *masak* 'to hold'). 10% were due to missing entries; and 6% were due to diacritization errors that can be fixed with regular expressions.

The difference in recall between MSA and EGY is striking but completely understandable given the differences in standardization traditions and the maturity of existing resources.

7 Conclusion and Future Work

We presented a new approach to modeling Arabic morphotactics and demonstrated its usefulness by creating a large-scale verbal analyzer for MSA and EGY using a common framework. All of our models and code will be publicly available. In the future, we plan to extend our work to all other POS classes in MSA and EGY, as well as target other dialects of Arabic. Some of the interesting challenges we want to address are noisy spelling, dialect-MSA intra-word code switching, and template-based backoff modeling.

References

Imad A. Al-Sughaiyer and Ibrahim A. Al-Kharashi. 2004. Arabic morphological analysis techniques: A comprehensive survey. *Journal of the American Society for Information Science and Technology*, 55(3):189–213.

Mohamed Altantawy, Nizar Habash, and Owen Rambow. 2011. Fast Yet Rich Morphological Analysis. In *Proceedings of the International Workshop on Finite-State Methods and Natural Language Processing (FSMNLP)*, Blois, France.

Ramy Baly, Hazem Hajj, Nizar Habash, Khaled Bashir Shaban, and Wassim El-Hajj. 2017. A sentiment treebank and morphologically enriched recursive deep models for effective sentiment analysis in Arabic. *ACM Transactions on Asian and Low-Resource Language Information Processing (TALLIP)*, 16(4):23.

Kenneth Beesley. 1996. Arabic Finite-State Morphological Analysis and Generation. In *Proceedings of the International Conference on Computational Linguistics (COLING)*, pages 89–94, Copenhagen, Denmark.

Kenneth Beesley, Tim Buckwalter, and Stuart Newton. 1989. Two-Level Finite-State Analysis of Arabic Morphology. In *Proceedings of the Seminar on Bilingual Computing in Arabic and English.*

Mohamed Boudchiche, Azzeddine Mazroui, Mohamed Ould Abdallahi Ould Bebah, Abdelhak Lakhouaja, and Abderrahim Boudlal. 2017. AlKhalil Morpho Sys 2: A robust Arabic morpho-syntactic analyzer. *Journal of King Saud University - Computer and Information Sciences*, 29(2):141–146.

Barli Bram. 2012. Three models of English morphology. *LLT Journal: A Journal on Language and Language Teaching*, 15(1):179–185.

Tim Buckwalter. 2002. Buckwalter Arabic morphological analyzer version 1.0. Linguistic Data Consortium (LDC) catalog number LDC2002L49, ISBN 1-58563-257-0.

Tim Buckwalter. 2004. Buckwalter Arabic Morphological Analyzer Version 2.0. LDC catalog number LDC2004L02, ISBN 1-58563-324-0.

Noam Chomsky and Morris Halle. 1968. *The sound pattern of English.* New York: Harper and Row.

Mona Diab, Nizar Habash, Owen Rambow, and Ryan Roth. 2013. LDC Arabic treebanks and associated corpora: Data divisions manual. *arXiv preprint arXiv:1309.5652.*

David Graff, Mohamed Maamouri, Basma Bouziri, Sondos Krouna, Seth Kulick, and Tim Buckwalter. 2009. Standard Arabic Morphological Analyzer (SAMA) Version 3.1. Linguistic Data Consortium LDC2009E73.

Nizar Habash. 2004. Large Scale Lexeme Based Arabic Morphological Generation. In *Proceedings of Traitement Automatique des Langues Naturelles (TALN)*, pages 271–276, Fez, Morocco.

Nizar Habash, Fadhl Eryani, Salam Khalifa, Owen Rambow, Dana Abdulrahim, Alexander Erdmann, Reem Faraj, Wajdi Zaghouani, Houda Bouamor, Nasser Zalmout, Sara Hassan, Faisal Al shargi, Sakhar Alkhereyf, Basma Abdulkareem, Ramy Eskander, Mohammad Salameh, and Hind Saddiki. 2018. Unified guidelines and resources for Arabic dialect orthography. In *Proceedings of the Language Resources and Evaluation Conference (LREC)*, Miyazaki, Japan.

Nizar Habash, Ramy Eskander, and Abdelati Hawwari. 2012. A Morphological Analyzer for Egyptian Arabic. In *Proceedings of the Workshop of the Special Interest Group on Computational Morphology and Phonology (SIGMORPHON)*, pages 1–9, Montréal, Canada.

Nizar Habash and Owen Rambow. 2006. MAGEAD: A morphological analyzer and generator for the Arabic dialects. In *Proceedings of the International Conference on Computational Linguistics and the Conference of the Association for Computational Linguistics (COLING-ACL)*, pages 681–688, Sydney, Australia.

Nizar Habash, Abdelhadi Soudi, and Tim Buckwalter. 2007. On Arabic Transliteration. In A. van den Bosch and A. Soudi, editors, *Arabic Computational Morphology: Knowledge-based and Empirical Methods*, pages 15–22. Springer, Netherlands.

Nizar Y Habash. 2010. *Introduction to Arabic natural language processing.* Morgan & Claypool Publishers.

Charles F Hockett. 1954. Two models of grammatical description. *Word*, 10(2-3):210–234.

Mans Hulden and Younes Samih. 2012. Conversion of procedural morphologies to finite-state morphologies: a case study of Arabic. In *Proceedings of the 10th International Workshop on Finite State Methods and Natural Language Processing*, pages 70–74.

Go Inoue, Salam Khalifa, and Nizar Habash. 2022. Morphosyntactic tagging with pre-trained language models for Arabic and its dialects. In *Findings of the Association for Computational Linguistics: ACL 2022*, pages 1708–1719, Dublin, Ireland. Association for Computational Linguistics.

George Kiraz. 1994. Multi-tape Two-level Morphology: A Case study in Semitic Non-Linear Morphology. In *Proceedings of the International Conference on Computational Linguistics (COLING)*, pages 180–186, Kyoto, Japan.

Mohamed Maamouri, Ann Bies, Tim Buckwalter, and Wigdan Mekki. 2004. The Penn Arabic Treebank: Building a Large-Scale Annotated Arabic Corpus. In *Proceedings of the International Conference on Arabic Language Resources and Tools*, pages 102–109, Cairo, Egypt.

Mohamed Maamouri, Ann Bies, Seth Kulick, Dalila Tabessi, and Sondos Krouna. 2012. Egyptian Arabic Treebank DF Parts 1-8 V2.0 - LDC catalog numbers LDC2012E93, LDC2012E98, LDC2012E89, LDC2012E99, LDC2012E107, LDC2012E125, LDC2013E12, LDC2013E21.

Ossama Obeid, Nasser Zalmout, Salam Khalifa, Dima Taji, Mai Oudah, Bashar Alhafni, Go Inoue, Fadhl Eryani, Alexander Erdmann, and Nizar Habash. 2020. CAMeL tools: An open source python toolkit for Arabic natural language processing. In *Proceedings of The 12th Language Resources and Evaluation Conference*, pages 7022–7032, Marseille, France. European Language Resources Association.

Arfath Pasha, Mohamed Al-Badrashiny, Mona Diab, Ahmed El Kholy, Ramy Eskander, Nizar Habash, Manoj Pooleery, Owen Rambow, and Ryan Roth. 2014. MADAMIRA: A fast, comprehensive tool for morphological analysis and disambiguation of Arabic. In *Proceedings of the Language Resources and Evaluation Conference (LREC)*, pages 1094–1101, Reykjavik, Iceland.

Otakar Smrž. 2007. *Functional Arabic Morphology. Formal System and Implementation*. Ph.D. thesis, Charles University in Prague, Prague, Czech Republic.

Dima Taji, Salam Khalifa, Ossama Obeid, Fadhl Eryani, and Nizar Habash. 2018. An Arabic Morphological Analyzer and Generator with Copious Features. In *Proceedings of the Fifteenth Workshop on Computational Research in Phonetics, Phonology, and Morphology (SIGMORPHON)*, pages 140–150.

Wajdi Zaghouani, Behrang Mohit, Nizar Habash, Ossama Obeid, Nadi Tomeh, Alla Rozovskaya, Noura Farra, Sarah Alkuhlani, and Kemal Oflazer. 2014. Large Scale Arabic Error Annotation: Guidelines and Framework. In *Proceedings of the Language Resources and Evaluation Conference (LREC)*, Reykjavik, Iceland.

Nasser Zalmout and Nizar Habash. 2017. Don't throw those morphological analyzers away just yet: Neural morphological disambiguation for Arabic. In *Proceedings of the Conference on Empirical Methods in Natural Language Processing (EMNLP)*, pages 704–713, Copenhagen, Denmark.

Nasser Zalmout and Nizar Habash. 2019. Joint diacritization, lemmatization, normalization, and fine-grained morphological tagging. *arXiv preprint arXiv:1910.02267*.

The SIGMORPHON 2022 Shared Task on Morpheme Segmentation

Khuyagbaatar Batsuren[1] Gábor Bella[2] Aryaman Arora[3] Viktor Martinovic[4]
Kyle Gorman[5] Zdeněk Žabokrtský[6] Amarsanaa Ganbold[1] Šárka Dohnalová[6]
Magda Ševčíková[7] Kateřina Pelegrinová[6] Fausto Giunchiglia[2] Ryan Cotterell[8]
Ekaterina Vylomova[9]
[1]National University of Mongolia [2]University of Trento [3]Georgetown University
[4]University of Vienna [5]Graduate center, City University Of New York [6]Charles University
[7]University of Ostrava [8]ETH Zürich [9]University of Melbourne

Abstract

The SIGMORPHON 2022 shared task on morpheme segmentation challenged systems to decompose a word into a sequence of morphemes and covered most types of morphology: compounds, derivations, and inflections. Subtask 1, word-level morpheme segmentation, covered 5 million words in 9 languages (Czech, English, Spanish, Hungarian, French, Italian, Russian, Latin, Mongolian) and received 13 system submissions from 7 teams and the best system averaged 97.29% F1 score across all languages, ranging English (93.84%) to Latin (99.38%). Subtask 2, sentence-level morpheme segmentation, covered 18,735 sentences in 3 languages (Czech, English, Mongolian), received 10 system submissions from 3 teams, and the best systems outperformed all three state-of-the-art subword tokenization methods (BPE, ULM, Morfessor2) by 30.71% absolute. To facilitate error analysis and support any type of future studies, we released all system predictions, the evaluation script, and all gold standard datasets.[1]

System	type	motivation	segmentation
BPE	surface	sta.	in I val I uable
Morfessor2	surface	sta. & lin.	in I valuable
DeepSPIN-3	canonical	sta. & lin.	in I value I able

Table 1: Structural differences of subword tokenization (BPE), morphological segmentation (Morfessor2), and morpheme segmentation (DeepSPIN-3 – subtask 1 winning system); acronyms: sta. - statistics and lin. - linguistic

1 Introduction

Many NLP applications, such as machine translation or question answering, require *subword tokenization*, i.e. splitting words into a sequence of substrings (Mielke et al., 2021). Such tokenizers are trained by an unsupervised algorithm, usually either Byte-Pair Encoding (BPE; Gage 1994; Sennrich et al. 2016) or Unigram Language Modeling (ULM; Kudo 2018). To give a few examples, contemporary language models RoBERTa (Liu et al., 2019) and GPT-3 (Brown et al., 2020) use a byte-level BPE (Radford et al., 2019) while XLNet (Yang et al., 2019) relies on ULM. These subword tokenization algorithms are not linguistically motivated but are rather based on statistical co-occurrences. Therefore, unsupervised and semi-supervised methods for morphological segmentation (Creutz and Lagus, 2005) have emerged in parallel, state-of-the-art methods of this kind being Morfessor variants (Grönroos et al., 2014, 2020). Ataman et al. (2017) and Schwartz et al. (2020) find that Morfessor-based language models can outperform BPE-based ones. Matthews et al. (2018); Nzeyimana and Rubungo (2022) show that enriching BPE with morphological analyzers can be beneficial for translation, while many others (Domingo et al., 2018; Macháček et al., 2018; Schwartz et al., 2020; Saleva and Lignos, 2021) find no conclusive improvements over BPE for machine translation.

One of the core problems is that the state-of-the-art morphological segmentation and subword tokenization algorithms provide "surface-level" segmentation, which has several theoretical drawbacks with respect to "canonical" segmentation (e.g., segmented substrings are not considered as meaningful as morphemes). Cotterell et al. (2016) provided formal definitions for both: given a word w, its "surface" segmentation is a sequence of *surface substrings* the concatenation of which is w, e.g., *funniest* $\rightarrow$ *funn-i-est*. The purpose of canonical segmentation (Kann et al., 2016; Girrbach, 2022), on the other hand, is not only computing surface segmentation but also restoring standardized forms of morphemes, e.g., *funniest* $\rightarrow$ *fun-y-est*. More detailed structural distinctions between these segmentation types are shown in Table 1.

However, state-of-the-art studies in canonical segmentations have been limited to very low num-

[1]`https://github.com/sigmorphon/2022SegmentationST`

19th SIGMORPHON Workshop on Computational Research in Phonetics, Phonology, and Morphology, pages 103 - 116

Lang	word	segmentation	category
eng	sheepiness	sheep @@y @@ness	010
	pokers	poke @@er @@s	110
hun	időpontod	idő @@pont @@od	101
	szőttetek	sző @@tt @@etek	100
mon	харах	харах	000
	гэмтлийг	гэмтэх @@л @@ийг	110

Table 2: Training samples for Subtask 1. Each sample consists of a word, its canonical segmentation, and a category encoding word formation processes.

bers of languages with sufficiently rich morphological resources (Kurimo et al., 2010a,b; Cotterell et al., 2016; Kann et al., 2018). With the goal of advancing research in this direction, we present a *morpheme segmentation shared task* and provide large-scale datasets over nine languages, evaluation metrics, and morphological annotations of five million word formations. In this, we rely on the latest release of UniMorph (Batsuren et al., 2022) which has introduced morpheme segmentations and derivational data from MorphyNet (Batsuren et al., 2021b). The resulting shared task is a follow-up to past morphological segmentation shared tasks such as "MorphoChallenge" (Kurimo et al., 2007, 2008, 2009) or "Multilingual parsing" (Zeman et al., 2017, where lemmatization as segmentation is a subtask).

2 Task and Evaluation Details

2.1 Subtask 1: Word-level Morpheme Segmentation

In subtask 1, participating systems were asked to segment a given word into a sequence of morphemes. The participants were initially provided with examples of segmentation to train and finetune their systems, as shown in Table 2. Each instance in the training set is a triplet consisting of a word, a sequence of morphemes, and a morphological category specifying the types of word formation (see Table 3). The morphological category is an optional feature that can only be used to oversample or undersample the training dataset (the word frequencies are imbalanced across the morphological categories, e.g., Italian has 431 compound words and 253K inflections). The test data only contained the initial word itself.

Key points of this subtask are:

- The task is focusing on canonical segmentation, i.e. given an input word, participants had to predict *a sequence of morphemes*. In canonical segmentation, the participating systems need to reconstruct internal morphophonological processes involved in word formation. For example, the word "intensive" will be decomposed into the base form "intens***e***" and the adjectival siffix '@@ive" (note that the ending '***e***' of the base word is inferred here);
- As shown in Table 4, the task is multilingual, with seven high-resource languages (English, Spanish, Hungarian, French, Italian, Russian, Latin) and two low-resource languages (Czech and Mongolian);
- The annotated corpus data represents a variety of morphological phenomena, including inflection, derivation, compounding (Table 4);
- A large-scale coverage as segmentations of five million words.

2.2 Subtask 2: Sentence-level Morpheme Segmentation

The second subtask is a context-dependent morpheme segmentation and focuses on resolving ambiguity in segmentations. Consider the following example containing a Mongolian homonym:

(1) Гэрт эмээ хоол хийв
Гэр @@т эмээ хоол хийх @@в
Home.DAT grandma meal cook.PRS.PRF
'Grandma just cooked a meal at home.'

(2) Би өдөр эмээ уусан
Би өдөр эм @@ээ уух @@сан
I afternoon medicine.PSSD take.PST
'Afternoon I took my medicine.'

where "эмээ" is a homonym of two different words; in the first sentence, it is "grandmother", and in the second sentence — an inflected form of "medicine". Thus, the form in the second case can be segmented. However, the modern subword segmentation tools consider no contextual differences in word forms.

Key points of this subtask are:

- Morpheme segmentation is context-dependent;
- We organize it for three languages: English, Czech, and Mongolian;
- For Czech and Mongolian we asked native speakers to manually annotate the data. The details of data collection are provided in Section 3.

Category	Infl.	Deri.	Comp.	Description	English example (input ==> output)
000	-	-	-	Root words (free morphemes)	progress ==> progress
100	✓	-	-	Inflection only	prepared ==> prepare @@ed
010	-	✓	-	Derivation only	intensive ==> intense @@ive
001	-	-	✓	Compound only	hotpot ==> hot @@pot
101	✓	-	✓	Inflection and Compound	wheelbands ==> wheel @@band @@s
011	-	✓	✓	Derivation and Compound	tankbuster ==> tank @@bust @@er
110	✓	✓	-	Inflection and Derivation	urbanizes ==> urban @@ize @@s
111	✓	✓	✓	Inflection, Derivation, Compound	trackworkers ==> track @@work @@er @@s

Table 3: Morphological categories and descriptions of segmented words in subtask 1

Category	English	Spanish	Hungarian	French	Italian	Russian	Czech	Latin	Mongolian
000	101938	15843	6952	13619	21037	2921	-	50338	1604
100	126544	502229	410662	105192	253455	221760	-	831991	7266
010	203102	18449	24923	67983	41092	72970	-	0	2201
001	16990	248	3320	1684	431	259	-	0	5
101	13790	458	101189	478	317	1909	-	0	35
011	5381	82	1654	506	140	328	-	0	0
110	106570	346862	323119	126196	237104	481409	-	0	7855
111	3059	343	54279	186	158	2658	-	0	0
total words	577374	884514	926098	382797	553734	784214	38682	882329	18966

Table 4: Word statistics across morphological categories on subtask 1

Language	train	dev	test
Czech	1,000	500	500
English	11,007	1,783	1,845
Mongolian	1,000	500	600

Table 5: The number of samples in each language in Subtask 2.

2.3 Evaluation

In order to evaluate and compare the systems, we used four metrics: (i) ***precision***, the ratio of correctly predicted morphemes over all predicted morphemes; (ii) ***recall***, the ratio of correctly predicted morphemes over all gold-label morphemes; (iii) ***f-measure***, the harmonic mean of the precision and recall; (iv) ***edit distance*** - average Levenshtein distance between the predicted output and the gold instance. For convenience, we provided the python tool[2] to evaluate these metrics on both subtasks. In addition, for subtask 1 this tool also provided detailed results across the morphological categories.

3 Data

We collected our morphological data from various sources to account for all types of morphology: derivational, inflectional, compounding. We also collected base forms. For derivational and inflectional morphology, we have used the segmentation data from UniMorph 4.0 (Batsuren et al., 2022) and MorphyNet (Batsuren et al., 2021b). UniMorph contains inflectional paradigms collected from linguistic sources as well as Wiktionary, while MorphyNet represents derivations scraped from various editions of Wiktionary. Compounds and base forms were also extracted from Wiktionary (see Section 3.2 for more details on the data extraction). We then used the data to produce morpheme segmentations for seven high-resource languages. For Czech and Mongolian, as low-resource languages, we asked native speakers and linguists to develop the resources (Section 3.3 provides more details). For English sentence data, we have used the universal dependency treebank of English (Silveira et al., 2014).

3.1 Data Statistics

The data for the shared task was moderately multilingual, containing nine unique languages of five genera including Germanic, Italic, Slavic, Mongolic, and Uralic. In subtask 1, we have over 5 million samples of morpheme segmentations that cover nine languages over nine morphological categories, as shown in Table 4. In subtask 2, Table 5 displays the data statistics of three languages.

3.2 Extraction from Wiktionary

Language-specific editions of Wiktionary contain a considerably large amount of derivations and compounds.

Compound extraction rules were applied to the

[2] `https://github.com/sigmorphon/2022SegmentationST/tree/main/evaluation`

etymology sections of Wiktionary entries to collect the Morphology template usages, such as for the English *newspaper*:

Equivalent to **news** + **paper**.

where we have a morphology entry from the Wiktionary XML dump as follows:

{{compound | en | news | paper}}

Most of compound entries use "compound" etymology template while some cases use "affix" templates, e.g., *basketball* and *volleyball*.

Root (and base) word extraction is a two-step procedure. In the first step we collected words, inherited from earlier phases of corresponding languages. For example, English 'book' is traced back to the Middle English 'bok', according to the etymology section of Wiktionary. We extracted 279,173 words from 6 languages from CogNet, a cognate database containing 8.1 million cognate pairs of 335 languages from Wiktionary (Batsuren et al., 2019a, 2021a). In the second step, we filtered out 116,863 words from the earlier extracted derivational and compound data, resulting in 162,310 root words in 6 languages. Similar Wiktionary data extraction procedures have been applied to a wide range of linguistic data, e.g., etymology (Fourrier and Sagot, 2020), multilingual lexicons - DBnary (Sérasset, 2015) and Yawipa (Wu and Yarowsky, 2020).

3.3 Collecting data for Czech and Mongolian

We had two languages with limited amount of data, Czech and Mongolian. For each language, we used a different development methodology than for the other seven languages (with larger amount of available data).

Mongolian: we asked two linguists (who are also native speakers of Mongolian) to annotate morpheme segmentations of 3,810 words from Mongolian WordNet (Batsuren et al., 2019b). After manual annotation, we received 1,604 base forms, 2201 derived forms, and 5 compounds. To account for inflectional morphology, we have used the Mongolian transducer tool (Munkhjargal et al., 2016) to generate inflected forms of the 3,810 annotated words. In total, we collected morpheme segmentations of 18,966 Mongolian words for subtask 1. For subtask 2, the same two linguists annotated 2,100 Mongolian sentences.

Czech: we merged hand-segmented word forms from four sources for the purpose of subtask 1: (a) segmentations previously created within DeriNet (Vidra et al., 2019), a project aimed at capturing derivational relations in Czech (9,508 word forms), (b) segmentations of Czech verb lemmas imported from a partially digitized version of a printed dictionary (Slavíčková et al. 2017; 13,162 word forms in addition, i.e. not counting overlaps), (c) segmentations available in the MorfCzech dataset (Pelegrinová et al., 2021), mostly extracted from dictionaries and grammar books existing for Czech (additional 11,137 word forms), and (d) word forms that we annotated newly in order to reach complete coverage of Czech subtask 2 sentences (see below; additional 4,887 word forms). In total, the subtask 1 dataset contains 38,694 unique Czech word forms segmented to morphs.

All annotations were performed by native speakers with linguistic education, and underwent careful harmonization if the input resources disagreed, as well as numerous consistency checks. However, because of rich allomorphy in Czech, we have not been able to merge allomorph sets under more abstract umbrella morphemes so far, and thus words are represented as sequences of morphs (whose concatenation perfectly matches the original word forms), not of morphemes.

The Czech subtask 2 dataset contains in total 2,000 sentences from the Czech subset of Universal Dependencies (de Marneffe et al. 2021; more specifically, 1000, 500, and 500 first sentences from the train, dev, and test sections, respectively, of the Prague Dependency Treebank subset of UD 2.9). Given that homonymy resulting in different morph boundaries is extremely rare in Czech, words are segmented basically regardless of their contexts.

3.4 Data Splits

From each language's collection of morpheme segmentations in subtask 1, we sampled 80% for the training, 10% for development, and 10% for test sets.[3] All splits of subtask 1 are balanced w.r.t. the nine morphological categories, described in Table 3. While sampling the training and development sets for the subtask 1, we excluded words that were present in the test sentences of subtask 2. This was done in order to avoid situations when the subtask 1 data could directly influence the results of subtask 2 (since we allowed the multi-task learnings between both subtasks).

[3] All the data splits can be obtained from `https://github.com/sigmorphon/2022SegmentationST/tree/main/data`

Team	Description	System	Neural	Ensemble	Data+	Multilingual	Multi-task
			System features				
Baseline	(Schuster and Nakajima, 2012)	`WordPiece*`	-	-	-	-	-
	(Kudo, 2018)	`ULM*`	-	-	-	-	-
	(Virpioja et al., 2013)	`Morfessor2*`	-	-	-	-	-
AUUH	(Rouhe et al., 2022)	`AUUH_A*`	✓	-	✓	✓	✓
		`AUUH_B*`	✓	-	-	✓	✓
		`AUUH_C`	✓	-	✓	-	✓
		`AUUH_D`	✓	-	-	-	✓
		`AUUH_E*`	✓	-	✓	-	-
		`AUUH_F*`	✓	-	-	-	-
CLUZH	(Wehrli et al., 2022)	`CLUZH`	✓	✓	-	-	-
		`CLUZH-1`	✓	✓	-	-	-
		`CLUZH-2`	✓	✓	-	-	-
		`CLUZH-3`	✓	✓	-	-	-
DeepSPIN	(Peters and Martins, 2022)	`DeepSPIN-1`	✓	-	-	-	-
		`DeepSPIN-2`	✓	-	-	-	-
		`DeepSPIN-3`	✓	-	-	-	-
GU	(Levine, 2022)	`GU-1`	✓	-	✓	-	-
		`GU-2`	✓	-	✓	-	-
NUM DI	(Zundui and Avaajargal, 2022)	`NUM DI`	✓	-	-	-	-
JB132	(Bodnár, 2022)	`JB132`	-	-	-	-	-
Tü Seg	(Girrbach, 2022)	`Tü_Seg-1`	✓	-	-	-	-
		`Tü_Seg-2`	✓	-	-	-	✓

Table 6: The list of participating systems submitted to the shared task and baseline systems; Systems marked with * are submitted to both subtasks

4 Baseline Systems

The shared task provided predictions and results of baseline systems to participants that covered all languages and both subtasks. We chose three baseline systems: First is `WordPiece`, one of the state-of-the-art subword tokenization algorithms used in BERT (Devlin et al., 2019), which is based on Schuster and Nakajima (2012) and somewhat resembles BPE (Sennrich et al., 2016). Second is `ULM` (Unigram Language Model Kudo (2018)), another popular subword tokenization, used in XLNet (Yang et al., 2019). Third is `Morfessor2`, one of the state-of-the-art unsupervised morphological segmentations (Virpioja et al., 2013).

In future shared tasks, we aim to include more state-of-the-art tokenization tools including other Morfessor variants (Grönroos et al., 2014; Ataman et al., 2017; Grönroos et al., 2020), BPE-dropout (Provilkov et al., 2019), dynamic programming encoding (DPE) (He et al., 2020) or its variant (Hiraoka et al., 2021; Song et al., 2022), multi-view subword regularization (Wang et al., 2021), Charformer (Tay et al., 2021), space-treatment variants of BPE and ULM (Gow-Smith et al., 2022).

5 System Descriptions

The SIGMORPHON 2022 Shared Task on Morpheme Segmentation received submissions from 7 teams with members from 10 universities and institutes. Many teams submitted more than one system while some focused on a specific set of languages like Romance. In total, we had 24 unique systems over two subtasks, including the baseline system. More system details can be seen in Table 6.

AUUH Researchers at the Aalto University and the University of Helsinki produced six submission systems: two were transformer models and four were bidirectional GRU models created with several innovations of Morfessor feature enrichment, multi-task learning, and multilingual learning. Morfessor (Creutz and Lagus, 2002, 2007) is the famous language-independent unsupervised and semi-supervised segmentation tool and has a big family of Morfessor variants (Virpioja et al., 2013; Grönroos et al., 2014; Ataman et al., 2017; Grönroos et al., 2020). They have used the first variant of Morfessor (Creutz and Lagus, 2005) for enriching input words along with their Morfessor subword segmentations. AUUH_A, AUUH_C, AAUH_E systems used this Morfessor-based feature enrichment. The key innovation of AUUH

System	ces	eng	fra	ita	lat	rus	mon	hun	spa	macro avg.
WordPiece	20.42	23.06	12.66	9.08	8.84	13.81	14.58	24.00	16.57	15.89
ULM	23.71	32.32	16.08	10.65	10.42	15.67	25.82	31.27	19.58	20.61
Morfessor2	29.43	37.65	22.38	9.02	14.53	17.71	37.80	40.96	20.64	25.57
AUUH_A*	93.65	92.32	-	-	-	-	98.19	-	-	94.72
AUUH_B*	93.85	93.20	-	-	-	-	98.31	-	-	95.12
AUUH_E*	90.71	87.10	90.78	92.39	98.71	94.33	96.06	-	-	92.87
AUUH_F	90.28	86.40	90.81	92.56	98.85	93.68	95.32	98.34	97.25	**93.72**
CLUZH	93.81	92.70	94.80	96.93	99.37	98.62	98.12	98.54	98.74	**96.85**
DeepSPIN-1	93.42	92.29	91.66	96.01	99.37	98.75	98.03	98.56	98.79	96.32
DeepSPIN-2	**93.88**	93.39	95.29	**97.47**	99.36	99.30	98.00	98.68	99.02	97.15
DeepSPIN-3	93.84	**93.63**	**95.73**	97.43	**99.38**	**99.35**	**98.51**	**98.72**	**99.04**	**97.29**
GU-1*	-	-	83.44	88.69	-	-	-	-	-	86.07
GU-2*	-	-	83.38	87.49	-	-	-	-	95.95	88.94
JB132	64.65	65.43	46.20	33.44	91.39	50.55	57.82	72.64	43.39	**58.39**
NUM DI*	-	83.56	-	89.55	-	-	85.59	95.91	-	88.65
Tü_Seg-1	93.38	90.51	93.76	95.73	99.37	98.21	97.02	98.59	97.93	**96.06**

Table 7: Subtask 1 word-level results by system: The f-measure performance of systems by language; and macro average f-measure of all languages in the last column. Systems marked with * are partial submissions of a specific language set. The performances in bold are best performance of corresponding languages.

systems was multilingual and multi-task traning. They used a similar preprocessing technique (Johnson et al., 2017) to distinguish tasks and languages from one another, and then trained multilingual neural models which work on both subtasks. Their transformer-based multilingual and multi-task model, AUUH_B was the subtask 2 winning system (by its macro average f-measure) and also quite competitive with the subtask 1 winning systems on its partial three-language submissions.

CLUZH Researchers at the University of Zurich ensembled four submissions (Wehrli et al., 2022) by extending their previous neural hard-attention transducer models (Makarov and Clematide, 2018b,a, 2020). For subtask 1, they submit the following strong ensemble **CLUZH** composed of 3 models without encoder dropout and 2 models with encoder dropout of 0.15. In the sentence-level subtask 2, they submitted three ensembles, and treated this problem as the word-level problem by tokenizing sentences into words. They have also used POS tags as additional features to provide a light for the context of words. All individual models have an encoder dropout probability of 0.25 and vary only in their use of features: **CLUZH-1** with 3 models without POS features, **CLUZH-2** with 3 models with POS tag features, and **CLUZH-3** with combined all the models from CLUZH-1 and CLUZH-2. In overall, the **CLUZH-3** system was the subtask 2 winning system (by winning two out of three languages) and in subtask 1 **CLUZH** was the only system, outranked one (DeepSPIN-1) of three DeepSPIN systems.

DeepSPIN Researchers submitted three neural seq2seq models: (1) **DeepSPIN-1**, a character-level LSTM with soft attention (Bahdanau et al., 2014) with softmax trained with cross-entropy loss; (2) **DeepSPIN-2**, a character-level LSTM with soft attention in which softwax is replaced with its sparser version, 1.5-entmax (Peters and Martins, 2019); (3) **DeepSPIN-3**, a subword-level transformer (Vaswani et al., 2017) with the proposed 1.5-entmax, in which subword segments are modelled using ULM (Kudo, 2018). This design was one of most innovative architectures among all submitted systems. The authors previously experimented with the 1.5-entmax function on other tasks, demonstrating its utility, especially in the tasks with less uncertainty in the search space (e.g., compared to language modelling or machine translation) such as morphological and phonological modelling (Peters and Martins, 2020). The final results of this year's shared task confirm these observations: **DeepSPIN-2** and **DeepSPIN-3** achieve superior results and are the winner of the shared task.

GU One team from Georgetown University produced two submissions for three Romance languages of the word-level subtask, based on the GRU-based encoder-decoder model (Levine, 2022). In initial attempts, they tried to use additional features from the Wiktionary lists of prefixes and suf-

inf.	drv.	cmp.	eng	fra	ita	rus	mon	hun	spa	macro avg.
-	-	-	**83.80** CLUZH	84.08 DeepSPIN-3	82.69* DeepSPIN-3	82.56* DeepSPIN-1	93.37 JB132	**85.52** DeepSPIN-3	83.58 DeepSPIN-2	83.6 DeepSPIN-3
-	-	✓	93.23 AUUH_A	**81.80** CLUZH	**58.10*** CLUZH	**77.67** DeepSPIN-2	100.00 all systems	85.89 DeepSPIN-3	**57.89*** DeepSPIN-3	**78.60** DeepSPIN-3
-	✓	-	94.12 DeepSPIN-3	87.36* DeepSPIN-3	94.62 DeepSPIN-3	91.4 DeepSPIN-3	**92.41** DeepSPIN-3	94.96 DeepSPIN-3	92.47 DeepSPIN-3	92.48 DeepSPIN-3
✓	-	-	91.29* CLUZH	96.37 CLUZH	96.27 CLUZH	99.75 DeepSPIN-3	99.66 DeepSPIN-3	98.31 DeepSPIN-3	98.81 DeepSPIN-2	96.97 DeepSPIN-3
-	✓	✓	95.74 DeepSPIN-2	80.61 DeepSPIN-3	70.59* DeepSPIN-3	92.13 DeepSPIN-3	- -	89.82 DeepSPIN-3	97.3 DeepSPIN-3	87.65 DeepSPIN-3
✓	-	✓	96.89 DeepSPIN-3	96.60 DeepSPIN-2	94.97 DeepSPIN-3	100 DeepSPIN-3	100 all systems	98.71 DeepSPIN-3	96.15 DeepSPIN-1	97.45 DeepSPIN-3
✓	✓	-	97.54 DeepSPIN-3	99.03 DeepSPIN-3	99.23 DeepSPIN-3	99.97 DeepSPIN-3	99.74 DeepSPIN-3	99.41 DeepSPIN-2	99.75 DeepSPIN-3	99.24 DeepSPIN-3
✓	✓	✓	97.13 DeepSPIN-3	100 DeepSPIN-3	100 DeepSPIN-2	99.88 DeepSPIN-2	- -	99.28 DeepSPIN-2	97.04 DeepSPIN-2	98.23 DeepSPIN-2

Table 8: Subtask 1 word-level results by morphological category: f-measure performance of best performing system on a corresponding language and a category; Numbers in bold are worst performance of their corresponding language. Performances marked with * are worst performances of their morphological category.

fixes to train the model. However, such additional features decreased the main performances across morphological categories, so they excluded these features from the final submissions. Later on, they focus on data sharing between Romance languages. In French, the training data were augmented with four morphological category data from Italian and Spanish training and development datasets. These categories include non-inflection categories of `000`, `001`, `010`, `011`. With these experiments, they made minor improvements to these three languages. For these results, more research is needed to understand that transfer learning is useful.

NUM DI A single submission from the National University of Mongolia (Zundui and Avaajargal, 2022) is a transformer-based neural model. Their model architecture is simple as single-layered encoder-decoder classic architecture. All the hyper-parameter settings are same as fairseq's standard tutorial tool. Their submission is also limited by four languages of subtask 1 due to human error.

JB132 The Charles University team (Bodnár, 2022) designed the Hidden Markov model, trained with the expectation-maximization algorithm. This model architecture has two sub-models. The first sub-model takes words as input and converts them into candidate morphemes. The second sub-model takes candidate morphemes and generates morphs as output. The first sub-model has three generators for accounting prefixes, root words, and suffixes. It is the only system not using neural methods among all submitted systems and the system's prediction is interpretable and can be useful for error analysis.

Tü Seg The University of Tübingen (Girrbach, 2022) team submitted two systems for each of subtasks. Both systems extend the sequence-labeling method proposed by (Hellwig and Nehrdich, 2018; Li and Girrbach, 2022). Their systems are very innovative and unique among all other neural models for considering the main segmentation task as a sequence-labeling task. All other neural systems used seq2seq architecture. Their neural model used a plain two-layer BiLSTM architecture. By its design, Tü Seg systems have at least two advantages over the main seq2seq alternative: (a) the number of parameters is much fewer, so the model can be trained fast and process quickly; (b) the system predictions are more interpretable compared to other neural systems and can help with the error analyses of high-resource datasets.

6 The System Results

All system results can be found and downloaded from the shared task GitHub page.[4]

6.1 Subtask 1 word-level results

Relative system performance of subtask 1 is provided in Table 7 which shows each system's f-measure by languages. The best performance of each language from submitted systems is in bold.

Two teams exploited external resources in some form: AUUH and GU. In general, any relative performance gained was minimal. AUUH submitted two systems that used additional resources, they received extra 1% compared to the team's other

[4]`https://github.com/sigmorphon/2022SegmentationST/tree/main/results`

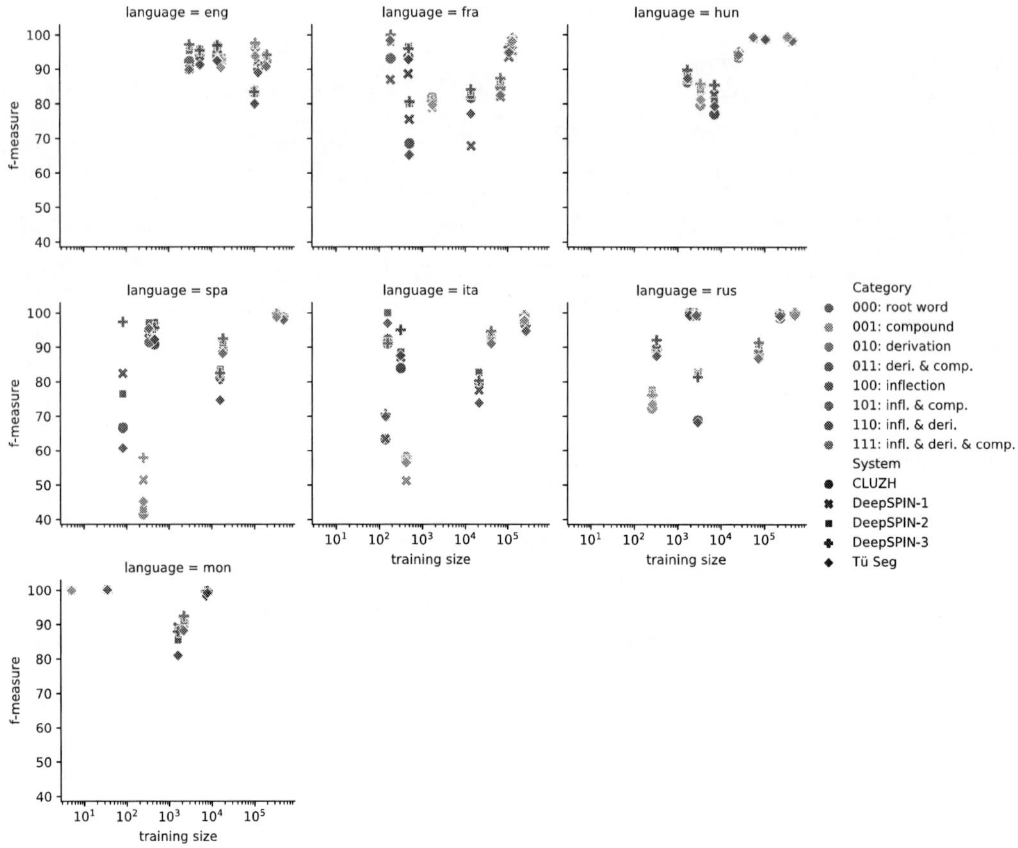

Figure 1: Impact of training sizes over languages and morphological categories: Results from top5-ranked systems of word-level subtask 1

systems. Similarly, GU and their submitted systems saw some minimal improvements over the performances. This details can be seen from their system description paper (Levine, 2022).

Only two of all the systems submitted to subtask 1 were multilingual and multi-task learning at same time. These two systems were proposed by AUUH team, but partial-language submissions were for English, Czech, and Mongolian. The important insight from this experiment is that the multi-task and multilingual learning approaches are quite beneficial for the task because their partial performances are quite competitive with the winning systems, DeepSPIN-3, DeepSPIN-2, and CLUZH.

Impact of training size: In subtask 1, the training datasets' sizes vary across languages and morphological categories. It might have impacted the top-ranked systems. Therefore, we plotted the top5-ranked systems over training size and f-measure performance across morphological categories, as shown in Figure 1. Here, in high-resource setting (as greater than 10^5) in all morphological categories, any of the top5-ranked systems always achieves 80% f-measure greater than 80%.

The root words are present in all types of resources settings from high to low. All the systems in this category of root words achieved no more than 85.5% f-measure except for Mongolian.

The two inflectional categories `100` and `110` are always in high-resource setting, having more than 10^6 training instances (except for two low-resource languages Czech and Mongolian). All systems achieved their best system performance over these two categories, compared to other categories.

Impact of word length: In many NLP tasks, the length of the input sequence is strongly correlated with the difficulty of their tasks (Yin et al., 2017; Wu et al., 2018). So, we present how the

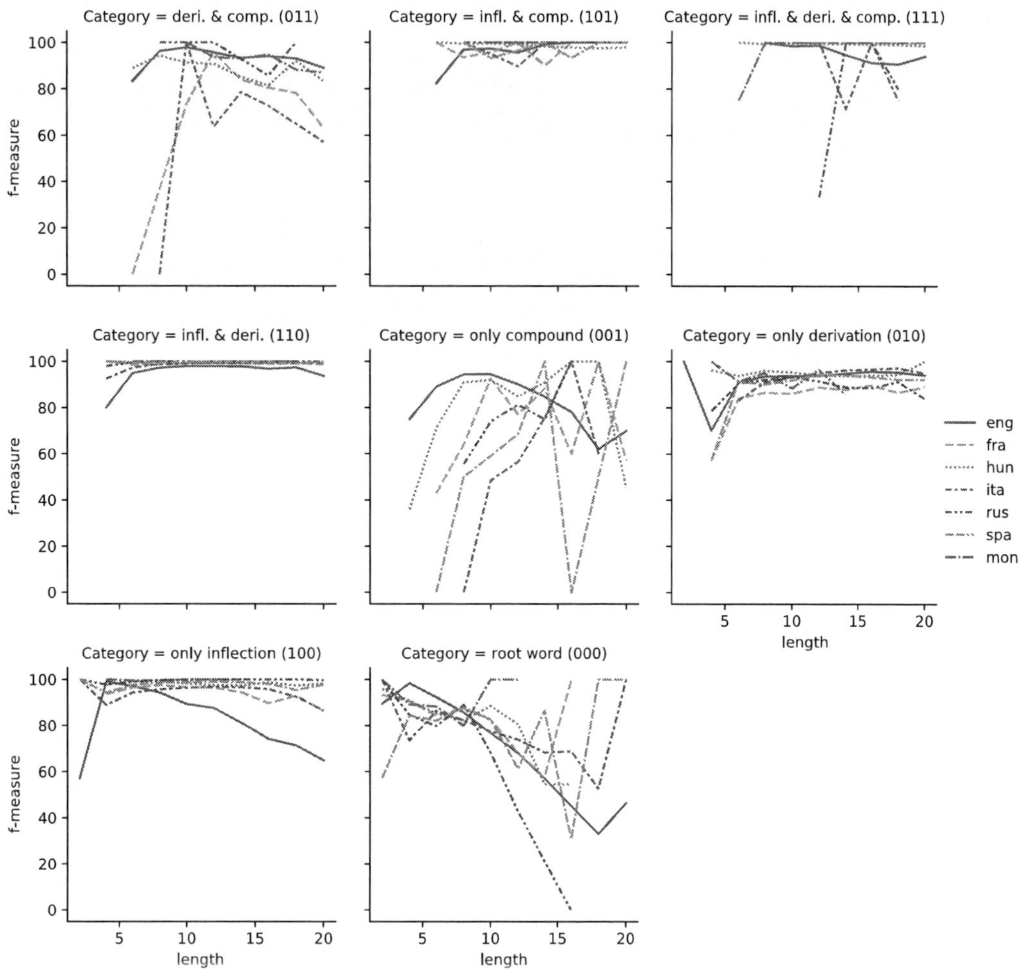

Figure 2: Impact of word length over languages and morphological categories: Results from DeepSPIN-3, the winning system of subtask 1, word-level morpheme segmentation

DeepSPIN-3's (subtask 1 winning system) performance relates to the word length across languages and morphological categories. Figure 2 shows various related facts: (i) for root words `000`, overall performance decreases across languages with increasing word length; (ii) inflectional morphology is systematically far more productive than other morphological categories, so this fact is reproduced here: the main inflectional category `100` has consistently high performance across languages and word lengths.

Difficulty of morphological categories: Even though the top-ranking systems perform very well on their own, other systems may have some complementary information across morphological categories. Therefore, we listed the best-performing systems for combinations of each language and each morphological category in Table 8. In the table, the lowest scores in corresponding languages are provided in bold. For instance, English root words (83.80 f-measure) are much harder to predict than other morphological categories in English. The hardest morphological categories are roots `000`, compounds `001`, and derivation and compound words `011`. The winning system, DeepSPIN-3 (marked with + in Figure 1), is consistently winning in these three categories across languages. Another observation from Figure 2 is that compound and root words are getting harder to predict across languages with the increase of word length. Also, identifying inflections from short

System	Czech				English				Mongolian				Macro avg.	
	P	R	F_1	Lev.	P	R	F_1	Lev.	P	R	F_1	Lev.	F_1	Lev.
WordPiece	38.47	31.45	34.61	17.88	62.02	65.13	63.53	5.54	19.82	29.20	23.62	29.19	40.59	17.54
ULM	41.98	30.39	35.26	16.39	62.32	69.24	65.60	5.68	38.79	35.58	37.12	20.76	45.99	14.28
Morfessor2	49.89	36.95	42.45	13.09	54.61	69.75	61.25	6.00	50.88	45.91	48.26	17.16	50.65	12.08
AUUH_A	89.70	87.53	88.60	4.97	96.66	95.78	96.22	1.86	83.49	80.94	82.19	5.42	89.00	4.08
AUUH_B	91.89	89.00	90.42	3.96	**96.82**	**95.79**	**96.31**	**1.39**	83.74	81.46	82.59	5.16	**89.77**	**3.50**
AUUH_C	50.60	69.19	58.45	71.37	84.77	71.67	77.67	19.13	79.07	73.45	76.15	17.33	70.76	35.94
AUUH_D	45.07	67.82	54.15	80.67	93.29	83.41	88.07	10.58	77.99	74.15	76.02	17.88	72.75	36.38
AUUH_E	57.39	67.22	61.92	55.92	95.23	76.82	85.04	12.36	73.34	72.01	72.67	24.88	73.21	31.05
AUUH_F	62.36	43.82	51.47	61.84	91.50	74.84	82.34	13.30	75.50	59.22	66.38	33.91	66.73	36.35
CLUZH-1	92.03	90.69	91.35	1.93	89.74	89.20	89.47	9.86	82.98	81.48	82.22	5.28	87.68	5.69
CLUZH-2	92.41	91.13	91.76	1.87	89.71	89.22	89.47	9.79	83.29	81.83	82.55	5.19	87.93	5.62
CLUZH-3	**92.63**	**91.35**	**91.99**	**1.80**	89.83	89.25	89.54	9.84	**83.71**	**82.07**	**82.88**	**5.10**	88.14	5.58
Tü_Seg-2	89.52	88.42	88.97	2.50	87.83	89.58	88.69	1.78	69.59	67.55	68.55	9.85	82.07	4.71

Table 9: Subtask 2 sentence-level results: F-measure across 3 languages

words (word length < 5) is one of the unsolved challenges in all languages (except for English), as shown in Figure 2.

6.2 Subtask 2 sentence-level results

Relative system performance is described in Table 9, showing all four evaluation metrics by each combination of system and language. In the sentence-level subtask 2, we have two winners: CLUZH-3 (won two out of three languages) and AUUH_B (F1 89.77 as maximum macro- average among submissions).

The performance of systems in the sentence-level subtask significantly decreased by 15% in Mongolian compared to the results of the word-level subtask. One reason is that all submitted systems treated this problem as a zero-shot solution of word-level subtask 1, and mostly ignored its context by their design.

7 Future Directions

The submitted systems achieved unexpectedly high accuracy across nine languages. This result suggests that the neural systems may have more capabilities beyond segmenting morphemes. For the next year, we plan to modify the task design and enrich the dataset with more fine-grained analysis. For example, *truckdrivers* $\rightarrow$ *truck @@drive @@er @@s* $\rightarrow$ *truck $$drive @@er ##s* where $$ is compound, @@ is derivation, and ## is inflection. In another direction, we will explore possibilities of adapting other morphological resources including word-formation resources (Zeller et al., 2013; Talamo et al., 2016; Vidra et al., 2019; Vodolazsky, 2020) or segmentation resources, UniSegments (Žabokrtský et al., 2022; Žabokrtský et al., 2022). Our shared task team welcomes continued contributions from the community.

8 Conclusion

The SIGMORPHON 2022 Shared Task on Morpheme Segmentation significantly expanded the problem of morphological segmentation, making it more linguistically plausible. In this task, seven teams submitted 23 systems for two subtasks in total of nine languages, achieving at minimum F1 30.71 improvement over the three baselines of the state-of-the-art subword tokenization and morphological segmentation tools, being used to train large language models, e.g., XLNet (Yang et al., 2019). The results suggest many directions for improving morpheme segmentation shared task.

Acknowledgements

We thank Garrett Nicolai and Eleanor Chodroff for their advice and support. The authors also thank Ben Peters and Simon Clematide for their invaluable contributions and advice, including developing the evaluation tool and early detection of data errors.

References

Rie Kubota Ando and Tong Zhang. 2005. A framework for learning predictive structures from multiple tasks and unlabeled data. *Journal of Machine Learning Research*, 6:1817–1853.

Galen Andrew and Jianfeng Gao. 2007. Scalable training of L1-regularized log-linear models. In *Proceedings of the 24th International Conference on Machine Learning*, pages 33–40.

Duygu Ataman, Matteo Negri, Marco Turchi, and Marcello Federico. 2017. Linguistically motivated vocabulary reduction for neural machine translation from turkish to english.

Dzmitry Bahdanau, Kyunghyun Cho, and Yoshua Bengio. 2014. Neural machine translation by jointly learning to align and translate. *arXiv preprint arXiv:1409.0473*.

Khuyagbaatar Batsuren, Gábor Bella, and Fausto Giunchiglia. 2019a. Cognet: A large-scale cognate database. In *Proceedings of the 57th annual meeting of the association for computational linguistics*, pages 3136–3145.

Khuyagbaatar Batsuren, Gábor Bella, and Fausto Giunchiglia. 2021a. A large and evolving cognate database. *Language Resources and Evaluation*.

Khuyagbaatar Batsuren, Gábor Bella, and Fausto Giunchiglia. 2021b. MorphyNet: a large multilingual database of derivational and inflectional morphology. In *Proceedings of the 18th SIGMORPHON Workshop on Computational Research in Phonetics, Phonology, and Morphology*, pages 39–48, Online. Association for Computational Linguistics.

Khuyagbaatar Batsuren, Amarsanaa Ganbold, Altangerel Chagnaa, and Fausto Giunchiglia. 2019b. Building the Mongolian WordNet. In *Proceedings of the 10th Global Wordnet Conference*, pages 238–244, Wroclaw, Poland. Global Wordnet Association.

Khuyagbaatar Batsuren, Omer Goldman, Salam Khalifa, Nizar Habash, Witold Kieraś, Gábor Bella, Brian Leonard, Garrett Nicolai, Kyle Gorman, Yustinus Ghanggo Ate, Maria Ryskina, Sabrina J. Mielke, Elena Budianskaya, Charbel El-Khaissi, Tiago Pimentel, Michael Gasser, William Lane, Mohit Raj, Matt Coler, Jaime Rafael Montoya Samame, Delio Siticonatzi Camaiteri, Esaú Zumaeta Rojas, Didier López Francis, Arturo Oncevay, Juan López Bautista, Gema Celeste Silva Villegas, Lucas Torroba Hennigen, Adam Ek, David Guriel, Peter Dirix, Jean-Philippe Bernardy, Andrey Scherbakov, Aziyana Bayyr-ool, Antonios Anastasopoulos, Roberto Zariquiey, Karina Sheifer, Sofya Ganieva, Hilaria Cruz, Ritván Karahóğa, Stella Markantonatou, George Pavlidis, Matvey Plugaryov, Elena Klyachko, Ali Salehi, Candy Angulo, Jatayu Baxi, Andrew Krizhanovsky, Natalia Krizhanovskaya, Elizabeth Salesky, Clara Vania, Sardana Ivanova, Jennifer White, Rowan Hall Maudslay, Josef Valvoda, Ran Zmigrod, Paula Czarnowska, Irene Nikkarinen, Aelita Salchak, Brijesh Bhatt, Christopher Straughn, Zoey Liu, Jonathan North Washington, Yuval Pinter, Duygu Ataman, Marcin Wolinski, Totok Suhardijanto, Anna Yablonskaya, Niklas Stoehr, Hossep Dolatian, Zahroh Nuriah, Shyam Ratan, Francis M. Tyers, Edoardo M. Ponti, Grant Aiton, Aryaman Arora, Richard J. Hatcher, Ritesh Kumar, Jeremiah Young, Daria Rodionova, Anastasia Yemelina, Taras Andrushko, Igor Marchenko, Polina Mashkovtseva, Alexandra Serova, Emily Prud'hommeaux, Maria Nepomniashchaya, Fausto Giunchiglia, Eleanor Chodroff, Mans Hulden, Miikka Silfverberg, Arya D. McCarthy, David Yarowsky, Ryan Cotterell, Reut Tsarfaty, and Ekaterina Vylomova. 2022. Unimorph 4.0: Universal morphology.

Jan Bodnár. 2022. Jb132 submission to the sigmorphon 2022 shared task 3 on morphological segmentation. In *19th SIGMORPHON Workshop on Computational Research in Phonetics, Phonology, and Morphology*.

Tom Brown, Benjamin Mann, Nick Ryder, Melanie Subbiah, Jared D Kaplan, Prafulla Dhariwal, Arvind Neelakantan, Pranav Shyam, Girish Sastry, Amanda Askell, et al. 2020. Language models are few-shot learners. *Advances in neural information processing systems*, 33:1877–1901.

Ryan Cotterell, Tim Vieira, and Hinrich Schütze. 2016. A joint model of orthography and morphological segmentation. Association for Computational Linguistics.

Mathias Creutz and Krista Lagus. 2002. Unsupervised discovery of morphemes. In *Proceedings of the ACL-02 Workshop on Morphological and Phonological Learning*, pages 21–30.

Mathias Creutz and Krista Lagus. 2005. *Unsupervised morpheme segmentation and morphology induction from text corpora using Morfessor 1.0*. Helsinki University of Technology Helsinki.

Mathias Creutz and Krista Lagus. 2007. Unsupervised models for morpheme segmentation and morphology learning. *ACM Transactions on Speech and Language Processing (TSLP)*, 4(1):1–34.

Marie-Catherine de Marneffe, Christopher Manning, Joakim Nivre, and Daniel Zeman. 2021. Universal dependencies. *Computational Linguistics*, 47(2):255–308.

Jacob Devlin, Ming-Wei Chang, Kenton Lee, and Kristina Toutanova. 2019. BERT: Pre-training of deep bidirectional transformers for language understanding. In *Proceedings of the 2019 Conference of the North American Chapter of the Association for Computational Linguistics: Human Language Technologies, Volume 1 (Long and Short Papers)*, pages 4171–4186, Minneapolis, Minnesota. Association for Computational Linguistics.

Miguel Domingo, Mercedes Garcıa-Martınez, Alexandre Helle, Francisco Casacuberta, and Manuel Herranz. 2018. How much does tokenization affect neural machine translation? *arXiv preprint arXiv:1812.08621*.

Clémentine Fourrier and Benoît Sagot. 2020. Methodological aspects of developing and managing an etymological lexical resource: Introducing etymdb 2.0. In *LREC 2020-12th Language Resources and Evaluation Conference*.

Philip Gage. 1994. A new algorithm for data compression. *C Users Journal*, 12(2):23–38.

Leander Girrbach. 2022. Sigmorphon 2022 shared task on morpheme segmentation submission description: Sequence labelling for word-level morpheme segmentation. In *19th SIGMORPHON Workshop on Computational Research in Phonetics, Phonology, and Morphology*.

Edward Gow-Smith, Harish Tayyar Madabushi, Carolina Scarton, and Aline Villavicencio. 2022. Improving tokenisation by alternative treatment of spaces. *arXiv preprint arXiv:2204.04058*.

Stig-Arne Grönroos, Sami Virpioja, and Mikko Kurimo. 2020. Morfessor em+ prune: Improved subword segmentation with expectation maximization and pruning. *arXiv preprint arXiv:2003.03131*.

Stig-Arne Grönroos, Sami Virpioja, Peter Smit, and Mikko Kurimo. 2014. Morfessor flatcat: An hmm-based method for unsupervised and semi-supervised learning of morphology. In *Proceedings of COLING 2014, the 25th International Conference on Computational Linguistics: Technical Papers*, pages 1177–1185.

Xuanli He, Gholamreza Haffari, and Mohammad Norouzi. 2020. Dynamic programming encoding for subword segmentation in neural machine translation. In *Proceedings of the 58th Annual Meeting of the Association for Computational Linguistics*, pages 3042–3051.

Oliver Hellwig and Sebastian Nehrdich. 2018. Sanskrit word segmentation using character-level recurrent and convolutional neural networks. In *Proceedings of the 2018 conference on empirical methods in natural language processing*, pages 2754–2763.

Tatsuya Hiraoka, Sho Takase, Kei Uchiumi, Atsushi Keyaki, and Naoaki Okazaki. 2021. Joint optimization of tokenization and downstream model. In *Findings of the Association for Computational Linguistics: ACL-IJCNLP 2021*, pages 244–255.

Melvin Johnson, Mike Schuster, Quoc V Le, Maxim Krikun, Yonghui Wu, Zhifeng Chen, Nikhil Thorat, Fernanda Viégas, Martin Wattenberg, Greg Corrado, et al. 2017. Google's multilingual neural machine translation system: Enabling zero-shot translation. *Transactions of the Association for Computational Linguistics*, 5:339–351.

Katharina Kann, Ryan Cotterell, and Hinrich Schütze. 2016. Neural morphological analysis: Encoding-decoding canonical segments. In *Proceedings of the 2016 Conference on Empirical Methods in Natural Language Processing*, pages 961–967, Austin, Texas. Association for Computational Linguistics.

Katharina Kann, Jesus Manuel Mager Hois, Ivan Vladimir Meza-Ruiz, and Hinrich Schütze. 2018. Fortification of neural morphological segmentation models for polysynthetic minimal-resource languages. In *Proceedings of the 2018 Conference of the North American Chapter of the Association for Computational Linguistics: Human Language Technologies, Volume 1 (Long Papers)*, pages 47–57, New Orleans, Louisiana. Association for Computational Linguistics.

Taku Kudo. 2018. Subword regularization: Improving neural network translation models with multiple subword candidates. In *Proceedings of the 56th Annual Meeting of the Association for Computational Linguistics (Volume 1: Long Papers)*, pages 66–75, Melbourne, Australia. Association for Computational Linguistics.

Mikko Kurimo, Mathias Creutz, and Matti Varjokallio. 2007. Unsupervised morpheme analysis evaluation by a comparison to a linguistic gold standard-morpho challenge 2007. In *CLEF (Working Notes)*.

Mikko Kurimo, Ville Turunen, and Matti Varjokallio. 2008. Overview of morpho challenge 2008. In *Workshop of the Cross-Language Evaluation Forum for European Languages*, pages 951–966. Springer.

Mikko Kurimo, Sami Virpioja, Ville Turunen, and Krista Lagus. 2010a. Morpho challenge 2005-2010: Evaluations and results. In *Proceedings of the 11th Meeting of the ACL Special Interest Group on Computational Morphology and Phonology*, pages 87–95.

Mikko Kurimo, Sami Virpioja, Ville T Turunen, Graeme W Blackwood, and William Byrne. 2009. Overview and results of morpho challenge 2009. In *Workshop of the Cross-Language Evaluation Forum for European Languages*, pages 578–597. Springer.

Mikko Kurimo, Sami Virpioja, Ville T Turunen, et al. 2010b. Proceedings of the morpho challenge 2010 workshop. In *Morpho Challenge Workshop; 2010; Espoo*. Aalto University School of Science and Technology.

Lauren Levine. 2022. Sharing data by language family: Data augmentation for romance language morpheme segmentation. In *19th SIGMORPHON Workshop on Computational Research in Phonetics, Phonology, and Morphology*.

Jingwen Li and Leander Girrbach. 2022. Word segmentation and morphological parsing for sanskrit. *arXiv preprint arXiv:2201.12833*.

Yinhan Liu, Myle Ott, Naman Goyal, Jingfei Du, Mandar Joshi, Danqi Chen, Omer Levy, Mike Lewis, Luke Zettlemoyer, and Veselin Stoyanov. 2019. Roberta: A robustly optimized bert pretraining approach. *arXiv preprint arXiv:1907.11692*.

Dominik Macháček, Jonáš Vidra, and Ondřej Bojar. 2018. Morphological and language-agnostic word segmentation for nmt. In *International Conference on Text, Speech, and Dialogue*, pages 277–284. Springer.

Peter Makarov and Simon Clematide. 2018a. Imitation learning for neural morphological string transduction. *arXiv preprint arXiv:1808.10701*.

Peter Makarov and Simon Clematide. 2018b. Uzh at conll-sigmorphon 2018 shared task on universal morphological reinflection. Association for Computational Linguistics.

Peter Makarov and Simon Clematide. 2020. CLUZH at SIGMORPHON 2020 shared task on multilingual grapheme-to-phoneme conversion. In *Proceedings of the 17th SIGMORPHON Workshop on Computational Research in Phonetics, Phonology, and Morphology*, pages 171–176, Online. Association for Computational Linguistics.

Austin Matthews, Graham Neubig, and Chris Dyer. 2018. Using morphological knowledge in open-vocabulary neural language models. In *Proceedings of the 2018 Conference of the North American Chapter of the Association for Computational Linguistics: Human Language Technologies, Volume 1 (Long Papers)*, pages 1435–1445.

Sabrina J Mielke, Zaid Alyafeai, Elizabeth Salesky, Colin Raffel, Manan Dey, Matthias Gallé, Arun Raja, Chenglei Si, Wilson Y Lee, Benoît Sagot, et al. 2021. Between words and characters: A brief history of open-vocabulary modeling and tokenization in nlp. *arXiv preprint arXiv:2112.10508*.

Zoljargal Munkhjargal, Altangerel Chagnaa, and Purev Jaimai. 2016. Morphological transducer for mongolian. In *International Conference on Computational Collective Intelligence*, pages 546–554. Springer.

Antoine Nzeyimana and Andre Niyongabo Rubungo. 2022. Kinyabert: a morphology-aware kinyarwanda language model. *arXiv preprint arXiv:2203.08459*.

Kateřina Pelegrinová, Viktor Elšík, Radek Čech, and Ján Mačutek. 2021. MorfoCzech. LINDAT/CLARIAH-CZ digital library at the Institute of Formal and Applied Linguistics (ÚFAL), Faculty of Mathematics and Physics, Charles University.

Ben Peters and André F. T. Martins. 2020. One-size-fits-all multilingual models. In *Proceedings of the 17th SIGMORPHON Workshop on Computational Research in Phonetics, Phonology, and Morphology*, pages 63–69, Online. Association for Computational Linguistics.

Ben Peters and André F. T. Martins. 2022. Beyond characters: Subword-level morpheme segmentation. In *19th SIGMORPHON Workshop on Computational Research in Phonetics, Phonology, and Morphology*.

Ben Peters and André FT Martins. 2019. IT–IST at the sigmorphon 2019 shared task: Sparse two-headed models for inflection. In *Proceedings of the 16th Workshop on Computational Research in Phonetics, Phonology, and Morphology*, pages 50–56.

Ivan Provilkov, Dmitrii Emelianenko, and Elena Voita. 2019. Bpe-dropout: Simple and effective subword regularization. *arXiv preprint arXiv:1910.13267*.

Alec Radford, Jeffrey Wu, Rewon Child, David Luan, Dario Amodei, Ilya Sutskever, et al. 2019. Language models are unsupervised multitask learners. *OpenAI blog*, 1(8):9.

Mohammad Sadegh Rasooli and Joel R. Tetreault. 2015. Yara parser: A fast and accurate dependency parser. *Computing Research Repository*, arXiv:1503.06733. Version 2.

Aku Rouhe, Stig-Arne Grönroos, Sami Virpioja, Mathias Creutz, and Mikko Kurimo. 2022. Morfessor-enriched features and multilingual training for canonical morphological segmentation. In *19th SIGMORPHON Workshop on Computational Research in Phonetics, Phonology, and Morphology*.

Jonne Saleva and Constantine Lignos. 2021. The effectiveness of morphology-aware segmentation in low-resource neural machine translation. In *Proceedings of the 16th Conference of the European Chapter of the Association for Computational Linguistics: Student Research Workshop*, pages 164–174, Online. Association for Computational Linguistics.

Mike Schuster and Kaisuke Nakajima. 2012. Japanese and korean voice search. In *2012 IEEE international conference on acoustics, speech and signal processing (ICASSP)*, pages 5149–5152. IEEE.

Lane Schwartz, Francis Tyers, Lori Levin, Christo Kirov, Patrick Littell, Chi-kiu Lo, Emily Prud'hommeaux, Hyunji Hayley Park, Kenneth Steimel, Rebecca Knowles, et al. 2020. Neural polysynthetic language modelling. *arXiv preprint arXiv:2005.05477*.

Rico Sennrich, Barry Haddow, and Alexandra Birch. 2016. Neural machine translation of rare words with subword units. In *Proceedings of the 54th Annual Meeting of the Association for Computational Linguistics (Volume 1: Long Papers)*, pages 1715–1725.

Gilles Sérasset. 2015. Dbnary: Wiktionary as a lemon-based multilingual lexical resource in rdf. *Semantic Web*, 6(4):355–361.

Natalia Silveira, Timothy Dozat, Marie-Catherine de Marneffe, Samuel Bowman, Miriam Connor, John Bauer, and Christopher D. Manning. 2014. A gold standard dependency corpus for English. In *Proceedings of the Ninth International Conference on Language Resources and Evaluation (LREC-2014)*.

Eleonora Slavíčková, Jaroslava Hlaváčová, and Patrice Pognan. 2017. Retrograde morphemic dictionary of czech - verbs. LINDAT/CLARIAH-CZ digital library at the Institute of Formal and Applied Linguistics (ÚFAL), Faculty of Mathematics and Physics, Charles University.

Haiyue Song, Raj Dabre, Chenhui Chu, Sadao Kurohashi, and Eiichiro Sumita. 2022. Self-supervised dynamic programming encoding for neural machine translation.

Luigi Talamo, Chiara Celata, and Pier Marco Bertinetto. 2016. Derivatario: An annotated lexicon of italian derivatives. *Word Structure*, 9(1):72–102.

Yi Tay, Vinh Q Tran, Sebastian Ruder, Jai Gupta, Hyung Won Chung, Dara Bahri, Zhen Qin, Simon Baumgartner, Cong Yu, and Donald Metzler. 2021. Charformer: Fast character transformers via gradient-based subword tokenization. *arXiv preprint arXiv:2106.12672*.

Ashish Vaswani, Noam Shazeer, Niki Parmar, Jakob Uszkoreit, Llion Jones, Aidan N Gomez, Łukasz Kaiser, and Illia Polosukhin. 2017. Attention is all you need. *Advances in neural information processing systems*, 30.

Jonáš Vidra, Zdeněk Žabokrtský, Magda Ševčíková, and Lukáš Kyjánek. 2019. Derinet 2.0: Towards an all-in-one word-formation resource. In *Proceedings of the Second International Workshop on Resources and Tools for Derivational Morphology (DeriMo 2019)*, pages 81–89, Praha, Czechia. ÚFAL MFF UK.

Sami Virpioja, Peter Smit, Stig-Arne Grönroos, Mikko Kurimo, et al. 2013. Morfessor 2.0: Python implementation and extensions for morfessor baseline.

Daniil Vodolazsky. 2020. Derivbase. ru: A derivational morphology resource for russian. In *Proceedings of The 12th Language Resources and Evaluation Conference*, pages 3937–3943.

Xinyi Wang, Sebastian Ruder, and Graham Neubig. 2021. Multi-view subword regularization. In *Proceedings of the 2021 Conference of the North American Chapter of the Association for Computational Linguistics: Human Language Technologies*, pages 473–482.

Silvan Wehrli, Simon Clematide, and Peter Makarov. 2022. Cluzh at sigmorphon 2022 shared tasks on morpheme segmentation and inflection generation. In *19th SIGMORPHON Workshop on Computational Research in Phonetics, Phonology, and Morphology*.

Wei Wu, Houfeng Wang, Tianyu Liu, and Shuming Ma. 2018. Phrase-level self-attention networks for universal sentence encoding. In *Proceedings of the 2018 Conference on Empirical Methods in Natural Language Processing*, pages 3729–3738.

Winston Wu and David Yarowsky. 2020. Computational etymology and word emergence. In *Proceedings of the 12th Language Resources and Evaluation Conference*, pages 3252–3259, Marseille, France. European Language Resources Association.

Zhilin Yang, Zihang Dai, Yiming Yang, Jaime Carbonell, Russ R Salakhutdinov, and Quoc V Le. 2019. Xlnet: Generalized autoregressive pretraining for language understanding. *Advances in neural information processing systems*, 32.

Wenpeng Yin, Katharina Kann, Mo Yu, and Hinrich Schütze. 2017. Comparative study of cnn and rnn for natural language processing. *arXiv preprint arXiv:1702.01923*.

Zdeněk Žabokrtský, Nyati Bafna, Jan Bodnár, Lukáš Kyjánek, Emil Svoboda, Magda Ševčíková, Jonáš Vidra, Sachi Angle, Ebrahim Ansari, Timofey Arkhangelskiy, Khuyagbaatar Batsuren, Gábor Bella, Pier Marco Bertinetto, Olivier Bonami, Chiara Celata, Michael Daniel, Alexei Fedorenko, Matea Filko, Fausto Giunchiglia, Hamid Haghdoost, Nabil Hathout, Irina Khomchenkova, Victoria Khurshudyan, Dmitri Levonian, Eleonora Litta, Maria Medvedeva, S. N. Muralikrishna, Fiammetta Namer, Mahshid Nikravesh, Sebastian Padó, Marco Passarotti, Vladimir Plungian, Alexey Polyakov, Mihail Potapov, Mishra Pruthwik, Ashwath Rao B, Sergei Rubakov, Husain Samar, Dipti Misra Sharma, Jan Šnajder, Krešimir Šojat, Vanja Štefanec, Luigi Talamo, Delphine Tribout, Daniil Vodolazsky, Arseniy Vydrin, Aigul Zakirova, and Britta Zeller. 2022. Universal segmentations 1.0 (UniSegments 1.0). LINDAT/CLARIAH-CZ digital library at the Institute of Formal and Applied Linguistics (ÚFAL), Faculty of Mathematics and Physics, Charles University.

Britta Zeller, Jan Šnajder, and Sebastian Padó. 2013. Derivbase: Inducing and evaluating a derivational morphology resource for german. In *Proceedings of the 51st Annual Meeting of the Association for Computational Linguistics (Volume 1: Long Papers)*, pages 1201–1211.

Daniel Zeman, Martin Popel, Milan Straka, Jan Hajic, Joakim Nivre, Filip Ginter, Juhani Luotolahti, Sampo Pyysalo, Slav Petrov, Martin Potthast, et al. 2017. Conll 2017 shared task: Multilingual parsing from raw text to universal dependencies. In *CoNLL 2017 Shared Task: Multilingual Parsing from Raw Text to Universal Dependencies*, pages 1–19. Association for Computational Linguistics.

Tsolmon Zundui and Chinbat Avaajargal. 2022. Word-live morpheme segmentation using transformer neural network. In *19th SIGMORPHON Workshop on Computational Research in Phonetics, Phonology, and Morphology*.

Zdeněk Žabokrtský, Niyati Bafna, Jan Bodnár, Lukáš Kyjánek, Emil Svoboda, Magda Ševčíková, and Jonáš Vidra. 2022. Towards Universal Segmentations: UniSegments 1.0. In *Proceedings of the 13th International Conference on Language Resources and Evaluation (LREC 2018)*, Marseille, France. European Language Resources Association (ELRA).

Sharing Data by Language Family: Data Augmentation for Romance Language Morpheme Segmentation

Lauren Levine
Georgetown University
Department of Linguistics
lel76@georgetown.edu

Abstract

This paper presents a basic character level sequence-to-sequence approach to morpheme segmentation for the following Romance languages: French, Italian, and Spanish. We experiment with adding a small set of additional linguistic features, as well as with sharing training data between sister languages for morphological categories with low performance in single language base models. We find that while the additional linguistic features were generally not helpful in this instance, data augmentation between sister languages did help to raise the scores of some individual morphological categories, but did not consistently result in an overall improvement when considering the aggregate of the categories.

1 Introduction

Morpheme segmentation is a task in which individual words are divided into meaningful sub-units called morphemes. It is a difficult task, particularly in synthetic languages which have more complex morphological systems, but morphological analysis is an important sub-component of various downstream NLP related tasks, such as lexicography, terminology management, and semantic parsing. Previous approaches to morpheme segmentation include unsupervised methods (Creutz and Lagus, 2007), and more recently there have been neural approaches (Wang et al., 2016).

This paper is a submission to the SIGMORPHON 2022 shared task on morpheme segmentation, which aims to benefit the NLP community with improvements for subword-based tokenization through morpheme segmentation (Batsuren et al., 2022). The shared task includes word-level and sentence-level morpheme segmentation subtasks for various development languages. We focus on the subtask for word-level morpheme segmentation, specifically for the three Romance languages among the development languages: French, Italian, and Spanish. In this paper, we experiment with adding character based features to a sequence to sequence neural model, and we also experiment with sharing training data between sister languages.

The structure of the of the paper is as follows: In Section 2 we give an overview of the base system architecture of our approach. Section 3 describes the character based features we experimented with during development, and Section 4 describes our methods for data sharing between sister languages. Section 5 presents the results from our various models, and Section 6 provides the accompanying discussion. Finally, Section 7 offers a brief conclusion.

2 System Architecture[1]

We take a character-level sequence-to-sequence approach as the base architecture for our morpheme segmentation models. We base our approach on a simple recurrent model in the Keras[2] framework and adapted the base model to fit the needs of the word-level morpheme segmentation task. The encoder and decoder for the model each contain a single GRU layer. The batch size was 64 and the latent dimension of the encoding space was 256. All models were trained with early stopping with a max of 30 epochs. Base models for each of our focus languages (French, Italian, Spanish) were trained on this architecture using only the language specific training data provided by the shared task for the word-level subtask. The performance of these models is described in Section 5.2.

3 Additional Features

While sequence-to-sequence neural models have a tremendous ability to learn patterns that are la-

[1] https://github.com/lauren-lizzy-levine/2022SegmentationST.git

[2] https://keras.io/examples/nlp/lstm_seq2seq/

19th SIGMORPHON Workshop on Computational Research in Phonetics, Phonology, and Morphology, pages 117 - 123
July 14, 2022

tent in the raw text data on which the models are trained, there is still value in leveraging additional knowledge sources to provide features that may be linguistically important to morpheme segmentation that cannot be gleaned from the raw text of the training data alone. This is particularly true for languages where training data is limited and for morphological categories that are represented with low frequency in the data.

In order to train extra features in sequence to sequence modeling, we can combine our features into a single input vector with the individual input character representations (Sundaramoorthy, 2017). We do this by concatenating vectorized character input with a vectorized representation of our character based features. For simplicity's sake, we experimented with a series presence/absence features, which could be represented with a binary 1 or 0 encoding and easily concatenated to the one-hot representation of the text of the input character.

We experimented with adding a series of binary features to indicate whether the substrings that would be created by making a morpheme boundary at a given character would contain a known prefix or suffix. We created character based features for the following rules (Yes-1, No-0):

If the given character were the start of a new morpheme:

1. Is the string to the left of the boundary a prefix?
2. Is the string to the right of the boundary a suffix?
3. Does a substring to the left (ending at the morpheme boundary) contain a prefix?
4. Does a substring to the left (ending at the morpheme boundary) contain a suffix?
5. Does a substring to the right (starting from the morpheme boundary) contain a prefix?
6. Does a substring to the right (starting from the morpheme boundary) contain a suffix?

For instance, the word *enthrallments* would have the feature vector *000001* for the character *m*, as visualized in Figure 1. This is because *ment* is a known suffix that starts a character *m* where we are imagining a morpheme boundary to be, which means that "Yes" is the answer for question six. The answer for the rest of the questions is "No", so the rest of the digits in the vector are *0*.

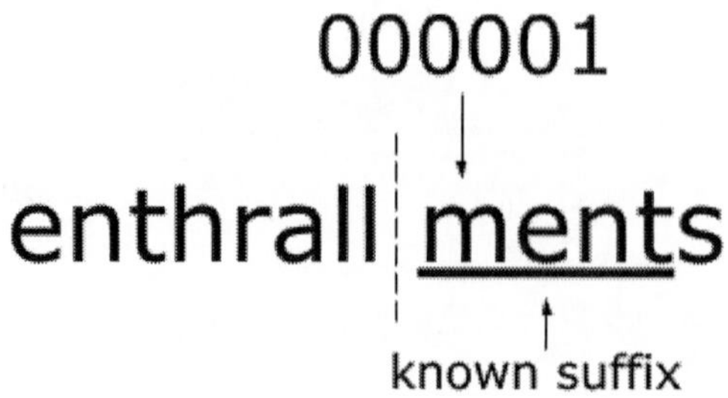

Figure 1: Visualization for the feature vector and corresponding potential morpheme boundary for the character *m* in the word *enthrallments*.

Such short feature vectors were generated for every character in every word of the provided data sets for our focus languages by referencing against previously complied language specific prefix[3] and suffix[4] lists compiled from Wiktionary.

We created various models with subsets of the training data and tested on subsets the development data for validation in order to gauge the merit of these features. In this instance, the inclusion of various combinations of the above features frequently led to degradation in performance compared to our base models when evaluated on the development data. As such, the features described above were not included in our final models trained on the full data set for most of our focus languages. For the sake of comparison, in Section 5.3 we include the results of a model trained on the full French training data which also incorporates a subset of the features outlined above. This model shows marginal improvement over the base French model on the test data.

4 Sister Language Data Sharing

Data augmentation for low-resource languages has been well researched area for various NLP tasks, such as machine translation (Fadaee et al., 2017) and speech recognition (Ragni et al., 2014). While data is provided by the shared task for all of the development languages, the number of training instances varies considerably, both in total amount and in the proportion of different morphological categories attested. Sharing data between languages is one means of evening out the representation of these underrepresented morphological cate-

[3]https://en.wiktionary.org/wiki/Category:Prefixes_by_language

[4]https://en.wiktionary.org/wiki/Category:Suffixes_by_language

Word Class	Description
000	Root words
001	Compound only
010	Derivation only
011	Derivation and Compound
100	Inflection only
101	Inflection and Compound
110	Inflection and Derivation
111	Inflection, Derivation, Compound

Table 1: Word class codes for morphological categories in training and development data.

gories. This type of data sharing is an instance of transductive transfer learning, where the domains are initially distinct (different languages), but the task in question remains the same (morpheme segmentation), and the knowledge in one domain is used to increase the task performance in the other domain (Pan and Yang, 2010).

Sister languages descend from a common ancestral language and are as such part of the same language family. Languages from the same language family are more likely to bear a strong resemblance to one another with regard to various linguistic aspects, including morphological structure, than sets of unrelated languages.

Our focus languages in this paper (French, Italian, and Spanish) are all a part of the Romance language family, and as such, we may posit that they share enough similarity in their morphological structure for there to be some benefit in sharing data between the languages during training.

In order to test this conjecture, we make a comparison between base models for each of our focus languages, which only contain training data from one language, and augmented models, which are trained on the full training data for one language and supplemented with training data from the other two Romance languages for select morphological categories.

For several of the development languages, including all three Romance languages, training and development data for the word-level subtask included additional annotation which indicated the morphological category of the word, and the evaluation scripts provided by that shared task also offered a breakdown by morphological category. The morphological categories provided in the shared task data are shown in Table 1.

In order to decide which morphological categories should be augmented with data from sister languages for each of the Romance languages, we evaluate our base models, which were each only trained with data from one language. For each language, we examine the base model's performance on the development data for the task, and we identify the four morphological categories with the lowest performance. For these categories, we add supplemental data from the other two Romance languages to train our augmented models. The identification of these categories for each of our augmented models and the results of their performance is detailed in Section 5.4.

5 Results

The shared task for word-level morpheme segmentation uses precision, recall, and F-measure as evaluation metrics for correctly predicted morphemes, as well as the average Levenshtein edit distance between the predicted instance and the reference instance. Overall scores are reported, as well as scores for individual morphological categories. The following subsections go through the baseline results provided by the shared task for our focus languages, as well as the results for our models. All scores are on the test data sets for individual languages. Overall, we find that all of our models make a significant improvement over the baseline.

5.1 Baseline

The baseline results given by the shared task for the Romance languages in the word-level subtask are all the results of Multilingual BERT Tokenizer (cased). Below are the overall baselines for French, Italian, and Spanish scored on the test data:

Lang.	P	R	F	Dist.
French	11.35	14.30	12.66	4.28
Italian	8.04	10.43	9.08	5.35
Spanish	15.59	17.68	16.57	5.21

5.2 Base Models

Base models for French, Italian, Spanish were trained on the architecture described in Section 2. Each model was trained on the entire training data for a single language. The results on the test data for each language broken down by morphological category are shown below. We note that these base models greatly outperform the baseline models from the previous sub-section.

French				
Cat.	P	R	F	Dist.
000	37.51	54.99	44.60	1.45
001	33.24	36.98	35.01	3.70
010	63.59	63.99	63.79	2.03
011	35.11	26.14	29.97	6.35
100	83.49	88.05	85.71	0.59
101	80.00	75.68	77.78	1.35
110	92.96	90.24	91.58	0.62
111	77.92	67.42	72.29	3.32
all	83.06	83.70	83.38	0.98

Italian				
Cat.	P	R	F	Dist.
000	39.94	57.44	47.12	1.53
001	23.40	22.92	23.16	4.27
010	71.93	71.99	71.96	1.68
011	32.43	26.67	29.27	6.43
100	84.04	88.18	86.06	0.64
101	47.56	42.86	45.09	4.80
110	93.86	91.28	92.55	0.60
111	48.39	31.91	38.46	6.27
all	87.21	87.77	87.49	0.78

Spanish				
Cat.	P	R	F	Dist.
000	44.16	61.50	51.41	1.23
001	13.11	13.79	13.45	4.72
010	68.93	65.43	67.13	1.59
011	36.36	21.05	26.67	7.67
100	95.27	96.25	95.76	0.23
101	86.24	77.25	81.50	1.31
110	98.35	97.32	97.83	0.18
111	93.67	86.05	89.70	2.00
all	96.00	95.90	95.95	0.27

Looking at the results above, we see that the relative performance on the different morphological categories amongst the three languages is relatively stable. All three of the languages have the highest scores on the *Inflection and Derivation (110)* category, followed by the *Inflection only (100)* category. For all three languages, the two lowest performing morphological categories are *Compound only (001)* and *Derivation and Compound (011)*.

We also note that the overall scores for each language relative to one another correlates to the size of the training data available: French has the least training data available, while Spanish has the most, and correspondingly, the overall scores for Spanish are the highest and the overall scores for French are the lowest. A table of the word category distributions within the shared task data for the three languages can be viewed in Appendix A. Predictions for all three of these models on the test data for their respective languages were submitted to the shared task (System GU-2).

5.3 Feature Model

As noted in Section 3, smaller trials during development indicated that the inclusion of the additional features we experimented with led to a degradation in performance. As such, we did not train a full set of feature models for all of our focus languages. For the sake of comparison, we trained a model on the full French training data with the first two features in our feature set:

If the given character were the start of a new morpheme:

1. Is the string to the left of the boundary a prefix?
2. Is the string to the right of the boundary a suffix?

The results for this model on the French development data are shown below. We note that in this instance there is marginal improvement when compared to the results of the French base model in the previous sub-section (gains/losses from the base model are listed in parentheses). Predictions from this model were not submitted to the shared task.

French	with	Features		
Cat.	P	R	F	Dist.
000	37.47	56.09	44.93	1.51
	(-0.04)	(+1.10)	(+0.33)	(+0.06)
001	28.95	32.54	30.64	3.90
	(-4.29)	(-4.44)	(-4.37)	(+0.40)
010	63.87	64.95	64.40	2.00
	(+0.28)	(+0.96)	(+0.43)	(-0.03)
011	35.10	30.11	32.42	6.35
	(-0.01)	(+4.97)	(+2.45)	(+0.00)
100	84.97	89.12	86.99	0.56
	(+1.48)	(+1.07)	(+1.28)	(-0.03)
101	76.54	68.24	79.14	1.83
	(-3.46)	(-7.44)	(+1.36)	(+0.48)
110	93.04	90.16	91.58	0.60
	(+0.08)	(-0.08)	(+0.00)	(-0.02)
111	83.53	79.78	81.61	2.21
	(+5.61)	(+12.36)	(+9.32)	(-1.11)
all	83.45	84.13	83.79	0.96
	(+0.39)	(+0.43)	(+0.41)	(-0.02)

5.4 Augmented Models

The augmented models for each language were trained with additional data from the other two Romance languages. The morphological categories that were chosen to be augmented for each language were selected by identifying the lower performing morphological categories (bottom 4 categories) in the results of the base models on the development data for each language (listed in full in Appendix B). For selected categories, all of the training data from the other two Romance languages in those same categories was added to the training data of the original language to train the augmented model. For each language below, we identify the morphological categories that were augmented and list the results of the augmented model's performance on the test data of the original language (gains/losses from each language's respective base model are listed in parentheses). Predictions for the French and Italian models on the test data for their respective languages were submitted to the shared task (System GU-1).

French:

According to the results of the base model on the development data, the following categories had the lowest performance: *root words (000)*, *compound only (001)*, *derivation only (010)*, and *inflection only (011)*. The categories were augmented with Italian and Spanish training data from the same categories.

Cat.	P	R	F	Dist.
000	49.76 (+12.25)	67.40 (+12.41)	57.25 (+12.65)	1.03 (-0.42)
001	26.97 (-6.27)	28.40 (-8.58)	27.67 (-7.34)	3.99 (+0.29)
010	63.09 (-0.50)	61.71 (-2.28)	62.39 (-1.40)	1.98 (-0.05)
011	42.14 (+7.03)	33.52 (+7.38)	37.34 (+7.37)	5.45 (-0.90)
100	85.31 (+1.82)	88.90 (+0.85)	87.07 (+1.36)	0.53 (-0.06)
101	72.99 (-7.01)	67.57 (-8.11)	70.18 (-7.60)	1.83 (+0.48)
110	92.50 (-0.46)	89.39 (-0.85)	90.92 (-0.66)	0.62 (+0.00)
111	80.52 (+2.60)	69.66 (+2.24)	74.70 (+2.41)	3.00 (-0.32)
all	83.66 (+0.60)	83.21 (-0.49)	83.44 (+0.06)	0.93 (-0.05)

Comparing the above table to the base model results for French, we see that the augmented category *root words (000)* increases by the largest amount: +12.25 (P), +12.41 (R), +12.65 (F), -0.42 (Dist.). All of the scores for the other morphological categories either raise or fall by smaller margins. The sizable jump for *root words (000)* is likely do to the fact that it is a larger morphological class in the training data sets of our languages.

Italian:

According to the results of the base model on the development data, the following categories had the lowest performance: *compound only (001)*, *derivation and compound (011)*, *inflection and compound (101)*, and *inflection, derivation, compound (111)*. The categories were augmented with French and Spanish training data from the same categories.

Cat.	P	R	F	Dist.
000	42.75 (+2.81)	60.93 (+3.49)	50.25 (+3.13)	1.42 (-0.11)
001	18.00 (-5.40)	18.75 (-4.17)	18.37 (-4.79)	4.48 (+0.21)
010	73.48 (+1.55)	74.32 (+2.33)	73.90 (+1.94)	1.56 (-0.12)
011	34.21 (+1.78)	28.89 (+2.22)	31.33 (+2.06)	6.07 (-0.36)
100	85.67 (+1.63)	89.48 (+1.30)	87.54 (+1.48)	0.57 (-0.07)
101	54.02 (+6.46)	51.65 (+8.79)	52.81 (+7.72)	3.37 (-1.43)
110	94.68 (+0.82)	92.14 (+0.86)	93.39 (+0.84)	0.53 (-0.07)
111	63.64 (+15.25)	44.68 (+12.77)	52.50 (+14.04)	5.64 (-0.63)
all	88.41 (+1.20)	88.97 (+1.20)	88.69 (+1.20)	0.70 (-0.08)

Comparing the above table to the base model results for Italian, we see that the overall results increase by a small margin: +1.20 (P), +1.20 (R), +1.20 (F), -0.08 (Dist.). All of the morphological categories had slight increases from the base model, except for the *compound only (001)* category.

Spanish:

According to the results of the base model on the development data, the following categories had the lowest performance: *root words (000)*, *compound only (001)*, *derivation only (010)*, and *inflection only (011)*. The categories were augmented with French and Italian training data from the same categories.

Cat.	P	R	F	Dist.
000	59.24 (+15.08)	75.03 (+13.53)	66.21 (+14.80)	0.82 (-0.41)
001	9.09 (-4.02)	8.62 (-5.17)	8.85 (-4.60)	3.97 (-0.75)
010	65.12 (-3.81)	59.96 (-5.47)	62.43 (-4.70)	1.72 (+0.13)
011	35.71 (-0.65)	26.32 (+5.27)	30.30 (+3.63)	7.33 (-0.34)
100	94.79 (-0.48)	95.69 (-0.56)	95.24 (-0.52)	0.24 (+0.01)
101	81.38 (-4.87)	72.51 (-4.74)	76.69 (-4.81)	1.68 (+0.37)
110	98.06 (-0.29)	96.86 (-0.46)	97.46 (-0.37)	0.20 (+0.02)
111	92.31 (-1.36)	83.72 (-2.33)	87.80 (-1.90)	2.22 (+0.22)
all	95.72 (-0.28)	95.35 (-0.55)	95.53 (-0.42)	0.29 (+0.02)

Comparing the above table to the base model results for Spanish, we see that the augmented category *root words (000)* increases by a notable amount: +15.08 (P), +13.53 (R), +14.80 (F), -0.41 (Dist.). All of the scores for the other morphological categories fall by a notable margin. The sizable jump for *root words (000)* is likely do to the fact that it is a larger morphological class in the training data sets of our languages. The gains from the *root words* category do not balance out the losses from the other morphological classes, and we see a loss in the overall scores.

6 Discussion

While all of base models made significant improvements from the baseline scores provided for the word-level subtask, we note that our additional experimentation resulted in only modest improvements. We also note that our experimenting with additional features frequently led to score degradation on the development data.

We did not expect to see the general degradation in our scores with the inclusion of the known affix presence/absence based features that we saw in our experiments predicting on the development data. However, we did see the marginal improvement we expected in the results of the fully trained French model predicting on the test data, as described in Section 5.3. On possible explanation for these inconsistent results is that the inclusion of single character or two character affixes created feature vectors with too many false positives to be of use in the model's learning for our small scales experiments predicting on the development data. Further error analysis is needed to conclude the reason for such inconsistency. The fact that the improvements seen in fully trained French model were marginal suggest that the base architecture of our models may be independently capable of learning information encoded in our linguistic features.

The sharing of language data between sister languages gave modest gains in our experiments, indicating that there is some potential to leverage available data from morphologically similar languages for morpheme segmentation. In future experiments we want to experiment with different methods of deciding what/how much data should be shared in order to maximize this potential. Additionally, rather than just assuming that being in the same language family indicates enough morphological similarity between languages for data sharing to be of use, we believe that is would be beneficial to make a closer study of the morphological similarities and differences between sets of languages that will be used for data sharing.

7 Conclusion

In this paper we presented a basic approach to morpheme segmentation at the word-level for the SIGMORPHON 2022 shared task for French, Italian, and Spanish. All of our presented models considerably improved upon the baselines for the shared task. While the extra character based features we experimented with generally did not prove useful in this instance, we did find some evidence that sharing data between morphologically similar languages could result in minor improvements in the segmentation of words in morphological categories which were augmented with additional data.

References

Khuyagbaatar Batsuren, Gábor Bella, Aryaman Arora, Viktor Martinović, Kyle Gorman, Zdeněk Žabokrtský, Amarsanaa Ganbold, Šárka Dohnalová, Magda Ševčíková, Kateřina Pelegrinová, Fausto Giunchiglia, Ryan Cotterell, and Ekaterina Vylomova. 2022. The sigmorphon 2022 shared task on morpheme segmentation. In *19th SIGMORPHON Workshop on Computational Research in Phonetics, Phonology, and Morphology*.

Mathias Creutz and Krista Lagus. 2007. Unsupervised models for morpheme segmentation and morphology learning. *ACM Transactions on Speech and Language Processing (TSLP)*, 4(1):1–34.

Marzieh Fadaee, Arianna Bisazza, and Christof Monz. 2017. Data augmentation for low-resource neural machine translation. *arXiv preprint arXiv:1705.00440*.

Sinno Jialin Pan and Qiang Yang. 2010. A survey on transfer learning. *IEEE Transactions on Knowledge and Data Engineering*, 22(10):1345–1359.

Anton Ragni, Kate M Knill, Shakti P Rath, and Mark JF Gales. 2014. Data augmentation for low resource languages. In *INTERSPEECH 2014: 15th Annual Conference of the International Speech Communication Association*, pages 810–814. International Speech Communication Association (ISCA).

Shiva Sundaramoorthy. 2017. A novel approach to feed and train extra features in seq2seq (tensorflow amp; pytorch).

Linlin Wang, Zhu Cao, Yu Xia, and Gerard De Melo. 2016. Morphological segmentation with window lstm neural networks. In *Thirtieth AAAI Conference on Artificial Intelligence*.

A Language Data Statistics (word counts)

Word Class	French	Italian	Spanish
000	13619	21037	15843
001	1684	431	248
010	67983	41092	18449
011	506	140	82
100	105192	253455	502229
101	478	317	458
110	126196	237104	346862
111	186	158	343
Total Words	382797	553734	884514

B Performance of Base Models on the Development Data

French				
Cat.	P	R	F	Dist.
000	36.56	54.63	43.80	1.45
001	32.61	36.01	34.23	3.46
010	63.28	63.48	63.38	2.07
011	29.58	24.56	26.84	6.67
100	84.21	88.54	86.32	0.57
101	85.14	82.89	84.00	0.79
110	92.99	90.25	91.60	0.61
111	83.13	78.41	80.70	2.11
all	83.18	83.75	83.47	0.97

Italian				
Cat.	P	R	F	Dist.
000	43.08	60.93	50.47	1.40
001	25.26	25.53	25.40	4.06
010	70.97	71.73	71.35	1.73
011	26.67	27.91	27.27	6.07
100	84.15	88.18	86.12	0.64
101	56.96	49.45	52.94	3.07
110	93.84	91.16	92.48	0.60
111	66.67	55.32	60.47	4.64
all	87.21	87.75	87.48	0.78

Spanish				
Cat.	P	R	F	Dist.
000	43.87	60.82	50.97	1.24
001	15.79	15.52	15.65	3.34
010	67.63	64.62	66.09	1.67
011	18.18	10.53	13.33	5.17
100	95.32	96.27	95.79	0.23
101	87.23	80.79	83.89	1.10
110	98.36	97.30	97.83	0.18
111	86.67	77.38	81.76	2.44
all	95.99	95.87	95.93	0.27

SIGMORPHON 2022 Shared Task on Morpheme Segmentation Submission Description: Sequence Labelling for Word-Level Morpheme Segmentation

Leander Girrbach
University of Tübingen, Germany
leander.girrbach@student.uni-tuebingen.de

Abstract

We propose a sequence labelling approach to word-level morpheme segmentation. Segmentation labels are edit operations derived from a modified minimum edit distance alignment. We show that sequence labelling performs well for "shallow segmentation" and "canonical segmentation", achieving 96.06 f1 score (macro-averaged over all languages in the shared task) and ranking 3rd among all participating teams. Therefore, we conclude that sequence labelling is a promising approach to morpheme segmentation.

1 Introduction

This paper describes our participation in the SIGMORPHON 2022 Shared Task on Morpheme Segmentation (Batsuren et al., 2022a). Building on previous work on word segmentation and transliteration by Hellwig and Nehrdich (2018), we propose a sequence labelling approach to morpheme segmentation.

The shared task consists of 2 tracks: Word-level morpheme segmentation and sentence-level morpheme segmentation. Data for this shared task was taken from (Batsuren et al., 2021) and (Batsuren et al., 2022b). Although our approach is applicable to both word-level and sentence-level morpheme segmentation, we focus on word-level segmentation. We only evaluate the zero-shot performance of our word-only segmentation models on sentence-level morpheme segmentation.

Sequence labelling approaches can claim several advantages over the main alternative, namely (neural) encoder-decoder approaches: Sequence labelling does not require beam search for inference, may allow for smaller models, and defines a direct alignment between the input and predictions. The latter property may make models more interpretable and help with error analysis. However, sequence labelling is less flexible than encoder-decoder approaches and requires special handling of cases where the input and target sequences are of different length. However, due to the local structure of morphology, sequence labelling may be sufficient to model morpheme segmentation despite being less expressive than encoder-decoder approaches.

2 Related Work

Morpheme segmentation is a well-established task in computational linguistics (cf. Mager et al. (2020)). Recently, two definitions of morpheme segmentations have emerged: "Shallow segmentation" and "canonical segmentation" (Kann et al., 2016). "Shallow" segmentation means segmenting the input word surface string into morphemic substrings. This kind of segmentation is called "shallow", because no orthographic restoration of morphemes to their "canonical" form is performed (Cotterell et al., 2016). "Canonical segmentation", instead, attempts to restore a standardised form of morphemes. As noted by Kann et al. (2016), this is necessary for synthetic languages where multiple morphemes may be merged. Another source of morpheme merging may arise from phonological or orthographic constraints of the language. The present shared task features both shallow segmentation data (e.g. Czech, Latin), and canonical segmentation (e.g. Italian, English). Since canonical segmentation is a strict generalisation of shallow segmentation, methods that work for all languages in this shared task have to be able to perform canonical segmentation.

However, shallow segmentation allows for a conceptually easier approach, namely sequence labelling (Ruokolainen et al., 2013; Sorokin, 2019). Canonical segmentation has hitherto been defined as a sequence-to-sequence task (Kann et al., 2016; Mager et al., 2020). Of course, various improvements for the sequence-to-sequence setup have been proposed, for example reranking of output hypotheses (Kann et al., 2016), multi task learn-

19th SIGMORPHON Workshop on Computational Research in Phonetics, Phonology, and Morphology, pages 124 - 130
July 14, 2022

ing (Kann et al., 2018), pointer-generator networks (Sharma et al., 2018), and imitation learning (Makarov and Clematide, 2018).

In fact, Sorokin (2019) explicitly doubts that canonical segmentation can be approached as a sequence labelling task. However, other approaches have already worked towards approaching canonical segmentation as a sequence labelling task: Cotterell et al. (2016) take a middle ground by allowing only for a maximum number of insertions. Ribeiro et al. (2018) train a model to first predict insertion positions in the input sequence. Then, they use a sequence labelling model on the augmented input string to predict the labels. While similar to our approach, we augment the labels instead of the input string. Therefore, our method remains end-to-end trainable. Finally, Hellwig and Nehrdich (2018) propose a sequence labelling approach to Sanskrit word segmentation, which includes restoring original forms that have been merged due to a phonological process called Sandhi.

Therefore, our work extends the method proposed by Hellwig and Nehrdich and thereby shows that canonical morpheme segmentation can be approached effectively as a sequence labelling task.

3 Method

3.1 Data preprocessing

We propose an adaption of the Sanskrit word segmentation method by Hellwig and Nehrdich (2018) for word-level morpheme segmentation. The main idea is to redefine morpheme segmentation as a sequence labelling task. In particular, for each character in the input word, we predict an edit operation. Edit operations can be copying, deletion, or substitution. Here, insertion is a special case of substitution. An example is in Table 1.

In order to redefine morpheme segmentation as a sequence labelling task, we need alignments of input words and the segmented morphemes. We propose to align words and morphemes by the Needleman-Wunsch algorithm (Needleman and Wunsch, 1970) with the following parameters: Only equal characters can be matched, and we set the gap cost to 0. Here, we treat all morphemes as one sequence of characters. From all alignments with maximum score according to the Needleman-Wunsch algorithm (i.e. minimum edit distance), we choose the alignment with the maximum sum of squared lengths of contiguous aligned segments. The idea is to copy longer morphemes directly from the input word and insert shorter morphemes. Furthermore, we want to avoid splitting predicted morphemes. Instead, we want to copy as many complete morphemes from the input word as possible. An example is in Table 2.

After having aligned words to their respective morphemes, we obtain data for sequence labelling in the following way: Word characters that are aligned to corresponding characters in the morpheme string are copied. Word characters that are aligned to gaps in the morpheme string are deleted. Morpheme separation characters and possible following characters to complete a morpheme are aligned to gaps in the input word. We prepend these to the label of the input word character following the gap. Remaining morpheme string characters (which do not appear behind a morpheme separation character) that are aligned to gaps in the input word are appended to the label of the next input word character before the gap. In Table 3, we show the resulting labels for the English word "entabulates". Note that our eventual labelling makes more use of copying than the simple edit operation example given in Table 1.

3.2 Models

For sequence labelling, we use a plain 2-layer BiLSTM model. For each position of the input sequence, the model predicts exactly one edit operation. Ground-truth labels for supervised training are derived as explained in Section 3.1.

Our submission is produced by single models (i.e. no ensembling) trained in a supervised fashion. Models have 2 layers with 256 hidden units each. We apply dropout with probability 0.1 after the first BiLSTM layer. We use the AdamW optimizer (Loshchilov and Hutter, 2019) with initial learning rate 0.001 and weight decay 0.001. We divide the learning rate by 2 after 3 epochs without improvement of word error rate (WER) on the development set. Note that WER is a stricter metric than f1 score and edit distance, which are the shared task's official evaluation metric. Each model is trained for 50 epochs with batch size 32, but we only keep the checkpoint with lowest WER on the development set.

3.3 Zero-shot sentence-level segmentation

For sentence-level segmentation, we proceed in the following way: Since all sentence-level languages (Czech, English, Mongolian) are also part of the word-level track, we can use our models from the

e	n	t	a	b	u	l	a	t	e	s
e	n	␣@@t	a	b		le	␣@@a	t	e	␣@@s
C	C	S	C	C	D	S	S	C	C	S

Table 1: Edit operation to transduce "entabulates" to its morphemic segment string "en␣@@table␣@@ate␣@@s". "␣@@" is the morpheme separation symbol in the given data, "S" means substitution, "C" means copy, and "D" means deletion.

m	a	m	m	a	␣	@	@	a	r	e	␣	@	@	e	r	a	n	n	o
m	a	m	m											e	r	a	n	n	o
m	a	m	m							e					r	a	n	n	o

Table 2: Example for different alignments of the Italian word "mammare" to its morpheme segmentation string "mamma␣@@are␣@@eranno". The upper alignment is preferred, because it contains longer contiguous aligned subsequences.

word-level track for sentence-level segmentation. We retrieve all space-separated tokens from the sentence-level test data and segment each token individually, thus creating a dictionary mapping tokens to their word-level segmentation. Then, we replace each token in the sentence by the segmentation according to the word-only dictionary. Tokens that only consist of punctuation are copied directly from the input sentence without any segmentation.

This method obviously ignores all sentence-level information that could help with disambiguating multiple possible segmentations. However, we still find it interesting to see how well a word-level-only segmentation model performs on the sentence level for the different languages.

4 Results

Word-level segmentation Official test set results[1] for word-level segmentation are in Table 4. f1 score is greater than 0.9 for all languages. In terms of macro-averaged f1 score, our submission ranks 3rd out of 5 participating teams (excluding baseline) who submit predictions for all languages.

In our results, we do not see any trends regarding a relationship between number of generated labels and performance. The language with weakest performance, English, has the 2nd highest number of generated labels, but the language with highest number of generated labels, Russian, is the language with second best performance. Czech, the number with the lowest number of generated labels, is the language with 3rd worst performance, but Latin, the language with 2nd lowest number of generated labels, is the language with best performance. This suggests that our data preprocessing method does not obscure the segmentation difficulty inherent in a language.

Remember that differences in the amounts of labels is due to different annotation approaches in the data: For Czech and Latin, only "shallow" morpheme boundaries are annotated, i.e. where morpheme boundaries are in the input string. For other languages, restored morphemes are annotated that are contracted when forming the word. For example, the English word "entabulates" is segmented as "en␣@@table␣@@ate␣@@s" where "u" is inserted to form the word, but the "e" in "table" is deleted.

Sentence-level segmentation Official test set results for sentence-level segmentation are in Table 5. Sentence-level performance is worse than word-level performance for all languages. While the decrease in performance is still moderate for English and Czech, we see a very high decrease in performance for Mongolian. This suggests that the number of ambiguous tokens in English and Czech is relatively not very high, while a lot of ambiguous words exist in Mongolian.

5 Error Analysis

Frequent Errors As claimed in Section 1, our proposed sequence labelling method allows for direct comparison of the predicted labels to labels created by our preprocessing. Here, we provide a short analysis of the most frequent errors made by our English word segmentation model. To this end, we apply the preprocessing method described in Section 3.1 to the test set released by the shared

[1]Taken from `https://github.com/sigmorphon/2022SegmentationST/tree/main/results`

e	n	t	a	b	u	l	a	t	e	s
C	C	␣@@ + C	C	C	D	C + e	␣@@ + C	C	C	␣@@ + C

Table 3: Labels generated by our data preprocessing method for English word "entabulates" with morpheme segment string "en␣@@table␣@@ate␣@@s". Our labels allow for special symbols (C = copy, D = delete) and arbitrary string insertions. Labels do not have to contain special symbols. "+" here means concatenation and is not to be read as part of the label.

Lang.	Dis.	P	R	F1	# Lbls
ces	0.18	93.95	92.81	93.38	2
eng	0.25	90.51	90.52	90.51	1740
fra	0.28	93.56	93.96	93.76	1275
hun	0.11	98.21	98.97	98.59	442
spa	0.11	97.88	97.98	97.93	1311
ita	0.20	95.50	95.97	95.73	850
lat	0.01	99.35	99.39	99.37	4
rus	0.15	98.16	98.26	98.21	1809
mon	0.10	96.91	97.13	97.02	442
Avg.	0.15	96.00	96.11	96.06	

Table 4: Official word-level results for our system (all languages). Dis is edit distance, P is precision, R is recall, and F1 is f1 score. # Lbls is the number of labels generated by our data preprocessing method (see Section 3.1).

Lang.	Dis.	P	R	F1
ces	2.50	89.52	88.42	88.97
eng	1.78	87.83	89.58	88.69
mon	9.85	69.59	67.55	68.55

Table 5: Official sentence-level results for our system (all languages). Dis is edit distance, P is precision, R is recall, and F1 is f1 score.

b	i	o	m	e
C	C	C	␣@@o + C	C
C	C + o	␣@@ + C	C	C

Table 6: An example where different labels result in the same (correct) segmentation: "biome" ⟶ "bio␣@@ome".

task organisers after the submission deadline. Then, we calculate a confusion matrix of the labels predicted by our model and the labels created by the preprocessing method.

First, however, we want to note that in few cases even incorrect predictions may lead to correct segmentations. This is due to ambiguity in the alignments. For example, consider the test item "biome" with ground truth segmentation "bio @@ome". In Table 6 we show that our model's prediction differs from the generated alignment, but the resulting segmentations are identical. In the English test set, this is the case for 118 words, so we do not think this is a problem for our subsequent error analysis. In total, there are 8615 words ($\approx$ 15% of all test words) with incorrect segmentation.

The most common errors are predicting morpheme boundaries where actually no morpheme boundaries are, i.e. predicting "␣@@ + C" instead of "C", which happens 3820 times, and missing to predict morpheme boundaries, i.e. predicting "C" instead of "␣@@ + C", which happens 3786 times. An example is "lemming": Our models predicts "lem␣@@ing" instead of "lemming". A morpheme boundary was overlooked in "sanity": Our model predicts "sanity" instead of "sane␣@@ity".

The next most frequent errors are missing to insert an "e", i.e. predicting "C" instead of "C+e", which happens 499 times, and inserting a superfluous "e", i.e. predicting "C + e" instead of "C", which happens 414 times. For example, our model predicts "wok␣@@ism" instead of "woke␣@@ism" for "wokism" and "ominouse␣@@ity" instead of "ominous␣@@ity" for "ominosity".

The last error type in the top 5 most frequent errors is not deleting an input character, i.e. predicting "C" instead of "D", which happens 448 times. For example, our model predicts "charr␣@@y" instead of "char␣@@y" for "charry".

Please note that there can be multiple errors in the predictions for a single input word. However, in most cases (5873), there is only one incorrectly predicted label. In 2008 cases, there are 2 incorrectly predicted labels. The extreme case is "alsakharovite", for which 9 of the predicted labels are incorrect: Our model simply predicts to copy each character, but the ground truth is given as "Aleksey␣@@ite". This shows that our model struggles with proper names, which is not surprising.

In conclusion, this analysis shows that the largest gains in performance can be expected from improving the shallow part of segmentation, while there are fewer individual morpheme reconstruction errors. Therefore, a possible future extension of our proposed model is switching to a multi task setting, where one task is to predict morpheme boundaries and the other task is to reconstruct partial or missing morphemes. In the setting evaluated here, these tasks are approached jointly.

Label Embeddings Additionally, we inspect the learned (English) label embeddings and try to see whether any patterns emerge. To this end, we retrieve the 50 most frequent labels (accounting for 98% of all labels in the dataset excluding the simple copy label) and their label embeddings (columns in the final linear prediction layer). We cluster the label embeddings by affinity propagation. The advantage of affinity propagation is that we do not have to specify the number of clusters. We use the scikit-learn implementation of affinity propagation (Pedregosa et al., 2011) with default parameters. The discovered clusters are in Table 7.

In total, the clustering generates 7 clusters, of which 4 clusters contain multiple labels and 3 clusters contain only 1 label. No cluster is completely pure, but we can observe the following trends: Cluster 0 mostly represents morpheme boundary labels followed by a copy operation, i.e. "insert morpheme boundary before this character". Cluster 2 mostly represents substitutions and Clusters 1 and 3 mostly represent insertions. We cannot say anything definite about the 1 element clusters.

From these observations we conclude that the model learns to distinguish different edit operations (insertion, substitution) and also learns to distinguish inserting morpheme boundaries from other edit operations. This provides further evidence that changing our approach to a multi task setting may be worth exploring.

Generalisation to Unseen Substitutions Finally, we want to address the problem that the finite number of labels generated by our data preprocessing method (see Section 3.1) may not allow the model to generalise to substitutions not seen in the training data.[2] To collect evidence concerning this problem, again for the English test set, we find all words that cannot be generated by our model because generating them would require labels that were not generated from the training data. In total, we find 35 such words (of 57755 test words in total). Furthermore, upon manual inspection, we find many of these cases either caused by proper names with irregular or non-English segmentation, for example "Staffie" is segmented as "Stafford␣@@shire␣@@ie" or "Lebos" is segmented as "Lebanon␣@@ese␣@@o␣@@s", or annotation errors, for example "unlid" is segmented (in the gold data) as "un#Etymology_2␣@@lid" or "perfosfamide" is segmented as "hydroperoxy␣@@fosfamide". However, we also discover a genuine problem of our model, namely that it does not have any labels to generate hyphens ("-"). This proves that the problem can be substantial, if there had been more hyphenated words in the test data.

On the other hand, hyphens do not appear as character in any train set segmentation, so it is generally hard to anticipate peculiarities of the test set. The case of proper names could perhaps be handled by external resources, but this does not scale well.

Summing up, we acknowledge that this is an issue not solved entirely by our approach. However, it does not cause many problems for this shared task. This being said, this shared task provides a lot of data for the featured languages, so the missing label problem may become more serious for low resource languages or settings.

One step towards approaching this issue could be not only generating labels from one alignment of the word to its morpheme segmentation string (see Section 3.1), but from multiple alignments. This could potentially also regularise the model or allow for different training strategies than the standard supervised training. Another possibility could be to equip the model with the ability to generate new

[2]We thank the reviewers for pointing out this problem.

Cluster ID	Labels
0	"C", "␣@@ + C", "␣@@e + C", "␣@@a + C", "␣@@i + C", "␣@@o + C", "C + t", "␣@@l + C", "D + n", "␣@@ + C + e", "C + ␣@@s", "C + te", "C + ic", "␣@@is + C", "␣@@i + C + e", "C + m", "␣@@en + C", "␣@@a + C + e", "C + l", "␣@@t + C"
1	"D + y", "D + ␣@@y", "C + um", "D + e", "C + s", "D + e␣@@y", "D + o", "D + a", "D + d"
2	"C + e", "C + y", "C + a", "C + o", "C + us", "C + on", "D + sis", "C + ion", "C + ous", "D + p"
3	"D", "D + i", "C + ␣@@y", "D + is", "D + x", "C + n", "D + s"
4	"C + ne"
5	"D + ce"
6	"D + de"

Table 7: Clusters of labels discovered by affinity propagation clustering of the label embeddings of the 50 most frequent English labels.

labels, for example by predicting a fixed number of label subsymbols from each input character. Symbols could be blanks, unigrams, or ngrams. This would relax the constraint that labels have to be entirely known beforehand, while maintaining a sequence labelling setup.

6 Conclusion

We presented a sequence labelling approach for word-level morpheme segmentation. Models trained with this approach yield strong performance on all languages (word-level) despite of not using ensembling and using a simple BiLSTM encoder. Error analysis for English reveals that the model is often only wrong in 1 single place, struggles with proper names, and most frequently errors are caused by incorrect prediction of morpheme boundaries.

Acknowledgements

We thank Çağrı Çöltekin for providing access to computation resources and giving feedback on a draft version of this paper. We thank the task organisers for organising this shared task. Finally, we thank the reviewers for their helpful comments and suggestions.

References

Khuyagbaatar Batsuren, Gábor Bella, and Fausto Giunchiglia. 2021. MorphyNet: a large multilingual database of derivational and inflectional morphology. In *Proceedings of the 18th SIGMORPHON Workshop on Computational Research in Phonetics, Phonology, and Morphology*, pages 39–48, Online. Association for Computational Linguistics.

Khuyagbaatar Batsuren, Gábor Bella, Aryaman Arora, Viktor Martinović, Kyle Gorman, Zdeněk Žabokrtský, Amarsanaa Ganbold, Šárka Dohnalová, Magda Ševčíková, Kateřina Pelegrinová, Fausto Giunchiglia, Ryan Cotterell, and Ekaterina Vylomova. 2022a. The sigmorphon 2022 shared task on morpheme segmentation. In *19th SIGMORPHON Workshop on Computational Research in Phonetics, Phonology, and Morphology*.

Khuyagbaatar Batsuren, Omer Goldman, Salam Khalifa, Nizar Habash, Witold Kieraś, Gábor Bella, Brian Leonard, Garrett Nicolai, Kyle Gorman, Yustinus Ghanggo Ate, et al. 2022b. Unimorph 4.0: Universal morphology. *arXiv preprint arXiv:2205.03608*.

Ryan Cotterell, Tim Vieira, and Hinrich Schütze. 2016. A joint model of orthography and morphological segmentation. In *Proceedings of the 2016 Conference of the North American Chapter of the Association for Computational Linguistics: Human Language Technologies*, pages 664–669, San Diego, California. Association for Computational Linguistics.

Oliver Hellwig and Sebastian Nehrdich. 2018. Sanskrit word segmentation using character-level recurrent and convolutional neural networks. In *Proceedings of the 2018 Conference on Empirical Methods in Natural Language Processing*, pages 2754–2763, Brussels, Belgium. Association for Computational Linguistics.

Katharina Kann, Ryan Cotterell, and Hinrich Schütze. 2016. Neural morphological analysis: Encoding-decoding canonical segments. In *Proceedings of the 2016 Conference on Empirical Methods in Natural Language Processing*, pages 961–967, Austin, Texas. Association for Computational Linguistics.

Katharina Kann, Jesus Manuel Mager Hois, Ivan Vladimir Meza-Ruiz, and Hinrich Schütze. 2018. Fortification of neural morphological segmentation models for polysynthetic minimal-resource languages. In *Proceedings of the 2018 Conference of the North American Chapter of the Association for Computational Linguistics: Human Language Technologies, Volume 1 (Long Papers)*, pages 47–57, New Orleans, Louisiana. Association for Computational Linguistics.

Ilya Loshchilov and Frank Hutter. 2019. Decoupled weight decay regularization. In *7th International Conference on Learning Representations, ICLR 2019, New Orleans, LA, USA, May 6-9, 2019*. OpenReview.net.

Manuel Mager, Özlem Çetinoğlu, and Katharina Kann. 2020. Tackling the low-resource challenge for canonical segmentation. In *Proceedings of the 2020 Conference on Empirical Methods in Natural Language Processing (EMNLP)*, pages 5237–5250, Online. Association for Computational Linguistics.

Peter Makarov and Simon Clematide. 2018. Neural transition-based string transduction for limited-resource setting in morphology. In *Proceedings of the 27th International Conference on Computational Linguistics*, pages 83–93, Santa Fe, New Mexico, USA. Association for Computational Linguistics.

Saul B Needleman and Christian D Wunsch. 1970. A general method applicable to the search for similarities in the amino acid sequence of two proteins. *Journal of molecular biology*, 48(3):443–453.

F. Pedregosa, G. Varoquaux, A. Gramfort, V. Michel, B. Thirion, O. Grisel, M. Blondel, P. Prettenhofer, R. Weiss, V. Dubourg, J. Vanderplas, A. Passos, D. Cournapeau, M. Brucher, M. Perrot, and E. Duchesnay. 2011. Scikit-learn: Machine learning in Python. *Journal of Machine Learning Research*, 12:2825–2830.

Joana Ribeiro, Shashi Narayan, Shay B. Cohen, and Xavier Carreras. 2018. Local string transduction as sequence labeling. In *Proceedings of the 27th International Conference on Computational Linguistics*, pages 1360–1371, Santa Fe, New Mexico, USA. Association for Computational Linguistics.

Teemu Ruokolainen, Oskar Kohonen, Sami Virpioja, and Mikko Kurimo. 2013. Supervised morphological segmentation in a low-resource learning setting using conditional random fields. In *Proceedings of the Seventeenth Conference on Computational Natural Language Learning*, pages 29–37, Sofia, Bulgaria. Association for Computational Linguistics.

Abhishek Sharma, Ganesh Katrapati, and Dipti Misra Sharma. 2018. IIT(BHU)–IIITH at CoNLL–SIGMORPHON 2018 shared task on universal morphological reinflection. In *Proceedings of the CoNLL–SIGMORPHON 2018 Shared Task: Universal Morphological Reinflection*, pages 105–111, Brussels. Association for Computational Linguistics.

Alexey Sorokin. 2019. Convolutional neural networks for low-resource morpheme segmentation: baseline or state-of-the-art? In *Proceedings of the 16th Workshop on Computational Research in Phonetics, Phonology, and Morphology*, pages 154–159, Florence, Italy. Association for Computational Linguistics.

Beyond Characters: Subword-level Morpheme Segmentation

Ben Peters[†] and **André F. T. Martins**[†‡*]
[†]Instituto de Telecomunicações, Instituto Superior Técnico, Lisbon, Portugal
[‡]LUMLIS (Lisbon ELLIS Unit), Lisbon, Portugal
[*]Unbabel, Lisbon, Portugal
benzurdopeters@gmail.com, andre.t.martins@tecnico.ulisboa.pt

Abstract

This paper presents DeepSPIN's submissions to the SIGMORPHON 2022 Shared Task on Morpheme Segmentation. We make three submissions, all to the word-level subtask. First, we show that entmax-based sparse sequence-to-sequence models deliver large improvements over conventional softmax-based models, echoing results from other tasks. Then, we challenge the assumption that models for morphological tasks should be trained at the character level by building a transformer that generates morphemes as sequences of unigram language model-induced subwords. This subword transformer outperforms all of our character-level models and wins the word-level subtask. Although we do not submit an official submission to the sentence-level subtask, we show that this subword-based approach is highly effective there as well.

1 Introduction

Nearly all neural models for morphological and phonological NLP tasks operate at the character level. This is a natural design choice because there is usually a monotonic alignment between source and target characters. Although often successful, character-level models do not leverage the fact that words contain longer substrings, such as roots and affixes, that can often be copied all at once. They also go against the grain of modern NLP, in which most systems for other tasks are trained on sequences of subword units induced by an unsupervised algorithm, usually either byte-pair encoding (BPE; Sennrich et al., 2016) or unigram language modeling (ULM; Kudo, 2018). Although subword units should not be adopted just because they are widespread, they should not be ignored either, especially given the great amount of effort that has gone into integrating morphological inductive biases into subword tokenization (Park et al., 2020; Tan et al., 2020; Huck et al., 2017; Weller-Di Marco and Fraser, 2020; Banerjee and Bhattacharyya, 2018).

We demonstrate that subword-level modeling *does* work for morpheme segmentation through our submissions to the SIGMORPHON 2022 Shared Task on Morpheme Segmentation (Batsuren et al., 2022). Our subword-level model, an entmax transformer with sampled ULM tokenizations, outperforms our character-level submissions and wins the word-level subtask. Because it generates morphemes as subword sequences, it also offers a way to combine the advantages of subword tokenization (a fixed-size vocabulary, compression) with the advantages of conventional morpheme segmentation (segments do not cross morpheme boundaries).

In all, we submit three models to the task:

- DeepSPIN-1 is a character-level RNN-based sequence-to-sequence model trained to minimize cross entropy. Although intended as a strong baseline, this model still finishes fourth overall with an average F-measure of 96.32.
- DeepSPIN-2 is a character-level sparse sequence-to-sequence model with entmax. It records the best F-measure on 2 of 9 languages, which finishing second overall with an average F-measure of 97.15.
- DeepSPIN-3 is a subword-level entmax transformer trained with subword regularization. It records the best F-measure on 7 of 9 languages, and wins the word-level subtask with an average F-measure of 97.29.

We then retrain DeepSPIN-3 on the combined word- and sentence-level data. Although this model is unofficial, it outperforms the winners of the sentence-level subtask for all three languages.

2 Model

In our experiments, we use both attentional LSTM (Bahdanau et al., 2015) and transformer (Vaswani

19th SIGMORPHON Workshop on Computational Research in Phonetics, Phonology, and Morphology, pages 131 - 138

et al., 2017) sequence-to-sequence models. Regardless of those internal details, at time step i the model predicts a next-target-token distribution $p_{\boldsymbol{\theta}}(\cdot \mid x, y_{<i})$ conditioned on a source sequence x and a target history $y_{<i}$. In most sequence-to-sequence systems, $p_{\boldsymbol{\theta}}(\cdot \mid x, y_{<i})$ is computed with softmax (Bridle, 1990), and x and y consist of sequences of characters. In this work, we depart from these defaults by replacing softmax with 1.5-entmax (Peters et al., 2019), and by tokenizing into subwords instead of characters.

Entmax and its loss. Language models, including sequence-to-sequence models, produce a normalized probability distribution at teach time step. To do this, they need a function $\mathbb{R}^n \to \triangle^n$: that is, a function that maps an arbitrary vector of real numbers to a vector in the n-dimensional probability simplex $\triangle^n := \{\boldsymbol{p} \in \mathbb{R}^n \colon \boldsymbol{p} \geq 0, \mathbf{1}^\top \boldsymbol{p} = 1\}$. The standard choice of function is softmax, which is **dense**: it assigns strictly positive probabilities to all outcomes. However, there is another option, the α-entmax transformation (Peters et al., 2019). Entmax, parameterized by a scalar $\alpha \geq 1$, computes

$$\alpha\text{-entmax}(\boldsymbol{z}) := \underset{\boldsymbol{p} \in \triangle^n}{\mathsf{argmax}}\, \boldsymbol{p}^\top \boldsymbol{z} + \mathsf{H}_\alpha(\boldsymbol{p}), \tag{1}$$

where $\mathsf{H}_\alpha(\boldsymbol{p})$ is the Tsallis α-entropy (Tsallis, 1988), defined in Appendix A. When $\alpha = 1$, this recovers softmax; for $\alpha > 1$, it can return **sparse** vectors, enabling models that can completely rule out some outcomes by assigning them zero probability. Exact algorithms exist for $\alpha \in \{1.5, 2\}$, while approximations exist in the general case. Because sparse probabilities are incompatible with the standard cross entropy loss, it is necessary to train with the entmax loss, defined

$$\mathsf{L}_\alpha(y, \boldsymbol{z}) := (\boldsymbol{p}^\star - \boldsymbol{e}_y)^\top \boldsymbol{z} + \mathsf{H}_\alpha(\boldsymbol{p}^\star), \tag{2}$$

where $\boldsymbol{p}^\star = \alpha\text{-entmax}(\boldsymbol{z})$ and $\boldsymbol{e}_y$ is a one-hot vector whose nonzero index is y. When $\alpha = 1$, this recovers cross entropy. Entmax-based sparse sequence-to-sequence models have been shown to work well on machine translation (Peters et al., 2019; Peters and Martins, 2021) as well morphological (Peters and Martins, 2019) and phonological (Peters and Martins, 2020) tasks. Beyond the top-line results, they have also been shown to be better calibrated than models trained with cross entropy loss (Peters and Martins, 2021).

sausagemakers	sausage|make|er|s
_sa us age makers	_sa us age _| make _| er _| s

Figure 1: The English word "sausagemakers" segmented with character-level tokenization (top) and the ULM model used by DeepSPIN-3 (bottom).

Tokenization. In morpheme segmentation, x and y are typically treated as character sequences. Character-level modeling is attractive because of the mostly monotonic alignments between source and target characters, and because it keeps vocabularies and embedding matrices small. However, multi-character sequences in words, such as "make" or "er" in Figure 1, often function as single units. Therefore, we use ULM (Kudo, 2018) to induce a subword tokenization. ULM is a top-down technique: the tokenization model is initialized with a large vocabulary of overlapping subwords. The parameters of a unigram model over this vocabulary are then estimated using expectation maximization and the lowest-scoring subword types are pruned. This process is repeated until the desired vocabulary size is reached. For any string, a ULM model licenses a **lattice of subword tokenizations**. The highest-scoring tokenization can be computed efficiently with the Viterbi algorithm (Viterbi, 1967). Tokenizations can also be sampled from the model, enabling subword regularization. ULM has been shown to produce tokens that more closely correspond to **meaningful linguistic units** (Bostrom and Durrett, 2020) than the more widespread BPE (Sennrich et al., 2016; Gage, 1994). An example ULM tokenization is shown in Figure 1: while completely merging the frequent morpheme "make" on the target side, it is also able to decompose the less frequent "sausage" into smaller units.

2.1 Implementation details

Training and decoding procedure. We trained with early stopping in all experiments, validating after each epoch. Our validation metric was the mean Levenshtein distance[1] between the gold segmentation and the model's prediction when decoding with a beam size of 5. Training was ended if the model failed to improve for five consecutive

[1]A more conventional choice would be to validate with force-decoded loss. However, this is problematic in our case for two reasons: first, we experiment with two different loss functions, and the values they return are not comparable; second, in a subword-level model there are several subword sequences that represent the same morpheme sequence, but force decoding would return the loss of only one of them.

epochs. We used only the official task data to train our models. We report the configuration with the highest validation set F-measure. We decoded with a beam size of 5 unless otherwise noted.

Software packages. We implemented all neural models with Fairseq (Ott et al., 2019), which we augmented with the pytorch implementation of entmax.[2] We used the BPE and ULM implementation from sentencepiece (Kudo and Richardson, 2018).

3 Word-level Subtask

Our three submissions to the word-level subtask can be divided into two parts. First, we present character-level LSTM-based models trained with cross entropy loss (DeepSPIN-1) and 1.5-entmax loss (DeepSPIN-2). These models are similar to models that performed well at past shared tasks and serve as strong supervised baselines for morpheme segmentation. Second, we implement subword-level transformer[3] models (DeepSPIN-3).

Additional baselines. Although the BERT tokenizer is the official task baseline, we find that its performance is (perhaps unsurprisingly) extremely weak. Therefore, we include three additional unsupervised/semi-supervised baselines. The first two are based on BPE and ULM, with models trained on the concatenation of source and target data. The vocabulary size was selected by development set F-measure from the values $\{2000, 4000, \ldots, 32000\}$. The third extra baseline is Morfessor 2.0 (Smit et al., 2014), for which we treated the task data as supervised annotations and used no additional unlabeled data. Our DeepSPIN-1 submission can also be thought of as a strong supervised baseline: its architecture is similar to Kann et al. (2016)'s system, which to our knowledge was the first to apply encoder-decoder models to canonical morpheme segmentation.

3.1 Character-level LSTM

Hyperparameters. We trained RNN-based models with a plateau-based learning rate schedule, using the hyperparameter ranges shown in Table 1. Due to the much smaller training sets for Czech and Mongolian than the other languages, we different batch sizes for them than the other languages.

Hyperparameters	Values
Embedding size	512
Hidden size	{512, 1024}
Layers	{1, 2}
Dropout	0.3
Batch size (Low)	{16, 32, 64}
Batch size (High)	{256, 512}
Learning rate	{.001, .0005, .0001}

Table 1: Hyperparameters for DeepSPIN-1 and DeepSPIN-2. Brackets indicate values that were determined by grid search. The 'Low' languages are Czech and Mongolian, while all others are 'High'.

The learning rate was reduced by a factor of 10 if the model failed to improve for two consecutive epochs. RNN models were trained for a maximum of 150,000 parameter updates.

3.2 Subword-level Transformer

Hyperparameters. We trained transformers with the inverse square root learning schedule and the hyperparameters in Table 3. The size of feedforward layers was always 4 times the embedding size. All models used 6 layers in the encoder and decoder, with 8 attention heads per layer, and were trained for up to 400,000 parameter updates.

Subword vocabulary. For each language, we trained a ULM model on the concatenation of the source and target training corpora. The vocabulary size was set at 2000 for Czech and Mongolian, and 8000 for the other languages.[4] We performed **subword regularization** at training time by sampling source and target subword sequences. Ideally, we would have generated new subword samples on the fly, as described in (Kudo, 2018). However, Fairseq expects data to be preprocessed in advance, so instead we concatenated several copies of the training data (100 for Czech and Mongolian, 10 for other languages) with different sampled tokenizations.

3.3 Results and discussion

We report results in terms of F-measure (Table 2). Regardless of metric, DeepSPIN-3 and DeepSPIN-2 finish first and second among all submitted systems. On a per-language basis, DeepSPIN-3 has the best F-measure for 7 of 9 languages, while DeepSPIN-2 has the best for the remaining two.

[2] `https://github.com/deep-spin/entmax`

[3] We also tried character-level transformers with the same hyperparameters, but these performed much worse. Future work should investigate why it remains challenging to train character-level transformers.

[4] This is not a principled choice. We found that 8000 seemed to work well for most languages. Due to the limited size of the Czech and Mongolian corpora, we used a smaller vocabulary for them. Future research should exhaustively explore subword vocabulary sizes for morpheme segmentation.

Model	ces	eng	fra	hun	ita	lat	mon	rus	spa	avg.
BERT	20.42	23.06	12.66	24.00	9.08	8.84	14.58	13.81	16.57	15.89
BPE	27.76	20.86	20.08	37.95	10.15	9.46	35.84	9.53	20.33	21.33
ULM	50.51	52.55	38.90	67.77	24.68	73.36	44.39	31.65	34.94	46.53
Morfessor	65.18	64.38	45.56	75.34	36.38	90.23	56.97	40.15	42.60	57.42
DeepSPIN-1	93.42	92.29	91.66	98.56	96.01	99.37	98.03	98.75	98.79	96.32
DeepSPIN-2	**93.88**	93.39	95.29	98.68	**97.47**	99.36	98.00	99.30	99.02	97.15
DeepSPIN-3	93.84	**93.63**	**95.73**	**98.72**	97.43	**99.38**	**98.51**	**99.35**	**99.04**	**97.29**
Best Other	93.85	93.20	94.80	98.59	96.93	99.37	98.31	98.62	98.74	96.85

Table 2: Test set F-measure results for baselines and our submissions. Numbers in boldface are the best among any submission to the task, not only ours. Per-language Best Other results are the best of any system, while the Best Other system averaged over languages is CLUZH (Wehrli et al., 2022).

Hyperparameters	Values
Embedding size	{256, 512}
Dropout	{0.1, 0.3}
Batch tokens (mon)	1024
Batch tokens (others)	8192
Warmup steps	{4000, 8000}

Table 3: Hyperparameters for subword models.

Model	ces	eng	mon	avg.
BERT	34.61	63.53	23.62	40.59
BPE	43.31	64.74	40.95	49.67
ULM	58.03	71.20	48.69	59.31
Morfessor	72.79	78.74	51.21	67.58
DeepSPIN-sent	**93.23**	**98.24**	**83.59**	**91.69**
Task winner	91.99	96.31	82.88	89.77

Table 4: Results for DeepSPIN's unofficial sentence-level system and the per-language task winners. The overall task winner is AUUH_B (Rouhe et al., 2022).

In terms of baselines, our results also support the claim that ULM is more morphologically faithful than BPE (Bostrom and Durrett, 2020), while neither matches Morfessor 2.0.

4 Unofficial Sentence-level Subtask Model

Although we did not submit to the sentence-level subtask due to time and computation restraints, we were able to train subword-level models similar to DeepSPIN-3 after the conclusion of the task. This system, which we dub DeepSPIN-Sent, uses the same hyperparameter grid as DeepSPIN-3. It is trained on the concatenation of data from the word-level and sentence-level subtasks. Our model does not make use of sentence context: each word in a sentence is presented as a separate example.

Our results are shown in Table 4 alongside the task winners and baselines trained on the same data as DeepSPIN-Sent. Our model outperforms the official task winner for all three languages.

5 Analysis

5.1 Does subword regularization matter?

DeepSPIN-3 uses subword regularization for both its source and target sequences. But is this an important part of its design? While source side regularization is generally considered beneficial, the situation on the target side is more controversial: Provilkov et al. (2020) suggest that target-side BPE-dropout only helps in lower-data settings, and alternate strategies have been developed to replace it on the target side (He et al., 2020). However, these experiments only compared BPE-based methods, not ULM, and only evaluated on machine translation. In order to evaluate the importance of subword regularization in our case, we trained English segmentation models that vary in their use of subword regularization, while keeping the same hyperparameter grid as DeepSPIN-3. Table 5 shows that subword regularization appears to be beneficial for both the source and target.

5.2 How difficult is search?

For a sequence-to-sequence model, the difficulty of the inference time search problem depends strongly on the task. In high-uncertainty tasks like machine translation, the highest-scoring hypothesis is often

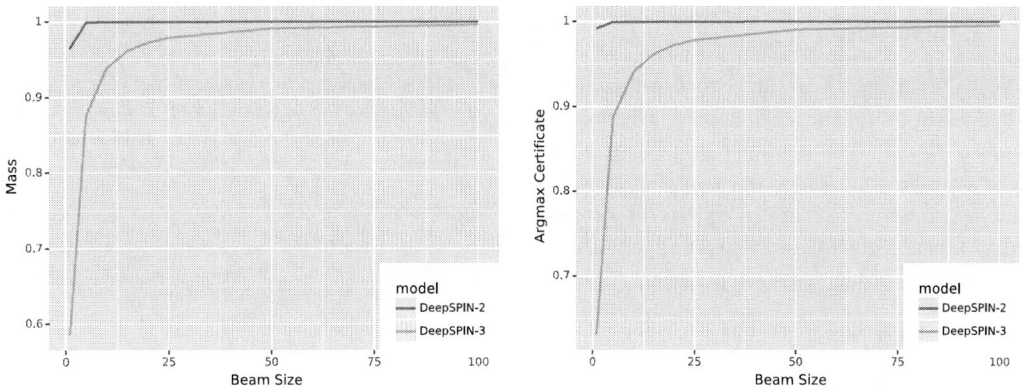

Figure 2: The average probability mass in the beam (left) and rate at which search returns an argmax certificate (right) as a function of beam size for character (DeepSPIN-2) and subword (DeepSPIN-3) models on the English word-level development set.

Subword Reg.	F-measure
neither	92.69
target	93.09
source	93.30
both	**93.83**

Table 5: English development set F-measure with varying subword regularization configurations. The "both" configuration is our official DeepSPIN-3 submission.

inadequate (Stahlberg and Byrne, 2019); strong performance is due to the helpful biases of beam search (Meister et al., 2020). In contrast, less uncertain tasks like morphological inflection often concentrate probability into a few hypotheses, making it easy for beam search to find the argmax (Peters and Martins, 2019; Forster et al., 2021).

Character-based segmentation is a low-uncertainty task: usually, a sequence has only one reasonable segmentation, or a handful at most. Indeed, as we show for the English word-level development set in Figure 2, DeepSPIN-2 concentrates more than 96% of probability mass into the greedy hypothesis on average, an amount that increases to nearly 99.9% at a beam size of 5. The story is different for subword-based models: DeepSPIN-3 concentrates an average of 58.5% of the probability mass in the greedy hypothesis and 87.6% in the hypotheses found with a beam width of 5. By increasing the beam size further, nearly all of the probability mass can be recovered.

Besides the raw amount of probability in the beam hypotheses, it is also possible to obtain a **certificate** that the argmax has found if the single-best beam hypothesis probability is greater than the combined probability mass of every hypothesis outside the beam. The rate at which an argmax certificate is found for DeepSPIN-2 and DeepSPIN-3 is shown in Figure 2. As expected, DeepSPIN-3 returns an argmax certificate less frequently than DeepSPIN-2 with a narrow beam, but the gap closes as the beam size increases.

6 Related Work

Given the widely-observed shortcomings of unsupervised subword units for handling morphology (Amrhein and Sennrich, 2021; Bostrom and Durrett, 2020; Ács, 2019; Mielke et al., 2021), several works have attempted to replace these units with a more morphologically-principled representation for downstream tasks. Although this sometimes means completely replacing the unsupervised subwords (Ataman et al., 2017; Schwartz et al., 2020), other works have adopted a pipeline approach in which unsupervised subwords are applied to a morphological analysis (Park et al., 2020; Tan et al., 2020; Huck et al., 2017; Weller-Di Marco and Fraser, 2020; Banerjee and Bhattacharyya, 2018). These techniques are attractive because unsupervised subword techniques are empirically very effective, and removing them entirely risks losing benefits such as their compressive capacity (Gallé, 2019). Although DeepSPIN-3 is similar to these combined approaches, it is not a pipeline: a single neural model predicts both the subword sequence and the location of the morpheme boundaries.

7 Conclusion

We implemented several sequence-to-sequence models for morpheme segmentation, showing that sparse entmax losses outperform cross entropy. Our strongest model, which won the word-level subtask, is a transformer that generates morphemes as sequences of subword units, unlike traditional character-level segmentation models.

Acknowledgments

This work was supported by the European Research Council (ERC StG DeepSPIN 758969), by the P2020 programs MAIA and Unbabel4EU (LISBOA-01-0247-FEDER-045909 and LISBOA-01-0247-FEDER-042671), and by the Fundação para a Ciência e Tecnologia through contract UIDB/50008/2020.

References

Judit Ács. 2019. Exploring bert's vocabulary. *Blog Post.*

Chantal Amrhein and Rico Sennrich. 2021. How suitable are subword segmentation strategies for translating non-concatenative morphology? In *Findings of the Association for Computational Linguistics: EMNLP 2021*, pages 689–705, Punta Cana, Dominican Republic. Association for Computational Linguistics.

Duygu Ataman, Matteo Negri, Marco Turchi, and Marcello Federico. 2017. Linguistically motivated vocabulary reduction for neural machine translation from turkish to english. *The Prague Bulletin of Mathematical Linguistics*, 108(1):331–342.

Dzmitry Bahdanau, Kyunghyun Cho, and Yoshua Bengio. 2015. Neural machine translation by jointly learning to align and translate. In *Proc. ICLR*.

Tamali Banerjee and Pushpak Bhattacharyya. 2018. Meaningless yet meaningful: Morphology grounded subword-level NMT. In *Proceedings of the Second Workshop on Subword/Character LEvel Models*, pages 55–60, New Orleans. Association for Computational Linguistics.

Khuyagbaatar Batsuren, Gábor Bella, Aryaman Arora, Viktor Martinović, Kyle Gorman, Zdeněk Žabokrtský, Amarsanaa Ganbold, Šárka Dohnalová, Magda Ševčíková, Kateřina Pelegrinová, Fausto Giunchiglia, Ryan Cotterell, and Ekaterina Vylomova. 2022. The sigmorphon 2022 shared task on morpheme segmentation. In *19th SIGMORPHON Workshop on Computational Research in Phonetics, Phonology, and Morphology*. Association for Computational Linguistics.

Kaj Bostrom and Greg Durrett. 2020. Byte pair encoding is suboptimal for language model pretraining. In *Findings of the Association for Computational Linguistics: EMNLP 2020*, pages 4617–4624, Online. Association for Computational Linguistics.

John S Bridle. 1990. Probabilistic interpretation of feedforward classification network outputs, with relationships to statistical pattern recognition. In *Neurocomputing*, pages 227–236. Springer.

Martina Forster, Clara Meister, and Ryan Cotterell. 2021. Searching for search errors in neural morphological inflection. In *Proceedings of the 16th Conference of the European Chapter of the Association for Computational Linguistics: Main Volume*, pages 1388–1394, Online. Association for Computational Linguistics.

Philip Gage. 1994. A new algorithm for data compression. *C Users Journal*, 12(2):23–38.

Matthias Gallé. 2019. Investigating the effectiveness of BPE: The power of shorter sequences. In *Proceedings of the 2019 Conference on Empirical Methods in Natural Language Processing and the 9th International Joint Conference on Natural Language Processing (EMNLP-IJCNLP)*, pages 1375–1381, Hong Kong, China. Association for Computational Linguistics.

Xuanli He, Gholamreza Haffari, and Mohammad Norouzi. 2020. Dynamic programming encoding for subword segmentation in neural machine translation. In *Proceedings of the 58th Annual Meeting of the Association for Computational Linguistics*, pages 3042–3051, Online. Association for Computational Linguistics.

Matthias Huck, Simon Riess, and Alexander Fraser. 2017. Target-side word segmentation strategies for neural machine translation. In *Proceedings of the Second Conference on Machine Translation*, pages 56–67, Copenhagen, Denmark. Association for Computational Linguistics.

Katharina Kann, Ryan Cotterell, and Hinrich Schütze. 2016. Neural morphological analysis: Encoding-decoding canonical segments. In *Proceedings of the 2016 Conference on Empirical Methods in Natural Language Processing*, pages 961–967, Austin, Texas. Association for Computational Linguistics.

Taku Kudo. 2018. Subword regularization: Improving neural network translation models with multiple subword candidates. In *Proceedings of the 56th Annual Meeting of the Association for Computational Linguistics (Volume 1: Long Papers)*, pages 66–75, Melbourne, Australia. Association for Computational Linguistics.

Taku Kudo and John Richardson. 2018. SentencePiece: A simple and language independent subword tokenizer and detokenizer for neural text processing. In *Proceedings of the 2018 Conference on Empirical Methods in Natural Language Processing: System Demonstrations*, pages 66–71, Brussels, Belgium. Association for Computational Linguistics.

Clara Meister, Ryan Cotterell, and Tim Vieira. 2020. If beam search is the answer, what was the question? In *Proceedings of the 2020 Conference on Empirical Methods in Natural Language Processing (EMNLP)*, pages 2173–2185, Online. Association for Computational Linguistics.

Sabrina J Mielke, Zaid Alyafeai, Elizabeth Salesky, Colin Raffel, Manan Dey, Matthias Gallé, Arun Raja, Chenglei Si, Wilson Y Lee, Benoît Sagot, and Samson Tan. 2021. Between words and characters: A brief history of open-vocabulary modeling and tokenization in nlp. *arXiv preprint arXiv:2112.10508*.

Myle Ott, Sergey Edunov, Alexei Baevski, Angela Fan, Sam Gross, Nathan Ng, David Grangier, and Michael Auli. 2019. fairseq: A fast, extensible toolkit for sequence modeling. In *Proceedings of the 2019 Conference of the North American Chapter of the Association for Computational Linguistics (Demonstrations)*, pages 48–53, Minneapolis, Minnesota. Association for Computational Linguistics.

Kyubyong Park, Joohong Lee, Seongbo Jang, and Dawoon Jung. 2020. An empirical study of tokenization strategies for various Korean NLP tasks. In *Proceedings of the 1st Conference of the Asia-Pacific Chapter of the Association for Computational Linguistics and the 10th International Joint Conference on Natural Language Processing*, pages 133–142, Suzhou, China. Association for Computational Linguistics.

Ben Peters and André F. T. Martins. 2019. IT–IST at the SIGMORPHON 2019 shared task: Sparse two-headed models for inflection. In *Proceedings of the 16th Workshop on Computational Research in Phonetics, Phonology, and Morphology*, pages 50–56, Florence, Italy. Association for Computational Linguistics.

Ben Peters and André F. T. Martins. 2020. One-size-fits-all multilingual models. In *Proceedings of the 17th SIGMORPHON Workshop on Computational Research in Phonetics, Phonology, and Morphology*, pages 63–69, Online. Association for Computational Linguistics.

Ben Peters and André F. T. Martins. 2021. Smoothing and shrinking the sparse Seq2Seq search space. In *Proceedings of the 2021 Conference of the North American Chapter of the Association for Computational Linguistics: Human Language Technologies*, pages 2642–2654, Online. Association for Computational Linguistics.

Ben Peters, Vlad Niculae, and André F. T. Martins. 2019. Sparse sequence-to-sequence models. In *Proceedings of the 57th Annual Meeting of the Association for Computational Linguistics*, pages 1504–1519, Florence, Italy. Association for Computational Linguistics.

Ivan Provilkov, Dmitrii Emelianenko, and Elena Voita. 2020. BPE-dropout: Simple and effective subword regularization. In *Proceedings of the 58th Annual Meeting of the Association for Computational Linguistics*, pages 1882–1892, Online. Association for Computational Linguistics.

Aku Rouhe, Stig-Arne Grönroos, Sami Virpioja, Mathias Creutz, and Mikko Kurimo. 2022. Morfessor-enriched features and multilingual training for canonical morphological segmentation. In *19th SIGMORPHON Workshop on Computational Research in Phonetics, Phonology, and Morphology*. Association for Computational Linguistics.

Lane Schwartz, Francis Tyers, Lori Levin, Christo Kirov, Patrick Littell, Chi-kiu Lo, Emily Prud'hommeaux, Hyunji Hayley Park, Kenneth Steimel, Rebecca Knowles, Jeffrey Micher, Lonny Strunk, Han Liu, Coleman Haley, Katherine J. Zhang, Robbie Jimmerson, Vasilisa Andriyanets, Aldrian Obaja Muis, Naoki Otani, Jong Hyuk Park, and Zhisong Zhang. 2020. Neural polysynthetic language modelling. Final Report of the Neural Polysynthetic Language Modelling Team at the 2019 Frederick Jelinek Memorial Summer Workshop.

Rico Sennrich, Barry Haddow, and Alexandra Birch. 2016. Neural machine translation of rare words with subword units. In *Proceedings of the 54th Annual Meeting of the Association for Computational Linguistics (Volume 1: Long Papers)*, pages 1715–1725, Berlin, Germany. Association for Computational Linguistics.

Peter Smit, Sami Virpioja, Stig-Arne Grönroos, and Mikko Kurimo. 2014. Morfessor 2.0: Toolkit for statistical morphological segmentation. In *Proceedings of the Demonstrations at the 14th Conference of the European Chapter of the Association for Computational Linguistics*, pages 21–24, Gothenburg, Sweden. Association for Computational Linguistics.

Felix Stahlberg and Bill Byrne. 2019. On NMT search errors and model errors: Cat got your tongue? In *Proceedings of the 2019 Conference on Empirical Methods in Natural Language Processing and the 9th International Joint Conference on Natural Language Processing (EMNLP-IJCNLP)*, pages 3356–3362, Hong Kong, China. Association for Computational Linguistics.

Samson Tan, Shafiq Joty, Lav Varshney, and Min-Yen Kan. 2020. Mind your inflections! Improving NLP for non-standard Englishes with Base-Inflection Encoding. In *Proceedings of the 2020 Conference on Empirical Methods in Natural Language Processing (EMNLP)*, pages 5647–5663, Online. Association for Computational Linguistics.

Constantino Tsallis. 1988. Possible generalization of Boltzmann-Gibbs statistics. *Journal of Statistical Physics*, 52:479–487.

Ashish Vaswani, Noam Shazeer, Niki Parmar, Jakob Uszkoreit, Llion Jones, Aidan N Gomez, Łukasz Kaiser, and Illia Polosukhin. 2017. Attention is all you need. In *Proc. NeurIPS*.

Andrew Viterbi. 1967. Error bounds for convolutional codes and an asymptotically optimum decoding algorithm. *IEEE transactions on Information Theory*, 13(2):260–269.

Silvan Wehrli, Simon Clematide, and Peter Makarov. 2022. Cluzh at sigmorphon 2022 shared tasks on morpheme segmentation and inflection generation. In *19th SIGMORPHON Workshop on Computational Research in Phonetics, Phonology, and Morphology*. Association for Computational Linguistics.

Marion Weller-Di Marco and Alexander Fraser. 2020. Modeling word formation in English–German neural machine translation. In *Proceedings of the 58th Annual Meeting of the Association for Computational Linguistics*, pages 4227–4232, Online. Association for Computational Linguistics.

A Tsallis Entropy

$$\mathsf{H}_\alpha(\boldsymbol{p}) := \begin{cases} \frac{1}{\alpha(\alpha-1)} \sum_j \left(p_j - p_j^\alpha\right), & \alpha \neq 1, \\ -\sum_j p_j \log p_j, & \alpha = 1 \end{cases}$$

Word-level Morpheme segmentation using Transformer neural network

Tsolmon Zundui and **Chinbat Avaajargal**
National University of Mongolia
tsolmonz@num.edu.mn, chinbat.carl@gmail.com

Abstract

This paper presents the submission of team NUM DI to the SIGMORPHON 2022 Task on Morpheme Segmentation Part 1, word-level morpheme segmentation. We explore the transformer neural network approach to the shared task. We develop monolingual models for world-level morpheme segmentation and focus on improving the model by using various training strategies to improve accuracy and generalization across languages.

1 Introduction

Morphological analysis is the heart of nearly all natural language processing tasks, such as sentiment analysis, machine translation, information retrieval, etc. Such natural language processing tasks become infeasible without any morphological analysis. One reason is the sparsity resulting from a high number of word forms that introduce out-of-vocabulary (OOV). Morphological segmentation is a way to deal with language sparsity by introducing the standard segments within the words rather than dealing with word forms (having multiple morphemes).

Morpheme segmentation is a type of morphological analysis in which words are divided into surface forms of morphemes, for example, successfulness = success @@ful @@ness. Automated morpheme segmentation was studied in the early years of natural language development (NLP). However, significant progress has been made in recent years in using various machine learning techniques.

Since morphemes are the smallest meaningful language units, information about the morphemic structure of words is already used in various NLP applications and additional tasks, including machine translation and recognition of semantically related words (cognates).

In this paper, we proposes a supervised method for word-level morphological segmentation using a transformer neural network. The task of machine translation has seen significant progress in recent times with the advent of Transformer-based models (Vaswani et al., 2017) for this year's SIGMORPHON 2022 shared task on morpheme segemntation (Batsuren et al., 2022a) which at the word level, participants will be asked to segment a given word into a sequence of morphemes. Input words contains all types of word forms: root words, derived words, inflected words, and compound words. However, to the best of our knowledge, there has not been work that applies such morpheme segmentation transformer-based models.

The paper is organized as follows: Section 2 addresses the related work on supervised morpheme segmentation, Section 3 describes the data used in training, Section 5 describes the model architecture, and section 6 presents the experiment results.

2 Related work

Z. Harris in (Harris, 1970) proposed the earliest method of morpheme segmentation. It detects morpheme boundaries by letter variety statistics (LVS) (Çöltekin, 2010). Morfessor system (Creutz and Lagus, 2007), (Smit et al., 2014) exploits unsupervised machine learning methods to be trained on a large unlabelled text. Another kind of semi-supervised machine learning for morpheme segmentation (Ruokolainen et al., 2014) was based on conditional random fields; the task was considered as sequential classifying and labeling letters of a given the word. A pure supervised method with significantly better quality for the twofold task of morpheme segmentation with classification was proposed in (Sorokin and Kravtsova, 2018); it was effective due to applying a convolutional neural network and training on the representative labeled data. The model outperforms all previous morpheme segmentation models, giving F-measure up

19th SIGMORPHON Workshop on Computational Research in Phonetics, Phonology, and Morphology, pages 139 - 143
July 14, 2022

to 98% on morpheme boundaries. Recent works developed two more supervised machine learning models for morpheme segmentation with classification for Russian words (Bolshakova and Sapin, 2019a), (Bolshakova and Sapin, 2019b). The first is based on decision trees with gradient boosting, while the second applies Bi-LSTM neural network. However, they were developed for morpheme segmentation applied CNN, Bi-LSTM, not applied transformer neural network. Therefore, to study possible ways to build a more broad supervised model with a transformer neural network.

3 Data

A dataset for this task, the organizer integrated all basic types of morphological databases (including UniMorph (Kirov et al., 2018; McCarthy et al., 2020; Batsuren et al., 2022b) – inflectional morphology; MorphyNet (Batsuren et al., 2021) – derivational morphology; Universal Dependencies (Nivre et al., 2017) and ten editions of Wiktionary – compound morphology and root words) cover 9 languages. 8 of these languages were available initially, while 1 surprise language, Mongolia, was released one week before the submission deadline. Each language had split a train and a development sample. The amount of data for the different languages vary in size, from 18966 (Mongolian) to 926098 (Hungarian). Each sample occupies a single line and consists of input word, the corresponding morpheme sequence, and the corresponding morphological category. Except for Spanish, eight languages have morphological word categories shown in table 1. All the data is available on the Github[1] page.

(1) **Example Training Set**

```
pentazole penta @@azo @@ole 010
nyala nyala 000
biots biot @@s 100
```

(2) **Example Development Set**

```
newspaper new @@s @@paper 011
players play @@er @@s 110
congruity congruent @@ity 010
```

(3) **Example Test Set**

```
hyperonym
distance
```

[1]https://github.com/sigmorphon/2022SegmentationST

To preprocess the dataset, we used the fairseq command-line tool to binarize the training data, making it easy for developers and researchers to directly run operations from the terminal.

4 Model architecture

We use the character level Transformer implementation of *fairseq* (Ott et al., 2019). Our model is composed of one encoder input word, and one decoder output segmentation of the word. We train a monolingual word segmentation model for each given language with identical parameters, 50 epochs, 1 encoder layer, 1 decoder layer, 0.0001 learning rate, using the Adam optimizer (Kingma and Ba, 2014) and the cross-entropy loss. Various hyperparameters of our Transformer model were experimentally tested in several experiments. The resulted model has the encoder and decoder layer with 128 hidden units, and the batch size is 32. Encoder and decoder more layers slightly improve the quality (less than 0.5%), but the model became too heavy both for training and evaluation. We also use created checkpoints to save the checkpoint the latest and the best ones. It is also a safe guard in case the training gets disrupted due to some unforeseen issue.

4.1 Evaluation

For the word-level segmentation shared task, the following evaluation metrics are provided.

- Precision: fraction of correctly predicted morphemes on all predicted morphemes
- Recall: ratio of correctly predicted morphemes on all gold morphemes
- F-measure: the harmonic mean of the precision and recall
- Edit distance: average Levenshtein distance between the predicted output and the gold instance.

We compare our results with the baseline model, in which the multilingual Bert tokenizer is shown in table 2.

5 Results

Results of the evaluation are shown in Table 2, where the leftmost column stands for the ISO-639 language code, the next one for the number of train data, the next one for the number of test data, rest

Word class	Description	Example
000	Root words	Vivian - Vivian
001	Compound only	snowfight - snow @@fight
010	Derivation only	unafraid - un @@afraid
011	Derivation and Compound	peacekeeper - peace @@keep @@er
100	Inflection only	descendents - descendent @@s
101	Inflection and Compound	setbacks - set @@back @@s
110	Inflection and Derivation	brandishing - brand @@ish @@ing
111	Inflection, Derivation, Compound	faultfinders - fault @@find @@er @@s

Table 1: Word categories.

Lang.	Train size	Test size	Models	Precision	Recall	F-measure	Distance
eng	458692	57755	Transformer	84.02	83.12	83.56	0.48
			Baseline	20.99	28.79	24.28	2.69
ces	30694	4000	Transformer	88.49	87.52	88.00	0.35
			Baseline	22.10	19.72	20.84	2.94
fra	252671	31588	Transformer	87.48	84.14	85.78	0.72
			baseline	11.08	14.00	12.37	4.32
hun	742239	95278	Transformer	96.33	95.50	95.91	0.21
			baseline	20.88	27.81	23.85	3.54
ita	369208	46153	Transformer	90.38	88.74	89.55	0.58
			baseline	8.12	10.54	9.18	5.35
lat	705862	88234	Transformer	97.03	95.68	96.35	0.08
			baseline	6.76	13.17	8.94	4.14
mon	15171	1900	Transformer	87.99	83.32	85.59	0.58
			baseline	5.89	10.59	7.57	4.51
rus	627367	78425	Transformer	95.6	93.42	94.5	0.46
			baseline	13.23	14.13	13.67	7.62
spa	688673	86088	Transformer	96.33	94.33	95.32	0.29
			baseline	15.76	17.91	16.76	5.20

Table 2: Comparison of our model and baseline for morpheme segmentation

of the columns stand for the evaluation metrics provided by shared task. It is clearly seen that our model performs much better in all evaluation metrics than the baseline model. We expected rich morphological language models to get lower scores than others. However, the results show that the English word segmentation model has a lower recall, precision, and f-measure scores than other language models; even Mongolian has fewest training data. In all metrics, the Latin word segmentation model had the highest score. All models trained on more than 60,000 training data have more than 90 points in the recall, precision, and f-measure score. In table 3, we compare the f-measure score of our model with team DeepSPIN-3 (Peters and Martins, 2022). Although our model performed poorly in all languages, it performed competitively.

6 Conclusion

We have presented the monolingual models for morpheme segmentation in 9 languages. Our model run outperforms the baseline. Even though our models as implemented prior to submission failed to attain reasonable evaluations scores on the word-level morpheme segmentation task, our results indicate that our model has the potential to have a better performance after fine-tuning and the good performance of our model under varying morphological complexity languages.

In future work, we plan on exploring multilingual word-level morpheme segmentation a model.

Language	Teams	F-measure
eng	NUM DI	83.56
	DeepSPIN-3	**93.63**
ces	NUM DI	88.0
	DeepSPIN-3	**93.84**
fra	NUM DI	85.78
	DeepSPIN-3	**95.73**
hun	NUM DI	95.91
	DeepSPIN-3	**98.72**
ita	NUM DI	89.55
	DeepSPIN-3	**97.43**
lat	NUM DI	96.35
	DeepSPIN-3	**99.38**
mon	NUM DI	85.59
	DeepSPIN-3	**98.51**
rus	NUM DI	94.5
	DeepSPIN-3	**99.35**
spa	NUM DI	95.32
	DeepSPIN-3	**99.04**

Table 3: Comparison of our model and model of the best team for word-level morpheme segmentation

Author contribution

All authors equally contributed to this work.

Acknowledgement

Thanks to Chinbat Avaajargal for dedicated work on this task. Thanks to several anonymous reviewers for their constructive feedback.

References

Khuyagbaatar Batsuren, Gábor Bella, and Fausto Giunchiglia. 2021. Morphynet: a large multilingual database of derivational and inflectional morphology. In *Proceedings of the 18th SIGMORPHON Workshop on Computational Research in Phonetics, Phonology, and Morphology*, pages 39–48.

Khuyagbaatar Batsuren, Gábor Bella, Aryaman Arora, Viktor Martinović, Kyle Gorman, Zdeněk Žabokrtský, Amarsanaa Ganbold, Šárka Dohnalová, Magda Ševčíková, Kateřina Pelegrinová, Fausto Giunchiglia, Ryan Cotterell, and Ekaterina Vylomova. 2022a. The sigmorphon 2022 shared task on morpheme segmentation. In *19th SIGMORPHON Workshop on Computational Research in Phonetics, Phonology, and Morphology*.

Khuyagbaatar Batsuren, Omer Goldman, Salam Khalifa, Nizar Habash, Witold Kieraś, Gábor Bella, Brian Leonard, Garrett Nicolai, Kyle Gorman, Yustinus Ghanggo Ate, Maria Ryskina, Sabrina J. Mielke, Elena Budianskaya, Charbel El-Khaissi, Tiago Pimentel, Michael Gasser, William Lane, Mohit Raj, Matt Coler, Jaime Rafael Montoya Samame, Delio Siticonatzi Camaiteri, Esaú Zumaeta Rojas, Didier López Francis, Arturo Oncevay, Juan López Bautista, Gema Celeste Silva Villegas, Lucas Torroba Hennigen, Adam Ek, David Guriel, Peter Dirix, Jean-Philippe Bernardy, Andrey Scherbakov, Aziyana Bayyr-ool, Antonios Anastasopoulos, Roberto Zariquiey, Karina Sheifer, Sofya Ganieva, Hilaria Cruz, Ritván Karahóğa, Stella Markantonatou, George Pavlidis, Matvey Plugaryov, Elena Klyachko, Ali Salehi, Candy Angulo, Jatayu Baxi, Andrew Krizhanovsky, Natalia Krizhanovskaya, Elizabeth Salesky, Clara Vania, Sardana Ivanova, Jennifer White, Rowan Hall Maudslay, Josef Valvoda, Ran Zmigrod, Paula Czarnowska, Irene Nikkarinen, Aelita Salchak, Brijesh Bhatt, Christopher Straughn, Zoey Liu, Jonathan North Washington, Yuval Pinter, Duygu Ataman, Marcin Wolinski, Totok Suhardijanto, Anna Yablonskaya, Niklas Stoehr, Hossep Dolatian, Zahroh Nuriah, Shyam Ratan, Francis M. Tyers, Edoardo M. Ponti, Grant Aiton, Aryaman Arora, Richard J. Hatcher, Ritesh Kumar, Jeremiah Young, Daria Rodionova, Anastasia Yemelina, Taras Andrushko, Igor Marchenko, Polina Mashkovtseva, Alexandra Serova, Emily Prud'hommeaux, Maria Nepomniashchaya, Fausto Giunchiglia, Eleanor Chodroff, Mans Hulden, Miikka Silfverberg, Arya D. McCarthy, David Yarowsky, Ryan Cotterell, Reut Tsarfaty, and Ekaterina Vylomova. 2022b. Unimorph 4.0: Universal morphology.

Elena Bolshakova and Alexander Sapin. 2019a. Bi-lstm model for morpheme segmentation of russian words. In *Conference on Artificial Intelligence and Natural Language*, pages 151–160. Springer.

Elena Bolshakova and Alexander Sapin. 2019b. Comparing models of morpheme analysis for russian words based on machine learning. In *Proc. of the International Conference Dialogue*, volume 2019, pages 104–113.

Çağrı Çöltekin. 2010. Improving successor variety for morphological segmentation. *LOT Occasional Series*, 16:13–28.

Mathias Creutz and Krista Lagus. 2007. Unsupervised models for morpheme segmentation and morphology learning. *ACM Transactions on Speech and Language Processing (TSLP)*, 4(1):1–34.

Zellig S Harris. 1970. Morpheme boundaries within words: Report on a computer test. In *Papers in Structural and Transformational Linguistics*, pages 68–77. Springer.

Diederik P Kingma and Jimmy Ba. 2014. Adam: A method for stochastic optimization. *arXiv preprint arXiv:1412.6980*.

Christo Kirov, Ryan Cotterell, John Sylak-Glassman, Géraldine Walther, Ekaterina Vylomova, Patrick Xia, Manaal Faruqui, Sabrina J Mielke, Arya D McCarthy,

Sandra Kübler, et al. 2018. Unimorph 2.0: universal morphology. *arXiv preprint arXiv:1810.11101*.

Arya D McCarthy, Christo Kirov, Matteo Grella, Amrit Nidhi, Patrick Xia, Kyle Gorman, Ekaterina Vylomova, Sabrina J Mielke, Garrett Nicolai, Miikka Silfverberg, et al. 2020. Unimorph 3.0: Universal morphology.

Joakim Nivre, Željko Agić, Lars Ahrenberg, Lene Antonsen, Maria Jesus Aranzabe, Masayuki Asahara, Luma Ateyah, Mohammed Attia, Aitziber Atutxa, Liesbeth Augustinus, et al. 2017. Universal dependencies 2.1.

Myle Ott, Sergey Edunov, Alexei Baevski, Angela Fan, Sam Gross, Nathan Ng, David Grangier, and Michael Auli. 2019. fairseq: A fast, extensible toolkit for sequence modeling. *arXiv preprint arXiv:1904.01038*.

Ben Peters and André F. T. Martins. 2022. Beyond characters: Subword-level morpheme segmentation. In *19th SIGMORPHON Workshop on Computational Research in Phonetics, Phonology, and Morphology*.

Teemu Ruokolainen, Oskar Kohonen, Sami Virpioja, and Mikko Kurimo. 2014. Painless semi-supervised morphological segmentation using conditional random fields. In *Proceedings of the 14th Conference of the European Chapter of the Association for Computational Linguistics, volume 2: Short Papers*, pages 84–89.

Peter Smit, Sami Virpioja, Stig-Arne Grönroos, Mikko Kurimo, et al. 2014. Morfessor 2.0: Toolkit for statistical morphological segmentation. In *The 14th Conference of the European Chapter of the Association for Computational Linguistics (EACL), Gothenburg, Sweden, April 26-30, 2014*. Aalto University.

Alexey Sorokin and Anastasia Kravtsova. 2018. Deep convolutional networks for supervised morpheme segmentation of russian language. In *Conference on Artificial Intelligence and Natural Language*, pages 3–10. Springer.

Ashish Vaswani, Noam Shazeer, Niki Parmar, Jakob Uszkoreit, Llion Jones, Aidan N Gomez, Łukasz Kaiser, and Illia Polosukhin. 2017. Attention is all you need. *Advances in neural information processing systems*, 30.

Morfessor-enriched features and multilingual training for canonical morphological segmentation

Aku Rouhe[◇] **Stig-Arne Grönroos**[♡♠] **Sami Virpioja**[♡]
Mathias Creutz[♡] **Mikko Kurimo**[◇]
[◇] Department of Signal Processing and Acoustics, Aalto University, Finland
[♡] Department of Digital Humanities, University of Helsinki, Finland
[♠] Silo.AI, Finland
[♡] name.surname@helsinki.fi
[◇] name.surname@aalto.fi

Abstract

In our submission to the SIGMORPHON 2022 Shared Task on Morpheme Segmentation, we study whether an unsupervised morphological segmentation method, Morfessor, can help in a supervised setting. Previous research has shown the effectiveness of the approach in semi-supervised settings with small amounts of labeled data. The current tasks vary in data size: the amount of word-level annotated training data is much larger, but the amount of sentence-level annotated training data remains small. Our approach is to pre-segment the input data for a neural sequence-to-sequence model with the unsupervised method. As the unsupervised method can be trained with raw text data, we use Wikipedia to increase the amount of training data. In addition, we train multilingual models for the sentence-level task. The results for the Morfessor-enriched features are mixed, showing benefit for all three sentence-level tasks but only some of the word-level tasks. The multilingual training yields considerable improvements over the monolingual sentence-level models, but it negates the effect of the enriched features.

1 Introduction

Current use of subword segmentation in neural natural language processing (NLP) with unsupervised segmentation methods such as BPE (Sennrich et al., 2015), SentencePiece (Kudo and Richardson, 2018), and Morfessor (Creutz and Lagus, 2002; Virpioja et al., 2013) mainly focuses on finding short and frequent subwords that give good performance in the NLP application, while putting less weight on linguistic correctness. The level of segmentation varies by the frequency of the word: frequent words retain their affixes, while rare words, such as rare proper names, are heavily segmented into syllable-like units or even characters. These methods typically perform *surface* segmentation, meaning that the subwords can be concatenated back into the surface form of the word without any transformation to account for phonological processes

$$\text{e.g.}\quad profibrotic \mapsto pro + fibr + ot + ic.$$

However, when linguistic fidelity is of importance—for example because the segments are analyzed statistically as opposed to using a neural model—a supervised segmentation method may be more suitable. The goal is to output morphemes, the smallest meaning-bearing linguistic units. In *canonical morphological segmentation* (Kann et al., 2016), instead of segmenting into surface forms of morphemes, the different allomorphs are mapped into a single canonical form, reversing any phonological changes.

$$\text{e.g.}\quad profibrotic \mapsto pro + fibre + osis + ic.$$

It is not always possible to give a single correct analysis for any particular surface form. A surface form may be homonymous, with inflections or derivations from two or more lemmas. In order to disambiguate the meanings to choose a single analysis from several alternatives, it is necessary to use the surrounding sentence context. In Task 2 of this shared task, such sentence level segmentation is performed.

$$\begin{aligned}\text{e.g.}\quad & she\quad rose\quad up \mapsto she\quad rise + ed\quad up\\ & a\quad red\quad rose \mapsto a\quad red\quad rose.\end{aligned}$$

Word-level morpheme segmentation is more widely studied than sentence-level morpheme segmentation. In part, the focus on word level segmentation is due to the historically limited ability of models to exploit all of the available context. With neural sequence to sequence (seq2seq) models, this limitation can easily be lifted. Limited availability of labeled data for the sentence level task provides

19th SIGMORPHON Workshop on Computational Research in Phonetics, Phonology, and Morphology, pages 144 - 151
July 14, 2022 ©2022 Association for Computational Linguistics

a second reason for the popularity of word-level segmentation.

This work presents the AUUH (Aalto University - University of Helsinki) team submission to the SIGMORPHON 2022 Shared Task on Morpheme Segmentation (Batsuren et al., 2022). In this shared task, the imbalance of training data persists. For the word-level Task 1, there is ample training data, ranging from 15 000 labeled words for the lowest resourced language, Mongolian, to hundreds of thousands of words for the higher resourced languages. Task 1 has between 3 and 30 times as much data as in sentence-level Task 2. In addition to the labeled data, an order of magnitude more unlabeled data can easily be sourced.

Considering that these types of data are available in very different amounts, there is an opportunity to improve especially the sentence-level performance by exploiting the other types of data. In this work, we use large amounts of unlabeled data to enrich the input with features from an unsupervised segmentation model. This feature set augmentation approach, which combines the strengths of generative and discriminative models, has previously been applied for word-level surface segmentation (Ruokolainen et al., 2014; Grönroos et al., 2019). Additionally, we use the word-level labeled data through multi-task and multi-lingual training.

Our systems are fully data-driven and language-independent, requiring no linguistic resources beyond the training data. All the software used in the systems has open-source implementations.

2 Methods

Our approach for the shared tasks consists of a neural seq2seq model, enrichment of data with features learned in an unsupervised manner, and multi-task and multilingual training. We submitted six different configurations, which we refer to as Systems A–F in the following.

2.1 Seq2seq model

We apply a sequence-to-sequence (seq2seq) model to map from character sequences to character sequences. In our baseline models, the input is the character sequence of the surface form of the word. In our enriched models, the surface form is augmented with predicted segmentation boundary symbols. In all cases, the output is the sequence of canonical morphemes and segmentation boundary symbols, decoded on character level. We treat the boundary marker "@@" as a single symbol[1]. In the original output format, the morphemes are separated by a space, which we simply ignore in the seq2seq data and add back in the detokenization step. Our seq2seq models are implemented using the Marian NMT (Junczys-Dowmunt et al., 2018) Neural Machine Translation framework.

Even though the amount of data is of a standard size for segmentation, it is small compared to typical machine translation data sets. Therefore, when designing the neural network architectures, we experiment with neural architectures from the literature on low-resource neural machine translation.

Following Sennrich and Zhang (2019), our models C–F use a bidirectional GRU bideep (Miceli Barone et al., 2017) architecture. We modify the architecture slightly by lowering the embedding dimension from 512 to 128, as we have a character-level model instead of a subword model.

Inspired by Araabi and Monz (2020), we try reducing the capacity of Transformer-base (Vaswani et al., 2017) to better suit the small data setting, reducing the number of layers in both encoder and decoder to 5, reducing the feed-forward dimension to 512, reducing the number of attention heads to 2, increasing dropout to 0.3, adding 0.1 target dropout (and in our implementation 0.1 source dropout as well), and increasing label smoothing to 0.5. However, in preliminary experiments this performed worse than Transformer-base. Instead, a smaller Transformer-base modification, which we title Transformer-base$_{mod}$, where we reduce the feed-forward dimension to 1024, and add 0.1 source and target dropout, yields our best Transformer results in preliminary experiments.

For the monolingual word-level tasks we use the bideep GRU architecture, as that architecture worked reliably even with limited data. For the multi-task, multi-lingual models A–B, which are trained with considerably more data overall, we use the Transformer-base$_{mod}$ architecture.

The seq2seq models are trained for 50 epochs with the cross-entropy loss, with early stopping based on validation criterion improvement stalling. As a validation criterion, we use the official evaluation F-measure. This choice yielded consistent improvements over the cross-entropy criterion in preliminary experiments.

[1] For clarity, represented later in the paper as a single symbol @.

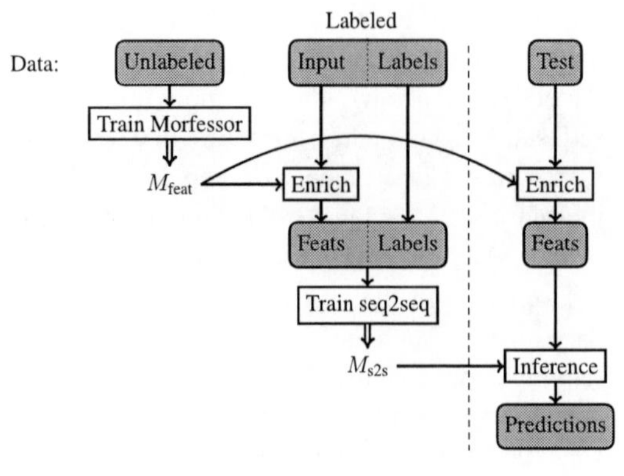

Figure 1: Feature enrichment process.

2.2 Enrichment with unsupervised features

The feature enrichment process is shown in Figure 1. For training the unsupervised features, the training data consists of a large word list extracted from an unlabeled corpus. Morfessor Baseline (Creutz and Lagus, 2002; Virpioja et al., 2013), an unsupervised generative model, is trained using the unlabeled data only.

The words in the labeled training set are first presegmented using the Morfessor Baseline model. The predicted segmentation is turned into features by adding a reserved unicode character at the predicted segmentation boundaries, and then concatenating to form the new input string.

For example, the input string *"subneural"* is segmented by Morfessor as

$$subneural \mapsto s\ u\ b\ \sqcup\ n\ e\ u\ r\ a\ l.$$

The seq2seq model then takes this feature representation as input, and outputs the canonical segmentation:

$$s\ u\ b \sqcup n\ e\ u\ r\ a\ l \mapsto s\ u\ b\ @\ n\ e\ u\ r\ o\ n\ @\ a\ l.$$

At decoding time a two-step procedure is used: first the features for the desired words are produced using the Morfessor Baseline model. The final segmentation can then be decoded from the seq2seq model.

The idea is that the features from the unsupervised generative model allow the statistical patterns found in the large unannotated data to be exploited. Two tasks remain for the seq2seq model to learn: determining when the predictions of Morfessor are reliable in order to correct its mistakes, and finding the mapping from predicted surface morphemes to the canonical forms of morphemes. We hypothesize that these two tasks are easier to learn as part of a pipeline system, compared to learning the mapping from the unsegmented surface form into canonical morphemes directly as an end-to-end task.

2.2.1 Morfessor

Morfessor is a family of language-independent unsupervised and semi-supervised morpheme segmentation models. The first variant, later called Morfessor Baseline, was introduced by Creutz and Lagus (2002). It is an unsupervised algorithm that makes use of a context-insensitive maximization criterion based on unigram probabilities. A Python implementation and extensions were provided by Virpioja et al. (2013) with further improvements by Grönroos et al. (2020). Further unsupervised variants introduce context-sensitive segmentation, identifying possible prefixes, stems and suffixes as a biproduct. The so-called Morfessor Categories-MAP model (Creutz and Lagus, 2005, 2007) produces a hierarchical segmentation structure, which later evolved into a flat structure in Morfessor FlatCat (Grönroos et al., 2014). Kohonen et al. (2010) extended to semi-supervised learning for situations where small amounts of linguistic gold standard analyses are available.

In this work, we focus on using Morfessor Baseline, leaving comparison of different Morfessor variants for future work.

2.2.2 Training data

For training the Morfessor models, we use the official word-level training sets, sentence-level training sets for the languages that had them available, and, in addition, Wikipedia dumps from 2022-04-01. The word-level data is added as is. From the sentence-level data, we include tokens that contained only letters in a script suitable for the language (Cyrillic for Mongolian, and Latin for English and Czech). Wikipedia dumps are processed with `wikiextractor` (Attardi, 2015). Only those tokens that have the correct script (Cyrillic for Mongolian and Russian, Latin for the rest) are included. In addition, to further reduce non-words and foreign words, we restrict word length to 40, word frequency to 3 for English and 2 for the rest, and either include only lowercase words (English) or lowercase the words (rest).

Finally, the words from the different sources are combined together for training Morfessor. The

	Wikipedia	Task 1	Task 2	total
labels	unlabeled	word-level	sentence-level	
ces	1097041	30694	4890	1107515
eng	466490	458692	15700	779878
fra	1502818	252671	0	1649688
hun	1356328	742239	0	1937213
ita	1171105	369208	0	1417499
lat	224277	705862	0	914135
mon	101136	15171	4961	108668
rus	2148379	627367	0	2483749
spa	1402977	688672	0	1942361

Table 1: Numbers of unique word forms in the training data sets.

frequencies of the words are ignored in training. Table 1 shows the numbers of unique word forms in the data sets.

We observe that with the exception of the Czech language, all subtasks of this shared task consist of canonical segmentation. For some words, the label sequence concatenates directly into the surface form, i.e. the canonicalization mapping of each morpheme is the identity function. The proportion of training words having this property vary by language, from 7.6% for Italian to 99.7% for Latin. However, for the Czech language, all the words in the training data have this property of concatenating directly into the surface form. As the Czech language does exhibit allomorphy (see e.g. Ševčíková, 2018), we conclude that the task for Czech was surface segmentation rather than canonical segmentation.

2.2.3 Hyper-parameter tuning

We use grid search to find the optimal corpus weight hyper-parameter for the Morfessor models. We test values in the range from 0.001 to 2.0. The word-level development sets are used for evaluation. However, the official evaluation scripts expect canonical segmentation, while Morfessor produces surface segmentation. Thus we rely on the EMMA-2 evaluation method and maximize the F_1-score between the model and reference segmentations.[2] EMMA-2, proposed by Virpioja et al. (2011), is a variant of the EMMA (Evaluation Metric for Morphological Analysis) introduced by Spiegler and Monson (2010). Both methods solve the problem of comparison of two different label sets by creating a mapping between the predicted and reference labels. The original EMMA method finds one-to-one assignment between the labels using the Hungarian algorithm, but the computational complexity prevents using it for large test sets. In contrast, EMMA-2 makes separate one-to-many assignments when calculating the precision and recall.

2.3 Multi-task and multilingual training

We train models that use two types of multi-task objectives. In the first one, we combine the word-level Task 1 with the sentence-level Task 2. In the second one, we train a multilingual model with the concatenation of all languages available in Task 2.

To distinguish tasks from each other, we use task selector tokens prefixed to the input, similar to Johnson et al. (2017). The language selector token is first, if used, and then in word tasks a special token is used. Sentence tasks do not have a separate selector token: no selector token implies a sentence task.

The multilingual model is then finetuned for an additional 50 epochs on each individual language. In a preliminary experiment, the additional training time did not by itself yield a better model. In finetuning, the sentence-level and word-level multi-task objective was kept. We finetuned models separately with word- and sentence-level validation data.

2.4 Systems

Table 2 lists the differences between the systems.

In the official competition, some of our submitted systems were trained on slightly different data than we intended, due to human error, and some

[2]Implementation available at `https://github.com/svirpioj/morphometrics`.

	Morfessor features	Architecture	Multilingual	Multitask
System A	✓	Transformer-base$_{mod}$	✓	✓
System B	–	Transformer-base$_{mod}$	✓	✓
System C	✓	Bideep GRU	–	✓
System D	–	Bideep GRU	–	✓
System E	✓	Bideep GRU	–	–
System F	–	Bideep GRU	–	–

Table 2: Differences between the six submitted systems.

systems were missing simply due to running out of time. The results in this description paper have been produced with corrected systems. The results that changed, or were added after the competition deadline, are marked with the symbol $\star$ in the tables.

3 Results

Tables 3 and 4 list the results of Tasks 1 and 2 respectively. Systems A and B, C and D, and E and F each form comparable pairs, where the former (e.g. System A) uses Morfessor-enriched features, and the latter (e.g. System B) is the same system without enriched features. In the result tables, these comparable pairs are separated with horizontal divider lines.

Some of our systems have the highest score of all shared task participants in specific subcategories of the evaluation. Our system B has the highest F_1-score (96.31%) and lowest Levenshtein distance (1.39) for the English sentence-level task. Our system A has the highest F_1-score (93.23%) for the English word-level evaluation category 001, i.e. compound words without inflectional or derivational affixes.

Tables 5 and 6 show Task 1 results by morphological category, for systems A–B and E–F respectively. For English, Russian, and Hungarian, the system using the Morfessor-enriched features performs better for most categories involving compounding, in particular the 001 category (only compounding). Of the languages in this shared task, only Hungarian and English vocabularies contain a substantial portion of compound words (17.32% and 6.79% respectively).

4 Discussion

The multilingual model without Morfessor-enriched features (System B) gives the best results in both tasks for the three languages (ces, eng, mon) for which we trained such a system. When using multilingual training, the Morfessor-enriched features are not beneficial. The unsupervised features may be less useful with the increased amount of training data in the multilingual setup, and varying granularities of the unsupervised segmentations for the different languages could confuse the multilingual model.

Without multilingual training, the results for enriched features are inconclusive for the word-level task, but clearly beneficial for the sentence-level task. The enriched features give better results for 5 languages (ces, eng, rus, mon, hun) in Task 1 and all three languages (ces, eng, mon) in Task 2.

Consistent with previous work (Grönroos et al., 2019), we find that Morfessor-features are useful for modeling the boundary between compound parts, which is challenging for supervised discriminative models on their own.

Except for the corpus weight hyper-parameter of the Morfessor model, we did not tune many parameters of the setup, such as thresholds for the words in the Wikipedia dumps, different weightings for the corpora, or use of the word frequencies in Morfessor training. More extensive optimization could lead to some improvements for the unsupervised features. It would also be possible to use the part of the data, for which the canonical morphemes correspond to surface morphemes as annotations for training semi-supervised Morfessor variants (Kohonen et al., 2010).

It is possible that using a different β for the F_β-score may result in better tuning. Finding the optimal value for β is left for future work. While computationally more burdensome, instead of searching for the best F_β-score of EMMA-2 for Morfessor's output, some parameters could also be optimized on the results of the final seq2seq model.

	ces	eng	fra	ita	lat	rus	mon	hun	spa
System A†	93.65	92.32	-	-	-	-	98.19	-	-
System B	⋆**93.68**	⋆**93.24**	-	-	-	-	⋆**98.29**	-	-
System E†	**90.71**	**87.10**	90.78	92.39	98.71	**94.33**	**96.06**	⋆**98.36**	⋆96.22
System F	90.28	86.40	**90.81**	**92.56**	**98.85**	93.68	95.32	98.34	**97.25**

Table 3: Word-level (Task 1) results (F1-measure [%]) on the official test sets. Results marked with ⋆ were not submitted to the official competition. Systems marked with † use Morfessor features.

	ces	eng	mon
System A†	88.60	96.22	82.19
System B	**90.42**	**96.31**	**82.59**
System C†	⋆**59.77**	⋆**93.44**	⋆**74.08**
System D	⋆59.08	88.07	⋆71.82
System E†	**61.92**	**85.04**	**72.67**
System F	51.47	82.34	66.38

Table 4: Sentence-level (Task 2) results (F1-measure [%]) on the official test sets. Results marked with ⋆ were not submitted to the official competition. Systems marked with † use Morfessor features.

5 Conclusions

We find that Morfessor-enriched features are beneficial for the sentence-level tasks, but see mixed results for the word-level tasks. The multilingual training yields considerable improvements for both tasks, but it negates the effect of the enriched features.

Category	Inflection	Derivation	Compounding	System	eng	mon
000	–	–	–	A†	80.39	87.16
000	–	–	–	B	⋆**82.63**	⋆**87.76**
001	–	–	✓	A†	**93.23**	100.00
001	–	–	✓	B	⋆93.02	⋆100.00
010	–	✓	–	A†	93.35	91.39
010	–	✓	–	B	⋆**93.86**	⋆**91.46**
011	–	✓	✓	A†	**95.60**	–
011	–	✓	✓	B	⋆94.98	–
100	✓	–	–	A†	89.27	99.35
100	✓	–	–	B	⋆**89.97**	⋆**99.69**
101	✓	–	✓	A†	94.03	100.00
101	✓	–	✓	B	⋆**95.76**	⋆100.00
110	✓	✓	–	A†	95.51	**99.56**
110	✓	✓	–	B	⋆**96.91**	⋆99.50
111	✓	✓	✓	A†	92.51	–
111	✓	✓	✓	B	⋆**94.33**	–

Table 5: Task 1 results for Systems A and B by morphological category (subsets of words containing inflection, derivation, compounding, or combinations of these). System A marked with † uses Morfessor features.

Acknowledgments

This work was funded by the European Research Council (ERC) under the EU's Horizon 2020 research and innovation program (FoTran project, agreement № 771113) and the Academy of Finland grant 345790 in ICT 2023 programme's project "Understanding speech and scene with ears and eyes". We also thank the CSC-IT Center for Science Ltd., for computational resources.

References

Ali Araabi and Christof Monz. 2020. Optimizing transformer for low-resource neural machine translation. In *Proceedings of the 28th International Conference on Computational Linguistics*, pages 3429–3435.

Giuseppe Attardi. 2015. Wikiextractor. `https://github.com/attardi/wikiextractor`.

Khuyagbaatar Batsuren, Gábor Bella, Aryaman Arora, Viktor Martinović, Kyle Gorman, Zdeněk Žabokrtský, Amarsanaa Ganbold, Šárka Dohnalová, Magda Ševčíková, Kateřina Pelegrinová, Fausto Giunchiglia, Ryan Cotterell, and Ekaterina Vylomova. 2022. The sigmorphon 2022 shared task on morpheme segmentation. In *19th SIGMORPHON Workshop on Computational Research in Phonetics, Phonology, and Morphology*.

Mathias Creutz and Krista Lagus. 2002. Unsupervised discovery of morphemes. In *Proceedings of the ACL-02 Workshop on Morphological and Phonological Learning (MPL)*, volume 6, pages 21–30, Philadelphia, Pennsylvania, USA. Association for Computa-

Category	Inflection	Derivation	Compounding	System	eng	fra	ita	rus	mon	hun	spa
000	–	–	–	E†	**76.34**	65.96	63.35	**63.38**	83.78	⋆**98.29**	⋆56.95
000	–	–	–	F	72.59	**66.32**	**64.34**	59.85	**87.76**	81.41	**63.69**
001	–	–	✓	E†	**90.85**	74.40	39.53	**65.35**	100.00	⋆**80.25**	⋆**17.14**
001	–	–	✓	F	89.61	**78.01**	**41.38**	57.73	100.00	80.09	14.95
010	–	✓	–	E†	**87.56**	**78.88**	84.11	80.88	**87.63**	⋆**93.21**	⋆67.10
010	–	✓	–	F	87.07	78.43	**84.75**	**80.96**	84.02	92.62	**75.87**
011	–	✓	✓	E†	**92.50**	**76.60**	50.67	**83.33**	–	⋆**86.52**	⋆41.38
011	–	✓	✓	F	90.79	73.43	**54.55**	78.48	–	85.55	**43.75**
100	✓	–	–	E†	84.48	91.21	**90.70**	**93.75**	**98.62**	⋆97.83	⋆96.52
100	✓	–	–	F	**84.91**	**91.22**	90.28	93.02	97.87	**97.87**	**97.12**
101	✓	–	✓	E†	**95.09**	77.46	59.04	**80.31**	100.00	⋆98.39	⋆44.44
101	✓	–	✓	F	91.03	**79.30**	**66.67**	78.86	100.00	**98.47**	**83.95**
110	✓	✓	–	E†	**89.37**	96.05	95.82	**95.83**	**97.09**	⋆99.29	⋆97.71
110	✓	✓	–	F	89.07	**96.25**	**96.22**	95.15	96.57	**99.30**	**98.64**
111	✓	✓	✓	E†	89.72	**89.89**	**72.94**	83.07	–	⋆**99.09**	⋆88.20
111	✓	✓	✓	F	**85.77**	85.55	67.47	**84.14**	–	98.81	**89.57**

Table 6: Task 1 results for Systems E and F by morphological category (subsets of words containing inflection, derivation, compounding, or combinations of these). System E marked with † uses Morfessor features. Results marked with ⋆ were not submitted to the official competition.

tional Linguistics.

Mathias Creutz and Krista Lagus. 2005. Inducing the morphological lexicon of a natural language from unannotated text. In *Proceedings of the International and Interdisciplinary Conference on Adaptive Knowledge Representation and Reasoning (AKRR'05)*, pages 106–113, Espoo, Finland.

Mathias Creutz and Krista Lagus. 2007. Unsupervised models for morpheme segmentation and morphology learning. *ACM Transactions on Speech and Language Processing*, 4(1).

Stig-Arne Grönroos, Sami Virpioja, and Mikko Kurimo. 2019. North Sámi morphological segmentation with low-resource semi-supervised sequence labeling. In *Proceedings of the Fifth International Workshop on Computational Linguistics for Uralic Languages*, pages 15–26.

Stig-Arne Grönroos, Sami Virpioja, and Mikko Kurimo. 2020. Morfessor EM+Prune: Improved subword segmentation with expectation maximization and pruning. In *Proceedings of the 12th Language Resources and Evaluation Conference*, Marseilles, France. ELRA.

Stig-Arne Grönroos, Sami Virpioja, Peter Smit, and Mikko Kurimo. 2014. Morfessor FlatCat: An HMM-based method for unsupervised and semi-supervised learning of morphology. In *Proceedings of COLING 2014, the 25th International Conference on Computational Linguistics*, pages 1177–1185, Dublin, Ireland. Association for Computational Linguistics.

Melvin Johnson, Mike Schuster, Quoc V. Le, Maxim Krikun, Yonghui Wu, Zhifeng Chen, Nikhil Thorat, Fernanda Viégas, Martin Wattenberg, Greg Corrado, Macduff Hughes, and Jeffrey Dean. 2017. Google's multilingual neural machine translation system: Enabling zero-shot translation. *Transactions of the Association for Computational Linguistics*, 5:339–351.

Marcin Junczys-Dowmunt, Roman Grundkiewicz, Tomasz Dwojak, Hieu Hoang, Kenneth Heafield, Tom Neckermann, Frank Seide, Ulrich Germann, Alham Fikri Aji, Nikolay Bogoychev, André F. T. Martins, and Alexandra Birch. 2018. Marian: Fast neural machine translation in C++. In *Proceedings of ACL 2018, System Demonstrations*, pages 116–121, Melbourne, Australia. Association for Computational Linguistics.

Katharina Kann, Ryan Cotterell, and Hinrich Schütze. 2016. Neural morphological analysis: Encoding-decoding canonical segments. In *Proceedings of the 2016 Conference on Empirical Methods in Natural Language Processing (EMNLP)*, pages 961–967. Association for Computational Linguistics.

Oskar Kohonen, Sami Virpioja, and Krista Lagus. 2010. Semi-supervised learning of concatenative morphology. In *Proceedings of the 11th Meeting of the ACL Special Interest Group on Computational Morphology and Phonology*, SIGMORPHON '10, page 78–86, USA. Association for Computational Linguistics.

Taku Kudo and John Richardson. 2018. SentencePiece: A simple and language independent subword tokenizer and detokenizer for neural text processing. In *Proceedings of the 2018 Conference on Empirical Methods in Natural Language Processing: System Demonstrations*, pages 66–71, Brussels, Belgium. Association for Computational Linguistics.

Antonio Valerio Miceli Barone, Jindrich Helcl, Rico Sennrich, Barry Haddow, and Alexandra Birch. 2017. Deep architectures for neural machine translation. In *Second Conference on Machine Translation*, pages 99–107. Association for Computational Linguistics.

Teemu Ruokolainen, Oskar Kohonen, Sami Virpioja, and Mikko Kurimo. 2014. Painless semi-supervised morphological segmentation using conditional random fields. In *European Chapter of the Association for Computational Linguistics (EACL)*, pages 84–89, Gothenburg, Sweden. Association for Computational Linguistics.

Rico Sennrich, Barry Haddow, and Alexandra Birch. 2015. Neural machine translation of rare words with subword units. In *Proceedings of the Annual Meeting of the Association for Computational Linguistics (ACL)*.

Rico Sennrich and Biao Zhang. 2019. Revisiting low-resource neural machine translation: A case study. In *Proceedings of the 57th Annual Meeting of the Association for Computational Linguistics*, pages 211–221.

Magda Ševčíková. 2018. Modelling morphographemic alternations in derivation of Czech. *The Prague Bulletin of Mathematical Linguistics*, 110(1):7–42.

Sebastian Spiegler and Christian Monson. 2010. EMMA: A novel evaluation metric for morphological analysis. In *Proceedings of the 23rd International Conference on Computational Linguistics (Coling 2010)*, pages 1029–1037, Beijing, China. Coling 2010 Organizing Committee.

Ashish Vaswani, Noam Shazeer, Niki Parmar, Jakob Uszkoreit, Llion Jones, Aidan N. Gomez, Lukasz Kaiser, and Illia Polosukhin. 2017. Attention is all you need. In *Advances in Neural Information Processing Systems*, pages 6000–6010.

Sami Virpioja, Peter Smit, Stig-Arne Grönroos, and Mikko Kurimo. 2013. Morfessor 2.0: Python implementation and extensions for Morfessor Baseline. Report 25/2013 in Aalto University publication series SCIENCE + TECHNOLOGY, Department of Signal Processing and Acoustics, Aalto University, Helsinki, Finland.

Sami Virpioja, Ville T Turunen, Sebastian Spiegler, Oskar Kohonen, and Mikko Kurimo. 2011. Empirical comparison of evaluation methods for unsupervised learning of morphology. *Traitement Automatique des Langues*, 52(2):45–90.

JB132 submission to the SIGMORPHON 2022 Shared Task 3 on Morphological Segmentation

Jan Bodnár
Charles University, Faculty of Mathematics and Physics, Prague, Czech Republic
bodnar@ufal.mff.cuni.cz

Abstract

This paper describes the JB132 submission to the SIGMORPHON 2022 Shared Task 3 on Morpheme Segmentation. In this paper we describe probabilistic model trained with the Expectation-Maximization algorithm, we provide the results and analyze sources of errors and general limitations of our approach. The model was implemented within our own modular probabilistic framework.

1 Introduction

This paper describes JB132 submission to Shared Task on Morphological segmentation, which is the task of segmentation of words to the smallest units carrying meaning - morphemes (e.g. prefixes, root, suffixes).

Our general approach was to create our own modular framework for probabilistic models trained via Expectation-Maximization, so that we can quickly test large number of various model architectures.

We designed various probabilistic models, described them within the framework and tested them across languages. In this paper we provide the description of the best model architecture. Since the algorithm achieves poor results, we further analyze its outputs and describe causes of errors it makes.

2 Task

The Shared Task focused on both morphological segmentation of solitary words (Task 1) and words in sentences (Task 2), but we have only participated in Task 1. The training data spanned across 9 languages (Czech, English, French, Hungarian, Spanish, Italian, Latin, Russian, Mongolian) and contained tens of thousands to hundreds of thousands training samples.

The structure and complexity of input data varied. The Czech words were segmented to morphs (*absorbovat ab-sorb-ova-t*), while e.g. Spanish and Russian data contained segmentation to morphemes, including change of root and presence of morphemes that were used in the derivation of the word but now only map to null morphs (encuestéis encuesta-ar-éis; автоматизируемые автомат-изм-ировать-уем-ый-ые).

3 Related Work

Probabilistic models are commonly used in morphological segmentation, although often focused on morphs instead of morphemes and trained in unsupervised or weakly supervised settings. There are three (sometimes overlapping) groups of probabilistic models used for segmentation: the first group are Bayesian models, which rely on complex generative stories, including even prior distributions of numbers of morphemes of words or prior distribution of morpheme frequencies. An interesting example of this approach is (Snyder and Barzilay, 2008), which experimented with a joint multilingual model for several related languages and showed that it can improve the resulting segmentation in unsupervised setting.

The second group are Maximum a posteriori probability (= Minimum description length) models. These models try to find the best compression of words (including the size of the compression model's parameters) and are usually optimized via some kind of local optimization. Models of this type are e.g. (Creutz and Lagus, 2002) and (Goldsmith, 2006), which also use morpheme lexicons, but unlike our model consider size of the dictionary part of the loss function.

The last group are Expectation-Maximization models such as (Creutz and Lagus, 2004),(Grönroos et al., 2020), which tend to make use of simpler loss functions that further simplify when EM is applied and thus allow for faster computation.

19th SIGMORPHON Workshop on Computational Research in Phonetics, Phonology, and Morphology, pages 152 - 156
July 14, 2022 ©2022 Association for Computational Linguistics

4 Solution

Our approach was to create a modular framework for probabilistic models optimized via the Expectation-Maximization algorithm. We then described various architectures within this framework and tried to find the one that works the best across the languages.

Our final architecture consists of two main parts: word→morpheme generator (Fig. 1) which models the structure of words as sequence of morphemes and the morpheme→morphs model (Fig. 2) which models the morpheme realization.

Each of those parts is trained separately and they are then merged together.

4.1 Word→Morphemes model

The goal of this model is to learn the high level structure of the word. The final version of this model (Fig. 1) uses Hidden Markov Model with hidden three states - prefix, root, suffix (only the transitions to the same or later state are allowed). Each of the states has an independent output model - Prefix outputs either one of the prefix morphemes in its morpheme dictionary or a string generated by a letter unigram character model (to generate the unknown morphemes). Root and suffix work on the same principle.

The morpheme dictionaries were obtained from the training dataset using a simple heuristic for identification of the root morpheme (roots tend to be long and infrequent compared to the affixes. Morphemes in front of a root are prefixes, morphemes behind it are suffixes).

After initialization, the model was trained on the second column of the dataset - we simply concatenated the morphemes and trained the model to split them back. This allowed the model to learn the morphemic structure of words.

The model is trained via EM - we first let the model find the most probable way of generating the word in a recursive manner: If we ask some module to generate subword beginning with i-th letter, then it uses itself and its submodules to find the most likely ways of generating the following 1, 2, 3, ... letters. Then it returns us the descriptions of such ways of generation.

With this recursive principle the top-most module will give us the likelihood of the best generation of the whole word and the recursive description (tree) describing how the modules generated it (e.g. the tree describes that HMM module first visited its prefix state, which used the Dictionary module and Boundary module to generate its substring, where the Dictionary module used prefix re-, etc).

In the maximization phase, we use these collected description trees and we let them go through the probabilistic model from top: The top most module will analyze the trees and find out how often it e.g. transitioned from prefix state to itself or to root. It then takes the remainders of the trees and sends them to the lower layers, which again take their own information to update their own parameters and send the rest below, etc.

4.2 Morpheme→Morph model

We then created the morpheme→morph model. We model the morpheme realization simply by assigning each morpheme a list of morphs (strings) it could generate, altogether with probabilities of generation (Fig. 2 top).

To train the model we first need to create a candidate set of potential morphs for each morpheme - we take all substrings of original words. We then remove the substrings that do not co-occur with the morpheme sufficiently frequently to be reasonable candidates. Then we run the training procedure which finds the actual correct morphs: We train the probabilities of morpheme generating a given morph (Fig. 2 bottom). For each training sample we take sequence of morphemes, replace the root morpheme with a universal root generator and find the best mapping of morphemes to morphs so that the sequence of morphemes generates the original word. When we do this on a large amount of samples simultaneously, we can observe the probabilities that a given morpheme generates a given morph and we can use this information to update the morpheme generators - this can be interpreted as just another form of EM optimization and we ran it for multiple epochs. Once the training finished, we removed the morphs with low likelihood.

4.3 Final model

After joining the word→morphemes and morpheme→morph models we simply let the model find the most likely way of generating the word and give us the tree describing the generation (as discussed in the 4.1 chapter).

This generation tree is then analyzed and we look for the positions of the Boundary modules and for the Morpheme modules, which tells us the resulting segmentation.

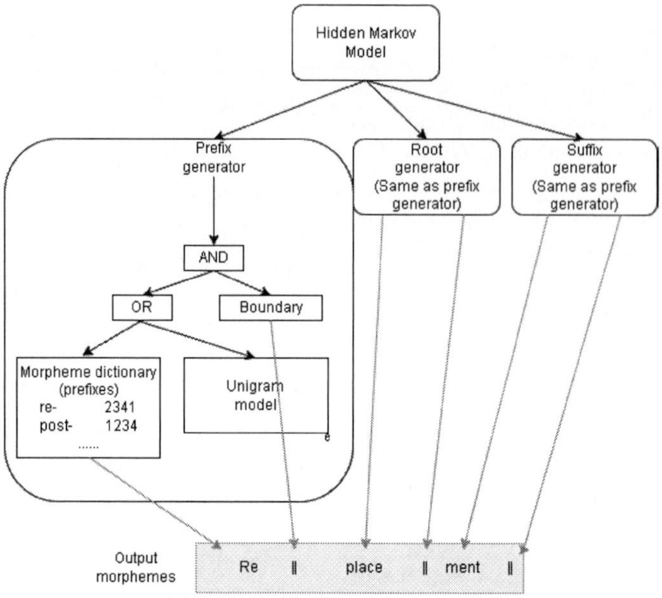

Figure 1: The architecture of word→morpheme model. Prefix-, Root-, and Suffix- generators are the same except for the dictionary. The uni-gram models generate string as combination of randomly selected letters (each letter has its probability). In the last phase of training, we will transform this model from generating morphemes to generating morphs: at first, morpheme dictionary just outputs the morpheme string for morpheme i (e.g. -s) with likelihood P[i]. After the transformation, it will output morpheme→morph model of morpheme i instead. This model will be then used to match the morphs (e.g. -s, -es, -en) in the input word. Boundary is a special sub-module that matches boundaries in the training phase and marks predicted boundaries in the inference phase

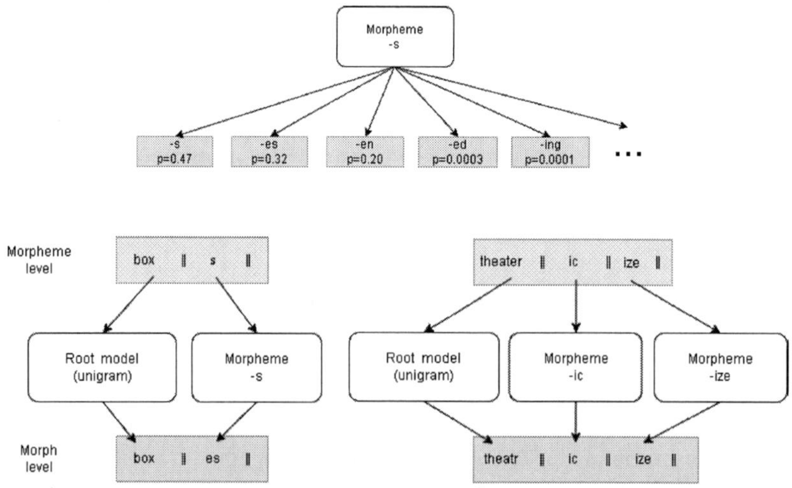

Figure 2: The architecture of morpheme→morph model (top) and the process of its training (bottom). The model describes generation of a morph as random choice among fixed candidates on the basis of trained probabilities. The training procedure works in such a way that it picks a word segmented to morphemes (red), uses it as a guideline for choice of morpheme models and looks for the best way how to use these morpheme models to generate the not segmented version of the word (green)

5 Results

The systems were evaluated via morpheme precision and recall. Precision is defined as the number of correctly predicted morphemes divided by total number of predicted morphemes. Recall is defined as the number of correctly predicted morphemes divided by total number of morphemes in the golden segmentation.

The following table summarizes our F-scores on the languages, as they were measured by the organizers of the Shared Task in (Batsuren et al., 2022).

Lang.	F1	Lang.	F1
Ces	64.65	Lat	91.39
Eng	65.43	Mon	57.82
Fra	46.20	Rus	50.55
Hun	72.64	Spa	43.39
Ita	33.44		

We can see that the model achieves relatively good results only on Latin (which was segmented to morphs) and not on other languages.

5.1 Error Analysis

This model was unable to achieve results comparable with the other approaches. We think that the main causes are following:

1. 1) Inability to capture the root changes, i.e. to transform the original root into its morpheme. (ENG: *emulations = emulate-ion-s*; SPA: *tricotemos = tricotar-emos*; ITA: *piastrellavamo = piastrellare-avamo*)

2. Missing context - the algorithm does not take surrounding letters into account when inserting a morph and it does not make use of joint probabilities of morphemes. Among other problems it also results in using a wrong morpheme for the generation of a morph (FRA: *recréerions = re-créer-erions* vs. *présidions = présider-ions*)

3. Morphemes with empty morph - probabilistic model of this type cannot generate morpheme from nothing (FRA: *agrémentant = agrér-ment-er-ant*). We would have to rely on joint probabilities of morphemes to derive it.

4. Under-segmentation - when we look at the results of the model on the Czech data (which are only segmented to morphs, not morphemes), then we notice that we discovered only 70% of boundaries between morphemes, but we have 95% precision on the boundary discovery. This was likely a consequence of removal of single letter morphemes from the model. Czech has tendency to use them frequently, as e.g. in *chyt-a-l-a*, or *bý-v-a-l-ý*, but they may cause problems with over-segmentation, as in *minim-al-iz-ova-t*, so it would be better to use a model that either groups the short morphs or incorporates joint probabilities of morphemes.

5. Root boundary detection - the model seems to have trouble detecting beginning and end of the root. When training the word→morphemes model we have observed that adding root dictionary (with roots extracted from the set of training morphemes) highly improves the segmentation accuracy. The problem is, that this dictionary cannot be directly transferred to the word→morphemes→morphs model, because root morphs in words are different from root morphemes in the dictionary, so some intermediate layer would be required.

6 Conclusion & Future Work

Our submission to the shared task on morphological segmentation was a modular probabilistic model trained via EM. The model has achieved poor results and the error analysis shows that a big amount of modifications will be needed in order to improve the results. Especially, the addition of more contextual information will be necessary. It also remains unclear how to handle differences between root morphs and root morphemes with this type of model.

7 Acknowledgement

This work was supported by the Grant No. START/HUM/010 of Grant schemes at Charles University (reg. No. CZ.02.2.69/0.0/0.0/19_073/0016935), the LINDAT/CLARIAH-CZ project of the Ministry of Education Youth and Sports of the Czech Republic (project LM2018101), and by the SVV project No. 260 575.

It was using language resources developed, stored, and distributed by the LINDAT/CLARIAH-CZ project.

References

Khuyagbaatar Batsuren, Gábor Bella, Aryaman Arora, Viktor Martinović, Kyle Gorman, Zdeněk Žabokrtský, Amarsanaa Ganbold, Šárka Dohnalová, Magda Ševčíková, Kateřina Pelegrinová, Fausto Giunchiglia, Ryan Cotterell, and Ekaterina Vylomova. 2022. The sigmorphon 2022 shared task on morpheme segmentation. In *19th SIGMORPHON Workshop on Computational Research in Phonetics, Phonology, and Morphology*.

Mathias Creutz and Krista Lagus. 2002. Unsupervised discovery of morphemes. In *Proceedings of the ACL-02 Workshop on Morphological and Phonological Learning*, pages 21–30. Association for Computational Linguistics.

Mathias Creutz and Krista Lagus. 2004. Induction of a simple morphology for highly-inflecting languages. In *Proceedings of the 7th meeting of the acl special interest group in computational phonology: Current themes in computational phonology and morphology*, pages 43–51.

John Goldsmith. 2006. An algorithm for the unsupervised learning of morphology. *Natural language engineering*, 12(4):353–371.

Stig-Arne Grönroos, Sami Virpioja, and Mikko Kurimo. 2020. Morfessor em+ prune: Improved subword segmentation with expectation maximization and pruning. *arXiv preprint arXiv:2003.03131*.

Benjamin Snyder and Regina Barzilay. 2008. Unsupervised multilingual learning for morphological segmentation. In *Proceedings of ACL-08: HLT*, pages 737–745, Columbus, Ohio. Association for Computational Linguistics.

SIGMORPHON–UniMorph 2022 Shared Task 0: Modeling Inflection in Language Acquisition

Jordan Kodner and **Salam Khalifa**
Stony Brook University
Department of Linguistics and Institute for Advanced Computational Science
Stony Brook, NY USA
`{jordan.kodner,salam.khalifa}@stonybrook.edu`

Abstract

This year's iteration of the SIGMORPHON-UniMorph shared task on "human-like" morphological inflection generation focuses on generalization and errors in language acquisition. Systems are trained on data sets extracted from corpora of child-directed speech in order to simulate a natural learning setting, and their predictions are evaluated against what is known about children's developmental trajectories for three well-studied patterns: English past tense, German noun plurals, and Arabic noun plurals. Three submitted neural systems were evaluated together with two baselines. Performance was generally good, and all systems were prone to human-like over-regularization. However, all systems were also prone to non-human-like over-irregularization and nonsense productions to varying degrees. We situate this behavior in a discussion of the Past Tense Debate.[1]

1 Introduction

The overarching goal of this subtask of the 2022 SIGMORPHON-UniMorph shared task on morphological inflection, in contrast with this year's and previous years' typologically informed subtasks, was to provide insight into how current state-of-the-art morphological inflection models relate to human language acquirers, to what extent they behave similarly or differently, and in what respects they perform better or worse. As such, the task was designed to be cognitively informative while still approachable for the NLP morphology community. This was achieved in two ways: First, nested training sets of increasing size were extracted from corpora of child-directed speech, following (Belth et al., 2021), allow us to approximate learning trajectories with batch learning models that are typical in the field today rather than incremental models which might better approximate the child language acquisition setting. Second, supervision with semantic features substitutes for semantic information which children in real acquisition settings would certainly glean from their linguistic and environmental experiences. While this simplified the task considerably, it also permitted us to focus on the act of generating correct forms in the absence of other learning confounds.

1.1 Historical Background

The acquisition of morphological patterns has been heavily investigated for decades from both experimental and computational perspectives. The acquisition of English past tense in particular was the original locus of the so-called "Past Tense Debate," with implications not only for the nature of cognitive morphological representations (*single-route* or *dual-route*), but also for the nature of cognitive representations and computations more generally (symbolic or non-symbolic, distributed or not). The debate kicked off in earnest following the publication of an early connectionist (psychologically-inspired feed-forward artificial neural network) model for past tense learning (Rumelhart and McClelland, 1986). The model did not explicitly handle regular and irregular patterns differently (it was single-route), yet it performed reasonably well given the computing power and neural network know-how available at the time.

A response by Pinker and Prince (Pinker and Prince, 1988), who instead advocated for a symbolic model of past tense learning and representation in which regular and irregular forms were handled separately (a dual-route model) was the first in what turned into many years and dozens of papers worth of discussion. As the years passed, they expanded to encompass morphological patterns in other languages as well, particularly pluralization of German nouns. See McClelland and Patterson (2002) and Pinker and Ullman (2002) for surveys of the debate.

[1] Data, evaluation scripts, and predictions are available at: `https://github.com/sigmorphon/2022InflectionST`

19th SIGMORPHON Workshop on Computational Research in Phonetics, Phonology, and Morphology, pages 157 - 175
July 14, 2022

Modern deep neural systems are in many ways the spiritual and technological successors to the connectionists. Given the success of such models on a wide range of tasks in NLP, it is possible that modern neural morphology models could overcome many of the drawbacks of their predecessors. A recent paper (Kirov and Cotterell, 2018) made this argument to the computational linguistics community. Given the critical responses and responses to the responses so far (Corkery et al., 2019; McCurdy et al., 2020; Belth et al., 2021; Beser, 2021; Dankers et al., 2021), it is fair to say that the debate has been reignited.

1.2 Contribution of the Shared Task

The SIGMORPHON inflection shared task paradigm (Cotterell et al., 2016, 2017, 2018; McCarthy et al., 2019; Vylomova et al., 2020; Pimentel et al., 2021) is well-suited for assessing the behavior of morphological learning systems. Developing a greater understanding of the ways in which systems are or are not human-like can help explain why their prediction accuracy is so good and also direct us towards areas of improvement. The Past Tense Debate and the developmental research that came out of it provides a backdrop over which we can evaluate the systems.

This is the second year that the SIGMORPHON shared task on morphological inflection is running a "human-like" generalization task. Last year's task[2] investigated the extent to which computational systems matched adult acceptability ratings on *wug tests* presented in English, German, Dutch and Russian. Such a task is suited for testing systems' ability to form human-like analogies between phonologically related forms in a laboratory setting. However, the task is not suitable for answering the questions addressed this year.

Adults appear to approach wug tests differently from children (Schütze, 2005), with many adults treating it as a game that requires clever analogies (Derwing and Baker, 1977). This difference is observed in the original wug test study (Berko, 1958), in which adults readily produced analogical past forms *glung* and *glang* for *gling* on analogy with verbs like *sting-stung* and *sing-sung*, while 83 of 86 young children either produced *glinged* or refused to answer. It is not clear to what extent this is a difference in child and adult linguistic representations or an artifact of experimental design. It is also not entirely clear to what extent gradient acceptability ratings are the result of the gradient experimental prompts, since they may drive test subjects to spread responses over a wider range than they would otherwise (Parducci and Perrett, 1971).[3] See Yang (2020) for additional discussion.

Since this task sought to compare computational morphology learning systems to child learners, we took a different approach. Teams were asked to train inflection models as for previous SIGMORPHON shared tasks but on data drawn from corpora of child directed speech, the input that children receive during acquisition. Systems made predictions on real words rather than nonce words, simulating the experience of children who need to produce never before heard forms for lemmas that they already know. These outputs were compared to what is known about children's learning trajectories and errorful productions.

Three inflectional patterns, English past tense, German noun plurals, and Arabic noun plurals, were chosen because they have been heavily studied from a developmental perspective and have been subject to computational cognitive modeling research. The acquisition of English past tense and German noun pluralization in particular have received renewed interest in recent years, and while less work has been conducted on this aspect of Arabic, we believe that it will make for an elucidating challenge case going forward. The remainder of this section briefly summarizes some relevant findings for English, German, and Arabic.

1.3 English Past Tense

The general state of the English past tense system is a familiar one. There is a clearly productive general default *regular* suffix *-ed* (subject to phonologically-conditioned allomorphy) which applies to the vast majority of verbs and new coinings, as well as several much less frequent patterns usually described as *irregular*. Many of these irregulars indicate past tense through a stem vowel mutation (the so-called *strong verbs* paralleled in other Germanic languages), for example, *sing-sang*, *sting-stung*, *bite-bit*, and *ride-rode*. Others combine a stem mutation with a coronal suffix (the so-called *semi-weak* verbs, where regular *-ed* verbs

[2] 2021 description and data available here: https://github.com/sigmorphon/2021Task0

[3] Armstrong et al. (1983) presents a stark example of this, finding that participants would gradiently rate integers for their "evenness" given the opportunity, even though the even/odd distinction is completely binary.

are *weak*) including *keep-kept*, *sleep-slept* and *tell-told*. There are also a few one-off suppletive forms, most notably *go-went*.

There is a clear distinction to be made between the single overwhelming majority default pattern, and the rest. Nevertheless, the irregulars as a whole tend to fall in the high end of the frequency range and so are over-represented in the input. As a result, children identify *-ed* as productive later than one may expect given its high type frequency. They acquire it around age three (Berko, 1958; Marcus et al., 1992). It is hard to say exactly what verbal vocabulary size this age corresponds to since there is quite a lot of variation among individuals, but Marcus et al. (1992, ch. 5) report that Sarah and Adam from the Brown Corpus (Brown et al., 1973) have produced 300-350 unique verbs by age three.

Children's novel productions exhibit an asymmetry between *over-regularizations*, which are over-applications of the default pattern (e.g., **goed*, **feeled*) and *over-irregularizations*, which apply irregular patterns to regular verbs (e.g., *fry-*frew* by analogy with *fly-flew* or *peep-*pept* by analogy with *keep-kept* and *sleep-slept*).

The former error type is far more common than the latter, both in English and in other languages. Studies of past tense errors in English learners have found over-irregularization rates of under 0.2% (Xu and Pinker, 1995), but over-regularization rates orders of magnitiude higher between 8 and 10% (Maratsos, 2000; Yang, 2002; Maslen et al., 2004). Similar findings have been observed in German past participle production with under 1% over-irregularization and about 10% over-regularization (Clahsen and Rothweiler, 1993), and a similar ratio in Spanish verbal production (Clahsen et al., 1992; Mayol, 2007). See Marcus et al. (1992) for more discussion. Nevertheless, for all their strengths, over-irregularization has been a persistent challenge for single-route models since the early connectionist days. Early connectionist models were also prone to producing nonsense, for example *mail-membled* (Xu and Pinker, 1995).

Despite its mundanity, the English past tense system provides a valuable test case for models of morphology acquisition. That said, it does have a major drawback. Since there is only one apparently productive global default pattern, and that pattern applies to the overwhelming majority of types, a naive model that performs simple frequency matching is expected to perform quite well on English.

Corpus	*-e*%	*-(e)n*%	*-er*%	*-∅*%	*-s*%
CELEX	27	48	4	17	4
UniMorph	34.4	37.3	2.9	19.2	4.0

Table 1: Type distribution of German noun plural types in CELEX (Baayen et al., 1993) reported in Sonnenstuhl and Huth (2002), and in UniMorph as reported in McCurdy et al. (2020). 2.1% of UniMorph nouns have "other" plural forms.

While type frequency is certainly the most important factor in the acquisition of productive generalizations (Aronoff, 1976; MacWhinney, 1978; Bybee, 1985; Baayen, 1993; Elman, 1998; Pierrehumbert, 2003; Yang, 2016), this obscures potential differences between dramatically different learning models. German noun pluralization was introduced into the Past Tense Debate because it has a much more even distribution of inflectional patterns.

1.4 German Noun Plurals

Unlike English past tense, the German noun plural system has several relatively frequent pluralization patterns: *-(e)n*, *-e*, *-er*, *-∅* and *-s* with distributions summarized in Table 1. Pluralization may be further indicated with Umlaut, or the fronting of certain vowels. There are three Umlaut patterns which are clearly indicated in German orthography: (*a*→*ä*, *o*→*ö*, *u*→*ü*). Suffixing and Umlaut appear to be largely orthogonal, so some recent computational modeling work has focused only on the former (McCurdy et al., 2020; Belth et al., 2021).

It is clear that German noun plurals do not have a high-frequency global default like English. However, some plural forms appear to be defaults for nouns that meet certain conditions. Feminine nouns, for example, productively pluralize with -*(e)n*, where the vowel is subject to phonologically conditioned allomorphy (Wiese, 1996). Several phonotactic properties are also shown to correlate with pluralization type preferences (Zaretsky and Lange, 2015).

While the *-s* plural is the least frequent of the language's pluralization types, it has attracted considerable theoretical attention because it nevertheless appears to be a case of a minority default pattern (Clahsen, 1990; Marcus et al., 1995; Sonnenstuhl and Huth, 2002). The *-s* plural is the plural of last resort that speakers fall back on when the conditions for other plurals are not met, however, unlike English *-ed*, it is not particularly frequent. As a result, it serves as a means of differentiating learning models which rely naively on type frequency from ones which leverage type frequency to learn more underlyingly complex morphological systems.

Developmental studies show that children do successfully learn this system around the same age that English past tense is acquired. Children learn *-e -∅*, and *-(e)n* by the time they know 100 words, and while *-er* and *-s* are learned later, they are acquired reliably around 500 words (Elsen, 2002). Over-application of *-(e)n* is the most common error type followed by over-application of *-e*, though even *-s* and *-er* are overproduced (Elsen, 2002).

1.5 Arabic Noun Plurals

Finally, we introduce Arabic noun pluralization as another challenge case. Arabic nouns may form plurals in two ways: by suffixation (so-called *sound plurals*) or by stem mutation (so-called *broken plurals*). There are two sound plural suffixes, a feminine *-āt*, and a masculine *-ūn* (*-īn, -ū, or -ī* depending on a nominal's case and state). The relationship between gender and sound plural ending is reliable but not exceptionless. In particular, some masculine nouns, generally non-human masculine nouns, take the feminine sound plural, e.g., *imtiḥān-imtiḥān-āt* 'exam.' Noun gender can be determined with agreement – pronouns, adjectives, and verbs all agree with nouns in gender, so masculine nouns taking feminine plurals are a clear morphological mismatch.

Broken plurals can be divided into many subclasses by which templatic pattern defines the output of their stem mutations. In Modern Standard Arabic (MSA), there are approximately 30 broken plural patterns (McCarthy and Prince, 1990), though the exact count depends on the level of abstraction assumed for the templatic pattern. Some classes of singular templates are known to take specific plural patterns, e.g., *maktab* (maCCaC) 'desk, office' → *makātib* (maCāCiC). On the other hand, different singular patterns can take the same plural pattern, e.g., both *kitāb* (CiCāC) 'book' and *sarīr* (CaCīC) 'bed' are pluralized as *kutub* and *surur* (CuCuC), respectively. This results in a very complex system. There are many theoretical accounts which seek to explain and predict the mappings betwen singular and broken plural patterns. McCarthy and Prince (1990), for example, group the broken plural patterns according to prosodic shapes and concluded that the iambic pattern is a productive one. However, some of their findings have been challenged (Gaskell and Marslen-Wilson, 2001; Haddad, 2008).

The Arabic pluralization system is quite elaborate, and it is not completely acquired by children until primary school age, however, most properties of the system are acquired much earlier, in line with the timelines observed for English and German (Ravid and Farah, 1999). Using a wug test paradigm, Ravid and Farah (1999) demonstrate that children follow *u*-shaped learning trajectories due to transient over-regularization in the direction *broken* → *sound*, and over-regularization in the direction MASC *sound* → FEM *sound*. The vast majority of child production errors belong to one of these two types, an asymmetry consistent with strong tendency for over-regularization rather than over-irregularization observed for other languages.

Dawdy-Hesterberg and Pierrehumbert (2014) present a series of related exemplar learning models and apply them to Arabic data. Their systems are generally successful at learning Arabic plural patterns, but they show fewer MASC *sound* → FEM *sound* and far more *sound* → *broken* errors than are observed in children. Exemplar learners are a kind of single-route learner, so this lack of asymmetry in error types may be expected given what has been observed for English.

2 Task Description

This task was organized very similarly to other iterations of the inflection task from the participants' perspective in order to encourage cross-submissions with this year's large scale generalization inflection task (Kodner et al., 2022). Participants were asked to design supervised learning systems which could predict an inflected form given a lemma and a morphological feature set corresponding to an inflectional category or cell in a morphological paradigm. They were provided with several nested training sets as well as a development set and test set for each language. The train and dev sets consisted of (`lemma, inflected, feature set`) triples, while the inflected forms were held out from the test set.

Initially, only training and development sets were available to participants. They were expected to design, train, and tune their models on this data. Shortly before the submission deadline, test sets with held-out inflections were released. In contrast with the large-scale subtask and previous iterations, only three languages were investigated which could be evaluated in detail: American English, Standard German, and Modern Standard Arabic. Several nested training sets were released for each language in increments of 100 items. Participants were asked to return predictions from models trained on each training size.

3 Data Preparation

Data sets for (American) English and (Standard) German were extracted from the CHILDES collection of child-directed speech (CDS) corpora (MacWhinney, 2000). CHILDES contains several types of corpora with various types of annotation. English was sourced from the Brown (Brown et al., 1973)[4] and Brent (Brent and Siskind, 2001) corpora. These contain free dialogue between caregivers and their children alternating with lines of morphological annotation. In (1), `*MOT` indicates that this utterance was produced by the child's mother and `%mor` indicates that the following line contains POS tags, lemmas, and morphological features. However, "words" in morphological annotation lines do not consistently line up one-to-one with tokens in dialogue lines, so it is not feasible to match lemma-feature pairs to inflected forms. To accomplish this, features were converted into UniMorph format, and `(lemma, inflected, features)` triples were extracted from English UniMorph (McCarthy et al., 2020).

(1) **Adam `021016.cha` 571-572** (Brown, 1973)

```
*MOT: what are you writing ?
%mor: pro:int|what aux|be&PRES
  pro:per|you part|write-PRESP ?
```

One advantage of CHILDES is that it presents vocabulary that a typical child is likely exposed to during the acquisition process, and since it contains dialogue, it can also be used to make reasonable frequency estimates of child-directed speech. In NLP terms, it is a reasonable approximation of the training set over which children learn morphological inflection. See Kodner (2022) for more information. 2,054 nouns were sampled from CHILDES weighted by their CHILDES frequencies, and their plurals were extracted from UniMorph. 454 of these items were sampled uniformly and reserved as the development set. 600 of the remainder were uniformly sampled from the remainder and set aside as the test set. The remaining 1,000 was used as the maximum training set. Smaller nested subsets in increments of 100 were sampled from these, weighted by noun lemma frequencies in CHILDES such that each larger subset was a superset of the smaller.

Training and test were sampled uniformly with respect to one another to guarantee that the test set would contain interesting test items. Another reasonable approach would have been to sample the 1,000 training items by frequency from the entire data set and then sample the test items from the remainder in order to yield a training set containing more frequent items and a test set containing less frequent items. Since item token frequency correlates with age of acquisition (Goodman et al., 2008), this would correspond to a realistic scenario where systems predict later-acquired forms from their knowledge of earlier acquired forms. However, English past tense irregulars (i.e., non-*ed* pasts), are heavily skewed towards the high end of a Zipfian frequency distribution, so such an approach would not yield many interesting test items.

The German data set was created in much the same way as the English with CDS frequency information sourced from the CHILDES Leo corpus (Behrens, 2006) and nominative plural forms matched from German UniMorph. Gender is known to be a predictor for plural forms (Wiese, 1996), so the German UniMorph features were augmented with MASC, FEM, or NEUT gender tags converted from the CHILDES annotation lines. These were split into 600 training items, 500 development items, and 600 test items with the same frequency-weighted algorithm that was applied to English. The intersection of nouns extracted from Leo and nouns present in UniMorph was relatively small, so the largest training set that could be extracted only contains 600 items.

Ideally, the Arabic data set would also be extracted from a CDS corpus in order to get a reasonable estimation of a child's vocabulary. Colloquial Arabic varieties are unfortunately considered to be low-resourced in terms of available linguistic resources, so even though there are several dialectal CDS corpora (Kern et al., 2009; Alqattan, 2015; Salama and Alansary, 2017), they do not provide morphological annotations useful to the task in hand. Thus, we selected Modern Standard Arabic (MSA) for the shared task. Even though it has virtually no native speakers and no CDS corpora, it is

[4] This is a classic CDS corpus built by Roger Brown. It is not to be confused with the classic NLP Brown Corpus developed at Brown University (Kučera and Francis, 1967).

well-resourced and exhibits the same kinds of morphological patterns present across Arabic varieties. A reasonable workaround for the lack of CDS is to estimate a child size corpus from a given non-CDS corpus through lemma frequencies. This will most likely contain high frequency lexemes that typically do not appear in CDS corpora but will likely cover a similar distribution of morphological phenomena (Kodner, 2019).

For this shared task, the Arabic data set was sourced from the Penn Arabic Treebank (PATB) (Maamouri et al., 2004), which is a morphologically and syntactically annotated news corpus of MSA. The corpus is written using standard Arabic orthography and it is fully diacritized. Diacritization include short vowels, specific case and state markings, and gemination. Arabic text without diacritization does not mark these critical phonological segments and thus would not be useful for the task at hand. Despite including fine-grained morphological annotations, PATB lacks the annotations of functional (grammatical) gender and number in addition to rationality (animacy). Therefore, a version that has been enriched with additional features through the CALIMA_{MSA} morphological analyzer (Taji et al., 2018) was used. Plural inflections that reflect state and case were normalized to a single inflection since only pluralization was under investigation for this task.

The 2,000 most frequent plural nouns were extracted according to their lemma frequencies from the TRAIN split of PATB (Diab et al., 2013). These were then split into a training set of 1,000 items, a development set of 343 items, and a test set of 600 items using the same algorithm that split English and German. An animacy feature HUM or NON-HUM was added was added to each noun, since it is known to impact nominal inflection patterns (McCarthy and Prince, 1990).

4 Systems

The same neural and non-neural baselines were provided for this task and the 2022 typologically diverse inflection shared task. The neural system `Neural`, Wu et al. (2021), is a character-level transformer. It is identical to the system `CHR-TRM` which was used in the 2021 task with identical hyperparameters. The non-neural system, `NonNeur`, is identical to the non-neural baseline made available in 2021 and 2020.[5] Three systems were submitted, the first and last of which were also submitted to the large scale generalization task:

`CLUZH` (Silvan Wehrli and Makarov, 2022): Universität Zürich's system is identical to the one submitted to this year's large scale generalization subtask (Kodner et al., 2022). Their submission is a character-level transducer which operates over edit actions: insertion, deletion, substitution, and copy. They implement true mini-batch training for a substantial speed up, rendering the system more practical on larger training sets.

`HeiMorph` (Ramarao et al., 2022): The team from Heinrich-Heine-Universität Düsseldorf developed a system with a self-attention Transformer architecture with bigram hallucination. Submitted models were trained on the enriched data setsthat include either 1,000 or 10,000 bigram-aware hallucinated word pairs, generated separately for each training set size. The system was implemented with Fairseq, a Pytorch-based tool.

`OSU` (Elsner and Court, 2022): OSU's system is identical to the one submitted to this year's large scale generalization subtask. This inflection system is a transformer whose input is augmented with an analogical exemplar showing how to inflect a different word into the target cell. In addition, alignment-based heuristic features indicate how well the exemplar is likely to match the output.

5 Evaluation

Whole-form accuracy was employed as the primary quantitative evaluation, though several further analyses were carried out by partitioning data over grammatical gender and other factors. Performance was good overall but showed some points of divergence from human behavior. This section provides an analysis for each of the shared task's three languages.

5.1 English Past Tense

As expected given its majority default pattern, performance across all systems was higher on English than the other languages. Table 2 summarizes the results. `CLUZH` in particular achieved most of its performance already on 100 training items, while `HeiMorph` and the neural baseline show the most substantial gains as the training size increases.

[5] Available here: `https://github.com/sigmorphon/2022InflectionST/tree/main/baselines/nonneural`

#Train	CLUZH	HeiM	OSU	*Neural*	*NonN*
Avg.	**85.67**	65.65	81.48	70.12	80.60
100	**80.33**	50.50	67.67	21.67	68.17
200	**82.33**	68.17	75.00	46.83	75.67
300	**83.17**	64.83	78.50	62.83	77.50
400	**83.50**	46.17	81.67	72.83	80.00
500	**85.67**	69.17	81.67	78.17	81.17
600	**87.83**	69.17	83.50	82.33	83.17
700	**87.00**	69.33	85.00	84.00	84.00
800	**87.83**	70.33	85.17	83.17	84.33
900	**90.33**	71.50	88.00	84.50	85.50
1000	**88.67**	77.33	**88.67**	84.83	**86.50**
Ortho	**91.17**	82.0	90.67		

Table 2: English: Overall percent exact match training size for submitted systems and baselines. *Ortho* are accuracy at 1000 when stem-final spelling errors are not penalized.

CLUZH	Match	Other	Reg	*-ed*	?
100	4.65	4.65	88.37	88.37	2.33
500	9.3	6.98	83.72	83.72	0.0
1000	9.3	6.98	83.72	83.72	0.0

HeiM	Match	Other	Reg	*-ed*	?
100	9.3	18.6	58.14	69.77	2.33
500	6.98	37.21	46.51	51.16	4.65
1000	2.33	9.3	76.74	81.4	6.98

OSU	Match	Other	Reg	*-ed*	?
100	9.3	27.91	53.49	55.81	6.98
500	11.63	9.3	67.44	74.42	4.65
1000	2.33	4.65	88.37	90.7	2.33

Table 3: Error type analysis for English irregular verbs. *Match* = % correct. *Other* = % other plausible strong and weak irregulars. *Reg* = % "correct" regularized. *-ed* = % forms ending in -ed. *?* = other nonsense output

Since English orthography is notoriously complex, evaluating this task on written English presents an unnecessary additional burden on the systems. And though few errors could be clearly attributed to orthography in practice, some were found. In particular, some systems occasionally failed to follow orthographic rules regarding the doubling of word-final consonants. For example, systems produced **enthraled* instead of expected *enthralled* and **payed* for *paid*. These are spelling mistakes, though the latter is actually attested in Early Modern English texts. The final line in Table 2, *Ortho*, evaluates the submitted systems at 1,000 training when these particular errors are not penalized.

The performance of each system rises 2-5 points when these errors are ignored. There is, however, one cause for concern. 557 of 600 test items form regular *-ed* pasts, so a baseline system which always predicts *-ed* should achieve 92.83% accuracy in the *Ortho* evaluation. No system outperformed this baseline.

Table 3 investigates the role that over-regularization played in driving errors at 100, 500, and 1,000 training. Numbers for other training sizes are available in Table 15 in the Appendix. The *Match* column presents the percent of gold irregulars which were correctly predicted. These values are appropriately low given that these patterns are generally unpredictable in English. The *Other* column indicates the percent of gold irregulars which were subject to other plausible irregular patterns (e.g., OSU produced *bring-?brang*, which is incorrect according to the gold standard *brought*[6]). The sum of these two columns is the proportion of gold irregulars that were predicted to be irregular. HeiMorph and OSU produced substantially more irregular forms than CLUZH.

Columns *Reg* and *-ed* indicate the rate of over-regularization. *Reg* is the proportion of gold irregular items that were inflected as "correct" regular past forms (e.g., *buy-*buyed, bleed-*bleeded*). This was the majority for each system at each training size, though CLUZH performed more over-regularization. The *-ed* adds predictions that included *-ed* but were still incorrect (e.g., *forgive-*forgaved* for expected *forgave*). *?* counts outputs that qualify as nonsense in some way (e.g., *seek-*sougk* for expected *sought*.)

Overall, the systems all clearly show a tendency towards over-regularization. The systems clearly learn an *-ed* rule and apply it readily. In fact, all the systems, especially CLUZH, are *too* good from a developmental perspective. They begin applying *-ed* the majority of the time after only 100 training instances, well ahead of children.

Table 4 and the full version Table 16 in the Appendix quantify over-irregularization. *Match* indicates percent of gold regular *-ed* verbs inflected correctly. *SorW* is the proportion gold regular verbs inflected according to some strong or semi-weak irregular pattern, for example OSU *ply-*plew*, CLUZH *spike-*spake*, and HeiMorph *top-*topt*. *SC+ed* is the proportion of gold regular verbs that received an *-ed* suffix but were also subjected to some stem vowel change (e.g., OSU *fine-*founed*), and *Irreg* is the sum total of irregularized gold regular verbs. *?* again indicates nonsense outputs

[6]This particular error is interesting. *Brang* does exist dialectally in American English.

CLUZH	Match	SorW	SC+*ed*	Irreg	?
100	99.1	0.9	0.0	0.9	0.0
500	97.49	2.51	0.0	2.51	0.0
1000	97.49	2.51	0.0	2.51	0.0

HeiM	Match	SorW	SC+*ed*	Irreg	?
100	63.91	12.93	0.72	14.9	21.18
500	80.43	15.44	0.72	16.88	2.69
1000	88.15	5.39	0.18	6.46	5.39

OSU	Match	SorW	SC+*ed*	Irreg	?
100	79.17	8.98	3.77	15.44	5.39
500	90.66	3.05	0.9	4.85	4.49
1000	97.49	1.26	0.36	1.62	0.9

Table 4: Error type analysis for English regular verbs. *Match* = % correct or orthographic. *SorW* = % well-formed strong or semi-weak irregular. *SC+ed* = % *-ed* is present but with a vowel change. *Irreg* = % all plausibly irregular patterns. *?* = nonsense output

	-ed	→*a*	→*u*	Other	?
Gold	2	2	3	1	–
CLUZH	4	1	3	0	0
HeiM	8	0	0	0	0
OSU	8	0	0	0	0

Table 5: Inflection type for English monosyllabic *-ing* verbs at 1,000 training. *-ed* = regular. →*a* = *sing-sang*-type. →*u* = *sting-stung*-type. *Other* = other inflection (*bring-brought* in the gold standard). *?* = nonsense inflection.

including *ski-*soa*, *crush-*crushi*, and *test-*tsot*.[7]

CLUZH produced by far the least over-irregularized forms at smaller training sizes, while the other systems produced substantially more. A qualitative error analysis revealed some interesting patterns. Every system extended the semi-weak shortening pattern of *keep-kept* to the lemmas such as *cheep* or *beep*, producing **bept* or **chept*. OSU and the neural baseline extended the *think-thought* pattern to monosyllabic verbs beginning with *consonant-h*, producing pairs such as *whiz-*whought* and *thin-*thought*. These are clear examples of unnatural over-irregularization behavior.

Finally, the monosyllabic *-ing* verbs were investigated as an illustrative study. Since it is not possible to predict the correct past forms of the *-ing* test items in a principled way, systems were expected to fail by raw accuracy. Thus, this makes for an interesting case for a more detailed analysis. There were six such items in the training data and eight in the test data. Lists of training and test items is provided in (2)-(3)[8] along with the smallest training sample in which the training items appeared.

(2) **Training**

```
300 swing-swung
300 sing-sang
700 thing-thinged
800 ding-dinged
800 sling-slung
900 cling-clung
```

(3) **Test**

```
sting-stung       bring-brought
fling-flung       king-kinged
ring-rang         spring-sprang
ping-pinged       string-strung
```

Even though the number of irregular *-ing* verbs increases with training size, over-regularization to *-ed* is the most common output at 1,000 training. HeiMorph and OSU "correctly" over-regularize all eight test items at 1,000 training. CLUZH over-regularizes half the forms and prefers *-ung* forms for three of the others (4). This ratio makes sense if the system is matching the training data, which has more *-ung* pasts than *-ang* pasts.

(4) **CLUZH *-ing* predictions at 1000 training**

```
sting-stung       bring-bringed
fling-flinged     king-kinged
ring-rang         spring-sprung
ping-pinged       string-strung
```

There was much more variety at smaller training sizes, including an aamusing incorrect production generated by the OSU system: it produced the present-past pair *ping-*pong*. Overall, systems showed a preference for over-regularization relative to over-irregularization, especially apparent for CLUZH. Nevertheless, they all produced orders of magnitude more over-irregularization than observed during child development as described in the Introduction. In particular, systems picked up on the semi-weak shortening pattern, over-applied *-ought*, and applied stem changes of various sorts even when simultaneously applying *-ed*. All systems showed super-human performance in their acquisition of *-ed*, productively applying it after only 100 training examples, when a human child might produce *-ed* only after learning a few hundred verbs (Brown, 1973).

[7]The neural baseline produced several instances of metathesis, especially at smaller training sizes. Examples include *flitter-*filtered*, *bark-*braked*, *sand-*snad*, *dodge-*dogde*, *clink-*clikned*, *own-*won*, *sell-*sleled*, *spring-*sprigned*, and *erase-*reased* at 100 vs. *erase-*earsed* at 200.

#Train	CLUZH	HeiM	OSU	*Neural*	*NonN*
Avg.	**76.72**	67.03	72.11	58.33	74.81
100	**72.67**	59.00	66.50	18.67	63.67
200	**74.67**	63.50	69.17	51.00	71.50
300	**76.17**	66.33	72.00	62.00	**76.00**
400	**78.17**	69.00	74.00	68.83	**78.00**
500	**78.50**	71.00	76.00	74.17	**79.50**
600	**80.17**	73.33	75.00	75.33	**80.17**
Suff.	**89.00**	85.83	85.67		
Uml.	**90.67**	88.83	90.17		

Table 6: German: Overall percent exact match training size for submitted systems and baselines. *Suff.* are accuracy at 600 when only suffix type is evaluated. *Uml.* are accuracy at 600 when only Umlaut is evaluated.

CLUZH	Gold NC	Gold Umlaut
Pred NC	**506 (96.93%)**	40 (51.28%)
Pred Umlaut	16 (3.07%)	**38 (48.72%)**

HeiMorph	Gold NC	Gold Umlaut
Pred NC	492 (94.25%)	37 (47.44%)
Pred Umlaut	30 (5.75%)	41 (52.56%)

OSU	Gold NC	Gold Umlaut
Pred NC	503 (96.36%)	40 (51.28%)
Pred Umlaut	19 (3.64%)	**38 (48.72%)**

Table 7: German Umlaut/No Change confusion matrices at 600 training

Set	*-e%*	*-(e)n%*	*-er%*	*-∅%*	*-s%*	#
Train200	29.5	46.5	2.0	20.0	2.0	200
Train600	27.8	38.0	3.0	26.7	4.6	600
TrainF	2.8	96.2	0.0	0.5	0.5	212
TrainM	45.4	7.3	1.5	41.2	4.5	262
TrainN	33.3	4.0	11.1	40.5	11.1	126
Test	30.5	36.7	2.8	24.8	5.2	600
TestF	3.5	95.0	0.0	0.0	1.5	201
TestM	48.9	9.2	0.3	35.9	5.6	284
TestN	32.2	2.6	13.9	40.9	10.4	115

Table 8: Distribution of German plural suffixes in the 200 training set, and by gender in the 600 training and test sets.

5.2 German Noun Pluralization

Performance on German, summarized in Table 6, was generally good but lower than for English at equivalent training sizes. This may be because German noun pluralization does not have an overwhelming majority pattern. CLUZH achieved the highest accuracies of any of the submitted systems, though it performed roughly on par with the non-neural baseline at training sizes 300 and above. All systems except for the neural baseline achieved most of their performance after only 100 training items – CLUZH in particular reached 90% of its final performance.

Two additional accuracy measures are reported in Table 6 for the submitted systems. *Suff* refers to test accuracy in the 600 training condition when only the suffix type is evaluated rather than exact match. This measure is more lenient because Umlaut and any other alternations do not need to be generated correctly. As expected, each system achieves a higher *Suff* score than exact match score at 600. HeiMorph shows the largest increase of 12.5 points. *Uml.* refers to test accuracy in the 600 training condition when only the presence of absence of Umlaut is evaluated. 522, or 87% of test items do not form plurals with additional Umlaut, so a baseline system that ignored the process altogether would achieve 87%. Each system surpassed this baseline by a small amount.

Table 7 presents Umlaut confusion matrices for each submitted system. Each system shows a similar pattern of under-application of Umlaut. Only HeiMorph applies Umlaut in more than half of the cases where it should apply, but only barely. Each system also occasionally over-applies Umlaut, with HeiMorph exhibiting the highest over-application rate at 5.75%.

Table 8 presents the overall and by-gender distribution of each pluralization suffix in the training and test sets. Counts for *-en* and *-n* are collapsed, since they are phonologically predictable allomorphs. These can be compared to the CELEX and UniMorph distributions presented in Table 1.

All systems are more accurate when the gold pluralization suffix is one of the three more common (*-e*, *-(e)n*, *-∅*) than one of the two less common (*-er*, *-s*). This is summarized in the confusion matrices provided in Tables 9-10 for training sizes 200 and 600. OSU and HeiMorph produces some forms containing miscellaneous stem-internal errors, marked as *?* in the confusion matrices, such as a *j* > *t* mutation in **Kabeltaue* as the plural of *Kabeljau*, but these were much rarer, and much more limited, than what was observed in their English predicitions. CLUZH did not produce any. *-er* and *-s* plurals were under-produced by each system. In both cases, each system usually applied *-e* instead. For example, CLUZH produced **Grase* instead of expected *Gräser* as the plural of *Gras*.

Comparing this to findings about the time course of children's plural pattern acquisition (Elsen, 2002), each system appears to acquire productive *-e* and *-(e)n* as early as expected, as evidenced by

[8]Some of these have alternative past forms in actual speech. Only a single form was chosen for each in the data set.

CLUZH	G -*e*	G -(*e*)*n*	G -*er*	G -∅	G -*s*	Sum
P -*e*	**166**	17	17	2	27	229
P -(*e*)*n*	7	**198**	0	2	4	211
P -*er*	0	0	0	0	0	0
P -∅	10	5	0	**145**	0	160
P -*s*	0	0	0	0	0	0
P ?	0	0	0	0	0	0
Sum	183	220	17	149	31	600

HeiM	G -*e*	G -(*e*)*n*	G -*er*	G -∅	G -*s*	Sum
P -*e*	110	8	7	6	15	146
P -(*e*)*n*	22	192	0	5	6	225
P -*er*	3	0	1	1	2	7
P -∅	42	14	7	133	7	203
P -*s*	3	4	2	1	**1**	11
P ?	3	2	0	3	0	8
Sum	183	220	17	149	31	600

OSU	G -*e*	G -(*e*)*n*	G -*er*	G -∅	G -*s*	Sum
P -*e*	159	16	14	5	28	222
P -(*e*)*n*	10	183	0	0	2	195
P -*er*	0	2	**3**	0	0	5
P -∅	10	10	0	139	0	159
P -*s*	1	0	0	0	0	1
P ?	3	9	0	5	1	18
Sum	183	220	17	149	31	600

Table 9: German inflection confusion matrices at 200 training for FEM nouns only, disregarding Umlaut. *G* = Gold, *P* = Prediction.

CLUZH	G -*e*	G -(*e*)*n*	G -*er*	G -∅	G -*s*	Sum
P -*e*	**168**	16	13	0	18	215
P -(*e*)*n*	6	**198**	0	1	2	207
P -*er*	0	0	3	0	0	3
P -∅	8	5	0	**148**	0	161
P -*s*	1	1	1	0	**11**	14
P ?	0	0	0	0	0	0
Sum	183	220	17	149	31	600

HeiM	G -*e*	G -(*e*)*n*	G -*er*	G -∅	G -*s*	Sum
P -*e*	154	13	12	4	16	199
P -(*e*)*n*	14	194	0	0	4	212
P -*er*	4	0	**4**	1	4	13
P -∅	9	10	0	142	1	162
P -*s*	1	1	1	0	3	6
P ?	1	2	0	2	3	8
Sum	183	220	17	149	31	600

OSU	G -*e*	G -(*e*)*n*	G -*er*	G -∅	G -*s*	Sum
P -*e*	155	19	13	1	18	206
P -(*e*)*n*	7	184	0	0	2	193
P -*er*	2	0	3	1	0	6
P -∅	11	10	1	142	1	165
P -*s*	2	1	0	1	8	12
P ?	6	6	0	4	2	18
Sum	183	220	17	149	31	600

Table 10: German inflection confusion matrices for each submitted system at 600 training disregarding Umlaut. *G* = Gold, *P* = Prediction.

over-application after 200 training. This is contrasted with -*er*, -*s*, which they rarely produce after 200 training but produce (still insufficiently frequently) at 600 training. These results are broadly consistent with what is observed developmentally, with the caveat that -*er*, -*s* are proportionately less frequent in the small training sets than the large ones (Table 8).

Since analyzing suffix confusions as a whole obscures some patterns, Tables 18-20 are provided in the Appendix which present confusion matrices partitioned by gender. Every system effectively learns that -(*e*)*n* is the appropriate ending for feminine nouns, and as observed in Table 18, most errors among feminines can be attributed to over-application of this ending.

Overall, systems show some consistency with the developmental patterns evaluated here. What the systems do learn, they learn on appropriate amounts of training data. However, they continue to greatly under-produce the infrequent but apparently minority default -*s* pattern. Further work needs to be done, along the lines of recent papers published on this topic (McCurdy et al., 2020; Belth et al., 2021; Dankers et al., 2021) to determine whether or not the submitted systems are behaving in a human-like manner.

5.3 Arabic Noun Pluralization

Arabic proved to be the most challenging of the three languages: summarized in Table 11, no system achieved more than 67% accuracy on any training size. This result is to be expected, since Arabic noun pluralization is more complex than the other phenomena evaluated. As for English, some errors were determined to be very minor and primarily orthographic. Not penalizing these errors yields the *Minor* line in the table, for which each system shows a 4-5-point increase. The line *S*F*S*M*B* additionally does not penalize broken-to-broken errors as long as the applied broken pattern is itself valid. This increases performance by another 6-9 points, indicating that predicting the correct broken pattern for an item was challenging compared to determining whether to apply a broken pattern at all. Since there are so many broken patterns, this is not surprising. Nevertheless, accuracies in this most permissive evaluation are still lower than for German or English.

Noun gender and rationality are known to correlate with plural formation in Arabic, so Table 12 presents the distribution of items by gender and rationality in the training and test sets. Masculine sound plurals are the least frequent, and masculine

#Train	CLUZH	HeiM	OSU	*Neural*	*NonN*
Avg.	**59.63**	55.37	57.53	52.70	33.70
100	**45.67**	41.83	34.00	14.83	28.33
200	**54.83**	45.67	49.17	41.67	28.33
300	**54.17**	48.67	53.33	51.00	29.00
400	**58.33**	49.83	54.17	52.83	31.67
500	**62.00**	59.67	61.00	57.17	34.83
600	63.17	62.83	**64.00**	61.50	35.50
700	**64.67**	60.33	63.83	62.50	36.33
800	**63.33**	62.17	63.83	61.33	37.33
900	64.33	63.33	**66.67**	60.83	37.33
1000	**65.83**	59.33	65.33	63.33	38.33
Minor	**69.67**	63.67	68.83		
SFSMB	75.50	71.00	**76.00**		

Table 11: Arabic: Overall percent exact match training size for submitted systems and baselines. *Minor* are accuracy at 1000 training when errors deemed to be minor or orthographic are ignored. *SFSMB* are accuracy at 1000 training when confusion between broken patterns is not penalized.

Set	SF	SM	B	#
Train	424	140	434	998
Train F	222	0	85	307
Train M	202	140	349	691
Train HUM	24	129	84	237
Train NHUM	400	11	350	761
Test	257	62	281	600
Test F	156	0	73	229
Test M	101	62	208	371
Test HUM	15	50	43	108
Test NHUM	242	12	238	492

Table 12: Distribution of Arabic plural types suffixes by gender and rationality in the 1000-training and test sets. Two irregular forms in the training set, *ðāt* 'self' and *ḥabb* 'seeds,' are excluded from this table.

nouns (as determined through agreement) are more diverse than feminines in their plural forms. About two thirds of feminine nouns take the feminine sound plural and all of the remainder take a broken plural. A plurality of rational nouns take the masculine sound plural, while non-rational nouns, which account for nearly five sixths of the data, are split about evenly between feminine sound and broken plurals with very few masculine sound plurals.

Table 13 presents confusion matrices for each plural type for each system. Breakdowns by gender and rationality can be found in Tables 22-25 in the Appendix. Each system over-produced feminine sound plurals at the expense of masculine sound and broken, but they varied in their production of masculine sound and broken plurals. This extended across gender and rationality.

Prior work evaluated children and a computational system according to their distributions of sound-to-sound, sound-to-broken, broken-to-sound, and broken-to-broken errors (Ravid and Farah, 1999; Dawdy-Hesterberg and Pierrehumbert, 2014). Table 14 provides such a breakdown for each system at 1,000 training, and Table 21 in the Appendix provides further breakdowns by gender and rationality. Each system's error types follow the same frequency order: broken-to-sound is the most frequent followed by broken-to-broken, sound-to-broken, and sound-to-sound errors.

CLUZH	Gold SF	Gold SM	Gold B	Sum
Pred SF	**213**	5	52	270
Pred SM	2	**51**	16	69
Pred B	38	4	**206**	248
Pred ?	4	2	7	13
Sum	257	62	281	600

HeiM	Gold SF	Gold SM	Gold B	Sum
Pred SF	**227**	7	72	306
Pred SM	3	43	15	61
Pred B	18	5	177	200
Pred ?	9	7	17	33
Sum	257	62	281	600

OSU	Gold SF	Gold SM	Gold B	Sum
Pred SF	218	8	49	275
Pred SM	5	50	15	70
Pred B	29	2	202	233
Pred ?	5	2	15	22
Sum	257	62	281	600

Table 13: Arabic inflection confusion matrices for each submitted system at 1000 training.

	S→S	S→B	B→S	B→B
CLUZH	7	42	68	52
HeiM	10	23	87	65
OSU	13	31	64	57

Table 14: Arabic error types at 1000 training.

This is quite unlike children, who overwhelmingly produce broken-to-sound and sound-to-sound errors (in both cases, mostly to feminine sound). It is also different from the (Dawdy-Hesterberg and Pierrehumbert, 2014) exemplar models in that broken-to-broken were much more common. Nevertheless, those exemplar models and the neural models submitted here both greatly over-produce sound-to-broken errors. The lack of to-broken errors among children, similar to the lack of over-irregularization in English, suggests that these are memorized patterns rather than ones that are productively applied. Thus, to-broken errors can be seen as a kind of over-irregularization.

6 Discussion

This year's shared task investigated the performance of neural systems on an inflection task designed to mimic language acquisition. Training data was mostly sourced from the CHILDES collection of child-directed speech corpora and extracted by frequency to represent early linguistic input, and systems produced past forms and plurals for real words, simulating children producing novel (to them) forms of lemmas that they know from daily life.

This was a challenging task characterized by small training data and complex patterns. Nevertheless, systems performed well in terms of raw accuracy. American English past tense forms proved the easiest, followed by Standard German noun plurals, then Modern Standard Arabic noun plurals. In some ways, the submitted systems actually outperformed children – they all learned the productive *-ed* pattern for English past tense after only 100 training items, far earlier than what is reported for children. Systems also achieved most of their performance on very small data. Superhuman performance on very small data is a valuable property for real-world NLP applications.

Compared to early connectionist systems, modern neural morphology learners produce far fewer nonsense forms of the *mail-membled* type, though this still remains a problem, even in the largest training conditions evaluated here. This is consistent with the findings of Gorman et al. (2019), which found that what they called "silly" errors were still present in the productions of the 2017 task, but they were majorly reduced compared to early work.

Systems "successfully" over-regularized the English *-ed* past, the most frequent German noun plural types, and the Arabic feminine sound plural. This is is a human-like tendency, however it cannot be said whether this indicates deep understanding of the paradigms or a simple case of frequency matching. Systems under-applied rarer German noun plural types even at the largest training size, which may imply the latter, but more work would need to be done to confirm this.

The most significant weakness of all three systems uncovered by this analysis is persistent inhuman over-irregularization. Though rates of over-irregularization varied significantly on English, all systems produced far more instances of it than child learners, and the problem was starker for Arabic. All three systems dramatically overproduced sound-to-broken and broken-to-broken errors which are rare in child productions. Broken plural patterns are apparently no more productive than English strong verb mutations, so their over-application has to be seen as over-irregularization.

Though Gorman et al. (2019) did not categorize errors in these cognitively-minded terms, they did find evidence for over-irregularization in their analysis. They noted, for example, that one system over-applied Spanish diphthongization, a pattern that applies to many verbs. The pattern is frequent but unpredictable – many verbs that could be subject to diphthongization are not. The pattern is apparently lexicalized and unproductive, and children under-apply it if anything (Mayol, 2007), thus the over-application is an instance of over-irregularization.

All of the systems evaluated this year happen to be neural *single-route* models that do not make an explicit distinction between regular and irregular items. No *dual-route* models were submitted for comparison. While all systems performed well, they showed the clear hallmarks of such models, in particular a tendency to over-produce over-irregularization. All of the technical improvements over the decades have greatly improved overall prediction accuracy, but single-route models are still single-route models.

What do these results tell us about human cognition? Even if the systems had shown very human-like performance, we could not therefore conclude that they are good models of cognition. As summarized recently in Guest and Martin (2021), that line of reasoning is backward. Prediction is not explanation. We would need to first justify the assertion that these are theoretically plausible cognitive models. Only then, if these systems were effective representations of cognition, then we should expect them behave in a human-like manner.

What studies like this do provide is insight into state-of-the-art morphological learning models with ever-improving prediction capabilities. Inasmuch as humans are the gold-standard in language learning and language use, one possible reason for current progress is that models are making predictions for more human-like reasons. The results here show that that intuition does not necessarily hold. The systems evaluated in this shared task were on the whole successful in their predictions but did not behave in a especially human-like manner.

Acknowledgements

We would like to thank shared task organizer Ekaterina Vylomova for her advice on logistics as well as Ellen Broselow, Jeff Heinz, and Charles Yang for their comments on this overview paper. The neural baseline system was trained on the Stony Brook SeaWulf HPC cluster, maintained by Research Computing and Cyberinfrastructure, and the Institute for Advanced Computational Science at Stony Brook University and made possible by NSF grant #1531492.

References

Shaima Alqattan. 2015. *Early phonological acquisition by Kuwaiti Arabic children*. Ph.D. thesis, Newcastle University.

Sharon L. Armstrong, Lila R. Gleitman, and Henry Gleitman. 1983. What some concepts might not be. *Cognition*, 13(3):263–308.

Mark Aronoff. 1976. *Word formation in generative grammar*. MIT Press, Cambridge, MA.

Harald Baayen. 1993. On frequency, transparency and productivity. In *Yearbook of morphology 1992*, pages 181–208. Springer, Dordrecht.

R Harald Baayen, Richard Piepenbrock, and H Van Rijn. 1993. The celex lexical database (cd-rom). linguistic data consortium. *Philadelphia, PA: University of Pennsylvania*.

Heike Behrens. 2006. The input–output relationship in first language acquisition. *Language and cognitive processes*, 21(1-3):2–24.

Caleb A Belth, Sarah RB Payne, Deniz Beser, Jordan Kodner, and Charles Yang. 2021. The greedy and recursive search for morphological productivity. In *Proceedings of the Annual Meeting of the Cognitive Science Society*, volume 43.

Jean Berko. 1958. The child's learning of english morphology. *Word*, 14(2-3):150–177.

Deniz Beser. 2021. Falling through the gaps: Neural architectures as models of morphological rule learning. In *Proceedings of the Annual Meeting of the Cognitive Science Society*, volume 43.

Michael Brent and Jay Siskind. 2001. The role of exposure to isolated words in early vocabulary development. *Cognition*, 81(1):31–44.

Roger Brown. 1973. *A first language: The early stages*. Harvard University Press, Cambridge, MA.

Roger Brown, Courtney B. Cazden, and Ursula Bellugi. 1973. The child's grammar from I to III. In Charles A. Ferguson and Daniel I. Slobin, editors, *Studies of child language development*, pages 295–333. Holt, Rinehart and Winston, New York.

Joan L Bybee. 1985. *Morphology: A study of the relation between meaning and form*. John Benjamins, Amsterdam.

Harald Clahsen. 1990. Constraints on parameter setting: A grammatical analysis of some acquisition in stages in German child language. *Language Acquisition*, 1(4):361–391.

Harald Clahsen and Monika Rothweiler. 1993. Inflectional rules in children's grammars: Evidence from German participles. In *Yearbook of morphology 1992*, pages 1–34. Springer.

Harald Clahsen, Monika Rothweiler, Andreas Woest, and Gary Marcus. 1992. Regular and irregular inflection in the acquisition of German noun plurals. *Cognition*, 45:225–255.

Maria Corkery, Yevgen Matusevych, and Sharon Goldwater. 2019. Are we there yet? encoder-decoder neural networks as cognitive models of english past tense inflection. In *Proceedings of the 57th Conference of the Association for Computational Linguistics, ACL*, pages 3868–3877.

Ryan Cotterell, Christo Kirov, John Sylak-Glassman, Géraldine Walther, Ekaterina Vylomova, Arya D. McCarthy, Katharina Kann, Sabrina J. Mielke, Garrett Nicolai, Miikka Silfverberg, David Yarowsky, Jason Eisner, and Mans Hulden. 2018. The CoNLL–SIGMORPHON 2018 shared task: Universal morphological reinflection. In *Proceedings of the CoNLL–SIGMORPHON 2018 Shared Task: Universal Morphological Reinflection*, pages 1–27, Brussels. Association for Computational Linguistics.

Ryan Cotterell, Christo Kirov, John Sylak-Glassman, Géraldine Walther, Ekaterina Vylomova, Patrick Xia, Manaal Faruqui, Sandra Kübler, David Yarowsky, Jason Eisner, and Mans Hulden. 2017. CoNLL-SIGMORPHON 2017 shared task: Universal morphological reinflection in 52 languages. In *Proceedings of the CoNLL SIGMORPHON 2017 Shared Task: Universal Morphological Reinflection*, pages 1–30, Vancouver. Association for Computational Linguistics.

Ryan Cotterell, Christo Kirov, John Sylak-Glassman, David Yarowsky, Jason Eisner, and Mans Hulden. 2016. The SIGMORPHON 2016 shared Task—Morphological reinflection. In *Proceedings of the 14th SIGMORPHON Workshop on Computational Research in Phonetics, Phonology, and Morphology*, pages 10–22, Berlin, Germany. Association for Computational Linguistics.

Verna Dankers, Anna Langedijk, Kate McCurdy, Adina Williams, and Dieuwke Hupkes. 2021. Generalising to german plural noun classes, from the perspective of a recurrent neural network. In *Proceedings of the 25th Conference on Computational Natural Language Learning*, pages 94–108.

Lisa Garnand Dawdy-Hesterberg and Janet Breckenridge Pierrehumbert. 2014. Learnability and generalisation of arabic broken plural nouns. *Language, cognition and neuroscience*, 29(10):1268–1282.

Bruce L Derwing and William J Baker. 1977. The psychological basis for morphological rules. In John Macnamara, editor, *Language learning and thought*, pages 85–110. Academic Press, New York.

Mona Diab, Nizar Habash, Owen Rambow, and Ryan Roth. 2013. LDC Arabic treebanks and associated corpora: Data divisions manual. *arXiv preprint arXiv:1309.5652*.

Jeffrey Elman. 1998. Generalization, simple recurrent networks, and the emergence of structure. In *Proceedings of the twentieth annual conference of the Cognitive Science Society*, pages 543–548, Mahwah, NJ. Lawrence Erlbaum.

Hilke Elsen. 2002. The acquisition of German plurals. In *Morphology 2000: Selected Papers from the 9th Morphology Meeting, Vienna, 25-27 February 2000*, volume 218, page 117. John Benjamins Publishing.

Micha Elsner and Sara K. Court. 2022. OSU at SIGMORPHON 2022: Analogical Inflection With Rule Features. In *Proceedings of the SIGMORPHON 2022 Shared Task: Morphological Inflection*, Seattle. North American Chapter of the Association for Computational Linguistics.

M. Gareth Gaskell and William D. Marslen-Wilson. 2001. Lexical ambiguity resolution and spoken word recognition: Bridging the gap. *Journal of Memory and Language*, 44(?):325–349.

Judith C Goodman, Philip S Dale, and Ping Li. 2008. Does frequency count? parental input and the acquisition of vocabulary. *Journal of child language*, 35(3):515–531.

Kyle Gorman, Arya D McCarthy, Ryan Cotterell, Ekaterina Vylomova, Miikka Silfverberg, and Magdalena Markowska. 2019. Weird inflects but ok: Making sense of morphological generation errors. In *Proceedings of the 23rd Conference on Computational Natural Language Learning (CoNLL)*, pages 140–151.

Olivia Guest and Andrea E Martin. 2021. On logical inference over brains, behaviour, and artificial neural networks. *PsyArXiv preprint 10.31234/osf.io/tbmcg*.

Youssef A. Haddad. 2008. Pseudometathesis in Three Standard Arabic Broken-Plural Templates. *Word Structure*, 1:135–155.

Sophie Kern, Barbara Davis, and Inge Zink. 2009. From babbling to first words in four languages: Common trends across languages and individual differences.

Christo Kirov and Ryan Cotterell. 2018. Recurrent neural networks in linguistic theory: Revisiting pinker and prince (1988) and the past tense debate. *Transactions of the Association for Computational Linguistics*, 6:651–665.

Jordan Kodner. 2019. Estimating child linguistic experience from historical corpora. *Glossa*, 4(1):122.

Jordan Kodner. 2022. Computational models of morphological learning. In *Oxford Research Encyclopedia of Linguistics*.

Jordan Kodner, Salam Khalifa, Khuyagbaatar Batsuren, Hossep Dolatian, Ryan Cotterell, Faruk Akkuş, Antonios Anastasopoulos, Taras Andrushko, Aryaman Arora, Nona Atanelov, Gábor Bella, Elena Budianskaya, Yustinus Ghanggo Ate, Omer Goldman, David Guriel, Silvia Guriel-Agiashvili, Ritvan Karahodja, Witold Kieraś, Andrew Krizhanovsky, Natalia Krizhanovsky, Igor Marchenko, Magdalena Markowska, Polina Mashkovtseva, Maria Nepomniashchaya, Daria Rodionova, Karina Sheifer, Alexandra Serova, Anastasia Yemelina, Jeremiah Young, and Ekaterina Vylomova. 2022. SIGMORPHON-UniMorph 2022 Shared Task 0: Generalization and Typologically Diverse Morphological Inflection. In *Proceedings of the SIGMORPHON 2022 Shared Task: Morphological Inflection*, Seattle. North American Chapter of the Association for Computational Linguistics.

Henry Kučera and W Nelson Francis. 1967. *Computational analysis of present-day American-English*. Brown University Press, Providence, RI.

Mohamed Maamouri, Ann Bies, Tim Buckwalter, and Wigdan Mekki. 2004. The Penn Arabic Treebank: Building a large-scale annotated Arabic corpus. In *NEMLAR conference on Arabic language resources and tools*, volume 27, pages 466–467, Cairo.

Brian MacWhinney. 1978. The acquisition of morphophonology. *Monographs of the Society for Research in Child Development*, pages 1–123.

Brian MacWhinney. 2000. *The CHILDES Project: Tools for analyzing talk. transcription format and programs*, volume 1. Psychology Press.

Michael Maratsos. 2000. More overregularizations after all: New data and discussion on Marcus, Pinker, Ullman, Hollander, Rosen & Xu. *Journal of Child Language*, 27(1):183–212.

Gary Marcus, Ursula Brinkmann, Harald Clahsen, Richard Wiese, and Steven Pinker. 1995. German inflection: The exception that proves the rule. *Cognitive psychology*, 29(3):189–256.

Gary F Marcus, Steven Pinker, Michael Ullman, Michelle Hollander, T John Rosen, Fei Xu, and Harald Clahsen. 1992. Overregularization in language acquisition. *Monographs of the society for research in child development*.

Robert JC Maslen, Anna L Theakston, Elena VM Lieven, and Michael Tomasello. 2004. A dense corpus study of past tense and plural overregularization in English. *Journal of Speech, Language, and Hearing Research*, 47(1319-1333).

Laia Mayol. 2007. Acquisition of irregular patterns in Spanish verbal morphology. In *Proceedings of the twelfth ESSLLI Student Session*, pages 1–11, Dublin.

Arya D. McCarthy, Christo Kirov, Matteo Grella, Amrit Nidhi, Patrick Xia, Kyle Gorman, Ekaterina Vylomova, Sabrina J. Mielke, Garrett Nicolai, Miikka Silfverberg, Timofey Arkhangelskiy, Nataly Krizhanovsky, Andrew Krizhanovsky, Elena Klyachko, Alexey Sorokin, John Mansfield, Valts Ernštreits, Yuval Pinter, Cassandra L. Jacobs, Ryan Cotterell, Mans Hulden, and David Yarowsky. 2020. UniMorph 3.0: Universal Morphology. In *Proceedings of the 12th Language Resources and Evaluation Conference*, pages 3922–3931, Marseille, France. European Language Resources Association.

Arya D. McCarthy, Ekaterina Vylomova, Shijie Wu, Chaitanya Malaviya, Lawrence Wolf-Sonkin, Garrett Nicolai, Christo Kirov, Miikka Silfverberg, Sabrina J. Mielke, Jeffrey Heinz, Ryan Cotterell, and Mans Hulden. 2019. The SIGMORPHON 2019 shared task: Morphological analysis in context and cross-lingual transfer for inflection. In *Proceedings of the 16th Workshop on Computational Research in Phonetics, Phonology, and Morphology*, pages 229–244, Florence, Italy. Association for Computational Linguistics.

John J. McCarthy and Alan S. Prince. 1990. Foot and Word in Prosodic Morphology: The Arabic Broken Plural. *Natural Language & Linguistic Theory*, 8:209–283.

James L. McClelland and Karalyn Patterson. 2002. Rules or connections in past-tense inflections: What does the evidence rule out? *Trends in Cognitive Sciences*, 6(11):465–472.

Kate McCurdy, Sharon Goldwater, and Adam Lopez. 2020. Inflecting when there's no majority: Limitations of encoder-decoder neural networks as cognitive models for german plurals. In *Proceedings of the 58th Annual Meeting of the Association for Computational Linguistics, ACL*, pages 1745–1756.

Allen Parducci and Linda F. Perrett. 1971. Category rating scales: Effects of relative frequency of stimulus values. *Journal of Experimental Psychology*, 89(2):427–452.

Janet B Pierrehumbert. 2003. On frequency, transparency and productivity. In *Probabilistic Linguistics*, pages 177–228. MIT Press, Cambridge, MA.

Tiago Pimentel, Maria Ryskina, Sabrina J. Mielke, Shijie Wu, Eleanor Chodroff, Brian Leonard, Garrett Nicolai, Yustinus Ghanggo Ate, Salam Khalifa, Nizar Habash, Charbel El-Khaissi, Omer Goldman, Michael Gasser, William Lane, Matt Coler, Arturo Oncevay, Jaime Rafael Montoya Samame, Gema Celeste Silva Villegas, Adam Ek, Jean-Philippe Bernardy, Andrey Shcherbakov, Aziyana Bayyr-ool, Karina Sheifer, Sofya Ganieva, Matvey Plugaryov, Elena Klyachko, Ali Salehi, Andrew Krizhanovsky, Natalia Krizhanovsky, Clara Vania, Sardana Ivanova, Aelita Salchak, Christopher Straughn, Zoey Liu, Jonathan North Washington, Duygu Ataman, Witold Kieraś, Marcin Woliński, Totok Suhardijanto, Niklas Stoehr, Zahroh Nuriah, Shyam Ratan, Francis M. Tyers, Edoardo M. Ponti, Grant Aiton, Richard J. Hatcher, Emily Prud'hommeaux, Ritesh Kumar, Mans Hulden, Botond Barta, Dorina Lakatos, Gábor Szolnok, Judit Ács, Mohit Raj, David Yarowsky, Ryan Cotterell, Ben Ambridge, and Ekaterina Vylomova. 2021. Sigmorphon 2021 shared task on morphological reinflection: Generalization across languages. In *Proceedings of the 18th SIGMORPHON Workshop on Computational Research in Phonetics, Phonology, and Morphology*, pages 229–259, Online. Association for Computational Linguistics.

Steven Pinker and Alan Prince. 1988. On language and connectionism: Analysis of a parallel distributed processing model of language acquisition. *Cognition*, 28(1-2):73–193.

Steven Pinker and Michael T. Ullman. 2002. The past and future of the past tense. *Trends in Cognitive Science*, 6(11):456–463.

Akhilesh Kakolu Ramarao, Yulia Zinova, Kevin Tang, and Ruben van de Vijver. 2022. HeiMorph at SIGMORPHON 2022 Shared Task on Morphological Acquisition Trajectories. In *Proceedings of the SIGMORPHON 2022 Shared Task: Morphological Inflection*, Seattle. North American Chapter of the Association for Computational Linguistics.

Dorit Ravid and Rola Farah. 1999. Learning about noun plurals in early palestinian arabic. *First Language*, 19(56):187–206.

David E Rumelhart and James L McClelland. 1986. On learning the past tenses of english verbs.

Heba Salama and Sameh Alansary. 2017. Lexical growth in egyptian arabic speaking children: A corpus based study. *The Egyptian Journal of Language Engineering*, 4(1):29–34.

Carson T. Schütze. 2005. Thinking about what we are asking speakers to do. In Stephan Kepser and Marga Reis, editors, *Linguistic evidence: Empirical, theoretical, and computational perspectives*, pages 457–485. Mouton de Gruyter, Berlin.

Simon Clematide Silvan Wehrli and Peter Makarov. 2022. CLUZH at SIGMORPHON 2022 Shared Tasks on Morpheme Segmentation and Inflection Generation. In *Proceedings of the SIGMORPHON 2022 Shared Task: Morphological Inflection*, Seattle. North American Chapter of the Association for Computational Linguistics.

Ingrid Sonnenstuhl and Axel Huth. 2002. Processing and representation of german-n plurals: A dual mechanism approach. *Brain and Language*, 81(1-3):276–290.

Dima Taji, Salam Khalifa, Ossama Obeid, Fadhl Eryani, and Nizar Habash. 2018. An Arabic morphological analyzer and generator with copious features. In *Proceedings of SIGMORPHON.*

Ekaterina Vylomova, Jennifer White, Elizabeth Salesky, Sabrina J. Mielke, Shijie Wu, Edoardo Maria Ponti, Rowan Hall Maudslay, Ran Zmigrod, Josef Valvoda, Svetlana Toldova, Francis Tyers, Elena Klyachko, Ilya Yegorov, Natalia Krizhanovsky, Paula Czarnowska, Irene Nikkarinen, Andrew Krizhanovsky, Tiago Pimentel, Lucas Torroba Hennigen, Christo Kirov, Garrett Nicolai, Adina Williams, Antonios Anastasopoulos, Hilaria Cruz, Eleanor Chodroff, Ryan Cotterell, Miikka Silfverberg, and Mans Hulden. 2020. SIGMORPHON 2020 shared task 0: Typologically diverse morphological inflection. In *Proceedings of the 17th SIGMORPHON Workshop on Computational Research in Phonetics, Phonology, and Morphology*, pages 1–39, Online. Association for Computational Linguistics.

Richard Wiese. 1996. *The phonology of German.* Clarendon, Oxford.

Shijie Wu, Ryan Cotterell, and Mans Hulden. 2021. Applying the transformer to character-level transduction. In *Proceedings of the 16th Conference of the European Chapter of the Association for Computational Linguistics: Main Volume*, pages 1901–1907, Online. Association for Computational Linguistics.

Fei Xu and Steven Pinker. 1995. Weird past tense forms. *Journal of Child Language*, 22(3):531–556.

Charles Yang. 2002. *Knowledge and learning in natural language.* Oxford University Press on Demand.

Charles Yang. 2016. *The price of linguistic productivity: How children learn to break the rules of language.* MIT press.

Charles Yang. 2020. Saussurean rhapsody: Systematicity and arbitrariness in language. In *The Oxford Handbook of the Lexicon*. Oxford University Press, USA.

Eugen Zaretsky and Benjamin P Lange. 2015. No matter how hard we try: Still no default plural marker in nonce nouns in modern high german. In *A blend of MaLT: Selected contributions from the Methods and Linguistic Theories Symposium*, pages 153–178.

A Additional Analysis

The tables in this appendix present additional analyses referenced in the paper.

CLUZH	Match	SorW	SC+*ed*	Irreg	?
100	99.1	0.9	0.0	0.9	0.0
200	99.28	0.72	0.0	0.72	0.0
300	99.82	0.18	0.0	0.18	0.0
400	99.46	0.54	0.0	0.54	0.0
500	97.49	2.51	0.0	2.51	0.0
600	96.41	3.59	0.0	3.59	0.0
700	96.77	3.05	0.0	3.23	0.0
800	97.67	2.33	0.0	2.33	0.0
900	99.28	0.72	0.0	0.72	0.0
1000	97.49	2.51	0.0	2.51	0.0

HeiM	Match	SorW	SC+*ed*	Irreg	?
100	63.91	12.93	0.72	14.9	21.18
200	80.97	9.69	0.18	14.18	4.85
300	79.17	10.77	0.54	14.72	6.1
400	63.2	3.77	0.36	5.75	31.06
500	80.43	15.44	0.72	16.88	2.69
600	82.05	13.46	0.9	15.26	2.69
700	81.87	13.82	0.36	14.54	3.59
800	81.87	10.77	0.36	11.13	7.0
900	80.79	10.77	0.0	11.31	7.9
1000	88.15	5.39	0.18	6.46	5.39

OSU	Match	SorW	SC+*ed*	Irreg	?
100	79.17	8.98	3.77	15.44	5.39
200	87.97	4.13	1.8	7.18	4.85
300	91.74	3.41	0.9	5.21	3.05
400	92.82	2.33	0.18	3.23	3.95
500	90.66	3.05	0.9	4.85	4.49
600	92.82	3.77	0.36	4.31	2.87
700	93.36	3.05	0.36	3.77	2.87
800	94.61	3.59	0.0	3.59	1.8
900	97.49	1.8	0.0	1.8	0.72
1000	97.49	1.26	0.36	1.62	0.9

Table 15: Error type analysis for English regular verbs. *Match* = % correct or orthographic. *SorW* = % well-formed strong or weak irregular. *SC+ed* = % *-ed* is present but with a vowel change. *Irreg* = % all plausibly irregular patterns. *?* = nonsense output

CLUZH	Match	Other	Reg	*-ed*	?
100	4.65	4.65	88.37	88.37	2.33
200	2.33	4.65	93.02	93.02	0.0
300	2.33	4.65	93.02	93.02	0.0
400	2.33	2.33	95.35	95.35	0.0
500	9.3	6.98	83.72	83.72	0.0
600	13.95	4.65	81.4	81.4	0.0
700	6.98	4.65	83.72	86.05	2.33
800	9.3	4.65	86.05	86.05	0.0
900	4.65	2.33	93.02	93.02	0.0
1000	9.3	6.98	83.72	83.72	0.0

HeiM	Match	Other	Reg	*-ed*	?
100	9.3	18.6	58.14	69.77	2.33
200	11.63	9.3	69.77	74.42	4.65
300	13.95	18.6	55.81	62.79	4.65
400	9.3	9.3	60.47	81.4	0.0
500	6.98	37.21	46.51	51.16	4.65
600	11.63	39.53	32.56	41.86	6.98
700	9.3	30.23	51.16	58.14	2.33
800	4.65	20.93	60.47	72.09	2.33
900	6.98	16.28	60.47	74.42	2.33
1000	2.33	9.3	76.74	81.4	6.98

OSU	Match	Other	Reg	*-ed*	?
100	9.3	27.91	53.49	55.81	6.98
200	9.3	11.63	69.77	79.07	0.0
300	11.63	20.93	62.79	67.44	0.0
400	4.65	11.63	72.09	81.4	2.33
500	11.63	9.3	67.44	74.42	4.65
600	9.3	13.95	65.12	76.74	0.0
700	6.98	9.3	74.42	79.07	4.65
800	4.65	16.28	72.09	76.74	2.33
900	4.65	6.98	83.72	88.37	0.0
1000	2.33	4.65	88.37	90.7	2.33

Table 16: Error type analysis for English irregular verbs. *Match* = % correct. *Other* = % other plausible strong and weak irregulars. *Reg* = % "correct" regularized. *-ed* = % forms ending in -ed. *?* = other nonsense output

CLUZH	#	*-ed*	$\rightarrow a$	$\rightarrow u$	NC	Other	?
100	8	8	0	0	0	0	0
200	8	8	0	0	0	0	0
300	8	8	0	0	0	0	0
400	8	8	0	0	0	0	0
500	8	6	1	1	0	0	0
600	8	6	1	1	0	0	0
700	8	7	0	1	0	0	0
800	8	7	0	1	0	0	0
900	8	7	0	1	0	0	0
1000	8	4	1	3	0	0	0

HeiM	#	*-ed*	$\rightarrow a$	$\rightarrow u$	NC	Other	?
100	8	8	0	0	0	0	0
200	8	8	0	0	0	0	0
300	8	6	0	0	1	0	1
400	8	7	0	0	0	0	1
500	8	4	0	0	4	0	0
600	8	5	0	0	3	0	0
700	8	4	0	0	4	0	0
800	8	8	0	0	0	0	0
900	8	8	0	0	0	0	0
1000	8	8	0	0	0	0	0

OSU	#	*-ed*	$\rightarrow a$	$\rightarrow u$	NC	Other	?
100	8	8	0	0	0	0	0
200	8	8	0	0	0	0	0
300	8	4	2	2	0	0	0
400	8	3	1	2	0	2	0
500	8	7	0	1	0	0	0
600	8	5	1	1	0	1	0
700	8	7	0	1	0	0	0
800	8	7	0	1	0	0	0
900	8	7	0	1	0	0	0
1000	8	8	0	0	0	0	0

Table 17: Inflection type for English monosyllabic *-ing* verbs. *-ed* = regular. $\rightarrow a$ = *sing-sang*-type. $\rightarrow u$ = *sting-stung*-type. NC = no change. Other = other strong inflection. ? = nonsense inflection.

CLUZH	G -*e*	G -(*e*)*n*	G -*er*	G -∅	G -*s*	Sum
P -*e*	1	0	0	0	0	1
P -(*e*)*n*	6	**191**	0	0	2	199
P -*er*	0	0	0	0	0	0
P -∅	0	0	0	0	0	0
P -*s*	0	0	0	0	**1**	1
P ?	0	0	0	0	0	0
Sum	7	191	0	0	3	201

HeiM	G -*e*	G -(*e*)*n*	G -*er*	G -∅	G -*s*	Sum
P -*e*	0	0	0	0	0	0
P -(*e*)*n*	7	190	0	0	3	200
P -*er*	0	0	0	0	0	0
P -∅	0	0	0	0	0	0
P -*s*	0	0	0	0	0	0
P ?	0	1	0	0	0	1
Sum	7	191	0	0	3	201

OSU	G -*e*	G -(*e*)*n*	G -*er*	G -∅	G -*s*	Sum
P -*e*	**2**	5	0	0	1	8
P -(*e*)*n*	3	181	0	0	2	186
P -*er*	1	0	0	0	0	1
P -∅	0	0	0	0	0	0
P -*s*	0	0	0	0	0	0
P ?	1	5	0	0	0	6
Sum	7	191	0	0	3	201

Table 18: German inflection confusion matrices at 600 training for FEM nouns only, disregarding Umlaut. *G* = Gold, *P* = Prediction.

CLUZH	G -*e*	G -(*e*)*n*	G -*er*	G -∅	G -*s*	Sum
P -*e*	**134**	14	1	0	9	158
P -(*e*)*n*	0	**7**	0	0	0	7
P -*er*	0	0	0	0	0	0
P -∅	4	5	0	**102**	0	111
P -*s*	1	0	0	0	**7**	8
P ?	0	0	0	0	0	0
Sum	139	26	1	102	16	284

HeiM	G -*e*	G -(*e*)*n*	G -*er*	G -∅	G -*s*	Sum
P -*e*	126	12	1	1	11	151
P -(*e*)*n*	7	4	0	0	1	12
P -*er*	1	0	0	0	0	1
P -∅	4	10	0	99	1	114
P -*s*	1	0	0	0	2	3
P ?	0	0	0	2	1	3
Sum	139	26	1	102	16	284

OSU	G -*e*	G -(*e*)*n*	G -*er*	G -∅	G -*s*	Sum
P -*e*	125	13	1	0	9	148
P -(*e*)*n*	4	3	0	0	0	7
P -*er*	0	0	0	0	0	0
P -∅	5	10	0	99	0	114
P -*s*	1	0	0	0	6	7
P ?	4	0	0	3	1	8
Sum	139	26	1	102	16	284

Table 19: German inflection confusion matrices at 600 training for MASC nouns only, disregarding Umlaut. *G* = Gold, *P* = Prediction.

CLUZH	G -*e*	G -(*e*)*n*	G -*er*	G -∅	G -*s*	Sum
P -*e*	**33**	2	12	0	9	56
P -(*e*)*n*	0	0	0	1	0	1
P -*er*	0	0	3	0	0	3
P -∅	4	0	0	**46**	0	50
P -*s*	0	1	1	0	**3**	5
P ?	0	0	0	0	0	0
Sum	37	3	16	47	12	115

HeiM	G -*e*	G -(*e*)*n*	G -*er*	G -∅	G -*s*	Sum
P -*e*	28	1	11	3	5	48
P -(*e*)*n*	0	0	0	0	0	0
P -*er*	3	0	**4**	1	4	12
P -∅	5	0	0	43	0	48
P -*s*	0	1	1	0	1	3
P ?	1	1	0	0	2	4
Sum	37	3	16	47	12	115

OSU	G -*e*	G -(*e*)*n*	G -*er*	G -∅	G -*s*	Sum
P -*e*	28	1	12	1	8	50
P -(*e*)*n*	0	0	0	0	0	0
P -*er*	1	0	3	1	0	5
P -∅	6	0	1	43	1	51
P -*s*	1	1	0	1	2	5
P ?	1	1	0	1	1	4
Sum	37	3	16	47	12	115

Table 20: German inflection confusion matrices at 600 training for NEUT nouns only, disregarding Umlaut. *G* = Gold, *P* = Prediction.

	S→S	S→B	B→S	B→B
CLUZH F	7	29	45	48
HeiM F	1	9	21	3
OSU F	2	13	23	0
CLUZH M	0	13	23	4
HeiM M	9	14	66	62
OSU M	11	18	41	57
CLUZH HUM	0	3	16	14
HeiM HUM	0	4	15	15
OSU HUM	2	1	15	16
CLUZH NHUM	7	39	52	38
HeiM NHUM	10	19	72	50
OSU NHUM	11	30	49	41

Table 21: Arabic error types at 1000 training by gender and rationality.

CLUZH	Gold SF	Gold SM	Gold B	Sum
Pred SF	139	0	23	162
Pred SM	0	0	0	0
Pred B	13	0	49	62
Pred ?	4	0	1	5
Sum	156	0	73	229

HeiM	Gold SF	Gold SM	Gold B	Sum
Pred SF	**140**	0	21	161
Pred SM	1	0	0	1
Pred B	9	0	**51**	60
Pred ?	6	0	1	7
Sum	156	0	73	229

OSU	Gold SF	Gold SM	Gold B	Sum
Pred SF	138	0	23	161
Pred SM	2	0	0	2
Pred B	13	0	45	58
Pred ?	3	0	5	8
Sum	156	0	73	229

Table 22: Arabic inflection confusion matrices for each submitted system at 1000 training. FEM nouns only.

CLUZH	Gold SF	Gold SM	Gold B	Sum
Pred SF	74	5	29	108
Pred SM	2	**51**	16	69
Pred B	25	4	**157**	186
Pred ?	0	2	6	8
Sum	101	62	208	371

HeiM	Gold SF	Gold SM	Gold B	Sum
Pred SF	**87**	7	51	145
Pred SM	2	43	15	60
Pred B	9	5	126	140
Pred ?	3	7	16	26
Sum	101	62	208	371

OSU	Gold SF	Gold SM	Gold B	Sum
Pred SF	80	8	26	114
Pred SM	3	50	15	68
Pred B	16	2	**157**	175
Pred ?	2	2	10	14
Sum	101	62	208	371

Table 23: Arabic inflection confusion matrices for each submitted system at 1000 training. MASC nouns only.

CLUZH	Gold SF	Gold SM	Gold B	Sum
Pred SF	**14**	0	1	15
Pred SM	0	**48**	15	63
Pred B	1	2	**24**	27
Pred ?	0	0	3	3
Sum	15	50	43	108

HeiM	Gold SF	Gold SM	Gold B	Sum
Pred SF	12	0	0	12
Pred SM	0	43	15	58
Pred B	2	2	16	20
Pred ?	1	5	12	18
Sum	15	50	43	108

OSU	Gold SF	Gold SM	Gold B	Sum
Pred SF	13	2	0	15
Pred SM	0	47	15	62
Pred B	1	0	**24**	25
Pred ?	1	1	4	6
Sum	15	50	43	108

Table 24: Arabic inflection confusion matrices for each submitted system at 1000 training. HUM nouns only.

CLUZH	Gold SF	Gold SM	Gold B	Sum
Pred SF	199	5	51	255
Pred SM	2	**3**	1	6
Pred B	37	2	182	**221**
Pred ?	4	2	4	10
Sum	242	12	238	492

HeiM	Gold SF	Gold SM	Gold B	Sum
Pred SF	**215**	7	72	294
Pred SM	3	0	0	3
Pred B	16	3	161	180
Pred ?	8	2	5	15
Sum	242	12	238	492

OSU	Gold SF	Gold SM	Gold B	Sum
Pred SF	205	6	49	260
Pred SM	5	**3**	0	8
Pred B	28	2	178	208
Pred ?	4	1	11	16
Sum	242	12	238	492

Table 25: Arabic inflection confusion matrices for each submitted system at 1000 training. NHUM nouns only.

SIGMORPHON–UniMorph 2022 Shared Task 0: Generalization and Typologically Diverse Morphological Inflection

Jordan Kodner[1] **Salam Khalifa**[1] **Khuyagbaatar Batsuren**[2] **Hossep Dolatian**[1]
Ryan Cotterell[3] **Faruk Akkuş**[4] **Antonios Anastasopoulos**[5] **Taras Andrushko**[6]
Aryaman Arora[7] **Nona Atanelov** **Gábor Bella**[8] **Elena Budianskaya**[9]
Yustinus Ghanggo Ate[10,11] **Omer Goldman**[12] **David Guriel**[12] **Simon Guriel**
Silvia Guriel-Agiashvili **Witold Kieraś**[13] **Andrew Krizhanovsky**[14]
Natalia Krizhanovsky[14] **Igor Marchenko**[6] **Magdalena Markowska**[1]
Polina Mashkovtseva[6] **Maria Nepomniashchaya**[6] **Daria Rodionova**[6] **Karina Sheifer**[6,9]
Alexandra Serova[6] **Anastasia Yemelina**[6] **Jeremiah Young**[15] **Ekaterina Vylomova**[16]

[1]Stony Brook University [2]National University of Mongolia [3]ETH Zürich
[4]University of Massachusetts-Amherst [5]George Mason University
[6]Higher School of Economics [7]Georgetown University [8]University of Trento
[9]Institute of Linguistics, Russian Academy of Sciences [10]STKIP Weetebula
[11]Australian National University [12]Bar-Ilan University
[13]Institute of Computer Science, Polish Academy of Sciences
[14]Karelian Research Centre of the Russian Academy of Sciences
[15]University of Oregon [16]University of Melbourne
`jordan.kodner@stonybrook.edu` `vylomovae@unimelb.edu.au`

Abstract

The 2022 SIGMORPHON–UniMorph shared task on large scale morphological inflection generation included a wide range of typologically diverse languages: 33 languages from 11 top-level language families: Arabic (Modern Standard), Assamese, Braj, Chukchi, Eastern Armenian, Evenki, Georgian, Gothic, Gujarati, Hebrew, Hungarian, Itelmen, Karelian, Kazakh, Ket, Khalkha Mongolian, Kholosi, Korean, Lamahalot, Low German, Ludic, Magahi, Middle Low German, Old English, Old High German, Old Norse, Polish, Pomak, Slovak, Turkish, Upper Sorbian, Veps, and Xibe. We emphasize generalization along different dimensions this year by evaluating test items with unseen lemmas and unseen features separately under small and large training conditions. Across the six submitted systems and two baselines, the prediction of inflections with unseen features proved challenging, with average performance decreased substantially from last year. This was true even for languages for which the forms were in principle predictable, which suggests that further work is needed in designing systems that capture the various types of generalization required for the world's languages.[1]

[1]Data, evaluation scripts, and predictions are available at: `https://github.com/sigmorphon/2022InflectionST`

1 Introduction

Generalization, the ability to extend patterns from known to unknown items, is a critical part of morphological competence. Morphological systems, both human and machine, must be able to recognize and produce novel items as new words are encountered. Every learner, every speaker, and any system intended for general use constantly encounters new words, both new coinings and existing words that are new to them.

The centrality of generalization is emphasized by the morphological sparsity that pervades language use. Inflected forms, lemmas, and inflectional categories are all sparsely distributed and highly skewed in any input sample, following long-tailed, often Zipfian, frequency distributions (Chan, 2008). This has serious implications for learning, since the overwhelming majority of lemmas, if present at all in the input, will only be attested in a fraction of their possible forms. This is true even for a language like English, with only five inflected forms per verb and two per noun, and the problem only grows as a language's paradigms increase in size and complexity.

The test paradigm that the SIGMORPHON inflection shared tasks have employed since 2016 (Cotterell et al., 2016, 2017, 2018; McCarthy et al., 2019; Vylomova et al., 2020; Pimentel et al., 2021)

19th SIGMORPHON Workshop on Computational Research in Phonetics, Phonology, and Morphology, pages 176 - 203
July 14, 2022

provides one test bed for generalization in morphological learning systems. The shared tasks leverage the UniMorph Database (Kirov et al., 2018; McCarthy et al., 2020; Batsuren et al., 2022), which provides data sets for an ever-growing range of typologically diverse morphologies.

In principle, there are at least two kinds of generalization which can be evaluated in our UniMorph-based test paradigm: generalization to unseen lemmas, and generalization to unseen inflectional categories (i.e., unseen feature sets). Contrasting seen and unseen lemmas and categories yields four different test conditions: 1) prediction of the form of a novel combination of a seen lemma and seen feature set, 2) prediction given a seen lemma but novel feature set, 3) prediction given a seen feature set but novel lemma, and 4) the prediction of a form when both the lemma and feature set are novel.

This year's shared task include 33 languages from 11 top-level language families with a particular focus on Eastern Europe, Central Asia, and Siberia: Arabic (Modern Standard), Assamese, Braj, Chukchi, Eastern Armenian, Evenki, Georgian, Gothic, Gujarati, Hebrew, Hungarian, Itelmen, Karelian, Kazakh, Ket, Khalkha Mongolian, Kholosi, Korean, Lamahalot, Low German, Ludic, Magahi, Middle Low German, Old English, Old High German, Old Norse, Polish, Pomak, Slovak, Turkish, Upper Sorbian, Veps, and Xibe. Many of these were included last year, but we hoped that running them again would provide further insights into generalization.

1.1 Motivation for Generalization Task

Generalization to the unseen is a challenging task, the feasibility of which should be sensitive to the organization of a given language's morphology. For a language with rampant unpredictable stem mutations or suppletion, it may not always be possible to generalize patterns accurately to unseen lemmas, but one would hope that a system could generalize well for a language with invariant stems or highly irregular stem changes. Similarly, it may not be possible for a system to generalize to unseen categories for a highly fusional language where forms cannot be predicted from their component features, but it should be possible for highly agglutinative languages where roughly each feature corresponds to its own morphological operation or for a language with a high degree of syncretism in which the expression of an unseen inflectional category is likely the same as one that has already been learned. This was shown to be feasible in practice for Nen, a Papuan language with a large degree of syncretism (Muradoglu et al., 2020).

Feature Set	*guakamole*
N;ACC;SG	?
N;ACC;PL	*guakamoleleri*
N;DAT;SG	*guakamoleye*
N;DAT;PL	?
N;ACC;PL;PSS3S	*guakamolelerini*
N;DAT;PL;PSS3S	*guakamolelerine*
...	...

Table 1: A partial paradigm for Turkish *guakamole* 'guacamole,' illustrating inference for novel feature sets in an agglutinative language.

Previous iterations of this shared task have looked at some aspects of this problem, but none made this a focus. Last year's task (Pimentel et al., 2021) reported separate performance numbers for seen and unseen lemmas, but did not control for seen/unseen feature overlap. The 2018 task (Cotterell et al., 2018), sampled train and test sets with frequency weighting from Wikipedia, which made for a more naturalistic sparse sampling setting, but did not control for either kind overlap. In preparation for this year's iteration, we found that the proportion of test items with seen feature sets varied greatly across languages in the 2018 task and may have been a major driver of performance.

For example, the best performing system on Turkish, consistently scored just under the proportion of test items with seen feature sets at each training size (Table 2), even though Turkish is a agglutinative language for which generalization to unseen categories should be possible. Table 1 provides a partial noun paradigm from Turkish UniMorph which illustrates why this type of generalization should be possible. Say the feature sets N;ACC;SG and N;DAT;PL were never attested in training, but the lemma *guakamole* was. It should be possible to deduce their forms anyway – this would be a fair homework problem for an undergraduate course.

Looking at the table, *-ler-* corresponds to PL here, ∅ to SG, and *-in-* to PSS3S. Both forms with ACC end in *-i*, while DAT seems to correspond to *-ye* in the singular and *-e* in the plural. From this alone, one can correctly infer that N;DAT;PL should be *guakamole-ler-e*, while N;ACC;SG should be *guakamole-yi* or maybe *guakamole-i*. The former is indeed correct: *y*-insertion is well attested elsewhere in the language and would certainly be present with other lemmas and with other feature sets containing ACC. While unseen Turkish inflectional categories are not completely predictable, since they also contain some morphological eccentricities which obscure predictability, "could an undergraduate solve it?" is a good rule of thumb for whether generalization to unseen feature sets is a feasible task.

Performance was divergent on closely related languages whose test sets' feature set overlaps differed. Turkish and Azeri are closely related Oghuz Turkic languages with some mutual intelligibility (Salehi and Neysani, 2017) and very similar morphological paradigms, nevertheless, scores for Azeri during the 2018 task were much higher than for Turkish. Table 3 shows feature overlap and performance for Azeri. It is tempting to propose that Azeri scores were higher than Turkish scores because overlap proportions were higher.

Taken together, this suggests two things. First, the proportion of test items with feature sets attested in training is an uncontrolled factor in the data that could be driving performance in a way that obscures language-internal factors. Second, this could suggest that the systems of the day were not able to generalize across inflectional categories,[2] but a more focused evaluation would be needed to investigate these hypotheses. We perform such an investigation this year.

Turkish	Overlap%	Best Acc%	Δ
Low	39.600	39.500	-0.1
Medium	94.100	90.700	-3.4
High	100	98.500	-1.5

Table 2: Comparison of best 2018 system accuracy on Turkish low-, medium-, and high-train conditions and percent of test items with feature sets attested during training.

Azeri	Overlap%	Best Acc%	Δ
Low	71.000	65.000	-6.0
Medium	99.000	96.000	-3.0
High	100	100	0

Table 3: Comparison of best 2018 system accuracy on Azeri low-, medium-, and high-train conditions and percent of test items with feature sets attested during training.

[2]Recent work has shown that lemma overlap is also an important predictor of performance (Goldman et al., 2022), but an analysis of 2018 results suggests that feature set overlap is an even better predictor (see Appendix A).

2 Task Description

From the participants' perspective, this task was organized very similarly to previous iterations. Participants were asked to design supervised learning systems which could predict an inflected form given a lemma and a morphological feature set corresponding to an inflectional category or cell in a morphological paradigm. They were provided with a small, and data permitting, large training set, as well as a development set and test set for each language. The train and dev sets consisted of (`lemma`, `inflected`, `feature set`) triples, while the inflected forms were held out from the test set.

Data was made available to participants in two phases. In the first phase, train and dev sets were provided, with the expectation that model development and tuning be carried out primarily on these languages. In the second phase, test sets were released for all languages during the evaluation phase. Teams produced predicted inflected forms for each test set. They were given the opportunity to submit two sets of predictions from two separate models, one trained on the small training sets and one trained on the large training sets, with the latter being a super set of the former.

3 Description of Languages

This section provides brief descriptions of each language that was newly included or newly updated for this year's task. Further information about returning languages can be found in previous years' papers (Vylomova et al., 2020; Pimentel et al., 2021). Table 4 summarizes the list of languages and provides citation and attribution information.

3.1 Armenian (Indo-European)

Armenian is an independent branch of the Indo-European family. Its oldest attested form is Old Armenian or Classical Armenian (∼5th century). It has two modern standardized varieties: Western Armenian and **Eastern Armenian**. Western Armenian is a diasporic language that developed in the Ottoman Empire, while Eastern Armenian is the official language of the Republic of Armenia (Dum-Tragut, 2009). Inflection is largely agglutinative, with some residues of Indo-European fusional morphology. For verb morphology, verbs fall into different conjugation classes. Most tenses are formed via periphrasis via a non-finite converb and a finite auxiliary, though some tenses are synthetic. Nouns

Family	Subfamily	ISO 639-2	Language	Source of Data	Annotators
Afro-Asiatic	Semitic	ara	Modern Standard Arabic	Taji et al. (2018)	Salam Khalifa Nizar Habash
		heb	Hebrew	Wiktionary	Omer Goldman
Austronesian	Malayo-Polynesian	slp	Lamahalot	Nagaya (2012)	Yustinus Ghanggo Ate
Chukotko-Kamchatkan	Northern	ckt	Chukchi	Chuklang; Tyers and Mishchenkova (2020)	Karina Sheifer Maria Ryskina
	Southern	itl	Itelmen		Karina Sheifer Sofya Ganieva Matvey Plugaryov
Indo-European	Armenian	hye	Eastern Armenian	Wiktionary	Hossep Dolatian
	Germanic	got	Gothic	Wiktionary	Khuyagbaatar Batsuren
		nds	Low German	Wiktionary	Jeremiah Young
		gml	Middle Low German	Wiktionary	"
		ang	Old English	Wiktionary	Khuyagbaatar Batsuren
		goh	Old High German	Wiktionary	Jeremiah Young
		non	Old Norse	Wiktionary	"
	Indic	asm	Assamese	Wiktionary	Khuyagbaatar Batsuren Aryaman Arora Shyam Ratan
		bra	Braj	Kumar et al. (2018)	Ritesh Kumar Aryaman Arora
		guj	Gujarati	Wiktionary	Khuyaagbaatar Batsuren
		hsi	Kholosi	Arora and Etebari (2021)	Aryaman Arora
		mag	Magahi	Kumar et al. (2014)	Mohit Raj, Ritesh Kumar
	Slavic	pol	Polish	Woliński et al. (2020); Woliński and Kieraś (2016)	Witold Kieraś Marcin Woliński
		poma	Pomak	Jusúf Karahóğa et al. (2022)	Ritvan Karahodja Antonios Anastasopoulos
		slo	Slovak	Hajič and Hric (2017)	Witold Kieraś
		hsb	Upper Sorbian	Fraser (2020)	Taras Andrushko Igor Marchenko
Kartvelian		kat	Georgian	Guriel et al. (2022)	David Guriel Simon Guriel Silvia Guriel-Agiashvili Nona Atanelov
Koreanic		kor	Korean	Wiktionary	Maria Nepomniashchaya Daria Rodionova Anastasia Yemelina
Mongolic	Central	khk	Khalkha Mongolian	Munkhjargal et al. (2016); Batsuren et al. (2019)	Khuyagbaatar Batsuren
Tungusic	Northern	evn	Evenki	Kazakevich and Klyachko (2013)	Elena Klyachko
	Southern	hsb	Xibe	Zhou et al. (2020)	"
Turkic	Kipchak	kaz	Kazakh	(Nabiyev, 2015; Turkicum, 2019), Polish Wiktionary	Eleanor Chodroff Khuyagbaatar Batsuren
	Oghuz	tur	Turkish	Wiktionary	Omer Goldman Duygu Ataman
Uralic	Ugric	hun	Hungarian	Wiktionary	Judit Ács Khuyagbaatar Batsuren Gábor Bella, Ryan Cotterell Christo Kirov Andrew Krizhanovsky Natalia Krizhanovsky
	Finnic	krl	Karelian	Boyko et al. (2021, VepKar)	Elizabeth Salesky
		lud	Ludic	Boyko et al. (2021, VepKar)	" " "
		vep	Veps	Boyko et al. (2021, VepKar)	" " "
Yeniseian	Northern	ket	Ket	Ket corpus	Elena Budianskaya Polina Mashkovtseva Alexandra Serova

Table 4: Languages presented in this year's shared task

fall into different declension classes, based on the choice of plural and case suffixes.

3.2 Finno-Ugric (Uralic)

Finno-Ugric is a branch of Uralic, a language family with around 25 million native speakers spread between Northern Russia, Scandinavia, and Hungary. The majority of them are agglutinating and extensively use suffixes. They are also known for a relatively rich grammatical case system. Verbs are inflected for number, person, tense, and mood. Phonologically, these languages often present vowel harmony and palatalization.

Hungarian, with its 13 million native speakers, is the most widely spoken Uralic language. Hungarian is an agglutinative language with a rich set of affixes expressing derivation or inflection, such as in the verb. Another feature of Hungarian morphology, adding to its complexity from a computational perspective, is vowel harmony: the vowels of certain affixes adapt to those of the stem (Rounds, 2009). Compounding in Hungarian is frequent and productive, leading to further complexity in its morphological analysis (Kiefer and Nemeth, 2019).

Karelian and Ludic are two closely related Finnic varieties spoken in Russian and Finnish Karelia and the regions around Lakes Onega and Ladoga. The data for both languages, along with Veps returning from last year, has been collected as part of the VepKar project (Boyko et al., 2021) and includes multiple dialects. Typical of Finnic, these languages are highly agglutinative, present vowel harmony processes, and overtly express well over ten cases on nominals and adjectives. Ludic is often described as a dialect of Karelian, although it has certain unique features such as the presence of a reflexive conjugation (Novak et al., 2019) and the use of the full temporal paradigm of the conditional. It is seriously endangered, with about 150 remaining speakers.[3]

3.3 Georgian (Kartvelian)

Kartvelian, or South Caucasian, languages are primarily spoken in the South Caucasus with no demonstrable genetic relation to other languages in the region. Georgian, an official language of Georgia, has about four million speakers worldwide. Georgian morphology is mostly agglutinative. Nouns have number (singular/plural), but no grammatical gender. Its grammatical case system is relatively rich, having seven cases. Nouns are declined for number and case. Verbs exhibit polypersonal agreement (incorporating the number and the person of both subject and objects). In addition, verbs are divided into 4 classes: transitive, intransitive, indirect, and medial, and present many irregularities.

3.4 Germanic (Indo-European)

The Germanic family constitutes one of the primary branches of Indo-European. It in turn contains three sub-branches. The West Germanic sub-branch includes English, Dutch, and German, among others. The North Germanic sub-branch contains the Germanic languages of Scandinavia. The East Germanic sub-branch is extinct and contained Gothic. At a high level, Germanic morphology is similar to that of other Indo-European branches, but it does diverge in some key ways (Ringe, 2017). Germanic languages, particularly in the past, had an inherited three-way gender distinction, an inherited three-way number system, and overt inflectional case systems, all reduced to some degree from Indo-European. Nominals fall into several inflectional classes with different case/number expressions.[4] The 2020 shared task revealed some major inconsistencies in the data (Vylomova et al., 2020). In this iteration, the data has been re-extracted and checked.

Gothic is an extinct East Germanic language. Nearly the entire extant Gothic corpus comes from a partial translation of the Christian Bible by bishop Wulfila. Gothic is in many ways more conservative than other Germanic languages. It lacks Umlaut, which is a type of vowel alternation on nouns and verbs present in the rest of the family, but it retains reduplicated perfects, and it sometimes uses the accusative as a vocative case. Data for Gothic was sourced from Wiktionary and contains both Gothic script and Latin transcriptions.

Old English, Old High German, and Old Norse were three closely related West and North Germanic languages and early attested ancestors of modern English, High German varieties, and liv-

[3] https://lyydi.net/

[4] Five of the six Germanic languages presented this year are historical. They no longer have living speakers, and their corpora are of a fixed size. Paradigms were initially extracted from Wiktionary. Given the highly skewed long-tailed distributions of inflected forms, lemmas, and inflected categories (Chan, 2008), which do not differ in historical corpora (Kodner, 2019), the large majority of potential inflected forms, even for known lemmas, are not attested in the historical record. As such, most of the forms in the full paradigms available on Wiktionary are generated and not actually attested. This is likely not a major concern for the purpose of this task, but the caveat must be expressed.

ing North Germanic languages today. Inflectional classes in these languages are often less transparent than in Gothic due to successive sound changes obscuring their basis.

Middle Low German was a collection of West Germanic dialects spoken along the southern North Sea coast. It was a major trade language, the lingua franca of the Hanseatic League during the European Medieval period. The language retains overt case distinctions on nominals, but it shows a greater degree of syncretism than earlier Germanic languages. This trend of increased syncretism extends to the verbal system as well (Lasch, 1914).

Low German is a collection of West Germanic varieties descended from Middle Low German occupying an intermediate space in a dialect continuum between Dutch and High German. Varieties exist in a state of diglossia, mostly with Standard German, a High German variety. Several million native speakers remain in the 21st century, though numbers are declining. Outside of Europe, Low German is spoken in some diaspora communities including Mennonite groups in the Americas.

3.5 Hebrew (Semitic)

The Semitic languages, a branch of the larger Afro-Asiatic family, are spoken by over 300 million people across North Africa and Southwest Asia. Hebrew is a Northwest Semitic language with around 5 million native speakers, spoken mainly in Israel. Typically of Semitic, Hebrew makes heavy use of *templatic* non-concatenative morphology (Coffin and Bolozky, 2005). Verbs are expressed through triliteral consonant roots which occupy slots in a template of vowels. Verbs occupy inflectional classes called *binyanim* in Hebrew. Person, number, and tense marking is indicated primarily with affixation. Both prefixation and suffixation are applied depending on the tense. Nouns and adjectives indicate gender and number through suffixation, sometimes with stem mutations. Verbs, nouns, and propositions may take possessive or pronominal object clitics. In the current shared task we introduce a vocalized version of Hebrew that has been recently added to the UniMorph.

3.6 Indic, or Indo-Aryan (Indo-European)

Indic is a branch of Indo-Iranian, itself a primary branch of Indo-European. The family has a long history, with a large attested corpus of Vedic and Classical Sanskrit. It currently has over 800 million speakers extending through all countries in South Asia. Morphologically conservative languages express a three-way gender distinction and case on nouns, tense, aspect, mood, number, and person on verbs. Inflectional morphology is primarily suffixing. Some languages possess overt formality distinctions on verbs.

Assamese is mainly spoken in the northeast Indian state of Assam, with over 20 million native speakers. While gender is not grammatically marked, Assamese presents a rich system of noun classifiers. The Assamese data has been extracted from the English edition of Wiktionary. **Gujarati** (Baxi et al., 2021) is spoken predominantly in the Indian state of Gujarat, with over 50 million native speakers. **Kholosi** is an under-documented Indo-Aryan language spoken in two villages (Kholus and Gotav) in Hormozgan Province, Iran. The data has been collected during field work (Arora and Etebari, 2021).

3.7 Ket (Yeniseian)

Yeniseian languages were historically spoken along the Yenisei River region of central Siberia. Ket, the only living member, is critically endangered, with only about 60 remaining speakers at any level of linguistic competence. The language presents mainly agglutinative morphology, with extensive use of suffixes, prefixes, and infixes. Although verbal conjugation and noun declension systems are well-developed, the boundaries between word classes are fuzzy (Verner, 1997). Noun classes differentiate between masculine and non-masculine in the singular, animate and inanimate in the plural. The grammatical case system contains between 8 and 10 cases depending on the analysis. Ket verbs express polypersonal agreement, with the case and number of all arguments reflected on the verb.

The data for Ket was sourced from a text collection compiled during the field work of the Laboratory for Computational Lexicography of the Moscow State University, that took place between 2004 and 2009. It contains word forms from twelve categories, seven of which (ADJ, NUM, ADV, INTJ, ADP, PART, CONJ) are invariable.

3.8 Khalkha Mongolian (Mongolic)

The Mongolic language family has 5.200 million active speakers of 14 language varieties, which are actively spoken in Mongolia, Russia, China, and Afghanistan. The Khalkha Mongolian is de facto the official national language of Mongolia and both the most widely spoken and most-known member of the Mongolic language family. Khalkha Mongolian is an agglutinative language with a rich set of suffixes, but no prefixes. It also expresses complex vowel harmony patterns (Jaimai et al., 2005).

3.9 Korean (Koreanic)

Korean, spoken by about 80 million people, is often described as a language isolate. However, the Jeju dialect, spoken on the southern island of Jeju is highly divergent and often considered its own language. The language expresses limited inflectional morphology on nominals. Verbs express valency, tense, aspect, mood, and various dimensions of formality through suffixation. The current dataset consists of mostly predicates, so the resulting lemmas are mainly verbs and a smaller number of adjectives.

3.10 Lamahalot (Austronesian)

Lamahalot, or Solor, is one of the Central-Malayo-Polynesian languages, a proposed branch in the Malayo-Polynesian within Austronesian. As of 2010, it had about 200,000 native speakers, primarily on the eastern part of Flores Island, and neighboring islands of Flores (Solor, Adonara, Lembata, and Alor). Nearby Papuan languages have had a significant influence on this language phonologically and syntactically (Nagaya, 2011; Arka, 2007; Klamer, 2002, 2009). The language has several dialects. We use data mainly from the Lewotobi dialect (Nagaya, 2011) spoken by about 6,000 people in Kecamatan Ile Bura, East Flores. Morphologically, Lamaholot is a nearly isolating language (each word typically has one morpheme) with a small inventory of affixes (mostly prefixes and a handful of suffixes) and clitics (mainly enclitics). This language has two salient morphological features, namely agreement and nominalization.

3.11 Slavic (Indo-European)

Slavic, another primary branch of Indo-European, contains approximately 20 languages, with half of them having over 1 million speakers. The languages are spoken in Central and Eastern Europe, the Balkans, and Russia. They are traditionally divided into three branches: East Slavic (incl. Belarusian, Russian, Rusyn, and Ukrainian), West Slavic (incl. Czech, Kashubian, Polish, Silesian, Slovak, and Upper and Lower Sorbian, among others), and South Slavic (incl. varieties of Bosnian-Croatian-Montenegrin-Serbian, varieties of Macedonian and Bulgarian including Pomak, and Slovenian).

Slavic morphology is generally typical of Indo-European, with several inflectional classes for both verbs and nouns, nominal inflection by case, number, and three genders. It elaborates Indo-European verbal inflectional paradigms marking aspect, tense, number, person, and sometimes gender.

Slovak (Mistrík, 1988), and **Upper Sorbian** are two closely related West Slavic languages. Masculine nouns additionally mark animacy, which is often described as a part of the gender system of these languages. The case systems of both languages are fairly similar, however in Slovak, vocative is usually syncretic with nominative. Upper Sorbian retains a dual number and has a greater variety of verbal past forms than other West Slavic languages. The Slovak data was obtained by automatic conversion of extensive inflectional dictionaries used for morphological analysis to the UniMorph scheme.[5] The data for Upper Sorbian was combined from WMT and online grammars.[6]

Pomak is a South Slavic language, a dialect of Southeastern Bulgarian spoken in Greece and European Turkey. It has around 30,000 speakers as of 2021 but lacks standardized orthography (Jusúf Karahóğa et al., 2022). Bulgarian and Macedonian varieties are unusual among Slavic for having mostly lost case marking on nouns and for marking voice synthetically on verbs.

4 Data Preparation

All data for this task is provided in standard UniMorph format, with training items consisting of (`lemma`, `inflected form`, `morphosyntactic features`) triples. Since the goal of the task is to predict inflected forms, the test set was presented as (`lemma`, `features`) pairs. Data was canonicalized as in previous years using `https://github.com/unimorph/um-canonicalize`, which ensures consistent ordering of the features in the feature sets.

4.1 Training-Test Overlap

As always, we ensured that there are no lemma-feature set pairs that occur in both the training and test sets. However, since test items contain both lemmas and features, other overlaps between training and test are possible. This year's data splitting algorithm aimed to control for the four logically

[5] `https://github.com/unimorph/slk`

[6] `https://www.statmt.org/wmt20/unsup_and_very_low_res/`, `https://baltoslav.eu/hsb/`

possible licit types of lemma and feature overlap, which define four kinds of test items:

Both Overlap: Both the lemma and feature set of a training pair are attested in the training set (but not together in the same triple)

Lemma Overlap: A test pair's lemma is attested in training, but its feature set is novel

Feature Overlap: A test pair's feature set is attested in training, but its lemma is novel

Neither Overlap: A test pair is entirely unattested in training. Both its lemma and features are novel.

For illustration, consider the sample training and test sets provided in (1)-(2). In this example, each test pair exhibits a different kind of overlap.

(1) **Example Training Set**

```
eat  eating  V;V.PTCP;PRS
run  ran     V;PST
```

(2) **Example Test Set**

```
eat  V;PST       <-- both
run  V;NFIN      <-- lemma
see  V;PST       <-- feature
go   V;PRS;3;SG  <-- neither
```

4.2 Data Splits

The data set for each language was split into training, development, and test sets. For languages with sufficiently large corpora, both large and small training sets were produced with the small set being a subset of the large one. We aimed for 7,000/1,000/2,000-item large train/dev/test splits and a 700-item small train split when possible, but splits for most languages were somewhat smaller in practice. Chukchi, Kholosi, Lamahalot, and Xibe in particular were too small to extract even full small training sets, while Braj, Gujarati, Itelmen, Ket, Low German, Magahi, Middle Low German, Old High German, Upper Sorbian were too small to extract large training sets. Split sizes are summarized in Table 5.[7]

[7]Triples which shared their lemma and feature set with another item in the data were removed after splitting, which is why some languages fall short of 7,000/1,000/2,000 splits.

4.3 Motivation for Data Splitting

The sampling script attempts to control the size of each overlap category in the test set. The challenge here is controlling for both *lemma overlap* and *feature overlap* simultaneously. Since no frequency information is provided in the UniMorph annotation scheme, any uniform sampling over triples, controlling for *lemma overlap* or otherwise, will tend to drive *feature overlap* to near 100%. This is unnatural. Since both lemmas and inflectional categories tend to follow long-tailed sparse frequency distributions in real language (Chan, 2008, ch. 3), a naturalistic split weighted by token frequencies of individual items will tend to oversample high frequency lemmas and inflectional categories (i.e., feature sets), and undersample most others. This skewed sampling should yield a mix of overlap types in the test set. This is what was achieved in 2018, though the ratios of overlap types were uncontrolled. In contrast, this year's data splitting achieves a controlled mixture of overlap types even in the absence of frequency information.

4.4 Splitting Process

The algorithm began by randomly partitioning a language's feature sets into OVERLAPPABLE and NON-OVERLAPPABLE sets and uniformly sampling the large training set from only those triples that contain feature sets in OVERLAPPABLE. If there were not enough triples with with feature sets in OVERLAPPABLE for a given language, then the OVERLAPPABLE partition was increased incrementally until enough training triples could be sampled. If there was insufficient data to create the large training set, then the small training set was sampled this way instead. If there was enough data, then the small training set was down-sampled uniformly from the large training set.

The test set was sampled from the remaining items, with half drawn from triples with feature sets in OVERLAPPABLE and half from triples with feature sets in NON-OVERLAPPABLE features. The development set was drawn from the remainder in the same fashion.

As summarized in Table 5, this approach resulted in a much more even mixtures of overlapping pairs at both training sizes than is achieved by sampling that does not take *feature overlap* into account, though the actual ratios varied by language due to corpus-specific and language-specific factors. In controlling for *feature overlap*, a good mixture of *lemma overlap* items is achieved simultaneously. Since most languages provide ample attestation of each overlap type, we could evaluate on each overlap type individually to gauge models' generalization abilities across both the lemma and inflectional category dimensions. Additionally, in aiming for a more uniform ratio of overlap types across languages, overall performance on each language is more directly comparable.

5 Baseline Systems

The organizers provided one neural and one non-neural baseline system. The neural system, `Neural`, is a character-level transformer (Wu et al., 2021). It is identical to the system `CHR-TRM` which was used in the 2021 task. The non-neural system, `NonNeur`, is identical to the non-neural baseline made available in 2020 and 2021.[8]

6 Submitted Systems

`CLUZH` (Silvan Wehrli and Makarov, 2022): The CLUZH team adapted their earlier model, character-level neural transducer, to work on large datasets (Makarov and Clematide, 2020). The model has previously shown superior performance, especially in low-resource scenarios. This year, the team optimized the training procedure using mini-batches. They only relied on the teacher-forcing approach, i.e., using gold labels rather than what was predicted during the training phase. Morphosyntactic features were treated individually, and their embeddings were summed. The team explored performance of the model across various task settings and demonstrated its ability to capture feature behaviour better than other team's models, especially in the small training condition. The system is identical to the one submitted to this year's acquisition-inspired subtask (Kodner and Khalifa, 2022).

`OSU` (Elsner and Court, 2022): OSU's system is identical to the one submitted to this year's acquisition-inspired subtask. This inflection system is a transformer whose input is augmented with an analogical exemplar model showing how to inflect a different word into the target cell. In addition, alignment-based heuristic features indicate how well the exemplar is likely to match the output. The system works only when examples of the target cell are present in the training set and can serve as exemplars; otherwise, it outputs the lemma as a placeholder. Thus, the system's scores are expected to be higher for the *feature overlap* and *both overlap* evaluation categories and very low when the target cell is unknown.

`TüMorph-Main` (Merzhevich et al., 2022): TüMorph's neural system is a modification of the character-level adaptation of transformer to morphology from Wu et al. (2021). In particular, the team trained the transformer to predict a distribution over states of FST (whose states are characters) rather than character sequences themselves. The model is scored third on both the small and large training settings.

`TüMorph-FST` (Merzhevich et al., 2022): As their second submission, the team manually developed FSTs using grammars and corresponding UnMorph repositories. Since that requires more human labour and linguistic competence, the team focused only on three languages: Chukchi, Kholosi, and Upper Sorbian. The resulting FST models outperformed all other submitted systems on two of three languages. The authors confirm earlier observations from Beemer et al. (2020) that such systems are able to reach superior results compared to neural ones, especially in low-resource scenarios and high morphological complexity, but require substantially more human working hours.

`UBC` (Yang et al., 2022): The UBC team proposed enriching the character-level transformer of Wu et al. (2021) with reverse positional embeddings to better account for suffixing, one of the most common word formation processes. In addition, the team explored a synthetic data augmentation technique proposed by Anastasopoulos and Neubig (2019) and student-forcing (Nicolai and Silfverberg, 2020), a training strategy where the model outputs are replaced with gold labels for some percentage of samples to alleviate exposure bias. Data augmentation leads to significant improvements, especially in the small training condition, confirming its utility. The student forcing training also provides a certain accuracy gain but presents mixed results when used together with data hallucination.

`Flexica` (Scherbakov and Vylomova, 2022) is a modified version of the non-neural system submitted to the SIGMORPHON 2020 Shared Task on morphological reinflection (Scherbakov, 2020). The system is based on refined alignment patterns between lemmas and inflected forms. In this year's submission, grammatical tag interchangeability learning was added to address smaller fea-

[8] Available here: `https://github.com/sigmorphon/2022InflectionST/tree/main/baselines/nonneural`

Language	Train/Dev/Test Split Sizes				Test/Small Train Overlaps				Test/Large Train Overlaps			
	#Small	#Large	#Dev	#Test	#Both	#Lemma	#Feats	#Neither	#Both	#Feat	#Lemma	#Neither
ang	700	7000	866	1969	158	217	815	779	697	821	278	173
ara	700	7000	988	1995	84	93	843	975	549	529	447	470
asm	700	7000	996	1990	416	498	558	518	979	990	12	9
bra	700	–	365	734	64	161	146	363	–	–	–	–
ckt	167	–	22	46	0	16	1	29	–	–	–	–
evn	700	7000	959	1743	1	519	2	1221	3	1065	0	675
gml	700	–	229	358	42	316	0	0	–	–	–	–
goh	700	–	986	1877	713	800	199	165	–	–	–	–
got	700	7000	994	1994	146	174	836	838	825	795	169	205
guj	700	–	994	1941	764	823	204	150	–	–	–	–
heb	700	7000	1000	2000	419	454	581	546	1000	1000	0	0
hsb	240	–	40	80	0	13	3	64	–	–	–	–
hsi	70	–	15	30	1	18	0	11	–	–	–	–
hun	700	7000	1000	2000	40	40	949	971	308	315	692	685
hye	700	7000	1000	2000	145	158	838	859	678	715	322	285
itl	700	–	572	1083	85	191	449	358	–	–	–	–
kat	630	7000	1000	2000	162	406	721	711	816	832	184	168
kaz	700	7000	998	1994	375	510	609	500	966	992	28	8
ket	700	–	85	137	13	48	14	62	–	–	–	–
khk	700	7000	996	1980	205	284	788	703	976	985	17	2
kor	700	7000	987	1964	221	245	748	750	886	925	83	70
krl	700	7000	998	1996	148	174	844	830	804	816	192	184
lud	700	7000	991	1976	87	105	880	904	775	297	212	692
mag	700	–	215	430	45	107	105	173	–	–	–	–
nds	700	–	963	1900	813	936	106	45	–	–	–	–
non	700	7000	992	1991	362	442	609	578	931	964	61	35
pol	700	7000	1000	2000	8	11	847	1134	61	70	939	930
poma	700	7000	921	1999	17	14	980	988	169	172	830	828
sjo	700	–	350	1857	184	286	754	633	–	–	–	–
slk	700	7000	1000	2000	4	5	869	1122	56	47	944	953
slp	240	–	40	79	2	56	3	18	–	–	–	–
tur	700	7000	1000	2000	333	575	469	623	874	869	126	131
vep	700	7000	995	1993	42	58	936	957	412	428	583	570

Table 5: Training, development, and test data sizes along with overlap sizes between small training and test and between large training and test. Items were exlcuded post-hoc from dev and test if there were multiple triples with the same lemma and features.

ture overlap. The system learns transformation patterns based on maximal continuous matches between lemma and inflected forms. The extraction of a pattern from an inflection sample starts with finding the longest common substring and then recurrently continues to the remaining parts until no more common characters can be found. Then, each of such extracted patterns is augmented with a set of more concrete patterns. Concrete patterns are produced from abstract ones by replacing some 'wildcard' characters back with concrete characters observed in a training sample. At prediction time, an inflected form is inferred by choosing a pattern that matches the respective lemma and yields a maximum score.

7 Results and Evaluation

Performance was evaluated by exact match accuracy. Macro-averages across languages on the entire test set and partitioned over the four overlap types are provided in Table 6. Results by language for both small and large training conditions are provided in Tables 14-18 in Appendix B.

A few points stand out immediately. First, overall performance is much lower this year compared to last year's similar task. During the 2021 iteration, all systems achieved over 90% accuracy on most of languages, while this year, no system achieves over 72% average in either training condition. This task was designed to be particularly challenging because the test set required systems to make predictions with only partial information. The results bore out this expectation.

Flexica, the only general non-neural submitted system, surpasses the non-neural baseline, but does not surpass 40% overall accuracy in either training condition. Being a hand-built system, TüMorph-FST outperformed all other systems on two of three languages that it was developed for.

As expected, all systems that submitted full or nearly full predictions for both the small and large training conditions performed substantially better with more training data. CLUZH, TüMorph-Main, UBC, and the neural baseline each improved by over ten points, while Flexica and the non-neural baseline showed smaller gains of around four points.

UBC achieved the highest performance of any system in either training condition. To understand why this is, it is necessary to look at a breakdown of performance by overlap type. The system is more resilient to novel feature sets than any other except for the hand-built FSTs.

System	Small Training Condition Overall	Both	Lemma	Feature	Neither	Large Training Condition Overall	Both	Lemma	Feature	Neither
CLUZH	56.871	**77.308**	31.269	**77.966**	43.255	67.853	**90.991**	41.425	**87.171**	60.300
Flexica	34.406	59.503	6.390	61.616	14.562	38.243	66.846	4.985	73.007	21.337
OSU	*47.688*	*79.310*	*8.565*	*82.308*	*44.133*	46.734	89.565	4.843	85.308	16.768
TüM-FST	*67.308*	*100.00*	*55.319*	*75.000*	*72.115*	–	–	–	–	–
TüM-Main	*41.591*	*58.907*	*18.597*	*62.469*	*27.613*	57.627	77.995	34.916	76.009	48.720
UBC	**57.234**	75.963	**35.519**	74.201	**46.060**	**71.259**	89.503	**50.583**	85.063	**66.224**
Neural	47.626	65.027	24.929	66.539	35.601	62.391	80.462	42.166	77.627	55.563
NonNeur	33.321	58.475	5.566	59.969	14.431	37.583	67.434	4.843	72.283	16.768

Table 6: Macro-average accuracy for each system. Three systems (OSU, TüMorph-Main, and TüMorph-FST) only submitted predictions for a subset of languages in the small training condition, so their numbers (italicized) are not directly comparable to the others. Flexica and NonNeur are non-neural.

7.1 Analysis by Overlap Partition

A breakdown by overlap partition reveals some consistent trends. As expected, *neither overlap* items proved challenging, since systems had to infer the forms for simultaneously novel lemmas and novel feature sets. Surprisingly, all systems performed better on *neither overlap* items than *lemma overlap* items. It is not clear why this would be, since it is observed on average for many but not all of the tested systems. It may be an artifact of the data splitting algorithm favoring balancing feature overlap over lemma overlap. However, the results are consistent with the observation over the 2018 data that systems struggle generalizing across feature sets more so than generalizing over lemmas.

They perform better on generalizations across lemmas to such an extent that the proportion of items with feature overlap in the test set washes out the effect of seen and unseen lemmas. Tables 7-8 illustrate this point quantitatively. Table 7 compares average performance on test items with feature sets attested in training (*both overlap* ∪ *feature overlap* items) with test items with novel feature sets (*neither overlap* ∪ *lemma overlap* items). All systems perform better on items with attested feature sets, but the gap in performance varies greatly from UBC's 32 points in the small training condition to OSU's 79 points in the large training condition. OSU's drop in performance is expected because it outputs the lemma when the feature set is unknown. In these cases it makes correct predictions exactly when the inflected form is identical to the lemma, pointing to a degree of syncretism in the data.

Table 8 shows the same, but for test items with lemmas attested during training *both overlap* ∪ *lemma overlap* items) and test items with novel feature sets (*neither overlap* ∪ *feature overlap* items). Every system actually performs *worse* on the attested lemma items than the novel lemma items. The penalty of novel feature sets overpowers gains incurred by attested lemmas.

Features System	Small Train Seen	Small Train Novel	Large Train Seen	Large Train Novel
CLUZH	77.790	39.417	89.753	47.874
OSU	*80.573*	*21.174*	88.186	8.918
TüM-FST	*80.000*	*66.887*	–	–
TüM-Main	*61.521*	*24.797*	77.351	39.633
UBC	74.672	42.684	88.064	55.928
Flexica	60.916	12.894	68.757	10.614

Table 7: Macro-Average performance for submitted systems on test items with attested feature sets (*both overlap* and *feature overlap*) and items with novel feature sets (*lemma overlap* and *neither overlap* types). Italicized small training results were calculated over partial submissions.

Lemma System	Small Train Seen	Small Train Novel	Large Train Seen	Large Train Novel
CLUZH	50.175	59.690	65.399	72.764
OSU	*38.248*	*62.811*	45.821	48.560
TüM-FST	*56.250*	*72.222*	–	–
TüM-Main	*35.442*	*44.116*	55.752	61.378
UBC	52.128	59.384	69.407	74.962
Flexica	28.629	37.309	35.378	44.300

Table 8: Macro-Average performance for submitted systems on test items with attested lemmas (*both overlap* and *lemma overlap*) and items with novel lemmas (*feature overlap* and *neither overlap* types). Italicized small training results were calculated over partial submissions.

Tables 6-7 together elucidate a clear difference between CLUZH and UBC. While the former outperforms the latter on items with seen feature sets, the latter outperforms the former on itsems with novel feature sets. This means that UBC outperformed CLUZH on this data set because it is better suited for generalization to unseen features, something that would likely been hidden if tested on previous years' data.

However, there is a sense in which testing on items with novel feature sets is not entirely fair for all languages. In highly fusional languages in particular, it may not actually be possible to predict the mapping from a set of semantic features to a particular inflection given what is known about the member features. On the other hand, it should be solvable for a canonically agglutinative language where each member feature contributes one piece of the inflected form like "beads on a string." Thus, it could be possible that the lower aggregate performance observed on novel feature test items is not due to a failure of generalization in the systems but rather the impossible nature of the task.

Table 9 tests this hypothesis. It shows average performance only on languages considered to be primarily agglutinative: Chukchi, Evenki, Georgian, Hungarian, Itelmen, Karelian, Kazakh, Ket, Korean, Ludic, Mongolian, Turkish, Veps, and Xibe. Further information can be gleaned from performance on each language individually as reported in Tables 14-18 in Appendix B.

In principle, a system should be able to infer the appropriate morphological operations for unseen feature sets in these languages, as was illustrated for Turkish in Table 1. While this is not a perfect test, since real agglutinative languages also contain some morphological eccentricities which obscure predictability, "could an undergraduate solve it?" does apply. It provides a clear result: the gap between performance on test items attested and novel features does not generally improve even for these languages where it should, if the unfairness of the task were driving decreased performance on fusional languages. This shows that generalization to novel feature sets, that is, to previously unattested inflectional categories, remains a legitimate concern for nearly all the systems.

7.2 Results by Part-of-Speech

As in previous years, the data employed for this task contains items from several parts-of-speech. Languages vary considerably in how much inflection they apply to different POS categories. As such, collapsing over POS categories can obscure interesting patterns. Tables 19-26 provide results for test items tagged with the four most common part-of-speech features in this year's data: verb (V), noun (N), adjective (ADJ), and participle (V.PTCP). Given the overall challenging nature of this year's task, performance across POS categories is generally weaker than what was reported for last year.

Features	**Small Train**		**Large Train**	
System	**Seen**	**Novel**	**Seen**	**Novel**
CLUZH	78.837	34.118	90.198	40.657
OSU	*77.800*	*30.376*	88.497	13.456
TüM-FST	*100.00*	*17.778*	–	–
TüM-Main	*61.730*	*14.816*	74.667	29.433
UBC	75.994	39.232	89.213	49.799
Flexica	60.885	11.386	69.173	10.094

Lemma	**Small Train**		**Large Train**	
System	**Seen**	**Novel**	**Seen**	**Novel**
CLUZH	44.850	56.649	62.082	66.201
OSU	*30.012*	*61.435*	45.315	53.753
TüM-FST	*6.250*	*26.667*	–	–
TüM-Main	*28.956*	*37.569*	48.871	53.093
UBC	50.439	57.022	67.471	68.427
Flexica	22.361	36.604	35.123	41.965

Table 9: Macro-Average performance for submitted systems on seen and unseen feature and lemma items *for agglutinative languages only*. Compare to Tables 7-8. Italicized small training accuracies were calculated over partial submissions.

8 Error Analysis by Language

This section contains qualitative error analysis for six languages from five different top-level families.

8.1 Arabic

As shown in Table 17, none of the systems outperformed either of the baselines in the *overall* partition in the large training setting.

15% of the lemmas in the test set were not inflected correctly by all the systems. Nouns (N) made up the majority of those errors (47.8%). Focusing on the noun majority, errors included inaccurate plurals, minor orthographic errors, and "reasonable" confusion of different state and possession features. The plural inflection errors follow a similar pattern to those in this year's acquisition-inspired subtask. See Kodner and Khalifa (2022) for more in-depth analysis. Orthographic errors include minor common mistakes resulting from missing orthotactic operations or an alternative spelling in the gold form. Lastly, there seems to be some confusion between SPEC, DEF, PSSD tags[9] in the dual and masculine plural forms since both those suffixes inflect for case and state. This confusion is mainly due to the existence of possible different forms of the same lemma sharing the same feature set or vice versa in the training data.

On the other hand, all systems correctly inflected 29% of the lemmas. In this case, 55% of those

[9]For more details about the state, case, and possession tags, please see the mapping description here: https://github.com/unimorph/ara#ara_atb

cases are adjectives (ADJ). This is not very surprising since adjectives in Arabic are more regular than nouns in pluralization in particular. Most of the plurals in this set are those ending with the feminine plural suffix, which does not inflect for case and state the same way the masculine plural suffix does. On the other hand, most of the masculine adjectives are singular and therefore the case and state inflections are easier.

In the small training setting, systems follow a similar trend, shown in Table 14. However, there is a higher percentage of verbs (V) among the lemmas that all systems inflected incorrectly. This is expected since verbal paradigms in Modern Standard Arabic tend to be very large in size, therefore, more sparsity in smaller training sets.

8.2 Armenian

Armenian orthography is quite close to the pronunciation of words. But all four models had issues when the triggers for inflectional allomorphy were from phonology, semantics, or morphological classes.[10]

The different learning models had problems in respecting the rather close correspondence between the orthography and phonology. For example, given a word with a final orthographic <a> like <anjny**a**> 'personable', adding a vowel-initial suffix sequence like *-i-s* (-GEN-POSS2SG) triggers a glide in both the orthography and pronunciation: <anjny**ayis**>. All four models incorrectly generated a glideless form for this word <*anjny**ais**>.

There were also cases of transparent phonological-conditioned allomorphy that caused errors. The definite suffix is <-n> after vowels, but <-ə> after consonants. Given a vowel-final word like <moře**ni**> 'raspberry,' the definite form should thus be <moře**nin**>, yet all four models made some type of error. The `Flexica` model used an entirely different ablative suffix *-ic'*, while the other three models used the wrong definite allomorph -ə. This allomorphy rule is exceptionless and is fully transparent from the reformed Armenian orthography. These errors suggest that the models didn't fully exploit the phonological properties that are reflected in the orthography. It is possible that such errors would reduce if the models incorporated some level of phonological information, such as by making the input forms be transcribed forms, and by having the models have a priori knowledge of cross-linguistic phonological feature systems.

Some errors were unavoidable and are due to phonology-semantics interactions. The plural suffix is <-er> after monosyllabic words, but <-ner> after polysyllabic words. For example, the monosyllabic word <nyut'> 'material' takes the plural <nyut'**-er**>. But if a word is an endocentric compound, then the plural suffix must count the number of syllables in the second stem of the word (the head). For example, the word <šparanyut'> 'makeup' is an endocentric compound of <špar> 'makeup' and <nyut'>. Its plural unambiguously takes *-er* because of the transparent semantic connections between the compound and the monosyllabic second stem. But all four models incorrectly generated the polysyllabic-selecting suffix *-ner*. It is not surprising that all four models made errors of this type. To avoid such errors, the models would need access to semantic information of the compound, and to also access the semantics of other words in the lexicon (the stems).

Some errors were due to purely morphological under-learning. Armenian has many different declension and conjugation classes. The different models made over-regularization mistakes, whereby they used regular inflectional suffixes over irregular ones. Sometimes the use of a suffix triggers morphological alternations in the stem. The models however preferred to keep the shape of the stem constant. Such 'mistakes' are common in colloquial speech, but they are absent in the prescriptive declension patterns that the Wiktionary data uses.

8.3 Hungarian

The richness of the Hungarian inflection system made prediction hard for all systems. While most errors show failures of generalization, many are attributable to genuinely hard, i.e., irregular or weakly systematic, forms of inflection. Mistakes due to vowel harmony are very frequent, as the vowels to be used in inflections are often unpredictable and can only be judged in terms of frequency in everyday use. Thus, **megtilt+enélek* is clearly ungrammatical (it should be *megtilt+análak*), but forms such as *szellős+ök* or *objektív+től*, not present in the gold standard, are actually used. Another recurrent mistake is the presence or ab-

[10] Transliteration is the Hübschmann-Meillet-Benveniste (HMB) system: `https://en.wiktionary.org/wiki/Wiktionary:Armenian_transliteration`. Forms in <angled brackets> are transliterations.

sence of the *-j-* in possessives where, again, systematicity is weak: in *siketfajd+(j)a*, the form without the *-j-* is not acceptable, but in other cases (*hangár+(j)aitok*, *tranzisztor+(j)a*) native speakers may accept either form. Unsurprisingly, all systems tended to fail over irregular inflections, such as hard-to-predict (but frequently used) inflectional classes, such as *low vowel nouns* (singular *út* but plural *utak*) or *v-stems* (singular *ló* but plural *lovak*). Finally, homonymy can also explain apparent mistakes, such as *szél* that means both *wind* and *edge*: in the first case its plural is *szelek* while in the second case it is *szélek*.

8.4 Khalkha Mongolian

Mongolian inflectional suffixes are highly unambiguous given a lemma's POS feature. Every inflectional suffix often belongs to only one morphological feature (Denwood, 2011; Munkhjargal et al., 2016). For example, Mongolian *-iin* belongs only to the genitive case while German *-s* suffix has two meanings by making the inflectional forms of either the genitive case or plural nouns. In this sense of low ambiguity, it is not surprising to see that the all participating systems have zero accuracy over the *lemma overlap* settings in Tables 15 and 18.

8.5 Polish

Performance on Polish was decent overall. In the small training condition, `CLUZH` managed to achieve nearly 91% on the *lemma overlap* items. While number decreased to 84% in the large training condition, which likely suggests that the *lemma overlap* test partitions contained coincidentally easy items, it does demonstrate generalization. Not all systems succeeded on the *lemma overlap* items. `OSU`, `Flexica`, and the non-neural baseline showed the usual performance drop.

Masculine genitive singular inflection proved challenging. There are two possible endings, *-u* and *-a*, but their distribution is unpredictable. As a classic example of paradigmatic gaps, native speakers themselves frequently disagree on which ending to apply (Dąbrowska, 2001). Then it is unsurprisingly that systems sometimes predict the wrong ending. For example `CLUZH` produced **przystępa* for *przystępu* as the genitive singular of *przystęp*. It also produced *filungu* instead of *filunga* as the genitive singular of *filung*, which is a known variant form in the language, but not the one presented in the gold standard data.

Systems also confuse masculine and feminine forms or inflect the wrong case. They also misapply *yers*, or palatalization, a pervasive process in Polish and in Slavic more generally. These types of errors were also identified in an error analysis of the 2017 task in Gorman et al. (2019). See that paper for more information.

8.6 Turkish

Turkish exhibits both front/back and rounding harmony. Harmony mismatches are a major source of errors on the language. For example, `Flexica` produces **dokumalisin*, a front/back violation for expected *dokumalısın*, and `CLUZH` produces a rounding violation **yoldurtmışım* for *yoldurtmuşum*. `Flexica`, the only non-neural submitted system particularly strugged in this area.

Voicing assimilation, which can occur intervocalically and at some morpheme boundaries, also proved to be challenging. For example, `Flexica` and `CLUZH`, the stem *çıldırt-* ends in voiceless stop, therefore the consonant of the following past tense suffix should be devoiced and realized as [t], however, in these three systems it remains [d], thus resulting in forms like **çıldırtdım mı* for expected *çıldırttım mı*. `CLUZH` and `Flexica` do not perform intervocalic voicing for *akrebinizi* from *akrep* and instead produce **akrepinizi*. Similarly no system except for `TüMorph-Main` correctly produces *asidi* from *asit*. They instead produce **asiti*. Related to this, systems sometimes fail to insert epenthetic glides between vowels in hiatus.

Sometimes systems produce commission errors, substituting a morpheme with one absent in the feature set. For example, for `CLUZH` in the small training condition, the case marking is wrong for the lemma *balta*: instead of producing the genitive *-ın*, it adds the ablative *-dan* even though the GEN feature is present. The same issue holds in quite a few lines as well. For example, for `Flexica`, the features contain GEN, but the system generates it with dative case (along with a vowel harmony error as in Hungarian), thus producing **havai fişeklara* instead of the expected form *havai fişeklerin*. All systems struggle significantly on items with unseen feature sets. This is interesting, because Turkish should have been one of the languages most conducive to generalization over unseen feature sets. The systems may not be associating the features in a set with their corresponding agglutinative realizations.

9 Discussion

This year's shared task investigated two dimensions of generalization in morphological inflection: generalization over lemmas and generalization over inflectional categories. Test items with lemmas or feature sets that were attested in training were evaluated separately from those with novel lemmas or feature sets to gain a better understanding of generalization. This proved to be a challenging version of the task, as performance is substantially lower across systems compared to previous years.

We carried on the tradition of including a range of typologically diverse languages in the task. From the perspective of the two dimensions of generalization, different morphological paradigms could prove more or less challenging. In particular, it is more reasonable to expect a system to generalize to an unseen feature set if the form of the corresponding inflectional category is in some way derived from forms associated with each of the member features. Similarly, a language with relatively invariant stem forms and little unpredictable stem-conditioned realization of inflectional categories should be conducive to generalization across lemmas, while a language with more stem changes or lexically arbitrary inflectional classes should prove more challenging.

Two major patterns emerged which held across systems. First, overall averages were lower than previous years in which overlaps between lemmas and features in training and test were left uncontrolled. The task was challenging. Second, performance test items with novel feature sets was almost uniformly weaker than performance on test items with novel lemmas. This was true for all systems and still held true for agglutinative languages which stood the best chance of generalization across feature sets.

9.1 Implications for Future Work

The results of this year's shared tasks have some implications for future systems and future shared tasks. First, since overlap type has a major effect on performance, cross-linguistic differences in performance in morphological inflection tasks may sometimes be driven by these distributions rather language-internal. Since these overlaps were hardly evaluated in previous years, a reanalysis of prior years' shared tasks along these lines may uncover interesting results. Related to this, train/test/dev splits created by uniform sampling of UniMorph will not only lead to uncontrolled overlap ratios, but will tend to drive feature overlap unrealistically high when training sets are large. This year's shared task provided an algorithm to make splits more uniformly with respect to overlap types, and it is recommended that future tasks also control for and separately analyze overlap types.

Second, both lemmas and inflectional categories are sparsely distributed in natural language use. As a result, systems in use in the real world will likely be asked to produce inflections for which lemmas or feature sets were not previously attested in their training. As focus grows on low-resource languages and language revitalization, a wide range of morphological typologies, including polysynthetic systems, will have to be reckoned with. The ability to generalize to unseen feature sets will become increasingly critical. Yet, there is a general weakness in generalization across inflectional categories in today's systems. Every system showed serious performance degradation. This was even true for agglutinative languages. Nevertheless, systems do appear to have generalized to unseen feature sets to a significant degree, and `CLUZH` and `UBC`, which showed similar overall performance, differed in their ability to handle unseen feature sets in particular. Thus, we believe there is reason for optimism and that there are real-world performance gains to be had by further developing this type of generalization.

Acknowledgements

We would like to thank Garrett Nicolai, Maria Ryskina, Ben Ambridge, Jeff Heinz, and all those who provided valuable advice and logistical support in the early stages of this project, Judit Ács, Duygu Ataman, Zigniew Bronk, Eleanor Chodroff, Sofya Ganieva, Włodzimierz Gruszczyński, Nizar Habash, Jan Hajič, Jan Hric, Ritvan Karahodja, Christo Kirov, Elena Klyachko, Ritesh Kumar, Vahagn Petrosyan, Matvey Plugaryov, Mohit Raj, Maria Ryskina, Elizabeth Salesky, Zygmunt Saloni, Danuta Skowrońska, Marcin Woliński, and Robert Wołosz, who prepared and authored lexicons used in this project, as well as Jeff Heinz, Sarah Payne, and Charles Yang, who provided feedback on this overview paper. The neural baseline system was trained on the SeaWulf HPC cluster maintained by RCC, and IACS at Stony Brook University and made possible by NSF grant #1531492.

References

Antonios Anastasopoulos and Graham Neubig. 2019. Pushing the limits of low-resource morphological inflection. In *Proceedings of the 2019 Conference on Empirical Methods in Natural Language Processing and the 9th International Joint Conference on Natural Language Processing (EMNLP-IJCNLP)*, pages 984–996, Hong Kong, China. Association for Computational Linguistics.

I Wayan Arka. 2007. Creole genesis and extreme analyticity in Flores languages. In *the 5th International East Nusantara Conference on Language and Culture (ENUS)*, Kupang.

Aryaman Arora and Ahmed Etebari. 2021. Kholosi dictionary.

Khuyagbaatar Batsuren, Amarsanaa Ganbold, Altangerel Chagnaa, and Fausto Giunchiglia. 2019. Building the Mongolian WordNet. In *Proceedings of the 10th Global Wordnet Conference*, pages 238–244, Wroclaw, Poland. Global Wordnet Association.

Khuyagbaatar Batsuren, Omer Goldman, Salam Khalifa, Nizar Habash, Witold Kieraś, Gábor Bella, Brian Leonard, Garrett Nicolai, Kyle Gorman, Yustinus Ghanggo Ate, Maria Ryskina, Sabrina J. Mielke, Elena Budianskaya, Charbel El-Khaissi, Tiago Pimentel, Michael Gasser, William Lane, Mohit Raj, Matt Coler, Jaime Rafael Montoya Samame, Delio Siticonatzi Camaiteri, Esaú Zumaeta Rojas, Didier López Francis, Arturo Oncevay, Juan López Bautista, Gema Celeste Silva Villegas, Lucas Torroba Hennigen, Adam Ek, David Guriel, Peter Dirix, Jean-Philippe Bernardy, Andrey Scherbakov, Aziyana Bayyr-ool, Antonios Anastasopoulos, Roberto Zariquiey, Karina Sheifer, Sofya Ganieva, Hilaria Cruz, Ritván Karahóǧa, Stella Markantonatou, George Pavlidis, Matvey Plugaryov, Elena Klyachko, Ali Salehi, Candy Angulo, Jatayu Baxi, Andrew Krizhanovsky, Natalia Krizhanovskaya, Elizabeth Salesky, Clara Vania, Sardana Ivanova, Jennifer White, Rowan Hall Maudslay, Josef Valvoda, Ran Zmigrod, Paula Czarnowska, Irene Nikkarinen, Aelita Salchak, Brijesh Bhatt, Christopher Straughn, Zoey Liu, Jonathan North Washington, Yuval Pinter, Duygu Ataman, Marcin Wolinski, Totok Suhardijanto, Anna Yablonskaya, Niklas Stoehr, Hossep Dolatian, Zahroh Nuriah, Shyam Ratan, Francis M. Tyers, Edoardo M. Ponti, Grant Aiton, Aryaman Arora, Richard J. Hatcher, Ritesh Kumar, Jeremiah Young, Daria Rodionova, Anastasia Yemelina, Taras Andrushko, Igor Marchenko, Polina Mashkovtseva, Alexandra Serova, Emily Prud'hommeaux, Maria Nepomniashchaya, Fausto Giunchiglia, Eleanor Chodroff, Mans Hulden, Miikka Silfverberg, Arya D. McCarthy, David Yarowsky, Ryan Cotterell, Reut Tsarfaty, and Ekaterina Vylomova. 2022. Unimorph 4.0: Universal morphology.

Jatayu Baxi, Dr Bhatt, et al. 2021. Morpheme boundary detection & grammatical feature prediction for Gujarati: Dataset & model. *arXiv preprint arXiv:2112.09860.*

Sarah Beemer, Zak Boston, April Bukoski, Daniel Chen, Princess Dickens, Andrew Gerlach, Torin Hopkins, Parth Anand Jawale, Chris Koski, Akanksha Malhotra, Piyush Mishra, Saliha Muradoglu, Lan Sang, Tyler Short, Sagarika Shreevastava, Elizabeth Spaulding, Testumichi Umada, Beilei Xiang, Changbing Yang, and Mans Hulden. 2020. Linguist vs. machine: Rapid development of finite-state morphological grammars. In *Proceedings of the 17th SIGMORPHON Workshop on Computational Research in Phonetics, Phonology, and Morphology*, pages 162–170, Online. Association for Computational Linguistics.

Tatyana Boyko, Nina Zaitseva, Natalya Krizhanovskaya, Andrew Krizhanovsky, Irina Novak, Natalia Pellinen, Alexandra Rodionova, and Elizaveta Trubina. 2021. The linguistic corpus VepKar is a language refuge for the Baltic-Finnish languages of Karelia. *Transactions of the Karelian Research Centre of the Russian Academy of Sciences*, (7):100–115.

Erwin Chan. 2008. *Structures and distributions in morphological learning*. Ph.D. thesis, University of Pennsylvania, Philadelphia, PA.

Edna Amir Coffin and Shmuel Bolozky. 2005. *A reference grammar of Modern Hebrew*. Cambridge University Press.

Ryan Cotterell, Christo Kirov, John Sylak-Glassman, Géraldine Walther, Ekaterina Vylomova, Arya D. McCarthy, Katharina Kann, Sabrina J. Mielke, Garrett Nicolai, Miikka Silfverberg, David Yarowsky, Jason Eisner, and Mans Hulden. 2018. The CoNLL–SIGMORPHON 2018 shared task: Universal morphological reinflection. In *Proceedings of the CoNLL–SIGMORPHON 2018 Shared Task: Universal Morphological Reinflection*, pages 1–27, Brussels. Association for Computational Linguistics.

Ryan Cotterell, Christo Kirov, John Sylak-Glassman, Géraldine Walther, Ekaterina Vylomova, Patrick Xia, Manaal Faruqui, Sandra Kübler, David Yarowsky, Jason Eisner, and Mans Hulden. 2017. CoNLL-SIGMORPHON 2017 shared task: Universal morphological reinflection in 52 languages. In *Proceedings of the CoNLL SIGMORPHON 2017 Shared Task: Universal Morphological Reinflection*, pages 1–30, Vancouver. Association for Computational Linguistics.

Ryan Cotterell, Christo Kirov, John Sylak-Glassman, David Yarowsky, Jason Eisner, and Mans Hulden. 2016. The SIGMORPHON 2016 shared Task—Morphological reinflection. In *Proceedings of the 14th SIGMORPHON Workshop on Computational Research in Phonetics, Phonology, and Morphology*, pages 10–22, Berlin, Germany. Association for Computational Linguistics.

Ewa Dąbrowska. 2001. Learning a morphological system without a default: The Polish genitive. *Journal of child language*, 28(3):545–574.

Ann Denwood. 2011. Template and morphology in Khalkha Mongolian—and beyond? In *Living on the Edge*, pages 543–562. De Gruyter Mouton.

Jasmine Dum-Tragut. 2009. *Armenian: Modern Eastern Armenian*. Number 14 in London Oriental and African Language Library. John Benjamins Publishing Company, Amsterdam/Philadelphia.

Micha Elsner and Sara K. Court. 2022. OSU at SIGMORPHON 2022: Analogical Inflection With Rule Features. In *Proceedings of the SIGMORPHON 2022 Shared Task: Morphological Inflection*, Seattle. North American Chapter of the Association for Computational Linguistics.

Alexander Fraser. 2020. Findings of the WMT 2020 shared tasks in unsupervised MT and very low resource supervised MT. In *Proceedings of the Fifth Conference on Machine Translation*, pages 765–771. Association for Computational Linguistics.

Omer Goldman, David Guriel, and Reut Tsarfaty. 2022. (un)solving morphological inflection: Lemma overlap artificially inflates models' performance. In *Proceedings of the 60th Annual Meeting of the Association for Computational Linguistics (Volume 2: Short Papers)*, pages 864–870, Dublin, Ireland. Association for Computational Linguistics.

Kyle Gorman, Arya D McCarthy, Ryan Cotterell, Ekaterina Vylomova, Miikka Silfverberg, and Magdalena Markowska. 2019. Weird inflects but ok: Making sense of morphological generation errors. In *Proceedings of the 23rd Conference on Computational Natural Language Learning (CoNLL)*, pages 140–151.

David Guriel, Omer Goldman, and Reut Tsarfaty. 2022. Morphological reinflection with multiple arguments: An extended annotation schema and a Georgian case study. In *Proceedings of the 60th Annual Meeting of the Association for Computational Linguistics*, Dublin, Ireland. Association for Computational Linguistics.

Jan Hajič and Jan Hric. 2017. MorfFlex SK 170914. LINDAT/CLARIAH-CZ digital library at the Institute of Formal and Applied Linguistics (ÚFAL), Faculty of Mathematics and Physics, Charles University.

Purev Jaimai, Tsolmon Zundui, Altangerel Chagnaa, and Cheol-Young Ock. 2005. PC-KIMMO-based description of Mongolian morphology. *Journal of Information Processing Systems*, 1(1):41–48.

Ritván Jusúf Karahóğa, Panagiotis G. Krimpas, Vivian Stamou, Vasileios Arampatzakis, Dimitrios Karamatskos, Vasileios Sevetlidis, Nikolaos Constantinides, Nikolaos Kokkas, George Pavlidis, and Stella Markantonatou. 2022. Morphologically annotated corpora of Pomak. In *Proceedings of the Fifth Workshop on the Use of Computational Methods in the Study of Endangered Languages*, pages 179–186, Dublin, Ireland. Association for Computational Linguistics.

Olga Kazakevich and Elena Klyachko. 2013. Creating a multimedia annotated text corpus: a research task (sozdaniye multimediynogo annotirovannogo kor- pusa tekstov kak issledovatelskaya protsedura). In *Proceedings of International Conference Computational linguistics*, pages 292—-300.

Ferenc Kiefer and Boglarka Nemeth. 2019. *Compounds and multi-word expressions in Hungarian: Compounds and Multi-Word Expressions*, pages 337–358. De Gruyter.

Christo Kirov, Ryan Cotterell, John Sylak-Glassman, Géraldine Walther, Ekaterina Vylomova, Patrick Xia, Manaal Faruqui, Sabrina J. Mielke, Arya McCarthy, Sandra Kübler, David Yarowsky, Jason Eisner, and Mans Hulden. 2018. UniMorph 2.0: Universal Morphology. In *Proceedings of the Eleventh International Conference on Language Resources and Evaluation (LREC 2018)*, Miyazaki, Japan. European Language Resources Association (ELRA).

Marian Klamer. 2002. Typical features of Austronesian languages in Central/Eastern Indonesia. *Oceanic Linguistics*, 41:250–263.

Marian Klamer. 2009. The use of language data in comparative research: A note on Blust (2008) and Onvlee (1984). *Oceanic Linguistics*, 250-263.

Jordan Kodner. 2019. Estimating child linguistic experience from historical corpora. *Glossa: a journal of general linguistics*, 4(1).

Jordan Kodner and Salam Khalifa. 2022. SIGMORPHON-UniMorph 2022 Shared Task 0: Modeling Inflection in Language Acquisition. In *Proceedings of the SIGMORPHON 2022 Shared Task: Morphological Inflection*, Seattle. North American Chapter of the Association for Computational Linguistics.

Ritesh Kumar, Bornini Lahiri, and Deepak Alok. 2014. Developing LRs for Non-scheduled Indian Languages: A Case of Magahi. In *Human Language Technology Challenges for Computer Science and Linguistics*, Lecture Notes in Computer Science, pages 491–501. Springer International Publishing, Switzerland. Original-date: 2014.

Ritesh Kumar, Bornini Lahiri, Deepak Alok Atul Kr. Ojha, Mayank Jain, Abdul Basit, and Yogesh Dawar. 2018. Automatic identification of closely-related Indian languages: Resources and experiments. In *Proceedings of the 4th Workshop on Indian Language Data Resource and Evaluation (WILDRE-4)*, Paris, France. European Language Resources Association (ELRA).

Agathe Lasch. 1914. *Mittelniederdeutsche Grammatik*. Max Niemeyer Verlag.

Peter Makarov and Simon Clematide. 2020. CLUZH at SIGMORPHON 2020 shared task on multilingual grapheme-to-phoneme conversion. In *Proceedings of the 17th SIGMORPHON Workshop on Computational Research in Phonetics, Phonology, and Morphology*, pages 171–176, Online. Association for Computational Linguistics.

Arya D. McCarthy, Christo Kirov, Matteo Grella, Amrit Nidhi, Patrick Xia, Kyle Gorman, Ekaterina Vylomova, Sabrina J. Mielke, Garrett Nicolai, Miikka Silfverberg, Timofey Arkhangelskiy, Nataly Krizhanovsky, Andrew Krizhanovsky, Elena Klyachko, Alexey Sorokin, John Mansfield, Valts Ernštreits, Yuval Pinter, Cassandra L. Jacobs, Ryan Cotterell, Mans Hulden, and David Yarowsky. 2020. UniMorph 3.0: Universal Morphology. In *Proceedings of the 12th Language Resources and Evaluation Conference*, pages 3922–3931, Marseille, France. European Language Resources Association.

Arya D. McCarthy, Ekaterina Vylomova, Shijie Wu, Chaitanya Malaviya, Lawrence Wolf-Sonkin, Garrett Nicolai, Christo Kirov, Miikka Silfverberg, Sabrina J. Mielke, Jeffrey Heinz, Ryan Cotterell, and Mans Hulden. 2019. The SIGMORPHON 2019 shared task: Morphological analysis in context and cross-lingual transfer for inflection. In *Proceedings of the 16th Workshop on Computational Research in Phonetics, Phonology, and Morphology*, pages 229–244, Florence, Italy. Association for Computational Linguistics.

Tatiana Merzhevich, Nkonye Gbadegoye, Leander Girrbach, Jingwen Li, and Ryan Soh-Eun Shim. 2022. Modelling Morphological Inflection with Data-Driven and Rule-Based Approaches. In *Proceedings of the SIGMORPHON 2022 Shared Task: Morphological Inflection*, Seattle. North American Chapter of the Association for Computational Linguistics.

J. Mistrík. 1988. *A Grammar of Contemporary Slovak*. Slovenské pedagogické nakladatel'stvo.

Zoljargal Munkhjargal, Altangerel Chagnaa, and Purev Jaimai. 2016. Morphological transducer for Mongolian. In *International Conference on Computational Collective Intelligence*, pages 546–554. Springer.

Saliha Muradoglu, Nicholas Evans, and Ekaterina Vylomova. 2020. Modelling verbal morphology in Nen. In *Proceedings of the The 18th Annual Workshop of the Australasian Language Technology Association*, pages 43–53, Virtual Workshop. Australasian Language Technology Association.

Temir Nabiyev. 2015. *Kazakh Language: 101 Kazakh Verbs*. Preceptor Language Guides, Online.

Naonori Nagaya. 2011. *The Lamaholot language of Eastern Indonesia*. Ph.D. thesis, Rice University, Houston, TX.

Naonori Nagaya. 2012. *The Lamaholot language of eastern Indonesia*. Ph.D. thesis, Rice University.

Garrett Nicolai and Miikka Silfverberg. 2020. Noise isn't always negative: Countering exposure bias in sequence-to-sequence inflection models. In *Proceedings of the 28th International Conference on Computational Linguistics*, pages 2837–2846, Barcelona, Spain (Online). International Committee on Computational Linguistics.

I Novak, M Penttonen, A Ruuskanen, and L Siilin. 2019. Karel'skiy yazyk v grammatikakh (Karelian in grammars). *Sravnitel'noe issledovanie foneticheskoy I morfologicheskoy sistem–Petrozavodsk: KarRC RAS*, page 22.

Tiago Pimentel, Maria Ryskina, Sabrina J. Mielke, Shijie Wu, Eleanor Chodroff, Brian Leonard, Garrett Nicolai, Yustinus Ghanggo Ate, Salam Khalifa, Nizar Habash, Charbel El-Khaissi, Omer Goldman, Michael Gasser, William Lane, Matt Coler, Arturo Oncevay, Jaime Rafael Montoya Samame, Gema Celeste Silva Villegas, Adam Ek, Jean-Philippe Bernardy, Andrey Shcherbakov, Aziyana Bayyr-ool, Karina Sheifer, Sofya Ganieva, Matvey Plugaryov, Elena Klyachko, Ali Salehi, Andrew Krizhanovsky, Natalia Krizhanovsky, Clara Vania, Sardana Ivanova, Aelita Salchak, Christopher Straughn, Zoey Liu, Jonathan North Washington, Duygu Ataman, Witold Kieraś, Marcin Woliński, Totok Suhardijanto, Niklas Stoehr, Zahroh Nuriah, Shyam Ratan, Francis M. Tyers, Edoardo M. Ponti, Grant Aiton, Richard J. Hatcher, Emily Prud'hommeaux, Ritesh Kumar, Mans Hulden, Botond Barta, Dorina Lakatos, Gábor Szolnok, Judit Ács, Mohit Raj, David Yarowsky, Ryan Cotterell, Ben Ambridge, and Ekaterina Vylomova. 2021. SIGMORPHON 2021 shared task on morphological reinflection: Generalization across languages. In *Proceedings of the 18th SIGMORPHON Workshop on Computational Research in Phonetics, Phonology, and Morphology*, pages 229–259, Online. Association for Computational Linguistics.

Donald A Ringe. 2017. *From Proto-Indo-European to Proto-Germanic*, volume 1. Oxford University Press.

Carol Rounds. 2009. *Hungarian: An essential grammar*. Routledge.

Mohammad Salehi and Aydin Neysani. 2017. Receptive intelligibility of Turkish to Iranian-Azerbaijani speakers. *Cogent Education*, 4(1):1326653.

Andreas Scherbakov. 2020. The UniMelb submission to the SIGMORPHON 2020 shared task 0: Typologically diverse morphological inflection. In *Proceedings of the 17th SIGMORPHON Workshop on Computational Research in Phonetics, Phonology, and Morphology*, pages 177–183.

Andrey Scherbakov and Ekaterina Vylomova. 2022. Morphology is not just a Naïve Bayes! In *Proceedings of the SIGMORPHON 2022 Shared Task: Morphological Inflection*, Seattle. North American Chapter of the Association for Computational Linguistics.

Simon Clematide Silvan Wehrli and Peter Makarov. 2022. CLUZH at SIGMORPHON 2022 Shared

Tasks on Morpheme Segmentation and Inflection Generation. In *Proceedings of the SIGMORPHON 2022 Shared Task: Morphological Inflection*, Seattle. North American Chapter of the Association for Computational Linguistics.

Dima Taji, Salam Khalifa, Ossama Obeid, Fadhl Eryani, and Nizar Habash. 2018. An Arabic morphological analyzer and generator with copious features. In *Proceedings of the Fifteenth Workshop on Computational Research in Phonetics, Phonology, and Morphology*, pages 140–150, Brussels, Belgium. Association for Computational Linguistics.

Turkicum. 2019. *The Kazakh Verbs: Review Guide*. Preceptor Language Guides, Online.

Francis Tyers and Karina Mishchenkova. 2020. Dependency annotation of noun incorporation in polysynthetic languages. In *Proceedings of the Fourth Workshop on Universal Dependencies (UDW 2020)*, pages 195–204.

G.K. Verner. 1997. Jeniseiskije jazyki. *Jazyki mira. Paleoasiatskije jazyki.*, pages 169–177.

Ekaterina Vylomova, Jennifer White, Elizabeth Salesky, Sabrina J. Mielke, Shijie Wu, Edoardo Maria Ponti, Rowan Hall Maudslay, Ran Zmigrod, Josef Valvoda, Svetlana Toldova, Francis Tyers, Elena Klyachko, Ilya Yegorov, Natalia Krizhanovsky, Paula Czarnowska, Irene Nikkarinen, Andrew Krizhanovsky, Tiago Pimentel, Lucas Torroba Hennigen, Christo Kirov, Garrett Nicolai, Adina Williams, Antonios Anastasopoulos, Hilaria Cruz, Eleanor Chodroff, Ryan Cotterell, Miikka Silfverberg, and Mans Hulden. 2020. SIGMORPHON 2020 shared task 0: Typologically diverse morphological inflection. In *Proceedings of the 17th SIGMORPHON Workshop on Computational Research in Phonetics, Phonology, and Morphology*, pages 1–39, Online. Association for Computational Linguistics.

Marcin Woliński and Witold Kieraś. 2016. The online version of grammatical dictionary of Polish. In *Proceedings of the Tenth International Conference on Language Resources and Evaluation (LREC'16)*, pages 2589–2594, Portorož, Slovenia. European Language Resources Association (ELRA).

Marcin Woliński, Zygmunt Saloni, Robert Wołosz, Włodzimierz Gruszczyński, Danuta Skowrońska, and Zbigniew Bronk. 2020. *Słownik gramatyczny języka polskiego*, 4th edition. Warsaw. `http://sgjp.pl`.

Shijie Wu, Ryan Cotterell, and Mans Hulden. 2021. Applying the transformer to character-level transduction. In *Proceedings of the 16th Conference of the European Chapter of the Association for Computational Linguistics: Main Volume*, pages 1901–1907, Online. Association for Computational Linguistics.

Changbing Yang, Ruixin Yang, Garrett Nicolai, and Miikka Silfverberg. 2022. Generalizing Morphological Inflection Systems to Unseen Lemmas. In *Proceedings of the SIGMORPHON 2022 Shared Task: Morphological Inflection*, Seattle. North American Chapter of the Association for Computational Linguistics.

He Zhou, Juyeon Chung, Sandra Kübler, and Francis Tyers. 2020. Universal dependency treebank for Xibe. In *Proceedings of the Fourth Workshop on Universal Dependencies (UDW 2020)*, pages 205–215.

A Lemma and Feature Overlap in 2018

Under the hypothesis that systems struggle at generalization to novel lemmas or feature sets, the proportion of test items which are novel should serve as a performance ceiling. Tables 2-3 show an apparent ceiling effect for two closely related highly agglutinative languages, Turkish and Azeri. This appendix provides performance and ceiling numbers for both lemma and feature overlap for the best performing system on each language on the low training size condition in the 2018 inflection task (Cotterell et al., 2018). This condition was chosen for illustration because it showed the most language-to-language variation in overlaps.

Tables 10-11 show a ceiling effect for feature overlap in the low training condition in 2018 task. The best systems manage to surpass the hypothesized ceiling for only 17 of 104 languages, most of which are agglutinative. In contrast, lemma overlap, shown in Tables 12-13, does not seem to produce a ceiling effect. The best systems surpass it for 74 of 104 languages, which can only possible if the systems possess a significant ability to generalize to unseen lemmas.

Language	F Overlap%	Acc%	Δ
Adyghe	98.3	90.6	-7.7
Albanian	54.8	36.4	-18.4
Arabic	54.2	45.2	-9.0
Armenian	**55.3**	**64.9**	**9.6**
Asturian	**65.2**	**74.6**	**9.4**
Azeri	71.0	65.0	-6.0
Bashkir	98.0	77.8	-20.2
Basque	**5.6**	**13.3**	**7.7**
Belarusian	86.3	33.4	-52.9
Bengali	83.0	72.0	-11.0
Breton	74.0	72.0	-2.0
Bulgarian	66.1	62.9	-3.2
Catalan	86.9	72.5	-14.4
Classical Syriac	**95.0**	**96.0**	**1.0**
Cornish	68.0	40.0	-28.0
Crimean Tatar	98.0	91.0	-7.0
Czech	56.7	46.5	-10.2
Danish	96.2	87.7	-8.5
Dutch	95.2	69.3	-25.9
English	100.	91.8	-8.2
Estonian	70.3	35.2	-35.1
Faroese	85.7	49.8	-35.9
Finnish	58.1	25.7	-32.4
French	85.5	66.6	-18.9
Friulian	89.0	79.0	-10.0
Galician	73.0	61.1	-11.9
Georgian	93.8	88.2	-5.6
German	79.6	67.1	-12.5
Greek	57.7	32.3	-25.4
Greenlandic	100.	80.0	-20.0
Haida	**45.0**	**63.0**	**18.0**
Hebrew	82.4	56.7	-25.7
Hindi	**38.8**	**78.0**	**39.2**
Hungarian	78.9	48.2	-30.7
Icelandic	92.2	56.2	-36.0
Ingrian	100.	46.0	-54.0
Irish	82.7	37.7	-45.0
Italian	82.8	57.4	-25.4
Kabardian	99.0	92.0	-7.0
Kannada	74.0	61.0	-13.0
Karelian	**88.0**	**94.0**	**6.0**
Kashubian	100.	68.0	-32.0
Kazakh	100.	86.0	-14.0
Khakas	100.	86.0	-14.0
Khaling	**22.0**	**33.8**	**11.8**
Kurmanji	90.2	87.4	-2.8
Ladin	77.0	72.0	-5.0
Latin	52.3	33.1	-19.2
Latvian	80.1	57.3	-22.8
Lithuanian	65.4	32.6	-32.8
Livonian	73.0	35.0	-38.0
Lower Sorbian	75.9	54.3	-21.6

Table 10: Difference between proportion of 2018 test set items with *feature overlap* and best performance in the low training condition (Adyghe-Lower Sorbian). Bolded rows indicate better percent correct than overlap.

Language	F Overlap%	Acc%	Δ
Macedonian	79.2	68.8	-10.4
Maltese	99.0	49.0	-50.0
Mapudungun	88.0	86.0	-2.0
Middle French	86.7	84.5	-2.2
Middle High German	94.0	84.0	-10.0
Middle Low German	92.0	54.0	-38.0
Murrinhpatha	98.0	38.0	-60.0
Navajo	88.9	20.8	-68.1
Neapolitan	90.0	89.0	-1.0
Norman	88.0	66.0	-22.0
Northern Sami	69.1	35.8	-33.3
North Frisian	85.0	45.0	-40.0
Norwegian Bokmaal	99.3	90.1	-9.2
Norwegian Nynorsk	98.3	83.6	-14.7
Occitan	91.0	77.0	-14.0
Old Armenian	47.4	42.0	-5.4
Old Church Slavonic	97.0	53.0	-44.0
Old English	81.0	46.5	-34.5
Old French	65.8	46.2	-19.6
Old Irish	46.0	8.0	-38.0
Old Saxon	68.3	46.6	-21.7
Pashto	59.0	48.0	-11.0
Persian	**54.7**	**67.6**	**12.9**
Polish	75.9	49.4	-26.5
Portuguese	**73.7**	**75.8**	**2.1**
Quechua	**21.4**	**70.2**	**48.8**
Romanian	79.4	46.2	-33.2
Russian	80.2	53.5	-26.7
Sanskrit	68.9	58.0	-10.9
Scottish Gaelic	100.	74.0	-26.0
Serbo Croatian	**34.5**	**44.8**	**10.3**
Slovak	90.0	51.8	-38.2
Slovene	70.8	58.0	-12.8
Sorani	**38.2**	**40.1**	**1.9**
Spanish	82.7	73.2	-9.5
Swahili	**39.0**	**72.0**	**33.0**
Swedish	95.0	79.0	-16.0
Tatar	98.0	90.0	-8.0
Telugu	**86.0**	**96.0**	**10.0**
Tibetan	100.	58.0	-42.0
Turkish	39.6	39.5	-0.1
Turkmen	100.	90.0	-10.0
Ukrainian	85.4	57.1	-28.3
Urdu	**41.3**	**72.5**	**31.2**
Uzbek	**75.0**	**92.0**	**17.0**
Venetian	88.5	78.8	-9.7
Votic	94.0	34.0	-60.0
Welsh	88.0	55.0	-33.0
West Frisian	100.	56.0	-44.0
Yiddish	100.	87.0	-13.0
Zulu	43.5	33.0	-10.5

Table 11: Difference between proportion of 2018 test set items with *feature overlap* and best performance in the low training condition (Macedonian-Zulu). Bolded rows indicate better percent correct than percent overlap.

B Full Results by Language

This section provides performance breakdowns by overlap type for each individual language for both small training (Tables 14-16) and large training (17-18) conditions. Data partition sizes can be found in Table 5.

C Performance by Part-of-Speech

This section provides performance breakdowns by part-of-speech for both small training (Tables 19-22) and large training (Tables 23-26) conditions. Information on the four most common parts-of-speech in the data overall: verbs V, nouns N, adjectives ADJ, and participles V.PTCP is provided. Results for TüMorph-FST are provided separately in Table 27.

Language	L Overlap%	Acc%	Δ
Adyghe	**4.6**	**90.6**	**86.0**
Albanian	**26.3**	**36.4**	**10.1**
Arabic	**3.4**	**45.2**	**41.8**
Armenian	**2.2**	**64.9**	**62.7**
Asturian	**22.0**	**74.6**	**52.6**
Azeri	**36.0**	**65.0**	**29.0**
Bashkir	**8.7**	**77.8**	**69.1**
Basque	87.8	13.3	-74.5
Belarusian	**10.2**	**33.4**	**23.2**
Bengali	**53.0**	**72.0**	**19.0**
Breton	86.0	72.0	-14.0
Bulgarian	**5.4**	**62.9**	**57.5**
Catalan	**5.5**	**72.5**	**67.0**
Classical Syriac	**47.0**	**96.0**	**49.0**
Cornish	100.	40.0	-60.0
Crimean Tatar	**4.0**	**91.0**	**87.0**
Czech	**3.4**	**46.5**	**43.1**
Danish	**3.2**	**87.7**	**84.5**
Dutch	**1.4**	**69.3**	**67.9**
English	**0.5**	**91.8**	**91.3**
Estonian	**12.8**	**35.2**	**22.4**
Faroese	**3.0**	**49.8**	**46.8**
Finnish	**0.2**	**25.7**	**25.5**
French	**1.6**	**66.6**	**65.0**
Friulian	**42.0**	**79.0**	**37.0**
Galician	**17.8**	**61.1**	**43.3**
Georgian	**3.0**	**88.2**	**85.2**
German	**0.8**	**67.1**	**66.3**
Greek	**2.1**	**32.3**	**30.2**
Greenlandic	100.	80.0	-20.0
Haida	100.	63.0	-37.0
Hebrew	**17.4**	**56.7**	**39.3**
Hindi	**33.1**	**78.0**	**44.9**
Hungarian	**0.6**	**48.2**	**47.6**
Icelandic	**2.2**	**56.2**	**54.0**
Ingrian	94.0	46.0	-48.0
Irish	**2.7**	**37.7**	**35.0**
Italian	**1.5**	**57.4**	**55.9**
Kabardian	**33.0**	**92.0**	**59.0**
Kannada	**51.0**	**61.0**	**10.0**
Karelian	100.	94.0	-6.0
Kashubian	88.0	68.0	-20.0
Kazakh	100.	86.0	-14.0
Khakas	**76.0**	**86.0**	**10.0**
Khaling	**18.1**	**33.8**	**15.7**
Kurmanji	**1.1**	**87.4**	**86.3**
Ladin	**47.0**	**72.0**	**25.0**
Latin	**0.9**	**33.1**	**32.2**
Latvian	**1.4**	**57.3**	**55.9**
Lithuanian	**9.3**	**32.6**	**23.3**
Livonian	40.0	35.0	-5.0
Lower Sorbian	**10.3**	**54.3**	**44.0**

Table 12: Difference between proportion of 2018 test set items with *lemma overlap* and best performance in the low training condition (Adyghe-Lower Sorbian). Bolded rows indicate better percent correct than overlap.

Language	L Overlap%	Acc%	Δ
Macedonian	**0.8**	**68.8**	**68.0**
Maltese	54.0	49.0	-5.0
Mapudungun	100.	86.0	-14.0
Middle French	**17.5**	**84.5**	**67.0**
Middle High German	98.0	84.0	-14.0
Middle Low German	78.0	54.0	-24.0
Murrinhpatha	98.0	38.0	-60.0
Navajo	**17.9**	**20.8**	**2.9**
Neapolitan	96.0	89.0	-7.0
Norman	100.	66.0	-34.0
North Frisian	88.0	45.0	-43.0
Northern Sami	**6.3**	**35.8**	**29.5**
Norwegian Bokmaal	**2.1**	**90.1**	**88.0**
Norwegian Nynorsk	**1.5**	**83.6**	**82.1**
Occitan	**43.0**	**77.0**	**34.0**
Old Armenian	**3.7**	**42.0**	**38.3**
Old Church Slavonic	53.0	53.0	0.0
Old English	**10.3**	**46.5**	**36.2**
Old French	**5.9**	**46.2**	**40.3**
Old Irish	90.0	8.0	-82.0
Old Saxon	**18.4**	**46.6**	**28.2**
Pashto	**35.0**	**48.0**	**13.0**
Persian	**30.3**	**67.6**	**37.3**
Polish	**1.6**	**49.4**	**47.8**
Portuguese	**2.2**	**75.8**	**73.6**
Quechua	**17.0**	**70.2**	**53.2**
Romanian	**4.0**	**46.2**	**42.2**
Russian	**0.4**	**53.5**	**53.1**
Sanskrit	**13.3**	**58.0**	**44.7**
Scottish Gaelic	80.0	74.0	-6.0
Serbo Croatian	**0.9**	**44.8**	**43.9**
Slovak	**10.4**	**51.8**	**41.4**
Slovene	**5.3**	**58.0**	**52.7**
Sorani	52.5	40.1	-12.4
Spanish	**2.5**	**73.2**	**70.7**
Swahili	78.0	72.0	-6.0
Swedish	**1.0**	**79.0**	**78.0**
Tatar	**5.0**	**90.0**	**85.0**
Telugu	100.	96.0	-4.0
Tibetan	80.0	58.0	-22.0
Turkish	**2.6**	**39.5**	**36.9**
Turkmen	**84.0**	**90.0**	**6.0**
Ukrainian	**5.9**	**57.1**	**51.2**
Urdu	76.9	72.5	-4.4
Uzbek	100.	92.0	-8.0
Venetian	**24.3**	**78.8**	**54.5**
Votic	92.0	34.0	-58.0
Welsh	**39.0**	**55.0**	**16.0**
West Frisian	61.0	56.0	-5.0
Yiddish	**7.0**	**87.0**	**80.0**
Zulu	**18.9**	**33.0**	**14.1**

Table 13: Difference between proportion of 2018 test set items with *lemma overlap* and best performance in the low training condition (Macedonian-Zulu). Bolded rows indicate better percent correct than percent overlap.

Lang	Partition	CLUZH	Flexica	OSU	TüM FST	TüM Main	UBC	Neural	NonNeur
ang	overall	**54.241**	37.075	–	–	45.962	51.346	49.822	33.215
	both	70.253	58.861	–	–	66.456	**72.785**	68.354	43.671
	lemma	38.710	17.512	–	–	34.562	38.710	**42.396**	8.756
	features	**70.307**	61.350	–	–	58.282	66.503	61.350	58.037
	neither	**38.511**	12.709	–	–	32.092	34.660	36.072	11.938
ara	overall	**66.566**	32.581	–	–	62.857	47.870	65.965	22.757
	both	71.429	50.000	–	–	67.857	60.714	**75.000**	39.286
	lemma	63.441	9.677	–	–	61.290	54.839	**65.591**	0
	features	**74.614**	58.719	–	–	71.530	52.313	70.700	47.568
	neither	59.487	10.667	–	–	55.077	42.256	**61.128**	2.051
asm	overall	**57.286**	30.452	–	–	38.995	55.025	54.673	26.231
	both	**74.760**	57.692	–	–	63.702	68.029	70.192	47.115
	lemma	40.562	0	–	–	23.494	44.177	**47.189**	1.807
	features	**72.043**	65.591	–	–	56.093	65.771	61.649	56.452
	neither	**43.436**	0	–	–	15.637	**43.436**	41.892	0.386
bra	overall	**60.354**	58.856	57.902	–	53.134	56.131	55.041	57.902
	both	26.562	26.562	25.000	–	21.875	25.000	**28.125**	21.875
	lemma	21.739	17.391	18.012	–	16.770	**22.360**	20.497	18.012
	features	74.658	**76.027**	71.233	–	67.808	68.493	66.438	72.603
	neither	**77.686**	76.033	76.033	–	68.871	71.625	70.523	76.033
ckt	overall	13.043	10.870	10.870	19.565	8.696	**21.739**	6.522	13.043
	both	0	0	0	0	0	0	0	0
	lemma	0	0	0	6.250	12.500	**18.750**	12.500	0
	features	**100.00**	**100.00**	0	**100.00**	0	**100.00**	0	**100.00**
	neither	17.241	13.793	17.241	**24.138**	6.897	20.690	3.448	17.241
evn	overall	28.514	3.328	–	–	23.867	**34.481**	29.260	25.014
	both	**100.00**	**100.00**	–	–	**100.00**	**100.00**	**100.00**	**100.00**
	lemma	14.258	2.312	–	–	15.992	**22.736**	21.580	9.441
	features	**50.000**	**50.000**	–	–	0	**50.000**	**50.000**	0
	neither	34.480	3.604	–	–	27.191	**39.394**	32.432	31.613
gml	overall	**56.704**	26.257	20.950	–	–	44.693	42.737	22.067
	both	88.095	71.429	33.333	–	–	88.095	**97.619**	40.476
	lemma	**52.532**	20.253	19.304	–	–	38.924	35.443	19.620
	features	–	–	–	–	–	–	–	–
	neither	–	–	–	–	–	–	–	–
goh	overall	**60.629**	40.224	52.637	–	52.158	59.03	56.420	42.568
	both	84.853	66.620	**87.237**	–	76.578	81.487	84.151	63.114
	lemma	**32.500**	8.875	15.125	–	26.500	31.875	30.125	15.125
	features	93.970	90.955	**95.980**	–	69.849	91.457	75.377	87.437
	neither	52.121	16.970	32.727	–	49.697	**54.545**	41.212	32.727
got	overall	51.204	18.154	–	–	47.693	**61.384**	60.582	38.816
	both	78.082	36.301	–	–	81.507	**89.041**	86.986	72.603
	lemma	26.437	5.747	–	–	34.483	**52.299**	50.575	4.023
	features	76.196	32.057	–	–	68.660	**78.349**	76.675	71.292
	neither	26.730	3.699	–	–	23.628	41.527	**42.005**	7.757
guj	overall	**66.924**	47.141	49.253	–	40.855	63.112	39.979	48.429
	both	**96.728**	86.518	96.073	–	64.136	94.895	63.743	93.717
	lemma	**34.143**	5.468	1.580	–	17.861	30.741	12.272	1.580
	features	**94.118**	90.686	91.667	–	59.804	91.667	69.118	92.647
	neither	**58.000**	16.000	14.667	–	22.667	40.000	31.333	14.667
heb	overall	**40.850**	19.250	–	–	31.150	35.150	39.650	14.750
	both	77.804	44.630	–	–	66.826	71.838	**81.862**	28.640
	lemma	5.066	0.220	–	–	0.881	0.441	1.322	**6.167**
	features	74.182	33.907	–	–	57.487	68.675	**75.904**	20.482
	neither	**6.777**	0	–	–	0.916	0.183	0.549	5.128
hsb	overall	15.000	13.750	8.750	**83.750**	7.500	3.750	5.000	10.000
	both	–	–	–	–	–	–	–	–
	lemma	7.692	0	0	**61.538**	0	0	0	0
	features	**100.00**	66.667	66.667	66.667	66.667	0	33.333	**100.00**
	neither	12.500	14.062	7.812	**89.062**	6.250	4.688	4.688	7.812

Table 14: Partitioned test performance in the small training condition (ang-hsb). No *feature overlap* or *neither overlap* items for gml and no *both overlap* items for hsb were included in the test set.

Lang	Partition	CLUZH	Flexica	OSU	TüM FST	TüM Main	UBC	Neural	NonNeur
hsi	overall	16.667	13.333	20.000	**96.667**	0	13.333	0	20.000
	both	0	0	0	**100.00**	0	0	0	0
	lemma	11.111	5.556	16.667	**94.444**	0	16.667	0	16.667
	features	–	–	–	–	–	–	–	–
	neither	27.273	27.273	27.273	**100.00**	0	9.091	0	27.273
hun	overall	60.000	25.900	–	–	51.850	61.750	**65.000**	23.900
	both	85.000	60.000	–	–	85.000	85.000	**90.000**	52.500
	lemma	40.000	0	–	–	27.500	45.000	**65.000**	0
	features	80.295	51.423	–	–	71.338	**80.400**	78.925	47.313
	neither	39.959	0.618	–	–	32.441	43.254	**50.360**	0.824
hye	overall	82.350	39.250	–	–	61.450	**86.250**	64.750	38.750
	both	**95.862**	80.690	–	–	52.414	95.172	51.724	82.759
	lemma	67.722	0	–	–	43.038	**74.684**	45.570	3.165
	features	**91.050**	79.714	–	–	68.377	89.737	69.093	76.611
	neither	74.272	0	–	–	59.604	**83.469**	66.240	0.931
itl	overall	33.333	31.210	31.487	–	33.056	**34.441**	34.257	28.163
	both	42.353	41.176	43.529	–	47.059	43.529	**48.235**	28.235
	lemma	3.141	0	0	–	3.665	**6.283**	**6.283**	0
	features	65.702	65.702	**66.370**	–	60.802	62.138	59.465	61.247
	neither	6.704	2.235	1.676	–	10.615	12.570	**14.246**	1.676
kat	overall	59.200	34.350	–	–	47.800	51.800	**60.200**	43.600
	both	51.852	43.210	–	–	51.852	48.148	**57.407**	53.704
	lemma	16.995	3.695	–	–	7.389	14.532	**23.399**	6.404
	features	**95.284**	73.925	–	–	92.372	90.430	93.620	94.730
	neither	**48.383**	9.705	–	–	24.754	34.740	47.961	10.689
kaz	overall	61.735	34.203	–	–	55.165	**65.747**	55.667	42.879
	both	**96.800**	64.800	–	–	83.467	**96.800**	83.467	85.611
	lemma	36.471	1.569	–	–	30.392	**45.098**	31.373	0
	features	98.686	70.115	–	–	94.745	97.701	95.567	**100.00**
	neither	16.200	0.800	–	–	11.000	**24.600**	11.000	0
ket	overall	33.577	18.978	**35.036**	–	13.139	26.277	10.949	32.847
	both	23.077	30.769	30.769	–	**38.462**	30.769	30.769	23.077
	lemma	**12.500**	0	**12.500**	–	2.083	2.083	0	**12.500**
	features	50.000	50.000	**57.143**	–	**57.143**	**57.143**	35.714	42.857
	neither	**48.387**	24.194	**48.387**	–	6.452	37.097	9.677	**48.387**
khk	overall	**41.768**	22.374	–	–	39.495	29.899	41.616	28.182
	both	83.902	48.293	–	–	89.268	61.951	**92.195**	56.098
	lemma	0	0	–	–	0	**0.352**	0	**0.352**
	features	**83.122**	43.655	–	–	76.015	58.629	80.584	55.584
	neither	0	0	–	–	0	0.284	0	**0.569**
kor	overall	**50.509**	30.957	–	–	17.821	44.348	23.523	28.870
	both	**70.588**	59.276	–	–	41.176	57.466	54.299	55.656
	lemma	**33.061**	0.408	–	–	18.776	**33.061**	28.163	0
	features	**71.658**	62.433	–	–	20.989	62.968	25.134	59.358
	neither	**29.200**	1.200	–	–	7.467	25.600	11.333	0
krl	overall	41.333	23.497	–	–	10.421	**45.842**	16.182	5.411
	both	**68.919**	37.838	–	–	16.216	**68.919**	22.297	1.351
	lemma	19.540	1.149	–	–	2.299	**27.011**	9.195	0.575
	features	63.389	45.735	–	–	16.588	**63.744**	22.986	8.886
	neither	18.554	3.012	–	–	4.819	**27.470**	9.639	3.614
lud	overall	87.702	88.006	–	–	46.559	84.565	46.609	**88.715**
	both	91.954	95.402	–	–	93.103	93.103	91.954	**96.552**
	lemma	**18.095**	16.190	–	–	2.857	17.143	3.810	**18.095**
	features	94.091	95.227	–	–	93.977	95.114	93.409	**95.909**
	neither	**89.159**	88.606	–	–	0.996	81.305	1.659	**89.159**
mag	overall	**64.419**	58.140	57.209	–	51.163	56.744	51.163	55.349
	both	**53.333**	44.444	37.778	–	31.111	51.111	40.000	31.111
	lemma	**15.888**	4.673	4.673	–	5.607	7.477	3.738	4.673
	features	**86.667**	83.810	83.810	–	76.190	80.952	79.048	79.048
	neither	**83.815**	79.191	78.613	–	69.364	73.988	66.474	78.613

Table 15: Partitioned test performance in the small training condition (hsi-mag). No *feature overlap* items were included in the hsi test set.

Lang	Partition	CLUZH	Flexica	OSU	TüM FST	TüM Main	UBC	Neural	NonNeur
nds	overall	47.789	31.316	34.947	–	21.947	**50.421**	25.789	16.053
	both	65.560	46.863	**72.079**	–	38.376	67.897	43.665	32.226
	lemma	32.799	16.239	1.603	–	7.906	**36.859**	10.256	1.603
	features	57.547	48.113	**59.434**	–	29.245	52.830	34.906	26.415
	neither	15.556	**24.444**	0	–	0	11.111	4.444	0
non	overall	48.820	39.126	–	–	47.313	52.436	**55.902**	30.638
	both	61.602	50.276	–	–	56.630	62.431	**69.613**	47.238
	lemma	37.330	22.851	–	–	47.738	49.548	**58.824**	5.430
	features	**63.054**	61.248	–	–	49.918	61.741	56.322	60.755
	neither	34.602	21.280	–	–	38.408	38.581	**44.637**	7.785
pol	overall	71.800	43.300	–	–	53.850	**78.350**	59.250	30.100
	both	75.000	87.500	–	–	**100.00**	**100.00**	**100.00**	87.500
	lemma	**90.909**	9.091	–	–	72.727	**90.909**	72.727	0
	features	85.596	70.130	–	–	61.393	**86.423**	65.289	68.123
	neither	61.287	23.280	–	–	47.707	**72.046**	54.321	1.587
poma	overall	50.975	29.315	–	–	45.873	46.023	**51.426**	22.311
	both	**70.588**	64.706	–	–	58.824	47.059	**70.588**	52.941
	lemma	42.857	21.429	–	–	42.857	35.714	**50.000**	0
	features	**61.020**	44.694	–	–	55.816	54.388	57.041	42.245
	neither	40.789	13.563	–	–	35.830	37.854	**45.547**	2.328
sjo	overall	71.998	65.751	68.174	–	54.496	**76.737**	58.643	67.905
	both	71.739	73.370	70.652	–	70.652	75.543	**76.087**	68.478
	lemma	36.014	20.280	24.476	–	27.273	**50.699**	36.713	24.476
	features	**93.103**	91.512	91.512	–	89.257	92.971	89.125	91.379
	neither	63.191	53.397	59.400	–	20.695	**69.510**	27.172	59.400
slk	overall	74.500	51.600	–	–	56.05	**84.100**	61.000	38.450
	both	**75.000**	**75.000**	–	–	50.000	**75.000**	50.000	**75.000**
	lemma	**80.000**	60.000	–	–	**80.000**	**80.000**	**80.000**	20.000
	features	87.457	83.774	–	–	65.823	**89.413**	67.664	82.739
	neither	64.439	26.560	–	–	48.396	**80.036**	55.793	4.100
slp	overall	29.114	8.861	6.329	–	12.658	**30.380**	15.190	5.063
	both	**100.00**	**100.00**	**100.00**	–	**100.00**	**100.00**	**100.00**	**100.00**
	lemma	25.000	3.571	0	–	10.714	**28.571**	16.071	0
	features	**66.667**	33.333	**66.667**	–	33.333	33.333	33.333	33.333
	neither	**27.778**	11.111	5.556	–	5.556	**27.778**	0	5.556
tur	overall	61.250	18.350	–	–	19.250	**85.800**	34.600	16.600
	both	80.18	54.655	–	–	17.718	**95.796**	28.228	51.952
	lemma	58.957	0	–	–	10.087	**89.391**	24.000	0
	features	72.068	39.446	–	–	37.740	**85.501**	51.173	31.983
	neither	45.104	0	–	–	14.607	**77.368**	35.313	1.445
vep	overall	40.291	20.622	–	–	27.446	**42.097**	35.575	21.325
	both	**54.762**	47.619	–	–	42.857	52.381	45.238	40.476
	lemma	25.862	1.724	–	–	15.517	**32.759**	24.138	1.724
	features	**56.624**	40.598	–	–	39.850	53.632	46.154	40.385
	neither	24.556	1.045	–	–	15.361	**30.930**	25.496	3.03

Table 16: Partitioned test performance in the small training condition (nds-vep).

Lang	Partition	CLUZH	Flexica	OSU	TüM Main	UBC	Neural	NonNeur
ang	overall	**64.855**	41.138	44.540	60.945	59.980	61.097	43.118
	both	82.496	73.171	80.488	82.066	80.918	**83.070**	78.479
	lemma	**48.356**	11.693	10.840	42.509	41.778	41.048	10.840
	features	**76.619**	64.388	73.741	71.942	74.101	73.381	68.705
	neither	**53.179**	14.451	12.717	45.665	39.306	47.977	12.717
ara	overall	75.890	37.544	40.902	75.338	67.218	**78.546**	26.917
	both	79.964	66.302	80.874	**81.603**	74.317	81.239	52.823
	lemma	73.913	10.397	1.323	71.834	71.078	**77.316**	1.323
	features	81.655	65.548	78.747	78.523	65.548	**81.879**	50.783
	neither	67.872	7.872	2.766	68.936	56.170	**73.617**	2.766
asm	overall	70.653	34.271	43.467	63.065	75.628	**76.784**	31.859
	both	**90.807**	68.744	86.313	77.222	85.393	83.861	62.615
	lemma	50.909	0	1.111	49.091	65.758	**69.697**	1.111
	features	83.333	75.000	75.000	**91.667**	83.333	83.333	83.333
	neither	33.333	0	0	22.222	**88.889**	77.778	0
evn	overall	48.939	3.844	24.957	52.037	57.487	**57.717**	25.072
	both	**66.667**	**66.667**	0	**66.667**	**66.667**	**66.667**	**66.667**
	lemma	40.376	1.878	12.582	45.634	52.394	**53.427**	12.582
	features	–	–	–	–	–	–	–
	neither	62.370	6.667	44.593	62.074	**65.481**	64.444	44.593
got	overall	65.747	21.264	51.254	65.346	**73.370**	72.166	46.038
	both	95.515	38.182	**95.879**	93.333	95.758	95.758	84.606
	lemma	35.723	3.522	4.654	38.239	**52.201**	49.560	4.654
	features	92.899	41.420	**94.083**	91.716	91.716	93.491	87.574
	neither	40.000	5.366	17.073	36.098	**50.244**	47.317	17.073
heb	overall	**51.750**	28.000	50.000	47.900	43.950	48.450	20.350
	both	94.100	55.900	94.400	94.400	86.500	**96.600**	35.100
	lemma	**9.400**	0.100	5.600	1.400	1.400	0.300	5.600
	features	–	–	–	–	–	–	–
	neither	–	–	–	–	–	–	–
hun	overall	72.350	32.950	47.100	68.150	74.900	**77.200**	37.250
	both	**94.805**	64.286	94.156	94.481	93.831	**94.805**	75.000
	lemma	54.603	2.540	1.270	45.397	60.000	**61.905**	1.270
	features	93.497	62.861	93.064	92.775	91.474	**94.364**	73.121
	neither	49.051	2.628	0.584	41.898	56.496	**58.978**	0.584
hye	overall	86.05	42.750	48.900	66.700	**93.400**	69.800	44.850
	both	97.935	85.841	97.640	61.357	**98.083**	61.947	90.708
	lemma	72.448	0	1.818	55.105	**88.671**	60.280	1.818
	features	94.410	84.783	94.099	91.304	**94.720**	90.062	83.540
	neither	82.456	0	0	80.702	**92.632**	89.474	0
kat	overall	74.350	45.100	52.400	78.850	83.200	**87.250**	45.500
	both	95.098	79.289	94.608	95.956	**98.284**	97.426	77.696
	lemma	53.005	7.572	9.255	61.779	68.990	**77.163**	9.255
	features	96.739	95.652	96.739	96.739	96.739	**97.283**	96.739
	neither	54.762	9.524	12.500	60.714	65.476	**76.786**	12.500
kaz	overall	58.375	34.203	49.198	53.611	**65.747**	55.667	42.879
	both	96.170	67.702	**98.758**	89.959	97.516	90.683	85.611
	lemma	20.867	0.806	0	17.44	**34.375**	20.867	0
	features	**100.00**	71.429	96.429	96.429	92.857	96.429	**100.00**
	neither	0	0	0	0	**25.000**	0	0

Table 17: Partitioned results on large training (ang-kaz). No *feature overlap* evn items and no *feature overlap* or *both overlap* heb items were included in the test set.

Lang	Partition	CLUZH	Flexica	OSU	TüM Main	UBC	Neural	NonNeur
khk	overall	47.879	23.384	**49.242**	47.727	46.263	49.141	38.03
	both	95.492	46.619	97.746	95.184	92.316	**98.053**	75.102
	lemma	0	0	**0.508**	0	0	0	**0.508**
	features	**94.118**	47.059	**94.118**	**94.118**	88.235	**94.118**	88.235
	neither	0	0	0	0	0	0	0
kor	overall	51.833	33.198	29.990	47.556	54.684	**56.161**	32.332
	both	**79.007**	67.494	61.738	69.300	76.185	78.668	66.140
	lemma	25.946	0.865	0	28.000	35.351	**36.865**	0
	features	**71.084**	55.422	50.602	56.627	60.241	62.651	59.036
	neither	27.143	0	0	20.000	**31.429**	18.571	0
krl	overall	58.367	37.876	45.190	24.098	**64.429**	27.104	5.361
	both	**88.557**	72.264	87.811	29.975	88.06	31.468	4.478
	lemma	27.328	2.083	0.858	8.578	**39.828**	13.725	0.858
	features	**87.500**	69.792	85.938	57.812	85.417	57.812	20.833
	neither	33.696	13.043	13.043	32.065	**48.370**	35.326	13.043
lud	overall	73.077	89.221	**89.676**	50.506	72.419	52.986	89.372
	both	94.839	95.871	**96.774**	96.000	94.710	96.516	95.871
	lemma	21.212	**51.515**	**51.515**	11.111	39.057	20.202	**51.515**
	features	87.264	91.981	92.925	93.396	88.208	**94.340**	93.396
	neither	66.618	**97.110**	**97.110**	3.324	56.936	5.636	**97.110**
non	overall	76.896	47.162	48.016	79.759	**87.243**	84.982	37.318
	both	90.763	68.743	90.548	89.796	**93.340**	92.374	67.991
	lemma	63.900	25.207	5.705	70.851	**82.054**	78.838	5.705
	features	85.246	77.049	85.246	80.328	**90.164**	88.525	80.328
	neither	51.429	25.714	17.143	57.143	**62.857**	51.429	17.143
pol	overall	86.500	52.850	47.800	67.700	**90.950**	69.450	43.600
	both	91.803	78.689	90.164	77.049	**95.082**	78.689	85.246
	lemma	84.286	15.714	0	71.429	**87.143**	68.571	0
	features	**96.060**	85.942	94.888	74.015	95.740	74.441	86.262
	neither	76.667	20.538	1.075	60.430	**86.129**	63.871	1.075
poma	overall	60.430	33.867	36.568	58.829	61.481	**63.882**	24.462
	both	73.373	48.521	74.556	69.231	69.822	**75.148**	40.828
	lemma	46.512	12.791	1.744	47.674	50.581	**59.884**	1.744
	features	**76.145**	54.458	70.120	69.398	73.253	74.096	47.831
	neither	44.928	14.614	2.415	48.430	50.242	**52.174**	2.415
slk	overall	85.550	58.250	47.400	65.750	**93.950**	70.100	47.450
	both	87.500	87.500	**89.286**	57.143	**89.286**	57.143	87.500
	lemma	89.362	44.681	2.128	51.064	**95.745**	57.447	2.128
	features	93.538	90.042	92.161	70.445	**95.657**	71.081	92.373
	neither	77.335	25.708	2.833	62.329	**92.445**	70.514	2.833
tur	overall	87.200	35.600	48.500	33.600	**94.150**	39.650	36.400
	both	97.941	72.654	96.224	36.041	**98.398**	37.414	72.654
	lemma	80.667	0.345	0.230	23.360	**93.326**	31.415	0.230
	features	93.651	57.937	**95.238**	80.159	92.857	79.365	66.667
	neither	52.672	0.763	5.344	40.458	**72.519**	70.992	5.344
vep	overall	57.451	30.457	36.929	44.104	**62.268**	48.821	32.413
	both	**75.485**	58.01	72.330	55.825	70.146	57.039	64.078
	lemma	42.757	1.402	1.402	25.935	**54.907**	33.879	1.402
	features	**71.527**	58.834	69.983	57.461	68.782	59.177	60.377
	neither	41.053	3.333	4.211	35.614	**55.439**	43.509	4.211

Table 18: Partitioned results on large training (khk-vep).

Lang	#	CLUZH	Flexica	OSU	TüM-M	UBC
ang	483	43.478	36.025	–	32.091	58.799
ara	341	32.551	11.730	–	27.859	52.199
asm	809	38.072	14.339	–	31.397	51.545
bra	208	21.635	17.308	–	17.788	18.269
ckt	20	10.000	10.000	5.000	0	5.000
evn	504	5.952	0.794	–	12.103	30.556
gml	229	63.755	23.581	–	–	93.886
goh	976	48.053	29.611	–	36.578	83.402
got	1003	41.874	19.541	–	36.491	80.160
guj	1214	57.908	36.903	–	28.007	93.987
heb	1729	43.493	18.681	–	33.372	79.294
hsb	21	4.762	0	71.429	0	0
hsi	19	10.526	5.263	100.00	0	15.789
hun	370	33.243	23.784	–	27.027	60.000
hye	764	74.215	37.696	–	26.702	96.859
itl	401	6.484	3.741	–	6.484	9.975
kat	453	5.519	5.298	–	6.402	47.461
kaz	576	72.222	23.438	–	56.771	92.188
ket	38	5.263	2.632	–	0	2.632
khk	78	1.282	6.410	–	1.282	30.769
kor	918	64.488	34.423	–	23.203	63.834
krl	1595	41.944	22.696	–	6.959	72.727
lud	903	85.050	86.157	–	1.661	91.251
mag	175	28.571	14.286	–	13.714	33.143
nds	880	43.523	37.273	–	28.636	75.114
non	585	41.709	34.188	–	39.316	60.000
pol	501	66.267	46.307	–	30.539	81.238
poma	747	54.217	27.711	–	49.665	63.989
sjo	297	29.630	10.438	–	35.690	56.902
slk	660	75.455	54.848	–	17.121	87.121
slp	63	26.984	6.349	–	12.698	57.143
tur	1446	65.698	19.018	–	11.549	91.978
vep	740	31.081	20.000	–	12.027	62.703

Table 19: Performance on verbs (V) in the small training condition

Lang	#	CLUZH	Flexica	OSU	TüM-M	UBC
ang	342	68.421	49.708	–	52.632	57.895
ara	833	67.827	31.933	–	65.306	49.340
asm	1103	73.255	44.152	–	44.968	70.898
bra	368	79.076	79.620	–	71.739	73.913
ckt	14	0	0	21.429	14.286	21.429
evn	867	45.559	0.231	–	35.409	47.174
gml	16	50.000	31.250	–	–	62.500
goh	839	77.116	54.470	–	71.514	75.924
got	206	34.466	12.136	–	28.155	43.204
guj	700	81.286	66.714	–	61.143	74.857
heb	226	28.761	27.434	–	20.354	28.761
hsb	37	16.216	10.811	91.892	8.108	2.703
hsi	5	40.000	40.000	100.00	0	20.000
hun	1287	64.180	28.127	–	55.245	63.403
hye	884	86.991	40.611	–	81.787	85.747
itl	217	49.309	50.230	–	54.839	54.378
kat	1505	74.684	42.724	–	59.801	64.518
kaz	1418	57.475	38.575	–	54.513	59.520
ket	44	18.182	15.909	–	18.182	20.455
khk	1847	44.721	23.714	–	42.285	32.052
krl	285	40.000	29.474	–	23.860	37.895
lud	878	91.230	90.774	–	90.319	91.344
mag	77	84.416	83.117	–	72.727	76.623
non	541	53.420	45.841	–	42.884	52.680
pol	259	63.707	69.884	–	55.212	65.251
poma	133	61.654	60.902	–	61.654	60.902
sjo	447	94.183	95.973	–	92.841	95.526
slk	111	65.766	63.964	–	54.955	63.063
slp	1	100.00	0	–	100.00	100.00
tur	538	50.929	16.543	–	40.335	73.978
vep	971	44.490	19.876	–	35.015	43.151

Table 20: Performance on verbs (N) in the small training condition

Lang	#	CLUZH	Flexica	OSU	TüM-M	UBC
ang	1085	57.512	35.484	–	52.535	57.419
ara	821	79.415	41.900	–	74.909	59.440
bra	69	57.971	55.072	–	55.072	59.420
ckt	1	0	0	100.00	0	0
evn	49	24.490	8.163	–	38.776	59.184
gml	78	57.692	39.744	–	–	50.000
got	309	59.547	12.945	–	58.900	67.961
hsb	18	22.222	27.778	77.778	16.667	5.556
hsi	4	0	0	75.000	0	0
hun	343	73.178	19.825	–	65.889	79.300
hye	315	94.603	38.730	–	89.206	93.651
itl	30	66.667	66.667	–	63.333	63.333
kat	42	83.333	47.619	–	64.286	73.810
ket	1	0	0	–	0	0
kor	221	69.683	42.534	–	21.267	57.466
krl	50	38.000	14.000	–	22.000	36.000
lud	105	92.381	92.381	–	92.381	90.476
mag	3	100.00	100.00	–	66.667	100.00
nds	887	49.605	21.082	–	13.191	55.919
non	652	50.920	35.583	–	56.748	58.896
pol	428	70.327	54.907	–	82.710	91.822
poma	242	66.529	54.959	–	58.678	60.744
sjo	2	0	0	–	0	50.000
slk	1142	75.569	48.862	–	77.758	87.916
tur	16	6.250	18.750	–	6.250	18.750
vep	233	54.506	26.180	–	45.064	57.082

Table 21: Performance on verbs (ADJ) in the small training condition

Lang	#	CLUZH	Flexica	OSU	TüM-M	UBC
ang	59	0	1.695	–	0	0
asm	78	30.769	3.846	–	33.333	23.077
ckt	2	50.000	50.000	50.000	0	50.000
evn	30	0	0	–	0	0
gml	31	12.903	6.452	–	–	12.903
goh	62	35.484	14.516	–	35.484	22.581
got	476	72.689	21.218	–	72.479	82.563
hun	12	25.000	33.333	–	33.333	8.333
hye	19	73.684	73.684	–	89.474	73.684
kor	127	63.780	45.669	–	15.748	48.031
krl	55	41.818	29.091	–	32.727	40.000
nds	133	63.910	60.150	–	36.090	55.639
non	213	50.235	46.479	–	51.643	53.521
pol	615	81.138	25.203	–	58.374	79.512
poma	875	42.400	18.857	–	36.800	37.371
sjo	246	33.333	15.041	–	25.203	40.244
slk	62	74.194	51.613	–	83.871	88.710
slp	8	50.000	25.000	–	12.500	50.000
vep	25	36.000	28.000	–	32.000	36.000

Table 22: Performance on verbs (V.PTCP) in the small training condition

Lang	#	CLUZH	Flexica	OSU	TüM-M	UBC
ang	483	62.733	45.963	52.174	51.967	51.346
ara	341	65.396	21.408	37.243	65.982	58.651
asm	809	65.760	20.643	38.072	54.141	67.367
evn	504	33.532	0.595	0	36.706	37.698
got	1003	52.044	20.538	47.856	54.337	64.806
heb	1729	52.747	27.357	50.781	48.120	44.997
hun	370	56.757	31.622	48.919	53.514	58.378
hye	764	80.628	42.670	50.131	32.068	92.016
kat	453	71.082	16.777	39.735	84.768	91.391
kaz	576	62.674	23.438	40.625	54.688	81.076
khk	78	11.538	8.974	14.103	12.821	11.538
kor	918	64.815	38.562	37.255	61.547	70.044
krl	1595	58.621	37.743	44.389	14.420	63.699
lud	903	53.045	87.375	88.372	3.765	51.717
non	585	69.231	38.632	38.120	72.308	80.513
pol	501	79.641	51.497	41.717	36.926	81.637
poma	747	60.241	34.806	42.704	65.060	63.989
slk	660	87.273	60.606	46.515	23.788	93.030
tur	1446	92.600	38.036	48.548	22.407	97.994
vep	740	54.730	29.459	31.486	17.432	59.865

Table 23: Performance on verbs (V) in the large training condition

Lang	#	CLUZH	Flexica	OSU	TüM-M	UBC
ang	342	80.117	54.094	58.772	73.977	71.053
ara	833	72.389	37.935	34.454	71.909	61.825
asm	1103	76.156	45.603	47.235	71.079	83.409
evn	867	65.052	0.231	43.599	68.166	73.818
got	206	61.165	20.874	56.796	52.427	58.738
heb	226	54.425	38.496	53.982	55.752	44.690
hun	1287	73.660	34.266	49.728	69.852	75.913
hye	884	90.498	43.439	50.113	88.575	94.796
kat	1505	75.083	53.223	55.880	77.010	80.731
kaz	1418	56.629	38.575	52.680	53.173	59.520
khk	1847	50.731	24.689	52.084	50.514	49.053
krl	285	58.246	38.947	48.772	64.912	71.228
lud	878	91.230	92.027	92.141	93.508	92.141
non	541	78.373	51.386	59.704	73.752	83.549
pol	259	79.923	74.903	62.934	81.467	84.942
poma	133	74.436	70.677	60.902	73.684	80.451
slk	111	76.577	74.775	72.973	80.180	78.378
tur	538	72.862	29.182	48.513	63.941	83.829
vep	971	59.423	29.763	40.886	58.805	62.925

Table 24: Performance on verbs (N) in the large training condition

Lang	#	CLUZH	Flexica	OSU	TüM-M	UBC
ang	1085	64.332	37.143	39.078	64.147	63.594
ara	821	83.800	43.849	48.965	82.704	76.248
evn	49	69.388	8.163	8.163	71.429	71.429
got	309	84.790	19.094	59.223	82.524	89.644
hun	343	84.257	29.446	35.277	77.551	88.921
hye	315	91.429	40.635	41.270	90.476	96.190
kat	42	83.333	59.524	64.286	80.952	83.333
kor	221	77.828	41.629	35.747	65.611	72.851
krl	50	64.000	36.000	54.000	68.000	70.000
lud	105	92.381	92.381	92.381	92.381	90.476
non	652	82.822	46.319	48.006	91.411	96.626
pol	428	83.645	58.645	55.140	96.028	99.065
poma	242	77.686	59.091	48.760	69.835	72.314
slk	1142	85.639	54.991	45.184	87.653	96.848
tur	16	81.250	31.250	43.750	25.000	93.750
vep	233	61.803	35.193	37.339	68.240	69.528

Table 25: Performance on verbs (ADJ) in the large training condition

Lang	#	CLUZH	Flexica	OSU	TüM-M	UBC
ang	59	3.390	0	0	0	0
asm	78	43.590	15.385	46.154	42.308	51.282
evn	30	3.333	0	0	10.000	16.667
got	476	84.244	24.370	50.840	82.983	87.185
hun	12	41.667	25.000	33.333	41.667	33.333
hye	19	78.947	78.947	78.947	94.737	78.947
kor	127	70.079	52.756	41.732	60.630	62.205
krl	55	50.909	41.818	50.909	52.727	49.091
non	213	76.056	62.441	45.540	79.812	86.385
pol	615	94.959	42.764	42.764	72.846	94.797
poma	875	53.829	20.571	24.343	48.343	53.600
slk	62	95.161	70.968	54.839	95.161	96.774
vep	25	52.000	44.000	48.000	52.000	64.000

Table 26: Performance on verbs (V.PTCP) in the large training condition

Lang	V	N	ADJ	V.PTCP
ckt	5.000	21.429	100.00	50.000
hsb	71.429	91.892	77.778	–
hsi	100.00	100.00	75.000	–

Table 27: TüMorph-FST results by POS. TüMorph-FST was only run on three languages, all in the small training condition.

SIGMORPHON 2022 Task 0 Submission Description:

Modelling Morphological Inflection with Data-Driven and Rule-Based Approaches

Tatiana Merzhevich[1], Nkonye Gbadegoye[1], Leander Girrbach[1], Jingwen Li[1], Ryan Soh-Eun Shim[2]

[1]Department of Linguistics, University of Tübingen

`{firstname.lastname}@student.uni-tuebingen.de`

[2]Institute for Natural Language Processing, University of Stuttgart

`soh-eun.shim@ims.uni-stuttgart.de`

Abstract

This paper describes our participation in the 2022 SIGMORPHON-UniMorph Shared Task on Typologically Diverse and Acquisition-Inspired Morphological Inflection Generation. We present two approaches: one being a modification of the neural baseline encoder-decoder model, the other being hand-coded morphological analyzers using finite-state tools (FST) and outside linguistic knowledge. While our proposed modification of the baseline encoder-decoder model underperforms the baseline for almost all languages, the FST methods outperform other systems in the respective languages by a large margin. This confirms that purely data-driven approaches have not yet reached the maturity to replace trained linguists for documentation and analysis especially considering low-resource and endangered languages.

1 Introduction

There are two tracks of the task of language Inflection Generation: Typologically Diverse Morphological (Re-)Inflection and (Automatic) Morphological Acquisition Trajectories. We only participate in the first track, Typologically Diverse Morphological (Re-)Inflection.

Here, the main goal is to predict inflected forms of a word by given lemmas and sets of morphological tags. In total, the task features 32 languages, for several of which both a low-resource scenario and a high resource scenario are proposed.

Our participation was split into two systems: One is a modification of the encoder-decoder baseline described in Wu et al. (2021), which is applied to all languages and resource settings.[1] The other system is based on hand-coded finite-state transducers for Chukchi (ckt), Upper Sorbian (hsb), and Kholosi (hsi).

The modification of the encoder-decoder baselines aims for better interpretability of predictions, but underperforms the baseline on almost all languages. The finite-state approaches yield very strong performance on the respective languages, however, their creation may have accidentally violated the train set / test set separation by usage of publicly available data UniMorph provided by Kirov et al. (2018) while constructing the transducers.

2 Methodology

2.1 Data-Driven Approach

In order to enable more explicit control of predicted forms and better interpretability, we propose a modification of the encoder-decoder baseline as in Wu et al. (2021). The main idea is as follows: We provide a directed graph whose states represent generated characters. Edges represent allowed transitions. This graph could be a full FST, or a simpler structure. Then, at each time-step, the encoder-decoder model predicts a distribution over states instead of characters as in the baseline model. While the difference may seem negligible, we argue there are several reasons why formulating the morphological prediction task in this way is useful: The provided graph can be used to control which sequences can be generated by disallowing illegal transitions during decoding. Also, the graph can be created and edited automatically or manually, which allows to inject expert knowledge. Here, different states may generate the same character, but in this way disambiguate possible trajectories through the graph. Finally, since each prediction can be directly mapped to a certain location in the graph topology, the model predictions can be interpreted relative to the given graph. If the graph is designed in a sufficiently informative way, this may allow better interpretation of predictions and also errors.

For training, each target form is converted to a path through the given graph and the characters are

[1]Unfortunately, we failed to submit results for Middle Low German (glm).

19th SIGMORPHON Workshop on Computational Research in Phonetics, Phonology, and Morphology, pages 204 - 211
July 14, 2022

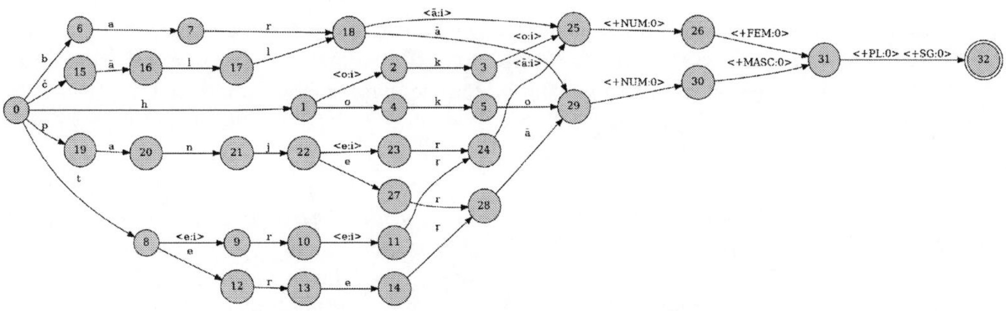

Fig. 1: Finite-state transducer for Kholosi numerals 1-5.

replaced by state identifiers. However, in order to simplify the provided graph, we may also define special states that allow the prediction of arbitrary characters, for example to predict base morphemes or copy them from the input lemma. In this case, we do not replace the respective characters with state identifiers. In any case, we train the baseline encoder-decoder model in the standard way but with modified targets.

The proposed idea is similar to learning weights of a FST as described in Rastogi et al. (2016). However, in our case, the encoder-decoder model does not have explicit access to the graph, but has to implicitly learn the possible transitions and their weights.

For this shared task, we were only able to test a simple but automatic way of constructing the proposed graph as auxiliary data structure for decoding: First, we align each paradigm in the train set, i.e. each set of forms with the same lemma, by iteratively aligning forms to the already aligned forms using the Needleman-Wunsch algorithm (Needleman and Wunsch, 1970) with column-sum as scoring metric. We replace all aligned substrings that are present in the lemma and all its forms by a placeholder symbol. This approach is similar to the method suggested in Forsberg and Hulden (2016). Finally, we use the same procedure to align the resulting forms of all paradigms.

Having obtained such alignments, each position in the multiple sequence alignment becomes a state in the graph. So far, we do not consider constraints on the edges, i.e. we effectively treat the graph as fully connected. However, in the future we would like to generate and evaluate more expressive auxiliary graphs.

2.2 Rule Based Approach

The morphological analyzers for three manually annotated languages were built using a finite-state compiler Foma (Hulden, 2009), which is based on lexicon and rules. The lexicon stores a list of words to which morphological analysis is applied. The rule transducers are established from regular expressions and applied to the list of identified word forms. For the system to perform better it is necessary to have a large lexical dataset to obtain higher accuracy of the morphological analysis performance. Therefore, we used the wordsets provided by the Universal Morphology project (UniMorph) (Kirov et al., 2018), which offers lists with lemmas, word forms and universal feature schemas with morphological categories.

Language	ISO	Speakers	Status
Chukchi	ckt	5.100	Threatened
Kholosi[2]	hsi	1.800	Unknown
Upper Sorbian	hsb	13.300	Threatened

Table 1: Manually annotated languages with their respective number of speakers and status (According to Eberhard et al. (2021)).

Chukchi Chukchi is a polysynthetic language spoken on the Chukotka Peninsula, in the northern part of the Russian Federation. It is composed of a rich inflectional and derivational morphology with progressive and regressive vowel harmony, productive incorporation, and extensive circumfixing across all its parts of speech described in Andriyanets and Tyers (2018). Chukchi is an ergative absolutive language with a highly complex system of verbal agreement constituting prefixal and suffixal components as stated in Bobaljik (1998).

[2]Data from Anonby and Bahmani (2016).

These components are commonly described as having some form of "split" ergativity such that prefixes show a nominative-accusative alignment, while suffixes show an absolutive-ergative bias (Wexler, 1982; Spencer, 2000).[3]

Chukchi also displays various types of perfective aspect as described in Volkov and Pupinina (2016). Examples of such are provided below.[4]

(1)	*etˀəm*	*Weɬwəne*	*ɣetuɬˀetɬinet*
	etˀəm	Weɬwə-ne	ɣe-tuɬˀet-ɬinet
	apparently	Weɬwə-ERG	PF-steal-3PL.PFV

'Apparently, Welwe stole them (deer)'

(2)	*ɣəm*	*tˀəɬɣˀi*	*ɣətkaɣtə*
	ɣəm	tˀəɬ-ɣˀi	ɣətka-ɣtə
	I.ABS	hurt-AOR.3SG	leg-ALL

'I hurt my leg'

(3)	*ɣənin*	*əneqej*
	ɣənin	əneqej
	your	old.brother.ABS.SG

ɣekeɬitkuɬin	*kaɬetkorak*	*?*
ɣe-keɬitku-ɬin	kaɬetkora-k	?
PFV-study-3SG.PFV	school-LOC	

'Did your older brother go to school ?'

A very critical set of rules incorporated into the FST were circumfixation and vowel harmony. Vowels in Chukchi are divided into two groups based on vowel height in addition to a schwa sound. The first group are the dominant vowels, which consist of letters э, о, а. The second group are the recessive vowels which are и, у, э (Andriyanets and Tyers, 2018). Both groups contain "э", which in both cases, are distinguished based on vowel harmony. Vowel harmony occurs progressively and regressively, influencing the entire word, thus morphological and phonological features can cause vowel changes in the stem and vice versa. For example, the verb "тэлпык", in the "V;PFV;IND;SG;3;PST" context becomes "гэтэлпылин".[5] While on the other hand, the verb "панрэватык" in the same context, becomes "гапанрэбатлен", thus changing the prefix-suffix combination "гэ..лин" into "га..лен", as a result of the dominant vowel "а" in the stem.

Chukchi also has morphological processes that on many occasions, result in the mutation or elision of letters. For example, the word "итык" changes to "титгъэк" in the "V;PFV;IND;SG;1;PST" context, thus resulting in the elision of the last two letters "ы" and "к".

The morphological and phonological analyzer accounts for some of the morphological and phonological processes in Chukchi. The finite state transducer for Chukchi adjectives can be seen in Figure 2.

Kholosi The Kholosi FST is additionally based on preliminary descriptions of the language's morphology. Since a systematic account of Kholosi morphology is yet to be published, we work exclusively with the work of Arora (2020), which is based on elicitation from a single native Kholosi speaker.

One interesting phenomenon is gender alternation with vowel harmony. Kholosi has two grammatical genders, which can be reflected by morphemes, `-o` for masculine and `-i` for feminine (Arora, 2020). In numerals, for instance, the feminine form always ends with `-i`. Hence we have a rule that transform the last character to an `i` when the `FEM` tag is expected. From the given five pairs of `MASC/FEM` numerals in the training data, we observe a change of non-`a/ā` vowels to `i`.

We also note the (notational) discrepancies among different data sources:[6] In the training data provided by the shared task, the numeral lemmas ends with an `ā` instead of an `o` which is different from what was proposed by Arora (2020).[7] We also found glossed sentences in Kholosi where instead of *baro* (or *barā*, depending on the data source), *bahro* is used for the masculine (lemma) form of the numeral *two*.[8]

The resulting numeral FST is shown in Figure 1. Adjectives can also inflect with respect to gender ac-

[3]Absolutive, as it is used traditionally, refers to the grouping of an intransitive subject and direct object of a transitive verb. Nominative here is reserved to indicate the grouping of the intransitive subject and transitive subject.

[4]This paper follows the Leipzig Glossing Rules (Can be accessed from: `https://www.eva.mpg.de/lingua/resources/glossing-rules.php`), with additionally AOR = aorist.

[5]The "л" sound is used as a substitute for the Cyrillic letter "El with hook".

[6]With possible errors inherited from UniMorph data: `V;IPFV;IND;SG;3;PRS` form of the verb *karen* is attested as *keraw* in glossed sentences but provided as *kerav* in train data, while the same forms for other verbs all observe an *-aw* suffix.

[7]Except the case of *hoko*, meaning *one*.

[8]Can be accessed from `https://aryamanarora.github.io/kholosi/sentences.html`

cording to Arora (2020), so similar rules are added to the adjective FST, although there are no feminine adjective forms provided in the training data at all.

Upper Sorbian Sorbian is a West Slavic language spoken in eastern Germany, in Saxony and Brandenburg (also called Lusatia). Sorbian demonstrate closeness with Czech and Polish, and at the same time shares certain features with South Slavic languages, such as the use of the double grammatical number with nouns, adjectives and verbs, as well as the use of specific forms of past tense. Unfortunately, due to the constant contact with German, Sorbian includes a large number of German loanwords in its standardized lexicon (Glaser, 2007).

According to Eberhard et al. (2021), the number of Upper Sorbian speakers estimated as no more than 13.000. Their community is fully bilingual, which means that if the rule of thumb proposed by Payne and Payne (1997) is applied, the Upper Sorbian might become extinct by the year 2070. However, the actual number of Sorbian speakers is based on estimations. According to the principles of minority law applicable in the Federal Republic of Germany, the commitment to a minority is free and not registered officially, as reported by Marti (2007).

3 Results

The data-driven approach earned third place for both small and large languages in part one of the shared task, although under-performing the neural baseline. The official preliminary results are available in Table 3.[9]

The rule based approach for three languages with relatively small datasets outperformed all other systems. However, the analyzers were not only built by the provided train data, but also with help of linguistic knowledge and UniMorph schemas, which in large encompassed the test set. The performance results are shown in Table 2.

Language	Result
Chukchi	19.565
Upper Sorbian	83.750
Kholosi	96.667

Table 2: Results (overall test scores) of the finite-state approach.

4 Discussion

The findings of our study follow up on the work of Beemer et al. (2020), where it was concluded that "it is very difficult in many cases to outperform a state-of-the-art neural network model without significant development effort and attention to nuanced morphophonological patterns". The finite-state grammars in Beemer et al. (2020) outperformed the seq2seq results only in languages with high morphophonological complexity such as Tagalog, and came at the cost of 5.5 manual working hours on average per week, over the course of 5 weeks.

Our work similarly required a high number of working hours, but was able to outperform other systems in low-resource scenarios precisely due to the reliance on the linguistic expertise of the FST creators. The trade-off we observe in our submission is therefore how much interpretability and intuition-guided modifications of a model is desired, where for sufficiently well-documented languages the benefit of FSTs may not be as obvious, but for scenarios where sufficient data may not be able to be collected, our submission would indicate that FSTs still maintain an edge over neural approaches.

Beemer et al. (2020) note that for certain languages the amount of inconsistencies makes it unlikely for a hand-written grammar to surpass neural systems, where certain rules were deemed irregular enough to not warrant treatment by their FSTs. We believe our study provides a partial defense for FSTs with precisely the same point: in cases where the amount of data is insufficient for neural models to infer the rules of low-resource languages, it is unlikely that the neural models can perform well without further data; for rule-based approaches, even with limited amount of data (e.g. due to a lack of orthography or access to native speakers), the models can always rely on linguistic knowledge to provide working solutions.

Our usage of data outside of the training set is also based on this concern: it is unlikely that there will be enough human resources for most of the world's languages to have enough data collected, but for the practical situation where a morphological analyzer is nevertheless needed, our results indicate that this approach still remains to be the most practical solution.

[9]Taken from `https://github.com/sigmorphon/2022InflectionST/blob/main/results/preliminary.md`

For our other submission where we experimented with a data-driven approach, we believe that it constitutes a step towards more interpretable encoder-decoder predictions, which in light of the above, may also stand as a future research direction, which could be beneficial for practical scenarios.

5 Conclusion

We presented two different approaches to morphological inflection, a data preprocessing method to be used in conjunction with standard encoder-decoder models and hand-coded finite-state methods. Despite the problems with both approaches, i.e. insufficient performance of the data-driven approach and large amounts of effort needed to engineer FSTs, we think that both have their benefits, as discussed in Section 4.

In particular we would like to note that the effort invested into creating FSTs expands computational resources for under-researched and low-resource languages and can be considered as a collaborative part in language revitalization as proposed in Pine and Turin (2017). Also, both approaches allow for future extensions, e.g. a big improvement of finite-state analyzers would be expansion of current lexicons with guessers for assigning possible stems and part-of-speech tags.

References

Vasilisa Andriyanets and Francis Tyers. 2018. A prototype finite-state morphological analyser for Chukchi. In *Proceedings of the Workshop on Computational Modeling of Polysynthetic Languages*, pages 31–40, Santa Fe, New Mexico, USA. Association for Computational Linguistics.

Erik Anonby and Hassan Mohebbi Bahmani. 2016. Shipwrecked and landlocked: Discovery of Kholosi, an Indo-Aryan language in south-west Iran. In Jila Ghomeshi, Carina Jahani, and Agnes Lenepveu-Hotz, editors, *Further Topics in Iranian Linguistics. Proceedings of the 5th International Conference on Iranian Linguistics, held in Bamberg on 24-26 August 2013*, volume 58 of *Cahiers de Studia Iranica*, pages 13–36. Peeters, Louvain.

Aryaman Arora. 2020. Historical Phonology and other Observations on Kholosi.

Sarah Beemer, Zak Boston, April Bukoski, Daniel Chen, Princess Dickens, Andrew Gerlach, Torin Hopkins, Parth Anand Jawale, Chris Koski, Akanksha Malhotra, Piyush Mishra, Saliha Muradoglu, Lan Sang, Tyler Short, Sagarika Shreevastava, Elizabeth Spaulding, Testumichi Umada, Beilei Xiang, Changbing Yang, and Mans Hulden. 2020. Linguist vs. machine: Rapid development of finite-state morphological grammars. In *Proceedings of the 17th SIGMORPHON Workshop on Computational Research in Phonetics, Phonology, and Morphology*, pages 162–170, Online. Association for Computational Linguistics.

Jonathan David Bobaljik. 1998. Pseudo-Ergativity in Chukotko-Kamchatkan Agreement Systems. *Recherches Linguistiques de Vincennes*, 27:21–44.

David M. Eberhard, Gary F. Simons, and Charles D. Fennig. 2021. *Ethnologue: Languages of the World. Twenty-fourth edition*, volume 16. SIL international, Dallas, TX.

Markus Forsberg and Mans Hulden. 2016. Learning Transducer Models for Morphological Analysis from Example Inflections. In *Proceedings of the SIGFSM Workshop on Statistical NLP and Weighted Automata*, pages 42–50, Berlin, Germany. Association for Computational Linguistics.

Konstanze Glaser. 2007. Minority languages and cultural diversity in Europe. In *Minority Languages and Cultural Diversity in Europe*. Multilingual matters.

Mans Hulden. 2009. Foma: a Finite-State Compiler and Library. In *EACL*.

Christo Kirov, Ryan Cotterell, John Sylak-Glassman, Géraldine Walther, Ekaterina Vylomova, Patrick Xia, Manaal Faruqui, Sabrina J. Mielke, Arya D. McCarthy, Sandra Kübler, David Yarowsky, Jason Eisner, and Mans Hulden. 2018. UniMorph 2.0: Universal Morphology.

Roland Marti. 2007. Lower Sorbian — twice a minority language. *International journal of the sociology of language*, 2007(183):31–51.

Saul B Needleman and Christian D Wunsch. 1970. A general method applicable to the search for similarities in the amino acid sequence of two proteins. *Journal of molecular biology*, 48(3):443–453.

Thomas E Payne and Thomas Edward Payne. 1997. *Describing morphosyntax: A guide for field linguists*. Cambridge University Press.

Aidan Pine and Mark Turin. 2017. *Language revitalization*. Oxford University Press.

Pushpendre Rastogi, Ryan Cotterell, and Jason Eisner. 2016. Weighting Finite-State Transductions With Neural Context. In *Proceedings of the 2016 Conference of the North American Chapter of the Association for Computational Linguistics: Human Language Technologies*, pages 623–633, San Diego, California. Association for Computational Linguistics.

Andrew Spencer. 2000. Agreement morphology in Chukotkan. *Amsterdam studies in the theory and history of linguistic science*, pages 191–222.

Oleg Volkov and Maria Pupinina. 2016. The category of perfect in chukotko-kamchatkan languages. *Acta Linguistica Petropolitana*, pages 535–568.

Paul Wexler. 1982. Bernard Comrie The Languages of the Soviet Union. *Language Problems and Language Planning*, 6(2):166–175.

Shijie Wu, Ryan Cotterell, and Mans Hulden. 2021. Applying the Transformer to Character-level Transduction. In *Proceedings of the 16th Conference of the European Chapter of the Association for Computational Linguistics: Main Volume*, pages 1901–1907, Online. Association for Computational Linguistics.

A Appendix

Language	Small	Large
ang	45.962	60.945
ara	62.857	75.338
asm	38.995	63.065
bra	53.134	-
ckt	8.696	-
evn	23.867	52.037
gml	*	-
goh	52.158	-
got	47.693	65.346
guj	40.855	-
heb	31.15	47.9
hsb	7.5	-
hsi	0.0	-
hun	51.85	68.15
hye	61.45	66.7
itl	33.056	-
kat	47.8	78.85
kaz	55.165	53.611
ket	13.139	-
khk	39.495	47.727
kor	17.821	47.556
krl	10.421	24.098
lud	46.559	50.506
mag	51.163	-
nds	21.947	-
non	47.313	79.759
pol	53.85	67.7
poma	45.873	58.829
sjo	54.496	-
slk	56.05	65.75
slp	12.658	-
tur	19.25	33.6
vep	27.446	44.104

Table 3: Results (overall accuracy of test set predictions) of data-driven approach for all languages. "-" means not part of this shared task. "*": We accidentally did not submit results for gml

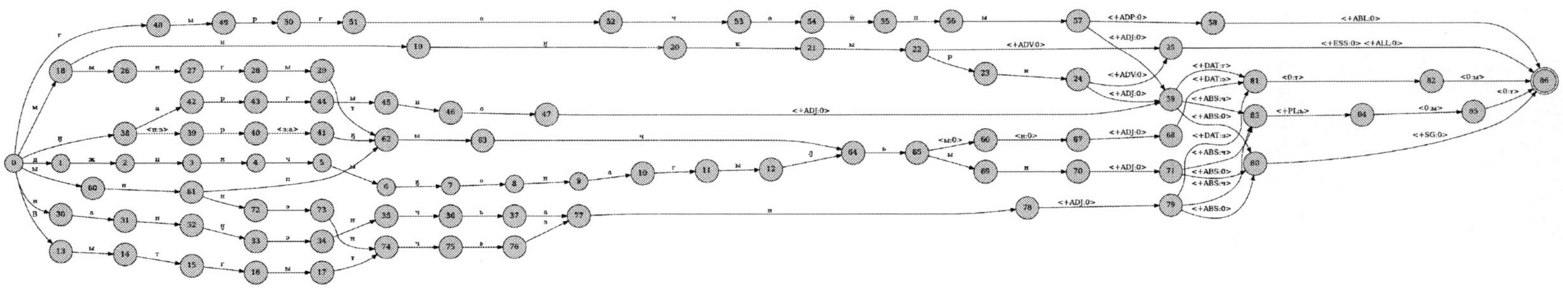

Fig. 2: Finite-state transducer for Chukchi adjectives.

CLUZH at SIGMORPHON 2022 Shared Tasks on Morpheme Segmentation and Inflection Generation

Silvan Wehrli **Simon Clematide** **Peter Makarov**
Department of Computational Linguistics
University of Zurich, Switzerland
silvan.wehrli@uzh.ch {simon.clematide,makarov}@cl.uzh.ch

Abstract

This paper describes the submissions of the team of the Department of Computational Linguistics, University of Zurich, to the SIGMORPHON 2022 Shared Tasks on Morpheme Segmentation and Inflection Generation. Our submissions use a character-level neural transducer that operates over traditional edit actions. While this model has been found particularly well-suited for low-resource settings, using it with large data quantities has been difficult. Existing implementations could not fully profit from GPU acceleration and did not efficiently implement mini-batch training, which could be tricky for a transition-based system. For this year's submission, we have ported the neural transducer to PyTorch and implemented true mini-batch training. This has allowed us to successfully scale the approach to large data quantities and conduct extensive experimentation. We report competitive results for morpheme segmentation (including sharing first place in part 2 of the challenge). We also demonstrate that reducing sentence-level morpheme segmentation to a word-level problem is a simple yet effective strategy. Additionally, we report strong results in inflection generation (the overall best result for large training sets in part 1, the best results in low-resource learning trajectories in part 2). Our code is publicly available.

1 Introduction

This paper describes our submissions to the following SIGMORPHON 2022 shared tasks:

SEGM Morpheme Segmentation (Batsuren et al., 2022):[1]

1. Word-level morpheme segmentation
2. Sentence-level morpheme segmentation

INFL Typologically Diverse and Acquisition-Inspired Morphological Inflection Generation:[2]

1. Typologically diverse morphological inflection (Kodner et al., 2022)
2. Morphological acquisition trajectories (Kodner and Khalifa, 2022)

Task	Input	Output
SEGM	hierarchisms	hierarch @@y @@ism @@s
INFL	sue V;PST	sued

Table 1: Examples of morpheme segmentation (SEGM) and inflection generation (INFL). SEGM involves predicting canonical forms of morphemes. The inputs for INFL consist of lemmas and UniMorph feature specifications.

All our submissions rely on the same neural hard-attention transducer architecture that has shown strong language-independent performance in a variety of character-level transduction tasks in morphology, grapheme-to-phoneme conversion, and text normalization (Makarov and Clematide, 2018, 2020a,b).

1.1 Morpheme Segmentation

The goal of this task is to design a system that splits words into morphemes (Table 1). Part 1 focuses on word-level morpheme segmentation (inputs are word types), part 2 on sentence-level morpheme segmentation (inputs are tokenized sentences). In part 1, there is a unique segmentation for every input word. This track provides very large datasets (in hundreds of thousands of training examples per language), allowing us to test the scalability of our system. In part 2, a word form may be segmented differently depending on the context. It offers an interesting setup to study, on the example of three languages (English, Czech, Mongolian), how important it is for a system to recognize and correctly handle this ambiguity. Our submission for part 2 tests this by using a word-level model (developed for part 1), optionally with part-of-speech (POS) tags as side input.

[1] https://github.com/sigmorphon/2022SegmentationST
[2] https://github.com/sigmorphon/2022InflectionST

19th SIGMORPHON Workshop on Computational Research in Phonetics, Phonology, and Morphology, pages 212 - 219
July 14, 2022

1.2 Inflection Generation

The SIGMORPHON–UniMorph 2022 shared task on typologically diverse and acquisition-inspired morphological inflection generation asks to predict an inflected word form given its lemma and a set of morphosyntactic features specified according to the UniMorph standard (Table 1). Part 1 consists of 32 languages with **small** training sets (mostly 700 items, but for 4 languages only 70 to 240 items) and 21 **large** training sets (exactly 7,000 items). Part 2 has an ablation-style setup for Arabic, English, and German: For each language, there is a dataset for each increment of 100, ranging from 100 to 600 (German) or 1,000 training samples (Arabic, English). The development set feature specifications are representative of the test set. Both tasks target the generalization capabilities of morphology learning systems by examining separately their test set performance on seen and unseen lemmas and feature specifications.

	training			**greedy decoding**	
	BL	**CLUZH**		**CLUZH**	
Batch size	GA	CPU	GPU	CPU	GPU
1	27.49	18.96	**5.02**	**6.49**	10.00
32	23.58	7.48	**0.25**	2.92	**0.73**
64	23.89	7.46	**0.16**	2.84	**0.47**
128	24.69	7.88	**0.13**	2.88	**0.33**
256	27.14	8.21	**0.12**	3.01	**0.26**
512	31.11	8.51	**0.12**	3.26	**0.23**

Table 2: Mini-batch training and greedy decoding speed for this year's implementation (*CLUZH*) vs the baseline (*BL*) of Makarov and Clematide (2020a) on the Armenian dataset of the SIGMOPRHON 2021 shared task on grapheme-to-phoneme conversion (Ashby et al., 2021). The BL models are trained on CPU using gradient accumulation (*GA*). All numbers are given in seconds and per 1,000 samples. The training times are averages of 20 epochs on the training set. The greedy decoding times are averages of 20 runs on the development set using a well-trained model. The CLUZH model hyper-parameters are identical to those of Makarov and Clematide (2020a).

2 Model Description

As a basis for all our submissions, we use a neural character-level transducer that edits the input string into the output string by a sequence of traditional edit actions: substitutions, insertions, deletion, and copy. The specific version of this approach was developed for grapheme-to-phoneme conversion (Makarov and Clematide, 2020a). Such neural transducers have typically performed well in morphological and related character-level transduction tasks in low to medium training data settings. Although they can be competitive in large-data regimes (Makarov and Clematide, 2018), their successful application to large data settings with appropriately large parameter sizes (cf. the Transformer-based models of Wu et al. (2021) have over 7M parameters) may also be limited by a specific implementation. In this year's submission, we scale the approach to large datasets by porting it to a different framework and making algorithmic improvements to training.

True mini-batch training. The training procedure for transition-based systems could be difficult to batch (Noji and Oseki, 2021; Ding and Koehn, 2019), which is why many systems are trained by gradient accumulation over individual samples (and possibly relying on library optimizations such as DyNet Autobatch (Neubig et al., 2017b)). This results in slow training for large data sets. In our implementation of true mini-batch training, we start by precomputing gold action sequences using an oracle character aligner. By doing so, alignments and gold actions for all decoding steps of all training samples are known a priori (as opposed to being computed on the fly, which would be useful when parameter updates are interleaved with sampling from the model distribution). This permits calling the unrolled version of the decoder. The resulting procedure dramatically speeds up training compared to gradient accumulation. Furthermore, our implementation supports batched greedy decoding. Table 2 gives an impression of these performance improvements: For a batch size of 32, training is around 3 times faster on a CPU and close to 100 times faster on a GPU. For a batch size of 512, training is faster by a factor of over 250 on a GPU. Additionally, the time needed for greedy decoding can be efficiently decreased on a GPU.[3]

Further model details. The latest implementation only uses teacher forcing. Specifically, it does not yet incorporate *roll-ins*, i.e. the model does not see its own predictions during training, which would improve generalizability by countering exposure bias (Pomerleau, 1989). We also add support

[3]Note that the precomputation of gold action sequences for the training data takes around 12 seconds per 1000 samples. However, this procedure is only required once per dataset as the precomputed output can be reused for any training run. In any case, the gains shown in Table 2 easily offset the additionally required time.

for features. Features are treated as atomic. For INFL, the features associated with an inflection input-output pair are passed through an embedding layer and then summed. For further details on the system and the oracle character aligner, we refer the reader to Makarov and Clematide (2020a).

3 Submission Details

For both tasks, we train separate models for each language and use the development set exclusively for model selection.

3.1 Morpheme Segmentation

Data preprocessing. Besides NFD normalization as a preprocessing step, we substitute the multi-character morpheme delimiter (" @@") by a single character unseen in the data to decrease the length of the output.

Sentence-level segmentation. We simplify part 2 of the SEGM task by reducing it to a word-level problem. Concretely, we split the input sentences into single word tokens and train the model on these word tokens, similarly to part 1. The single word predictions are then simply concatenated to form the original sentence. Since this completely neglects the context of the words, we have also experimented with POS tags as additional input features (Table 3). We use TreeTagger (Schmid, 1999) to obtain the features.[4] We also experimented with transducing entire sentences in one go, however this led to a substantial drop in accuracy.

Hyper-parameter search. For both parts, we have evaluated extensively various choices of optimizers, learning rate schedulers, batch size, encoder dropout. We found the Adam optimizer (Kingma and Ba, 2015) to work well, as well as the scheduler that reduces the learning rate whenever a development set metric plateaus. We settled on a batch size of 32 for all models, which offers a good trade-off between model performance and training speed.

[4]The parameter files are available at https://www.cis.uni-muenchen.de/˜schmid/tools/TreeTagger/.

Гэрт	**эмээ**	хоол	хийв	.
Гэр @@т	**эмээ**	хоол	хийх @@в	.
NN	**NN**	VB	VB	.
Grandmother cooked at home.				

Би	өдөр	**эмээ**	уусан	.
Би	өдөр	**эм** @@ээ	уух @@сан	.
PR	NN	**VB**	VB	.
Today I took my medicine.				

Table 3: SEGM part 2 with POS features for Mongolian. The features inferred from the context using TreeTagger could help disambiguate the word form in bold.

Encoders. We use a 2-layer stacked LSTM as the encoder and experimented with encoder dropout. We also experimented extensively with a Transformer encoder (Vaswani et al., 2017). Despite considerable effort, we failed to make it work at the performance level of stacked LSTMs. Other hyperparameters (e.g. various embedding dimensions) are similar to the previous work (Makarov and Clematide, 2020a).

Decoding. For efficiency, we compute all the model outputs using mini-batch greedy decoding.

Ensembling. All our submissions are majority-vote ensembles. For part 1, we submit a 5-strong ensemble, **CLUZH**, composed of 3 models without encoder dropout and 2 models with encoder dropout of 0.1.[5]

For part 2, we submit three ensembles. All individual models have an encoder dropout probability of 0.25 and vary only in their use of features: **CLUZH-1** with 3 models without POS features, **CLUZH-2** with 3 models with POS tag features, and **CLUZH-3** with combines all the models from **CLUZH-1** and **CLUZH-2**.

3.2 Inflection Generation

Data preprocessing. For both parts, we apply NFD normalization to the input and split the UniMorph features at ";" by default. For languages that showed lower performance compared to the neural or non-neural baseline on the development set in part 1, we also computed models without NFD normalization and chose the best based on their development set performance. For Korean, we observed some Latin transliteration noise in the train/development set targets, which we removed before training. For Lamaholot (slp), we observed a very low accuracy (5%) on the development set compared to the neural baseline's 20% performance. By splitting UniMorph features at "+"

[5]Due to a mistake, the predictions by the models with dropout 0.1 were included twice, and a prepared model with dropout 0.25 was not used at all. However, the F1 macro-average over all the languages for the intended ensemble on the development set is only 0.08 points higher.

as well as ";",[6] we achieved better generalization for this low-resource language (only 240 training examples available).

Hyper-parameters. For small datasets in both parts: batch size 1, a patience of 30 epochs, one-layer encoder and decoder with hidden size 200, character and action embeddings of size 100, feature embeddings of size 50, the AdamW optimizer (Loshchilov and Hutter, 2019) with a learning rate of 0.0005 (half of the default value), the reduce-learning-rate-on-plateau scheduler with factor 0.75, and beam decoding with beam width 4. For a few languages whose development set performance was lower than that of the baselines, we computed models without NFD normalization and used those in case of improved accuracy.[7]

For large datasets in part 1, we made the following changes from the above: batch size 32, a patience of 20 epochs, action embeddings of size 200, a two-layer encoder with a hidden size of 1,000, a one-layer decoder with a hidden size of 2,000. In case of the development set performance was below that of any of the official baselines, we used some alternative hyper-parameters:[8] no NFD normalization, batch size 16, a one-layer encoder with a hidden size of 2,000, a one-layer decoder with a hidden size of 4,000, and the Adadelta optimizer (Zeiler, 2012) with the default learning rate. Hyper-parameters were not chosen using a systematic grid search or experimentation.

Convergence. For the small datasets in part 1 with default hyper-parameters and NFD normalization, we observe large differences in the number of epochs to convergence (mean 27.3, SD 22.8). For some languages, e.g. Chukchi (ckt), Ket (ket), and Ludian (lud), we see the best results on the first epoch, which typically means the model has just learned to copy the input to the output. For other languages, much larger or highly varying numbers of epochs to convergence are observed: Slovak (15-93), Karelian (13-88), Mongolian, Khalkha (19-61), and Korean (12-143).

For the large datasets in part 1 (7,000 training examples) with default hyper-parameters and NFD normalization, we observe a mean of 17.3 epochs to convergence (SD 16.0). For Ludian, even in the large setting, the first epoch with copying gave the best results. In contrast, Georgian could generally profit from more epochs (mean 36.8, SD 17.9).

Ensembling. Our submission for part 1 is a 5-strong majority-voting ensemble, and it is a 10-strong ensemble for part 2.

4 Results and Discussion

4.1 Morpheme Segmentation

Table 4 and Table 5 show our results for parts 1 and 2, respectively. Based on the macro-average F1 score over all languages, our submission for part 1 ranks third out of 7 full submissions. For part 2, our submission CLUZH-3 was declared the winner out of 10 full submissions.[9]

Dropout. The results for part 1 suggest that encoder dropout can help improve model performance. For some languages, the performance can improve by as much as 1% F1 score absolute.

Ensembling. Ensembling brings a clear improvement over single-best results. On average, the improvement is +0.55% on the development set and +0.53% on the test set (compared to the best single model result). The improvement on the English dataset is substantial: +1.64% and +1.84% on the development and test sets, respectively.

Gains from POS tags. The results for part 2 suggest that treating a sentence-level problem as word-level may be a simple yet powerful strategy for morpheme segmentation. The success of this strategy depends on the language and the data. The more segmentation ambiguity a language has, the more important the context is. Mongolian has the highest segmentation ambiguity (Table 6). Around $1/5$ of the tokens in the training data have at least two possible segmentations, whereas Czech and English exhibit little to no ambiguity. This may partially explain why the performance on the Mongolian data is the lowest. This also explains why using POS tags as additional features bring the biggest improvement for Mongolian: +0.29% and +0.27% on the development and test sets, based on the average of individual models. Using POS tags improves the prediction of ambiguous segmentation by an absolute 1.1% and 0.6% on the development and

[6] For instance, `V;ARGAC2P+ARGNO2P;SBJV` would be split into 4 separate features.

[7] Arabic, Gothic, Hungarian, and Old Norse.

[8] Arabic, Assamese, Evenki, Hungarian, Kazakh, Mongolian, Khalkha, and Old Norse.

[9] Our submission performed the best on two out of three languages (Czech and Mongolian). As it was beaten by another submission based on the macro F1 average, two submissions were declared winners.

Language	dropout = 0.0 (avg. of 3 models) dev	test	dropout = 0.1 (1 model) dev	test	dropout = 0.25 (1 model) dev	test	ensemble (5 models) dev	test	best other test
Czech	92.96	93.31	93.35	93.60	93.32	93.49	94.07	93.81	**93.88**
English	90.33	90.33	91.01	90.86	90.91	90.68	92.65	92.70	**93.63**
French	93.22	93.02	93.95	93.85	93.72	93.48	94.94	94.80	**95.73**
Hungarian	99.40	98.28	99.15	98.09	99.63	98.57	99.61	98.54	**98.72**
Spanish	97.79	97.78	98.57	98.61	98.53	98.56	98.71	98.74	**99.04**
Italian	95.54	95.54	96.15	96.19	96.02	96.11	96.93	96.93	**97.47**
Latin	99.20	99.20	99.30	99.26	99.30	99.23	99.40	99.37	**99.38**
Russian	97.52	97.54	96.38	96.43	96.65	96.54	98.58	98.62	**99.35**
Mongolian	98.21	97.73	98.47	97.80	98.47	97.90	98.53	98.12	**98.51**
AVG	96.02	95.86	96.26	96.08	96.28	96.06	97.05	96.85	**97.30**

Table 4: F1 scores for SEGM part 1.

Language	without features average (3 models) dev	test	ensemble (3 models) dev	test	with POS tags average (3 models) dev	test	ensemble (3 models) dev	test	combined ensemble (6 models) dev	test	best other test
Czech	94.06	90.90	94.54	91.35	94.15	91.15	94.45	91.76	94.72	**91.99**	91.76
English	98.12	89.27	98.31	89.47	98.18	89.29	98.38	89.47	98.41	89.54	**96.31**
Mongolian	85.95	81.57	87.06	82.22	86.24	81.84	87.26	82.55	87.62	**82.88**	82.59
AVG	92.71	87.25	93.30	87.68	92.86	87.43	93.36	87.93	93.58	88.14	**90.22**

Table 5: F1 scores for SEGM part 2. All models are trained with a dropout probability of 0.25.

Language	train 1	train ≥2	dev 1	dev ≥2
Czech	100%	0%	100%	0%
English	99.58%	0.42%	99.75%	0.25%
Mongolian	77.91%	22.09%	90.00%	10.00%

Table 6: Segmentation ambiguity in SEGM part 2: Relative frequency of unambiguous (1) vs ambiguous (≥ 2) word tokens.

dev ambiguous NF	dev ambiguous POS	dev all Δ	test ambiguous NF	test ambiguous POS	test all Δ
63.0%	64.1%	+0.11%	59.5%	60.1%	+0.06%

Table 7: Impact of POS features on Mongolian, SEGM part 2. *ambiguous* shows the average percentage of correctly predicted ambiguous segmentations for Mongolian. *NF* denotes models without features, *POS* denotes models using POS tags. *all* shows the absolute improvement for POS compared to NF, in relation to the whole dataset.

test sets for Mongolian (Table 7). When looking at the whole dataset, using POS features increases the relative number of correct predictions by 0.11% (development set) and 0.06% (test set) compared to not using the features. Using POS tags brings slight improvements and helps mitigate the loss of context.

PyTorch reimplementation. This year's system is a close reimplementation in PyTorch (Paszke et al., 2019) of our earlier CPU codebase using DyNet (Neubig et al., 2017a). It fully supports GPU utilization, allowing for efficient processing of large amounts of training data. Our code is publicly available.[10]

Token–type ratio. Another reason for the lower performance of Mongolian might lie in the high variance in the data: The Mongolian training dataset contains around 40% unique tokens (Table 8). This is around 4 times more than in the

Language	train total	train unique	dev total	dev unique
Czech	15,157	5,126	7,545	3,217
English	169,117	17,249	21,444	4,849
Mongolian	13,237	5,293	6,632	3,216

Table 8: Word counts in SEGM part 2: The total number of word forms and the number of unique words.

[10] https://github.com/slvnwhrl/il-reimplementation

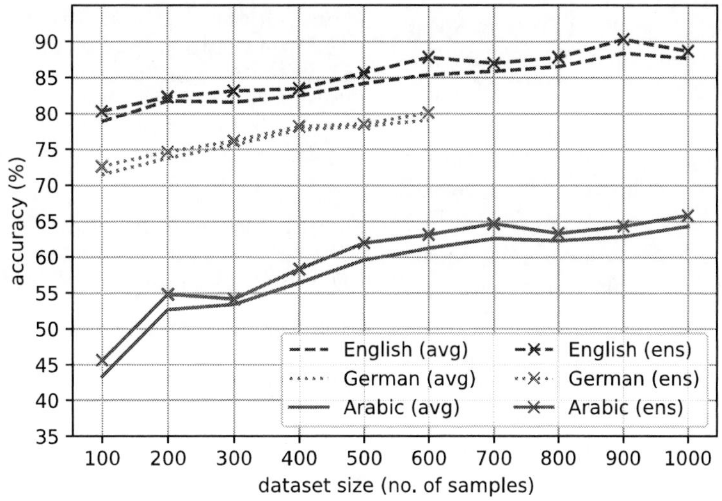

Figure 1: Test accuracy results for INFL part 2. avg=average, ens=10-strong ensemble.

System	Overall	seen status (± Lemma/Features) +L +F	+L −F	-L +F	-L −F
Small dataset setting					
CLUZH	56.87	77.31	31.27	**77.97**	43.26
Best	**74.76**	**81.64**	72.91	**77.97**	70.87
Δ	-17.89	-4.33	-41.64	0.00	-27.62
Large dataset setting					
CLUZH	**67.85**	**90.99**	41.43	**87.17**	**60.30**
Best	62.39	89.57	**42.17**	85.31	55.56
Δ	5.46	1.43	-0.74	1.86	4.74

Table 9: Test results (accuracy macro-averaged over languages) for INFL part 1 split by training dataset size: large (7,000 training examples) vs small (up to 700 examples). Δ shows the difference between our submission and the best competitor covering the full set of languages.

English dataset. This makes the learning problem much harder, which is further exacerbated by the relatively small size of the data (compared to English).

4.2 Inflection Generation

The part 1 test set results are shown in Table 9. Given the large number of languages, we discuss the average accuracy on small and large training sets. An important goal for this shared task was to assess a system's performance on test data subsets defined by whether both the lemma and the feature specification were seen in the training data (+L +F in the Table), whether only the lemma (+L, -F), or only the feature specification (-L, +F) were seen, or whether neither of them (-L -F) appeared in the training data.

Small datasets. On the small datasets, our system only excels on the -L +F subset, meaning it is strong in modeling the behaviour of features. In the small dataset setting, the best competitor system, UBC, has an extremely strong performance in case the lemma is known (+L). It would be interesting to know what kind of information or data augmentation UBC uses: The neural baseline, which utilizes data augmentation, has a much lower performance (24.9%) than our submission. Overall, our submission with a 5-strong ensemble achieves the second-best result of the submissions covering all languages.

Large datasets. In the large dataset setting, our submission shows the best performance overall. On the subset with seen lemmas and unseen features (+L -F), the neural baseline is the only system with slightly better results. This indicates that our system's modeling of lemmas is not yet optimal. The information flow in our architecture maybe dominated by the features (they are fed into the decoder at every action prediction step) and the aligned input character, and it may not have the best representation of the input lemma as a whole.

Trajectories. The test set results for part 2 are shown in Figure 1. Our 10-strong ensemble was the clear overall winner in this low-resource track. It beats the best competing approaches by a substantial margin on the per-language average: Arabic 59.6% accuracy (best competitor OSU 57.5%), German 76.7% (non-neural baseline 74.8%), English 85.7% (OSU 81.5%).

Individual model performance varies, and the majority-vote ensembling improved the scores by 1.4% absolute on average on the test set. Interestingly, the difference between the average model performance and the ensemble performance does not get smaller with larger training sets.

The correlation between the increasing number of training examples and the improving test set performance is almost perfect for the average performance. Ensembles are slightly less stable.

5 Conclusion

This paper presents the submissions of the Department of Computational Linguistics, University of Zurich, to the SIGMOPRHON 2022 morpheme segmentation and inflection generation shared tasks. We build on the previous architecture, the neural transducer over edit actions, porting it to a new deep learning framework and implementing GPU-optimized mini-batch training. This permits scaling the system to large training datasets, as demonstrated by strong performance in both shared tasks.

We show that reducing sentence-level morpheme segmentation to a word-level problem is a viable strategy. Conditioning on POS tags brings further improvements. We leave it to future work to explore more powerful representations of context. We experimented with a Transformer-based encoder for morpheme segmentation, and while the initial results were not satisfactory, we intent to pursue this further. In inflection generation, we note problems with capturing unseen lemmas, despite otherwise strong performance across data regimes.

References

Lucas F.E. Ashby, Travis M. Bartley, Simon Clematide, Luca Del Signore, Cameron Gibson, Kyle Gorman, Yeonju Lee-Sikka, Peter Makarov, Aidan Malanoski, Sean Miller, Omar Ortiz, Reuben Raff, Arundhati Sengupta, Bora Seo, Yulia Spektor, and Winnie Yan. 2021. Results of the Second SIGMORPHON Shared Task on Multilingual Grapheme-to-Phoneme Conversion. In *Proceedings of the 18th SIGMORPHON Workshop on Computational Research in Phonetics, Phonology, and Morphology*.

Khuyagbaatar Batsuren, Gábor Bella, Aryaman Arora, Viktor Martinović, Kyle Gorman, Zdeněk Žabokrtský, Amarsanaa Ganbold, Šárka Dohnalová, Magda Ševčíková, Kateřina Pelegrinová, Fausto Giunchiglia, Ryan Cotterell, and Ekaterina Vylomova. 2022. The sigmorphon 2022 shared task on morpheme segmentation. In *19th SIGMORPHON Workshop on Computational Research in Phonetics, Phonology, and Morphology*.

Shuoyang Ding and Philipp Koehn. 2019. Parallelizable stack long short-term memory. In *Proceedings of the Third Workshop on Structured Prediction for NLP*.

Diederik P. Kingma and Jimmy Ba. 2015. Adam: A Method for Stochastic Optimization. In *3rd International Conference on Learning Representations, ICLR 2015, San Diego, CA, USA, May 7-9, 2015, Conference Track Proceedings*.

Jordan Kodner and Salam Khalifa. 2022. SIGMORPHON-UniMorph 2022 Shared Task 0: Modeling Inflection in Language Acquisition. In *Proceedings of the SIGMORPHON 2022 Shared Task: Morphological Inflection*.

Jordan Kodner, Salam Khalifa, Khuyagbaatar Batsuren, Hossep Dolatian, Ryan Cotterell, Faruk Akkuş, Antonios Anastasopoulos, Taras Andrushko, Aryaman Arora, Nona Atanelov, Gábor Bella, Elena Budianskaya, Yustinus Ghanggo Ate, Omer Goldman, Simon Guriel, Silvia Guriel-Agiashvili, Jan Hajič, Jan Hric, Ritvan Karahodja, Witold Kieraś, Andrew Krizhanovsky, Natalia Krizhanovsky, Igor Marchenko, Magdalena Markowska, Polina Mashkovtseva, Maria Nepomniashchaya, Daria Rodionova, Elizabeth Salesky, Karina Sheifer, Alexandra Serova, Anastasia Yemelina, Jeremiah Young, and Ekaterina Vylomova. 2022. SIGMORPHON-UniMorph 2022 Shared Task 0: Generalization and Typologically Diverse Morphological Inflection. In *Proceedings of the SIGMORPHON 2022 Shared Task: Morphological Inflection*.

Ilya Loshchilov and Frank Hutter. 2019. Decoupled weight decay regularization. In *7th International Conference on Learning Representations, ICLR 2019, New Orleans, LA, USA, May 6-9, 2019*.

Peter Makarov and Simon Clematide. 2018. Imitation learning for neural morphological string transduction. In *Proceedings of the 2018 Conference on Empirical Methods in Natural Language Processing*.

Peter Makarov and Simon Clematide. 2020a. CLUZH at SIGMORPHON 2020 Shared Task on Multilingual Grapheme-to-Phoneme Conversion. In *Proceedings of the 17th SIGMORPHON Workshop on Computational Research in Phonetics, Phonology, and Morphology*.

Peter Makarov and Simon Clematide. 2020b. Semi-supervised contextual historical text normalization. In *Proceedings of the 58th Annual Meeting of the Association for Computational Linguistics*.

Graham Neubig, Chris Dyer, Yoav Goldberg, Austin Matthews, Waleed Ammar, Antonios Anastasopoulos, Miguel Ballesteros, David Chiang, Daniel Clothiaux, Trevor Cohn, Kevin Duh, Manaal Faruqui, Cynthia Gan, Dan Garrette, Yangfeng Ji, Lingpeng Kong, Adhiguna Kuncoro, Gaurav Kumar, Chaitanya Malaviya, Paul Michel, Yusuke Oda, Matthew Richardson, Naomi Saphra, Swabha Swayamdipta, and Pengcheng Yin. 2017a. Dynet: The dynamic neural network toolkit. *arXiv preprint arXiv:1701.03980*.

Graham Neubig, Yoav Goldberg, and Chris Dyer. 2017b. On-the-fly Operation Batching in Dynamic Computation Graphs. In *Advances in Neural Information Processing Systems*, volume 30.

Hiroshi Noji and Yohei Oseki. 2021. Effective batching for recurrent neural network grammars. In *Findings of the Association for Computational Linguistics: ACL-IJCNLP 2021*.

Adam Paszke, Sam Gross, Francisco Massa, Adam Lerer, James Bradbury, Gregory Chanan, Trevor Killeen, Zeming Lin, Natalia Gimelshein, Luca Antiga, Alban Desmaison, Andreas Kopf, Edward Yang, Zachary DeVito, Martin Raison, Alykhan Tejani, Sasank Chilamkurthy, Benoit Steiner, Lu Fang, Junjie Bai, and Soumith Chintala. 2019. Pytorch: An imperative style, high-performance deep learning library. In *Advances in Neural Information Processing Systems 32*.

Dean A Pomerleau. 1989. Alvinn: An autonomous land vehicle in a neural network. In *Proceedings of the Conference on Neural Information Processing Systems*.

H. Schmid. 1999. Improvements in Part-of-Speech Tagging with an Application to German. In *Natural Language Processing Using Very Large Corpora*, Text, Speech and Language Technology.

Ashish Vaswani, Noam Shazeer, Niki Parmar, Jakob Uszkoreit, Llion Jones, Aidan N Gomez, Łukasz Kaiser, and Illia Polosukhin. 2017. Attention is All you Need. In *Advances in Neural Information Processing Systems*, volume 30.

Shijie Wu, Ryan Cotterell, and Mans Hulden. 2021. Applying the transformer to character-level transduction. In *Proceedings of the 16th Conference of the European Chapter of the Association for Computational Linguistics: Main Volume*.

Matthew D Zeiler. 2012. ADADELTA: an adaptive learning rate method. arXiv:1212.5701.

OSU at SigMorphon 2022: Analogical Inflection With Rule Features

Micha Elsner and **Sara Court**
Department of Linguistics
Ohio State University
`melsner0@gmail.com` and `court.22@osu.edu`

Abstract

OSU's inflection system is a transformer whose input is augmented with an analogical exemplar showing how to inflect a different word into the target cell. In addition, alignment-based heuristic features indicate how well the exemplar is likely to match the output. OSU's scores substantially improve over the baseline transformer for instances where an exemplar is available, though not quite matching the challenge winner. In Part 2, the system shows a tendency to over-apply the majority pattern in English, but not Arabic.

1 Introduction

Many theories of inflection production propose a central role for memorized word forms in shaping the outcomes for unknown or weakly represented words (Bybee, 1995). In such memory-based models, speakers retrieve *exemplar* forms A from memory for which the outcomes B are known and use them to predict the outcome for a word C via a process of analogical reasoning: *exemplar source* A : *exemplar target* B :: *source* C : *target* D. This type of analogical reasoning is detectable in historical changes (Sims-Williams, 2021) and in experiments with nonce-words (Dąbrowska, 2008), and underlies some influential computational models of inflection (Albright and Hayes, 2003; Daelemans, 2002). Recently, Elsner (2021) and Liu and Hulden (2020) show that transformer models for inflection prediction can also benefit from access to exemplars.

OSU's inflection prediction system[1] builds on this recent work, also using a transformer for prediction, but adds a heuristic set of "rule features" intended to make the system more flexible in its use of analogical reasoning. Rule features are necessary because the source-target pair C : D may not correspond directly to the exemplar pair due to morphophonological alternations or inflection class mismatch. Consider an analogy from Anglo-Saxon, *ēþel : ēþle :: ġelīca : ġelīcan* ("homeland", "equal".DAT.SG), for which the target suffixes do not match. Below is a prediction instance and its desired output, based on previous work:

(1) ġelīca DAT.SG ēþel : ēþle → ġelīcan

When instances like this are common in training, the relative unreliability of the exemplar information leads the system to concentrate on the output cell label DAT.SG and ignore the exemplar, which results in performance very similar to a transformer baseline without exemplars. To prevent this, we augment training examples to indicate whether the desired output matches or mismatches the exemplar; these augmented features are predicted by the transformer at test time (see Section 3). For example, we can add features indicating that the exemplar has a suffix which does not match, so that the system can learn whether to attend to it:

(2) ġelīca DAT.SG ēþel : ēþle SUFF REPLACE.SUFF
→ ġelīcan

In pilot experiments, systems trained with these features behaved qualitatively differently from the baseline, reacting more to exemplar information and producing a wider variety of outputs when the exemplar was varied.

2 Results

OSU entered systems for both Part 1 (multilingual inflection; Kodner et al. (2022)) and Part 2 (learning trajectories: Kodner and Khalifa (2022)). However, we did not attempt all parts of the Part 1 task. First, we ran each language from Part 1 with the largest available dataset; we submitted results for the **small** partition only for languages which

[1] https://github.com/melsner/transformerbyexample

19th SIGMORPHON Workshop on Computational Research in Phonetics, Phonology, and Morphology, pages 220 - 225
July 14, 2022 ©2022 Association for Computational Linguistics

	Overall	Both	Cell
Small part.	47.688	79.31	82.308
Large part.	46.734	89.565	85.308
Large winner	67.853	90.991	87.171
Large neural base	62.391	80.462	77.627

Table 1: Official results for Task 0, Part 1: score overall, score for items with known lemma and cell, score for items with unknown lemma and known cell.

lacked a **large** training set. Second, our system relies on being able to recall an exemplar with a known output for the target cell. Thus, we did not attempt instances for which the target cell was unseen (**lemma-only** and **neither**); for such instances, we output the original lemma as a placeholder prediction.

Our results overall (Table 1) reflect our inability to make predictions on unknown cells. However, for known cells, performance is fairly close to the challenge winner CLUZH, though the differences are statistically significant. Moreover, the system comfortably outperforms the neural baseline. This is particularly interesting since the baseline uses the same transformer model, Wu et al. (2021), for predictions; only the instance generation and training procedure differ. Nonetheless, the system improves by almost 10% absolute when the cell is known.

OSU surpassed the neural baseline in the known cell, unknown lemma condition by 1% absolute or more on Armenian, Karelian, Polish, Slovak, Turkish and Veps (for all these except Armenian, the improvement was at least 10%). It performed worse than baseline on Arabic, Assamese, Hungarian, Korean, Ludic, Old Norse and Pomak (with a 12% drop on Korean)[2]. There is no obvious typological pattern in these results. Two Slavic languages (Polish and Slovak) performed excellently while a third (Pomak) underperformed; similarly, one Finnic language (Karelian) performed well while another (Ludic) did not. While several underperforming languages used non-Latin scripts, which can cause trouble for inflector models (Murikinati et al., 2020), OSU was the best-performing system on Gothic, with some words written in Gothic script and others in Latin characters, and also performed well on Khalkha Mongolian, written in Cyrillic, and on Hebrew.

Task 2 (learning trajectories) did not involve

[2]Our development score for this condition in Korean is 80.679%; our test score is 50.602%, suggesting there may be a dataset mismatch.

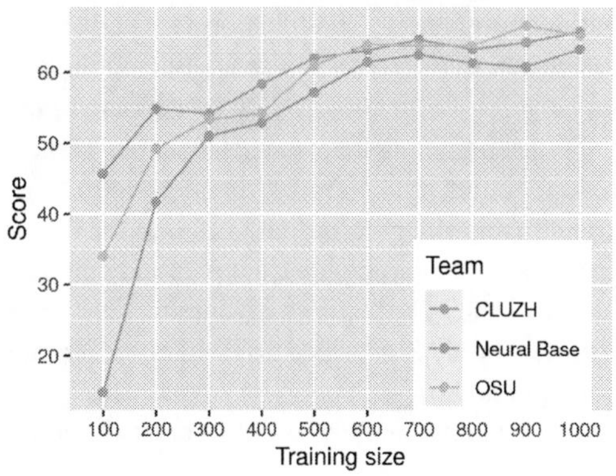

Figure 1: Comparative learning trajectories for Arabic (Task 2).

held-out cells, but did vary the amount of training data. A representative set of learning curves for Arabic is shown in Figure 1; curves for English and German are qualitatively similar. Our system experiences a rapid rise in performance between 100 and 300 training items, with diminishing returns around 600 items. We attribute poor early performance to under-regularization; unlike in Part 1, we did not use cross-lingual training, which helps to regularize small-data inflectors (Kann et al., 2017).

3 System design

Training using the OSU system involves the following steps: (1) generation of training instances, (2) training a language-agnostic string edit model, (3) multilingual training, (4) language-specific fine-tuning. Each training instance includes the input lemma, the morphosyntactic features of the output cell, the language and the language family (each encoded as a character), the exemplar lemma and form (separated by a diacritic), and the rule features. Rule features for training instances are generated by aligning the lemma and output form as in Ahlberg et al. (2015), aligning the exemplar and its output, and then comparing the two. Looking only at the lemma and output, we generate features to indicate whether there is a prefix, a suffix, a stem-internal edit, or no edit. Based on the comparison, we indicate whether prefix/suffix/stem edits are identical between source-target pairs, contain some but not all matching characters, or are disjoint. For instance, the pair *fill* $\sim$ *filled* (suffix *-ed*) with exemplar *die* $\sim$ *died* (suffix *-d*) would be marked SUFFIX to indicate the rule type and SIMILAR.SUFFIX to indicate that the edits match partly but not completely. The transformer is not forced to obey these features when generating outputs, but uses them to learn how to attend to the exemplar.

For each training item, we generate one instance for inflection prediction (with rule features generated using the gold output) and one for feature prediction, containing the exemplar and cell label, but with the rule features as output. The transformer thus learns to predict a likely alignment configuration for each query/exemplar pair. For example, a feature prediction instance corresponding to Example (2) would be:

(3) ġelīca DAT.SG ēþel : ēþle PREDICT.FEATS $\rightarrow$ SUFF REPLACE.SUFF

Language-agnostic string edit instances for step (2) (random strings with prefixes, suffixes or internal edits) were generated as in Elsner (2021). In step (3), we trained all languages together for 18 hours (during which we ran 57 epochs). We then trained sub-models by language family, but since many families this year had only one or two representatives, we decreased this training process to only 5 epochs, anticipating that it would make little difference. Finally, we trained for 50 more epochs on the individual language training sets. The learning model itself is a transformer with settings from Wu et al. (2021).

Inference is a multistep process involving the following steps: (1) generation of multiple test instances with different exemplars, (2) prediction of rule features for each instance, (3) prediction of inflected forms for each instance, (4) majority voting to produce a single inflected output. In step (1), we sampled 5 random exemplars from the training set for each test item; the exemplar output was always drawn from exactly the same morphosyntactic cell as the target output.[3] We generated an instance for each test item $\times$ exemplar. We used the transformer in feature prediction mode to produce rule features for each instance (step 2), then concatenated these rule features with the inputs to produce inflection instances. By re-running the transformer on these augmented instances, we output an inflected form for each instance (step 4). Finally, we chose the most likely output across the 5 exemplars as the model's final prediction, with ties broken at random.

[3]As stated, if a suitable exemplar cannot be found, we produce the input form as a placeholder prediction.

As an example of this process, suppose the instance *ġelīca* DAT.SG occurred in the test set, and we had selected the pair *ēþel : ēþle* as one of our five exemplars. We would first generate a feature prediction instance (example 3) and present it to the trained transformer. Suppose the transformer incorrectly assumed the suffix would be shared, and output SUFF SAME.SUFF (rather than REPLACE.SUFF). In step (3), we create an inflection instance using these predicted features:

(4) ġelīca DAT.SG ēþel : ēþle SUFF REPLACE.SUFF $\rightarrow$ ġelīcan

As with any pipelined prediction system, an error cascade may occur; the transformer may not decode this instance correctly due to the incorrect features proposed in the previous step. In any case, we would collect this output, and those of the four other exemplars, and select the most frequently proposed form as the final prediction.

System development was carried out before the shared task commenced, using datasets from SIGMORPHON 2020 (Vylomova et al., 2020); we made no effort to tune on the 2022 datasets.

4 Analysis

We analyze some outputs from Part 2 with an alignment-based analysis tool as in King et al. (2020); Gorman et al. (2019), leveraging some of the same code as our rule feature extractor. In English, the model shows a strong preference for over-applying the regular (*-ed*) suffix throughout the learning process; using the 100-example (severely under-regularized) dataset, the model produces suffixes 84% of the time, but by 200 examples, this rises to 90% and continues to rise slowly thereafter. Nearly all of the rise in accuracy is due to the model's gradual acquisition of orthographic allomorphs of *-ed*, such as *drum* ∼ *drummed*, first produced with 400 examples. No irregular allomorphs improve consistently, although some (*swear* ∼ *swore*, *grind* ∼ *ground*) are occasionally produced correctly. The zero past tense (*bet* ∼ *bet*) is produced less often as the dataset increases. In other experiments, we have observed that our model often produces zero outputs when trained with insufficient data; we believe our initial success with this class is the product of this tendency rather than learning.

The lack of generalization of irregular allomorphs is generally consistent with the claim of Xu and Pinker (1995) that infants rarely produce such errors. It is not clear from results on held-out data whether a "U-shaped curve" (Marcus et al., 1992) would appear, since this phenomenon results from over-application of the regular suffix to previously *memorized* irregulars and would require inspection of training outputs. It is also likely that the token, as well as type, frequency distribution of the training data matters for the acquisition of irregulars (Frank et al., 2020).

In Arabic, the model is able to learn suffixing 'sound' plurals starting from the first 100 words, and performs best on these examples overall, reaching over 80% accuracy on concatenative patterns when trained on all available data. The model initially struggles with nonconcatenative 'broken' plural forms, but shows consistent improvement as the amount of training data increases. The alignment method used to generate training instances groups alternations into microclasses, taking changes in short vowel diacritics into account. One of these classes, the CaCCaC ∼ CaCaaCiC class, containing nouns such as *maslak* ∼ *masaalik* 'path' (35 examples), reaches 100% accuracy with 600 words. Gradual improvement is also seen in nouns of the CaCaC ∼ 'aCCaaC class, for example *khtar* ∼ *akhtaar* 'danger' (50 examples), which goes from 2% accuracy using 100 words to 86% accuracy on the full dataset. Another interesting class is the CiCaa' ∼ 'aCCiya class, for example *binaa'* ∼ *'ibniya* 'building', with only 5 examples in the dataset. Unlike other microclasses of similar size which the model fails to ever learn, the model is able to accurately produce 4 of the 5 examples (80% accuracy) using the 600-word and 900-word datasets (although with 1,000 words the model only produces 1 of the 5). Other similar nouns, such as the CaCiiC ∼ 'aCCiCaa' pattern including *qariib* ∼ *aqribaa'* 'relative' (5 examples) are never learned by the model.

The model's performance reflects broad generalizations found in the literature on child acquisition of dialectal Arabic plural inflection. In general, while nonconcatenative 'broken' plural nouns are present in the speech of very young children, nonconcatenative inflection isn't productive until late preschool (Ravid and Farah, 1999), and a study on the acquisition of plural inflection in Egyptian Arabic found that children as old as 15 may commonly produce errors when inflecting broken plural nouns in the language (Omar, 2017). In their study on plural acquisition of native Arabic speakers across multiple age groups, Saiegh-Haddad et al. (2012) found that the feminine sound plural marker is acquired earlier and faster than broken plural inflection patterns, and that differences in the production of broken plural forms are affected both by speakers' familiarity with the singular form and the type frequency of its associated plural template. Both the human and machine acquisition trajectories are likely related to the sheer number of possible ways (i.e., 'templates') of nonconcatenatively relating singular and plural nouns in Semitic languages. There are comparatively far fewer productive suffixes in MSA (one feminine and one masculine) than there are templates (perhaps more than 70: Plunkett and Nakisa (1997)).

5 Conclusion and Future work

The competition alerts us to one obvious weak point: our inability to predict fillers for cells in which no training example is given. This is particularly problematic for languages with very large paradigms. Such paradigms generally involve some degree of agglutination (separatist exponence) which renders low-frequency cells predictable (Plank, 2017). The relationships between cells can be modeled by using multiple input forms to predict a target (Rathi et al., 2021). The ability to do this would be a valuable addition to our model.

While our system was not the best in the competition, we are encouraged to find that analogical examples allow a transformer inflector to achieve near-state-of-the-art results. An analogical model is both cognitively plausible and easy to implement, and the resulting system is substantially more robust and generalizable than the simple transformer baseline.

Acknowledgements

We thank Jordan Kodner, Salam Khalifa and all the SM'22 shared task organizers, and Andrea Sims for design discussions. All experiments were run on the Ohio Supercomputer (OSC, 1987).

References

Malin Ahlberg, Markus Forsberg, and Mans Hulden. 2015. Paradigm classification in supervised learning of morphology. In *Proceedings of the 2015 Conference of the North American Chapter of the Association for Computational Linguistics: Human Language Technologies*, pages 1024–1029, Denver,

Colorado. Association for Computational Linguistics.

Adam Albright and Bruce Hayes. 2003. Rules vs. analogy in english past tenses: A computational/experimental study. *Cognition*, 90(2):119–161.

Joan Bybee. 1995. Diachronic and typological properties of morphology and their implications for representation. In Laurie Beth Feldman, editor, *Morphological aspects of language processing*, pages 225–246. Erlbaum Hillsdale.

Ewa Dąbrowska. 2008. The effects of frequency and neighbourhood density on adult speakers' productivity with polish case inflections: An empirical test of usage-based approaches to morphology. *Journal of Memory and Language*, 58(4):931–951.

Walter Daelemans. 2002. A comparison of analogical modeling to memory-based language processing. In *Analogical modeling : an exemplar-based approach to language*, pages 157–179.

Micha Elsner. 2021. What transfers in morphological inflection? experiments with analogical models. In *Proceedings of the 18th SIGMORPHON Workshop on Computational Research in Phonetics, Phonology, and Morphology*, pages 154–166, Online. Association for Computational Linguistics.

Stella Frank, Kenny Smith, and Christine F. Cuskley. 2020. Learner dynamics in a model of wug inflection: integrating frequency and phonology. In *CogSci*.

Kyle Gorman, Arya D McCarthy, Ryan Cotterell, Ekaterina Vylomova, Miikka Silfverberg, and Magdalena Markowska. 2019. Weird inflects but ok: Making sense of morphological generation errors. In *Proceedings of the 23rd Conference on Computational Natural Language Learning (CoNLL)*, pages 140–151.

Katharina Kann, Ryan Cotterell, and Hinrich Schütze. 2017. One-shot neural cross-lingual transfer for paradigm completion. In *Proceedings of the 55th Annual Meeting of the Association for Computational Linguistics (Volume 1: Long Papers)*, pages 1993–2003, Vancouver, Canada. Association for Computational Linguistics.

David King, Andrea D. Sims, and Micha Elsner. 2020. Interpreting sequence-to-sequence models for Russian inflectional morphology. In *Proceedings of the Society for Computation in Linguistics (SCiL) 3*, pages Article 39, 402–411. Society for Computation in Linguistics.

Jordan Kodner and Salam Khalifa. 2022. SIGMORPHON-UniMorph 2022 Shared Task 0: Modeling Inflection in Language Acquisition. In *Proceedings of the SIGMORPHON 2022 Shared Task: Morphological Inflection*, Seattle. Association for Computational Linguistics.

Jordan Kodner, Salam Khalifa, Khuyagbaatar Batsuren, Hossep Dolatian, Faruk Akkuş, Antonios Anastasopoulos, Taras Andrushko, Aryaman Arora, Nona Atanelov, Elena Budianskaya, Bella Gábor, Yustinus Ghanggo Ate, Omer Goldman, Simon Guriel, Silvia Guriel-Agiashvili, Ritvan Karahodja, Andrew Krizhanovsky, Natalia Krizhanovsky, Igor Marchenko, Magdalena Markowska, Polina Mashkovtseva, Maria Nepomniashchaya, Daria Rodionova, Elizabeth Salesky, Alexandra Serova, Anastasia Yemelina, Jeremiah Young, and Ekaterina Vylomova. 2022. SIGMORPHON-UniMorph 2022 Shared Task 0: Generalization and Typologically Diverse Morphological Inflection. In *Proceedings of the SIGMORPHON 2022 Shared Task: Morphological Inflection*, Seattle. Association for Computational Linguistics.

Ling Liu and Mans Hulden. 2020. Analogy models for neural word inflection. In *Proceedings of the 28th International Conference on Computational Linguistics*, pages 2861–2878, Barcelona, Spain (Online). International Committee on Computational Linguistics.

Gary F Marcus, Steven Pinker, Michael Ullman, Michelle Hollander, T John Rosen, Fei Xu, and Harald Clahsen. 1992. Overregularization in language acquisition. *Monographs of the society for research in child development*, pages i–178.

Nikitha Murikinati, Antonios Anastasopoulos, and Graham Neubig. 2020. Transliteration for cross-lingual morphological inflection. In *Proceedings of the 17th SIGMORPHON Workshop on Computational Research in Phonetics, Phonology, and Morphology*, pages 189–197, Online. Association for Computational Linguistics.

Margaret K. Omar. 2017. *The Acquisition of Egyptian Arabic as a Native Language*. De Gruyter Mouton.

OSC. 1987. Ohio supercomputer center.

Frans Plank. 2017. Split morphology: How agglutination and flexion mix. *Linguistic Typology*, 21(2017).

Kim Plunkett and Ramin Charles Nakisa. 1997. A connectionist model of the arabic plural system. *Language and Cognitive processes*, 12(5-6):807–836.

Neil Rathi, Michael Hahn, and Richard Futrell. 2021. An information-theoretic characterization of morphological fusion. In *Proceedings of the 2021 Conference on Empirical Methods in Natural Language Processing*, pages 10115–10120, Online and Punta Cana, Dominican Republic. Association for Computational Linguistics.

Dorit Ravid and Rola Farah. 1999. Learning about noun plurals in early palestinian arabic. *First Language*, 19(56):187–206.

Elinor Saiegh-Haddad, Areen Hadieh, and Dorit Ravid. 2012. Acquiring noun plurals in palestinian arabic: Morphology, familiarity, and pattern frequency. *Language learning*, 62(4):1079–1109.

Helen Sims-Williams. 2021. Token frequency as a determinant of morphological change. *Journal of Linguistics*, online first.

Ekaterina Vylomova, Jennifer White, Elizabeth Salesky, Sabrina J. Mielke, Shijie Wu, Edoardo Maria Ponti, Rowan Hall Maudslay, Ran Zmigrod, Josef Valvoda, Svetlana Toldova, Francis Tyers, Elena Klyachko, Ilya Yegorov, Natalia Krizhanovsky, Paula Czarnowska, Irene Nikkarinen, Andrew Krizhanovsky, Tiago Pimentel, Lucas Torroba Hennigen, Christo Kirov, Garrett Nicolai, Adina Williams, Antonios Anastasopoulos, Hilaria Cruz, Eleanor Chodroff, Ryan Cotterell, Miikka Silfverberg, and Mans Hulden. 2020. SIGMORPHON 2020 shared task 0: Typologically diverse morphological inflection. In *Proceedings of the 17th SIGMORPHON Workshop on Computational Research in Phonetics, Phonology, and Morphology*, pages 1–39, Online. Association for Computational Linguistics.

Shijie Wu, Ryan Cotterell, and Mans Hulden. 2021. Applying the transformer to character-level transduction. In *Proceedings of the 16th Conference of the European Chapter of the Association for Computational Linguistics: Main Volume*, pages 1901–1907, Online. Association for Computational Linguistics.

Fei Xu and Steven Pinker. 1995. Weird past tense forms. *Journal of child language*, 22(3):531–556.

Generalizing Morphological Inflection Systems to Unseen Lemmas

Changbing Yang* **Ruixin (Ray) Yang*** **Garrett Nicolai** **Miikka Silfverberg**
University of British Columbia
`first.last@ubc.ca`

Abstract

This paper presents experiments on morphological inflection using data from the SIGMORPHON-UniMorph 2022 Shared Task 0: Generalization and Typologically Diverse Morphological Inflection. We present a transformer inflection system, which enriches the standard transformer architecture with reverse positional encoding and type embeddings. We further apply data hallucination and lemma copying to augment training data. We train models using a two-stage procedure: (1) We first train on the augmented training data using standard backpropagation and teacher forcing. (2) We then continue training with a variant of the scheduled sampling algorithm dubbed student forcing. Our system delivers competitive performance under the small and large data conditions on the shared task datasets.

1 Introduction

This paper presents experiments on morphological inflection using data from the SIGMORPHON-UniMorph Shared Task 0: Generalization and Typologically Diverse Morphological Inflection (Kodner et al., 2022).[1] Our system focuses on typologically diverse inflection generation, that is, the task of inflecting a lemma in a given form, which is specified by a morphosyntactic description (MSD). As an example, consider inflecting the English verb lemma *walk* in the past tense according to the MSD `VERB+PAST`, thereby generating the inflected form *walked*. The shared task investigates two data conditions: Under the *small data condition*, up to 700 training examples are provided. Under the *large data condition*, up to 7000 training examples are provided. Our system beats the official neural shared task baseline by more than 8%-points under both the small and large data conditions.

We apply *transformer models* (Vaswani et al., 2017b) to the inflection task. The model is trained to translate an input sequence consisting of lemma characters and an MSD, like:

`w, a, l, k, +VERB, +PAST`

into the inflected output sequence:

`w, a, l, k, e, d`

General purpose transformers were originally developed for machine translation, but they also deliver strong performance on morphology tasks (Wu et al., 2021). Nevertheless, we observe that the vanilla transformer architecture is not ideally suited for inflection: In contrast to machine translation, many inflectional phenomena are strongly positionally dependent, which is something that the vanilla transformer architecture does not adequately model. For example, phonological alternations often happen at affix boundaries and these typically occur either at the start or end of word forms. Whereas the positional encoding in the transformer architecture allows for uniquely conditioning on relative positions with regard to the start of the string, the same is not true for positions at the end of the input string. We, therefore, augment our transformers with *reverse positional encoding*, presented in Section 3.1, which allow the model to condition directly on the end of the input string.

In previous iterations of the SIGMORPHON inflection shared task (Pimentel et al., 2021; Vylomova et al., 2020; McCarthy et al., 2019; Cotterell et al., 2018, 2017, 2016), so called *lemma overlap*, where identical lemmas occur both in the training and test set, has caused inflated performance, resulting in near perfect inflection accuracy for many languages. Liu and Hulden (2022) and Goldman et al. (2022) show that more challenging data splits with low lemma overlap can cause significant reduction in inflection performance. The data in this

*The first two authors contributed equally.

[1]Note, our system is not an official shared task submission because we submitted our final results after the shared task deadline.

19th SIGMORPHON Workshop on Computational Research in Phonetics, Phonology, and Morphology, pages 226 - 235
July 14, 2022 ©2022 Association for Computational Linguistics

year's inflection task demonstrate varying lemma overlap, ranging from < 1% for Slovak under the small data condition to 100% for Hebrew under the large data condition but centering on lower overlap (see Appendix A for details). Accordingly, we decided to investigate different mechanisms which we hypothesized would improve generalization to unseen lemmas in the test set.

Data augmentation is a commonly used technique, which improves generalization in many NLP tasks. Here the gold standard training data is augmented with synthetic examples. Back-translation introduced for machine translation is perhaps the best known method (Sennrich et al., 2016), but has not been very successful in morphology tasks (Liu and Hulden, 2021). We instead use the *data hallucination* approach by Anastasopoulos and Neubig (2019), which synthesizes new training examples from existing gold standard training examples by identifying a (possibly discontinuous) word stem and replacing this with a random character sequence. In addition to data hallucination, we experiment with another data augmentation technique: *lemma copying* (Liu and Hulden, 2022), where the model is trained to copy input lemmas from the test set in order to adapt the model more closely to the test data. In our experiments, this method ultimately delivers better performance than data hallucination.

As a further attempt to improve generalization, we experiment with modifications of the standard *teacher forced* training procedure of inflection models. When applying teacher forcing during training, the model is allowed to rely on gold standard history for time steps 1 up to t, when predicting output at time step $t + 1$. This speeds up convergence considerably but can also result in sub-optimal performance due to so-called *exposure bias* (Wiseman and Rush, 2016), which is caused by a mismatch when conditioning on gold standard history during training and predicted history during test time. We take an alternative approach called *student forcing* (Nicolai and Silfverberg, 2020), which is an application of *scheduled sampling* (Bengio et al., 2015) for morphology tasks. Here model-predicted output history is substituted for the gold standard history for a subset of training examples in order to counteract exposure bias while simultaneously maintaining efficient training (see Figure 1). According to Nicolai and Silfverberg (2020), student forcing can improve inflection performance under low-resource conditions. Our experiments show that student forcing can deliver small improvements for some languages but does not outperform data hallucination. However, the techniques seem to be complementary; their combination provides improvements over plain data augmentation.

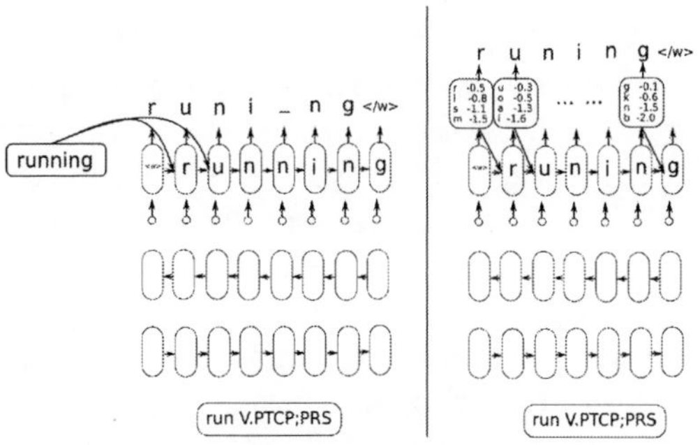

[Illustration from Nicolai and Silfverberg (2020)]

Figure 1: Teacher forcing (left) and student forcing (right); some connections have been left out to reduce clutter.

In summary, our main contributions are as follow:

1. We enrich the transformer architecture with reverse positional encoding in order to support the inflection task.
2. We investigate data hallucination and lemma copying as ways to prompt better generalization to lemmas missing from the training set.
3. We apply student forcing to counter exposure bias in inflection.

2 Related Work

Wu et al. (2021) present a systematic investigation of applying the transformer model to morphology tasks. They propose two changes to the general transformer architecture introduced by Vaswani et al. (2017b): (1) type embeddings, which are used to distinguish between input characters and morphosyntactic tags and (2) restricting positional encoding to the input characters, while encoding morphosyntactic tags in a position-agnostic manner. Another modification to the transformer architecture, which can improve performance on morphology tasks, is to add a so-called monotonicity loss (Rios et al., 2021). This can bias the transformer toward near-monotonic alignment between the input and output sequence, which is often the case in inflection.

We use data augmentation to improve generalization to unseen lemmas. This has become a standard technique in low-resource inflection in recent years. A common approach is to generate synthetic examples by first identifying word stems in gold standard examples and then replacing the stems with random character sequences (Anastasopoulos and Neubig, 2019; Silfverberg et al., 2017). Liu and Hulden (2022) introduce a more refined method to hallucinate synthetic stems, which aims to honor the phonology of the target language by generating sequences of random syllables rather than random characters. Kann and Schütze (2017) show that a simpler data augmentation method, where random strings or unlabeled word forms are copied from the input to the output, can also be effective. Liu and Hulden (2022) apply this approach to copying lemmas in the development and test set and show that this can lead to substantial gains in inflection accuracy. We apply their technique in Section 3.4. Other approaches to data augmentation in morphological inflection include: reframing the task as reinflection and generating reinflection examples from the existing inflection training data (Liu and Hulden, 2020), as well as generating new training examples using back-translation (Liu and Hulden, 2021), and self-training (Yu et al., 2020).

In addition to data augmentation, we also experiment with student forcing to improve generalization. As mentioned above, this is an application of scheduled sampling. Bengio et al. (2015) explore scheduled sampling for various sequence generation tasks (image captioning, constituency parsing and speech recognition). This is a curriculum learning approach (Bengio et al., 2009), where the model is gradually exposed to more of its own prediction errors during training, thereby counteracting exposure bias. The student forcing approach presented by Nicolai and Silfverberg (2020) is a slight simplification of this approach. Essentially, student forcing uses a fixed amount of model-predicted contexts throughout training instead of a curriculum approach.

3 Methods

In this section, we describe our contributions to the inflection task, before moving on to our experiments in subsequent sections.

3.1 Reverse Positional Encoding

The vanilla Transformer architecture, which serves as the basis for our system, accounts for the order of input and output tokens by pairing each token with a sinusoidal positional encoding (Vaswani et al., 2017a). This positional encoding captures relative distance from the *start* of the string, meaning that it is a *forward* positional encoding. In inflection tasks, it is, however, vital to encode not only distance from the start of the input string, but also distance to the *end* of the string.

For example, in English, the plural form of nouns ending in a strident like *s* is formed by appending an affix *-es* to the end of the noun (e.g. *class* $\rightarrow$ *class+es*) instead of the regular plural suffix *-s*. The alternation *s* $\rightarrow$ *es* always occurs at the penultimate position of the inflected form, which means that it is important to allow the model to directly refer to positions at the end of the strings. Because word length differs, this information is difficult to infer from a purely forward positional encoding.

We augment the vanilla transformer model in the Fairseq toolkit (Ott et al., 2019) with reverse positional encoding: Let $f_1, ..., f_n$ be the k-dimensional forward sinusoidal positional encoding vectors for a string of length n. We introduce k-dimensional reverse positional encoding vectors $b_1, ..., b_n$, where $r_i = f_{n-i+1}$. Our final positional encoding vectors are given by the $2k$-dimensional concatenation $[f_i; b_i]$. Following Wu et al. (2021), we only use positional encoding vectors for characters in the input lemma. For morphosyntactic tags, we instead use a special NULL vector. See Figure 2 for a representation of the reverse positional encoding.

3.2 Type Embeddings

Given an example like *bus*+NOUN+PL $\rightarrow$ *buses*, the input sequences to our inflection model consist of two token-types: lemma-characters like *b, u* and *s* and morphosyntactic tags like +NOUN and +PL. Following Wu et al. (2021), we use type embedding vectors e_{LEM} and e_{MSD} to distinguish between these token-types. The type vectors have the same dimensionality as the input embeddings. We sum them with token embedding vectors to compute input token representations. The vectors e_{LEM} and e_{MSD} are randomly initialized and are trained jointly with the rest of the inflection model. See Figure 2 for an illustration of type embeddings.

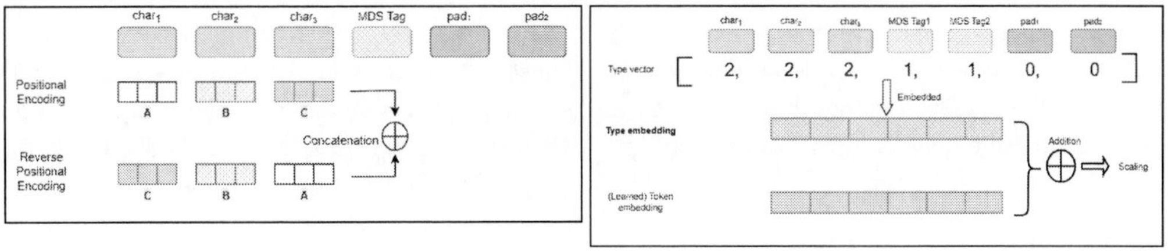

Figure 2: Illustration of reverse positional encoding and type embeddings. The left figure shows the encoding of source character positions from the backward pass, concatenated with the forward positional encoding. The right figure displays a type embedding built from an integer-encoded type vector that distinguishes the three possible types of an input token. The type embedding is then summed with the original token embedding and multiplied by a scaling factor.

	stem *stem*
Original triple	
lemma	π α ρ α κ ά μ π τ ω
+V;2;SG;IPFV;PST	π α ρ έ κ α μ π τ ε ς
Hallucinated	
lemma	π ξ ρ α κ ά μ ο τ ω
+V;2;SG;IPFV;PST	π ξ ρ έ κ α μ ο τ ε ς

[Illustration from Anastasopoulos and Neubig (2019)]

Figure 3: Illustration of the data hallucination method. Noise is introduced into the existing training examples by replacing the longest common subsequence of input and output forms with random character strings.

3.3 Data Hallucination

Under low-data conditions, encoder-decoder models are often strongly influenced by the target language model. Common character sequences which appear in the training data are more likely to be produced, even at the expense of ignoring the input example. In order to address this label bias, we augment the training data with hallucinated examples. We employ the approach proposed by Anastasopoulos and Neubig (2019). This method introduces noise into the existing training examples by replacing the longest common subsequence of input and output forms with random character strings, as shown in Figure 3.

Although the problem is more prevalent under low-data conditions, we experiment with adding synthetic examples to the original dataset under both the small and large data condition. Preliminary development experiments motivate the number of hallucinated forms. Accordingly, we use 7,000 synthetic examples for the small data set and 1,400 examples for the large training set.

3.4 Lemma Copying

The data hallucination method introduced by Anastasopoulos and Neubig (2019) can sometimes create invalid examples due to phonological alternations as noted by Samir and Silfverberg (2022). For example, given the English inflection example *like+VERB+PAST* → *liked*, their approach will first identify the longest common subsequence of the lemma and word form, that is, *like* and will then replace this with a random character sequence, for example *xyz*. This results in a synthetic example *xyz+VERB+PAST* → *xyzd*. Now, this example is erroneous since *-d* occurs as the English past tense marker for regular verbs only when the stem ends in *e*, which the syntetic stem *xyz* does not.

In order to avoid introducing errors during augmentation, we experiment with an alternative approach to data augmentation: so-called lemma copying, first presented by Liu and Hulden (2022). We augment the training set with artificial examples where a lemma is copied verbatim, e.g. *like*+`COPY` → *like*. Here we use the special `+COPY` tag to indicate copying. We collect lemmas for the copy examples from the input forms in the test set. Therefore, lemma copying can be seen as a domain adaptation technique, where we adapt the inflection model to the specific test input forms.

At a first glance, lemma copying might seem like an artificial technique, which will only be useful in a shared task setting where we have a fixed test set. However, even in real-world scenarios, we will often run the model on a fixed dataset of inputs.[2] It is, therefore, possible to either retrain the model on a combination of the original training data and test input forms, or fine-tune the model on lemma

[2]For example, we might want to inflect a set of baseforms from a dictionary.

copying.[3] It is also important to note that lemma copying does not use any additional labeled data for training the system. Neither does is make use of any additional unlabeled data, which would be unavailable at inference-time.

3.5 Student Forcing

Sequence-to-sequence architectures are very dependent on the context of generated items—it is their greatest strength, but can also lead to disjunctions between training and testing settings.

In very low data setups, exposure bias can overfit to the training data, as it observes a very small set of contexts. Although data hallucination has been shown to counter overfitting in such scenarios, we additionally adopt the student forcing approach described by Nicolai and Silfverberg (2020).

For a small number of instances (a tunable hyperparameter, *student-forced percentage* [SF-%], most effective between 10 and 30%), contextual cues from the target are replaced with hypotheses generated by the model. Hypotheses are typically generated via the standard inference method (in this case, a beam search with beam width 5). We explore several alternative methods to further allow the model to take advantage of the prediction space, including sampling from items that reach a probability threshold, a count threshold, and using multiple diverse beam groups. Development results suggested that sampling from the top 2 candidates yielded the best results, and is used for all experiments describing student forcing for the remainder of this paper.

Since hallucinated data makes up a significant portion of the training data (90% under the small data condition, and 17% under the large data condition), we anticipate the possibility that the model overfits to hallucinated data. In an attempt to counter overfitting, we apply student-forcing in a fine-tuning step after the initial data-augmented models have been trained.

4 Experiments and Results

Here, we describe our experiments on small and large training sets. Under both data conditions, we train models using the following procedure: We first augment the training data using data hallucination or lemma copying. We then train the model on the augmented data for a maximum of 20,000 steps without teacher forcing. We then identify the best checkpoint model based on development set accuracy and continue training this model with student forcing for an additional 1000 steps. When applying lemma copying, we have to train separate models for the development and test set: one model which augments the training set with lemmas from the development set and another one which augments with test lemmas. We first tune hyperparameters on the development set and then use this hyperparameter configuration when training the final model for the test set. Crucially, this allows us to avoid augmenting the training data both with development and test lemmas in order to not use extra data for tuning model parameters.

4.1 Original Data for Inflection Generation

Data across 33 languages are included in our experiments. We follow the training, development, and testing splits provided by the task organizers. Twenty of the languages contain two training conditions: small and large. Small training data range from 70 to 700 instances, where an instance is composed of a lemma, an MSD, and an inflected form. Most languages have 700 training instances, but Chukchi (ckt), Upper Sorbian (hsb), Kholosi (hsi), and Ket (ket) represent an even lower-resource condition. In the large training data condition, each language has 7,000 training instances. Generally, development splits contain approximately 1,000 instances, and test splits contain 2,000.

4.2 Model Architecture

We conduct our experiments with a modified version of Fairseq's (Ott et al., 2019) implementation of transformers (Vaswani et al., 2017b). The transformer architecture is enriched with reverse positional encoding and type embeddings, as we illustrated in Sections 3.1 and 3.2. We train our models with 4 layers in the encoder and decoder, each containing 4 attention heads. The embedding size is 256 and the hidden layer size is 1024. These hyperparameter settings roughly correspond to the values used by Wu et al. (2021) for character-level tasks.

We use the Adam optimizer with an initial learning rate of 0.001, and batch size 400. Prediction is performed with the best checkpoint model, according to the development accuracy, using a beam of width 5. All models are trained for a maximum of 20,000 updates. Fine-tuning then proceeds for a maximum of 1000 additional updates. Again, we

[3] In the current submission, we only investigate the retraining approach.

choose the best model as determined by development accuracy.

4.3 Main Results

Experiment	Small	Large
ST BASELINE	47.63	62.39
OUR BASELINE	47.93	69.57
HALL	53.83	69.19
COPY	56.64	70.66
COPY+SF	**57.23**	**71.26**
COPY+HALL	55.27	70.43

Table 1: Results on the test data under both small and large data conditions. ST BASELINE refers to the official neural shared task baseline and "Our Baseline" to our baseline transformer with reverse positional encoding and type embeddings. SF refers to student forcing, HALL to data hallucination and COPY to lemma copying.

We use micro averaged full-form accuracy to evaluate our predictions on development and test splits, including results both under the small and large data condition.[4] Average results across all languages are shown in Table 1.[5] See Kodner et al. (2022) for detailed results. The best results (Copy+SF) represent our official shared task submission.

Across both data conditions, our models outperform the official shared task neural baseline. Our modified Fairseq models with reverse positional encoding and type embeddings but without data augmentation (OUR BASELINE) perform slightly better than the official shared task baseline under the small training data condition, while on the large training set our modifications to the transformer architecture contribute a substantial improvement of around 7%-points.

Results from data hallucination HALL are mixed. Under the low data condition, it delivers a clear improvement of 5.90%-points over OUR BASELINE on the test set, but under the large data condition, it results in a small drop of 0.38%-points in inflection accuracy. In contrast, lemma copying delivers consistent improvements over OUR BASELINE under all data conditions. Under the small data condition, the COPY system delivers a substantial 8.71%-point improvement and a smaller improvement of 1.09%-points under the large data condition, outperforming HALL under both conditions. A combination of the data augmentation techniques COPY+HALL does not deliver improvements over plain lemma copying but outperforms HALL. In general, data augmentation is always more helpful under the low data condition.

Student forcing (COPY+SF) further boosts the performance of the COPY system for several languages, resulting in a 0.5%-points gain under both data conditions. Some languages show only modest improvement, such as Hebrew increasing from 34.6% to 35.2%, or even small decreases - Braj decreases from 56.1% to 56.0%. However, other improvements are much more noteworthy - Arabic increases from 43% to 47.9%, and Pomak from 44.2% to 46.0%. The trends are similar under the large data condition, although fewer languages are affected.

We take a closer look at the types of errors that are corrected by the COPY+SF model when compared to COPY. Concentrating on Evenki, we notice that the corrections made by student forcing are generally small - typically, the addition or removal of a single letter. For example, the 3rd person singular possessive form of *atirkanma* should be *atirkanman*. While the model prior to fine-tuning simply copies the lemma, COPY+SF corrects the error. Likewise, the 3rd person dative possessive form of *nadiśi* is predicted as *nadiśidun*, which is then corrected by student forcing to *nadiśidu:n*.

5 Discussion

The most prominent trend in our experiments is that lemma copying delivers sizable improvements in accuracy, particularly under the small data condition. It is also noteworthy that models trained on small training data using data augmentation(either hallucinated data or copied data) outperform models trained on large training data without data augmentation. Based on these results, it is clear that data augmentation is a crucial technique in low-resource inflection, delivering substantial improvements which parallel improvements from a significant additional annotation effort. This might allow researchers to kick-start development of morphology resources for low-resource languages using very little annotated data. Performance also seems to improve even under higher data conditions when lemma overlap in the training data and test data is small.

Student forcing delivers small improvements at best and is often harmful when combined with data augmentation. We do not have a good explanation

[4]This corresponds to the official evaluation metric of the SIGMORPHON 2022 inflection shared task.

[5]See Appendix B for results on the development set.

for this phenomenon at the current time. Based on our experimental results, we can conclude that data augmentation is a far more influential method for countering data sparsity.

It is interesting to see that our base inflector, trained without student forcing or data augmentation, outperforms the shared task baseline. Given that the baseline system is a character-level transformer (Wu et al., 2021), this might be attributable to our architectural innovation, namely reverse positional encoding. However, another difference between our system and the shared task baseline is that the baseline is a multilingual system, whereas our system is monolingual. Further investigation is required to tease apart these effects.

6 Conclusion

In this work, we advance the generation performance of inflectional forms with a joint effort including reverse positional encoding, data hallucination, copying lemmas, and student forcing. We improve the prediction accuracy by 9.6% and 8.6% above the official neural shared task baseline on the small and large test set respectively.

According to our results, the joint effect of reverse positional encoding, lemma copying, and student forcing results in the best performance. We investigate two data augmentation strategies: The effect of data augmentation is more evident when less annotated data is available for training.

Due to time constraints, many observed phenomena are still ripe for interpretation, including the role that sampling has in a space populated by artificial examples. Our findings suggest that not only is data hallucination beneficial for low-resource morphological inflection, but that it is a necessary step in the inflectional pipeline. That said, there is still room to improve. Even in the more challenging (and more realistic) setting present in this task, several languages are close to solved for inflection, but many still have significant room for improvement. We anticipate more focused investigations into the reasons why these languages remain so difficult for transformer models, even as the state of the art approaches new heights.

Acknowledgements

We want to thank Farhan Samir for useful discussions regarding scheduled sampling. We also want to thank the organizers of the shared task. This research was supported by funding from the National Endowment for the Humanities (Documenting Endangered Languages Fellowship) and the Social Sciences and Humanities Research Council of Canada (Grant 430-2020-00793). Any views/findings/conclusions expressed in this publication do not necessarily reflect those of SSHRC.

References

Antonios Anastasopoulos and Graham Neubig. 2019. Pushing the limits of low-resource morphological inflection. In *Proceedings of the 2019 Conference on Empirical Methods in Natural Language Processing and the 9th International Joint Conference on Natural Language Processing*, pages 984–996.

Samy Bengio, Oriol Vinyals, Navdeep Jaitly, and Noam Shazeer. 2015. Scheduled sampling for sequence prediction with recurrent neural networks. *Advances in neural information processing systems*, 28.

Yoshua Bengio, Jérôme Louradour, Ronan Collobert, and Jason Weston. 2009. Curriculum learning. In *Proceedings of the 26th annual international conference on machine learning*, pages 41–48.

Ryan Cotterell, Christo Kirov, John Sylak-Glassman, Géraldine Walther, Ekaterina Vylomova, Arya D. McCarthy, Katharina Kann, Sabrina J. Mielke, Garrett Nicolai, Miikka Silfverberg, David Yarowsky, Jason Eisner, and Mans Hulden. 2018. The CoNLL–SIGMORPHON 2018 shared task: Universal morphological reinflection. In *Proceedings of the CoNLL–SIGMORPHON 2018 Shared Task: Universal Morphological Reinflection*, pages 1–27.

Ryan Cotterell, Christo Kirov, John Sylak-Glassman, Géraldine Walther, Ekaterina Vylomova, Patrick Xia, Manaal Faruqui, Sandra Kübler, David Yarowsky, Jason Eisner, and Mans Hulden. 2017. CoNLL-SIGMORPHON 2017 shared task: Universal morphological reinflection in 52 languages. In *Proceedings of the CoNLL SIGMORPHON 2017 Shared Task: Universal Morphological Reinflection*, pages 1–30.

Ryan Cotterell, Christo Kirov, John Sylak-Glassman, David Yarowsky, Jason Eisner, and Mans Hulden. 2016. The sigmorphon 2016 shared task—morphological reinflection. In *Proceedings of the 14th SIGMORPHON Workshop on Computational Research in Phonetics, Phonology, and Morphology*, pages 10–22.

Omer Goldman, David Guriel, and Reut Tsarfaty. 2022. (un)solving morphological inflection: Lemma overlap artificially inflates models' performance. In *Proceedings of the 60th Annual Meeting of the Association for Computational Linguistics (Volume 2: Short Papers)*, pages 864–870.

Katharina Kann and Hinrich Schütze. 2017. Unlabeled data for morphological generation with character-based sequence-to-sequence models. In *Proceedings of the First Workshop on Subword and Character Level Models in NLP*, pages 76–81.

Jordan Kodner, Salam Khalifa, Khuyagbaatar Batsuren, Hossep Dolatian, Ryan Cotterell, Faruk Akkuş, Antonios Anastasopoulos, Taras Andrushko, Aryaman Arora, Nona Atanelov, Gábor Bella, Elena Budianskaya, Yustinus Ghanggo Ate, Omer Goldman, Simon Guriel, Silvia Guriel-Agiashvili, Jan Hajič, Jan Hric, Ritvan Karahodja, Witold Kieraś, Andrew Krizhanovsky, Natalia Krizhanovsky, Igor Marchenko, Magdalena Markowska, Polina Mashkovtseva, Maria Nepomniashchaya, Daria Rodionova, Elizabeth Salesky, Karina Sheifer, Alexandra Serova, Anastasia Yemelina, Jeremiah Young, and Ekaterina Vylomova. 2022. SIGMORPHON-UniMorph 2022 Shared Task 0: Generalization and Typologically Diverse Morphological Inflection. In *Proceedings of the SIGMORPHON 2022 Shared Task: Morphological Inflection*.

Ling Liu and Mans Hulden. 2020. Leveraging principal parts for morphological inflection. In *Proceedings of the 17th SIGMORPHON Workshop on Computational Research in Phonetics, Phonology, and Morphology*, pages 153–161.

Ling Liu and Mans Hulden. 2021. Backtranslation in neural morphological inflection. In *Proceedings of the Second Workshop on Insights from Negative Results in NLP*, pages 81–88.

Ling Liu and Mans Hulden. 2022. Can a transformer pass the wug test? tuning copying bias in neural morphological inflection models. In *Proceedings of the 60th Annual Meeting of the Association for Computational Linguistics (Volume 2: Short Papers)*, pages 739–749.

Arya D. McCarthy, Ekaterina Vylomova, Shijie Wu, Chaitanya Malaviya, Lawrence Wolf-Sonkin, Garrett Nicolai, Christo Kirov, Miikka Silfverberg, Sabrina J. Mielke, Jeffrey Heinz, Ryan Cotterell, and Mans Hulden. 2019. The SIGMORPHON 2019 shared task: Morphological analysis in context and cross-lingual transfer for inflection. In *Proceedings of the 16th Workshop on Computational Research in Phonetics, Phonology, and Morphology*, pages 229–244.

Garrett Nicolai and Miikka Silfverberg. 2020. Noise isn't always negative: Countering exposure bias in sequence-to-sequence inflection models. In *Proceedings of the 28th International Conference on Computational Linguistics*, pages 2837–2846.

Myle Ott, Sergey Edunov, Alexei Baevski, Angela Fan, Sam Gross, Nathan Ng, David Grangier, and Michael Auli. 2019. fairseq: A fast, extensible toolkit for sequence modeling. In *Proceedings of the 2019 Conference of the North American Chapter of the Association for Computational Linguistics (Demonstrations)*, pages 48–53.

Tiago Pimentel, Maria Ryskina, Sabrina J. Mielke, Shijie Wu, Eleanor Chodroff, Brian Leonard, Garrett Nicolai, Yustinus Ghanggo Ate, Salam Khalifa, Nizar Habash, Charbel El-Khaissi, Omer Goldman, Michael Gasser, William Lane, Matt Coler, Arturo Oncevay, Jaime Rafael Montoya Samame, Gema Celeste Silva Villegas, Adam Ek, Jean-Philippe Bernardy, Andrey Shcherbakov, Aziyana Bayyr-ool, Karina Sheifer, Sofya Ganieva, Matvey Plugaryov, Elena Klyachko, Ali Salehi, Andrew Krizhanovsky, Natalia Krizhanovsky, Clara Vania, Sardana Ivanova, Aelita Salchak, Christopher Straughn, Zoey Liu, Jonathan North Washington, Duygu Ataman, Witold Kieraś, Marcin Woliński, Totok Suhardijanto, Niklas Stoehr, Zahroh Nuriah, Shyam Ratan, Francis M. Tyers, Edoardo M. Ponti, Grant Aiton, Richard J. Hatcher, Emily Prud'hommeaux, Ritesh Kumar, Mans Hulden, Botond Barta, Dorina Lakatos, Gábor Szolnok, Judit Ács, Mohit Raj, David Yarowsky, Ryan Cotterell, Ben Ambridge, and Ekaterina Vylomova. 2021. SIGMORPHON 2021 shared task on morphological reinflection: Generalization across languages. In *Proceedings of the 18th SIGMORPHON Workshop on Computational Research in Phonetics, Phonology, and Morphology*, pages 229–259.

Annette Rios, Chantal Amrhein, Noëmi Aepli, and Rico Sennrich. 2021. On biasing transformer attention towards monotonicity. In *2021 Annual Conference of the North American Chapter of the Association for Computational Linguistics*.

Farhan Samir and Miikka Silfverberg. 2022. One wug, two wug+ s transformer inflection models hallucinate affixes. In *Proceedings of the Fifth Workshop on the Use of Computational Methods in the Study of Endangered Languages*, pages 31–40.

Rico Sennrich, Barry Haddow, and Alexandra Birch. 2016. Improving neural machine translation models with monolingual data. In *54th Annual Meeting of the Association for Computational Linguistics*, pages 86–96.

Miikka Silfverberg, Adam Wiemerslage, Ling Liu, and Lingshuang Jack Mao. 2017. Data augmentation for morphological reinflection. In *Proceedings of the CoNLL SIGMORPHON 2017 Shared Task: Universal Morphological Reinflection*, pages 90–99.

Ashish Vaswani, Noam Shazeer, Niki Parmar, Jakob Uszkoreit, Llion Jones, Aidan N Gomez, Ł ukasz Kaiser, and Illia Polosukhin. 2017a. Attention is all you need. In *Advances in Neural Information Processing Systems*, volume 30. Curran Associates, Inc.

Ashish Vaswani, Noam Shazeer, Niki Parmar, Jakob Uszkoreit, Llion Jones, Aidan N Gomez, Łukasz Kaiser, and Illia Polosukhin. 2017b. Attention is all you need. *Advances in neural information processing systems*, 30.

Ekaterina Vylomova, Jennifer White, Elizabeth Salesky, Sabrina J. Mielke, Shijie Wu, Edoardo Maria Ponti, Rowan Hall Maudslay, Ran Zmigrod, Josef Valvoda, Svetlana Toldova, Francis Tyers, Elena Klyachko, Ilya Yegorov, Natalia Krizhanovsky,

Paula Czarnowska, Irene Nikkarinen, Andrew Krizhanovsky, Tiago Pimentel, Lucas Torroba Hennigen, Christo Kirov, Garrett Nicolai, Adina Williams, Antonios Anastasopoulos, Hilaria Cruz, Eleanor Chodroff, Ryan Cotterell, Miikka Silfverberg, and Mans Hulden. 2020. SIGMORPHON 2020 shared task 0: Typologically diverse morphological inflection. In *Proceedings of the 17th SIGMORPHON Workshop on Computational Research in Phonetics, Phonology, and Morphology*, pages 1–39.

Sam Wiseman and Alexander M. Rush. 2016. Sequence-to-sequence learning as beam-search optimization. In *Proceedings of the 2016 Conference on Empirical Methods in Natural Language Processing*, pages 1296–1306.

Shijie Wu, Ryan Cotterell, and Mans Hulden. 2021. Applying the transformer to character-level transduction. In *Proceedings of the 16th Conference of the European Chapter of the Association for Computational Linguistics: Main Volume*, pages 1901–1907.

Xiang Yu, Ngoc Thang Vu, and Jonas Kuhn. 2020. Ensemble self-training for low-resource languages: Grapheme-to-phoneme conversion and morphological inflection. In *Proceedings of the 17th SIGMORPHON Workshop on Computational Research in Phonetics, Phonology, and Morphology*, pages 70–78.

A Lemma Overlap

Lemma overlap for small training data (in Table 3) and large training data (in Table 2) with the development and test sets. Lemma overlap is computed by dividing the number of examples, where the lemma occurs in the training set, with the total number of examples.

B Supplementary results

Table 4 shows the micro averaged inflection accuracy of each model on the development data.

	ang	ara	asm	evn	got	heb	hun	hye	kat	kaz	khk	kor	krl	lud	non	pol	poma	slk	tur	vep
dev	64.7	62.8	99.3	65.7	76.0	100.0	30.9	68.8	90.8	97.7	98.9	92.0	59.0	53.5	95.4	7.3	11.6	5.6	91.7	44.7
test	77.1	54.0	98.9	61.3	81.2	100.0	31.1	69.7	82.4	98.2	99.0	92.2	81.2	54.3	95.2	6.6	17.1	5.1	87.2	42.1

Table 2: Lemma overlap for the large training sets with the development and test data. Lemma overlap is computed as f/N, where f is the number of development/test examples, where the lemma is found in the training set and N is the total number of development/test examples.

	ang	ara	asm	bra	ckt	evn	gml	goh	got	guj	heb	hsb	hsi	hun	hye	itl	kat	kaz	ket
dev	14.2	13.3	45.4	25.8	27.3	36.7	100.0	78.7	13.7	83.7	45.5	20.0	73.3	3.1	14.7	27.8	52.3	97.7	57.6
test	19.0	8.9	45.9	30.7	34.8	29.8	100.0	80.6	16.0	81.8	43.6	16.2	63.3	4.0	15.2	25.5	28.4	98.2	44.5

	khk	kor	krl	lud	mag	nds	non	pol	poma	sjo	slk	slp	tur	vep
dev	26.1	23.1	10.1	12.5	36.7	90.7	38.9	0.5	1.5	32.3	0.6	65.0	50.5	7.2
test	24.7	23.7	16.1	9.7	35.3	92.1	40.4	0.9	1.6	25.3	0.4	72.2	45.4	5.0

Table 3: Lemma overlap for the small training sets with the development and test data.

Experiment	Small	Large
ST BASELINE	42.59	60.04
OUR BASELINE	43.52	67.37
HALL	49.28	67.49
COPY	52.41	68.57
COPY+SF	**53.36**	**68.99**
COPY+HALL	52.32	68.09

Table 4: Results on the development data under small and large data conditions. ST BASELINE refers to the official neural shared task baseline and "Our Baseline" to our baseline transformer with reverse positional encoding and type embeddings. SF refers to student forcing, HALL to data hallucination and COPY to lemma copying.

HeiMorph at SIGMORPHON 2022 Shared Task on Morphological Acquisition Trajectories

Akhilesh Kakolu Ramarao and **Yulia Zinova** and **Kevin Tang** and **Ruben van de Vijver**
Heinrich-Heine-University, Düsseldorf
{kakolura, yulia.zinova, kevin.tang, ruben.vijver}@hhu.de

Abstract

This paper presents the submission by the HeiMorph team to the SIGMORPHON 2022 task 2 of Morphological Acquisition Trajectories. Across all experimental conditions, we have found no evidence for the so-called U-shaped development trajectory. Our submitted systems achieve an average test accuracies of 55.5% on Arabic, 67% on German and 73.38% on English. We found that, bigram hallucination provides better inferences only for English and Arabic and only when the number of hallucinations remains low.

1 Introduction

Morphological inflection concerns generating the inflected word form given the lemma and a set of morphosyntactic descriptions. A morphology learner (human or machine) must be able to generalise patterns from extremely sparse data. Observations from morphology acquisition by children provides us with a glimpse of how learners generalise regular and irregular patterns differently and how the trajectories of pattern generalisations interact with a small but growing lexicon.

This paper describes our approach and results for Task 0 Part 2 of the SIGMORPHON 2022 shared task on morphological acquisition trajectories. Two main challenges of the task are that it covers two different inflectional patterns (past tense and noun plurals) over three languages and that there is only a small amount of training data ranging from as few as 100 samples to as many as 1,000 samples. This extreme data sparsity calls for the use of data hallucination techniques commonly used for low-resourced NLP development (Chen et al., 2021).

The neural baseline provided by the shared task is based on input-variant transformer (Wu et al., 2020) or the vanilla transformer with optional data augmentation (Anastasopoulos and Neubig, 2019).

We use a multi-headed self-attention Transformer with unigram-aware and bigram-aware data hallucinations.

Our models yielded an improved average test accuracy by 2.66% on Arabic, 8.69% on German, 4.5% on English, as compared with the neural baseline results.

2 Background and Data

The details of the task description can be found at `https://github.com/sigmorphon/2022InflectionST`. We use the data provided by the SIGMORPHON 2022 shared task (Part 2) (Kodner and Khalifa, 2022). The data features lemmas, inflections, and corresponding morphosyntactic description (MSD) using the uni-morph schema (Kirov et al., 2018). The data was released for English, German and Arabic. The specific inflectional patterns were the English past tense (Marcus et al., 1992), German noun plurals (Clahsen et al., 1992) and Arabic noun plurals (Dawdy-Hesterberg and Pierrehumbert, 2014).

3 System Description

In this section, we describe the neural network architecture, the data hallucination process and the submissions.

3.1 Neural Network architecture

All our models use the self-attention Transformer architecture (Vaswani et al., 2017) and implemented using the Fairseq (Ott et al., 2019) tool. Both the encoder and decoder have 4 layers with 4 attention heads, an embedding size of 256 and hidden layer size of 1,024. All models are trained with Adam optimizer (Kingma and Ba, 2014) with an initial learning rate of 0.001, batch size of 400, label smoothing as 0.1, gradient clip threshold as 1.0, and 4,000 warmup updates. All models are trained for a maximum of 3,000 optimizer updates, with checkpoints saved every 10 epochs. Beam search is used at decoding time with a beam width of 5.

19th SIGMORPHON Workshop on Computational Research in Phonetics, Phonology, and Morphology, pages 236 - 239
July 14, 2022 ©2022 Association for Computational Linguistics

The checkpoint with the smallest loss on the development data is chosen as the best model.

The inputs to each model are the individual characters of the lemma followed by their morpho-syntactic tags separated by # symbol. For example, for the English training triple (take, took, V;PST), the input to the model is t a k e <V;PRS> # <V;PST> and the output is t o o k.

3.2 Hallucinations

As has been shown in Anastasopoulos and Neubig (2019), adding hallucinated data boosts the learning process for small datasets. In the system described there, the hallucinated data is produced by 1) identifying a sequence of three or more consecutive characters that are aligned between the lemma and the inflected form and 2) randomly replacing the characters inside of this region by other characters from the language's alphabet. This replacement strategy produces is motivated by the label bias problem associated with the small dataset sizes. On the other hand, as a result the algorithm of Anastasopoulos and Neubig (2019) produces, among others, string pairs that lack vowels and have no resemblance to the original language data except for the inflected part. Our hypothesis was that such an approach may work well for languages with affixal morphology that is independent but may be less optimal for languages where the type of the inflection depends on the phonological properties of the stem (Haspelmath and Sims, 2013).

In order to check this hypothesis we have set up an alternative hallucination procedure. For each training set size, we compute a matrix of co-occurring characters and during the replacement step when a character from the alphabet is selected, we verify if this character occurred after the preceding character in the original train data. If yes, the replacement takes place, otherwise a new candidate character is selected.

As can be seen from the plots, the proposed bigram hallucination algorithm provides better results for English and Arabic data, if we do not produce too many hallucinations (1,000 hallucinations are better than 10,000, which was the original size in Anastasopoulos and Neubig (2019)).

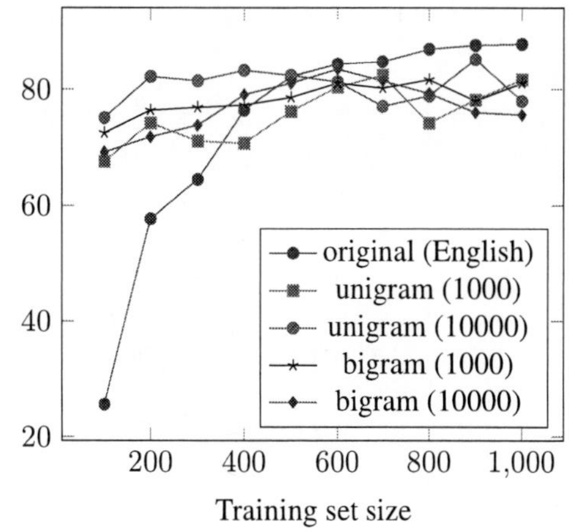

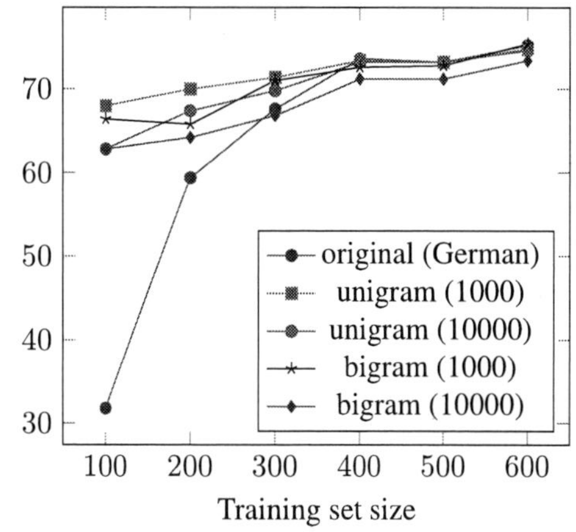

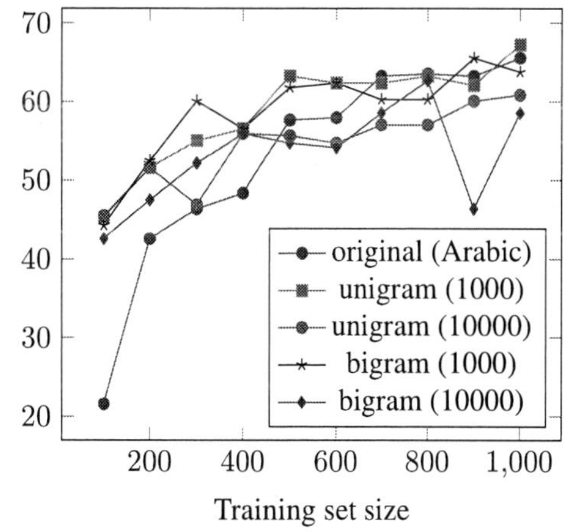

3.3 Development decision

We selected our submitted system based only on a subset of the experiments, since we did not have the full picture across all experimental conditions at the time. Concretely, we based our decisions on the models performance for German. We found that the training size of less than 500 samples yielded models that performed better on 10,000 hallucinations, while training size of 500 and above yielded

	Arabic		German		English	
	Accuracy	Distance	Accuracy	Distance	Accuracy	Distance
100	42.6	2.2	62.8	0.46	69.2	2.08
200	47.5	1.99	64.2	0.45	71.8	1.9
300	52.2	1.79	66.8	0.41	73.8	1.6
400	56	1.75	71.2	0.36	79.1	1.39
500	61.8	1.5	72.8	0.34	78.6	1.83
600	62.4	1.49	75.4	0.3	81.1	1.48
700	60.3	1.61			80.2	1.62
800	60.3	1.63			81.7	1.41
900	65.6	1.35			78	1.54
1000	63.8	1.64			81.1	1.2

Table 1: Accuracy and Levenshtein distance on the development set

	Arabic		German		English	
	Accuracy	Distance	Accuracy	Distance	Accuracy	Distance
100	41.833	2.24	59	0.52	65.2	0.93
200	45.667	2.07	63.5	0.48	67.5	0.59
300	48.667	2.02	66.333	0.43	71.1	0.62
400	49.833	2.1	69	0.41	76.3	0.91
500	59.667	1.6	71	0.38	70.8	0.58
600	62.833	1.5	73.33	0.33	75.5	0.58
700	60.333	1.57			74.3	0.49
800	62.167	1.53			78.7	0.59
900	63.333	1.52			74.7	0.6
1000	59.333	1.74			80	0.48

Table 2: Accuracy and Levenshtein distance on the test set

models that performed better on only 1,000 hallucinations. Based on this finding with German, at the time of the development, we assumed this trend would hold also for English and Arabic.

3.4 Submissions

The models trained with training size less than 500 were hallucinated with 10,000 samples and the rest of the models with 1,000 samples across the three languages.

As the models trained on the proposed bigram hallucination algorithm provides better results on the development set for English and Arabic with 1000 hallucinations across all training sizes, this would have been our alternate submission.

4 Results

Table 1 shows the performance of our models on the development set. Results on the test data from SIGMORPHON 2022 Task 0 with Levenshtein distance can be found in Table 2.

5 Conclusion

How do children learn morphology? It has often been noted that children start out using correct forms, followed by a period of regularlizing irregular forms, followed by mastery of the morphology (Tessier, 2019)–often called the U-shaped development. This development can be found in Arabic (Abdalla et al., 2012; Benmamoun et al., 2014; Ravid and Farah, 1999; Saiegh-Haddad et al., 2012), German (Marcus et al., 1995) and English (Marcus et al., 1992). In our simulations we have found no evidence for such a development. This is, in fact, a good thing. Assuming a U-shaped development in morphological acquisition is too coarse, as the literature says little if anything about the question whether the (very few) forms used by very young children are used in the correct morphosynatctic environment. Moreover, this literature assumes that learning morphology involves learning how forms map onto other forms, reminiscent of the paradigm cell filling problem (Ackerman and Malouf, 2013; Guzmán, 2020; Malouf, 2017)–for example, how does a singular form map onto a plural form? The role of meaning is very limited, often not more than a contrastive label. However, the fact that children gradually reduce the number of overgeneralizations of irregular forms can be explained by the way in which children learn which word forms are used to express which particular meanings (Ramscar et al., 2013).

Our experiment with restricting the hallucination process to generate forms that are phonotactically attested (bigram) in the training data revealed that its benefit was found only in very restricted conditions depending on the amount of hallucinated samples and the specific language (and presumably the inflectional pattern). Our findings are in agreement with the detailed error analyses of data hallucination techniques by Samir and Silfverberg (2022) which concluded that hallucination is not a one-size-fits-all technique and it must be used with caution and requires closer inspection depending on the type of morphological inflections.

Acknowledgements

We gratefully acknowledge the support of the central HPC system "HILBERT" at Heinrich-Heine-University, Düsseldorf.

References

Fauzia Abdalla, Khawla Aljenaie, Abdessatar Mahfoudhi, Edith L Bavin, and Letitia R Naigles. 2012. Plural noun inflection in kuwaiti arabic-speaking children with and without specific language impairment*. *Journal of child language*, 40(1):139–168.

Farrell Ackerman and Robert Malouf. 2013. Morphological organization: The low conditional entropy conjecture. *Language*, 89(3):429–464.

Antonios Anastasopoulos and Graham Neubig. 2019. Pushing the limits of low-resource morphological inflection. *arXiv preprint arXiv:1908.05838*.

Elabbas Benmamoun, Abdulkafi Albirini, Silvina A. Montrul, and Eman Saadah. 2014. Arabic plurals and root and pattern morphology in palestinian and egyptian heritage speakers. *Linguistic Approaches to Bilingualism*, 4(1):89–123.

Jiaao Chen, Derek Tam, Colin Raffel, Mohit Bansal, and Diyi Yang. 2021. An empirical survey of data augmentation for limited data learning in nlp.

Harald Clahsen, Monika Rothweiler, Andreas Woest, and Gary F Marcus. 1992. Regular and irregular inflection in the acquisition of german noun plurals. *Cognition*, 45(3):225–255.

Lisa Garnand Dawdy-Hesterberg and Janet Breckenridge Pierrehumbert. 2014. Learnability and generalisation of arabic broken plural nouns. *Language, cognition and neuroscience*, 29(10):1268–1282.

Naranjo Matías Guzmán. 2020. Analogy, complexity and predictability in the russian nominal inflection system. *Morphology*, pages 1–44.

Martin Haspelmath and Andrea Sims. 2013. *Understanding morphology*. Routledge.

Diederik P. Kingma and Jimmy Ba. 2014. Adam: A method for stochastic optimization.

Christo Kirov, Ryan Cotterell, John Sylak-Glassman, Géraldine Walther, Ekaterina Vylomova, Patrick Xia, Manaal Faruqui, Sabrina J Mielke, Arya D McCarthy, Sandra Kübler, et al. 2018. Unimorph 2.0: universal morphology. *arXiv preprint arXiv:1810.11101*.

Jordan Kodner and Salam Khalifa. 2022. SIGMORPHON-UniMorph 2022 Shared Task 0: Modeling Inflection in Language Acquisition. In *Proceedings of the SIGMORPHON 2022 Shared Task: Morphological Inflection*, Seattle. North American Chapter of the Association for Computational Linguistics.

Robert Malouf. 2017. Abstractive morphological learning with a recurrent neural network. *Morphology*, 27(4):431–458.

Gary F Marcus, Ursula Brinkmann, Harald Clahsen, Richard Wiese, and Steven Pinker. 1995. German inflection: The exception that proves the rule. *Cognitive psychology*, 29(3):189–256.

Gary F Marcus, Steven Pinker, Michael Ullman, Michelle Hollander, T John Rosen, Fei Xu, and Harald Clahsen. 1992. Overregularization in language acquisition. In *Monographs of the society for research in child development*. JSTOR.

Myle Ott, Sergey Edunov, Alexei Baevski, Angela Fan, Sam Gross, Nathan Ng, David Grangier, and Michael Auli. 2019. fairseq: A fast, extensible toolkit for sequence modeling. In *Proceedings of the 2019 Conference of the North American Chapter of the Association for Computational Linguistics (Demonstrations)*, pages 48–53, Minneapolis, Minnesota. Association for Computational Linguistics.

Michael Ramscar, Melody Dye, and Stewart M McCauley. 2013. Error and expectation in language learning: The curious absence of mouses in adult speech. *Language*, pages 760–793.

Dorit Ravid and Rola Farah. 1999. Learning about noun plurals in early palestinian arabic. *First Language*, 19(56):187–206.

Elinor Saiegh-Haddad, Areen Hadieh, and Dorit Ravid. 2012. Acquiring noun plurals in palestinian arabic: Morphology, familiarity, and pattern frequency. *Language Learning*, 62(4):1079–1109.

Farhan Samir and Miikka Silfverberg. 2022. One wug, two wug+ s transformer inflection models hallucinate affixes. In *Proceedings of the Fifth Workshop on the Use of Computational Methods in the Study of Endangered Languages*, pages 31–40.

Anne-Michelle Tessier. 2019. U-shaped development in error-driven child phonology. *Wiley Interdisciplinary Reviews: Cognitive Science*, 10(6):e1505.

Ashish Vaswani, Noam Shazeer, Niki Parmar, Jakob Uszkoreit, Llion Jones, Aidan N. Gomez, Lukasz Kaiser, and Illia Polosukhin. 2017. Attention is all you need.

Shijie Wu, Ryan Cotterell, and Mans Hulden. 2020. Applying the transformer to character-level transduction.

Morphology is not just a naive Bayes – UniMelb Submission to SIGMORPHON 2022 ST on Morphological Inflection

Andreas Scherbakov **Ekaterina Vylomova**
The University of Melbourne
andreas@softwareengineer.pro vylomovae@unimelb.edu.au

Abstract

The paper describes the Flexica team's submission to the SIGMORPHON 2022 Shared Task 1 Part 1: Typologically Diverse Morphological Inflection. Our team submitted a non-neural system that extracted transformation patterns from alignments between a lemma and inflected forms. For each inflection category, we chose a pattern based on its abstractness score. The system outperformed the non-neural baseline, the extracted patterns covered a substantial part of possible inflections. However, we discovered that such score that does not account for all possible combinations of string segments as well as morphosyntactic features is not sufficient for a certain proportion of inflection cases.

1 Introduction

Previous years' shared tasks on morphological reinflection demonstrated superior performance across a variety of typologically diverse languages, especially in high-resource setting (Cotterell et al., 2016, 2017, 2018; McCarthy et al., 2019; Vylomova et al., 2020; Pimentel et al., 2021). Still, in low-resource setting and languages with limited resources in which paradigms were only partially represented the accuracy numbers were much less optimistic (Vylomova et al., 2020; Pimentel et al., 2021). Recently, Goldman et al. (2022) experimented with the 2020 shared task data splitting it by lemmas and demonstrated the 30% accuracy drop on average among top-3 top ranked systems in that year's shared task. This motivated organizers of this year's shared task to focus on various aspects of morphological generalisation and conduct controlled experiments to evaluate systems' ability to predict inflected forms for unseen lemmas and morphosyntactic feature combinations.

In this paper, we describe a modification of our earlier model, Flexica (Scherbakov, 2020), that has been participated in the 2020 shared task (Vylomova et al., 2020).[1] We provide a summary of its modified version where we attempted to improve its pattern-based generalization ability. We added ability to reuse word forms observed at different combinations of grammatical tags. Also, we improved scoring mechanism to enable better fitting to rule-and-exception hierarchy which typically presents in a language, and to reduce noise in pattern selection.

2 Task Description

This year's shared task setting substantially differed from previous years in controlling the lemma and feature sets. More specifically, the training, development, and tests sets for the shared task were designed to assess various kinds of generalization. The shared task organizers considered four scenarios of overlap between the training and test sets : 1) both test lemma and feature set are observed in the training (but separately); 2) a test lemma is observed in the training set whereas the feature combination is entirely novel; 3) a feature combination is observed in the training set but the lemma is novel; 4) both a test pair's lemma and feature set are entirely novel and were not presented in the training set.

In addition, the training data sizes vary from 700 training instances in the small (low-resource) setting to 7,000 instance in the large (high-resource) setting. For some under-resourced languages the large setting contained fewer samples.

3 Data

3.1 Data Format

All shared task data are in UTF-8 and follow UniMorph annotation schema (Sylak-Glassman, 2016). Training and developments samples consist of a

[1] https://github.com/andreas-softwareengineer-pro/flexica

19th SIGMORPHON Workshop on Computational Research in Phonetics, Phonology, and Morphology, pages 240 - 246
July 14, 2022 ©2022 Association for Computational Linguistics

lemma, an inflected (target) form, and its morphosyntactic features (tags). Test samples omit the target form.

3.2 Languages

The shared task covered morphological paradigms for 33 typologically diverse languages representing 11 language families: Arabic (Modern Standard), Assamese, Braj, Chukchi, Eastern Armenian, Evenki, Georgian, Gothic, Gujarati, Hebrew, Hungarian, Itelmen, Karelian, Kazakh, Ket, Khalkha Mongolian, Kholosi, Korean, Lamahalot, Low German, Ludic, Magahi, Middle Low German, Old English, Old High German, Old Norse, Polish, Pomak, Slovak, Turkish, Upper Sorbian, Veps, and Xibe.

4 Baseline Systems

As in previous years' shared tasks, two types of baseline systems were provided: neural and non-neural. The **non-neural** baseline aligns extracts suffixes and prefixes based on lemma–form alignments, later associating them with corresponding morpholosyntatic features (Cotterell et al., 2017, 2018). As the **neural** baseline, organizers provided a character-level adaptation of transformer (Wu et al., 2021).

5 Evaluation

The systems submitted to the shared task were evaluated in terms of test accuracy between predicted and gold forms. Besides the overall accuracy, four categories were distinguished in the analytic data provided by organizers. Depending on whether a test sample lemma has been seen in the training set, and whether an exact tag combination ("feature") has been seen in the training set, a test sample might fall into one of the following four categories: "Lemma Overlap", "Feature Overlap", "Neither Overlap", or "Both Overlap".

6 System Description

6.1 Training

We implemented a non-neural system (**`Flexica`**) where an inflected form is inferred from string-to-string transformation patterns observed in training samples. We produce multiple transformation patterns per each training sample. Those patterns differ in their level of abstractness and also depend on string-to-string alignments between a lemma and an inflected form. Later on, we also distinguish two types of patterns, namely a *string* pattern abd a *transformation* pattern. A *string* pattern is a string which may consist of concrete characters and wildcards, e.g. `"u①nd"` pattern for the word "understand". A *transformation* pattern is a triple $(lemma\_pattern, tag \rightarrow form\_pattern)$ which is produced from $(lemma, tag \rightarrow form)$ training samples by replacing certain character subsequences with wildcards. $lemma\_pattern$ and $form\_pattern$ share the same wildcards within a transformation pattern.

In order to produce *transformation patterns* for a given training sample we follow the stages:

1. Find the longest common substring for a lemma and its form. Introduce a wildcard (character subsequence) ① and replace the matching part by the wildcard symbol. For example, an inflection `("observe", V;3;SG → "observes")` produces a pattern `("①", V;3;SG → "①s")`. If there are multiple longest matches, we produce as many transformation pattern variants. For example, `("bring", V;PST → "brang")` will result in two patterns at this stage, `("①ing", V;PST → "①ang")` and `("bri①", V;PST → "bra①")`. We recursively apply the above procedure to the remaining concrete subsequences, finding longest matches and adding new wildcards until no more matching fragments are available.[2] While doing so, we never nest wildcards into each other. We also reject lemma patterns where two or more wildcards would be immediately adjacent, because it would lead to excessive ambiguity in further matching.

   Note: although the process described above may seem to be proliferating, just a single pattern is produced for a vast majority of inflection samples, as they usually have a single longest match. A notable exception are languages with templatic morphology.

2. Produce patterns with various character refinements. At this stage, we partially "surrender" longest matches found at the alignment stage. We replace some characters

[2] We apply an upper threshold for the number of wildcards specifying its as a hyperparameter (usually 2 or 3), which does not affect prediction accuracy.

in wildcard groups back to their concrete values that were observed in a training sample. Once a character is reverted to its concrete value, a wildcard that contained it may be split into two wildcard groups or even disappear. The latter happens whenever a wildcard standing for an empty substring is produced. We do such for $0, 1..CCL$ characters selected in all possible combinations, where CCL is a limit of the concrete characters.[3] Transformation patterns such as (`"①e", V;3;SG → "①es"`), (`"①v②", V;3;SG → "①v②s"`), (`"o①v②e", V;3;SG → "o①v②es"`) constitute a non-exhaustive list of refinements for the pattern (`"①", V;3;SG → "①s"`) produced for an (`"observe", V;3;SG → "observe"`) sample.

We collect all unique patterns produced over a training corpus, finally constructing a trie database model in which data records are as follows: $l \rightarrow \{s \rightarrow \{t, c, d\}\}$ where l is a lemma pattern; s is an inflected form pattern; t is a grammatical tag combination; c is a number of training samples matching the transformation $(l, t\} \rightarrow s)$; d is a number of samples where lemma and tags match l and t, respectively, but the inflected form doesn't match s.

6.2 Inference

In order to predict an infected form for a $(lemma, tag)$ pair, our system finds all the transformation patterns that match the lemma (given any non-empty substring substitution for each wildcard group). Then it picks the transformation that yields the highest score. The score is hierarchical which means that a less significant score factor is considered if and only if all the factors of greater significance are in a tie. Here are the list of score factors, ordered by decreasing significance:

1. Penalty for the pattern abstractness, measured as count of characters substituted into wildcard groups. We include an extra "pad" character per group while calculating that sum;

2. Penalty for tag sets' mismatch (which is fixed per each mismatching tag) plus (optionally) a fixed "lump" amount for any two mismatching tag sets;[4]

3. *Representative* premium (optional), which is a fixed bonus assigned to transformations that are the most abstract while being correct representations of at least one training sample. This score component serves as a counterweight to the pattern abstractness score component described above. It may be seen as an adaptation of the idea of the most general paradigm (Hulden et al., 2014);

4. A (squashed) frequency f of transformation pattern occurrence in a training set for the given tag combination, minus double (squashed) frequency observed for alternative transformations for the same lemma pattern and tag combination.

7 Results

Tables 1 and 2 present accuracy across all the shared task's languages measured for the small and large settings, respectively. For `Flexica`, the column "B" stands for the basic option (without representative bonus), while the column "R" stands for the option with representative bonus. The official submission accuracy numbers are shown in the "Sb." column. Also, accuracy results for the non-neural and neural baselines ("BL") and best results across neural systems submitted to the shared task ("neural"/"max"), are presented for the reference.

We also explored some modifications to pattern scoring, but they did not affect performance much. In particular, we tried the following options:

- Increased penalty for impure patterns where different transformations were learnt for a given lemma pattern. The change resulted in approx. 1% accuracy increase for Middle Low German, although a nearly equal decrease happened in Old High German;

- We added an extra bonus for the exact match of grammatical tag combinations. Surprisingly, due to a notable sparseness of such combinations in the dataset we used, that

[3] In our officially reported results CCL is taken to be 3, because computations are too numerous for greater values. However, our observations suggest that this value is not sufficient, and increasing it enables better performance.

[4] We also considered using a variable tag-to-tag mismatch penalty which was proportional to a negative log-likelihood of tag interchangeability, but our experiments demonstrated lower accuracy for that option.

lang	non-neural					neural	
	Flexica				BL	max	BL
	B	R	Av.	Sb.			
ang	41	41	85	37	49	54	33
ara	31	31	70	32	65	66	22
asm	33	33	47	30	54	57	26
bra	55	56	82	58	55	60	57
ckt	21	21	29	10	6	21	13
evn	3	3	43	3	29	34	25
gml	27	27	92	26	42	56	22
goh	49	50	73	40	56	60	42
got	38	38	68	18	60	61	38
guj	47	47	61	47	39	66	48
heb	19	19	31	19	39	40	14
hsb	13	13	52	13	5	83	10
hsi	16	16	27	13	0	96	20
hun	26	26	58	25	65	61	23
hye	40	40	61	39	64	86	38
itl	30	30	53	31	34	34	28
kat	36	36	63	34	60	59	43
kaz	40	40	52	34	55	65	42
ket	21	21	42	18	10	35	32
khk	24	24	46	22	41	41	28
kor	32	31	57	30	23	50	28
krl	23	23	31	23	16	45	5
lud	88	87	91	88	46	87	88
mag	58	58	79	58	51	64	55
nds	29	29	62	31	25	50	16
non	35	35	71	39	55	52	30
pol	40	40	67	43	59	78	30
poma	29	29	49	29	51	50	22
sjo	55	55	90	65	58	76	67
slk	44	44	81	51	61	84	38
slp	7	7	51	8	15	30	5
tur	18	18	25	18	34	85	16
vep	20	20	41	20	35	42	21

Table 1: Accuracy (in %) measured in the small training condition. `B` - basic options; `R` - with a bonus score for "representative" patters; `Av.` - theoretical limit at a perfect pattern choice; `Sb.` - submitted version; `BL` - baseline; `max` - best among submitted systems

lang	non-neural					neural	
	Flexica				BL	max	BL
	B	R	Av.	Sb.			
ang	46	47	91	41	61	64	43
ara	37	37	79	37	78	75	26
asm	35	35	63	34	76	75	31
evn	3	3	70	3	57	57	25
got	44	44	80	21	72	73	46
heb	29	29	45	28	48	51	20
hun	34	34	75	32	77	74	37
hye	43	42	66	42	69	93	44
kat	32	32	75	45	87	83	45
kaz	40	40	52	34	55	65	42
khk	31	31	50	23	49	49	38
kor	33	34	63	33	56	54	32
krl	36	37	53	37	27	64	5
lud	83	78	93	89	52	89	89
non	41	41	86	47	84	87	37
pol	50	50	84	52	69	90	43
poma	34	34	65	33	63	61	24
slk	49	49	87	58	70	93	47
tur	36	36	53	35	39	94	36
vep	30	30	60	30	48	62	32

Table 2: Accuracy (in %) measured in the large training condition. `B` - basic options; `R` - with a bonus score for "representative" patters; `Av.` - theoretical limit at a perfect pattern choice; `Sb.` - submitted version; `BL` - baseline; `max` - best among submitted systems

change produced no significant difference, except for a minor accuracy increase for Gothic and Georgian.

- Tag combinations in some UniMorph inflection data files may denote multiple options. For instance, multiple tags corresponding to the same category may be included into a single combination, in which any of them is meant to be equally suitable for producing a given inflected form. In order to meet that an alternative tagging format, we tried a modified tag mismatch penalty. Namely, an absence of a target tag in a learnt tag combination is interpreted as "one unit" of tag mismatch. This option yields approximately the same performance as the previous one described.

As exact tag combinations were significantly sparse in training and test sets, the majority of mispredictions can be attributed to failures to inference tag interchangeability. Indeed, in most cases of misprediction a correct transformation was available in the learnt model, but it deemed to be irrelevant due to low "similarity" between the learnt tag combination and the target one. The "Av." column in Tables 1 and 2 shows the percentage of test samples where a correct transformation was available for the model. It tells the upper bound of accuracy that our system would have if the pattern selection mechanism worked perfectly.

8 Discussion

The system we explored in this paper relies on two simple hypotheses. According to the first one, a choice of inflection paradigm in most cases may be associated with some distinctive subsequence of characters in a lemma. The second hypothesis claims existence of a hierarchy of rules and exceptions in most languages, where each exception domain is fenced by a more concrete character pattern than one associated with an embracing general inflection rule. We note that our current approach only admits a very restrictive meaning for such a "concreteness", namely, the number of concrete characters in a template. Due to this substantial limitation, we only consider an *approximate* split of rule-specific domains.

While the analysis of predictions suggests this approach is generally reasonable, the distinguishing of relevant patterns from noise is challenging. Certain information-based criteria such as entropy, cross-entropy and the like did not work, mainly due to specific patterns being sparsely distributed in the dataset (especially small ones), so that majority of highly concrete patterns peaked the distribution of inflection transformations. On the other hand, many relevant generic patterns demonstrate rather disperse distributions due to numerous exceptions. As a result, it is not possible to easily link the entropy to the relevancy. We intentionally avoided imposing extra biases toward "known" common language rules in order to focus our exploration on the system's learning capability itself. Unfortunately, we have not yet found universal enough criteria to assess pattern relevance against inflection rules, so in this aspect the system should be considered as a work in progress. We attempted "promotion" of one maximally abstract pattern per training sample, that match the given sample and does not contradict any other observed samples. The underlying hypothesis was that every inflection paradigm is probably justified by a single "cause", where a "cause" in our restricted context stands for a distinct character pattern for a lemma. Therefore, it should be reasonable to restrict prediction selection to those transformation patterns which were proven to be correctly representing at least one training sample in the most generic way. However, our experiments disproved such an approach, because, as we already said above, relevance criteria based on distribution purity are fundamentally flawed.

Our system operates at character level without considering more generic classes of sub-patterns. However, it did not seem to be a significant issue in most languages. In other words, patterns needed for correct inflection have usually been successfully learnt in most languages (still, non necessarily with the same grammatical tag). However, there are numerous languages where correct patterns cannot be found for a large fraction of examples; this severely jeopardised the respective prediction rates. Besides the "genuinely" high morphological complexity of languages such as Veps, there also occurred some "technical" reasons for the pattern match missing, such as non-standardized scripting of spoken languages (Pomak, Evenki). It is our system's lack of a mechanism for the affix concatenation which was responsible for inferior results observed in agglutinative languages like Turkish of Hungarian, especially in their low-resource settings.

In the 2022 shared task, we faced a new challenge of extreme sparsity of grammatical tag combinations. A separate model per learnt tag combination does not work in such an environment. We allowed using transformation patterns observed at grammatical tag combinations different from a requested one, with a score penalty proportional to the number of different "atomic" tags (morphosyntatic features). From the inflection perspective, many grammatical tags are not as significant for a correct prediction as others are. This inspired us to use variable penalty per tag substitutions, which was proportional to a log-likelihood of observing the same transformation regardless whether a given tag is present, as measured over all learn transformation patterns, without considering other tags. For instance, in Polish, the animacy does not affect inflection paradigms much, and ignoring it would significantly increase the average accuracy of inference. However, to our surprise, according to the likelihood, some case tag substitutions occurred to be better candidates for being ignored. For instance, the dative and the instrumental cases produce same forms for a majority of Polish feminine nouns, therefore our predictor frequently chooses `INS` → `DAT` substitution, which is usually incorrect beyond the feminitive (instead of correct `ANIM` → `INAN`). Thus, such Bayesian approach, that considers tags independently, even failed to outperform a simplistic technique based on the "edit distance" between tag combinations. We did not yet consider more complex sub-combinations of tags, still the results definitely suggest one to do that way.

An excessive number of generated patterns is another challenge which yet needs to be addressed. Currently, our system unrolls all the combinations of concrete characters in lemma patterns until ultimately discriminative ones are found over a training set. This leads to huge proliferation of noisy patterns of no extra value. In practice, this fact prevents the system from considering longer subsequences of concrete characters where those subsequences could really help to delimit paradigm domains.

Summarizing our impressions from the experiments, we suggest that the system is primarily interesting as it prototypes a simple but efficient approach to the conversion of a sequence-to-sequence task into a "plain" classification task. In this view, further enhancements of the system may be broken into two separate directions. The first one concerns the pattern matching mechanism which would become less consuming, more generalized, based on incrementally collected "cues" (and, in such a way, borrowing features of the "soft attention"). Another direction, which is less specific, would be an exploration of better classification models to be used. Also, the principally optimistic results obtained in our experiments inspire us to attempt expanding the proposed multi-pattern approach into other sequence-to-sequence tasks beyond the reinflection one.

9 Conclusion

We developed a non-neural system for morphological inflection. We submitted it to the SIGMORPHON 2022 shared task 1, part 1. The system outperformed the non-neural baseline, still we discovered a fundamental insufficiency of simplistic approaches that rely on observed probabilities of particular transformation patterns.

Acknowledgements

We are deeply thankful to all the organizers of SIGMORPHON workshop and its re-inflection shared task, and to all the contributors to the UniMorph database, for the opportunity to participate in this inspirational contest and to carry out insightful experiments on amazingly diverse morphological corpora.

References

Ryan Cotterell, Christo Kirov, John Sylak-Glassman, Géraldine Walther, Ekaterina Vylomova, Arya D. McCarthy, Katharina Kann, Sebastian Mielke, Garrett Nicolai, Miikka Silfverberg, David Yarowsky, Jason Eisner, and Mans Hulden. 2018. The CoNLL–SIGMORPHON 2018 shared task: Universal morphological reinflection. In *Proceedings of the CoNLL–SIGMORPHON 2018 Shared Task: Universal Morphological Reinflection*, pages 1–27, Brussels. Association for Computational Linguistics.

Ryan Cotterell, Christo Kirov, John Sylak-Glassman, Géraldine Walther, Ekaterina Vylomova, Patrick Xia, Manaal Faruqui, Sandra Kübler, David Yarowsky, Jason Eisner, and Mans Hulden. 2017. CoNLL-SIGMORPHON 2017 shared task: Universal morphological reinflection in 52 languages. In *Proceedings of the CoNLL SIGMORPHON 2017 Shared Task: Universal Morphological Reinflection*, pages 1–30, Vancouver. Association for Computational Linguistics.

Ryan Cotterell, Christo Kirov, John Sylak-Glassman, David Yarowsky, Jason Eisner, and Mans Hulden. 2016. The SIGMORPHON 2016 shared Task—Morphological reinflection. In *Proceedings of the 14th SIGMORPHON Workshop on Computational Research in Phonetics, Phonology, and Morphology*, pages 10–22, Berlin, Germany. Association for Computational Linguistics.

Omer Goldman, David Guriel, and Reut Tsarfaty. 2022. (un)solving morphological inflection: Lemma overlap artificially inflates models' performance. In *Proceedings of the 60th Annual Meeting of the Association for Computational Linguistics (Volume 2: Short Papers)*, pages 864–870, Dublin, Ireland. Association for Computational Linguistics.

Mans Hulden, Markus Forsberg, and Malin Ahlberg. 2014. Semi-supervised learning of morphological paradigms and lexicons. In *Proceedings of the 14th Conference of the European Chapter of the Association for Computational Linguistics*, pages 569–578, Gothenburg, Sweden. Association for Computational Linguistics.

Arya D. McCarthy, Ekaterina Vylomova, Shijie Wu, Chaitanya Malaviya, Lawrence Wolf-Sonkin, Garrett Nicolai, Christo Kirov, Miikka Silfverberg, Sebastian J. Mielke, Jeffrey Heinz, Ryan Cotterell, and Mans Hulden. 2019. The SIGMORPHON 2019 shared task: Morphological analysis in context and cross-lingual transfer for inflection. In *Proceedings of the 16th Workshop on Computational Research in Phonetics, Phonology, and Morphology*, pages 229–244, Florence, Italy. Association for Computational Linguistics.

Tiago Pimentel, Maria Ryskina, Sabrina J. Mielke, Shijie Wu, Eleanor Chodroff, Brian Leonard, Garrett Nicolai, Yustinus Ghanggo Ate, Salam Khalifa, Nizar Habash, Charbel El-Khaissi, Omer Goldman,

Michael Gasser, William Lane, Matt Coler, Arturo Oncevay, Jaime Rafael Montoya Samame, Gema Celeste Silva Villegas, Adam Ek, Jean-Philippe Bernardy, Andrey Shcherbakov, Aziyana Bayyr-ool, Karina Sheifer, Sofya Ganieva, Matvey Plugaryov, Elena Klyachko, Ali Salehi, Andrew Krizhanovsky, Natalia Krizhanovsky, Clara Vania, Sardana Ivanova, Aelita Salchak, Christopher Straughn, Zoey Liu, Jonathan North Washington, Duygu Ataman, Witold Kieraś, Marcin Woliński, Totok Suhardijanto, Niklas Stoehr, Zahroh Nuriah, Shyam Ratan, Francis M. Tyers, Edoardo M. Ponti, Grant Aiton, Richard J. Hatcher, Emily Prud'hommeaux, Ritesh Kumar, Mans Hulden, Botond Barta, Dorina Lakatos, Gábor Szolnok, Judit Ács, Mohit Raj, David Yarowsky, Ryan Cotterell, Ben Ambridge, and Ekaterina Vylomova. 2021. SIGMORPHON 2021 shared task on morphological reinflection: Generalization across languages. In *Proceedings of the 18th SIGMORPHON Workshop on Computational Research in Phonetics, Phonology, and Morphology*, pages 229–259, Online. Association for Computational Linguistics.

Andreas Scherbakov. 2020. The UniMelb submission to the SIGMORPHON 2020 shared task 0: Typologically diverse morphological inflection. In *Proceedings of the 17th SIGMORPHON Workshop on Computational Research in Phonetics, Phonology, and Morphology*, pages 177–183.

John Sylak-Glassman. 2016. The composition and use of the universal morphological feature schema (unimorph schema). *Johns Hopkins University*.

Ekaterina Vylomova, Jennifer White, Elizabeth Salesky, Sabrina J. Mielke, Shijie Wu, Edoardo Maria Ponti, Rowan Hall Maudslay, Ran Zmigrod, Josef Valvoda, Svetlana Toldova, Francis Tyers, Elena Klyachko, Ilya Yegorov, Natalia Krizhanovsky, Paula Czarnowska, Irene Nikkarinen, Andrew Krizhanovsky, Tiago Pimentel, Lucas Torroba Hennigen, Christo Kirov, Garrett Nicolai, Adina Williams, Antonios Anastasopoulos, Hilaria Cruz, Eleanor Chodroff, Ryan Cotterell, Miikka Silfverberg, and Mans Hulden. 2020. SIGMORPHON 2020 shared task 0: Typologically diverse morphological inflection. In *Proceedings of the 17th SIGMORPHON Workshop on Computational Research in Phonetics, Phonology, and Morphology*, pages 1–39, Online. Association for Computational Linguistics.

Shijie Wu, Ryan Cotterell, and Mans Hulden. 2021. Applying the transformer to character-level transduction. In *Proceedings of the 16th Conference of the European Chapter of the Association for Computational Linguistics: Main Volume*, pages 1901–1907.

Author Index

Association for Computational Linguistics
209 N. Eighth Street
Stroudsburg, Pennsylvania 18360

ISBN 978-1-7138-5638-2

CURRAN ASSOCIATES INC.
proceedings.com